WeightWatchers®

NEW COMPLETE COOKBOOK
Bonus edition

WILEY

JOHN WILEY & SONS, INC.

Contents

BREAKFASTS

Apple and Almond Oatmeal A-3

Breakfast Fruit Compote with Yogurt
and Granola A-3

APPETIZERS

Artichoke, Spinach, and Sun-Dried
Tomato Dip A-4

Flank Steak Carnitas A-4

Island-Style Pork and Pineapple........... A-6

Mini-Meatballs in Sour Cream–Mustard
Sauce... A-6

SOUPS

Chickpea Soup with Rosemary and
Tomato.. A-7

Chicken and Rice Noodle Pho A-7

Hearty Root Vegetable–Beef Soup A-9

Yellow Split Pea Soup A-9

Creamy Black Bean Soup A-10

Garlicky White Bean Soup A-10

Roasted Cauliflower Soup A-12

Classic French Onion Soup A-12

MAIN DISHES

Tomato-Smothered Pot Roast A-14

Bell Pepper and Beef Stew, Tex Mex
Style A-14

Mediterranean Beef Stew A-15

Steak and Red Bean Soft Tacos........... A-15

Italian-Style Beef Rolls...................... A-17

Pork Chops with Golden Onions and
Prunes A-17

Boneless Pork Chops with Creamy
Mushrooms A-18

Pulled Pork and Slaw Sandwiches A-18

North African Lamb and Squash Stew... A-21

Mustard and Herb–Rubbed Leg of
Lamb A-21

Chicken in White Wine A-22

Curried Chicken with Vegetables A-22

Spiced Chicken Tagine A-23

Cioppino-Style Chicken A-23

Chicken with Mushrooms and Sage A-25

Kielbasa and Shrimp Jambalaya........... A-25

New Orleans Gumbo A-27

Halibut and Tomato Stew A-27

Indian-Spiced Shrimp with Red Lentils. A-28

Three Bean Chili................................ A-28

Vegetable Ragu with Pasta.................. A-29

DESSERTS

Tapioca Pudding with Vanilla and
Raspberries.................................... A-29

Chocolate-Espresso Bread Pudding....... A-30

Lemon-Lime Cheesecake A-30

Carrot-Molasses Steamed Pudding........ A-32

Apple-Cranberry Crisp A-32

Apple and Almond Oatmeal

serves 6

4 cups water
1 cup steel-cut oats
1 Granny Smith apple, peeled, cored,
    and shredded
¼ cup dried currants
¾ teaspoon ground cinnamon
½ teaspoon salt
1 cup vanilla almond milk
¼ cup pure maple syrup
2 tablespoons sliced almonds, toasted

1   Combine water, oats, apple, currants, cinnamon, and salt in 3½- or 4-quart slow cooker. Cover and cook until oats are very soft and mixture is thick and creamy, 7–8 hours on low.

2   Stir almond milk and maple syrup into slow cooker. Divide oatmeal among 6 bowls and sprinkle evenly with almonds.

PER SERVING (SCANT 1 CUP OATMEAL AND 1 TEASPOON ALMONDS): 207 grams, 139 Cal, 2 g Total Fat, 0 g Sat Fat, 0 g Trans Fat, 0 mg Chol, 225 mg Sod, 29 g Carb, 17 g Sugar, 3 g Fib, 3 g Prot, 30 mg Calc.
PointsPlus value: *4.*

▲ HEALTHY EXTRA

Start your day with the sweet smell of cinnamon, and add a healthy dose of vitamins by topping each serving of oatmeal with sliced strawberries and/or blueberries.

Breakfast Fruit Compote with Yogurt and Granola

serves 8

3 cups mixed dried fruit, such as peaches,
    pears, apples, and pitted prunes
2 navel oranges, peeled and cut into
    ½-inch rounds
1 lemon, peeled and cut into ½-inch rounds
1 cup water
¾ cup orange juice
2 tablespoons honey
3 (3-inch) cinnamon sticks
10 whole cloves
4 cups plain fat-free Greek yogurt
½ cup low-fat granola

1   Combine dried fruit, oranges, lemon, water, orange juice, honey, cinnamon sticks, and cloves in 3½- or 4-quart slow cooker. Cover and cook until fruit is softened, 7–8 hours on low. Discard cinnamon sticks and cloves.

2   Divide compote among 8 bowls. Top each serving with ½ cup yogurt and sprinkle evenly with granola.

PER SERVING (½ CUP FRUIT, ½ CUP YOGURT, AND 1 TABLESPOON GRANOLA): 286 grams, 280 Cal, 0 g Total Fat, 0 g Sat Fat, 0 g Trans Fat, 0 mg Chol, 148 mg Sod, 60 g Carb, 35 g Sugar, 6 g Fib, 13 g Prot, 134 mg Calc.
PointsPlus value: *7.*

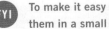 FYI   To make it easy to retrieve the cloves, tie them in a small square of cheesecloth before adding them to the slow cooker.

Artichoke, Spinach, and Sun-Dried Tomato Dip

serves 8

1 (14-ounce) can artichoke hearts, drained
    and finely chopped
½ (10-ounce) package frozen chopped
    spinach, thawed and squeezed dry
½ cup grated Parmesan cheese
½ cup reduced-fat mayonnaise
¼ cup light sour cream
2 scallions, thinly sliced
1 small garlic clove, minced
⅛ teaspoon cayenne
4 sun-dried tomatoes (not packed in oil),
    finely chopped

1   Combine all ingredients except sun-dried
tomatoes in 1½-quart slow cooker; mix well.
Cover and cook until Parmesan is melted and
dip is hot, 1–2 hours on high or 3–4 hours
on low.
2   Stir in sun-dried tomatoes. Serve hot or
warm.

PER SERVING (¼ CUP): 101 grams, 88 Cal, 5 g Total Fat,
2 g Sat Fat, 0 g Trans Fat, 7 mg Chol, 386 mg Sod,
9 g Carb, 2 g Sugar, 1 g Fib, 4 g Prot, 84 mg Calc.
PointsPlus value: *3.*

▲ HEALTHY EXTRA

Serve this flavorful dip with a variety of vegetable
scoopers, including Belgian endive leaves,
pieces of celery, pieces of red bell pepper, and
thickly sliced zucchini and/or English (seedless)
cucumber.

Flank Steak Carnitas

serves 8

1 pound flank steak, trimmed
1 cup beer
¼ cup orange juice
¼ cup lime juice
1 teaspoon dried oregano
½ teaspoon salt
¼ teaspoon cayenne
¼ teaspoon black pepper
8 (6-inch) corn tortillas, warmed
½ cup fat-free sour cream
½ cup tomato salsa or pico de gallo

1   Combine steak, beer, orange juice, lime
juice, oregano, salt, cayenne, and black pepper
in 5- or 6-quart slow cooker. Cover and cook
until steak is fork-tender, 4–5 hours on high or
8–10 hours on low.
2   Transfer steak to cutting board; discard all
but 2 tablespoons of cooking liquid. With two
forks, finely shred beef. Transfer to bowl and
stir in reserved cooking liquid.
3   Lay tortillas on work surface; top evenly
with shredded beef. Top each with 1 tablespoon sour cream and 1 tablespoon salsa. Roll
up tortillas to enclose filling.

PER SERVING (1 CARNITA): 147 grams; 183 Cal, 4 g Total Fat,
1 g Sat Fat, 0 g Trans Fat, 22 mg Chol, 285 mg Sod, 20 g
Carb, 1 g Sugar, 1 g Fib, 14 g Prot, 32 mg Calc.
PointsPlus value: *4.*

▲ HEALTHY EXTRA

Accompany these carnitas with bowls of chopped
red bell pepper and fresh cilantro leaves.

FLANK STEAK CARNITAS

Island-Style Pork and Pineapple

serves 8

1 pound pork tenderloin, trimmed and cut
    into ¾-inch pieces
2 tablespoons cornstarch
2 teaspoons canola oil
2 (8-ounce) cans pineapple chunks in juice,
    drained, juice from 1 can reserved
1 small red onion, chopped
1 red bell pepper, chopped
¼ cup ketchup
3 tablespoons white vinegar
2 tablespoons reduced-sodium soy sauce
1½ tablespoons light agave nectar
3 large garlic cloves, minced
2 tablespoons minced peeled fresh ginger
¼ cup coarsely chopped fresh cilantro

1   Combine pork and 1 tablespoon of cornstarch in large bowl; toss until pork is coated evenly. Heat oil in large nonstick skillet over medium heat. Add pork, in batches, and cook, turning, until browned, about 5 minutes per batch.

2   Combine remaining 1 tablespoon cornstarch, the pineapple chunks, reserved pineapple juice, onion, bell pepper, ketchup, vinegar, soy sauce, agave nectar, garlic, and ginger in 5- or 6-quart slow cooker; mix well. Stir in pork. Cover and cook until pork is fork-tender, 4–5 hours on high or 8–10 hours on low. Sprinkle with cilantro.

PER SERVING (½ CUP): 163 grams, 144 Cal, 3 g Total Fat,
1 g Sat Fat, 0 g Trans Fat, 37 mg Chol, 249 mg Sod, 18 g
Carb, 13 g Sugar, 1 g Fib, 13 g Prot, 19 mg Calc.
PointsPlus value: *4.*

 FYI Agave nectar extracted from the blue agave plant, is sweeter than honey.

Mini-Meatballs in Sour Cream–Mustard Sauce

serves 12

3 slices reduced-calorie bread, torn in pieces
½ pound ground skinless chicken breast
½ pound lean ground pork
1 large egg
1 small onion, finely chopped
2 tablespoons country-style Dijon mustard
½ teaspoon salt
¼ teaspoon black pepper
¼ teaspoon ground allspice
⅛ teaspoon ground nutmeg
½ cup reduced-sodium beef broth
½ cup light sour cream
2 tablespoons chopped fresh flat-leaf parsley

1   Preheat oven to 450°F. Spray large rimmed baking sheet with nonstick spray.

2   Put bread in food processor and pulse until fine crumbs are formed. Combine bread crumbs, chicken, pork, egg, onion, 1 tablespoon of mustard, the salt, pepper, allspice, and nutmeg in large bowl; stir until mixed well. With damp hands, form mixture into 36 (1-inch) meatballs. Place 1 inch apart on prepared baking sheet. Bake until lightly browned, about 15 minutes.

3   Transfer meatballs to 5- or 6-quart slow cooker. Whisk together broth and remaining 1 tablespoon mustard in small bowl; pour over meatballs. Cover and cook until meatballs are cooked through and sauce is slightly thickened, 1–2 hours on high or 3–4 hours on low. Stir in sour cream and sprinkle with parsley.

PER SERVING (3 MEATBALLS WITH 1 TABLESPOON
SAUCE): 64 grams, 87 Cal, 3 g Total Fat, 1 g Sat Fat,
0 g Trans Fat, 43 mg Chol, 211 mg Sod, 4 g Carb,
1 g Sugar, 0 g Fib, 9 g Prot, 27 mg Calc.
PointsPlus value: *2.*

Chickpea Soup with Rosemary and Tomato

serves 8

1 tablespoon olive oil
1 large onion, chopped
3 large garlic cloves, minced
2 teaspoons minced fresh rosemary
1 (15½-ounce) can chickpeas, rinsed
   and drained
3 carrots, diced
3 celery stalks with leaves, stalks diced
   and leaves chopped
¼ teaspoon black pepper
2 (32-ounce) containers reduced-sodium
   chicken broth
1 cup tiny whole wheat or whole-grain pasta
3 plum tomatoes, seeded and chopped
2 tablespoons chopped fresh parsley

1   Heat oil in large nonstick skillet over medium heat. Add onion and garlic; cook, stirring, until onion is softened, about 5 minutes. Stir in rosemary.
2   Transfer onion mixture to 5- or 6-quart slow cooker. Add chickpeas, carrots, celery, and pepper. Pour broth over chickpeas and vegetables. Cover and cook until vegetables are fork-tender, 4–5 hours on high or 8–10 hours on low.
3   Meanwhile, cook pasta according to package directions, omitting salt if desired. Drain and add to soup.
4   Ladle soup into 8 bowls. Sprinkle evenly with tomatoes and parsley.

PER SERVING (1½ CUPS): 407 grams, 166 Cal, 4 g Total Fat, 1 g Sat Fat, 0 g Trans Fat, 0 mg Chol, 231 mg Sod, 26 g Carb, 4 g Sugar, 4 g Fib, 9 g Prot, 49 mg Calc.
PointsPlus value: **4.**

Chicken and Rice Noodle Pho

serves 6

1 (1-pound) bone-in chicken breast, skinned
3 scallions, white and green parts separated
2 garlic cloves, unpeeled and lightly crushed
3 thick slices unpeeled fresh ginger
½ teaspoon salt
2 (32-ounce) containers reduced-sodium
   chicken broth
6 ounces rice stick noodles (vermicelli)
1 cup lightly packed mung bean sprouts
½ cup torn fresh basil and mint leaves
1 lime, cut into 6 wedges

1   Place chicken, white part of scallions, the garlic, ginger, and salt in 5- or 6-quart slow cooker; add broth. Cover and cook until chicken is fork-tender, 4–5 hours on high or 8–10 hours on low.
2   Meanwhile, cook noodles according to package directions. Drain and rinse under cold running water. Set aside.
3   With slotted spoon, transfer chicken to cutting board. When cool enough to handle, pull chicken from bone, then tear into bite-size pieces. Discard bone. Strain broth through large strainer set over slow cooker. Discard vegetables.
4   Return chicken to broth and add noodles. Cover and cook until heated through, about 10 minutes on high.
5   Thinly slice green part of scallions. Ladle soup into 6 bowls; top with bean sprouts, basil, mint, and scallions. Serve with lime.

PER SERVING (GENEROUS 1½ CUPS): 401 grams, 232 Cal, 3 g Total Fat, 1 g Sat Fat, 0 g Trans Fat, 34 mg Chol, 317 mg Sod, 28 g Carb, 1 g Sugar, 1 g Fib, 21 g Prot, 35 mg Calc.
PointsPlus value: **6.**

HEARTY ROOT VEGETABLE–BEEF SOUP

Hearty Root Vegetable–Beef Soup

serves 8

3 carrots, diced
2 parsnips, diced
2 onions, chopped
¾ cup pearl barley
1¼ pounds boneless beef chuck, trimmed
    and cut into ½-inch pieces
10 ounces cremini mushrooms, sliced
2 large garlic cloves, minced
¾ teaspoon salt
¼ teaspoon black pepper
6 cups reduced-sodium beef broth
4 cups water
¼ cup chopped fresh parsley

1   Place racks in upper and lower thirds of oven. Preheat oven to 450°F.
2   Combine carrots, parsnips, onions, and barley on rimmed baking sheet. Spray with nonstick spray and toss. Roast on lower oven rack, stirring, until vegetables are tender and browned, about 30 minutes.
3   Spray large nonstick roasting pan with nonstick spray. Spread beef in pan; roast on upper oven rack, turning, until browned, about 20 minutes.
4   Transfer beef with any accumulated juices and roasted vegetable mixture to 5- or 6-quart slow cooker. Add mushrooms, garlic, salt, and pepper. Pour broth and water over beef and vegetables. Cover and cook until beef and vegetables are fork-tender, 4–5 hours on high or 8–10 hours on low. Stir in parsley.

PER SERVING (1¾ CUPS): 497 grams, 245 Cal, 5 g Total Fat, 2 g Sat Fat, 0 g Trans Fat, 30 mg Chol, 324 mg Sod, 29 g Carb, 7 g Sugar, 6 g Fib, 22 g Prot, 66 mg Calc.
PointsPlus value: *6.*

Yellow Split Pea Soup

serves 6

1 (1-pound) package yellow split peas,
    picked over, rinsed, and drained
3 carrots, diced
3 celery stalks, diced
1 large onion, chopped
2 garlic cloves, minced
1 teaspoon dried oregano
½ teaspoon salt
¼ teaspoon black pepper
8 cups water
3 slices Canadian bacon, chopped
¼ cup chopped fresh parsley

1   Combine split peas, carrots, celery, onion, garlic, oregano, salt, and pepper in 5- or 6-quart slow cooker; pour water over split peas and vegetables. Cover and cook until split peas and vegetables are tender, 4–5 hours on high or 8–10 hours on low. Skim off any scum from soup; stir in Canadian bacon.
2   Ladle soup into 6 bowls. Sprinkle with parsley.

PER SERVING (ABOUT 1⅓ CUPS): 491 grams, 328 Cal, 3 g Total Fat, 0 g Sat Fat, 0 g Trans Fat, 7 mg Chol, 442 mg Sod, 56 g Carb, 5 g Sugar, 26 g Fib, 20 g Prot, 62 mg Calc.
PointsPlus value: *7.*

▲ HEALTHY EXTRA
Add 1 pound baby potatoes, scrubbed and diced, to the split pea mixture in step 1. This will increase the per-serving *PointsPlus* value by *1.*

Creamy Black Bean Soup
serves 8

1 tablespoon olive oil
2 onions, chopped
1½ teaspoons ground cumin
4 (15½-ounce) cans black beans, rinsed
    and drained
1 large baking potato, peeled and chopped
¼ teaspoon black pepper
6 cups reduced-sodium chicken broth
½ cup plain low-fat yogurt
8 thin slices lime
¼ cup lightly packed fresh cilantro leaves

1   Heat oil in large nonstick skillet over medium heat. Add onions and cook, stirring, until softened, about 5 minutes. Add cumin and cook, stirring, until fragrant, about 30 seconds.
2   Put beans in 5- or 6-quart slow cooker. Add onion mixture, potato, and pepper. Pour broth over beans and vegetables. Cover and cook until vegetables are fork-tender, 4–5 hours on high or 8–10 hours on low.
3   Puree soup, in batches, in blender or food processor. Return soup to slow cooker; cook on high until heated through, about 15 minutes.
4   Ladle soup into 8 bowls. Top each serving with 1 tablespoon yogurt, 1 lime slice, and cilantro.

PER SERVING (1½ CUPS): 507 grams, 272 Cal, 4 g Total Fat, 1 g Sat Fat, 0 g Trans Fat, 0 mg Chol, 768 mg Sod, 43 g Carb, 4 g Sugar, 11 g Fib, 16 g Prot, 125 mg Calc.
PointsPlus value: **6.**

 FYI The lime and cilantro add a bit of bright flavor to this robust Cuban soup.

Garlicky White Bean Soup
serves 8

2 onions, diced
2 carrots, diced
1½ cups diced butternut squash
2 large garlic cloves, minced
2 (15½-ounce) cans white kidney (cannellini)
    beans, rinsed and drained
1 (14½-ounce) can fire-roasted diced
    tomatoes, drained
1 fresh sage sprig
¼ teaspoon black pepper
2 (32-ounce) containers reduced-sodium
    chicken broth

1   Preheat oven to 450°F.
2   Combine onions, carrots, squash, and garlic on large rimmed baking sheet. Spray with olive oil nonstick spray; toss until coated. Roast, stirring occasionally, until vegetables are tender and lightly browned, about 30 minutes.
3   Combine vegetable mixture, beans, tomatoes, sage sprig, and pepper in 5- or 6-quart slow cooker. Pour broth over beans and vegetables. Cover and cook until vegetables are fork-tender, 4–5 hours on high or 8–10 hours on low. Discard sage sprig.

PER SERVING (1½ CUPS): 464 grams, 169 Cal, 1 g Total Fat, 0 g Sat Fat, 0 g Trans Fat, 0 mg Chol, 484 mg Sod, 29 g Carb, 7 g Sugar, 7 g Fib, 12 g Prot, 94 mg Calc.
PointsPlus value: **4.**

FYI Here's an easy way to peel garlic: Place a clove on a cutting board. With the side of a large knife, press down on the clove until it's slightly crushed and the skin splits. The skin will slip right off.

Roasted Cauliflower Soup

serves 8

1 head cauliflower, cored and cut into
    1-inch florets
2 onions, chopped
3 carrots, chopped
8 fresh parsley sprigs
1/2 teaspoon salt
1/4 teaspoon black pepper
2 (32-ounce) containers reduced-sodium
    chicken broth
1/2 cup grated Parmesan cheese

1   Preheat oven to 450°F.
2   Combine cauliflower, onions, and carrots
on large rimmed baking sheet. Spray with olive
oil nonstick stick spray and toss until coated.
Roast, stirring occasionally, until vegetables are
tender and lightly browned, about 30 minutes.
3   Transfer vegetables to 5- or 6-quart slow
cooker. Add parsley sprigs, salt, and pepper.
Pour broth over vegetables. Cover and cook
until vegetables are fork-tender, 4–5 hours on
high or 8–10 hours on low. Discard parsley
sprigs.
4   Puree soup, in batches, in blender or
food processor. Return soup to slow cooker
and cook on high until heated through, about
15 minutes.
5   Ladle soup into 8 bowls. Sprinkle evenly
with Parmesan.

PER SERVING (1 CUP SOUP AND 1 TABLESPOON
PARMESAN): 398 grams, 105 Cal, 3 g Total Fat, 1 g Sat Fat,
0 g Trans Fat, 4 mg Chol, 338 mg Sod, 14 g Carb,
6 g Sugar, 4 g Fib, 9 g Prot, 107 mg Calc.
PointsPlus value: *3.*

FYI   Roasting the vegetables caramelizes them,
which brings out all their natural sweetness
and gives this soup its deep flavor.

Classic French Onion Soup

serves 8

1 tablespoon + 1 teaspoon olive oil
3 pounds onions, thinly sliced
2 teaspoons sugar
1 tablespoon all-purpose flour
1 (32-ounce) container reduced-sodium
    beef broth
1 (32-ounce) container no-salt-added
    beef broth
1/4 teaspoon black pepper
3 ounces soft (mild) goat cheese,
    at room temperature
2 teaspoons chopped thyme
8 (3/8-inch) slices French baguette, toasted

1   Heat oil in large Dutch oven over medium
heat. Add onions and cook, stirring occasionally, about 10 minutes. Sprinkle sugar
over onions and cook, stirring occasionally,
until onions are deep golden brown and well
softened, about 35 minutes, adding a bit of
water to pot if onions seem dry. Stir in flour
and cook, stirring constantly, until flour is
lightly browned, about 2 minutes longer.
2   Transfer onions to 5- or 6-quart slow
cooker. Add broth and pepper. Cover and cook
until flavors are blended 4–5 hours on high or
8–10 hours on low.
3   Mix together goat cheese and chopped
thyme in small bowl. Spread cheese mixture
evenly over slices of toast. Ladle soup into
8 bowls; top each serving with a cheese toast.

PER SERVING (ABOUT 1¼ CUPS SOUP WITH 1 CHEESE
TOAST): 423 grams, 170 Cal, 5 g Total Fat, 2 g Sat Fat,
0 g Trans Fat, 5 mg Chol, 306 mg Sod, 22 g Carb,
8 g Sugar, 3 g Fib, 11 g Prot, 56 mg Calc.
PointsPlus value: *4.*

CLASSIC FRENCH ONION SOUP

Tomato-Smothered Pot Roast

serves 8

¼ cup all-purpose flour
1 teaspoon salt
½ teaspoon black pepper
1 (2¾-pound) bottom round beef roast,
    trimmed
1 tablespoon olive oil
2 onions, thinly sliced
4 garlic cloves, minced
½ cup dry red wine or water
1 (14½-ounce) can petite diced tomatoes
1 tablespoon chopped fresh thyme

1   Combine flour, salt, and pepper on sheet
of wax paper. Roll beef in seasoned flour,
shaking off excess.
2   Heat oil in large nonstick skillet over
medium heat. Add beef and cook until
browned on all sides, about 10 minutes.
Transfer to 5- or 6-quart slow cooker.
3   Add onions to skillet and cook, stirring,
until softened, about 5 minutes. Add garlic and
cook, stirring constantly, until fragrant, about
1 minute. Add wine and bring to boil, scraping
up browned bits from bottom of skillet.
Transfer to slow cooker; stir in tomatoes
and thyme.
4   Cover and cook until beef is fork-tender,
4–6 hours on high or 8–10 hours on low.
Transfer beef to cutting board; let stand
10 minutes. Cut beef into 16 slices and serve
with sauce.

**PER SERVING (2 SLICES BEEF AND 3 TABLESPOONS
SAUCE):** 228 grams, 317 Cal, 11 g Total Fat, 3 g Sat Fat,
0 g Trans Fat, 121 mg Chol, 459 mg Sod, 9 g Carb,
4 g Sugar, 1 g Fib, 41 g Prot, 33 mg Calc.
PointsPlus value: **8.**

Bell Pepper and Beef Stew, Tex Mex Style

serves 4

1 teaspoon canola oil
1 pound boneless beef chuck, trimmed and cut
    into 1½-inch chunks
1½ cups no-salt-added beef broth
1 large onion, coarsely chopped
1 (1.25-ounce) package low-sodium fajita
    seasoning mix
2–3 teaspoons chili powder
2 teaspoons ground cumin
2 garlic cloves, minced
2 red bell peppers, cut into 1-inch pieces
½ cup lightly packed fresh cilantro leaves
4 (6-inch) whole wheat tortillas, warmed

1   Heat oil in large nonstick skillet over
medium heat. Add beef, in batches, and cook,
until browned on all sides, about 6 minutes
per batch.
2   Transfer beef to 5- or 6-quart slow cooker.
Add broth to skillet; bring to boil, stirring
constantly to scrape brown bits from bottom
of skillet. Pour broth over beef. Add onion,
fajita seasoning mix, chili powder, cumin, and
garlic; mix well. Cover and cook until meat and
vegetables are fork-tender, 4–5 hours on high
or 8–10 hours on low.
3   About 40 minutes before cooking time is
up, stir bell peppers into slow cooker. Cover
and cook on high until the bell peppers are
tender, about 35 minutes. Stir in cilantro and
serve with tortillas.

PER SERVING (1 CUP STEW AND 1 TORTILLA):
304 grams, 283 Cal, 9 g Total Fat, 2 g Sat Fat,
0 g Trans Fat, 48 mg Chol, 813 mg Sod, 25 g Carb,
4 g Sugar, 10 g Fib, 30 g Prot, 40 mg Calc.
PointsPlus value: **7.**

Mediterranean Beef Stew

serves 6

1 pound bottom round steak, trimmed and
    cut into 1-inch chunks
4 leeks (white and light green parts only)
    halved lengthwise and sliced
1 fennel bulb, diced
4 large garlic cloves, minced
1 (28-ounce) can diced tomatoes
1 cup dry red wine or reduced-sodium
    beef broth
1 teaspoon dried thyme
½ teaspoon fennel seeds
1 bay leaf
¼ teaspoon salt
¼ teaspoon black pepper
2 teaspoons olive oil
1½ pounds cremini mushrooms, halved
½ cup pitted Kalamata olives,
    coarsely chopped
Grated zest of ½ orange

1   Combine beef, leeks, diced fennel, garlic,
tomatoes, wine, thyme, fennel seeds, bay leaf,
salt, and pepper in 5- or 6-quart slow cooker.
Cover and cook until beef is fork-tender,
4–5 hours on high or 8–10 hours on low.
2   About 20 minutes before cooking time
is up, heat oil in large nonstick skillet over
medium heat. Add mushrooms and cook,
stirring, until browned and liquid is evaporated,
about 5 minutes.
3   Stir mushrooms into beef mixture in
slow cooker. Cover and cook on high until
mushrooms are very tender, about 10 minutes
longer. Stir in olives and orange zest.

PER SERVING (1½ CUPS): 447 grams, 305 Cal, 10 g Total Fat,
3 g Sat Fat, 0 g Trans Fat, 36 mg Chol, 609 mg Sod, 25 g
Carb, 9 g Sugar, 4 g Fib, 21 g Prot, 115 mg Calc.
PointsPlus value: *8.*

Steak and Red Bean Soft Tacos

serves 6

1½ cups reduced-sodium beef broth
2 teaspoons chili powder
1 pound flank steak, trimmed
1½ cups chunky tomato salsa
½ cup canned red kidney beans, rinsed
    and drained
¼ cup lightly packed fresh cilantro leaves
1–2 jalapeño peppers, finely chopped
12 (6-inch) corn tortillas, warmed
6 tablespoons fat-free sour cream

1   Whisk together broth and chili powder in
5- or 6-quart slow cooker. Add steak. Cover
and cook until steak is fork-tender, 4–5 hours
on high or 8–10 hours on low.
2   Transfer steak to cutting board. Discard
all but ¼ cup of cooking liquid; wipe out slow
cooker. With two forks, finely shred beef.
Return beef to slow cooker and stir in reserved
cooking liquid, ¾ cup of salsa, the beans,
cilantro, and jalapeño. Cover and cook on high
until heated through, about 10 minutes.
3   Lay tortillas on work surface. Divide beef
mixture evenly among tortillas and top each
with 1 tablespoon sour cream. Fold tortillas in
half and serve with remaining ¾ cup salsa.

PER SERVING (2 TACOS AND 2 TABLESPOONS SALSA):
277 grams, 308 Cal, 7 g Total Fat, 2 g Sat Fat, 0 g Trans Fat,
29 mg Chol, 405 mg Sod, 38 g Carb, 3 g Sugar, 3 g Fib,
21 g Prot, 39 mg Calc.
PointsPlus value: *8.*

▲ HEALTHY EXTRA
Add some tasty fiber to this dish by lining each
tortilla with about ⅓ cup of broccoli slaw or
coleslaw.

ITALIAN-STYLE BEEF ROLLS

Italian-Style Beef Rolls

serves 6

¹⁄₂ cup dried currants
¹⁄₂ cup hot water
1 cup seasoned whole wheat bread crumbs
¹⁄₂ cup chopped fresh parsley
¹⁄₂ cup grated Parmesan cheese
1 teaspoon dried oregano
6 (¹⁄₄-pound) slices beef top round steak,
   trimmed (about ¹⁄₄-inch-thick)
¹⁄₄ teaspoon black pepper
1¹⁄₂ cups fat-free tomato sauce
¹⁄₄ cup thinly sliced fresh basil

1   Combine currants and hot water in small bowl; let stand 10 minutes. Drain, reserving ¹⁄₄ cup water.
2   Combine currants, bread crumbs, parsley, Parmesan, and oregano in bowl. Spray with nonstick spray; toss. Add enough of reserved water to moisten.
3   Place slices of steak between pieces of plastic wrap; pound to ¹⁄₈-inch thickness. Sprinkle steak with pepper. Sprinkle ¹⁄₄ cup of filling onto each slice of meat, leaving ¹⁄₂-inch border. From a short end, roll up slices. Tie with kitchen string.
4   Spray large nonstick skillet with nonstick spray; set over medium heat. Add beef and cook until browned, about 8 minutes.
5   Transfer rolls to 5- or 6-quart slow cooker. Add tomato sauce. Cover and cook until rolls are fork-tender, 3–4 hours on high or 6–8 hours on low. Remove strings. Spoon sauce over and sprinkle with basil.

PER SERVING (1 BEEF ROLL AND 3 TABLESPOONS SAUCE): 209 grams, 325 Cal, 11 g Total Fat, 4 g Sat Fat, 0 g Trans Fat, 54 mg Chol, 679 mg Sod, 24 g Carb, 13 g Sugar, 3 g Fib, 32 g Prot, 165 mg Calc.
PointsPlus value: **8.**

Pork Chops with Golden Onions and Prunes

serves 4

4 (¹⁄₄-pound) boneless pork loin chops,
   trimmed
³⁄₄ teaspoon salt
¹⁄₄ teaspoon black pepper
2 teaspoons olive oil
2 large onions, thinly sliced
12 pitted prunes, halved
12 apricots
³⁄₄ cup unsweetened apple juice
1 (3-inch) cinnamon stick
1 teaspoon dried thyme
2 tablespoons chopped fresh mint

1   Sprinkle pork chops with ¹⁄₄ teaspoon of salt and ¹⁄₈ teaspoon of pepper. Heat 1 teaspoon of oil in large nonstick skillet over medium heat. Add pork and cook, turning once, until browned, about 6 minutes. Transfer pork to plate.
2   Heat remaining 1 teaspoon oil in skillet. Add onions and remaining ¹⁄₂ teaspoon salt and ¹⁄₈ teaspoon pepper. Cook, stirring occasionally, until onions are softened and turn golden, 10–12 minutes.
3   Put prunes and apricots in bottom of 5- or 6-quart slow cooker. Place pork in single layer on top of dried fruit. Top with onions, apple juice, cinnamon stick, and thyme. Cover and cook until pork is fork-tender, 3–4 hours on high or 6–8 hours on low. Discard cinnamon stick. Sprinkle onion-fruit mixture with mint and serve with pork.

PER SERVING (1 PORK CHOP AND ¹⁄₂ CUP ONION-FRUIT MIXTURE): 244 grams, 309 Cal, 8 g Total Fat, 2 g Sat Fat, 0 g Trans Fat, 66 mg Chol, 487 mg Sod, 37 g Carb, 24 g Sugar, 4 g Fib, 23 g Prot, 65 mg Calc.
PointsPlus value: **8.**

Boneless Pork Chops with Creamy Mushrooms

serves 4

4 (¼-pound) boneless pork loin chops, trimmed
¼ teaspoon black pepper
1 (10.75-ounce) can reduced-sodium reduced-fat condensed cream of mushroom soup
¼ cup water
4 carrots, thinly sliced
1 large onion, thinly sliced
6 ounces white mushrooms, sliced
2 teaspoons Worcestershire sauce
½ teaspoon dried thyme
4 cups hot cooked yolk-free egg noodles
2 tablespoons chopped fresh parsley

1   Sprinkle pork chops with pepper. Spray large nonstick skillet with nonstick spray and set over medium heat. Add pork and cook, turning once, until browned, about 6 minutes.
2   Combine soup, water, carrots, onion, mushrooms, Worcestershire sauce, and thyme in 5- or 6-quart slow cooker; mix well. Place pork on top of vegetable mixture. Cover and cook until pork and vegetables are fork tender, 3–4 hours on high or 6–8 hours on low.
3   Serve with egg noodles sprinkled with parsley.

PER SERVING (1 PORK CHOP, ½ CUP VEGETABLE MIXTURE, AND 1 CUP NOODLES): 345 grams, 338 Cal, 8 g Total Fat, 2 g Sat Fat, 0 g Trans Fat, 69 mg Chol, 525 mg Sod, 37 g Carb, 8 g Sugar, 4 g Fib, 28 g Prot, 72 mg Calc.
PointsPlus value: *8.*

FYI   Save time in the kitchen by purchasing sliced mushrooms.

Pulled Pork and Slaw Sandwiches

serves 6

1½ pounds pork tenderloin, trimmed
1 cup barbecue sauce
1 onion, finely chopped
2 teaspoons chili powder
1½ cups lightly packed coleslaw mix
6 light hamburger buns, split and toasted

1   Spray ridged grill pan with nonstick spray and set over medium-high heat. Add pork and cook until browned on all sides, about 6 minutes. Transfer pork to cutting board. When cool enough to handle, cut into ¾-inch pieces.
2   Combine pork, barbecue sauce, onion, and chili powder in 5- or 6-quart slow cooker; mix well. Cover and cook until pork is fork-tender, 3–4 hours on high or 6–8 hours on low.
3   With two forks, shred pork. Place ¼ cup of coleslaw on bottom of each bun and top with ½ cup pork mixture. Cover with tops of buns.

PER SERVING (1 SANDWICH): 265 grams, 308 Cal, 4 g Total Fat, 1 g Sat Fat, 0 g Trans Fat, 76 mg Chol, 667 mg Sod, 39 g Carb, 16 g Sugar, 4 g Fib, 29 g Prot, 54 mg Calc.
PointsPlus value: *8.*

FYI   Browning the pork in a grill pan lends it an authentic smoky flavor.

PULLED PORK AND SLAW SANDWICHES

NORTH AFRICAN LAMB AND SQUASH STEW

North African Lamb and Squash Stew

serves 4

1 pound lean boneless lamb shoulder, trimmed and cut into 1½-inch chunks
3 large garlic cloves, minced
2 teaspoons ground cumin
½ teaspoon salt
¼ teaspoon cayenne
2 large carrots, cut into 1-inch chunks
1 large onion, chopped
2 large tomatoes, cut into 1-inch chunks
1 pound (1-inch chunks) peeled butternut squash
1 (14½-ounce) can reduced-sodium vegetable broth
½ cup frozen peas
8 small pimiento-stuffed green olives, sliced
¼ cup chopped fresh cilantro or mint
1 tablespoon lemon juice
2 cups hot cooked whole wheat couscous

1   Spray large nonstick skillet with nonstick spray and set over medium heat. Add lamb, in batches, and cook, until browned on all sides, about 6 minutes per batch. Add garlic, cumin, salt, and cayenne; cook 1 minute.

2   Put carrots and onion in 5- or 6-quart slow cooker. Add lamb and top with tomatoes and squash. Pour broth over. Cover and cook until lamb and vegetables are tender, 4–5 hours on high or 8–10 hours on low.

3   Stir in peas, olives, cilantro, and lemon juice. Cover and cook on high 10 minutes. Serve with couscous.

PER SERVING (1½ CUPS STEW AND ½ CUP COUSCOUS): 491 grams, 369 Cal, 10 g Total Fat, 4 g Sat Fat, 0 g Trans Fat, 89 mg Chol, 639 mg Sod, 41 g Carb, 9 g Sugar, 10 g Fib, 30 g Prot, 113 mg Calc. *PointsPlus* value: **9.**

Mustard and Herb–Rubbed Leg of Lamb

serves 6

2 teaspoons extra-virgin olive oil
2 pounds butterflied boneless leg of lamb, trimmed
2 tablespoons Dijon-style mustard
3 garlic cloves, minced
2 tablespoons chopped fresh rosemary
1 tablespoon chopped fresh thyme
½ teaspoon salt
¼ teaspoon black pepper
½ cup dry white wine or low-sodium beef broth

1   Heat 1 teaspoon of oil in large nonstick skillet over medium heat. Add lamb and cook until browned, about 8 minutes. Transfer lamb to cutting board, boned side down.

2   Mix together remaining 1 teaspoon oil, the mustard, garlic, rosemary, thyme, salt, and pepper in cup. Brush over top of lamb. Place lamb in 5- or 6-quart slow cooker.

3   Add wine to skillet and bring to boil, scraping up browned bits from bottom of pan. Pour wine mixture around lamb. Cover and cook until lamb is fork-tender, 3–4 hours on high or 6–8 hours on low.

4   Cut lamb into 12 slices.

PER SERVING (2 SLICES): 180 grams, 239 Cal, 9 g Total Fat, 3 g Sat Fat, 0 g Trans Fat, 97 mg Chol, 437 mg Sod, 2 g Carb, 0 g Sugar, 0 g Fib, 31 g Prot, 18 mg Calc. *PointsPlus* value: **6.**

▲ HEALTHY EXTRA

Turn this succulent lamb dish into a complete meal by serving it with baked tomato halves and steamed baby potatoes sprinkled with salt and grated lemon zest. One cooked 5-ounce potato per serving will increase the *PointsPlus* value by **3.**

Chicken in White Wine

serves 6

6 skinless chicken thighs, trimmed
½ teaspoon salt
¼ teaspoon black pepper
1 tablespoon olive oil
1½ cups thinly sliced green cabbage
1 onion, thinly sliced
1 cup baby-cut carrots
3 garlic cloves, peeled
1 cup dry white wine
½ cup reduced-sodium chicken broth
2 tablespoons tomato paste
⅓ cup water
2 tablespoons all-purpose flour

1   Sprinkle chicken with salt and pepper.
2   Heat oil in large nonstick skillet over medium heat. Add chicken and cook, until browned. Transfer to 5- or 6-quart slow cooker.
3   Add cabbage and onion to skillet; cook, stirring, until onion is softened, about 5 minutes. Transfer to slow cooker and top with carrots and garlic.
4   Whisk together wine, broth, and tomato paste in small bowl; pour over chicken. Cover and cook until chicken and carrots are fork-tender, 4–6 hours on high or 8–10 hours on low. Transfer chicken to deep platter.
5   Whisk together water and flour in small bowl until smooth. Whisk in about ¼ cup of hot stew liquid until blended, then stir flour mixture into slow cooker. Cover and cook on high until mixture bubbles and thickens, about 15 minutes. Spoon over chicken.

PER SERVING (1 CHICKEN THIGH AND ½ CUP VEGETABLES WITH SAUCE): 197 grams, 200 Cal, 8 g Total Fat, 2 g Sat Fat, 0 g Trans Fat, 49 mg Chol, 303 mg Sod, 9 g Carb, 3 g Sugar, 2 g Fib, 15 g Prot, 31 mg Calc.
PointsPlus value: **5.**

Curried Chicken with Vegetables

serves 6

2 teaspoons olive oil
2 large red onions, chopped
2 teaspoons curry powder
1 pound skinless boneless chicken breasts, cut into 1-inch pieces
3 small sweet potatoes (about 5 ounces each), peeled, halved lengthwise, and cut into ½-inch slices
1½ cups reduced-sodium vegetable broth
1 teaspoon salt
¼ teaspoon cayenne
1 (16-ounce) bag mixed frozen vegetables, thawed
3 cups hot cooked brown rice

1   Heat oil in large nonstick skillet over medium heat. Add onions and cook, stirring, until softened, about 5 minutes. Stir in curry powder and cook, stirring, until fragrant, about 1 minute longer.
2   Transfer onions to 5- or 6-quart slow cooker and top with chicken and potatoes.
3   Stir broth, salt, and cayenne into chicken mixture. Cover and cook until chicken and sweet potatoes are fork-tender, 4–6 hours on high or 8–10 hours on low.
4   About 20 minutes before cooking time is up, add thawed vegetables to slow cooker. Cover and cook on high until vegetables are tender, about 20 minutes longer.
5   Divide rice among 6 bowls and top evenly with curry mixture.

PER SERVING (1½ CUPS CURRY AND ½ CUP RICE): 340 grams, 300 Cal, 4 g Total Fat, 1 g Sat Fat, 0 g Trans Fat, 42 mg Chol, 485 mg Sod, 43 g Carb, 7 g Sugar, 5 g Fib, 20 g Prot, 60 mg Calc.
PointsPlus value: **7.**

Spiced Chicken Tagine

serves 6

3 large garlic cloves, peeled
½ teaspoon salt
3 zucchini, halved lengthwise and cut into
    ½-inch slices
1 (15½-ounce) can chickpeas, rinsed and
    drained
1 (14½-ounce) can diced tomatoes
1 cup reduced-sodium chicken broth
2 teaspoons ground ginger
1 teaspoon ground turmeric
1 teaspoon ground cinnamon
¼ teaspoon cayenne
6 bone-in chicken thighs, skinned and
    trimmed
1 (12-ounce) package whole wheat couscous

1   With side of large knife, mash together
garlic and salt until it forms a paste.
2   Combine zucchini, chickpeas, tomatoes,
broth, ginger, turmeric, cinnamon, cayenne,
and garlic paste in 5- or 6-quart slow cooker.
Add chicken and push it down into liquid.
Cover and cook until chicken is fork-tender,
4–6 hours on high or 8–10 hours on low.
3   About 20 minutes before cooking time is
up, cook couscous according to package
directions, omitting salt if desired.
4   Divide couscous among 6 plates and top
evenly with chicken. With slotted spoon, spoon
vegetable mixture over chicken. Discard liquid.

PER SERVING (1 CHICKEN THIGH, GENEROUS ¾ CUP
VEGETABLES, AND ¾ CUP COUSCOUS): 393 grams,
428 Cal, 8 g Total Fat, 2 g Sat Fat, 0 g Trans Fat,
49 mg Chol, 965 mg Sod, 65 g Carb, 5 g Sugar, 12 g Fib,
27 g Prot, 74 mg Calc.
PointsPlus value: *11.*

▲ HEALTHY EXTRA

End the meal on a sweet note by serving sliced
peaches sprinkled with sliced fresh mint.

Cioppino-Style Chicken

serves 8

8 chicken drumsticks (about 2¼ pounds),
    skinned
½ teaspoon salt
1 tablespoon olive oil
1 large onion, chopped
1 large red bell pepper, chopped
2 large celery stalks, thinly sliced
3 garlic cloves, minced
1 (14½-ounce) can petite diced tomatoes
1 cup dry white wine
¼ teaspoon red pepper flakes
¼ cup chopped fresh basil
2 tablespoons chopped fresh flat-leaf parsley

1   Sprinkle chicken with ¼ teaspoon of salt.
Heat oil in large nonstick skillet over medium
heat. Cook chicken, in batches, until browned
on all sides, about 8 minutes per batch.
Transfer chicken to 5- or 6-quart slow cooker.
2   Add onion, bell pepper, celery, and garlic
to skillet. Cook, stirring, until vegetables are
softened, about 5 minutes. Add vegetables,
tomatoes, wine, pepper flakes, and remaining
¼ teaspoon salt to slow cooker; mix well.
Cover and cook until chicken and vegetables
are fork-tender, 4–5 hours on high or
8–10 hours on low. Stir in basil and parsley.

PER SERVING (1 DRUMSTICK WITH ABOUT ⅓ CUP
SAUCE): 204 grams, 144 Cal, 4 g Total Fat, 1 g Sat Fat,
0 g Trans Fat, 48 mg Chol, 618 mg Sod, 7 g Carb,
3 g Sugar, 1 g Fib, 14 g Prot, 33 mg Calc.
PointsPlus value: *4.*

▲ HEALTHY EXTRA

Spooning this San Francisco–style chicken dish
over whole wheat pasta will make it heartier and
more satisfying (1 cup cooked whole wheat pasta
per serving will increase the *PointsPlus* value by *4*).

CHICKEN WITH MUSHROOMS AND SAGE

Chicken with Mushrooms and Sage

serves 6

1 (3½-pound) chicken, first two joints of
    wings discarded, cut into 6 pieces,
    and skinned
¾ teaspoon salt
¼ teaspoon black pepper
2 pounds leeks (white and light green parts
    only), halved lengthwise and sliced
½ pound cremini mushrooms, sliced
2 carrots, sliced
½ cup dry white wine or reduced-sodium
    chicken broth
4 teaspoons quick-cooking tapioca
1 teaspoon dried sage

1   Sprinkle chicken with ¼ teaspoon of salt
and ⅛ teaspoon of pepper. Spray large nonstick
skillet with nonstick spray and set over
medium heat. Add chicken, in batches, and
cook, turning, until browned, about 10 minutes
per batch.
2   Transfer chicken to 5- or 6-quart slow
cooker. Add leeks, mushrooms, and carrots
to skillet; cook, stirring occasionally, until
vegetables begin to soften, 4–5 minutes. Add
wine and cook about 2 minutes longer. Stir in
tapioca, sage, and remaining ½ teaspoon salt
and ⅛ teaspoon pepper.
3   Spoon vegetable mixture over chicken.
Cover and cook until chicken is fork-tender,
4–5 hours on high or 8–10 hours on low.

**PER SERVING (1 PIECE CHICKEN AND ½ CUP VEGETABLES
WITH ⅓ CUP BROTH):** 359 grams, 287 Cal, 4 g Total Fat,
1 g Sat Fat, 0 g Trans Fat, 89 mg Chol, 435 mg Sod,
28 g Carb, 8 g Sugar, 4 g Fib, 31 g Prot, 119 mg Calc.
PointsPlus value: **7.**

Kielbasa and Shrimp Jambalaya

serves 6

1 large onion, chopped
3 celery stalks, sliced
1 large green bell pepper, chopped
5 large garlic cloves, minced
2 teaspoons Creole seasoning
2 cups no-salt-added chicken broth
1 (14½-ounce) can no-salt-added diced
    tomatoes
½ pound turkey kielbasa, thinly sliced
1 cup long-grain white rice
1 pound medium shrimp, peeled and deveined

1   Combine onion, celery, bell pepper, garlic,
Creole seasoning, broth, and tomatoes in 5- or
6-quart slow cooker. Cover and cook until
vegetables are tender, 4–5 hours on high or
8–10 hours on low.
2   About 50 minutes before cooking time
is up, heat large nonstick skillet over medium
heat. Add kielbasa and cook, turning, until
browned, about 5 minutes.
3   Stir kielbasa and rice into slow cooker.
Cover and cook on high until rice is tender,
about 45 minutes. About 15 minutes before
rice is done, stir in shrimp. Cover and cook on
high until the shrimp are just opaque in center.

PER SERVING (ABOUT 1⅓ CUPS): 375 grams, 287 Cal,
5 g Total Fat, 1 g Sat Fat, 0 g Trans Fat, 179 mg Chol,
789 mg Sod, 33 g Carb, 5 g Sugar, 2 g Fib, 26 g Prot,
63 mg Calc.
PointsPlus value: **7.**

FYI   Here's an easy way to remove the seeds
and stem from a bell pepper: Stand the
pepper on a cutting board. With a large knife, slice
off the four "walls" of the pepper, then turn it on
its side and slice off the bottom.

NEW ORLEANS GUMBO

New Orleans Gumbo

serves 4

2½ tablespoons unsalted butter
3 tablespoons all-purpose flour
1 (14½-ounce) can no-salt-added diced
    tomatoes
1 (10-ounce) package frozen cut okra
1 cup no-salt-added chicken broth
1 small onion, chopped
1 small green bell pepper, diced
1 celery stalk, diced
2 teaspoons chopped fresh thyme or
    ¾ teaspoon dried thyme
1½ pounds large shrimp, peeled and deveined

1   Melt butter in small skillet over medium-high heat. Add flour and cook, stirring constantly with wooden spoon, until mixture turns reddish brown, about 5 minutes.
2   Combine butter mixture, tomatoes, okra, broth, onion, bell pepper, celery, and thyme in 5- or 6-quart slow cooker; mix well. Cover and cook until sauce thickens and vegetables are tender, 3–4 hours on high or 6–8 hours on low.
3   About 20 minutes before cooking time is up, stir shrimp into slow cooker. Cover and cook on high until shrimp are just opaque in center.

PER SERVING (ABOUT 1½ CUPS): 468 grams, 319 Cal, 10 g Total Fat, 5 g Sat Fat, 0 g Trans Fat, 357 mg Chol, 444 mg Sod, 16 g Carb, 7 g Sugar, 4 g Fib, 40 g Prot, 168 mg Calc.
PointsPlus value: *8.*

FYI   When fat and flour are cooked together it is called a roux (ROO). It is usually used to thicken soups and stews. A roux is cooked until white, light golden, or reddish brown, as in this gumbo. The longer it cooks, the richer its flavor and the more color it imparts to a dish.

Halibut and Tomato Stew

serves 8

1 (28-ounce) can diced tomatoes, drained
1 cup reduced-sodium vegetable broth
½ cup clam juice
¼ cup tomato paste
2 tablespoons red-wine vinegar
1 large onion, chopped
2 celery stalks, chopped
1 red bell pepper, chopped
3 garlic cloves, minced
1½ teaspoons Italian seasoning
1 teaspoon fennel seeds
½ teaspoon salt
¼ teaspoon red pepper flakes
¼ teaspoon black pepper
2 pounds halibut or monkfish, cut into
    1-inch chunks
1 pound escarole, thickly sliced

1   Combine tomatoes, broth, clam juice, tomato paste, vinegar, onion, celery, bell pepper, garlic, Italian seasoning, fennel seeds, salt, pepper flakes, and black pepper in 5- or 6-quart slow cooker; mix well. Cover and cook until sauce is simmering and tomatoes have softened, 2–3 hours on high.
2   Gently stir in halibut and escarole. Cover and cook on high until fish is just opaque in center, about 40 minutes longer.

PER SERVING (ABOUT 1¼ CUPS): 376 grams, 184 Cal, 3 g Total Fat, 0 g Sat Fat, 0 g Trans Fat, 37 mg Chol, 571 mg Sod, 12 g Carb, 6 g Sugar, 4 g Fib, 26 g Prot, 122 mg Calc.
PointsPlus value: *4.*

▲ **HEALTHY EXTRA**
Serve toasted slices of reduced-calorie whole wheat bread alongside each serving for sopping up the flavorful stew liquid (1 slice of reduced-calorie whole wheat bread per serving will increase the *PointsPlus* value by *1*).

Indian-Spiced Shrimp with Red Lentils

serves 6

2½ cups reduced-sodium chicken broth
1 cup red lentils, picked over, rinsed,
    and drained
1 large red onion, chopped
2 celery stalks, thinly sliced
2 tablespoons minced peeled fresh ginger
2 garlic cloves, minced
2 teaspoons ground cumin
1 teaspoon ground turmeric
½ teaspoon ground cinnamon
½ teaspoon black pepper
¼ teaspoon salt
2 pounds medium shrimp,
    peeled and deveined

1   Combine broth, lentils, onion, celery,
ginger, garlic, cumin, turmeric, cinnamon,
pepper, and salt in 5- or 6-quart slow cooker;
mix well. Cover and cook until bubbly and
aromatic, 2–3 hours on high or 4–6 hours
on low.
2   Stir in shrimp. Cover and cook on low
until shrimp are just opaque in center, about
15 minutes.

PER SERVING (ABOUT 1¼ CUPS): 331 grams, 300 Cal,
3 g Total Fat, 1 g Sat Fat, 0 g Trans Fat, 295 mg Chol,
491 mg Sod, 24 g Carb, 2 g Sugar, 6 g Fib, 43 g Prot,
100 mg Calc.
PointsPlus value: **7.**

FYI   Like your Indian food with a bit of heat?
Add ¼ teaspoon cayenne along with the
other spices in step 1.

Three Bean Chili

serves 6

1 (15½-ounce) can no-salt-added red kidney
    beans, rinsed and drained
1 (15½-ounce) can no-salt-added pinto
    beans, rinsed and drained
1 (14½-ounce) can no-salt-added
    diced tomatoes
1 cup frozen baby lima beans
1 (8-ounce) can tomato sauce
1 large onion, chopped
2 poblano peppers, chopped
4 garlic cloves, minced
2–4 tablespoons mild cayenne pepper sauce,
    such as Frank's
3 tablespoons chili powder
2 tablespoons honey
2 teaspoons ground cumin
¼ cup thinly sliced scallions

1   Combine kidney beans, pinto beans,
tomatoes, lima beans, tomato sauce, onion,
poblanos, garlic, pepper sauce, chili powder,
honey, and cumin in 5- or 6-quart slow cooker;
mix well. Cover and cook until vegetables are
fork-tender, 4–5 hours on high or 8–10 hours
on low.
2   Divide chili among 6 bowls and sprinkle
with scallions.

PER SERVING (ABOUT 1 CUP): 333 grams, 253 Cal,
2 g Total Fat, 0 g Sat Fat, 0 g Trans Fat, 0 mg Chol,
349 mg Sod, 49 g Carb, 12 g Sugar, 16 g Fib, 13 g Prot,
129 mg Calc.
PointsPlus value: **6.**

▲ HEALTHY EXTRA
Spoon this hearty meatless chili over brown rice
and sprinkle each serving with fat-free Cheddar
cheese (½ cup cooked brown rice and ¼ cup
shredded fat-free Cheddar cheese per serving will
increase the *PointsPlus* value by 4).

Vegetable Ragu with Pasta

serves 4

1 (14½-ounce) can diced tomatoes
¾ cup canned tomato sauce
¾ cup finely chopped white mushrooms
1 small onion, finely chopped
½ red bell pepper, finely chopped
1 small celery stalk, finely chopped
½ cup finely chopped fennel
1 large garlic clove, minced
1 teaspoon dried thyme
⅛ teaspoon black pepper
¼ cup reduced-fat (2%) milk
8 ounces whole wheat penne
¼ cup grated Parmesan cheese

1   Combine tomatoes, tomato sauce, mushrooms, onion, bell pepper, celery, fennel, garlic, thyme, and black pepper in 5- or 6-quart slow cooker. Cover and cook until vegetables are softened, about 3½ hours on low. Stir milk in and cook 30 minutes longer.

2   Meanwhile, cook pasta according to package directions, omitting salt if desired. Drain. Add pasta to ragu. Divide ragu-pasta mixture among 4 bowls; sprinkle with Parmesan.

PER SERVING (ABOUT 1½ CUPS WITH 1 TABLESPOON PARMESAN): 294 grams, 299 Cal, 4 g Total Fat, 1 g Sat Fat, 0 g Trans Fat, 6 mg Chol, 576 mg Sod, 55 g Carb, 9 g Sugar, 8 g Fib, 12 g Prot, 135 mg Calc. *PointsPlus* value: **7.**

▲ **HEALTHY EXTRA**
Start your meal off with a classic Italian salad of escarole dressed with fresh lemon juice and a sprinkling of black pepper and end with some fresh figs and a cup of espresso.

Tapioca Pudding with Vanilla and Raspberries

serves 6

2 cups low-fat (1%) milk
¾ cup fat-free half-and-half
⅓ cup + 2 tablespoons sugar
3 tablespoons quick-cooking tapioca
⅛ teaspoon salt
2 large eggs, separated
2 teaspoons vanilla extract
2 (6-ounce) containers fresh raspberries
Grated zest of ½ lemon

1   Combine milk, half-and-half, ⅓ cup of sugar, the tapioca, and salt in 4-quart slow cooker; mix well. Cover and cook 3 hours on high or 6 hours on low.

2   About 15 minutes before cooking time is up, whisk together egg yolks and vanilla in small bowl; stir in about ¼ cup of hot tapioca mixture until blended. Stir egg yolk mixture into slow cooker. Cover and cook on high until mixture simmers.

3   Meanwhile, with electric mixer on high, beat egg whites and 1 tablespoon of sugar in medium bowl until soft peaks form. Fold beaten egg whites into tapioca mixture until blended. Turn off slow cooker; cover and let stand about 5 minutes. Uncover and let pudding cool at least 15 minutes.

4   To serve, toss raspberries with lemon zest and remaining 1 tablespoon sugar. Divide tapioca pudding among 6 dessert dishes; top evenly with raspberry mixture.

PER SERVING (¾ CUP PUDDING AND ABOUT ⅓ CUP RASPBERRIES): 162 grams, 147 Cal, 2 g Total Fat, 1 g Sat Fat, 0 g Trans Fat, 74 mg Chol, 114 mg Sod, 27 g Carb, 16 g Sugar, 4 g Fib, 5 g Prot, 112 mg Calc. *PointsPlus* value: **4.**

Chocolate-Espresso Bread Pudding

serves 6

¾ cup low-fat (1%) milk
⅓ cup unsweetened cocoa
1 teaspoon instant espresso powder
1 ounce unsweetened chocolate, chopped
3 cups (¾-inch cubes) day-old firm
   white bread
1 cup fat-free half-and-half
2 large eggs, lightly beaten
1½ teaspoons vanilla extract
¾ cup packed light brown sugar

1   Whisk together milk, cocoa, and espresso powder in medium saucepan until blended. Add chocolate and set over medium heat. Cook, whisking constantly, until chocolate is melted, about 2 minutes. Remove saucepan from heat.

2   Put bread in 4-quart slow cooker.

3   Whisk together half-and-half, eggs, and vanilla in medium bowl until blended. Whisk egg mixture and brown sugar into chocolate mixture; pour over bread cubes and stir to coat well. Cover and cook until small knife inserted into center of pudding comes out clean, 2 hours on high or 4 hours on low. Serve warm or cold.

PER SERVING (¾ CUP): 129 grams, 217 Cal, 5 g Total Fat, 3 g Sat Fat, 0 g Trans Fat, 73 mg Chol, 107 mg Sod, 39 g Carb, 31 g Sugar, 2 g Fib, 6 g Prot, 132 mg Calc. *PointsPlus* value: **6.**

FYI If you prefer your chocolate desserts "straight," omit the espresso powder.

Lemon-Lime Cheesecake

serves 12

1½ tablespoons honey
⅔ cup chocolate wafer cookie crumbs
12 ounces light cream cheese (Neufchâtel),
   at room temperature
1 cup reduced-fat (2%) cottage cheese
½ cup sugar
1 tablespoon all-purpose flour
⅓ cup thawed lemonade concentrate
2 large egg whites + 1 egg yolk
1½ teaspoons grated lime zest

1   Spray 7-inch springform pan with nonstick spray. Put honey in medium microwavable bowl; microwave on High until honey is more fluid, about 15 seconds. Add crumbs; stir until moistened. Press onto bottom of pan. Place pan in 5- or 6-quart slow cooker (pan should not touch cooker).

2   Combine cream cheese, cottage cheese, sugar, and flour in food processor; pulse until blended. Add lemonade concentrate, egg whites, egg yolk, and lime zest; pulse until blended.

3   Pour batter over crust. Place double layer of paper towels on top of slow cooker, then place lid on top, pulling edges of towels taut so they don't touch batter. Cook 2 hours on high. Turn off slow cooker (do not uncover).

4   Let cheesecake stand until slow cooker is cool to touch, about 1 hour. Transfer cheese-cake to wire rack and let cool. Refrigerate until chilled, at least 2 hours.

PER SERVING (1/12 OF CAKE): 78 grams, 167 Cal, 8 g Total Fat, 4 g Sat Fat, 0 g Trans Fat, 40 mg Chol, 203 mg Sod, 19 g Carb, 15 g Sugar, 0 g Fib, 6 g Prot, 56 mg Calc. *PointsPlus* value: **5.**

FYI The paper towels absorb the moisture that accumulates inside the slow cooker.

LEMON-LIME CHEESECAKE

Carrot-Molasses Steamed Pudding

serves 12

²/₃ cup hot water
²/₃ cup chopped pitted dates
1²/₃ cups all-purpose flour
1 teaspoon baking powder
½ teaspoon baking soda
1 teaspoon ground cinnamon
⅓ cup unsalted butter, softened
½ cup packed light brown sugar
⅓ cup light molasses
1 large egg
¾ cup finely grated carrots

1   Spray 2-quart soufflé dish with nonstick spray. Place wire rack in 5- or 6-quart slow cooker.
2   Combine hot water and dates in glass measure. Whisk together flour, baking powder, baking soda, and cinnamon in bowl.
3   With electric mixer, beat butter, brown sugar, and molasses in bowl until light. Beat in egg. Stir in date mixture and carrots. Add flour mixture; scrape into pan.
4   Spray 12-inch square of heavy-duty foil with nonstick spray. Tightly cover springform pan with foil. Place in slow cooker. Add boiling water to come halfway up side of pan.
5   Cover and cook until toothpick inserted into center of pudding comes out clean, 3 hours on high. Turn off cooker; uncover and let cool. Remove pudding from slow cooker. Run knife around edge; unmold onto plate.

PER SERVING (¹⁄₁₂ OF PUDDING): 75 grams, 205 Cal, 6 g Total Fat, 3 g Sat Fat, 0 g Trans Fat, 31 mg Chol, 117 mg Sod, 37 g Carb, 22 g Sugar, 1 g Fib, 3 g Prot, 58 mg Calc.
PointsPlus value: **6.**

Apple-Cranberry Crisp

serves 8

2 tablespoons cold water
4 teaspoons cornstarch
½ cup packed brown sugar
4 Golden Delicious apples (about
      1½ pounds), peeled, cored, and sliced
1 cup fresh or thawed frozen cranberries
Grated zest of ½ lemon
1 tablespoon lemon juice
Pinch salt
1 tablespoon unsalted butter
¾ cup low-fat granola
2 tablespoons finely chopped walnuts

1   Stir together water and cornstarch in small bowl until smooth. Combine all but 1 tablespoon of brown sugar, the cornstarch mixture, apples, cranberries, lemon zest and juice, and salt in 4-quart slow cooker; mix well. With back of spoon, gently press apples to form even layer. Cover and cook until hot and bubbling, 2½ hours on high or 5 hours on low.
2   Transfer fruit mixture to serving dish; let cool 30 minutes.
3   Meanwhile, to make topping, combine butter and remaining 1 tablespoon brown sugar in medium microwavable bowl. Cook on High until butter is melted, about 15 seconds; stir until blended well. Stir in granola and walnuts until coated evenly with butter-sugar mixture. Sprinkle over fruit.

PER SERVING (ABOUT ⅓ CUP): 154 grams, 176 Cal, 4 g Total Fat, 1 g Sat Fat, 0 g Trans Fat, 4 mg Chol, 43 mg Sod, 38 g Carb, 28 g Sugar, 3 g Fib, 2 g Prot, 26 mg Calc.
PointsPlus value: **5.**

WeightWatchers®

NEW COMPLETE COOKBOOK

PAPPARDELLE WITH SHRIMP, PAGE 216

![WeightWatchers®]

NEW
COMPLETE
COOKBOOK

WILEY

JOHN WILEY & SONS, INC.

Published by John Wiley & Sons, Inc., Hoboken, New Jersey

Published simultaneously in Canada

For general information on our other products and services, or technical support, please contact our Customer Care Department within the United States at (800) 762-2974, outside the United States at (317) 572-3993 or fax (317) 572-4002.

Wiley publishes in a variety of print and electronic formats and by print-on-demand. Some material included with standard print versions of this book may not be included in e-books or in print-on-demand. If this book refers to media such as a CD or DVD that is not included in the version you purchased, you may download this material at http://booksupport.wiley.com. For more information about Wiley products, visit www.wiley.com.

For general information on our other products and services or to obtain technical support, please contact our Customer Care Department within the U.S. at 800-762-2974, outside the U.S. at 317-572-3993 or fax 317-572-4002.

Wiley also publishes its books in a variety of electronic formats. Some content that appears in print may not be available in electronic books.

COVER PHOTO Skillet Chicken with Cherry Tomatoes and Garlic (page 172)

Library of Congress Cataloging-in-Publication Data:

Weight Watchers new complete cookbook. -- Fourth edition bonus edition.
  pages cm
  Includes index.
  ISBN 978-1-118-47653-6 (loose-leaf), ISBN 978-1-118-47665-9 (ebk), ISBN 978-1-118-47666-6 (ebk), ISBN 978-1-118-47667-3 (ebk)
  1. Reducing diets--Recipes. 2. Low-calorie diet. I. Weight Watchers International. II. Title: New complete cookbook.
  RM222.2.W3218 2012b
  641.5'635--dc23

20120292453

Manufactured in China

10 9 8 7 6 5 4 3 2 1

ABOUT WEIGHT WATCHERS

Weight Watchers International, Inc. is the world's leading provider of weight-management services, operating globally through a network of company-owned and franchise operations. Weight Watchers holds nearly 45,000 meetings each week worldwide, at which members receive group support and education about healthful eating patterns, behavior modification, and physical activity. Weight-loss and weight-management results vary by individual. We recommend that you attend Weight Watchers meetings to benefit from the supportive environment and follow the comprehensive Weight Watchers program, which includes a food plan, an activity plan, and a behavioral component. **WeightWatchers.com** provides subscription weight management products, such as eTools and Weight Watchers Mobile and is the leading internet-based weight management provider in the world. In addition, Weight Watchers offers a wide range of products, publications (including **Weight Watchers Magazine** which is available on newsstands and in Weight Watchers meeting rooms), and programs for people interested in weight loss and control. For the Weight Watchers meeting nearest you, call **1-800-651-6000**. For information about bringing Weight Watchers to your workplace, call **1-800-8AT-WORK**.

Weight Watchers Publishing Group

VICE PRESIDENT, EDITORIAL DIRECTOR Nancy Gagliardi
CREATIVE DIRECTOR Ed Melnitsky
PHOTO DIRECTOR Deborah Hardt
MANAGING EDITOR Diane Pavia
FOOD EDITOR Eileen Runyan
EDITOR Deborah Mintcheff
NUTRITION CONSULTANTS Jacqueline Kroon and Patty Santelli
PHOTOGRAPHY Rita Maas, Romulo Yanes, Ann Stratton
FOOD STYLING Anne Disrude
PROP STYLING Lynda White

Wiley Publishing, Inc.

PUBLISHER Natalie Chapman
ASSOCIATE PUBLISHER Jessica Goodman
EXECUTIVE EDITOR Anne Ficklen
ASSISTANT EDITOR Charleen Barila
PRODUCTION MANAGER Michael Olivo
SENIOR PRODUCTION EDITOR Amy Zarkos
INTERIOR AND COVER DESIGNER Memo Productions, Inc.
MANUFACTURING MANAGER Kevin Watt

Contents

Introduction · *vii*

1   New Basics · 3

2   Breakfasts and Brunches · 35

3   Starters and Light Meals · 55

4   Salads—Sides and Main Dishes · 83

5   Soups—Starters and Main Dishes · 105

6   Beef, Pork, and Lamb · 131

7   Poultry · 163

8   Fish and Shellfish · 195

9   Vegetarian Main Dishes · 227

10 Vegetable Sides · 255

11 Grain and Bean Sides · 283

12 Slow-Cooker Classics · 305

13 Pizzas, Calzones, and Sandwiches · 321

14 Yeast Breads, Quick Breads, and Muffins · 343

15 Cakes, Pies, and More · 367

16 Fruit and Frozen Desserts, Puddings, and Sauces · 405

Index · *425*

Recipes by *PointsPlus* value · *434*

Introduction

Weight Watchers® is *the* world's leading provider of weight management services. For more than 45 years, the Weight Watchers program has been built on a consistently solid foundation of weight-loss science. This book, *Weight Watchers New Complete Cookbook*, is a comprehensive collection of over 500 delicious and nutrition-conscious recipes designed to help you follow the *PointsPlus*™ program—the latest program from Weight Watchers that has been scientifically proven to provide a weight-loss advantage. The following information about the basic philosophy of Weight Watchers—including our approach to weight loss (and the *PointsPlus* program), fitness, and behavior modification—can not only help you make the right choices for improving your overall health but also help your weight-loss efforts.

The Science Factor

The World Health Organization, the National Institute of Medicine, the National Institutes of Health, and the U.S. Surgeon General's Office—the most influential and knowledgeable organizations when it comes to weight and health issues—have convened panels of experts to evaluate the accumulated scientific research on these topics and condense it into reports identifying which methods are the most effective and nutritionally sound. Weight Watchers has embraced these reports, drawing from them and conducting extensive research of our own to devise an easy-to-learn and simple-to-follow weight-loss method.

While developing the *PointsPlus* program, as well as each of our previous programs, we've stayed committed to our members' well-being by never wavering from four principles:

1   Any program developed by Weight Watchers must promote healthy weight loss. This translates into a program designed to:
    - Produce a rate of weight loss of up to an average of two pounds per week after the first three weeks (when losses may be greater due to water loss).
    - Recommend food choices that not only are lower in calories but also meet current scientific guidelines for optimum nutrition in order to help reduce risk for chronic disease.
    - Construct a fitness and exercise plan that provides a full range of weight- and health-related benefits.
    - Maintain weight loss—the program goes beyond advising members how to *lose* excess weight and addresses how to keep it off as well.

2   In addition to being healthy, any Weight Watchers program must be realistic and practical, as well as livable and flexible. For example, each new member is encouraged to set a realistic goal—lose 5 percent to 10 percent of starting body weight—because a weight loss of just 10 percent translates into significant health benefits, and because modest starting goals in general help members experience success sooner.

3   Weight Watchers believes in imparting knowledge about its program, rather than shrouding it in mystery. Weight Watchers promotes such understanding, because it believes that members should learn not only what to do to lose weight but also why they are doing it. With this insight, people gain the confidence they need to make informed choices and to live by them.

4   Finally, again, every program created by Weight Watchers must be comprehensive. As mentioned, we do this by emphasizing changes in food intake, exercise habits, and other behaviors in a supportive environment.

And it's worked: Weight Watchers has helped millions of members lose weight. Our program is backed by scientific studies that have been published in well-known scientific journals, and has been recognized by the scientific community for that reason.*

Making It Work

It is often said that different paths can lead to the same destination, and this is never truer than when it refers to eating for healthy weight loss. Each person is unique when it comes to the foods that provide satisfaction, from preferred meals and times of day to dine, to food choices for sustained weight loss. Weight-loss success is all about finding a way to achieve the calorie deficit necessary for weight loss—that is, calories in versus calories out—without compromising one's lifestyle and preferences. That's why the program works: It gives Weight Watchers members the freedom to make their own choices while explaining the impact of each choice.

On the *PointsPlus* program, each member receives a personalized daily *PointsPlus* Target and each food has a *PointsPlus* value. *PointsPlus* values are calculated for foods based on their protein, fiber, fat, and carbohydrate content; the formula takes into account how these substances are processed by the body, for a complete picture of a food's impact on weight loss. To lose weight, a member simply tracks and tallies the *PointsPlus* values of foods he or she eats and does not exceed his or her daily *PointsPlus* Target.

PointsPlus values help members select foods that are satisfying and nutritious. And Weight Watchers Power Foods are filling, nutrient-packed *PointsPlus* value choices. Lower in sugar, saturated fat, and sodium, they're the best choices to help members meet the guidelines for good health.

Key Ingredients for Losing

Sustained weight loss comes not just from taking a holistic view of food, but also from taking a holistic view on healthy living in general. That's why the Weight Watchers program also includes physical activity, behavioral changes, and a supportive atmosphere.

Physical Activity: Weight Watchers provides members with a systematic approach to exercise during the entire weight-loss process. The levels and types of physical activity are based

---

*   Tsai AG, Wadden TA. (2005 Jan 4). Systematic review: an evaluation of major commercial weight loss programs in the United States. *Ann Intern Med. 142* (1):56–66.

on recommendations by the American College of Sports Medicine and the American Heart Association; we explain how to start with a safe amount of activity, and then build up to the amount necessary for weight maintenance.

Behavior: Lasting change begins on the inside and works its way out. The key to long-term weight management is figuring out which behaviors are getting in the way and learning how to develop constructive habits instead. To help members achieve this goal, based on exhaustive research, we've identified eight beneficial habits often possessed by successful members. New members take a quiz to determine which habits they should work on, and which they already have; all habits are discussed extensively in meetings. Plus, members receive another behavior booster at meetings: Weight Watchers Tools for Living. These techniques include strategies for helping to restructure internal thought processes in a way that enhances one's ability to make long-term behavioral changes.

Support: A member of Weight Watchers attends weekly meetings, which are conducted by a Weight Watchers Leader. All Leaders are successful members and have also undergone extensive training. In addition to being role models for current members, Leaders are sources of inspiration and information. Additional support is provided by other current members: Every Weight Watchers meeting is made up of people at different stages of their weight loss who are willing to share practical tips and talk about lessons learned from their experiences.

A Word About Weight Watchers Meetings

Weight Watchers meetings include a confidential weigh-in to monitor weight-loss progress; information about the *PointsPlus* program; and a discussion of a new topic related to basic

nutrition and good food choices, physical activity, or healthful habits. Many people who have achieved sustained weight loss with Weight Watchers tell us they believe attending meetings was the single biggest reason they were successful.

Why? Many people find that attending a weekly Weight Watchers meeting provides the structure necessary to maintain a high level of commitment. For example, the feelings of accountability that result from being weighed by another person also boost members' motivation. This is true not just for members who are losing weight, but also for members who are maintaining their weight losses. For this reason, Weight Watchers rewards certain successful members with Lifetime Membership. As long as a Lifetime Member weighs in monthly within two pounds of his or her weight goal, he or she can attend Weight Watchers meetings anywhere in the world at no cost. With this unique system, Weight Watchers can provide its Lifetime Members with the two things that predict sustained weight loss: continued weight monitoring and continued contact with those who supported their weight loss.

About Our Recipes

While losing weight isn't only about what you eat, Weight Watchers realizes the critical role it plays in your success and overall good health. That's why our philosophy is to offer great-tasting, easy recipes that are nutritious as well as delicious. We make every attempt to use wholesome ingredients and to ensure that our recipes fall within the recommendations of the U.S. Dietary Guidelines for Americans for a diet that promotes health and reduces the risk for disease. If you have special dietary needs, consult with your health-care professional for advice on a diet that is best for you and how to adapt these recipes to meet your specific nutritional needs.

To achieve these good-health goals and get the maximum satisfaction from the foods you eat, we suggest you keep the following information in mind while preparing our recipes.

The *PointsPlus*™ Program and Good Nutrition

- Recipes in this book have been developed for Weight Watchers members who are following the *PointsPlus* program. *PointsPlus* values are given for each recipe. They're assigned based on the amount of protein (grams), carbohydrates (grams), fat (grams), and fiber (grams), contained in a single serving of a recipe.

- Recipes include approximate nutritional information; they are analyzed for Calories (Cal), Total Fat, Saturated Fat (Sat Fat), Trans Fat, Cholesterol (Chol), Sodium (Sod), Total Carbohydrates (Total Carb), Total Sugar, Dietary Fiber (Fib), Protein (Prot), and Calcium (Calc). The nutritional values are calculated by registered dietitians, using nutrition analysis software.

- Substitutions made to the ingredients will alter the per-serving nutritional information and may affect the *PointsPlus* value.

- Our recipes meet Weight Watchers Good Health Guidelines for eating lean proteins and fiber-rich whole grains, and having at least five servings of vegetables and fruits and two servings of low-fat or fat-free dairy products a day, while limiting your intake of saturated fat, sugar, and sodium.

- Health agencies recommend limiting sodium intake. To stay in line with this recommendation, we keep sodium levels in our recipes reasonably low and, to boost flavor, we often include fresh herbs or a squeeze of citrus instead of salt. If you don't have to restrict your sodium, feel free to add a touch more salt as desired.

- ▲ Healthy Extra suggestions have a *PointsPlus* value of *0* unless otherwise stated.

- For more about the science behind lasting weight loss and other helpful information, please visit **weightwatchers.com/science**.

Shopping for Ingredients

As you learn to eat healthier and add more Power Foods to your meals, remember these tips for choosing foods wisely:

- Purchase lean meats and poultry, and trim them of all visible fat before cooking. When poultry is cooked with the skin on, we recommend removing the skin before eating. Nutritional information for recipes that include meat, poultry, and fish is based on cooked, skinless boneless portions (unless otherwise stated), with the fat trimmed.
- Whenever possible, our recipes call for seafood that is sustainable and deemed the most healthful for human consumption, so that your choice of seafood is not only good for the oceans but also good for you. For more information about the best seafood choices and to download a pocket guide, go to **montereybayaquarium.org** or **environmentaldefensefund.org**. For information about mercury and seafood go to **weightwatchers.com**.
- For best flavor, maximum nutrient content, and the lowest prices, buy fresh, local produce, such as vegetables, leafy greens, and fruits in season. Rinse them thoroughly before using and keep a supply of cut-up vegetables and fruits in your refrigerator for convenient, healthy snacks.
- Explore your market for whole grain products such as whole wheat and whole grain breads and pastas, brown rice, bulgur, barley, cornmeal, whole wheat couscous, oats, and quinoa to enjoy with your meals.

Preparation and Measuring

- Take a couple of minutes to read through the ingredients and directions before you start to prepare a recipe. This will prevent you from discovering midway through that you don't have an important ingredient or that the recipe requires several hours of marinating. And it's also a good idea to assemble all ingredients and utensils within easy reach before you begin a recipe.
- The success of any recipe depends on accurate weighing and measuring. The effectiveness of the Weight Watchers program and the accuracy of the nutritional analysis depend on correct measuring as well. Use the following techniques:
  - Weigh food such as meat, poultry, and fish on a food scale.
  - To measure liquids, use a standard glass or plastic measuring cup placed on a level surface. For amounts less than ¼ cup, use standard measuring spoons.
  - To measure dry ingredients, use metal or plastic measuring cups that come in ¼-, ⅓-, ½-, and 1-cup sizes. Fill the appropriate cup and level it with the flat edge of a knife or spatula. For amounts less than ¼ cup, use standard measuring spoons.

Icon Key

Basic
Intermediate
Advanced

New Basics

New Basics

4   Kitchen Tools
6   Healthy Pantry
8   Food Safety
10 How to Measure Ingredients
10 Sources

12 Classic Tomato Sauce
12 Spicy Tomato Sauce
13 No-Cook Summer Tomato Sauce
13 Roasted Tomato-Basil Sauce
14 Rich Cheese Sauce
14 Smoky Barbecue Sauce
16 Basil Pesto
17 Roasted Red Pepper Coulis
17 Chimichurri Sauce
18 Raita
18 Green Sauce
19 Tartar Sauce
19 Mango and Black Bean Salsa
21 Nectarine–Bell Pepper Salsa
21 Pico de Gallo
22 Cranberry-Walnut Relish
22 Mango Chutney
23 Basic Marinade
23 Hoisin-Ginger Marinade
24 Teriyaki Marinade
24 Dijon-Herb Marinade
25 Tandoori Yogurt Marinade
25 Citrus Marinade
26 Basic Dry Rub
26 Fennel, Lemon, and Black Pepper Rub
27 Cajun Dry Rub
27 Pepper Dry Rub
28 Jamaican Jerk Paste
28 Green Goddess Dressing
30 Italian Dressing
30 Honey-Mustard Dressing
30 Classic Vinaigrette
31 Asian Vinaigrette
31 Carrot-Ginger Dressing
32 Blue Cheese Dressing
32 Thousand Island Dressing

Kitchen Tools

With the right tools, any job is easier. When stocking your kitchen, buy the best-quality tools you can afford because you'll be using them almost every day.

Must Have

A **BOX GRATER** has a sturdy handle on top and four sides to finely or coarsely grate or shred vegetables, cheeses, and citrus zest.

A must-have tool for opening canned foods, the best-designed **CAN OPENERS** have a cushioned knob and handles for easy operation. Buy one with a stainless steel cutting blade.

Ideal for small amounts of juice, a **CITRUS REAMER** is a small cone-shaped tool with a pointed end and deep furrows. As a stand-in for a reamer, insert a fork into a lemon half and twist it to extract the juice.

A **COLANDER** lets you separate liquids from sol- ids. Use it for draining cooked pasta and vegetables, draining washed greens, or rinsing fresh berries.

COOLING RACKS allow air to circulate while baked goods cool. Round wire racks are good for cooling round cake layers. Large rectangular racks are perfect for cooling large quantities of cookies or large cakes.

Choose a **CUTTING BOARD** made of wood or plastic. Avoid ceramic, as it does not absorb the impact of the knife blade.

An **INSTANT-READ THERMOMETER** gives a temperature reading in a matter of seconds. The thermometer is inserted into the center of meat or poultry (without touching bone) to ensure that the food is cooked to the proper temperature (see page 9 for a chart of the minimum safe cooking temperatures).

KITCHEN SHEARS are ideal for cutting paper to line cake pans, cutting up raw chicken, clipping kitchen string, and mincing chives. Choose shears made of stainless steel.

To make sure your foods are cooked to the correct doneness, a **KITCHEN TIMER** is essential. Set the timer for the least amount of time to avoid overcooking.

Three **KNIVES** are essential: a **SMALL PARING KNIFE**, which is 3 to 4 inches long and used for peeling and slicing small foods; an 8- or 9-inch **CHEF'S KNIFE**, which is used for all basic chopping, dicing, and slicing; and a **SERRATED KNIFE**, for slicing bread.

A **LADLE** is essential for serving soup or stew or for adding broth to risotto without spilling.

To measure dry ingredients accurately, use a standard set of nesting **MEASURING** **CUPS** of ¼-, ⅓-, ½- and 1-cup sizes. To measure wet ingredients, use glass or plastic measuring cups. It is essential to have a 1-cup glass measure and nice to also have 2- and 4-cup measures.

MEASURING SPOONS come in nesting sets of ¼ teaspoon, ½ teaspoon, 1 teaspoon, and 1 tablespoon.

A **MEDIUM-SIZE WHISK** is a must-have for whipping up egg whites, mixing salad dressings, producing smooth gravies and sauces, and making pancake and quick-bread batters.

Nesting glass or stainless steel **MIXING BOWLS** are the workhorses of any kitchen. Plastic bowls are not recommended as they absorb both flavor and fat.

Use a **PASTRY BRUSH** for glazing breads and pastries, brushing syrup over warm cakes and muffins, or for basting meats and poultry.

There are several styles of **POTATO MASHERS**; all make quick work of mashing potatoes and other root vegetables.

ROLLING PINS come with and without handles: both styles work well. The heavier the pin, the less effort it takes to roll out dough.

A plastic **SALAD SPINNER** uses centrifugal force to remove most of the water from washed greens, herbs, or fresh berries. They are available in several sizes.

Use a coarse-mesh **SIEVE** for sifting flour, cocoa, and confectioners' sugar and a fine-mesh sieve for straining stocks and separating fruit purees from their seeds. It's a good idea to have a few sizes.

A **SLOTTED SPOON** makes it easy to lift a piece of pasta or a vegetable from boiling water to test for doneness.

SPATULAS come in different shapes for different tasks. A flat, wide metal spatula is good for turning fish, and a rubber spatula is best for mixing batters. A silicone (heatproof) spatula has the flexibility of a rubber spatula and can withstand temperatures up to 800°F.

SPRING-LOADED TONGS are the best tool for lifting and moving food and can be locked shut for easy storage. Use silicone-tipped tongs to prevent scratching nonstick cookware.

A **SWIVEL-BLADED VEGETABLE PEELER** makes quick work of peeling fruits and vegetables without removing too much peel or skin.

Have a few **WOODEN SPOONS** in your kitchen. They don't transfer heat, so your hand stays cool while stirring. And they won't scratch your pots.

Nice to Have

Perfect for making pan gravy, a **FAT SEPARATOR** has a sharply angled spout set at the base. The fat floats to the top of the separator so you can pour off the fat-free pan juices, leaving the fat behind.

A **GARLIC PRESS** is a hinged tool that squeezes garlic into smaller pieces than can be achieved by mincing.

Also called a vegetable slicer, the **MANDOLINE** is a sharp-bladed countertop tool that slices, cuts french fries, and juliennes firm fruits and vegetables.

The curved wires of a **PASTRY BLENDER**, a classic baking tool, easily cut butter and vegetable shortening into dry ingredients for biscuits, scones, and pie crusts, ensuring a flaky result.

Originally made for woodworkers to smooth the rough edges of wood, the handy **RASP GRATER** can be used for grating citrus zest, whole nutmeg, chocolate, and hard cheeses.

Healthy Pantry

Use these charts as a guide to storing staples safely. If a food doesn't have a sell-by date, affix a label to the package and mark the date you bought it so you'll know when it's past its prime.

SHELF STAPLES

FOOD	STORAGE TIME	STORAGE TIPS
Canned tuna and salmon	Unopened, 1 year; opened, 2 days refrigerated	After opening, immediately transfer to an airtight container and refrigerate.
Canned beans	Unopened, 1 year; opened, 3 days refrigerated	After opening, refrigerate in an airtight container; do not keep in the original can.
Brown rice (including basmati and jasmine)	6 months	Brown rice still has its nutritious bran layer intact. Because of the oil in the bran, brown rice will not keep as long as white rice.
Whole wheat pasta	1 year	Store in the original container in a cool, dry place.
Barley	6 months	For longer storage, store in an airtight container in the refrigerator for up to 1 year.
Oats	6 months	Store in the original container in a cool, dark place.
Whole wheat couscous	6 months	If you live in a humid climate, store in an airtight container.
Dried beans and lentils	1 year	Store in their original plastic bag. Never store in the refrigerator; beans can absorb moisture and spoil.
Honey, maple syrup, molasses	2 years	If sugar crystals form, place the container in warm water and stir until the crystals dissolve.
All-purpose flour	1 year at room temperature; up to 2 years frozen	Store in a cool, dry place.
Whole wheat flour	1–3 months at room temperature; 6 months refrigerated; 1 year frozen	Transfer to an airtight container to preserve its moisture content.
Granulated and confectioners' sugar	2 years	To protect against humidity, store in an airtight container.
Light and dark brown sugar	4–6 months	Brown sugar dries out quickly; store in an airtight container after opening the package.

FOOD	STORAGE TIME	STORAGE TIPS
Baking powder, baking soda	12–18 months	Store tightly covered in a cool, dry place.
Unsweetened cocoa	1 year	Store at room temperature in the original container.
Chocolate chips, baking chocolate	1 year	Store all chocolate in a cool, dry place. A white film sometimes appears on the surface caused by temperature fluctuations; it does not affect the taste or quality.
Nuts	Unopened can or jar, 1 year; opened, 3 months	Store in an airtight container.

REFRIGERATOR STAPLES

FOOD	STORAGE TIME	STORAGE TIPS
Pickles, olives, capers	Unopened, 1 year; opened, 1–2 months refrigerated	Keep the jar tightly capped; discard if salt crystals accumulate at the top of the jar.
Salsa	Unopened, 1 year; opened, 1 month refrigerated	If mold forms around the edge of the salsa, discard the entire jar.
Mustard, ketchup	Unopened, 1 year; opened, 3 months refrigerated	Since these condiments contain acid, they are less prone to spoilage and can be stored in the door (the warmest part) of the refrigerator.
Reduced-fat and fat-free mayonnaise	Unopened, 1 year; opened, 2 months refrigerated	For best quality and freshness, always check the "use-by" date on mayonnaise.
Reduced-sodium soy sauce	Unopened, 1 year; opened, 6 months refrigerated	Always store opened soy sauce in the refrigerator to preserve its flavor.
Worcestershire sauce	Unopened, 1 year; opened, 6 months refrigerated	Wipe off the bottle after each use to prevent drips in the refrigerator.
Jellies and jams	Unopened, 1 year; opened, 6 months refrigerated	Wipe off the rim of the jar before replacing the lid after each use to prevent sticky buildup.
Whole wheat tortillas	2 months	After opening, store tightly sealed in the original package in the refrigerator.

FREEZER STAPLES

FOOD	STORAGE TIME	STORAGE TIPS
Steaks and roasts	2–3 days refrigerated; 6–8 months frozen	Freeze in zip-close plastic freezer bags to maintain the maximum freshness.
Ground beef	1–2 days refrigerated; 3–4 months frozen	Always label and date so you eat the beef before it starts losing quality.
Pork chops	2–3 days refrigerated; 4–6 months frozen	Buy chops in a single-layer tray; freeze on the tray. Remove the packaging and put the frozen chops in a zip-close plastic freezer bag; return to the freezer. They will keep as individual servings.
Skinless, boneless chicken breasts	1–2 days refrigerated; 9 months frozen	Individually wrap chicken breasts in heavy-duty foil for easy thawing.
Skinless fish fillets	1 day refrigerated; 3 months frozen	Place fish in a sealed container in the refrigerator to stop the juices from dripping on other foods.
Peeled shrimp	1–2 days refrigerated; 3 months frozen	Don't freeze fresh shrimp. Most likely, they have already been frozen and thawed for retail sale.
Frozen fruits and vegetables	9 months	Store in the original bag or box.

Food Safety

Safe food handling starts at the grocery store and continues as you prepare food at home. At every step you need to minimize risk for contamination and food-borne illnesses. Here are a few guidelines to help keep you and your family safe.

Shop Wisely

- Place meats, poultry, and seafood inside plastic bags from the produce department before adding them to your cart. This prevents juices from dripping onto other foods and spreading bacteria.

- Open egg cartons to make sure the eggs are clean and that none of them have cracks. Inspect the eggs again once you get home and discard any that may have been damaged during transport.

- Inspect packaging on all foods. Make sure meat and poultry are tightly wrapped and fresh-cut vegetables are in sealed packages. Avoid canned foods that have dents, rust, or bulges. Squeeze frozen foods to ensure they are frozen solid.

Prep Smart

- Wash all fresh produce—even if the label says "prewashed"—before eating. Place greens in a large bowl of cold water and lift them out to drain in a colander. Place vegetables such as broccoli, cauliflower, green beans, and baby carrots in a colander and rinse under cold running water. Scrub sturdy produce such as apples, potatoes, and celery with a brush.
- Do not wash produce with soap or detergent. These products are not approved for use on food, and may leave residues.
- Always marinate foods in the refrigerator.

Clean Up

- Always wash your hands thoroughly before beginning any food preparation.
- Use hot, soapy water and a dishcloth to clean countertops and appliances. Wash dishcloths and towels often in hot water.

On Board

- Keep two cutting boards: one for meats, poultry, and seafood and one for produce.
- Either wood or plastic cutting boards are acceptable. Wash them in hot, soapy water after each use and dry thoroughly. To sanitize cutting boards, wash them in a solution of 1 tablespoon bleach mixed with 1 gallon of water.

Thaw Safely

- **Slow and Sure:** Thawing in the refrigerator is the safest method of defrosting foods. Count on about 12 hours to thaw 1 pound of steak, ground beef, pork chops, chicken, or shrimp.
- **Faster:** You can thaw a 1-pound portion of food in about 2 hours in cold water. To do so, place the food in a zip-close plastic bag with a watertight seal. Submerge the bag in cold water and change the water every 30 minutes until the food is thawed. Cook the food immediately after thawing.
- **Fastest:** To thaw food in the microwave, follow the manufacturer's directions. The thawing time will depend on the amount of food and the wattage of your microwave. Cook any food thawed in the microwave immediately.

Minimum Safe Cooking Temperatures

- Use an instant-read thermometer to ensure that cooked foods have reached a safe temperature.
- Insert the thermometer into the center of the food (without touching bone in roasts or poultry) to get an accurate reading. Follow the minimum safe cooking temperatures in the chart below.
- Wash the stem of the thermometer with hot, soapy water after each use.

TYPE OF FOOD	TEMPERATURE
Ground beef, pork, and lamb	160°F
Beef and lamb steaks, chops, or roasts	145°F (medium) 160°F (well-done)
Pork chops or roast	160°F
Fresh ham	160°F
Fully cooked ham (to reheat)	140°F
Chicken or turkey, whole, parts, or ground	165°F
Egg dishes	160°F
Leftovers and casseroles	165°F

How to Measure Ingredients

Here's some invaluable information about measuring so you'll get consistent results every time you cook or bake.

BUTTER The wrapper that butter comes in is premarked for tablespoons, ¼ cup, ⅓ cup, and ½ cup, so there is no need to measure it.

DRY INGREDIENTS Use standard dry measuring cups that come in nesting sets of ¼, ⅓, ½, and 1 cup. To measure flour, first stir it to aerate, then lightly spoon it into the desired size cup to overflowing. Level it off with the straight edge of a knife.

LIQUIDS Place a glass measuring cup with a spout on the counter and add the desired amount of liquid. Bend down to check the amount at eye level.

SOLID FATS AND BROWN SUGAR Use standard dry measuring cups. Firmly pack the ingredient into the cup, then level it off with the straight edge of a knife.

SPICES, HERBS, CITRUS ZEST, AND EXTRACTS Use standard measuring spoons that come in nesting sets of ¼, ½, and 1 teaspoon and 1 tablespoon. Fill the desired spoon with the ingredient, then level it off with the straight edge of a knife, if needed.

YOGURT AND SOUR CREAM Use standard dry measuring cups. Spoon the ingredient into a cup, and level it off with a rubber spatula.

Sources

Here are some reliable Web sites from leading resources for cooks everywhere.

ASIAN FOOD GROCER
1-888-482-2742 / www.asianfoodgrocer.com
miso, dried noodles, nori, panko, sushi rice, Sriracha

BOB'S RED MILL
1-800-553-2258 / www.bobsredmill.com
cereal, organic and non-organic flour, whole grains, seeds

D'ARTAGNAN
1-800-327-8246 / www.dartagnan.com
buffalo, duck, venison

KALUSTYAN'S
1-800-352-3451 / www.kalustyans.com
chili powder, citron, extracts and essences, flatbread, dried fruit, dried herbs, dried mushrooms, dried noodles, nuts, oil, saffron, spices, vinegar

KING ARTHUR FLOUR
1-800-827-6836 / www.kingarthurflour.com
bar chocolate, chocolate chips, cocoa, organic and non-organic flour (including white whole wheat), yeast

LOS CHILEROS DE NUEVO MEXICO
1-888-EAT-CHILE / www.loschileros.com
organic and non-organic dried chiles, chili powder, chipotles en adobo

PENZEYS SPICES
1-800-741-7787 / www.penzeys.com
dried whole chile peppers, chile powder, extracts and essences, filé powder, dried herbs, herbes de Provence, spices, vanilla beans

THE SPANISH TABLE
1-505-986-0243 / www.spanishtable.com
sweet, hot, and smoked paprika, paella pans, paella rice, saffron

WILLIAMS-SONOMA
1-877-812-6235 / www.williams-sonoma.com
herbes de Provence, Parmigiano-Reggiano, balsamic vinegar, demi-glace

THE RECIPES

Classic Tomato Sauce

serves 12

1 tablespoon extra-virgin olive oil
2 onions, chopped
4 garlic cloves, minced
2 (28-ounce) cans plum tomatoes, drained
    and broken up
1/4 cup tomato paste
1 teaspoon dried oregano
1 teaspoon salt
1/2 teaspoon black pepper

1   Heat oil in Dutch oven over medium heat.
Add onions and garlic; cook, stirring, until onions soften, about 5 minutes.
2   Add all remaining ingredients and bring
to boil. Reduce heat and simmer, partially
covered, until flavors are blended and sauce is
slightly thickened, about 25 minutes. Use or
refrigerate in covered container up to 5 days.

PER SERVING (½ CUP): 121 grams, 41 Cal, 1 g Total Fat,
0 g Sat Fat, 0 g Trans Fat, 0 mg Chol, 355 mg Sod,
7 g Total Carb, 4 g Total Sugar, 1 g Fib, 1 g Prot,
38 mg Calc.
PointsPlus value: *1*

▲ HEALTHY EXTRA

Spoon this classic tomato sauce over whole wheat
spaghetti for an easy and satisfying weeknight
supper (1 cup of cooked whole wheat spaghetti
with each serving will increase the *PointsPlus*
value by 4).

Spicy Tomato Sauce

serves 6

1 tablespoon extra-virgin olive oil
3 large garlic cloves, minced
1/4–1/2 teaspoon red pepper flakes
1 (28-ounce) can whole tomatoes in juice,
    drained and broken up
1/2 teaspoon salt
1/4 teaspoon black pepper

1   Heat oil in large saucepan over medium
heat. Add garlic and pepper flakes; cook, stirring, until garlic is fragrant, about 30 seconds.
2   Add all remaining ingredients to pot and
bring to boil. Reduce heat and simmer, partially
covered, until flavors are blended and sauce is
slightly thickened, about 20 minutes. Use or
refrigerate in covered container up to 5 days.

PER SERVING (½ CUP): 137 grams, 48 Cal, 3 g Total Fat,
0 g Sat Fat, 0 g Trans Fat, 0 mg Chol, 390 mg Sod,
6 g Total Carb, 3 g Total Sugar, 1 g Fib, 1 g Prot,
43 mg Calc.
PointsPlus value: *1*

FYI   Although the addition of red pepper flakes
is what makes this tomato sauce special, it
is also delicious without the added heat.

No-Cook Summer Tomato Sauce

serves 4

1 garlic clove, peeled
½ teaspoon salt
5 tomatoes, halved, seeded, and chopped
1 small red onion, chopped
2 tablespoons chopped fresh basil
1 tablespoon extra-virgin olive oil
1 teaspoon grated lemon zest
¼ teaspoon black pepper

1   With side of large knife, mash garlic with salt on cutting board until it forms a paste.
2   Stir together garlic paste and all remaining ingredients in medium bowl. Use or refrigerate in covered container up to 1 day.

PER SERVING (ABOUT ⅔ CUP): 202 grams, 79 Cal, 4 g Total Fat, 1 g Sat Fat, 0 g Trans Fat, 0 mg Chol, 298 mg Sod, 10 g Total Carb, 6 g Total Sugar, 2 g Fib, 2 g Prot, 32 mg Calc.
PointsPlus value: *2*

▲ HEALTHY EXTRA
Summer tomatoes give this sauce its great flavor. Enjoy it over broiled or grilled chicken breasts. A 3-ounce portion of cooked skinless, boneless chicken breast per serving will increase the *PointsPlus* value by *3*.

Roasted Tomato-Basil Sauce

serves 5

3 pounds plum tomatoes, quartered
     lengthwise
1 large sweet onion, such as Vidalia,
     thinly sliced
2 large garlic cloves, minced
¾ teaspoon salt
½ teaspoon dried oregano
¼ teaspoon black pepper
6 large fresh basil leaves, torn

1   Place racks in upper and lower thirds of oven. Preheat oven to 375°F. Spray 2 large non-stick baking pans with olive oil nonstick spray.
2   Divide tomatoes, onion, and garlic evenly between prepared pans. Sprinkle evenly with salt, oregano, and pepper; lightly spray with nonstick spray. Toss to mix well.
3   Roast, stirring once or twice, until tomatoes and onion are lightly browned and give off an intense, sweet aroma, about 50 minutes, rotating pans after 25 minutes.
4   Let vegetables cool slightly. Pulse in food processor, in batches, until slightly chunky. Use or refrigerate in covered container for up to 5 days.

PER SERVING (½ CUP): 298 grams, 69 Cal, 1 g Total Fat, 0 g Sat Fat, 0 g Trans Fat, 0 mg Chol, 374 mg Sod, 15 g Total Carb, 9 g Total Sugar, 4 g Fib, 3 g Prot, 24 mg Calc.
PointsPlus value: *2*

FYI   The natural sweetness of a Vidalia onion makes it the perfect complement for the tangy-sweet flavor of ripe tomatoes. If Vidalia—or other sweet onions—are not available, use 2 large yellow onions instead and sprinkle them with ½ teaspoon sugar.

Rich Cheese Sauce

serves 6

½ cup evaporated fat-free milk
3 tablespoons all-purpose flour
¾ cup low-fat (1%) milk
2 teaspoons Dijon mustard
½ teaspoon salt
½ cup shredded reduced-fat sharp
    Cheddar cheese
¼ teaspoon black pepper

1   Whisk together evaporated milk and flour in medium saucepan until smooth. Whisk in low-fat milk, mustard, and salt until blended. Bring to simmer over medium heat; cook, stirring, until slightly thickened, about 4 minutes.
2   Stir in Cheddar and pepper. Remove saucepan from heat and stir until cheese is melted and sauce is smooth. Use or refrigerate in covered container up to 3 days.

PER SERVING (3 TABLESPOONS): 68 grams, 76 Cal, 3 g Total Fat, 2 g Sat Fat, 0 g Trans Fat, 9 mg Chol, 56 mg Sod, 7 g Total Carb, 4 g Total Sugar, 0 g Fib, 6 g Prot, 170 mg Calc.
PointsPlus value: *2*

FYI   For a bit more zing, add a pinch of cayenne to the sauce along with the black pepper in step 2.

Smoky Barbecue Sauce

serves 8

1 tablespoon olive oil
1 onion, finely chopped
1 garlic clove, minced
2 cups ketchup
3 tablespoons dark brown sugar
1 tablespoon cider vinegar
1 tablespoon dark molasses
1 teaspoon chili powder
1 teaspoon dry mustard
½ teaspoon smoked paprika
¼ teaspoon ground ginger
⅛ teaspoon cayenne

1   Heat oil in medium saucepan over medium heat. Add onion and garlic; cook, stirring, until onion is softened, about 5 minutes.
2   Stir in all remaining ingredients and bring to boil. Reduce heat and simmer, covered, until sauce is thickened, about 10 minutes. Use or refrigerate in covered container up to 5 days.

PER SERVING (¼ CUP): 93 grams, 116 Cal, 2 g Total Fat, 0 g Sat Fat, 0 g Trans Fat, 0 mg Chol, 719 mg Sod, 26 g Total Carb, 15 g Total Sugar, 1 g Fib, 1 g Prot, 28 mg Calc.
PointsPlus value: *3*

FYI   If you prefer your barbecue sauce with more heat, increase the amount of chili powder and cayenne to taste.

SMOKY BARBECUE
SAUCE

TOASTING NUTS

1   *Preheat oven or toaster oven to 350°F.*

2   *Spread nuts in single layer in shallow baking pan.*

3   *Bake, shaking pan occasionally, until nuts are lightly browned and fragrant. Transfer nuts to plate to avoid overbrowning.*

Basil Pesto
serves 6

2 cups lightly packed fresh basil leaves (about 1 bunch)
3 tablespoons pine nuts
2 tablespoons water
1 tablespoon extra-virgin olive oil
2 garlic cloves, minced
¼ teaspoon salt
½ cup + 2 tablespoons grated Parmesan cheese

Combine all ingredients except Parmesan in food processor or blender and puree. Add cheese and pulse to mix. Transfer pesto to jar with tight-fitting lid; spray top of pesto with olive oil nonstick spray to prevent browning. Refrigerate up to 3 weeks.

PER SERVING (SCANT 3 TABLESPOONS): 35 grams, 87 Cal, 7 g Total Fat, 2 g Sat Fat, 0 g Trans Fat, 7 mg Chol, 253 mg Sod, 2 g Total Carb, 1 g Total Sugar, 1 g Fib, 5 g Prot, 140 mg Calc.
PointsPlus value: *2*

FYI   Here's a way to ensure that this pesto remains bright green. Plunge the whole basil leaves into a medium saucepan of boiling water for 1 minute to set the color. Drain and rinse under cold running water, then pat dry with paper towels. Follow the recipe as directed.

Roasted Red Pepper Coulis

serves 4

3 large red bell peppers
1 tablespoon extra-virgin olive oil
3 garlic cloves, minced
4 large fresh basil leaves, torn
2 teaspoons sherry vinegar
½ teaspoon salt
⅛ teaspoon black pepper

1   Preheat broiler. Line rack of broiler pan with foil.

2   Cut bell peppers in half; remove and discard seeds. Place peppers, cut side down, on prepared pan. Broil 5 inches from heat, without turning, until skin is blackened, about 10 minutes. Transfer peppers to large zip-close plastic bag; seal and let steam 10 minutes.

3   When cool enough to handle, peel peppers and cut into large pieces; transfer to food processor.

4   Heat oil in small skillet over medium heat. Add garlic and cook until fragrant, about 30 seconds. Add garlic and all remaining ingredients to food processor and puree. Use or refrigerate in covered container up to 2 days.

PER SERVING (¼ CUP): 132 grams, 67 Cal, 4 g Total Fat, 1 g Sat Fat, 0 g Trans Fat, 0 mg Chol, 294 mg Sod, 9 g Total Carb, 3 g Total Sugar, 3 g Fib, 1 g Prot, 17 mg Calc.
PointsPlus value: *2*

FYI   To give this versatile sauce a smoky flavor, add a drop or two of hickory liquid smoke to the food processor in step 4.

Chimichurri Sauce

serves 4

½ cup chopped fresh flat-leaf parsley
¼ cup chopped fresh cilantro
2 tablespoons chopped fresh basil
1 tablespoon olive oil
1 tablespoon red wine vinegar
1 pickled jalapeño pepper, seeded and minced

Stir together all ingredients in small bowl until mixed well. Serve at once or refrigerate in covered container up to 4 days.

PER SERVING (2 TABLESPOONS): 20 grams, 34 Cal, 3 g Total Fat, 1 g Sat Fat, 0 g Trans Fat, 0 mg Chol, 53 mg Sod, 1 g Total Carb, 0 g Total Sugar, 0 g Fib, 0 g Prot, 13 mg Calc.
PointsPlus value: *1*

FYI   Add some tomato goodness to this already flavorful chimichurri by stirring in 1 or 2 finely chopped moist-packed sun-dried tomatoes (not packed in oil).

Raita
serves 12

2 cups plain low-fat yogurt
2 cucumbers, peeled, seeded, shredded, and
    squeezed dry
½ jalapeño pepper, seeded and thinly sliced
2 tablespoons chopped fresh mint
1 teaspoon ground cumin
¾ teaspoon salt
¼ teaspoon ground coriander
¼ teaspoon black pepper

1   Spoon yogurt into coffee filter or cheese-cloth-lined sieve set over medium bowl; let stand until liquid drains off, about 20 minutes. Discard liquid.
2   Stir together strained yogurt and all remaining ingredients in medium bowl. Serve at once or refrigerate in covered container up to 1 day.

PER SERVING (¼ CUP): 90 grams, 33 Cal, 1 g Total Fat, 0 g Sat Fat, 0 g Trans Fat, 3 mg Chol, 176 mg Sod, 4 g Total Carb, 3 g Total Sugar, 1 g Fib, 3 g Prot, 85 mg Calc.
PointsPlus value: *1*

FYI   In India, raitas are served as a cooling counterbalance to the spicier offerings of a meal.

Green Sauce
serves 12

1 bunch watercress, trimmed
¾ cup reduced-fat mayonnaise
2 tablespoons chopped fresh flat-leaf parsley
1 teaspoon Dijon mustard
1 teaspoon lemon juice
½ teaspoon grated lemon zest
Pinch salt
Pinch black pepper

Put watercress in food processor and pulse until finely chopped. Transfer to serving bowl. Stir in all remaining ingredients until mixed well. Serve at once or refrigerate in covered container up to 3 days.

PER SERVING (1 TABLESPOON): 22 grams, 51 Cal, 5 g Total Fat, 1 g Sat Fat, 0 g Trans Fat, 5 mg Chol, 145 mg Sod, 1 g Total Carb, 0 g Total Sugar, 0 g Fib, 0 g Prot, 9 mg Calc.
PointsPlus value: *1*

FYI   If you have other fresh herbs on hand, such as basil or thyme, consider adding them to the sauce for additional flavor.

Tartar Sauce

serves 12

³/₄ *cup reduced-fat mayonnaise*
1 small shallot, finely chopped
1 tablespoon finely chopped fresh flat-leaf
    parsley
1 tablespoon finely chopped cornichons or
    gherkins
¹/₄ *teaspoon cornichon or gherkin liquid*
¹/₄ *teaspoon grated lemon zest*
Pinch black pepper

Stir together all ingredients in small bowl until
mixed well. Serve at once or refrigerate in
covered container up to 4 days.

PER SERVING (GENEROUS 1 TABLESPOON): 19 grams,
51 Cal, 5 g Total Fat, 1 g Sat Fat, 0 g Trans Fat,
5 mg Chol, 130 mg Sod, 1 g Total Carb, 0 g Total Sugar,
0 g Fib, 0 g Prot, 1 mg Calc.
PointsPlus value: *1*

▲ HEALTHY EXTRA

Tartar sauce is the perfect accompaniment for
cooked cod fillets. A 3-ounce portion of cooked
cod fillet with each serving will increase the
PointsPlus value by *2*.

Mango and Black Bean Salsa

serves 4

1 mango, peeled, pitted, and diced
1 small red onion, diced
¹/₂ *red bell pepper, diced*
¹/₂ *cup fresh or thawed frozen corn kernels*
¹/₂ *cup canned black beans, rinsed and*
    drained
2 tablespoons chopped fresh cilantro
2 tablespoons lime juice
¹/₄ *teaspoon sugar*
¹/₄ *teaspoon salt*
¹/₈ *teaspoon black pepper*

Stir together all ingredients in medium bowl
until mixed well. Cover and refrigerate at
least 30 minutes to allow flavors to blend. Use
within 1 day.

PER SERVING (ABOUT ¾ CUP): 136 grams, 88 Cal,
1 g Total Fat, 0 g Sat Fat, 0 g Trans Fat, 0 mg Chol,
208 mg Sod, 20 g Total Carb, 9 g Total Sugar, 4 g Fib,
2 g Prot, 21 mg Calc.
PointsPlus value: *2*

FYI Here's how to cut up a mango: Stand a
mango on its side. With a long, sharp knife,
cut off a lengthwise slice, cutting close to the pit.
Repeat on the other side. Cut the flesh into ¼-inch
dice, being careful not to cut through the skin.
Turn the mango halves inside out to separate the
cubes, then cut the cubes from the skin.

Nectarine–Bell Pepper Salsa

serves 6

3 small nectarines, pitted and diced
1 red bell pepper, diced
2 tablespoons chopped fresh cilantro
2 teaspoons olive oil
1 teaspoon lime juice
¼ teaspoon salt
⅛ teaspoon cayenne

Stir together all ingredients in small bowl until mixed well. Cover and refrigerate at least 30 minutes to allow flavors to blend. Use within 1 day.

PER SERVING (⅓ CUP): 91 grams, 52 Cal, 2 g Total Fat, 0 g Sat Fat, 0 g Trans Fat, 0 mg Chol, 98 mg Sod, 9 g Total Carb, 7 g Total Sugar, 2 g Fib, 1 g Prot, 6 mg Calc.
PointsPlus value: *1*

FYI You can substitute peaches for the nectarines and a yellow or orange bell pepper for the red pepper, if you like.

Pico de Gallo

serves 6

1 garlic clove, minced
½ teaspoon salt
2 large green heirloom or red tomatoes, halved, seeded, and finely chopped
1 small onion, finely chopped
¼ cup chopped fresh cilantro
1–2 jalapeño peppers, seeded and finely chopped
2 teaspoons lime juice

1   With side of large knife, mash garlic with salt on cutting board until it forms a paste.
2   Stir together garlic paste and all remaining ingredients in small bowl until mixed well. Cover and refrigerate at least 30 minutes to allow flavors to blend. Use within 1 day.

PER SERVING (⅓ CUP): 73 grams, 17 Cal, 0 g Total Fat, 0 g Sat Fat, 0 g Trans Fat, 0 mg Chol, 200 mg Sod, 4 g Total Carb, 2 g Total Sugar, 1 g Fib, 1 g Prot, 6 mg Calc.
PointsPlus value: *0*

▲   **HEALTHY EXTRA**
Spoon the salsa into Belgian endive leaves.

←
FROM TOP: NECTARINE–BELL PEPPER SALSA, MANGO AND BLACK BEAN SALSA (PAGE 19), PICO DE GALLO

Cranberry-Walnut Relish

serves 10

1 (12-ounce) bag fresh or thawed frozen
    cranberries
1 navel orange, unpeeled, cut into large
    chunks and seeds discarded
1/3 cup sugar
1 small red apple, unpeeled, cored, and
    finely chopped
1/4 cup chopped walnuts

Combine cranberries, orange, and sugar in
food processor and pulse until finely chopped.
Transfer to serving bowl. Stir in apple and
walnuts. Serve at once or refrigerate in covered
container up to 4 days.

PER SERVING (GENEROUS ¼ CUP): 68 grams, 75 Cal,
2 g Total Fat, 0 g Sat Fat, 0 g Trans Fat, 0 mg Chol,
1 mg Sod, 15 g Total Carb, 12 g Total Sugar, 2 g Fib,
1 g Prot, 12 mg Calc.
PointsPlus value: *2*

▲ HEALTHY EXTRA

Try this relish with slices of roasted turkey breast
the day after Thanksgiving. Two 2-ounce slices of
skinless roasted turkey breast with each serving
will increase the *PointsPlus* value by *4*.

Mango Chutney

serves 8

1 mango, peeled, pitted, and diced
1/2 Vidalia or other sweet onion, chopped
3/4 cup cider vinegar
1/2 cup sugar
1/2 cup golden raisins
4 dried California apricots, chopped
2 tablespoons dried currants
1 teaspoon grated lime zest
2 teaspoons lime juice
1 teaspoon grated peeled fresh ginger
1/2 (3-inch) cinnamon stick
3/4 teaspoon salt
1/4 teaspoon ground nutmeg
1/4 teaspoon ground allspice

1   Combine mango, onion, and vinegar in
heavy medium saucepan and bring to boil. Reduce heat and simmer until mango and onion
are cooked down slightly, about 15 minutes.
2   Stir all remaining ingredients into saucepan; return mixture to boil. Reduce heat and
simmer, stirring occasionally, until chutney is
thickened, about 45 minutes. Discard cinnamon stick. Serve at once or refrigerate in covered container up to 1 week.

PER SERVING (2 TABLESPOONS): 87 grams, 116 Cal,
0 g Total Fat, 0 g Sat Fat, 0 g Trans Fat, 0 mg Chol,
222 mg Sod, 30 g Total Carb, 28 g Total Sugar, 2 g Fib,
1 g Prot, 15 mg Calc.
PointsPlus value: *3*

Basic Marinade

serves 4

1 tablespoon olive oil
1 onion, thinly sliced
1 small carrot, thinly sliced
2 garlic cloves, thinly sliced
1 cup dry red wine
6 black peppercorns
2 fresh thyme sprigs or ½ teaspoon dried
    thyme
1 bay leaf

1   Heat oil in medium nonstick saucepan
over medium heat. Add onion, carrot, and garlic; cook, stirring, until onion is softened, about
5 minutes.
2   Add all remaining ingredients to saucepan;
bring to boil. Boil until slightly reduced, about
8 minutes. Pour marinade through sieve set
over medium bowl, pressing hard on solids to
extract as much liquid as possible; discard solids. Use or refrigerate in covered container up
to 4 days.

PER SERVING (¼ CUP): 52 grams, 54 Cal, 4 g Total Fat,
1 g Sat Fat, 0 g Trans Fat, 0 mg Chol, 6 mg Sod,
5 g Total Carb, 3 g Total Sugar, 1 g Fib, 1 g Prot,
16 mg Calc.
PointsPlus value: *2*

FYI   This piquant red wine–based marinade is
ideal for flavoring beef, lamb, chicken,
or pork. Be sure to cool the marinade completely
before combining it with meat. Marinate, covered,
in the refrigerator at least several hours or up to
overnight for a more intense flavor.

Hoisin-Ginger Marinade

serves 4

½ cup ketchup
2 tablespoons hoisin sauce
2 tablespoons reduced-sodium soy sauce
2 tablespoons unseasoned rice vinegar
1 (1-inch) piece fresh ginger, peeled and
    finely chopped
2 garlic cloves, minced

Stir together all ingredients in small bowl
until mixed well. Use or refrigerate in covered
container up to 1 week.

PER SERVING (2 TABLESPOONS): 58 grams, 57 Cal,
0 g Total Fat, 0 g Sat Fat, 0 g Trans Fat, 0 mg Chol,
788 mg Sod, 13 g Total Carb, 3 g Total Sugar, 1 g Fib,
1 g Prot, 11 mg Calc.
PointsPlus value: *1*

Teriyaki Marinade

serves 6

¼ *cup reduced-sodium soy sauce*
¼ *cup orange juice*
1 *tablespoon honey*
1 *tablespoon dark brown sugar*
1 *teaspoon Asian (dark) sesame oil*
1 *garlic clove, minced*
1 *tablespoon minced peeled fresh ginger*

Combine all ingredients in jar with tight-fitting lid; cover and shake well. Use or refrigerate up to 5 days.

PER SERVING (1½ TABLESPOONS): 30 grams, 39 Cal,
1 g Total Fat, 0 g Sat Fat, 0 g Trans Fat, 0 mg Chol,
405 mg Sod, 7 g Total Carb, 6 g Total Sugar, 0 g Fib,
1 g Prot, 4 mg Calc.
PointsPlus value: *1*

FYI This very flavorful marinade can take pork chops, salmon, shrimp, and chicken from plain to fabulous without a lot of effort.

Dijon-Herb Marinade

serves 6

2 *tablespoons olive oil*
2 *tablespoons Dijon mustard*
1 *tablespoon water*
1½ *teaspoons red wine vinegar*
2 *tablespoons finely chopped fresh rosemary*
1 *large shallot, finely chopped*
2 *garlic cloves, minced*
¾ *teaspoon dried oregano*

Combine all ingredients in small jar with tight-fitting lid; cover and shake well. Use or refrigerate up to 5 days.

PER SERVING (ABOUT 1½ TABLESPOONS): 17 grams,
50 Cal, 5 g Total Fat, 1 g Sat Fat, 0 g Trans Fat,
0 mg Chol, 127 mg Sod, 1 g Total Carb, 0 g Total Sugar,
0 g Fib, 1 g Prot, 15 mg Calc.
PointsPlus value: *1*

FYI Feel free to substitute other fresh herbs for the rosemary, including fresh thyme, tarragon, or chives.

Tandoori Yogurt Marinade

serves 4

1 small onion, coarsely chopped
4 garlic cloves, peeled
2 tablespoons minced peeled fresh ginger
1 tablespoon lemon juice
1 cup plain low-fat yogurt
1 teaspoon turmeric
$^1/_2$ teaspoon ground coriander
$^1/_2$ teaspoon ground cumin
$^1/_2$ teaspoon salt
$^1/_4$ teaspoon ground cinnamon
$^1/_4$ teaspoon black pepper
$^1/_8$ teaspoon ground cardamom
$^1/_8$ teaspoon ground cloves

Combine onion, garlic, ginger, and lemon juice in food processor or blender and puree. Add remaining ingredients and pulse until mixed well. Use or refrigerate in covered container up to 2 days.

PER SERVING ($^1/_3$ CUP): 83 grams, 55 Cal, 1 g Total Fat, 1 g Sat Fat, 0 g Trans Fat, 4 mg Chol, 336 mg Sod, 8 g Total Carb, 5 g Total Sugar, 1 g Fib, 4 g Prot, 128 mg Calc.
PointsPlus value: **1**

Tandoori marinades are best for adding flavor to chicken, lamb, or pork. Marinate for at least 4 hours or up to overnight.

Citrus Marinade

serves 4

$^1/_3$ cup orange or grapefruit juice
2 tablespoons chopped fresh flat-leaf parsley
2 tablespoons lemon or lime juice
1 tablespoon extra-virgin olive oil
1 teaspoon dried thyme
1 garlic clove, minced
$^1/_4$ teaspoon black pepper

Combine all ingredients in small jar with tight-fitting lid; cover and shake well. Use or refrigerate up to 5 days.

PER SERVING (ABOUT 2 TABLESPOONS): 35 grams, 44 Cal, 4 g Total Fat, 1 g Sat Fat, 0 g Trans Fat, 0 mg Chol, 2 mg Sod, 4 g Total Carb, 2 g Total Sugar, 0 g Fib, 0 g Prot, 14 mg Calc.
PointsPlus value: **1**

FYI Citrus and shellfish is a great combination. Use this marinade to flavor up peeled and deveined shrimp or scallops, then grill just until opaque in the center.

Basic Dry Rub

serves 12

3 tablespoons dark brown sugar
1 tablespoon chili powder
1 tablespoon ground cumin
1 tablespoon paprika
2 teaspoons dried oregano
2 teaspoons garlic powder
2 teaspoons onion powder
2 teaspoons salt

Combine all ingredients in small jar with tight-fitting lid. Use or store at room temperature up to 2 months.

PER SERVING (1 TABLESPOON): 7 grams, 22 Cal, 0 g Total Fat, 0 g Sat Fat, 0 g Trans Fat, 0 mg Chol, 397 mg Sod, 5 g Total Carb, 3 g Total Sugar, 1 g Fib, 0 g Prot, 16 mg Calc.
PointsPlus value: *0*

FYI This delicious all-purpose rub is as flavorful as it is easy to prepare. Stir up a double or triple batch so you have lots on hand whenever you need it.

Fennel, Lemon, and Black Pepper Rub

serves 4

1 garlic clove, minced
¼ teaspoon salt
1 tablespoon fennel seeds
1½ teaspoons black peppercorns
1 tablespoon grated lemon zest
2 teaspoons lemon juice
2 teaspoons olive oil

1   With side of large knife, mash garlic with salt on cutting board until it forms a paste.
2   Combine fennel seeds and peppercorns in spice grinder and process until finely ground. Transfer to small bowl. Add garlic paste and remaining ingredients, stirring until mixed well. Use or refrigerate in covered container up to 1 day.

PER SERVING (1 TABLESPOON): 10 grams, 30 Cal, 3 g Total Fat, 0 g Sat Fat, 0 g Trans Fat, 0 mg Chol, 143 mg Sod, 2 g Total Carb, 0 g Total Sugar, 1 g Fib, 0 g Prot, 24 mg Calc.
PointsPlus value: *1*

Cajun Dry Rub

serves 12

1 tablespoon black pepper
1 tablespoon white pepper
1 tablespoon dried thyme
1 tablespoon paprika
2 teaspoons dry mustard
2 teaspoons garlic powder
1 teaspoon salt
1/4–1/2 teaspoon cayenne

Combine all ingredients in small jar with tight-fitting lid. Use or store at room temperature up to 2 months.

PER SERVING (ROUNDED 1 TEASPOON): 4 grams, 10 Cal, 0 g Total Fat, 0 g Sat Fat, 0 g Trans Fat, 0 mg Chol, 195 mg Sod, 2 g Total Carb, 0 g Total Sugar, 1 g Fib, 1 g Prot, 13 mg Calc.
PointsPlus value: *0*

FYI Our robust rub is just like those used for Louisiana's famous blackened dishes, most notably, blackened redfish. Spread it on fish, shellfish, chicken, pork, or vegetables before grilling, broiling, or sautéing for a deeply flavored dark crust.

Pepper Dry Rub

serves 6

2 tablespoons cracked black peppercorns
2 tablespoons cracked white peppercorns
2 teaspoons ground coriander
2 teaspoons dark brown sugar
1 teaspoon salt
1/4 teaspoon red pepper flakes

Combine all ingredients in small jar with tight-fitting lid. Use or store at room temperature up to 2 months.

PER SERVING (2 TEASPOONS): 10 grams, 19 Cal, 0 g Total Fat, 0 g Sat Fat, 0 g Trans Fat, 0 mg Chol, 458 mg Sod, 4 g Total Carb, 2 g Total Sugar, 1 g Fib, 0 g Prot, 18 mg Calc.
PointsPlus value: *0*

FYI This dry rub, the perfect blend of salty, sweet, hot, and spicy, is excellent on steak, pork, and lamb chops.

Jamaican Jerk Paste

serves 4

3 Scotch bonnet or habanero peppers, seeded
    and coarsely chopped
6 scallions, sliced
3 tablespoons lime juice
1 tablespoon dark brown sugar
1 tablespoon minced peeled fresh ginger
1 tablespoon reduced-sodium soy sauce
1 tablespoon canola oil
2 garlic cloves, minced
1 teaspoon dried thyme
1 teaspoon ground allspice
½ teaspoon ground cinnamon
¼ teaspoon ground nutmeg

Combine all ingredients in blender or mini
food processor; pulse until it forms a coarse
paste. Use or refrigerate in covered container
up to 1 week.

PER SERVING (2 TABLESPOONS): 57 grams, 64 Cal,
4 g Total Fat, 0 g Sat Fat, 0 g Trans Fat, 0 mg Chol,
157 mg Sod, 8 g Total Carb, 4 g Total Sugar, 1 g Fib,
1 g Prot, 34 mg Calc.
PointsPlus value: *2*

FYI In the Jamaican tradition of jerk cooking,
pork or chicken is rubbed with a fiery spice
paste. It is then "jooked" with a stick to enable
the spices to penetrate the meat. The mix of
spices depends on the cook, but the blend usually
includes allspice, thyme, nutmeg, and intensely
hot Scotch bonnet or habanero peppers.

Green Goddess Dressing

serves 6

½ cup low-fat (1%) cottage cheese
¼ cup lightly packed tender watercress sprigs
    or fresh flat-leaf parsley leaves
3 tablespoons fat-free milk
2 tablespoons lemon juice
1 tablespoon snipped fresh dill
1 tablespoon snipped fresh chives
1 tablespoon reduced-fat mayonnaise
1 small garlic clove, minced
½ teaspoon anchovy paste

Combine all ingredients in blender and pulse
until smooth. Thin with 1 or 2 tablespoons of
water, if needed. Transfer dressing to small
bowl. Refrigerate, covered, at least 1 hour to
allow flavors to blend. Use or refrigerate in
covered container up to 2 days.

PER SERVING (2 TABLESPOONS): 37 grams, 28 Cal,
1 g Total Fat, 0 g Sat Fat, 0 g Trans Fat, 2 mg Chol,
229 mg Sod, 2 g Total Carb, 1 g Total Sugar, 0 g Fib,
3 g Prot, 29 mg Calc.
PointsPlus value: *1*

FYI Green Goddess Dressing was invented in
San Francisco's Palace Hotel in the 1920s
to commemorate a hit play of the same name. If
you're not a fan of anchovy, don't worry; the paste
adds a subtle layer of flavor without a trace of
fishiness.

GREEN GODDESS DRESSING

Italian Dressing

serves 4

¼ *cup reduced-sodium chicken broth*
1 *tablespoon chopped fresh basil*
1 *tablespoon white wine vinegar*
2 *teaspoons extra-virgin olive oil*
½ *teaspoon grated lemon zest*
½ *teaspoon salt*
1 *small garlic clove, minced*
¼ *teaspoon sugar*
¼ *teaspoon dried oregano, crumbled*
⅛ *teaspoon black pepper*

Combine all ingredients in small jar with tight-fitting lid. Cover and shake well. Use or refrigerate up to 1 week.

PER SERVING (2 TABLESPOONS): 21 grams, 26 Cal, 2 g Total Fat, 0 g Sat Fat, 0 g Trans Fat, 0 mg Chol, 298 mg Sod, 1 g Total Carb, 0 g Total Sugar, 0 g Fib, 0 g Prot, 6 mg Calc.
PointsPlus value: **1**

Honey-Mustard Dressing

serves 4

½ *cup plain fat-free yogurt*
4 *teaspoons Dijon mustard*
4 *teaspoons honey*
1 *tablespoon snipped fresh dill*
2 *teaspoons white wine vinegar*
½ *teaspoon sugar*
⅛ *teaspoon salt*
⅛ *teaspoon black pepper*

Combine all ingredients in small jar with tight-fitting lid. Cover and shake well. Use or refrigerate up to 1 week.

PER SERVING (3 TABLESPOONS): 44 grams, 43 Cal, 1 g Total Fat, 0 g Sat Fat, 0 g Trans Fat, 0 mg Chol, 216 mg Sod, 10 g Total Carb, 8 g Total Sugar, 0 g Fib, 2 g Prot, 46 mg Calc.
PointsPlus value: **2**

Classic Vinaigrette

serves 4

3 *tablespoons water*
2 *tablespoons balsamic vinegar*
2 *tablespoons red wine vinegar*
4 *teaspoons extra-virgin olive oil*
1 *heaping teaspoon Dijon mustard*
1 *shallot, minced*
1 *small garlic clove, minced*
½ *teaspoon salt*
¼ *teaspoon black pepper*

Combine all ingredients in small jar with tight-fitting lid; cover and shake well. Use or refrigerate up to 1 week.

PER SERVING (2 TABLESPOONS): 38 grams, 50 Cal, 5 g Total Fat, 1 g Sat Fat, 0 g Trans Fat, 0 mg Chol, 326 mg Sod, 2 g Total Carb, 1 g Total Sugar, 0 g Fib, 0 g Prot, 7 mg Calc.
PointsPlus value: **2**

FYI This vinaigrette is great on salads, but it also doubles as a tasty marinade for chicken or pork.

Asian Vinaigrette

serves 4

3 tablespoons reduced-sodium chicken broth
2 tablespoons unseasoned rice vinegar
1 tablespoon reduced-sodium soy sauce
2 teaspoons canola oil
2 teaspoons Asian (dark) sesame oil
1 teaspoon sugar
1 teaspoon minced peeled fresh ginger

Combine all ingredients in small jar with tight-fitting lid. Cover and shake well. Use or refrigerate up to 1 week.

PER SERVING (SCANT 2 TABLESPOONS): 27 grams,
49 Cal, 5 g Total Fat, 1 g Sat Fat, 0 g Trans Fat,
0 mg Chol, 155 mg Sod, 1 g Total Carb, 1 g Total Sugar,
0 g Fib, 0 g Prot, 1 mg Calc.
PointsPlus value: *1*

FYI Toss this Asian-inspired vinaigrette with packaged coleslaw mix, a handful of matchstick-cut carrots, and a sprinkling of chopped fresh parsley.

Carrot-Ginger Dressing

serves 8

$^1/_3$ cup shredded carrots
$^1/_4$ cup chopped shallots
2 teaspoons grated peeled fresh ginger
3 tablespoons seasoned rice vinegar
2 tablespoons water
1 teaspoon Asian (dark) sesame oil
$^1/_2$ teaspoon reduced-sodium soy sauce

Put carrots in mini food processor and pulse until finely ground. Add shallots and ginger; pulse until finely ground. Add vinegar and pulse until mixed. Transfer dressing to small bowl; stir in all remaining ingredients. Can be refrigerated in covered container up to 4 days.

PER SERVING (GENEROUS 1 TABLESPOON): 21 grams,
16 Cal, 1 g Total Fat, 0 g Sat Fat, 0 g Trans Fat,
0 mg Chol, 126 mg Sod, 3 g Total Carb, 2 g Total Sugar,
0 g Fib, 0 g Prot, 3 mg Calc.
PointsPlus value: *1*

FYI Use this boldly flavored dressing on coleslaw or mixed-green salads.

Blue Cheese Dressing

serves 6

1/2 cup low-fat buttermilk
2 tablespoons reduced-fat mayonnaise
1/2 cup reduced-fat crumbled blue cheese
2 teaspoons snipped fresh chives
1 small garlic clove, minced
Pinch cayenne

Whisk together buttermilk and mayonnaise in small bowl until smooth. Stir in all remaining ingredients. Use or refrigerate in covered container up to 3 days.

PER SERVING (2 TABLESPOONS): 38 grams, 65 Cal, 5 g Total Fat, 3 g Sat Fat, 0 g Trans Fat, 11 mg Chol, 219 mg Sod, 2 g Total Carb, 1 g Total Sugar, 0 g Fib, 3 g Prot, 84 mg Calc.
PointsPlus value: *2*

▲ HEALTHY EXTRA

Spoon this decadent dressing over thick wedges of iceberg lettuce surrounded by halved cherry tomatoes and sliced radishes.

Thousand Island Dressing

serves 4

3 tablespoons orange juice
3 tablespoons reduced-fat mayonnaise
2 tablespoons minced green bell pepper
2 tablespoons minced red bell pepper
2 tablespoons tomato paste
2 tablespoons plain fat-free yogurt
1 tablespoon drained prepared horseradish
1 tablespoon grated onion
1 teaspoon Dijon mustard
1/2 teaspoon chili powder
1/4 teaspoon black pepper

Combine all ingredients in small jar with tight-fitting lid. Cover and shake well. Use or refrigerate up to 4 days.

PER SERVING (1/4 CUP): 51 grams, 60 Cal, 4 g Total Fat, 1 g Sat Fat, 0 g Trans Fat, 4 mg Chol, 146 mg Sod, 5 g Total Carb, 3 g Total Sugar, 1 g Fib, 1 g Prot, 17 mg Calc.
PointsPlus value: *2*

FYI As the story goes, this popular dressing was created by the chef of the Drake Hotel in Chicago in the early part of the last century. When his wife saw the lumpy dressing, she commented that it resembled the Thousand Islands near Ontario, New York.

2

Breakfasts and Brunches

Breakfasts and Brunches

36   **Whole Grain French Toast**

36   **Stuffed French Toast**

38   **Whole Wheat–Buttermilk Waffles**

39   **Basic Pancakes**

41   **Walnut-Raisin Granola**

41   **Mixed Grain Porridge**

42   **Baked Fruit–Cinnamon Oatmeal**

42   **Scrambled Eggs with Smoked Salmon and Dill**

43   **Basic Omelette**

44   **Vegetable Scrambled Eggs**

44   **Roman Rice Frittata**

45   **Potato-Onion Frittata**

46   **Shrimp, Mushroom, and Tomato Frittata**

46   **Fried Eggs Tex Mex–Style**

47   **Tomato, Parmesan, and Egg–Topped Pizza**

49   **Creamy Ham and Arugula Crêpes**

49   **Crêpes**

50   **Greek Pita Pizzas with Spinach and Feta**

50   **Breakfast Tostadas**

52   **Cheese Quiche**

52   **Spinach and Cheese Quiche**

Whole Grain French Toast

serves 4

1 cup reduced-fat (2%) milk
¾ cup fat-free egg substitute
½ teaspoon vanilla extract
¼ teaspoon ground cinnamon
Pinch salt
8 slices whole grain bread

1   Whisk together milk, egg substitute, vanilla, cinnamon, and salt in shallow bowl or pie plate.
2   Generously spray large nonstick griddle or skillet with nonstick spray and set over medium heat.
3   Dip bread, 1 slice at a time, into milk mixture, turning to coat well on each side. Cook dipped bread, in batches if needed, until well browned, about 4 minutes per side, spraying griddle with nonstick spray between batches.

PER SERVING (2 SLICES FRENCH TOAST): 156 grams, 188 Cal, 4 g Total Fat, 2 g Sat Fat, 0 g Trans Fat, 4 mg Chol, 348 mg Sod, 26 g Total Carb, 6 g Total Sugar, 4 g Fib, 12 g Prot, 142 mg Calc. *PointsPlus* value: **5**

FYI   Be sure to thoroughly soak each slice of bread in the milk mixture, and cook it until well browned and slightly crisp on each side.

Stuffed French Toast

serves 4

⅓ cup dried cherries, chopped
1 tablespoon dark rum
8 slices challah or other egg bread
1 tablespoon finely chopped almonds
1 large egg
2 large egg whites
¼ cup low-fat buttermilk
1 teaspoon confectioners' sugar

1   Combine cherries and rum in cup; let soak about 10 minutes, stirring once or twice.
2   Meanwhile, spray nonstick baking sheet with nonstick spray and place in oven. Preheat oven to 400°F.
3   Place 4 slices of bread in shallow baking pan in single layer. Stir almonds into cherry mixture; sprinkle evenly over bread. Top each slice of bread with second slice of bread. Beat together egg, egg whites, and buttermilk in 2-cup glass measure. Pour evenly over stuffed bread, then turn bread over to coat evenly. Let stand 10 minutes, pressing edges of bread together to seal.
4   With wide spatula, transfer stuffed bread to preheated prepared baking sheet. Bake 10 minutes; turn over and bake until French toast is well browned and cooked through, about 6 minutes. Dust with confectioners' sugar.

PER SERVING (1 STUFFED TOAST): 144 grams, 319 Cal, 7 g Total Fat, 2 g Sat Fat, 0 g Trans Fat, 95 mg Chol, 457 mg Sod, 49 g Total Carb, 9 g Total Sugar, 3 g Fib, 13 g Prot, 111 mg Calc. *PointsPlus* value: **8**

FYI   If you don't happen to have a nonstick baking sheet, line a regular baking sheet with nonstick foil.

Whole Wheat– Buttermilk Waffles

serves 4

$^2/_3$ *cup whole wheat flour*
$^1/_4$ *cup all-purpose flour*
$^3/_4$ *teaspoon baking powder*
$^1/_2$ *teaspoon baking soda*
$^1/_4$ *teaspoon salt*
1 cup low-fat buttermilk
$^1/_4$ *cup fat-free egg substitute*
2 teaspoons canola oil
$^1/_4$ *cup pure maple syrup*

1   Spray waffle baker with nonstick spray. Preheat according to manufacturer's directions.
2   Whisk together whole wheat flour, all-purpose flour, baking powder, baking soda, and salt in medium bowl. Whisk together butter-milk, egg substitute, and oil in small bowl. Add buttermilk mixture to flour mixture, stirring just until batter is smooth.
3   When waffle baker is ready, ladle in ½ cup of batter. Close lid and bake until golden brown, about 5 minutes. Transfer waffle to plate and keep warm. Repeat with remaining batter, making a total of 4 waffles. Serve with maple syrup.

PER SERVING (1 WAFFLE AND 1 TABLESPOON MAPLE SYRUP): 128 grams, 205 Cal, 4 g Total Fat, 1 g Sat Fat, 0 g Trans Fat, 2 mg Chol, 498 mg Sod, 37 g Total Carb, 15 g Total Sugar, 3 g Fib, 7 g Prot, 116 mg Calc. *PointsPlus* value: **5**

Variations

Orange Waffles

Add grated zest of 1 small orange to the buttermilk mixture.

Vanilla Waffles

Add 1 teaspoon pure vanilla extract to the buttermilk mixture.

Double Maple Waffles

Add ½ teaspoon maple extract to the buttermilk mixture.

▲ HEALTHY EXTRA
Serve the waffles topped with sliced fresh strawberries or peaches.

Basic Pancakes

serves 6

2 cups all-purpose flour
1/3 cup sugar
2 tablespoons baking powder
1/4 teaspoon salt
2 1/2 cups low-fat (1%) milk
1/2 cup fat-free egg substitute
1 tablespoon canola oil

1   Whisk together flour, sugar, baking powder, and salt in medium bowl. Whisk together milk, egg substitute, and oil in small bowl. Add milk mixture to flour mixture, stirring just until flour mixture is moistened (batter will be lumpy).
2   Generously spray nonstick griddle with nonstick spray and set over medium heat. Pour scant 1/4 cupfuls of batter onto griddle. Cook until bubbles appear and edges of pancakes look dry, about 3 minutes. Turn pancakes over and cook until golden brown on second side, about 3 minutes longer. Transfer to platter and keep warm. Repeat with remaining batter, making a total of 24 pancakes.

PER SERVING (4 PANCAKES): 184 grams, 284 Cal,
4 g Total Fat, 1 g Sat Fat, 0 g Trans Fat, 6 mg Chol,
733 mg Sod, 51 g Total Carb, 16 g Total Sugar,
1 g Fib, 10 g Prot, 237 mg Calc.
PointsPlus value: **7**

Variations

Whole Wheat Pancakes

Substitute 1/2 cup whole wheat flour or white whole wheat flour for 1/2 cup of all-purpose flour, if you like.

PER SERVING (4 PANCAKES): 183 grams, 280 Cal,
4 g Total Fat, 1 g Sat Fat, 0 g Trans Fat, 6 mg Chol,
733 mg Sod, 50 g Total Carb, 16 g Total Sugar,
2 g Fib, 10 g Prot, 239 mg Calc.
PointsPlus value: **7**

Blueberry Pancakes

Stir 1 cup fresh or frozen blueberries into batter just until combined.

PER SERVING (4 PANCAKES): 209 grams, 298 Cal,
4 g Total Fat, 1 g Sat Fat, 0 g Trans Fat, 6 mg Chol,
733 mg Sod, 55 g Total Carb, 19 g Total Sugar,
2 g Fib, 10 g Prot, 238 mg Calc.
PointsPlus value: **7**

Buckwheat Pancakes

Substitute 1/2 cup buckwheat flour for 1/2 cup all-purpose flour.

PER SERVING (4 PANCAKES): 183 grams, 280 Cal,
5 g Total Fat, 1 g Sat Fat, 0 g Trans Fat, 6 mg Chol,
734 mg Sod, 50 g Total Carb, 17 g Total Sugar,
2 g Fib, 10 g Prot, 239 mg Calc.
PointsPlus value: **7**

WALNUT-RAISIN
GRANOLA

Walnut-Raisin Granola

serves 12

3 cups old-fashioned oats
1/3 cup chopped walnuts
1/3 cup raw pumpkin seeds
1/4 cup raw wheat germ
1/4 cup flaked sweetened coconut
1 tablespoon canola oil
1 teaspoon ground cinnamon
1/4 teaspoon salt
Grated zest of 1 orange
1/2 cup raisins

1   Preheat oven to 300°F. Spray 10½ × 15½-inch jelly-roll pan with nonstick spray.
2   Stir together all ingredients except raisins in large bowl. Spoon mixture into prepared baking pan and spread evenly.
3   Bake, stirring once, until golden brown, about 25 minutes. Stir in raisins and let cool completely in pan on wire rack. Can be stored in airtight container up to 1 month.

PER SERVING (⅓ CUP): 41 grams, 178 Cal,
8 g Total Fat, 1 g Sat Fat, 0 g Trans Fat, 0 mg Chol,
8 mg Sod, 22 g Total Carb, 7 g Total Sugar, 3 g Fib,
5 g Prot, 11 mg Calc.
PointsPlus value: *5*

Variation

Almond-Cranberry Granola
Substitute sliced or chopped almonds for walnuts and dried cranberries or chopped dried apricots for raisins.

Mixed Grain Porridge

serves 4

4 cups water
1/3 cup steel-cut oats
1/3 cup wheat berries
1/3 cup oat groats
1/2 teaspoon salt
1/4 cup golden raisins
1/4 cup dried cherries or cranberries
4 teaspoons brown sugar
1/2 cup reduced-fat (2%) milk, warmed

1   Combine water, steel-cut oats, wheat berries, oat groats, and salt in large saucepan and bring to boil. Reduce heat and simmer, stirring, until wheat berries and oat groats are softened and liquid is absorbed, about 40 minutes.
2   Remove saucepan from heat; stir in raisins and cherries. Spoon porridge evenly into 4 bowls; sprinkle evenly with brown sugar and top with milk.

PER SERVING (¾ CUP PORRIDGE, 1 TEASPOON SUGAR,
AND 2 TABLESPOONS MILK): 326 grams, 208 Cal,
2 g Total Fat, 0 g Sat Fat, 0 g Trans Fat, 2 mg Chol,
316 mg Sod, 44 g Total Carb, 17 g Total Sugar,
6 g Fib, 7 g Prot, 65 mg Calc.
PointsPlus value: *5*

FYI Once whole oats have been cleaned, toasted, hulled, and cleaned again, they are called oat groats. When oat groats are steamed and flattened, they are called old-fashioned (rolled) oats. Steel-cut oats, also known as Irish oatmeal or Scottish oats, are oat groats that have been cut into pieces but not rolled.

Baked Fruit–Cinnamon Oatmeal

serves 8

3 cups old-fashioned oats
1/2 cup chopped dried apricots
1/2 cup dried cranberries or blueberries
1/3 cup packed dark brown sugar
2 teaspoons baking powder
3/4 teaspoon ground cinnamon
1/4 teaspoon salt
1/2 cup plain fat-free yogurt
1 cup reduced-fat (2%) milk
1/2 cup applesauce
1/2 cup fat-free egg substitute
2 tablespoons canola oil
1 1/2 teaspoons vanilla extract

1   Preheat oven to 350°F. Lightly spray 8-inch square baking dish with nonstick spray.
2   Mix together oats, apricots, cranberries, all but 2 tablespoons of brown sugar, the baking powder, cinnamon, and salt in large bowl. Whisk together yogurt, 1/2 cup of milk, the applesauce, egg substitute, oil, and vanilla in medium bowl until smooth. Add yogurt mixture to oat mixture, stirring until combined well.
3   Spoon into prepared baking dish and spread evenly; sprinkle with remaining 2 tablespoons brown sugar. Bake oatmeal until toothpick inserted into center comes out clean, about 35 minutes. Let cool 10 minutes in baking dish on wire rack. Cut oatmeal into 8 equal portions and serve with remaining 1/2 cup milk.

PER SERVING (¾ CUP): 126 grams, 249 Cal, 6 g Total Fat, 1 g Sat Fat, 0 g Trans Fat, 2 mg Chol, 252 mg Sod, 44 g Total Carb, 21 g Total Sugar, 5 g Fib, 7 g Prot, 83 mg Calc.
PointsPlus value: **7**

Scrambled Eggs with Smoked Salmon and Dill

serves 6

2 teaspoons olive oil
1 small red onion, chopped
1 1/2 cups fat-free egg substitute
1/3 cup fat-free milk
1/4 teaspoon black pepper
1 (1/2-pound) piece smoked salmon, chopped
8 tablespoons reduced-fat sour cream
2 tablespoons snipped fresh dill

1   Heat oil in large nonstick skillet over medium heat. Add onion and cook, stirring, until softened, about 5 minutes.
2   Beat egg substitute, milk, and pepper in medium bowl. Add to skillet along with salmon. Cook until eggs begin to set, about 1 1/2 minutes, pushing egg mixture toward center of skillet to form large soft curds, cooking eggs until set, about 3 minutes longer.
3   Divide eggs evenly among 6 plates. Top each serving with dollop of sour cream and sprinkling of dill.

PER SERVING (SCANT 1 CUP EGGS AND 1½ TABLE-SPOONS SOUR CREAM): 141 grams, 122 Cal, 5 g Total Fat, 2 g Sat Fat, 0 g Trans Fat, 17 mg Chol, 897 mg Sod, 3 g Total Carb, 2 g Total Sugar, 0 g Fib, 14 g Prot, 64 mg Calc.
PointsPlus value: **3**

FYI   An opened carton of fat-free egg substitute can be refrigerated for up to 7 days, making it a handy staple. An unopened carton can be frozen for up to 1 year and thawed in the refrigerator. Do not refreeze.

Basic Omelette

serves 4

2 cups fat-free egg substitute
½ cup water
¼ teaspoon salt
Pinch black pepper

1   Whisk together all ingredients in medium bowl until frothy.
2   Generously spray heavy 10-inch nonstick skillet with nonstick spray and set over medium heat. When drop of water sizzles in pan, pour in generous ½ cup of egg mixture, tilting pan to coat bottom completely. Cook until eggs are almost set, about 3 minutes, gently lifting edge of eggs with silicone spatula to allow uncooked portion of egg to run underneath.
3   With spatula, fold omelette in half and slide onto plate. Repeat with remaining egg mixture, lightly spraying skillet before cooking each omelette.

PER SERVING (1 OMELETTE): 145 grams, 40 Cal,
0 g Total Fat, 0 g Sat Fat, 0 g Trans Fat, 0 mg Chol,
326 mg Sod, 0 g Total Carb, 0 g Total Sugar, 0 g Fib,
10 g Prot, 41 mg Calc.
PointsPlus value: *1*

Variations

Tomato and Goat Cheese Omelette

Seed and coarsely chop 2 tomatoes; toss with 2 teaspoons chopped fresh parsley and pinch each salt and black pepper. After egg mixture is set, sprinkle one-fourth of tomato mixture and generous 2 tablespoons crumbled soft goat cheese over half of omelette and fold over.

PER SERVING (1 OMELETTE): 215 grams, 71 Cal,
2 g Total Fat, 1 g Sat Fat, 0 g Trans Fat, 3 mg Chol,
393 mg Sod, 3 g Total Carb, 2 g Total Sugar, 1 g Fib,
12 g Prot, 67 mg Calc.
PointsPlus value: *2*

Canadian Bacon, Asparagus, and Scallion Omelette

Cook 1½ cups sliced asparagus in boiling water until tender, about 4 minutes. Drain, rinse under cold running water, and pat dry with paper towels. Transfer to small bowl and combine with 2 slices fully cooked Canadian bacon, thinly sliced, 2 scallions, thinly sliced, and pinch each salt and black pepper. After egg mixture is set, sprinkle one-fourth of asparagus mixture over half of omelette and fold over.

PER SERVING (1 OMELETTE): 231 grams, 78 Cal,
1 g Total Fat, 0 g Sat Fat, 0 g Trans Fat, 7 mg Chol,
708 mg Sod, 2 g Total Carb, 0 g Total Sugar, 1 g Fib,
15 g Prot, 60 mg Calc.
PointsPlus value: *2*

Mixed Mushroom–Herb Omelette

Spray medium nonstick skillet with nonstick spray and set over medium heat. Add ½ pound sliced mushrooms and pinch each dried thyme, salt, and black pepper; cook, stirring occasionally, until mushrooms release their juices and it evaporates, about 8 minutes. Stir in 1 tablespoon chopped fresh parsley. After egg mixture is set, sprinkle one-fourth of mushroom mixture over half of omelette and fold over.

PER SERVING (1 OMELETTE): 202 grams, 54 Cal,
0 g Total Fat, 0 g Sat Fat, 0 g Trans Fat, 0 mg Chol,
367 mg Sod, 2 g Total Carb, 1 g Total Sugar, 0 g Fib,
11 g Prot, 46 mg Calc.
PointsPlus value: *1*

Vegetable Scrambled Eggs

serves 4

4 large eggs
4 large egg whites
1/2 teaspoon salt
1 tablespoon olive oil
1/2 red bell pepper, chopped
1 cup sliced white mushrooms
2 scallions, thinly sliced
1/2 teaspoon dried thyme
1/8 teaspoon black pepper

1   Beat together eggs, egg whites, and 1/4 teaspoon of salt in medium bowl.
2   Heat oil in large nonstick skillet over high heat. Add bell pepper, mushrooms, scallions, thyme, remaining 1/4 teaspoon salt, and the black pepper; cook, stirring, until vegetables are softened, about 5 minutes.
3   Reduce heat to medium. Pour egg mixture into skillet. Cook until eggs begin to set, about 1 1/2 minutes, pushing egg mixture toward center of skillet to form large soft curds. Cook eggs until set, about 3 minutes longer.

PER SERVING (ABOUT 3/4 CUP): 138 grams, 129 Cal, 8 g Total Fat, 2 g Sat Fat, 0 g Trans Fat, 215 mg Chol, 414 mg Sod, 4 g Total Carb, 2 g Total Sugar, 1 g Fib, 10 g Prot, 33 mg Calc.
PointsPlus value: **3**

▲ **HEALTHY EXTRA**
For additional vegetable goodness, use 1 bell pepper and increase the amount of mushrooms to 1 1/2 cups.

Roman Rice Frittata

serves 4

1 tablespoon olive oil
1 onion, finely chopped
1 garlic clove, minced
1 cup fat-free egg substitute
1/2 cup hot cooked brown rice
2 dried figs, finely chopped
2 tablespoons grated Parmesan cheese
1/4 teaspoon dried thyme

1   Preheat broiler.
2   Heat oil in cast-iron or other ovenproof skillet and set over medium heat. Add onion and garlic; cook, stirring, until onion is softened, about 5 minutes.
3   Whisk egg substitute in medium bowl until frothy; stir in onion mixture and all remaining ingredients.
4   Wipe skillet clean. Spray with nonstick spray and set over medium heat; pour in egg mixture. Reduce heat to medium-low; cook until set on bottom, about 10 minutes.
5   Broil frittata 5 inches from heat until top is set and lightly browned, about 2 minutes. Slide frittata onto plate and cut into 4 wedges.

PER SERVING (1 WEDGE): 130 grams, 115 Cal, 5 g Total Fat, 1 g Sat Fat, 0 g Trans Fat, 2 mg Chol, 130 mg Sod, 12 g Total Carb, 4 g Total Sugar, 2 g Fib, 7 g Prot, 70 mg Calc.
PointsPlus value: **3**

FYI   A frittata is an Italian-style omelette. All the ingredients are combined with the eggs instead of being folded inside the omelette. Frittatas are easy to prepare and are delicious hot, warm, or at room temperature, making them ideal for company.

Potato-Onion Frittata

serves 6

6 large eggs
6 large egg whites
¾ teaspoon salt
¼ teaspoon black pepper
1 small red bell pepper, chopped
1 small onion, chopped
1 (14½-ounce) can sliced potatoes,
    rinsed and drained
¼ cup chopped fresh flat-leaf parsley

1   Preheat broiler.
2   Beat together eggs, egg whites, salt, and
black pepper in medium bowl.
3   Spray medium cast-iron or other ovenproof skillet with nonstick spray and set over
medium heat. Add bell pepper and onion; cook,
stirring, until softened, about 5 minutes. Add
potatoes, breaking up larger slices with side
of wooden spoon. Pour eggs over vegetables,
gently stirring to combine. Cook, lifting edge
of eggs with silicone spatula to allow uncooked
portion of egg to run underneath, until eggs are
almost set, about 4 minutes.
4   Broil frittata 5 inches from heat until top
is set and lightly browned, about 2 minutes.
Slide frittata onto plate; sprinkle with parsley
and cut into 6 wedges.

PER SERVING (1 WEDGE): 179 grams, 137 Cal,
5 g Total Fat, 1 g Sat Fat, 0 g Trans Fat, 215 mg Chol,
563 mg Sod, 13 g Total Carb, 1 g Total Sugar, 2 g Fib,
11 g Prot, 33 mg Calc.
PointsPlus value: *4*

▲ **HEALTHY EXTRA**
Add 1 cup of thinly sliced zucchini or mushrooms
to the skillet along with the bell pepper in step 3.

MINCING FRESH HERBS

1   *Pull leaves from stem of herb.*

2   *Gather leaves into pile on cutting
board. With large chef's knife, cut
across herbs to coarsely chop.*

3   *Place palm of hand on top of knife
blade. Rock knife up and down without lifting tip of knife from board until
herbs are minced.*

Shrimp, Mushroom, and Tomato Frittata

serves 4

½ ounce dried porcini mushrooms
4 large eggs
4 large egg whites
3 tablespoons grated Parmesan cheese
½ teaspoon salt
¼ teaspoon black pepper
1 tablespoon olive oil
1 cup grape tomatoes, halved
3 scallions, thinly sliced
2 garlic cloves, minced
1 teaspoon herbes de Provence
½ pound peeled and deveined cooked shrimp,
    coarsely chopped

1   Preheat broiler.
2   Put mushrooms in small bowl and add enough boiling water to cover by 1 inch. Let stand until softened, about 10 minutes. Drain mushrooms, then rinse under cool running water to remove any dirt. Chop mushrooms.
3   Beat together eggs, egg whites, Parmesan, salt, and pepper in medium bowl.
4   Heat oil in 10-inch cast-iron or other ovenproof skillet over medium-high heat. Add mushrooms and cook, stirring, until beginning to brown, about 5 minutes. Add tomatoes, scallions, garlic, and herbes de Provence; cook, stirring, until tomatoes begin to soften, about 3 minutes. Stir in shrimp. Pour egg mixture over mushroom mixture, stirring gently to combine. Reduce heat to medium and cook, lifting edge of eggs with silicone spatula to allow uncooked portion of egg to run underneath, until eggs are almost set, about 4 minutes.
5   Broil frittata 5 inches from heat until top is set and lightly browned, about 2 minutes. Slide frittata onto plate and cut into 4 wedges.

PER SERVING (1 WEDGE): 201 grams, 225 Cal, 10 g Total Fat, 3 g Sat Fat, 0 g Trans Fat, 333 mg Chol, 635 mg Sod, 6 g Total Carb, 2 g Total Sugar, 1 g Fib, 27 g Prot, 121 mg Calc. *PointsPlus* value: **6**

▲ **HEALTHY EXTRA**
Add 1 cup of steamed small broccoli florets to the skillet along with the tomatoes in step 4.

Fried Eggs Tex Mex–Style

serves 4

1 (16-ounce) tube prepared polenta,
    cut into 12 slices
1 (15½-ounce) can red kidney beans,
    rinsed and drained
1 cup salsa
4 large eggs
½ cup shredded reduced-fat pepper
    Jack cheese
2 tablespoons chopped fresh parsley

1   Preheat oven to 425°F. Spray baking sheet with nonstick spray.
2   Arrange polenta slices on prepared baking sheet in single layer; lightly spray with olive oil nonstick spray. Bake until heated through, about 20 minutes.
3   Meanwhile, combine beans and salsa in small saucepan; bring to boil. Reduce heat and simmer, covered, 10 minutes.
4   Spray large nonstick skillet with nonstick spray. Crack each egg into skillet and fry until whites are set and yolks begin to thicken, about 3 minutes. Remove skillet from heat; sprinkle eggs with pepper Jack and parsley. Cover skillet and let stand until cheese is melted, about 2 minutes.

5   To serve, place 3 polenta slices on each of 4 plates. Spoon beans evenly over polenta and top each serving with 1 egg.

PER SERVING (3 SLICES POLENTA, ½ CUP BEAN
MIXTURE, AND 1 EGG): 352 grams, 363 Cal,
8 g Total Fat, 3 g Sat Fat, 0 g Trans Fat, 223 mg Chol,
876 mg Sod, 54 g Total Carb, 6 g Total Sugar,
11 g Fib, 21 g Prot, 303 mg Calc.
PointsPlus value: **9**

FYI   Other beans and cheeses can be used with equally good results in this satisfying breakfast/brunch dish. Use pinto, small white, or black beans instead of the red kidney beans or substitute an equal amount of reduced-fat Cheddar, feta, or goat cheese for the pepper Jack cheese, if you like.

Tomato, Parmesan, and Egg–Topped Pizza

serves 4

2 teaspoons olive oil
1 small onion, finely chopped
1 (8-ounce) can tomato sauce
Pinch salt
Pinch black pepper
1 pound refrigerated whole wheat pizza dough
    or Whole Wheat Pizza Dough (page 322)
4 large eggs
2 tablespoons grated Parmesan cheese
2 tablespoons chopped fresh flat-leaf parsley

1   Spray large baking sheet with olive oil non-stick spray and sprinkle with cornmeal.
2   Heat oil in small nonstick skillet over medium heat. Add onion and cook, stirring, until softened, about 5 minutes. Stir in tomato

sauce, salt, and pepper; bring to boil. Transfer to small bowl.
3   Divide pizza dough into 4 equal pieces. On lightly floured work surface with lightly floured rolling pin, roll each piece of dough into 6-inch round; roll edge in to form 1-inch-high rim. Transfer dough rounds to prepared baking sheet; cover with clean kitchen towel. Let dough rise 30 minutes in warm place (80–85°F).
4   Meanwhile, preheat oven to 450°F.
5   Spoon tomato sauce mixture evenly over pizza dough rounds. Bake 7 minutes. Break 1 egg in center of each pizza and sprinkle evenly with 1 tablespoon of Parmesan. Bake just until whites are set and yolks begins to thicken, 8–10 minutes. Sprinkle pizzas evenly with parsley and remaining 1 tablespoon cheese.

PER SERVING (1 PIZZA): 243 grams, 386 Cal,
11 g Total Fat, 2 g Sat Fat, 0 g Trans Fat,
217 mg Chol, 934 mg Sod, 54 g Total Carb,
4 g Total Sugar, 7 g Fib, 16 g Prot, 92 mg Calc.
PointsPlus value: **10**

FYI   Make sure the rim of the pizza is 1-inch high, as the high rim prevents the eggs from sliding off the pizzas.

Creamy Ham and Arugula Crêpes

serves 6

½ cup reduced-fat tub-style cream cheese
2 tablespoons fat-free milk
2 scallions (green part only), thinly sliced
8 Crêpes [right]
8 (1-ounce) slices lean Black Forest ham
1 small bunch arugula, trimmed

1   Whisk together cream cheese and milk in small bowl until smooth. Stir in scallions.
2   Place 1 crêpe on work surface, prettiest side down. Spread 1 rounded tablespoon of cream cheese mixture over half of crêpe closest to you. Top with 1 slice of ham and ¼ cup of arugula; roll up jelly-roll style. Repeat, making a total of 8 filled crêpes. Cut 2 of the crêpes in thirds. Serve at room temperature.

PER SERVING (1⅓ FILLED CRÊPES): 149 grams, 176 Cal, 7 g Total Fat, 3 g Sat Fat, 0 g Trans Fat, 103 mg Chol, 563 mg Sod, 13 g Total Carb, 5 g Total Sugar, 1 g Fib, 15 g Prot, 156 mg Calc.
PointsPlus value: *5*

▲ HEALTHY EXTRA
Serve some tomato wedges alongside the crêpes.

Crêpes

serves 8

½ cup all-purpose flour
½ teaspoon ground nutmeg
¼ teaspoon salt
1 cup fat-free milk
2 large eggs, lightly beaten

1   Whisk together flour, nutmeg, and salt in medium bowl. Beat together milk and eggs in small bowl. Whisk milk mixture into flour mixture until smooth. Let stand 15 minutes.
2   Spray 8-inch nonstick skillet with nonstick spray and set over medium heat until drop of water sizzles in pan. Re-stir batter; pour scant ¼ cupful of batter into skillet, tilting pan to coat bottom completely. Cook until top is set and underside is golden brown, about 1½ minutes.
3   With spatula, loosen edge of crêpe and turn over. Cook until second side is lightly browned, about 25 seconds. Slide crêpe onto plate. Repeat with remaining batter, lightly spraying skillet before adding more batter, making a total of 8 crêpes.

PER SERVING (1 CRÊPE): 52 grams, 62 Cal, 2 g Total Fat, 1 g Sat Fat, 0 g Trans Fat, 54 mg Chol, 102 mg Sod, 8 g Total Carb, 2 g Total Sugar, 0 g Fib, 3 g Prot, 45 mg Calc.
PointsPlus value: *2*

FYI   Crêpes freeze well, so plan ahead and cook an extra batch. Layer the crêpes between sheets of wax paper, wrap in foil, and freeze up to 3 months. Thaw overnight in the refrigerator. Separating the crêpes between layers of wax paper makes it easy to remove as many crêpes as needed, but if you plan to use them all at once, the wax paper isn't necessary.

Greek Pita Pizzas with Spinach and Feta

serves 4

1 teaspoon olive oil
3 scallions, thinly sliced
2 garlic cloves, minced
¼ teaspoon dried oregano
¼ teaspoon salt
1 (10-ounce) package frozen chopped spinach, thawed and squeezed dry
⅓ cup crumbled reduced-fat soft goat cheese
¼ cup snipped fresh dill
2 whole wheat naan flatbreads
1 cup halved cherry tomatoes
¾ cup shredded part-skim mozzarella cheese

1   Preheat oven to 425°F.
2   Heat oil in large nonstick skillet over medium heat. Add scallions and cook, stirring frequently, until softened, about 4 minutes. Stir in garlic, oregano, and salt; cook, stirring, 1 minute. Stir in spinach and cook until heated through, about 2 minutes. Remove skillet from heat and stir in goat cheese and dill.
3   Place naan on ungreased baking sheet. Top each evenly with spinach mixture, spreading to edge. Sprinkle evenly with tomatoes; bake until naan are crisp on bottom and along edges, about 10 minutes.
4   Sprinkle pizzas evenly with mozzarella; bake just until cheese begins to soften, about 3 minutes. Cut each pizza in half.

PER SERVING (½ PIZZA): 195 grams, 246 Cal,
9 g Total Fat, 4 g Sat Fat, 0 g Trans Fat, 15 mg Chol,
531 mg Sod, 29 g Total Carb, 3 g Total Sugar, 7 g Fib,
15 g Prot, 280 mg Calc.
PointsPlus value: *6*

FYI   Naan is a type of flatbread popular in northern India, Pakistan, and Afghanistan.

Breakfast Tostadas

serves 4

4 small tomatoes, coarsely chopped
2 scallions, coarsely chopped
1 jalapeño pepper, seeded and coarsely chopped
3 tablespoons lightly packed fresh cilantro leaves
¼ teaspoon salt
1 teaspoon white vinegar
4 large eggs
4 (6-inch) fat-free corn tortillas, warmed
¼ cup shredded fat-free pepper Jack cheese
1 cup lightly packed tender watercress sprigs

1   To make salsa, combine tomatoes, scallions, jalapeño, cilantro, and salt in food processor; pulse until coarsely chopped. Transfer to small bowl.
2   Half fill large skillet with water and bring to boil. Add vinegar and reduce heat so water slowly simmers. Crack eggs, one at a time, and slip into water, waiting about 10 seconds before adding each additional egg. Poach eggs just until set, about 1 minute. With slotted spoon, transfer eggs, one at a time, to paper towel–lined plate to drain.
3   Place 1 tortilla on each of 4 plates and top each with watercress and 1 egg. Sprinkle each with 1 tablespoon pepper Jack and top with one-fourth of salsa.

PER SERVING (1 FILLED TORTILLA): 195 grams,
160 Cal, 5 g Total Fat, 2 g Sat Fat, 0 g Trans Fat,
216 mg Chol, 272 mg Sod, 18 g Total Carb,
3 g Total Sugar, 2 g Fib, 10 g Prot, 165 mg Calc.
PointsPlus value: *4*

▲ **HEALTHY EXTRA**
Toss cooked potatoes with salt and black pepper
(2 cooked small potatoes with each serving will
increase the *PointsPlus* value by *2*).

Cheese Quiche

serves 8

1 refrigerated pie crust (from 15-ounce box)
   or Pie Dough for Single Crust (page 383)
2 teaspoons butter
1 large onion, finely chopped
2 large eggs
2 large egg whites
½ cup shredded Gruyère cheese
1½ cups low-fat (1%) milk
½ teaspoon salt
⅛ teaspoon black pepper
Pinch ground nutmeg

1 Preheat oven to 425°F.
2 Press dough onto bottom and against side of 9-inch pie plate; crimp edge. Line dough with sheet of foil and fill with dried beans or rice. Bake 10 minutes. Remove foil with beans; bake until crust is golden, 5–10 minutes longer. Set aside on wire rack.
3 Reduce oven temperature to 350°F.
4 Melt butter in large nonstick skillet over medium heat. Add onion and cook, stirring, until golden, about 10 minutes.
5 Whisk together eggs, egg whites, ¼ cup of Gruyère, the milk, salt, pepper, and nutmeg in medium bowl. Spread onion over bottom of pie shell. Pour egg mixture over onion and sprinkle with remaining ¼ cup cheese.
6 Bake until quiche is golden and knife inserted into center comes out clean, about 35 minutes. Cut into 8 wedges and serve hot, warm, or at room temperature.

PER SERVING (1 WEDGE): 125 grams, 230 Cal, 14 g Total Fat, 6 g Sat Fat, 0 g Trans Fat, 71 mg Chol, 364 mg Sod, 19 g Total Carb, 3 g Total Sugar, 1 g Fib, 7 g Prot, 138 mg Calc.
PointsPlus value: **6**

Spinach and Cheese Quiche

serves 8

1 refrigerated pie crust (from 15-ounce box)
   or Pie Dough for Single Crust (page 383)
1 (12-ounce) can evaporated fat-free milk
⅓ cup low-fat (1%) cottage cheese
¼ cup grated Parmesan cheese
2 large eggs
3 large egg whites
½ teaspoon salt
¼ teaspoon black pepper
1 (10-ounce) package frozen chopped spinach, thawed and squeezed dry

1 Preheat oven to 425°F.
2 Press dough onto bottom and against side of 9-inch pie plate; crimp edge. Line dough with sheet of foil and fill with dried beans or rice. Bake 10 minutes. Remove foil with beans; bake until crust is golden, 5–10 minutes longer. Set aside on wire rack.
3 Whisk together evaporated milk, cottage cheese, Parmesan, eggs, egg whites, salt, and pepper in medium bowl until combined. Spread spinach evenly over bottom of pie shell; pour cheese mixture over top.
4 Bake quiche 15 minutes. Reduce oven temperature to 350°F. Bake until knife inserted into center comes out clean, about 20 minutes longer. Cut into 8 wedges and serve hot, warm, or at room temperature.

PER SERVING (1 WEDGE): 149 grams, 215 Cal, 9 g Total Fat, 3 g Sat Fat, 0 g Trans Fat, 57 mg Chol, 507 mg Sod, 23 g Total Carb, 6 g Total Sugar, 2 g Fib, 9 g Prot, 185 mg Calc.
PointsPlus value: **5**

3

Starters and Light Meals

Starters and Light Meals

56 Classic Guacamole
57 Hummus
57 Baba Ghanoush
58 Roasted Red Pepper Dip
58 White Bean Dip
59 Milanese-Style Tuna Spread
59 Caponata
60 Cheese Crisps
60 Cheese Straws
62 Deviled Eggs
62 Italian-Style Stuffed Mushrooms
63 Spinach-Stuffed Mushrooms
64 Keema Samosas
64 Spanakopita Triangles
65 Hot-and-Spicy Chickpea Cakes
66 Roasted Vegetable Crostini
66 Caramelized Garlic Toasts
68 Portobello and Ham Bruschetta
68 White Bean Bruschetta
69 Smoky Onion Tartlets
69 Lemon-Thyme Zucchini on Flatbread
70 White Bean, Bell Pepper, and Olive Pizzas
70 Nachos Grandes
72 California Sushi Rolls
73 Roasted Pepper and Tomato–Stuffed Eggplant Rollups
73 Antipasto Platter
74 Thai-Style Roast Beef Salad
74 Korean Steak on a Stick
76 Picadillo in Lettuce Leaves
76 Chicken Satay with Peanut Sauce
77 Stuffed Turkey Rollups
77 Duck and Goat Cheese Quesadillas
78 Tuna Seviche
78 Garlic Shrimp Tapas
80 Shrimp Cocktail with Horseradish Sauce
80 Vietnamese Lobster Summer Rolls with Dipping Sauce

PITTING AN AVOCADO

1 *Cut avocado lengthwise in half. Twist two halves to separate.*

2 *Run tip of soupspoon around pit and lift it out.*

3 *With spoon, scoop out pulp from each half in one piece; cut or mash as directed.*

Classic Guacamole

serves 6

1 large Hass avocado, halved and pitted
2 plum tomatoes, chopped
½ small onion, chopped
¼ cup chopped fresh cilantro
1 small jalapeño pepper, seeded and minced
1 tablespoon lime juice
½ teaspoon salt
¼ teaspoon black pepper

Scoop avocado pulp into small bowl and coarsely mash. Add all remaining ingredients, gently mixing until combined. Serve at once or press piece of plastic wrap directly onto surface to prevent browning. Store at room temperature and serve within 2 hours.

PER SERVING (¼ CUP): 59 grams, 58 Cal, 5 g Total Fat, 1 g Sat Fat, 0 g Trans Fat, 0 mg Chol, 200 mg Sod, 4 g Total Carb, 1 g Total Sugar, 2 g Fib, 1 g Prot, 6 mg Calc.
PointsPlus value: *2*

▲ HEALTHY EXTRA

Serve the guacamole with a platter of cut-up raw vegetables, such as thickly sliced zucchini or cucumber, bell pepper wedges, radish halves, Belgian endive leaves, and thickly sliced jumbo white mushrooms.

Hummus

serves 8

*1 (15½-ounce) can chickpeas, rinsed and
   drained*
3 garlic cloves, peeled
2 tablespoons tahini
2 tablespoons lemon juice
2 tablespoons olive oil
1 tablespoon water
½ teaspoon salt
⅛ teaspoon black pepper
1 or 2 drops hot sauce, preferably Tabasco
½ teaspoon paprika
Finely chopped fresh parsley

Combine all ingredients except paprika and
parsley in food processor and puree, adding a
bit more water if hummus is too thick. Transfer
hummus to serving dish; sprinkle with paprika
and parsley. Serve at once or refrigerate in
covered container up to 3 days.

PER SERVING (2 TABLESPOONS): 50 grams, 86 Cal,
6 g Total Fat, 1 g Sat Fat, 0 g Trans Fat, 0 mg Chol,
214 mg Sod, 7 g Total Carb, 0 g Total Sugar, 2 g Fib,
2 g Prot, 19 mg Calc.
PointsPlus value: *2*

▲ HEALTHY EXTRA

Hummus is traditionally accompanied by a basket
of warm pita breads. It is just as satisfying,
however, when served on small plates with thick
slices of cooked red potato. One 3-ounce red
potato, cooked and sliced, with each serving will
increase the *PointsPlus* value by *2.*

Baba Ghanoush

serves 8

1 (1-pound) eggplant
3 tablespoons lemon juice
2 tablespoons tahini
1 tablespoon extra-virgin olive oil
2 garlic cloves, minced
¾ teaspoon salt
¼ teaspoon black pepper

1   Preheat oven to 400° F. Line baking sheet
with foil; spray with nonstick spray.
2   With knife, pierce eggplant several times
and place on baking sheet. Bake, turning once,
until softened, about 45 minutes.
3   When eggplant is cool enough to handle,
peel off skin and remove stem. Cut eggplant
into chunks. Put eggplant in food processor and
puree. Add all remaining ingredients and pulse
to combine. Serve at once or refrigerate in covered container up to 4 days.

PER SERVING (¼ CUP): 59 grams, 52 Cal, 4 g Total Fat,
1 g Sat Fat, 0 g Trans Fat, 0 mg Chol, 221 mg Sod,
5 g Total Carb, 2 g Total Sugar, 1 g Fib, 1 g Prot,
11 mg Calc.
PointsPlus value: *2*

FYI To add some authentic smoky flavor to the
eggplant, soak 1 cup of apple or hickory
wood chips in water to cover for at least 30
minutes. Drain off the water and sprinkle the chips
over the hot coals if using a charcoal grill, or put
them into a small disposable foil pan with some
holes pricked in and set on top of the burners of a
gas grill. Grill the eggplant as directed.

Roasted Red Pepper Dip

serves 4

2 large red bell peppers
1 tablespoon extra-virgin olive oil
2 teaspoons tomato paste
2 teaspoons balsamic vinegar
1 garlic clove, minced
½ teaspoon salt
⅛ teaspoon black pepper
⅛ teaspoon cayenne

1   Line rack of broiler pan with foil and pre-heat broiler.
2   Cut bell peppers in half; remove and discard seeds. Arrange peppers, cut side down, on prepared pan. Broil 5 inches from heat until skin is blackened, about 10 minutes. Transfer peppers to large zip-close plastic bag; seal and let steam 10 minutes.
3   When cool enough to handle, peel peppers and cut into large pieces; put in food processor. Add all remaining ingredients and puree, adding a little water if mixture is too thick. Serve at once or refrigerate in covered container up to 4 days.

PER SERVING (¼ CUP): 92 grams, 58 Cal, 4 g Total Fat, 1 g Sat Fat, 0 g Trans Fat, 0 mg Chol, 295 mg Sod, 7 g Total Carb, 3 g Total Sugar, 2 g Fib, 1 g Prot, 10 mg Calc.
PointsPlus value: *2*

FYI   If you're short on time, use a 7-ounce jar of roasted red peppers packed in water. Drain the peppers, reserving the liquid. Proceed as directed in the recipe, adding some of the reserved pepper liquid if the dip is too thick.

White Bean Dip

serves 6

6 large garlic cloves, unpeeled
1 cup canned cannellini (white kidney) beans, rinsed and drained
¼ cup finely chopped red bell pepper
3 scallions, minced
2 tablespoons lemon juice
1 tablespoon extra-virgin olive oil
½ teaspoon salt
⅛ teaspoon cayenne

1   Preheat oven or toaster oven to 400°F.
2   Wrap garlic in foil and roast until very soft, about 30 minutes. Unwrap garlic and let cool.
3   When cool enough to handle, squeeze garlic from skins; put in food processor. Add all remaining ingredients and puree. Transfer to small bowl. Serve at once or refrigerate in covered container up to 2 days.

PER SERVING (ABOUT ¼ CUP): 67 grams, 63 Cal, 3 g Total Fat, 0 g Sat Fat, 0 g Trans Fat, 0 mg Chol, 249 mg Sod, 8 g Total Carb, 1 g Total Sugar, 2 g Fib, 2 g Prot, 24 mg Calc.
PointsPlus value: *2*

Milanese-Style Tuna Spread

serves 4

1 (5-ounce) can water-packed light tuna,
    drained and flaked
3 tablespoons reduced-fat mayonnaise
1 tablespoon lemon juice
1 tablespoon capers, drained
2 teaspoons reduced-sodium soy sauce
1½ teaspoons olive oil
⅛ teaspoon black pepper

Combine all ingredients in food processor or blender and process until smooth, scraping down side of bowl once or twice. Transfer to serving dish. Serve at once or refrigerate in covered container up to 2 days.

PER SERVING (¼ CUP): 57 grams, 101 Cal,
7 g Total Fat, 1 g Sat Fat, 0 g Trans Fat, 19 mg Chol,
388 mg Sod, 1 g Total Carb, 0 g Total Sugar, 0 g Fib,
9 g Prot, 6 mg Calc.
PointsPlus value: *3*

▲ HEALTHY EXTRA
Spread the tuna mixture into 4-inch lengths of celery hearts.

Caponata

serves 12

1 tablespoon olive oil
1 onion, chopped
3 garlic cloves, minced
2 celery stalks, diced
1 small eggplant (¾ pound), peeled and diced
⅓ cup water
1 large tomato, chopped
2 tablespoons golden raisins
1 tablespoon capers, drained
¾ teaspoon salt
¼ teaspoon black pepper
8 pitted green olives, sliced
4 large fresh basil leaves, thinly sliced

1   Heat oil in large nonstick skillet over medium heat. Add onion and garlic; cook, stirring, until onion is softened, about 5 minutes. Add celery and cook, stirring, until softened, about 4 minutes.

2   Add eggplant and water to skillet; cook, covered, 5 minutes. Stir in tomato, raisins, capers, salt, and pepper; cook, covered, stirring occasionally, 10 minutes. Uncover and cook until eggplant is softened, about 4 minutes longer.

3   Remove skillet from heat and stir in olives and basil. Let cool to room temperature. Serve at once or refrigerate in covered container up to 3 days.

PER SERVING (ABOUT ¼ CUP): 70 grams, 39 Cal,
2 g Total Fat, 0 g Sat Fat, 0 g Trans Fat, 0 mg Chol,
251 mg Sod, 6 g Total Carb, 3 g Total Sugar, 1 g Fib,
1 g Prot, 11 mg Calc.
PointsPlus value: *1*

FYI   This caponata freezes well. Transfer the cooled caponata to a freezer-safe container and freeze up to 3 months. Thaw overnight in the refrigerator or at room temperature.

Cheese Crisps

serves 8

1 cup shredded part-skim mozzarella cheese
3 tablespoons grated Parmesan cheese
1 tablespoon all-purpose flour
½ teaspoon dried thyme, crumbled
Pinch cayenne

1   Preheat oven to 400°F. Spray 2 baking
sheets with nonstick spray.
2   Stir together all ingredients in small bowl.
Drop cheese mixture by tablespoonfuls, at
least 2 inches apart, onto prepared baking
sheets. Bake crisps until cheese is melted and
edges are lightly browned, about 5 minutes.
3   Let crisps cool 1 minute on baking sheets.
With pancake spatula, transfer crisps to
double thickness of paper towels and let cool
completely. Crisps can be stored in airtight
container up to 2 days at room temperature.

PER SERVING (2 CRISPS): 17 grams, 48 Cal,
3 g Total Fat, 2 g Sat Fat, 0 g Trans Fat, 10 mg Chol,
101 mg Sod, 1 g Total Carb, 1 g Total Sugar, 0 g Fib,
4 g Prot, 119 mg Calc.
PointsPlus value: *1*

FYI   In Italy, these delicate and delectable
treats are called *frico*. They are usually
prepared only with Parmesan cheese, but we love
the combination of cheeses used in our version.

Cheese Straws

serves 16

1 cup all-purpose flour
½ teaspoon black pepper
⅛ teaspoon cayenne
5 tablespoons cold unsalted butter,
    cut into pieces
1 cup shredded extra-sharp Cheddar cheese
¼ cup grated Parmesan cheese
3–4 tablespoons cold water

1   Preheat oven to 375°F.
2   Combine flour, pepper, and cayenne in
food processor and pulse to mix. Scatter butter
on top of seasoned flour; pulse until mixture
resembles coarse crumbs. Scatter Cheddar and
Parmesan on top and drizzle with 3 tablespoons
of water; pulse until mixture forms a ball, adding remaining 1 tablespoon water, if needed.
3   Turn dough out onto lightly floured work
surface. With lightly floured rolling pin, roll
dough into 9-inch square. With pizza cutter or
knife, cut dough into 3 × ½-inch strips, making a total of 48 strips.
4   Place cheese strips about 1 inch apart on
ungreased large nonstick baking sheet. Bake
until golden, about 15 minutes. With wide
spatula, transfer cheese straws to wire racks
and let cool completely. Cheese straws can be
stored in airtight container up to 2 days.

PER SERVING (3 CHEESE STRAWS): 18 grams, 82 Cal,
6 g Total Fat, 3 g Sat Fat, 0 g Trans Fat, 16 mg Chol,
61 mg Sod, 6 g Total Carb, 0 g Total Sugar, 0 g Fib,
3 g Prot, 62 mg Calc.
PointsPlus value: *2*

Deviled Eggs

serves 4

4 large eggs
2 tablespoons reduced-fat mayonnaise
1 teaspoon cider vinegar
½ teaspoon Dijon mustard
Pinch salt
Pinch black pepper
Chopped fresh flat-leaf parsley or paprika

1   Place eggs and enough cold water to cover by at least 1 inch in medium saucepan; bring to boil. Immediately remove saucepan from heat and cover. Let stand 15 minutes. Pour off water and rinse eggs under cold running water until cool.
2   Peel eggs. Cut eggs lengthwise in half and remove yolks. Transfer yolks to small bowl and mash with fork until smooth. Add mayonnaise, vinegar, mustard, salt, and pepper; stir until mixed well.
3   Place egg whites on plate. Spoon yolk mixture evenly into egg white halves or spoon yolk mixture into pastry bag fitted with star tip and pipe into egg white halves. Sprinkle with parsley and serve or loosely cover and refrigerate up to 4 hours.

PER SERVING (2 DEVILED EGGS): 60 grams, 104 Cal, 8 g Total Fat, 2 g Sat Fat, 0 g Trans Fat, 215 mg Chol, 173 mg Sod, 1 g Total Carb, 1 g Total Sugar, 0 g Fib, 6 g Prot, 26 mg Calc.
PointsPlus value: *3*

Variations

Curried Deviled Eggs

Add ¼ teaspoon mild or hot curry powder to egg yolk mixture.

Horseradish Deviled Eggs

Add 1½ teaspoons drained prepared horseradish to egg yolk mixture and sprinkle eggs with snipped fresh dill instead of parsley.

Caviar Eggs

Top each deviled egg with ½ teaspoon caviar and omit parsley.

PER SERVING (2 DEVILED EGGS): 65 grams, 117 Cal, 9 g Total Fat, 2 g Sat Fat, 0 g Trans Fat, 246 mg Chol, 253 mg Sod, 1 g Total Carb, 1 g Total Sugar, 0 g Fib, 8 g Prot, 41 mg Calc.
PointsPlus value: *3*

Italian-Style Stuffed Mushrooms

serves 6

½ pound sweet Italian turkey sausages,
    casings removed
30 cremini mushrooms (about 1½ pounds),
    stems finely chopped
1 small onion, finely chopped
1 garlic clove, minced
¼ cup chopped fresh parsley
¼ cup plain dried bread crumbs
¼ cup grated Romano cheese
1 large egg white
½ teaspoon dried oregano
¼ teaspoon salt
⅛ teaspoon black pepper

1   Preheat oven to 350°F. Spray jelly-roll pan with nonstick spray.
2   To make mushroom filling, put sausages in medium nonstick skillet and set over medium-high heat. Cook, breaking them apart with wooden spoon, until no longer pink, about 5

minutes. Add mushroom stems, onion, and garlic; cook, stirring, until mushrooms begin to brown, about 6 minutes. Transfer to medium bowl and let cool about 5 minutes.

3   Add all remaining ingredients to sausage mixture, stirring to mix well. Spoon about 2½ teaspoons filling into each mushroom cap. Place stuffed mushrooms in prepared pan. Bake until mushrooms are tender and filling is heated through, about 20 minutes. Serve hot or warm.

PER SERVING (5 STUFFED MUSHROOMS): 92 grams, 91 Cal, 4 g Total Fat, 1 g Sat Fat, 0 g Trans Fat, 19 mg Chol, 355 mg Sod, 7 g Total Carb, 1 g Total Sugar, 1 g Fib, 8 g Prot, 34 mg Calc.
PointsPlus value: *2*

▲ HEALTHY EXTRA
Make these delectable stuffed mushrooms the centerpiece of an antipasto plate of grilled vegetables, including radicchio wedges, zucchini slices, cherry tomato skewers, and grilled halved or quartered Belgian endive.

Spinach-Stuffed Mushrooms
serves 4

1 (10-ounce) bag baby spinach, rinsed (do not dry)
1 large egg
⅓ cup crumbled soft goat cheese
2 tablespoons seasoned dried bread crumbs
2 tablespoons plain fat-free yogurt
2 tablespoons snipped fresh dill
¼ teaspoon salt
⅛ teaspoon black pepper
4 large portobello mushrooms, stems removed

1   Preheat oven to 400°F. Spray medium baking dish with olive oil nonstick spray.
2   Set large skillet over medium-high heat. Add spinach and cook, stirring, until wilted, about 3 minutes. Transfer to cutting board and let cool slightly. Chop spinach and transfer to large bowl; stir in all remaining ingredients except mushrooms.
3   Place mushrooms, stem side down, in prepared baking dish. Bake 5 minutes. Turn mushrooms over; fill evenly with spinach mixture. Bake until filling is heated through, about 15 minutes longer.

PER SERVING (1 MUSHROOM): 169 grams, 111 Cal, 3 g Total Fat, 2 g Sat Fat, 0 g Trans Fat, 58 mg Chol, 418 mg Sod, 14 g Total Carb, 2 g Total Sugar, 5 g Fib, 7 g Prot, 89 mg Calc.
PointsPlus value: *3*

FYI   Turn these tasty stuffed mushrooms into mini hors d'oeuvres by substituting about 16 medium white mushrooms for the portobellos.

Keema Samosas

serves 17

2 tablespoons canola oil
½ cup finely chopped onion
1 jalapeño pepper, seeded and finely chopped
2 garlic cloves, minced
1 teaspoon garam masala
¾ teaspoon Madras curry powder
¼ teaspoon turmeric
1 pound ground skinless chicken breast
¾ teaspoon salt
¼ cup chopped fresh cilantro
1 tablespoon lime juice
34 (3-inch) square wonton wrappers

1   To make filling, heat oil in large nonstick skillet over medium-high heat. Add onion, jalapeño, and garlic; cook until onion begins to soften, about 4 minutes. Stir in garam masala, curry powder, and turmeric; cook 30 seconds. Add chicken and sprinkle with salt; cook, breaking up chicken with wooden spoon, until no longer pink, about 5 minutes. Remove skillet from heat; let cool 10 minutes. Stir in cilantro and lime juice.

2   Preheat oven to 425°F. Spray baking sheet with nonstick spray.

3   Place 6 wonton wrappers on work surface. Put scant 1 tablespoon of filling in center of each wrapper. Moisten edges of wrappers with water. Fold each wrapper over filling to form triangle. Press edges firmly to seal. Place samosas on prepared baking sheet. Repeat with remaining filling and wrappers, making a total of 34 samosas.

4   Lightly spray samosas with nonstick spray. Bake until crisp and golden, about 6 minutes per side.

PER SERVING (2 SAMOSAS): 40 grams, 88 Cal, 2 g Total Fat, 0 g Sat Fat, 0 g Trans Fat, 16 mg Chol, 198 mg Sod, 10 g Total Carb, 0 g Total Sugar, 0 g Fib, 6 g Prot, 12 mg Calc.
PointsPlus value: *2*

FYI   Samosas are a great party food because they freeze beautifully. Prepare them as directed through step 3. Place the samosas on wax or parchment paper–lined baking sheets in a single layer and freeze until hard. Transfer to zip-close plastic freezer bags and freeze up to 2 months. To serve, thaw at room temperature for 15 minutes, then bake as directed.

Spanakopita Triangles

serves 8

²/₃ cup crumbled reduced-fat feta cheese
1 (10-ounce) package frozen chopped spinach, thawed and squeezed dry
3 scallions, chopped
¼ cup snipped fresh dill
1 large egg white
¼ teaspoon black pepper
8 (12 × 17-inch) sheets frozen phyllo dough, thawed
2 tablespoons unsalted butter, melted

1   Place oven rack in center of oven. Preheat oven to 375°F. Spray baking sheet with nonstick spray.

2   With fork, mash feta in medium bowl. Add spinach, scallions, dill, egg white, and pepper, stirring until mixed well.

3   Lay 1 phyllo sheet on work surface with long side facing you (keep remaining phyllo covered with damp paper towel and plastic wrap to keep it from drying out); spray with

olive oil nonstick spray. Top with another phyllo sheet and lightly spray. With pizza cutter or sharp knife, cut phyllo crosswise into 6 strips. Place scant 1 tablespoonful of spinach mixture at one end of each strip. Fold corner of phyllo up and over filling, then continue folding flag-style to form triangle.

4   Arrange filled triangles on prepared baking sheet. Repeat with remaining filling and phyllo sheets, making a total of 24 triangles. Lightly brush tops of triangles with melted butter. Bake until golden brown, about 25 minutes. Serve hot or warm.

PER SERVING (3 TRIANGLES): 74 grams, 98 Cal, 4 g Total Fat, 3 g Sat Fat, 0 g Trans Fat, 11 mg Chol, 268 mg Sod, 11 g Total Carb, 0 g Total Sugar, 2 g Fib, 5 g Prot, 61 mg Calc.
PointsPlus value: *3*

FYI The Spanakopita Triangles can be baked up to 3 hours in advance and set aside at room temperature up to several hours. Reheat in a 375°F oven until crisp and heated through, about 8 minutes.

Hot-and-Spicy Chickpea Cakes
serves 6

1 (15½-ounce) can chickpeas, rinsed and drained
⅓ cup light sour cream
¼ cup + 2 tablespoons cornmeal
4 garlic cloves, minced
1 teaspoon ground cumin
¾ teaspoon hot sauce, such as Tabasco
1½ cups salsa

1   Combine chickpeas, sour cream, 2 tablespoons of cornmeal, the garlic, cumin, and hot sauce in food processor and puree. Transfer to medium bowl; refrigerate, covered, until chilled, about 30 minutes.
2   Form chickpea mixture into 6 (3-inch) round cakes. Spread remaining ¼ cup cornmeal on sheet of wax paper; lightly coat cakes with cornmeal.
3   Spray large nonstick skillet with olive oil nonstick spray and set over medium heat. Add cakes and cook until browned on bottom, about 5 minutes. Spray cakes with nonstick spray: turn and cook until browned, about 5 minutes longer. Serve with salsa.

PER SERVING (1 CAKE AND ¼ CUP SALSA): 133 grams, 115 Cal, 2 g Total Fat, 1 g Sat Fat, 0 g Trans Fat, 4 mg Chol, 558 mg Sod, 20 g Total Carb, 3 g Total Sugar, 3 g Fib, 4 g Prot, 48 mg Calc.
PointsPlus value: *3*

Roasted Vegetable Crostini

serves 12

1 (1-pound) eggplant, cut into ½-inch dice
2 red bell peppers, finely chopped
2 zucchini, finely chopped
1 onion, sliced
2 tablespoons extra-virgin olive oil
1 teaspoon dried oregano
¾ teaspoon salt
¼ teaspoon black pepper
8 ounces Italian bread, cut into 24 thin slices
    and toasted
½ cup chopped fresh basil
12 pitted Kalamata olives, halved
¼ cup grated Parmesan cheese

1   Preheat oven to 425°F.
2   Toss together eggplant, bell peppers, zucchini, onion, oil, oregano, salt, and black pepper in large roasting pan. Spread to form single layer. Roast vegetables, stirring occasionally, until tender and browned along edges, about 45 minutes. Let cool to room temperature.
3   Spoon vegetable mixture evenly onto toasts. Sprinkle evenly with basil, olives, and Parmesan.

PER SERVING (2 CROSTINI): 136 grams, 149 Cal,
5 g Total Fat, 1 g Sat Fat, 0 g Trans Fat, 1 mg Chol,
417 mg Sod, 22 g Total Carb, 4 g Total Sugar, 3 g Fib,
4 g Prot, 62 mg Calc.
PointsPlus value: *4*

FYI   This tasty vegetable mixture is rather versatile. You can substitute an equal amount of thinly sliced fennel, yellow bell pepper, or radicchio for any of the vegetables called for.

Caramelized Garlic Toasts

serves 8

⅓ cup water
1 tablespoon honey
12 large garlic cloves, peeled
¼ teaspoon cayenne
Pinch salt
Pinch black pepper
2 tablespoons unsalted butter, softened
8 thin slices French bread, toasted

1   Combine water and honey in small saucepan; bring to simmer over medium-low heat. Add garlic and cook until softened, about 12 minutes. Add cayenne, salt, and pepper; cook until garlic turns deep golden, about 3 minutes.
2   Transfer garlic mixture to mini food processor. Add butter and process until smooth. Serve with toasts.

PER SERVING (1 TOAST AND 1 ROUNDED TEASPOON
GARLIC SPREAD): 40 grams, 127 Cal, 4 g Total Fat,
2 g Sat Fat, 0 g Trans Fat, 8 mg Chol, 210 mg Sod,
20 g Total Carb, 3 g Total Sugar, 1 g Fib, 3 g Prot,
33 mg Calc.
PointsPlus value: *3*

CLOCKWISE FROM BOTTOM LEFT: CARAMELIZED GARLIC TOASTS, ROASTED VEGETABLE CROSTINI, PORTOBELLO AND HAM BRUSCHETTA (PAGE 68)

Portobello and Ham Bruschetta

serves 4

4 large portobello mushrooms, stems removed
2 (½-inch) slices country bread, cut crosswise
    in half
1 garlic clove, halved
2 teaspoons extra-virgin olive oil
2 teaspoons reduced-sodium soy sauce
2 (1-ounce) slices lean Black Forest ham, cut
    in half
2 tablespoons grated Parmesan cheese

1   Spray grill rack with nonstick spray; pre-heat grill to medium or prepare medium fire using direct method.
2   Lightly spray mushrooms with nonstick spray. Place on grill rack and grill until lightly browned and tender, about 5 minutes per side. Transfer to plate.
3   Lightly spray both sides of slices of bread with nonstick spray. Place on grill rack and grill until golden brown, about 1 minute per side. Rub one side of each slice of bread with cut side of garlic and drizzle evenly with oil.
4   Slice mushrooms and divide among slices of bread; drizzle evenly with soy sauce. Top each bruschetta with 1 piece of ham; sprinkle with Parmesan.

PER SERVING (1 BRUSCHETTA): 98 grams, 107 Cal, 4 g Total Fat, 1 g Sat Fat, 0 g Trans Fat, 4 mg Chol, 329 mg Sod, 13 g Total Carb, 2 g Total Sugar, 2 g Fib, 6 g Prot, 51 mg Calc.
PointsPlus value: *3*

▲ HEALTHY EXTRA

Turn this Italian bruschetta into lunch by serving it with a salad of sliced radicchio, baby arugula, and Belgian endive dressed with a splash of lemon juice and a sprinkling of sea salt.

White Bean Bruschetta

serves 4

1 (15½-ounce) can cannellini (white kidney)
    beans, rinsed and drained
2 tablespoons chopped fresh flat-leaf parsley
Grated zest and juice of ½ lemon
2 teaspoons extra-virgin olive oil
¼ teaspoon salt
¼ teaspoon black pepper
1 garlic clove, cut in half
12 thin slices whole wheat Italian bread,
    toasted

1   Mash beans with 1 tablespoon of parsley, the lemon zest and juice, oil, salt, and pepper in medium bowl.
2   Rub cut side of garlic over one side of each slice of toasted bread. Top bread evenly with bean mixture and sprinkle with remaining 1 tablespoon parsley.

PER SERVING (3 BRUSCHETTA): 128 grams, 169 Cal, 2 g Total Fat, 1 g Sat Fat, 0 g Trans Fat, 0 mg Chol, 464 mg Sod, 33 g Total Carb, 2 g Total Sugar, 7 g Fib, 7 g Prot, 69 mg Calc.
PointsPlus value: *4*

FYI   Bruschetta (broo-SKEH-tah) is derived from the Italian word *bruscare*, which means "to roast over coals." Bruschetta is made by rubbing raw garlic over toasted slices of Italian bread then drizzling them with olive oil.

▲ HEALTHY EXTRA

Top each bruschetta with some chopped fresh tomato and sprinkle with thinly sliced fresh basil.

Smoky Onion Tartlets

serves 15

2 sweet onions, such as Vidalia (about 1³⁄₄ pounds), very thinly sliced
³⁄₄ teaspoon smoked paprika
³⁄₄ teaspoon salt
¹⁄₂ teaspoon black pepper
¹⁄₃ cup shredded Gruyère cheese
2 (2.1-ounce) packages frozen mini phyllo pastry shells (30 shells total)

1   To make filling, spray large nonstick skillet with nonstick spray and set over medium heat. Add onions and cook, stirring, until softened and deep golden, about 25 minutes. Stir in paprika, salt, and pepper. Remove skillet from heat and let cool 15 minutes.
2   Meanwhile, preheat oven to 350°F.
3   Stir Gruyère into cooled filling. Place pastry shells on ungreased baking sheet. Spoon about 1¹⁄₂ teaspoons onion mixture into each shell. Bake until pastry is lightly crisped and filling is heated through, 6–8 minutes. Serve hot or warm.

PER SERVING (2 TARTLETS): 26 grams, 51 Cal, 3 g Total Fat, 1 g Sat Fat, 0 g Trans Fat, 3 mg Chol, 150 mg Sod, 5 g Total Carb, 1 g Total Sugar, 0 g Fib, 1 g Prot, 28 mg Calc.
PointsPlus value: *1*

FYI   In order to caramelize the onions, you must cook them very slowly. This allows them enough time to get deeply colored and to bring out all their natural sweetness.

Lemon-Thyme Zucchini on Flatbread

serves 6

3 tablespoons lemon juice
1¹⁄₂ teaspoons extra-virgin olive oil
3 garlic cloves, minced
2 teaspoons chopped fresh thyme or ¹⁄₂ teaspoon dried
¹⁄₂ teaspoon salt
2 zucchini, cut crosswise in half, then lengthwise into ¹⁄₄-inch slices
3 whole wheat naan flatbreads
¹⁄₂ cup crumbled soft goat cheese, at room temperature

1   Combine lemon juice, oil, garlic, thyme, and salt in large zip-close plastic bag; add zucchini. Squeeze out air and seal bag; turn to coat zucchini. Let stand 30 minutes.
2   Spray grill rack with nonstick spray. Preheat grill to medium-high or prepare medium-high fire using direct method.
3   Place zucchini on grill rack and grill until tender, about 2 minutes per side. Transfer to plate. Place naan on grill rack and grill until lightly crisped on bottom, about 2 minutes. Turn naan over; sprinkle evenly with goat cheese and top with zucchini. Grill, covered, until naan are lightly charred on bottom, about 3 minutes longer. Cut naan crosswise in half.

PER SERVING (¹⁄₂ GARNISHED FLATBREAD): 118 grams, 158 Cal, 4 g Total Fat, 1 g Sat Fat, 0 g Trans Fat, 4 mg Chol, 240 mg Sod, 24 g Total Carb, 2 g Total Sugar, 5 g Fib, 8 g Prot, 34 mg Calc.
PointsPlus value: *4*

FYI   Packages of naan can be found in the specialty bread section in supermarkets.

White Bean, Bell Pepper, and Olive Pizzas

serves 8

3 cups lightly packed chopped romaine lettuce
1 cup grape tomatoes, halved
1 (8½-ounce) can quartered artichoke hearts, drained
1 cup canned cannellini (white kidney) beans, rinsed and drained
1 (7-ounce) jar roasted red bell peppers, drained and sliced
1 small onion, thinly sliced
12 pitted Kalamata olives, sliced
2 tablespoons lemon juice
1 tablespoon olive oil
½ teaspoon dried oregano
¼ teaspoon black pepper
4 (6-inch) whole wheat pita breads
½ cup crumbled fat-free feta cheese

1   Preheat oven to 425°F.
2   Meanwhile, toss together lettuce, tomatoes, artichoke hearts, beans, roasted peppers, onion, olives, lemon juice, oil, oregano, and black pepper in large bowl.
3   Place pita breads on ungreased baking sheet. Top each with 1¼ cups of salad and sprinkle with 2 tablespoons of feta. Bake until cheese is softened and lettuce is slightly wilted, about 5 minutes.

PER SERVING (½ PIZZA): 160 grams, 176 Cal,
4 g Total Fat, 0 g Sat Fat, 0 g Trans Fat, 0 mg Chol,
589 mg Sod, 30 g Total Carb, 3 g Total Sugar, 5 g Fib,
8 g Prot, 53 mg Calc.
PointsPlus value: **5**

▲ **HEALTHY EXTRA**
Add 1 cup sliced white mushrooms to the
vegetable mixture in step 2.

Nachos Grandes

serves 12

1 teaspoon canola oil
¼ pound ground skinless turkey breast
1 cup canned red kidney beans, rinsed and drained
1 small onion, finely chopped
1 (14-ounce) can diced green tomatoes with green chiles, drained
2 teaspoons Mexican or taco seasoning
6 ounces reduced-fat restaurant-style tortilla chips
¾ cup shredded reduced-fat Cheddar cheese
12 pitted black olives, sliced
¼ cup sliced pickled jalapeño peppers, drained
½ cup fat-free sour cream

1   Preheat oven to 425°F. Spray baking sheet with nonstick spray.
2   Heat oil in large nonstick skillet over medium-high heat. Add turkey, red kidney beans, and onion; cook, breaking turkey apart with wooden spoon, until no longer pink, about 3 minutes. Stir in tomatoes and Mexican seasoning; cook until slightly thickened, about 5 minutes. Keep warm.
3   Place tortilla chips on prepared baking sheet in single layer. Top evenly with turkey mixture; sprinkle evenly with Cheddar, olives, and jalapeños. Bake until cheese is melted, about 5 minutes. Pile nachos on serving platter. Serve with sour cream.

PER SERVING (¹⁄₁₂ OF NACHOS): 106 grams, 132 Cal,
3 g Total Fat, 1 g Sat Fat, 0 g Trans Fat, 11 mg Chol,
471 mg Sod, 19 g Total Carb, 2 g Total Sugar, 2 g Fib,
7 g Prot, 105 mg Calc.
PointsPlus value: **3**

NACHOS GRANDES

California Sushi Rolls

serves 8

2¼ cups water
2 cups sushi rice, rinsed and drained
½ cup seasoned rice vinegar
1 tablespoon sesame seeds, toasted
3 tablespoons warm water
2 tablespoons reduced-sodium soy sauce
2 teaspoons wasabi powder
1 teaspoon Asian (dark) sesame oil
1 teaspoon grated peeled fresh ginger
4 (7 × 8-inch) nori sheets
½ cucumber, peeled and cut into thick
    matchsticks
½ avocado, peeled, pitted, and cut into thick
    matchsticks
¼ pound surimi (imitation crab), cut into
    thick matchsticks

1   Combine water and rice in medium saucepan and bring to boil. Reduce heat and simmer,
covered, until rice is tender and liquid is absorbed, about 20 minutes. Transfer rice to large
bowl. Add vinegar and sesame seeds, stirring
until mixed well. Let rice mixture cool to room
temperature.
2   Meanwhile, to make dipping sauce, whisk
together warm water, soy sauce, wasabi, sesame oil, and ginger in serving bowl.
3   To make sushi rolls, place 1 nori sheet,
shiny side down, on sushi rolling mat with one
long side facing you. With damp hands spread
1 cup of seasoned rice over nori, leaving ½-
inch border at long side farthest away. Make
¼-inch-deep indentation along length of rice;
layer one-fourth of cucumber, avocado, and
surimi in indentation.
4   Holding filling in place with your fingers,
roll mat away from you until ends of nori over-
lap, forming tight cylinder. Applying gentle but

even pressure to mat, remove sushi roll from
mat. With very sharp knife, cut sushi into 6
pieces, wetting knife between cuts. Repeat
with remaining nori, rice, cucumber, avocado,
and surimi, making a total of 24 pieces of sushi. Serve with dipping sauce.

PER SERVING (3 PIECES SUSHI AND ABOUT
2 TEASPOONS DIPPING SAUCE): 165 grams, 180 Cal,
3 g Total Fat, 1 g Sat Fat, 0 g Trans Fat, 3 mg Chol,
272 mg Sod, 32 g Total Carb, 1 g Total Sugar, 2 g Fib,
5 g Prot, 6 mg Calc.
PointsPlus value: *5*

FYI   Nori, crisp, paper-thin sheets of dried
seaweed, can be found in health food and
specialty food stores. Once moistened with
sushi rice, the sheets become flexible and easy to
roll up.

Roasted Pepper and Tomato–Stuffed Eggplant Rollups

serves 4

¼ cup crumbled soft goat cheese
1 large plum tomato, chopped
⅓ cup chopped roasted red pepper
1 small onion, chopped
½ teaspoon dried oregano
½ teaspoon salt
¼ teaspoon black pepper
1 (1-pound) eggplant, cut lengthwise into 8
    slices
1 tablespoon extra-virgin olive oil
2 tablespoons chopped fresh mint

1   Stir together goat cheese, tomato, roasted pepper, onion, oregano, ¼ teaspoon of salt, and the black pepper in medium bowl.
2   Spray grill rack with olive oil nonstick spray. Preheat grill to medium-high or prepare medium-high fire using direct method.
3   Lightly spray eggplant slices with nonstick spray and sprinkle with remaining ¼ teaspoon salt. Place eggplant on grill rack and grill until well marked and tender, about 3 minutes per side. Transfer to plate; let cool.
4   To assemble rollups, spoon about 2 tablespoons of tomato mixture on wider end of each slice of eggplant. Roll up tightly and place, seam side down, on platter. Drizzle oil over rollups and sprinkle with mint.

PER SERVING (2 EGGPLANT ROLLS): 166 grams, 95 Cal, 5 g Total Fat, 2 g Sat Fat, 0 g Trans Fat, 3 mg Chol, 360 mg Sod, 11 g Total Carb, 6 g Total Sugar, 3 g Fib, 3 g Prot, 29 mg Calc.
PointsPlus value: *3*

Antipasto Platter

serves 12

2 tablespoons balsamic vinegar
1 tablespoon extra-virgin olive oil
1 garlic clove, minced
½ teaspoon black pepper
1 (9-ounce) package frozen artichoke hearts,
    cooked according to package directions
    and drained
12 thin slices prosciutto (about ¼ pound)
½ small cantaloupe, peeled, seeded, and cut
    into 12 wedges
2 ounces mozzarella cheese,
    cut into ½-inch dice
½ fennel bulb, thinly sliced
2 plum tomatoes, sliced
10 fresh basil leaves, thinly sliced
12 Kalamata olives
8 ounces Italian bread, cut into
    12 slices and toasted

1   Whisk together vinegar, oil, garlic, and pepper in medium bowl. Add artichoke hearts and toss to coat. Let stand 10 minutes.
2   Wrap slice of prosciutto around each cantaloupe wedge.
3   Drain artichoke hearts; reserve dressing. Pile artichokes at one end of large platter. Arrange prosciutto-wrapped melon at other end of platter and arrange mozzarella, fennel, and tomatoes in piles in middle. Drizzle reserved dressing and basil over cheese, fennel, and tomatoes. Scatter Kalamata olives on platter and serve with toasts.

PER SERVING (1/12 OF PLATTER): 101 grams, 133 Cal, 5 g Total Fat, 2 g Sat Fat, 0 g Trans Fat, 12 mg Chol, 389 mg Sod, 16 g Total Carb, 2 g Total Sugar, 2 g Fib, 6 g Prot, 58 mg Calc.
PointsPlus value: *3*

Thai-Style Roast Beef Salad

serves 6

3 tablespoons lime juice
1 tablespoon sugar
2 teaspoons Asian fish sauce
½ teaspoon Thai red curry paste
¾ pound thinly sliced lean roast beef, cut into thin strips
1 small carrot, grated
½ small red bell pepper, diced
1 tomato, halved, seeded, and diced
½ small red onion, thinly sliced
2 mini (Persian) cucumbers, thinly sliced
⅓ cup chopped fresh cilantro
¼ cup chopped fresh mint
6 large Boston lettuce leaves
¼ cup unsalted peanuts, chopped
Lime wedges

1   Whisk together lime juice, sugar, fish sauce, and curry paste in small bowl until sugar is dissolved.

2   Toss together roast beef, carrot, bell pepper, tomato, onion, cucumbers, cilantro, and mint in large bowl. Add lime juice mixture, tossing until mixed well.

3   Place 1 lettuce leaf on each of 6 plates and top each with about ¾ cup of roast beef mixture. Sprinkle evenly with peanuts and serve with lime wedges.

PER SERVING (1 STUFFED LETTUCE LEAF): 167 grams, 141 Cal, 5 g Total Fat, 1 g Sat Fat, 0 g Trans Fat, 27 mg Chol, 744 mg Sod, 12 g Total Carb, 7 g Total Sugar, 2 g Fib, 14 g Prot, 28 g Calc.
PointsPlus value: *4*

Korean Steak on a Stick

serves 8

1¼ pounds flank steak, thinly sliced
6 scallions, finely chopped
½ cup cider vinegar
¼ cup reduced-sodium soy sauce
¼ cup honey
2 tablespoons sugar
1 tablespoon grated peeled fresh ginger
2 garlic cloves, minced
2 teaspoons Asian fish sauce
1 teaspoon chili garlic sauce

1   Soak 16 (12-inch) wooden skewers in water at least 30 minutes.

2   Thread steak onto skewers dividing evenly; place in large baking dish. Stir together all remaining ingredients in small bowl; pour over meat, turning to coat. Cover and refrigerate at least 2 hours or up to 4 hours.

3   Spray broiler rack with nonstick spray and preheat broiler.

4   Drain marinade into small saucepan; bring to boil. Boil, stirring occasionally, until sauce is thickened, about 8 minutes.

5   Meanwhile, place skewers on broiler rack and broil 5 inches from heat, turning, until meat is browned, about 4 minutes per side. Arrange skewers on platter and drizzle evenly with sauce.

PER SERVING (2 SKEWERS): 101 grams, 162 Cal, 5 g Total Fat, 2 g Sat Fat, 1 g Trans Fat, 34 mg Chol, 469 mg Sod, 15 g Total Carb, 13 g Total Sugar, 0 g Fib, 15 g Prot, 14 mg Calc.
PointsPlus value: *4*

FYI   The Korean-style marinade can also be used to season flank steak, salmon fillets or steaks, pork ribs, chops, or tenderloin.

KOREAN STEAK ON A STICK

Picadillo in Lettuce Leaves

serves 8

1 onion, chopped
2 garlic cloves, minced
1 pound lean ground beef (7% fat or less)
¼ cup sliced pitted green olives
1 tablespoon chili powder
2 teaspoons ground cumin
¼ cup chopped fresh cilantro
2 tablespoons red wine vinegar
¾ teaspoon salt
¾ teaspoon black pepper
8 Boston lettuce leaves

1   Spray large nonstick skillet with nonstick spray and set over medium heat. Add onion and cook, stirring occasionally, until softened, about 5 minutes. Add garlic and cook, stirring frequently, until fragrant, about 30 seconds. Add beef and cook, breaking it apart with spoon, until browned, about 5 minutes.
2   Add olives, chili powder, and cumin to skillet; cook, stirring, 2 minutes. Add cilantro, vinegar, salt, and pepper; cook, stirring constantly, until vinegar is evaporated, about 30 seconds.
3   Spoon about ⅓ cup of picadillo onto each lettuce leaf and arrange on platter.

PER SERVING (1 FILLED LETTUCE LEAF): 83 grams, 99 Cal, 4 g Total Fat, 1 g Sat Fat, 0 g Trans Fat, 32 mg Chol, 223 mg Sod, 4 g Total Carb, 1 g Total Sugar, 1 g Fib, 12 g Prot, 19 mg Calc.
PointsPlus value: *2*

FYI   This flavorful beef mixture can be used as a stuffing for vegetables, including zucchini, tomatoes, bell peppers, and baby eggplant.

Chicken Satay with Peanut Sauce

serves 8

3 tablespoons creamy peanut butter
2 teaspoons sugar
2 garlic cloves, minced
2 tablespoons reduced-sodium soy sauce
1 tablespoon water
2 teaspoons rice wine vinegar
Several drops Sriracha (hot chili sauce)
1 tablespoon chopped fresh cilantro
2 (5-ounce) skinless boneless chicken breasts,
    each cut into 8 lengthwise strips

1   Soak 8 (12-inch) wooden skewers in water at least 30 minutes. Line rack of broiler pan with foil and spray with nonstick spray.
2   To make peanut sauce, whisk together peanut butter, sugar, and garlic in small bowl until smooth. Add soy sauce, water, vinegar, and Sriracha, whisking until blended. Transfer to serving bowl and sprinkle with cilantro.
3   Preheat broiler.
4   Thread chicken onto skewers and spray with nonstick spray. Arrange skewers on rack of broiler pan and broil 5 inches from heat until cooked through, about 4 minutes per side. Serve with peanut sauce.

PER SERVING (1 SKEWER AND ABOUT 1 TABLESPOON SAUCE): 39 grams, 81 Cal, 4 g Total Fat, 1 g Sat Fat, 0 g Trans Fat, 20 mg Chol, 200 mg Sod, 3 g Total Carb, 2 g Total Sugar, 0 g Fib, 9 g Prot, 7 mg Calc.
PointsPlus value: *2*

Stuffed Turkey Rollups

serves 4

1 yellow or orange bell pepper, cut into thin
   strips
4 (¼-pound) turkey cutlets
1 teaspoon chili powder
¼ teaspoon salt
4 scallions (green part only)

1   Preheat oven to 450°F.
2   Spread bell pepper strips on baking sheet
and lightly spray with nonstick spray. Roast until softened, about 10 minutes. Let cool.
3   Meanwhile, place cutlets on work surface
with long sides facing you. Sprinkle with chili
powder and salt; turn cutlets over. Arrange
one-fourth of bell pepper strips and scallions
across each cutlet and roll up to form 4 rolls.
(Ends of scallions and bell pepper strips should
protrude from each roll.) Secure rolls with
toothpicks.
4   Spray large cast-iron or ovenproof nonstick
skillet with nonstick spray and set over medium-
high heat. Add turkey rolls and cook until
browned on all sides, about 3 minutes. Transfer
skillet to oven and roast until turkey is cooked
through, about 10 minutes.

PER SERVING (1 ROLLUP): 163 grams, 145 Cal,
1 g Total Fat, 0 g Sat Fat, 0 g Trans Fat, 74 mg Chol,
412 mg Sod, 5 g Total Carb, 2 g Total Sugar, 1 g Fib,
28 g Prot, 25 mg Calc.
PointsPlus value: *3*

Duck and Goat Cheese Quesadillas

serves 8

1 (8-ounce) package white or cremini
   mushrooms, sliced
1 cup thinly sliced red onion
2 teaspoons chopped fresh thyme
   or ½ teaspoon dried
½ teaspoon salt
⅛ teaspoon black pepper
1 pound cooked duck breast, skin removed
   and breast thinly sliced
4 ounces soft goat cheese, crumbled
4 (8-inch) fat-free flour tortillas
½ cup chutney, such as Major Grey's

1   Spray large nonstick skillet with nonstick
spray; set over medium-high heat. Add mushrooms, onion, thyme, salt, and pepper; cook
until mushroom juice is evaporated, about 8
minutes. Transfer to bowl. Wipe skillet clean.
2   Layer one-fourth of duck, mushroom
mixture, and goat cheese on one half of each
tortilla; fold unfilled half of tortilla over filling.
Spray with nonstick spray.
3   Spray skillet with nonstick spray; set over
medium-high heat. Place 2 quesadillas, sprayed
side down, in skillet; cook, until browned
in spots, about 3 minutes. Spray quesadillas
with nonstick spray; turn. Cook until heated
through, about 2 minutes. Repeat. Cut each
quesadilla into 4 wedges; serve with chutney.

PER SERVING (2 WEDGES AND 1 TABLESPOON
CHUTNEY): 141 grams, 174 Cal, 5 g Total Fat,
2 g Sat Fat, 0 g Trans Fat, 88 mg Chol, 427 mg Sod,
12 g Total Carb, 2 g Total Sugar, 2 g Fib, 21 g Prot,
64 mg Calc.
PointsPlus value: *4*

Tuna Seviche
serves 4

*1 pound sushi-grade tuna, cut into ½-inch
   cubes*
⅔ cup lime juice
1 large tomato, seeded and chopped
1 small red onion, very thinly sliced
¼ cup chopped fresh cilantro
½–1 jalapeño pepper, seeded and minced
Grated zest of ½ orange
½ teaspoon salt

1   Mix together tuna and lime juice in large
glass bowl. Cover and refrigerate, stirring several times, until tuna is opaque, about 1 hour.
Drain tuna and transfer to serving bowl; discard marinade.
2   Add all remaining ingredients to tuna; toss
to mix well.

PER SERVING (½ CUP): 215 grams, 149 Cal,
1 g Total Fat, 0 g Sat Fat, 0 g Trans Fat, 51 mg Chol,
338 mg Sod, 7 g Total Carb, 3 g Total Sugar, 1 g Fib,
27 g Prot, 30 mg Calc.
PointsPlus value: *3*

▲ HEALTHY EXTRA
Pile the seviche evenly into 4 Boston or butter
lettuce cups for a special presentation.

Garlic Shrimp Tapas
serves 8

1 tablespoon olive oil
4 garlic cloves, minced
*24 large shrimp (about 1 pound), peeled and
   deveined*
¾ teaspoon dried oregano
⅛ teaspoon red pepper flakes

Heat oil in very large nonstick skillet over
medium heat. Add garlic and cook, stirring,
until fragrant, about 30 seconds. Increase heat
to medium-high; add shrimp and sprinkle with
oregano and pepper flakes. Cook, stirring, until
shrimp are just opaque throughout, about 2
minutes. Serve hot or warm.

PER SERVING (3 SHRIMP): 20 grams, 34 Cal,
2 g Total Fat, 0 g Sat Fat, 0 g Trans Fat, 32 mg Chol,
37 mg Sod, 1 g Total Carb, 0 g Total Sugar, 0 g Fib,
4 g Prot, 12 mg Calc.
PointsPlus value: *1*

FYI   To devein shrimp, cut a shallow slit along
the back of each peeled shrimp with a
small sharp knife and remove the dark vein. Rinse
the shrimp briefly under cold running water and
pat dry with paper towels.

TOP: GARLIC SHRIMP TAPAS
BELOW: VIETNAMESE LOBSTER SUMMER ROLLS
WITH DIPPING SAUCE (PAGE 80)

Shrimp Cocktail with Horseradish Sauce

serves 4

1 pound medium shrimp, peeled and deveined
½ cup light sour cream
¼ cup finely chopped onion
2 tablespoons drained chopped pimiento
1 tablespoon prepared horseradish
¼ teaspoon black pepper
2 cups lightly packed thinly sliced romaine
    lettuce
Lemon wedges

1   Bring large pot of water to boil. Add shrimp and cook, stirring once or twice, just until opaque in center, about 3 minutes. Drain in colander, then rinse under cold running water. Drain again. Pat dry with paper towels.

2   To make horseradish sauce, whisk together sour cream, onion, pimiento, horseradish, and pepper in small bowl.

3   Pile ½ cup of lettuce on each of 4 plates. Divide shrimp evenly among plates and top each serving with ¼ cup of sauce. Serve with lemon wedges.

PER SERVING (1 PLATE): 165 grams, 137 Cal, 4 g Total Fat, 2 g Sat Fat, 0 g Trans Fat, 178 mg Chol, 273 mg Sod, 5 g Total Carb, 3 g Total Sugar, 1 g Fib, 20 g Prot, 109 mg Calc.
PointsPlus value: *3*

Vietnamese Lobster Summer Rolls with Dipping Sauce

serves 8

2 tablespoons seasoned rice vinegar
2 tablespoons lime juice
2 tablespoons hoisin sauce
2 tablespoons minced peeled fresh ginger
1 tablespoon Asian fish sauce
8 (8-inch) rice-paper rounds
2 cups lightly packed thinly sliced romaine
    lettuce
⅓ cup lightly packed fresh mint leaves
⅓ cup lightly packed fresh cilantro leaves
⅓ cup lightly packed fresh basil leaves
½ pound cooked lobster meat, cut into
    ½-inch pieces

1   To make dipping sauce, whisk together vinegar, lime juice, hoisin sauce, ginger, and fish sauce in small bowl.

2   Soak rice-paper rounds, 1 at a time, in large bowl of hot water just until softened, 10–30 seconds. Drain on paper towels.

3   Toss together lettuce, mint, cilantro, and basil in medium bowl.

4   Place 4 softened rice-paper rounds on work surface. Put about ¼ cup of lobster meat along center of each wrapper; top each with ½ cup of lettuce mixture. Fold in sides of each wrapper and roll up tightly to enclose filling. Cut each roll in half on diagonal. Serve with dipping sauce.

PER SERVING (1 SUMMER ROLL AND GENEROUS 1 TABLESPOON SAUCE): 70 grams, 66 Cal, 1 g Total Fat, 0 g Sat Fat, 0 g Trans Fat, 21 mg Chol, 432 mg Sod, 9 g Total Carb, 1 g Total Sugar, 1 g Fib, 7 g Prot, 36 mg Calc.
PointsPlus value: *2*

4

Salads—Sides and Main Dishes

Salads—Sides and Main Dishes

84   Whole Leaf Caesar Salad with Golden Croutons
84   Beet, Apple, and Watercress Salad
85   Baby Romaine with Clementines and Pecans
85   Greek Islands Salad
87   Watermelon-Peach Salad with Ricotta Salata
87   Tomato, Sweet Onion, and Goat Cheese Salad
88   Orange and Red Onion Salad with Citrus Dressing
88   California Greens Salad with Baked Goat Cheese
89   Salad Niçoise
89   Salmon Salad with Horseradish
91   Rainbow Slaw
91   Radicchio, Cabbage, and Jicama Slaw
92   German Potato Salad
92   All-American Potato Salad
94   Wild Rice Salad with Pecans and Cranberries
94   Southwestern Black Bean Salad
95   Minted Tabbouleh
95   Quinoa-Fruit Salad
97   Grilled Thai Beef Salad
97   Roast Beef Salad with Arugula
98   Crispy Buffalo-Style Chicken Salad
98   Chinese Chicken Salad
99   Classic Chicken Salad
99   Wheat Berries with Smoked Turkey and Fruit
100   Tuna and White Bean Salad
100   Lobster Salad
101   California Seafood Salad
101   Quinoa, Black Bean, and Shrimp Salad
102   Pasta Salad Primavera
102   Tuscan Panzanella

Whole Leaf Caesar Salad with Golden Croutons

serves 6

1 cup cubes (¾-inch) whole grain bread
1 small garlic clove, peeled
¼ teaspoon salt
3 tablespoons reduced-sodium chicken broth
2 tablespoons grated Parmesan cheese
1 tablespoon extra-virgin olive oil
1 tablespoon reduced-fat mayonnaise
1 tablespoon chopped fresh flat-leaf parsley
1 teaspoon cider vinegar
1 teaspoon Dijon mustard
1 teaspoon anchovy paste
Pinch black pepper
8 cups lightly packed small romaine lettuce
 leaves

1   Preheat oven to 350°F.
2   Put bread cubes in bowl; spray with non-stick spray. Spread in baking pan. Bake until golden, about 10 minutes.
3   With side of knife, mash garlic with salt.
4   To make dressing, whisk together broth, 1 tablespoon of Parmesan, the oil, mayonnaise, parsley, vinegar, mustard, anchovy paste, garlic paste, and pepper in small bowl until blended.
5   Put romaine and croutons in large bowl; drizzle dressing over and toss to coat evenly. Divide salad evenly among 6 plates; sprinkle with remaining 1 tablespoon cheese.

PER SERVING (1⅓ CUPS): 91 grams, 66 Cal, 4 g Total Fat, 1 g Sat Fat, 0 g Trans Fat, 3 mg Chol, 235 mg Sod, 5 g Total Carb, 1 g Total Sugar, 2 g Fib, 3 g Prot, 61 mg Calc.
PointsPlus value: *2*

FYI   Using only the small inner romaine lettuce leaves makes this Caesar salad especially striking when mounded on plates.

Beet, Apple, and Watercress Salad

serves 6

1 bunch beets (about 1 pound), trimmed
1 Granny Smith apple, unpeeled, cored, and
 diced
1 bunch watercress, trimmed
3 tablespoons red wine vinegar
1 tablespoon olive oil
¼ teaspoon salt
⅛ teaspoon black pepper

1   Preheat oven to 400°F.
2   Wrap beets in foil and roast until tender, about 1 hour. Unwrap beets.
3   When beets are cool enough to handle, slip off their skins and dice. Toss together beets, apple, and watercress in salad bowl.
4   To make dressing, whisk together all remaining ingredients in small bowl until well blended. Drizzle dressing over salad and toss well to coat evenly.

PER SERVING (ABOUT ¾ CUP): 95 grams, 59 Cal, 2 g Total Fat, 0 g Sat Fat, 0 g Trans Fat, 0 mg Chol, 141 mg Sod, 9 g Total Carb, 6 g Total Sugar, 2 g Fib, 1 g Prot, 24 mg Calc.
PointsPlus value: *1*

FYI   If you prefer that the apple doesn't turn pink from the beets, put the apple in a small bowl and toss it with a small amount of the dressing. Pile the apple on top of the salad.

Baby Romaine with Clementines and Pecans

serves 4

2 tablespoons orange juice
2 teaspoons extra-virgin olive oil
¼ teaspoon salt
¼ teaspoon black pepper
6 cups lightly packed baby romaine lettuce
2 clementines, peeled and sectioned
¼ cup snipped fresh chives
2 tablespoons pecans, chopped and toasted

1   To make dressing, whisk together orange juice, oil, salt, and pepper in small bowl until well blended.
2   Toss together romaine, clementines, chives, and pecans in salad bowl. Drizzle dressing over and toss to coat evenly.

PER SERVING (ABOUT 2 CUPS): 136 grams, 78 Cal,
5 g Total Fat, 1 g Sat Fat, 0 g Trans Fat, 0 mg Chol,
153 mg Sod, 7 g Total Carb, 5 g Total Sugar, 3 g Fib,
2 g Prot, 42 mg Calc.
PointsPlus value: *2*

▲ HEALTHY EXTRA

If you are especially fond of clementines, use 4 instead of 2.

Greek Islands Salad

serves 6

2 tablespoons lemon juice
1 tablespoon extra-virgin olive oil
1 garlic clove, minced
½ teaspoon dried oregano, crumbled
¼ teaspoon black pepper
3 cups lightly packed torn romaine lettuce
1 large tomato, cut into thin wedges
1 mini (Persian) cucumber, thinly sliced
1 red bell pepper, cut into thin strips
½ red onion, thinly sliced
6 large pitted black olives, halved
¼ cup lightly packed fresh flat-leaf parsley
    leaves
¼ cup crumbled reduced-fat feta cheese

1   To make dressing, whisk together lemon juice, oil, garlic, oregano, and black pepper in small bowl until blended.
2   Toss together all remaining ingredients except feta in salad bowl. Drizzle dressing over and toss to coat evenly. Sprinkle with cheese.

PER SERVING (GENEROUS 1 CUP): 121 grams, 62 Cal,
4 g Total Fat, 0 g Sat Fat, 0 g Trans Fat, 2 mg Chol,
106 mg Sod, 6 g Total Carb, 3 g Total Sugar, 2 g Fib,
2 g Prot, 33 mg Calc.
PointsPlus value: *2*

▲ HEALTHY EXTRA

Use 4 cups of lightly packed torn romaine lettuce instead of 3 cups.

**WATERMELON-PEACH
SALAD WITH RICOTTA SALATA**

Watermelon-Peach Salad with Ricotta Salata

serves 4

1 (2-pound) piece seedless watermelon, rind
    removed and cut into ¾-inch dice
2 large peaches, pitted and cut into ¾-inch
    pieces
2 mini (Persian) cucumbers, thinly sliced
3 tablespoons champagne vinegar or white
    wine vinegar
¼ teaspoon salt
½ cup coarsely crumbled ricotta salata or feta
    cheese
1 scallion (white and light green parts only),
    cut into very thin strips

Toss together all ingredients except ricotta
salata and scallion in serving bowl; let stand 10
minutes. Sprinkle with cheese and scallion.

PER SERVING (GENEROUS 1 CUP): 258 grams, 133 Cal,
5 g Total Fat, 3 g Sat Fat, 0 g Trans Fat, 17 mg Chol,
359 mg Sod, 19 g Total Carb, 16 g Total Sugar, 2 g Fib,
4 g Prot, 113 mg Calc.
PointsPlus value: *4*

FYI Ricotta salata is made by salting and
pressing fresh ricotta cheese, then aging it
for a few months. The resulting cheese resembles
feta cheese but is more delicately flavored.

Tomato, Sweet Onion, and Goat Cheese Salad

serves 6

2 tablespoons champagne vinegar or white
    wine vinegar
1 tablespoon lemon juice
4 teaspoons olive oil
1 teaspoon Dijon mustard
½ teaspoon salt
¼ teaspoon black pepper
4 tomatoes, cut into wedges
1 sweet onion, cut into thin wedges
½ cup lightly packed fresh flat-leaf parsley
    leaves
2 ounces soft goat cheese, crumbled

1   To make dressing, whisk together vinegar,
lemon juice, oil, mustard, salt, and pepper in
small bowl until blended.
2   Toss together tomatoes, onion, and parsley
in large bowl. Drizzle dressing over and toss
to coat evenly. Divide salad evenly among 6
plates. Sprinkle evenly with goat cheese.

PER SERVING (1 SALAD): 144 grams, 86 Cal,
5 g Total Fat, 2 g Sat Fat, 0 g Trans Fat, 5 mg Chol,
257 mg Sod, 7 g Total Carb, 4 g Total Sugar, 2 g Fib,
3 g Prot, 39 mg Calc.
PointsPlus value: *2*

Orange and Red Onion Salad with Citrus Dressing

serves 4

2 (3-inch) strips orange zest, very thinly
    sliced
$^1/_3$ cup orange juice
4 teaspoons lemon juice
4 teaspoons lime juice
1 tablespoon extra-virgin olive oil
1 tablespoon balsamic vinegar
$^1/_2$ teaspoon Dijon mustard
Pinch salt
Pinch black pepper
2 cups lightly packed torn escarole or romaine
    lettuce
2 navel oranges, peeled and sectioned
1 carrot, grated
$^1/_2$ red onion, very thinly sliced

1   To make dressing, combine orange zest
and juice, lemon juice, lime juice, oil, vinegar,
mustard, salt, and pepper in small jar with
tight-fitting lid; cover and shake well.
2   Toss together all remaining ingredients in
salad bowl. Drizzle dressing over and toss to
coat evenly.

PER SERVING (ABOUT 1 CUP): 175 grams, 99 Cal,
4 g Total Fat, 1 g Sat Fat, 0 g Trans Fat, 0 mg Chol,
69 mg Sod, 17 g Total Carb, 12 g Total Sugar, 4 g Fib,
2 g Prot, 0 g Alcohol, 58 mg Calc.
PointsPlus value: *3*

FYI   The zest of citrus fruit consists of the
colorful, flavorful peel without any of the
bitter white pith still attached. To remove the
zest, use a vegetable peeler, then scrape off any
remaining pith with a small knife.

California Greens Salad with Baked Goat Cheese

serves 6

1 garlic clove, peeled
$^1/_2$ teaspoon salt
1 tablespoon extra-virgin olive oil
1 tablespoon lemon juice
1 tablespoon chopped fresh flat-leaf parsley
1 small shallot, minced
1 teaspoon Dijon mustard
$^1/_4$ teaspoon black pepper
3 tablespoons plain dried bread crumbs
2 tablespoons finely ground walnuts
2 ounces reduced-fat soft goat cheese, cut into
    6 rounds
1 large egg white, lightly beaten
6 cups lightly packed mixed baby salad greens

1   Preheat oven to 400°F. Spray baking sheet
with nonstick spray.
2   With side of large knife, mash garlic with
salt on cutting board until it forms a paste.
3   To make dressing, whisk together oil, lemon juice, parsley, shallot, mustard, pepper, and
garlic paste in small bowl until blended.
4   Mix crumbs and walnuts on wax paper.
Coat cheese with egg, then coat with crumb
mixture. Place on baking sheet; bake until
warm, about 5 minutes.
5   Meanwhile, put salad greens in large bowl;
drizzle dressing over and toss to coat evenly.
Divide salad evenly among 6 plates and top
with warm goat cheese round.

PER SERVING (1 SALAD): 89 grams, 75 Cal,
5 g Total Fat, 1 g Sat Fat, 0 g Trans Fat, 2 mg Chol,
309 mg Sod, 6 g Total Carb, 1 g Total Sugar, 1 g Fib,
3 g Prot, 48 mg Calc.
PointsPlus value: *2*

Salad Niçoise

serves 4

1¼ pounds small red potatoes, scrubbed
2 cups trimmed green beans
6 large Boston or butter lettuce leaves
4 cups lightly packed sliced romaine lettuce
2 (5-ounce) cans water-packed light tuna,
    drained and flaked
24 cherry tomatoes, halved
2 hard-cooked large eggs, peeled and
    quartered
6 large pitted black olives, sliced
4 anchovy fillets, rinsed and patted dry
2 tablespoons red wine vinegar
2 tablespoons lemon juice
1 tablespoon olive oil
¼ teaspoon salt
¼ teaspoon black pepper

1   Put potatoes in large saucepan and add
enough water to cover by 1 inch; bring to boil.
Reduce heat and simmer, partially covered,
until tender, about 12 minutes. With slotted
spoon, transfer potatoes to colander and cool
under cold running water; drain. Cut potatoes
into quarters.
2   Add green beans to same boiling water;
cook just until tender, about 6 minutes. Drain;
rinse under cold running water. Drain again.
3   Line platter with lettuce; arrange separate
mounds of potatoes, green beans, tuna, tomatoes, and eggs on top. Sprinkle olives over all
and top with anchovy fillets.
4   To make dressing, whisk together all remaining ingredients in small bowl until blended. Drizzle evenly over salad.

PER SERVING (ABOUT 3 CUPS): 502 grams, 362 Cal,
11 g Total Fat, 2 g Sat Fat, 0 g Trans Fat, 139 mg Chol,
673 mg Sod, 41 g Total Carb, 7 g Total Sugar, 7 g Fib,
27 g Prot, 103 mg Calc.
PointsPlus value: **9**

Salmon Salad with Horseradish

serves 4

1¼ pounds small white potatoes, scrubbed
1 (¾-pound) salmon fillet, skinned
½ cup cold water
1 yellow bell pepper, diced
1 dill pickle, thinly sliced
¼ cup snipped fresh chives
¾ cup plain fat-free yogurt
3 tablespoons prepared horseradish, drained
3 tablespoons reduced-fat mayonnaise
½ teaspoon salt
2 cups lightly packed baby arugula

1   Put potatoes in large saucepan and add
enough water to cover by 1 inch; bring to boil.
Reduce heat and simmer, partially covered,
until tender, about 12 minutes; drain. When
cool enough to handle, dice potatoes.
2   Meanwhile, put salmon in large skillet and
add water; bring to boil. Reduce heat and simmer, covered, until salmon is just opaque in
center, about 8 minutes. With slotted spoon,
transfer salmon to plate. Let cool completely,
then flake with fork.
3   Mix together salmon, potatoes, bell pepper, pickle, and chives in large bowl.
4   To make dressing, whisk yogurt, horseradish, mayonnaise, and salt in bowl. Pour dressing
over salmon mixture; toss to coat. Line platter
with arugula; top with salmon mixture.

**PER SERVING (GENEROUS 1 CUP SALMON SALAD WITH
½ CUP ARUGULA):** 339 grams, 317 Cal, 7 g Total Fat,
1 g Sat Fat, 0 g Trans Fat, 53 mg Chol, 725 mg Sod,
39 g Total Carb, 7 g Total Sugar, 4 g Fib, 24 g Prot,
114 mg Calc.
PointsPlus value: **8**

RAINBOW SLAW

Rainbow Slaw

serves 8

3 tablespoons reduced-fat mayonnaise
3 tablespoons light sour cream
3 tablespoons red wine vinegar
¾ teaspoon salt
¼ teaspoon black pepper
3 cups thinly sliced green cabbage
3 cups thinly sliced red cabbage
2 large carrots, grated
1 large orange, yellow, or red bell pepper,
    chopped
2 scallions, thinly sliced
¼ cup chopped fresh parsley

1   To make dressing, whisk together mayonnaise, sour cream, vinegar, salt, and black pepper in large bowl until smooth.
2   Add all remaining ingredients and toss until coated evenly. Cover and refrigerate at least 1 hour or up to overnight. Let stand at room temperature about 30 minutes before serving for the best flavor.

PER SERVING (1 CUP): 116 grams, 56 Cal, 3 g Total Fat, 1 g Sat Fat, 0 g Trans Fat, 4 mg Chol, 292 mg Sod, 8 g Total Carb, 4 g Total Sugar, 2 g Fib, 2 g Prot, 50 mg Calc.
PointsPlus value: *2*

FYI   The longer you allow the coleslaw to sit in the refrigerator, the softer it will become.

Radicchio, Cabbage, and Jicama Slaw

serves 4

2 cups thinly sliced Savoy cabbage
1 cup thinly sliced radicchio
¼ jicama, peeled and cut into matchsticks
½ yellow bell pepper, cut into thin strips
1 celery stalk, thinly sliced
2 tablespoons plain fat-free yogurt
2 tablespoons fat-free mayonnaise
1 tablespoon cider vinegar
1 teaspoon pickle relish
½ teaspoon grated lemon zest
¼ teaspoon salt
¼ teaspoon black pepper

1   Toss together cabbage, radicchio, jicama, bell pepper, and celery in large bowl.
2   To make dressing, whisk together all remaining ingredients in small bowl until combined. Drizzle over vegetables and toss to coat evenly. Cover and refrigerate until flavors are blended, at least 1 hour or up to 4 hours.

PER SERVING (GENEROUS 1 CUP): 136 grams, 45 Cal, 0 g Total Fat, 0 g Sat Fat, 0 g Trans Fat, 1 mg Chol, 247 mg Sod, 10 g Total Carb, 4 g Total Sugar, 4 g Fib, 2 g Prot, 37 mg Calc.
PointsPlus value: *1*

FYI   Jicama, a knobby root vegetable used in Mexican dishes, is very sweet and crunchy with a texture similar to water chestnuts. It is also delicious raw. Jicama can be found in supermarkets and Latino groceries. Choose smaller jicama, as the larger ones tend to be woody and tough.

German Potato Salad

serves 6

1 1/2 *pounds all-purpose potatoes, peeled*
1 *onion, finely chopped*
1 *celery stalk, finely chopped*
1/2 *green bell pepper, chopped*
3 *slices bacon, crisp cooked and crumbled*
1/2 *cup apple juice*
1/4 *cup cider vinegar*
1 *tablespoon all-purpose flour*
1/2 *teaspoon salt*
1/4 *teaspoon black pepper*

1   Put potatoes in large saucepan and add enough water to cover by 1 inch; bring to boil. Reduce heat and simmer, partially covered, until tender, about 20 minutes; drain.
2   When cool enough to handle, cut potatoes into 3/4-inch dice. Toss together warm potatoes, onion, celery, bell pepper, and bacon in serving bowl. Keep warm.
3   To make dressing, whisk together apple juice, vinegar, and flour in small saucepan until smooth; bring to boil, whisking constantly. Reduce heat and simmer, whisking, until thickened, about 4 minutes; stir in salt and black pepper. Drizzle hot dressing over potato mixture and toss to coat evenly. Serve warm.

PER SERVING (ABOUT 1 CUP): 179 grams, 132 Cal, 2 g Total Fat, 1 g Sat Fat, 0 g Trans Fat, 3 mg Chol, 260 mg Sod, 27 g Total Carb, 5 g Total Sugar, 3 g Fib, 3 g Prot, 26 mg Calc.
PointsPlus value: **3**

▲ **HEALTHY EXTRA**
Double the amount of celery and bell pepper for lots more crunch.

All-American Potato Salad

serves 8

2 *pounds small red potatoes, scrubbed and*
   halved
1 *cup fat-free mayonnaise*
1/3 *cup chopped fresh flat-leaf parsley*
4 *scallions, thinly sliced*
2 *small celery stalks with leaves, thinly sliced*
2 *teaspoons cider vinegar*
1 *teaspoon Dijon mustard*
1/2 *teaspoon salt*
1/4 *teaspoon black pepper*

1   Put potatoes in large saucepan and add enough water to cover by 1 inch; bring to boil. Reduce heat and simmer, partially covered, until potatoes are tender, about 8 minutes; drain.
2   Meanwhile, mix together all remaining ingredients in serving bowl. Add potatoes and toss to coat evenly. Let cool to room temperature. Serve at once or cover and refrigerate up to 2 days. Let stand at room temperature 30 minutes before serving.

PER SERVING (¾ CUP): 168 grams, 105 Cal, 0 g Total Fat, 0 g Sat Fat, 0 g Trans Fat, 0 mg Chol, 420 mg Sod, 23 g Total Carb, 3 g Total Sugar, 2 g Fib, 2 g Prot, 25 mg Calc.
PointsPlus value: **3**

ALL-AMERICAN POTATO SALAD

Wild Rice Salad with Pecans and Cranberries
serves 8

1¼ cups wild rice (about 8 ounces)
2 cups halved red, green, and/or black grapes
2 celery stalks with leaves, thinly sliced
6 tablespoons chopped fresh flat-leaf parsley
⅓ cup dried cranberries or dried cherries
¼ cup pecans, toasted and chopped
2 tablespoons white wine vinegar
1 tablespoon extra-virgin olive oil
1 teaspoon chopped fresh thyme
¾ teaspoon salt
½ teaspoon black pepper

1 Cook wild rice according to package directions. Drain and let cool
2 Meanwhile, mix together all remaining ingredients in serving bowl. Stir in rice. Serve at once or cover and refrigerate up to 6 hours.

PER SERVING (¾ CUP): 171 grams, 190 Cal, 5 g Total Fat, 1 g Sat Fat, 0 g Trans Fat, 0 mg Chol, 236 mg Sod, 34 g Total Carb, 11 g Total Sugar, 3 g Fib, 5 g Prot, 20 mg Calc.
PointsPlus value: **5**

FYI Despite its name, wild rice isn't actually a rice but a long-grain marsh grass that is native to the Great Lakes area. It is also commercially produced in other parts of the U.S. Be sure to cook wild rice just until the grains begin to open, so it is still nice and chewy. Overcooking will turn it mushy.

Southwestern Black Bean Salad
serves 4

1 (15½-ounce) can black beans, rinsed and drained
1 red onion, finely chopped
1 cup chopped roasted red pepper
½ cup thawed frozen corn kernels
½ cup chopped fresh cilantro
4 scallions, thinly sliced
1 jalapeño pepper, seeded and minced
4 teaspoons lime juice
4 teaspoons olive oil
2 garlic cloves, minced
¼ teaspoon salt
Pinch black pepper

Toss together all ingredients in serving bowl until mixed well. Serve at once or cover and refrigerate up to 2 days.

PER SERVING (ABOUT 1½ CUPS): 218 grams, 163 Cal, 5 g Total Fat, 1 g Sat Fat, 0 g Trans Fat, 0 mg Chol, 393 mg Sod, 25 g Total Carb, 6 g Total Sugar, 6 g Fib, 5 g Prot, 45 mg Calc.
PointsPlus value: **4**

FYI During the summer months when fresh corn is readily available and very tender, you can use raw corn instead of the frozen corn in this salad.

Minted Tabbouleh

serves 4

1 cup bulgur
1 cup boiling water
1 large tomato, halved, seeded, and chopped
2 mini (Persian) cucumbers, diced
2 celery stalks, diced
¹/₂ cup chopped fresh mint
¹/₂ cup chopped fresh parsley
1 tablespoon lemon juice
1 tablespoon extra-virgin olive oil
2 teaspoons ground cumin
¹/₂ teaspoon salt
¹/₈ teaspoon black pepper

1   Put bulgur in large bowl. Pour boiling water over and let stand until water is absorbed, about 30 minutes.
2   Add all remaining ingredients to bulgur; toss to mix well. Transfer to serving bowl. Serve at once or cover and refrigerate up to 2 days.

PER SERVING (ABOUT ½ CUP): 223 grams, 181 Cal,
4 g Total Fat, 1 g Sat Fat, 0 g Trans Fat, 0 mg Chol,
338 mg Sod, 33 g Total Carb, 2 g Total Sugar, 9 g Fib,
6 g Prot, 72 mg Calc.
PointsPlus value: *4*

▲   **HEALTHY EXTRA**
In the summer when tomatoes are at their most flavorful, use 2 instead of 1 in this salad.

Quinoa-Fruit Salad

serves 6

2 cups water
¹/₄ teaspoon salt
1 cup quinoa, rinsed and drained
¹/₃ cup chopped fresh mint
¹/₄ cup vanilla fat-free yogurt
2 tablespoons orange juice
1¹/₂ cups sliced hulled strawberries
2 kiwifruit, peeled and sliced
1 (11-ounce) can mandarin orange sections,
    drained

1   Combine water and salt in medium saucepan and bring to boil; stir in quinoa. Reduce heat and simmer, covered, until quinoa is translucent, about 15 minutes.
2   To make dressing, whisk together mint, yogurt, and orange juice until blended.
3   Combine strawberries, kiwifruit, and orange sections in serving bowl. Drizzle dressing over and toss to coat evenly. Add quinoa; toss to combine. Cover and refrigerate until well chilled, about 2 hours. Serve within 2 days.

PER SERVING (GENEROUS 1 CUP): 233 grams, 170 Cal,
2 g Total Fat, 0 g Sat Fat, 0 g Trans Fat, 0 mg Chol,
110 mg Sod, 34g Total Carb, 11 g Total Sugar, 4 g Fib,
6 g Prot, 64 mg Calc.
PointsPlus value: *4*

FYI   Quinoa (*KEEN-wah*) is considered an ancient grain, as it was a staple of the Incas, who called it the "mother grain." This tiny grain contains more protein than any other known grain and is a complete protein, since it contains all eight essential amino acids. When cooked, quinoa expands to four times its size.

GRILLED THAI BEEF SALAD

Grilled Thai Beef Salad

serves 4

3 teaspoons canola oil
2 (¼-pound) filets mignons, trimmed
¼ cup lime juice
2 teaspoons Asian fish sauce
2 teaspoons brown sugar
¼ teaspoon red pepper flakes
2 cups lightly packed mixed baby salad greens
1 cup bean sprouts
1 small cucumber, thinly sliced
½ cup matchstick-cut carrot
½ red onion, thinly sliced
½ cup lightly packed fresh mint leaves
½ cup lightly packed fresh cilantro leaves

1   Heat 2 teaspoons of oil in medium non-stick skillet over medium-high heat. Add beef and cook until instant-read thermometer inserted into side of steak registers 145°F for medium, about 4 minutes per side. Transfer to cutting board and let stand 5 minutes.
2   Meanwhile, to make dressing, whisk together lime juice, fish sauce, brown sugar, pepper flakes, and remaining 1 teaspoon oil in large bowl until blended. Add all remaining ingredients and toss to coat evenly.
3   Mound salad on platter. Cut steaks into ¼-inch slices, then lengthwise in half. Arrange on top of salad.

PER SERVING (2 CUPS): 185 grams, 148 Cal,
7 g Total Fat, 2 g Sat Fat, 1 g Trans Fat, 29 mg Chol,
273 mg Sod, 10 g Total Carb, 5 g Total Sugar, 3 g Fib,
12 g Prot, 61 mg Calc.
PointsPlus value: *4*

Roast Beef Salad with Arugula

serves 4

1 tablespoon balsamic vinegar
2 teaspoons Dijon mustard
¼ teaspoon black pepper
4 teaspoons extra-virgin olive oil
10 moist-packed sun-dried tomatoes (not
    packed in oil), finely chopped
1 tablespoon water
8 cups lightly packed baby arugula or regular
    arugula, trimmed
1 small red onion, thinly sliced
1 cup thinly sliced cremini mushrooms
½ pound thinly sliced lean roast beef, cut into
    strips
1 lemon, cut into 4 wedges

1   To make dressing, whisk together vinegar, mustard, and pepper in small bowl until blended; gradually whisk in oil, then stir in sun-dried tomatoes and water.
2   Toss together arugula and 1 tablespoon of dressing in large bowl; divide evenly among 4 plates. Combine onion and mushrooms in same bowl and toss with another tablespoon of dressing; pile evenly on top of arugula. Toss together roast beef and remaining dressing in same bowl; arrange on top of salads. Place a lemon wedge alongside each salad.

PER SERVING (1 SALAD): 145 grams, 141 Cal,
7 g Total Fat, 1 g Sat Fat, 0 g Trans Fat, 27 mg Chol,
757 mg Sod, 8 g Total Carb, 3 g Total Sugar, 2 g Fib,
14 g Prot, 81 mg Calc.
PointsPlus value: *4*

Crispy Buffalo-Style Chicken Salad

serves 4

¹/₃ cup crumbled reduced-fat blue cheese
¹/₄ cup + 1 tablespoon fat-free mayonnaise
¹/₄ cup fat-free sour cream
1 teaspoon white wine vinegar
³/₄ cup cornflake crumbs
1 pound chicken tenders
2 tablespoons buffalo wing sauce
5 cups lightly packed sliced romaine lettuce
1 cup lightly packed tender watercress sprigs
2 large tomatoes, chopped
2 scallions, sliced

1   Preheat oven to 450°F. Spray small baking pan with nonstick spray.
2   To make dressing, whisk together blue cheese, ¹/₄ cup of mayonnaise, the sour cream, and vinegar in small bowl until blended.
3   Spread cornflake crumbs on wax paper.
4   Toss together chicken, buffalo wing sauce, and remaining 1 tablespoon mayonnaise in medium bowl. Coat chicken, one piece at a time, with crumbs. Place chicken in prepared baking pan. Lightly spray with nonstick spray. Bake chicken until cooked through, about 5 minutes per side.
5   Toss together romaine, watercress, tomatoes, and scallions in serving bowl. Place chicken on top of salad.

PER SERVING (2 CUPS): 320 grams, 254 Cal, 4 g Total Fat, 2 g Sat Fat, 0 g Trans Fat, 68 mg Chol, 613 mg Sod, 25 g Total Carb, 7 g Total Sugar, 3 g Fib, 28 g Prot, 98 mg Calc.
PointsPlus value: **6**

Chinese Chicken Salad

serves 4

³/₄ cup plain fat-free yogurt
1 tablespoon creamy peanut butter
1 tablespoon rice wine vinegar
1 teaspoon Asian (dark) sesame oil
1 garlic clove, minced
2 cups cubed cooked chicken breast
1¹/₂ cups cooked cellophane noodles
6 scallions, cut into 1-inch lengths
1 red bell pepper, cut into thin strips
1 (8-ounce) can sliced water chestnuts, drained
2 cups lightly packed tender watercress sprigs or mixed baby salad greens
1 tablespoon sesame seeds, toasted

1   To make dressing, whisk together yogurt, peanut butter, vinegar, oil, and garlic in large bowl until blended.
2   Add all remaining ingredients except watercress and sesame seeds to dressing; toss to coat evenly.
3   Divide watercress evenly among 4 plates. Top evenly with chicken mixture and sprinkle with sesame seeds.

PER SERVING (ABOUT 2½ CUPS): 235 grams, 243 Cal, 7 g Total Fat, 1 g Sat Fat, 0 g Trans Fat, 61 mg Chol, 112 mg Sod, 20 g Total Carb, 5 g Total Sugar, 4 g Fib, 27 g Prot, 110 mg Calc.
PointsPlus value: **6**

Classic Chicken Salad

serves 4

$^1/_4$ *cup plain fat-free yogurt*
3 tablespoons reduced-calorie mayonnaise
1 tablespoon cider vinegar
2 teaspoons Dijon mustard
$^1/_2$ *teaspoon salt*
$^1/_4$ *teaspoon black pepper*
2$^1/_2$ cups cubed cooked chicken breast
2 celery stalks, chopped
2 tablespoons grated onion

1   To make dressing, whisk together yogurt, mayonnaise, vinegar, mustard, salt, and pepper in small bowl until blended.
2   Mix together chicken, celery, and onion in medium bowl. Add yogurt mixture, tossing to coat evenly. Cover and refrigerate at least 1 hour or up to 4 hours before serving.

PER SERVING (ABOUT 1 CUP): 154 grams, 201 Cal, 7 g Total Fat, 2 g Sat Fat, 0 g Trans Fat, 79 mg Chol, 543 mg Sod, 4 g Total Carb, 1 g Total Sugar, 1 g Fib, 29 g Prot, 48 mg Calc.
PointsPlus value: **5**

▲ **HEALTHY EXTRA**
Serve the chicken salad on a bed of Boston or butter lettuce leaves.

Wheat Berries with Smoked Turkey and Fruit

serves 4

2$^1/_4$ cups water
1 cup wheat berries, rinsed
1 ($^1/_2$-pound) piece smoked turkey, diced
2 nectarines, pitted and cut into $^1/_2$-inch pieces
1 Granny Smith apple, peeled, cored, and diced
$^1/_2$ *red onion, finely chopped*
$^1/_4$ *cup orange juice*
3 tablespoons cider vinegar
1 tablespoon Dijon mustard
1 tablespoon honey
$^1/_2$ *(10-ounce) bag baby spinach, coarsely chopped*

1   Bring water to boil in medium saucepan. Stir in wheat berries; reduce heat and simmer, covered, until wheat berries are tender and water is absorbed, 1$^1/_2$–2 hours. Fluff wheat berries with fork; let stand 5 minutes.
2   Mix together wheat berries, turkey, nectarines, apple, and onion in large bowl.
3   To make dressing, whisk together orange juice, vinegar, mustard, and honey in small bowl until blended. Drizzle dressing over wheat berry mixture; toss to coat evenly.
4   Line platter with spinach; top with wheat berry mixture.

PER SERVING (2 CUPS): 296 grams, 322 Cal, 3 g Total Fat, 0 g Sat Fat, 0 g Trans Fat, 24 mg Chol, 673 mg Sod, 62 g Total Carb, 18 g Total Sugar, 10 g Fib, 17 g Prot, 44 mg Calc.
PointsPlus value: **8**

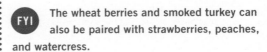 **FYI** The wheat berries and smoked turkey can also be paired with strawberries, peaches, and watercress.

Tuna and White Bean Salad

serves 4

1 (15½-ounce) can cannellini (white kidney)
    beans, rinsed and drained
2 (5-ounce) cans water-packed light tuna,
    drained and flaked
½ red onion, chopped
3 celery stalks, sliced
¼ cup chopped fresh parsley
3 tablespoons lemon juice
2 garlic cloves, minced
2 teaspoons dried sage
2 teaspoons olive oil
¼ teaspoon salt
¼ teaspoon black pepper

Mix together all ingredients in serving bowl
until combined well.

PER SERVING (ABOUT 1½ CUPS): 223 grams, 180 Cal,
3 g Total Fat, 1 g Sat Fat, 0 g Trans Fat, 21 mg Chol,
573 mg Sod, 15 g Total Carb, 2 g Total Sugar, 4 g Fib,
22 g Prot, 64 mg Calc.
PointsPlus value: **4**

▲ HEALTHY EXTRA
Serve 1 large tomato, thinly sliced, alongside the
tuna salad.

Lobster Salad

serves 4

1 pound cooked lobster meat, cut into chunks
1 pink grapefruit, peeled, sectioned, and
    coarsely chopped
1 navel orange, peeled, sectioned, and coarsely
    chopped
1½ cups cantaloupe balls
1 mango, peeled, pitted, and diced
2 cups lightly packed tender watercress sprigs
½ cup fat-free sour cream
3 tablespoons reduced-fat mayonnaise
2 teaspoons grated orange zest
¼ cup orange juice
¼ teaspoon salt
¼ teaspoon black pepper
2 tablespoons snipped fresh chives

1   Mix together lobster, grapefruit, orange,
cantaloupe, and mango in large bowl.
2   Line platter with watercress; mound lobster salad on top.
3   To make dressing, whisk together all
ingredients except chives in small bowl until
blended. Spoon over salad; sprinkle with chives.

PER SERVING (ABOUT 2½ CUPS): 405 grams, 291 Cal,
8 g Total Fat, 3 g Sat Fat, 0 g Trans Fat, 90 mg Chol,
738 mg Sod, 31 g Total Carb, 23 g Total Sugar, 3 g Fib,
26 g Prot, 167 mg Calc.
PointsPlus value: **8**

California Seafood Salad

serves 4

¼ cup clam-tomato or tomato juice
¼ cup lemon juice
4 teaspoons olive oil
1 tablespoon Worcestershire sauce
¼ teaspoon salt
¼ teaspoon black pepper
4 cups lightly packed torn red leaf lettuce
¼ pound cooked crabmeat, picked over
½ pound cooked medium shrimp, peeled and
    deveined, tails left on if desired
12 cherry tomatoes, halved
½ avocado, pitted, peeled, and diced
2 navel oranges, peeled and sectioned
1 cup croutons

1   To make dressing, whisk together clam-tomato juice, lemon juice, oil, Worcestershire sauce, salt, and pepper in small bowl.
2   Line platter with lettuce; mound crabmeat in center. Arrange shrimp, tomatoes, avocado, and oranges around crabmeat. Drizzle dressing over and scatter croutons on top.

PER SERVING (ABOUT 2 CUPS): 328 grams, 261 Cal,
10 g Total Fat, 1 g Sat Fat, 0 g Trans Fat, 141 mg Chol,
562 mg Sod, 23 g Total Carb, 10 g Total Sugar, 6 g Fib,
22 g Prot, 114 mg Calc.
PointsPlus value: **7**

FYI   To make the croutons, cut firm white bread into enough cubes to equal 1 cup and spread in a shallow baking pan. Spray with olive oil nonstick spray and toss to coat evenly. Bake the croutons in a 375°F oven, turning once or twice, until golden brown, about 6 minutes. Let cool.

Quinoa, Black Bean, and Shrimp Salad

serves 4

¾ cup quinoa, rinsed and drained
1½ cups water
1 teaspoon salt
1 cup frozen corn kernels, thawed
¾ pound large shrimp, peeled and deveined
1 (15½-ounce) can black beans, rinsed and
    drained
2 large peaches, pitted and coarsely chopped
2 tomatoes, coarsely chopped
2 celery stalks, chopped
¼ cup chopped fresh parsley
¼ cup chopped fresh cilantro
2 tablespoons lemon juice
2 teaspoons extra-virgin olive oil
Pinch cayenne

1   Combine quinoa, water, and ½ teaspoon of salt in medium saucepan; bring to boil. Reduce heat and simmer, covered, 12 minutes. Stir in corn and cook until quinoa is tender, about 2 minutes longer. Drain off any excess water and transfer quinoa mixture to large bowl; let cool.
2   Spray small nonstick skillet with nonstick spray and set over medium heat. Add shrimp and cook, stirring occasionally, until just opaque in center, about 3 minutes. Add to quinoa mixture.
3   Add all remaining ingredients and remaining ½ teaspoon salt to quinoa mixture; toss to mix well.

PER SERVING (ABOUT 2 CUPS): 429 grams, 385 Cal,
6 g Total Fat, 1 g Sat Fat, 0 g Trans Fat, 166 mg Chol,
974 mg Sod, 57 g Total Carb, 13 g Total Sugar, 11 g Fib,
29 g Prot, 110 mg Calc.
PointsPlus value: **10**

Pasta Salad Primavera

serves 4

2 tablespoons grated Parmesan cheese
4 teaspoons olive oil
1 tablespoon red wine vinegar
1 garlic clove, minced
1 teaspoon grated lemon zest
½ teaspoon salt
¼ teaspoon black pepper
2 cups cooked rotelle or penne
1 cup small broccoli florets, steamed until
    crisp-tender
1 cup small cauliflower florets, steamed until
    crisp-tender
12 cherry tomatoes, halved
½ red onion, finely chopped
¼ cup thinly sliced fresh basil

1   To make dressing, whisk together Parmesan, oil, vinegar, garlic, lemon zest, salt, and pepper in small bowl until blended.
2   Mix together all remaining ingredients in serving bowl. Drizzle dressing over and toss to coat evenly.

PER SERVING (ABOUT 1¾ CUPS): 224 grams, 188 Cal, 6 g Total Fat, 1 g Sat Fat, 0 g Trans Fat, 2 mg Chol, 408 mg Sod, 28 g Total Carb, 5 g Total Sugar, 4 g Fib, 7 g Prot, 70 mg Calc.
PointsPlus value: **5**

Tuscan Panzanella

serves 4

1 (8-ounce) loaf day-old Italian bread,
    cut or torn into large chunks
4 tomatoes, peeled and chopped
4 celery stalks, finely chopped
1 red onion, chopped
½ cup finely chopped fresh parsley
2 tablespoons red wine vinegar
4 teaspoons extra-virgin olive oil
2 garlic cloves, minced
½ teaspoon salt
¼ teaspoon black pepper
¼ cup chopped fresh basil

1   Put bread in large bowl and pour enough hot water over to moisten bread thoroughly; let stand until evenly soaked, about 3 minutes. Drain and squeeze dry; discard water. With your hands, tear bread into smaller pieces.
2   Toss together all remaining ingredients except basil in serving bowl until mixed well. Let stand until tomatoes release some of their juice, about 15 minutes. Add bread and basil; toss to mix.

PER SERVING (ABOUT 2 CUPS): 324 grams, 262 Cal, 7 g Total Fat, 1 g Sat Fat, 0 g Trans Fat, 0 mg Chol, 683 mg Sod, 43 g Total Carb, 7 g Total Sugar, 5 g Fib, 7 g Prot, 110 mg Calc.
PointsPlus value: **7**

▲ **HEALTHY EXTRA**
Stirring 12 ounces of diced cooked skinless boneless chicken breast into the salad will increase the per-serving *PointsPlus* value by *3*.

5

Soups—Starters and Main Dishes

Soups—Starters and Main Dishes

106 Basic Beef Stock
106 Basic Chicken Stock
107 Basic Vegetable Stock
107 Roasted Vegetable Stock
108 Borscht
108 Summertime Grilled Corn Soup
109 Chilled Cucumber-Yogurt Soup
111 French Onion Soup
111 Creamy Yellow Squash Soup with Chives
112 Mixed Mushroom Soup
112 South American–Style Pumpkin Soup
113 Fresh Tomato-Basil Soup
113 Roasted Tomato–Bell Pepper Soup
114 Butternut Squash and Sage Soup
115 Potato-Watercress Soup
115 Food Processor Gazpacho
116 Avgolemono Chicken Soup
116 Chinese Noodle Soup
118 Hot-and-Sour Soup
118 Bok Choy–Noodle Soup
119 Classic Minestrone
119 Ribollita
120 Matzo Ball Soup
120 Italian-Style Bean Soup
121 Best-Ever Black Bean Soup
121 Creamy Bean Soup
123 Mexican-Style Chicken-Corn Soup
123 Creamy Corn, Potato, and Bacon Soup
124 Yellow Split Pea Soup
124 African Peanut Soup
125 Lentil and Swiss Chard Soup
125 Classic Beef-Barley Soup
126 Quick Gumbo
126 Cioppino
128 Turkey Mulligatawny
128 Smoky Manhattan-Style Clam Chowder

Basic Beef Stock

makes 8 cups

4 pounds meaty beef neck bones or beef soup
    bones
12 cups water
1 large onion, cut into chunks
2 carrots, cut into 1-inch lengths
1 large celery stalk with leaves, cut into 1-
    inch pieces
1 large leek (white and pale green part only),
    sliced
1 small white turnip, coarsely chopped
8 fresh flat-leaf parsley sprigs
2 fresh thyme sprigs
1 bay leaf
12 black peppercorns
1½ teaspoons salt

1   Preheat oven to 400°F.
2   Place bones in shallow roasting pan. Roast
until beginning to brown, about 30 minutes.
3   Transfer bones to stockpot. Add all remaining ingredients; bring to simmer over medium heat. Gently simmer, partially covered, 2
hours, skimming off foam.
4   Line colander with double thickness of paper towels or cheesecloth; set over large bowl.
Strain stock, pressing hard on solids to extract
all juices; discard solids.
5   Let stock cool; refrigerate until fat rises to
surface and solidifies, at least 4 hours. Scrape
off fat; discard. Use stock at once or refrigerate
up to 2 days. Or transfer to 1-cup freezer containers and freeze up to 6 months.

PER SERVING (1 CUP): 198 grams, 15 Cal, 0 g Total Fat,
0 g Sat Fat, 0 g Trans Fat, 5 mg Chol, 440 mg Sod,
1 g Total Carb, 1 g Total Sugar, 0 g Fib, 2 g Prot,
0 mg Calc.
PointsPlus value: *0*

Basic Chicken Stock

makes 8 cups

4 pounds chicken wings or backs or a mix
12 cups water
1 large onion, quartered
2 carrots, coarsely chopped
2 large celery stalks with leaves, thickly sliced
1 large leek (white and pale green part only),
    sliced
8 fresh flat-leaf parsley sprigs
2 fresh thyme sprigs
12 black peppercorns
1½ teaspoons salt

1   Combine chicken and water in stockpot;
bring to simmer over medium heat, skimming
off foam that rises to surface. Add all remaining ingredients; reduce heat and simmer, partially covered, 2 hours, skimming off foam that
rises to surface.
2   Line colander with double thickness of paper towels or cheesecloth; set over large bowl.
Strain stock, pressing hard on solids to extract
all juices; discard solids.
3   Let stock cool; refrigerate until fat rises to
surface and solidifies, at least 4 hours. Scrape
off fat; discard. Use stock at once or refrigerate
up to 2 days. Or transfer to 1-cup freezer containers and freeze up to 6 months.

PER SERVING (1 CUP): 268 grams, 24 Cal, 1 g Total Fat,
0 g Sat Fat, 0 g Trans Fat, 4 mg Chol, 452 mg Sod,
2 g Total Carb, 1 g Total Sugar, 0 g Fib, 2 g Prot,
13 mg Calc.
PointsPlus value: *1*

Basic Vegetable Stock

makes 8 cups

1 tablespoon olive oil
4 onions, coarsely chopped
3 leeks (white and pale green part only),
    sliced
2 celery stalks with leaves, coarsely chopped
2 parsnips, coarsely chopped
1 carrot, coarsely chopped
12 cups water
6 large dried mushrooms
12 fresh flat-leaf parsley sprigs
6 fresh dill sprigs
12 black peppercorns
1½ teaspoons salt

1   Heat oil in stockpot over medium heat. Add onions, leeks, celery, parsnips, and carrot; cook, stirring occasionally, until vegetables begin to soften, about 10 minutes. Add all remaining ingredients; bring to simmer, skimming off any foam that rises to surface. Gently simmer, partially covered, 2 hours.
2   Line colander with double thickness of paper towels or cheesecloth; set over large bowl. Strain stock, pressing hard on solids to extract all juices; discard solids.
3   Use stock at once or let cool and refrigerate up to 2 days. Or transfer to 1-cup freezer containers and freeze up to 6 months.

PER SERVING (1 CUP): 258 grams, 25 Cal, 2 g Total Fat, 0 g Sat Fat, 0 g Trans Fat, 0 mg Chol, 446 mg Sod, 2 g Total Carb, 1 g Total Sugar, 1 g Fib, 0 g Prot, 11 mg Calc.
PointsPlus value: *1*

FYI   If you don't have large dried mushrooms on hand, substitute 12 large fresh white or cremini mushrooms, thickly sliced.

Roasted Vegetable Stock

makes 4 cups

6 onions, coarsely chopped
3 carrots, sliced
3 celery stalks, sliced
1 white turnip, sliced
4 large garlic cloves, peeled
1 tablespoon olive oil
1 cup dry white wine
10 cups water
2 large tomatoes, coarsely chopped
6 fresh flat-leaf parsley sprigs
2 fresh thyme sprigs
10 black peppercorns
1 bay leaf

1   Preheat oven to 400°F.
2   Toss together onions, carrots, celery, turnip, garlic, and oil in roasting pan. Roast, stirring occasionally, until vegetables are lightly browned, about 45 minutes.
3   Transfer vegetables to stockpot. Place roasting pan on stove across two burners over medium heat. Add wine and cook, scraping up browned bits from bottom of pan. Add to vegetables in stockpot. Add all remaining ingredients and gently simmer 1½ hours.
4   Line colander with double thickness of paper towels or cheesecloth; set over large bowl. Strain stock, pressing on solids to extract all juices; discard solids.
5   Use stock at once or let cool and refrigerate up to 2 days. Or transfer to 1-cup freezer containers and freeze up to 6 months.

PER SERVING (1 CUP): 288 grams, 49 Cal, 3 g Total Fat, 1 g Sat Fat, 0 g Trans Fat, 0 mg Chol, 28 mg Sod, 4 g Total Carb, 2 g Total Sugar, 1 g Fib, 1 g Prot, 22 mg Calc.
PointsPlus value: *1*

Borscht

serves 4

2 cups reduced-sodium chicken broth or Basic
    Chicken Stock (page 106)
1½ cups water
3 beets, peeled and grated
6 scallions, sliced
1 teaspoon light brown sugar
½ cup thinly sliced red cabbage
2 tablespoons snipped fresh dill
1 teaspoon grated lemon zest
2 tablespoons lemon juice
⅛ teaspoon black pepper
¼ cup light sour cream

1   Combine broth, water, beets, scallions,
and brown sugar in medium saucepan and bring
to boil. Reduce heat and simmer, covered, 15
minutes. Add cabbage and cook, covered, until
beets and cabbage are tender, about 5 minutes
longer. Remove saucepan from heat; let cool to
room temperature.
2   Stir dill, lemon zest and juice, and pepper
into borscht; transfer to covered container. Refrigerate until well chilled, at least 4 hours or
up to overnight.
3   Ladle soup evenly into 4 bowls. Top each
serving with dollop of sour cream.

PER SERVING (ABOUT 1 CUP BORSCHT AND
1 TABLESPOON SOUR CREAM): 323 grams, 66 Cal,
1 g Total Fat, 1 g Sat Fat, 0 g Trans Fat, 5 mg Chol,
382 mg Sod, 12 g Total Carb, 7 g Total Sugar, 3 g Fib,
4 g Prot, 52 mg Calc.
PointsPlus value: *2*

FYI   Beets are in the root vegetable family and
take a long time to become tender when
cooked. Therefore, in this recipe, the beets are
coarsely grated to greatly reduce the cooking time.

Summertime Grilled Corn Soup

serves 6

4 ears of corn
1 tablespoon olive oil
1 onion, chopped
1 (½-pound) Yukon Gold potato, peeled and
    cut into 1-inch chunks
2 (14½-ounce) cans reduced-sodium
    vegetable broth or 3½ cups Basic
    Vegetable Stock (page 107)
½ cup water
½ teaspoon dried thyme
¼ teaspoon salt
¼ teaspoon black pepper
¼ cup fat-free half-and-half

1   To prepare corn for grilling, pull back
husks and remove silk. Place husks back over
corn. Put corn in large bowl and add enough
water to cover. Let stand 20 minutes; drain.
2   Meanwhile, spray grill rack with nonstick
spray. Preheat grill to medium or prepare medium fire using direct method.
3   Place corn on grill rack and grill, turning, until corn is tender and husks are lightly
charred, about 20 minutes. When cool enough
to handle, remove husks. With long serrated
knife, cut off corn kernels. Reserve cobs.
4   Heat oil in large saucepan over medium
heat. Add onion and cook, stirring, until softened, about 5 minutes. Add reserved cobs and
all remaining ingredients except half-and-half;
bring to boil. Reduce heat and simmer, covered, until potato is tender, about 15 minutes.
Remove and discard cobs. Remove saucepan
from heat; let cool 5 minutes.

5   Puree soup, in batches if needed, in blender or food processor. Return soup to saucepan and stir in half-and-half; reheat over medium heat. Serve hot or transfer to covered container and refrigerate until well chilled, at least 4 hours or up to 2 days.

PER SERVING (1 CUP): 294 grams, 129 Cal, 3 g Total Fat, 0 g Sat Fat, 0 g Trans Fat, 0 mg Chol, 480 mg Sod, 22 g Total Carb, 6 g Total Sugar, 3 g Fib, 5 g Prot, 23 mg Calc.
PointsPlus value: **3**

FYI   Here is a great way to neatly remove corn kernels from their cob. Set a Bundt pan on the counter and set an ear of corn in the center tube, stem end down. Using a serrated knife, slice down to remove the kernels. The kernels will fall into the well of the pan.

Chilled Cucumber-Yogurt Soup

serves 4

2 English (seedless) cucumbers, peeled
1 (16-ounce) container plain fat-free yogurt
1 small garlic clove
2 teaspoons lemon juice
$\frac{1}{2}$ teaspoon salt
$\frac{1}{8}$ teaspoon black pepper
2 scallions, sliced
$\frac{1}{2}$ cup lightly packed fresh mint leaves, finely chopped

1   Dice enough cucumber to equal $\frac{1}{3}$ cup and set aside. Cut remaining cucumber into coarse chunks.
2   Combine yogurt, garlic, lemon juice, salt, pepper, and cucumber chunks in blender, in batches if needed, and puree. Add scallions and mint; blend until finely chopped. Pour into large bowl; stir in reserved diced cucumber. Cover and refrigerate until well chilled, at least 4 hours or up to overnight.

PER SERVING (GENEROUS 1 CUP): 249 grams, 72 Cal, 0 g Total Fat, 0 g Sat Fat, 0 g Trans Fat, 3 mg Chol, 363 mg Sod, 14 g Total Carb, 8 g Total Sugar, 2 g Fib, 7 g Prot, 179 mg Calc.
PointsPlus value: **2**

▲ HEALTHY EXTRA
Add some bright color and even more flavor to this soup by topping each serving with seeded and diced tomato.

FRENCH ONION SOUP

French Onion Soup

serves 4

2 teaspoons olive oil
6 onions, thinly sliced
1 teaspoon sugar
3 cups water
1 (14½-ounce) can reduced-sodium beef broth
    or 1¾ cups Basic Beef Stock (page 106)
¼ teaspoon salt
¼ teaspoon black pepper
4 (1-ounce) slices French bread, toasted
⅓ cup shredded Gruyère cheese

1   Heat oil in Dutch oven or large pot over medium-low heat. Add onions and sprinkle with sugar; cook, stirring frequently, until onions are deep brown, about 45 minutes.
2   Add water, broth, salt, and pepper to pot; bring to boil, scraping up browned bits from bottom of pan. Reduce heat and simmer, covered, 20 minutes.
3   Preheat broiler.
4   Set 4 flameproof bowls on baking sheet. Ladle soup evenly into bowls. Float 1 slice of bread in each bowl and sprinkle with rounded tablespoon Gruyère. Broil about 5 inches from heat until cheese is melted, about 2 minutes.

PER SERVING (1 BOWL): 480 grams, 175 Cal, 6 g Total Fat, 2 g Sat Fat, 0 g Trans Fat, 10 mg Chol, 468 mg Sod, 25 g Total Carb, 12 g Total Sugar, 4 g Fib, 7 g Prot, 140 mg Calc.
PointsPlus value: *5*

FYI   The key to success with this classic soup is to cook the onions very slowly until they have a chance to caramelize, which turns them a deep mahogany color and ensures a rich flavor.

Creamy Yellow Squash Soup with Chives

serves 4

2 teaspoons olive oil
1 onion, chopped
1 celery stalk, chopped
2 garlic cloves, minced
4 yellow squash or zucchini, thinly sliced
1½ cups reduced-sodium chicken broth or
    Basic Chicken Stock (page 106)
¼ teaspoon salt
¼ teaspoon black pepper
½ cup fat-free sour cream
2 tablespoons snipped fresh chives

1   Heat oil in large saucepan over medium heat. Add onion, celery, and garlic; cook until softened, about 5 minutes. Add squash, broth, salt, and pepper; bring to boil. Reduce heat and simmer, partially covered, 15 minutes. Remove saucepan from heat; let cool 5 minutes.
2   Puree soup, in batches if needed, in food processor or blender. Transfer soup to large bowl; cover and refrigerate until well chilled, at least 4 hours or up to overnight.
3   To serve, whisk sour cream into soup until blended. Ladle evenly into 4 bowls and sprinkle with chives.

PER SERVING (ABOUT 1 CUP): 376 grams, 115 Cal, 3 g Total Fat, 1 g Sat Fat, 0 g Trans Fat, 3 mg Chol, 420 mg Sod, 19 g Total Carb, 9 g Total Sugar, 5 g Fib, 6 g Prot, 102 mg Calc.
PointsPlus value: *3*

▲ **HEALTHY EXTRA**
Double the onion and celery and cook an extra minute or two.

Mixed Mushroom Soup

serves 6

2 teaspoons canola oil
1 large onion, chopped
2 celery stalks, chopped
1 pound mixed mushrooms, such as white,
    cremini, and shiitake, chopped (remove
    stems if using shiitakes)
1 tablespoon chopped fresh thyme or
    ½ teaspoon dried
2 tablespoons all-purpose flour
2 (14½-ounce) cans reduced-sodium
    vegetable broth or 3½ cups Roasted
    Vegetable Stock (page 107)
½ teaspoon salt
¼ teaspoon black pepper
1 cup fat-free half-and-half

1   Heat oil in Dutch oven or large pot over
medium heat. Add onion and celery; cook,
stirring, until softened, about 5 minutes. Add
mushrooms and thyme; cook, stirring, until
mushrooms are softened, about 5 minutes.
2   Sprinkle flour over mushrooms and cook,
stirring, 3 minutes. Add broth, salt, and pepper; bring to boil. Reduce heat and simmer,
covered, 20 minutes. Remove pot from heat;
let cool 5 minutes.
3   Puree soup, in batches if needed, in food
processor or blender. Return soup to pot. Stir
in half-and-half and reheat over medium heat.

PER SERVING (GENEROUS 1 CUP): 301 grams, 91 Cal,
2 g Total Fat, 0 g Sat Fat, 0 g Trans Fat, 0 mg Chol,
499 mg Sod, 13 g Total Carb, 6 g Total Sugar, 2 g Fib,
6 g Prot, 71 mg Calc.
PointsPlus value: *2*

South American–Style Pumpkin Soup

serves 8

2 teaspoons olive oil
1 large onion, chopped
2 teaspoons ground cumin
½ teaspoon ground cinnamon
⅛ teaspoon cayenne
5 cups reduced-sodium chicken broth or Basic
    Chicken Stock (page 106)
2 (15-ounce) cans pumpkin puree
½ cup unsweetened applesauce
¼ teaspoon black pepper
Grated zest of 1 lime
2 tablespoons lime juice

1   Heat oil in large saucepan over medium
heat. Add onion and cook, stirring, until
softened, about 5 minutes. Sprinkle cumin,
cinnamon, and cayenne over onion; cook, stirring, until fragrant, about 30 seconds. Remove
saucepan from heat; let cool 5 minutes.
2   Transfer onion mixture to food processor.
Add 1 cup of broth and puree. Return onion
mixture to pot; add remaining 4 cups broth
and all remaining ingredients except lime zest
and juice. Bring to boil over medium heat,
stirring occasionally. Reduce heat and simmer,
covered, about 3 minutes. Stir in lime zest and
juice just before serving.

PER SERVING (ABOUT 1 CUP): 295 grams, 74 Cal,
2 g Total Fat, 0 g Sat Fat, 0 g Trans Fat, 0 mg Chol,
396 mg Sod, 13 g Total Carb, 8 g Total Sugar, 5 g Fib,
4 g Prot, 30 mg Calc.
PointsPlus value: *2*

Fresh Tomato-Basil Soup

serves 6

2 teaspoons extra-virgin olive oil
½ cup chopped shallots
4 large tomatoes, coarsely chopped
1 cup reduced-sodium vegetable broth or
    Roasted Vegetable Stock (page 107)
½ teaspoon dried oregano
½ teaspoon salt
¼ teaspoon black pepper
2 cups fat-free milk
¼ cup tomato paste
1 cup fat-free half-and-half
¼ cup thinly sliced fresh basil

1   Heat oil in large saucepan over medium
heat. Add shallots and cook, stirring, until softened, about 5 minutes. Add tomatoes, broth,
oregano, salt, and pepper; bring to boil. Reduce
heat and simmer, covered, until tomatoes are
softened, about 6 minutes; let cool 5 minutes.
Puree, in batches if needed, in food processor
or blender. Return soup to pot.
2   Whisk together 1 cup of milk and the
tomato paste in small bowl until smooth. Stir
into soup along with remaining 1 cup milk,
half-and-half, and basil. Cook over medium-
low heat, stirring occasionally, until soup is
heated through, about 5 minutes (do not boil).

PER SERVING (ABOUT 1 CUP): 311 grams, 120 Cal,
2 g Total Fat, 0 g Sat Fat, 0 g Trans Fat, 2 mg Chol,
366 mg Sod, 19 g Total Carb, 12 g Total Sugar, 2 g Fib,
6 g Prot, 174 mg Calc.
PointsPlus value: *3*

▲ HEALTHY EXTRA
Stir 1½ cups cooked very small whole wheat pasta
into the soup along with the basil in step 3. The
per-serving *PointsPlus* value will increase by *1*.

Roasted Tomato–Bell Pepper Soup

serves 4

2 pounds plum tomatoes, halved lengthwise
1 red bell pepper, cut into strips
1 onion, sliced
2 large garlic cloves, chopped
2 teaspoons olive oil
1 (14½-ounce) can diced tomatoes
⅓ cup lightly packed fresh basil leaves, thinly
    sliced
½ teaspoon salt
¼ teaspoon black pepper

1   Preheat oven to 400°F.
2   Combine plum tomatoes, bell pepper,
onion, and garlic in large roasting pan. Drizzle
with oil and toss to coat evenly. Roast, tossing
occasionally, until tomatoes are softened and
lightly browned along edges, about 35 minutes.
Transfer to large saucepan.
3   Add diced tomatoes with their juice, all
but 1 tablespoon of basil, the salt, and black
pepper to saucepan; bring to boil. Reduce heat
and simmer, covered, 20 minutes. Remove
saucepan from heat; let cool 5 minutes.
4   Coarsely puree, in batches if needed, in
food processor or blender. If soup is too thick,
add a little water. Ladle soup evenly into 4
bowls and sprinkle with remaining 1 tablespoon basil.

PER SERVING (ABOUT 1 CUP): 376 grams, 106 Cal,
3 g Total Fat, 0 g Sat Fat, 0 g Trans Fat, 0 mg Chol,
442 mg Sod, 20 g Total Carb, 12 g Total Sugar, 5 g Fib,
3 g Prot, 44 mg Calc.
PointsPlus value: *3*

PREPARING BUTTERNUT SQUASH

1 With large chef's knife, cut off stem and cut squash lengthwise in half.

2 With soupspoon, scrape out and discard seeds and membranes.

3 Peel squash; cut or slice as directed.

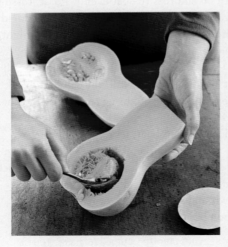

Butternut Squash and Sage Soup

serves 4

1 (2½- to 3-pound) butternut squash, peeled, seeded, and cut into 2-inch chunks
1 tablespoon olive oil
1 onion, chopped
1 large leek (white and pale green parts only), sliced
2 garlic cloves, minced
3 cups reduced-sodium vegetable broth or Basic Vegetable Stock (page 107)
1½ teaspoons dried sage, crumbled
¼ teaspoon black pepper
Pinch cayenne

1   Put squash in steamer basket; set into large saucepan over 1 inch boiling water. Cover and cook until squash is tender but still holds its shape, about 15 minutes.

2   Meanwhile, heat oil in large saucepan over medium heat. Add onion, leek, and garlic; cook, stirring, until softened, about 5 minutes. Add squash and all remaining ingredients; bring to boil. Reduce heat and simmer, covered, until squash is very soft, about 15 minutes. Remove saucepan from heat; let cool 5 minutes.

3   Puree soup, in batches if needed, in food processor or blender. Return soup to pot and reheat over medium heat.

PER SERVING (ABOUT 1½ CUPS): 487 grams, 192 Cal, 4 g Total Fat, 1 g Sat Fat, 0 g Trans Fat, 0 mg Chol, 366 mg Sod, 39 g Total Carb, 12 g Total Sugar, 10 g Fib, 4 g Prot, 158 mg Calc.
***PointsPlus* value: 5**

▲ **HEALTHY EXTRA**
Peel, core, and dice 1 large Granny Smith apple and add to the soup along with the squash in step 2.

Potato-Watercress Soup

serves 6

4 all-purpose potatoes, peeled and cut into
    ½-inch pieces
2 leeks (white and pale green part only),
    sliced
1 large onion, chopped
4½ cups reduced-sodium chicken broth or
    Basic Chicken Stock (page 106)
¼ teaspoon black pepper
½ bunch watercress, trimmed
½ cup fat-free half-and-half

1   Combine potatoes, leeks, onion, broth, and pepper in large pot; bring to boil. Reduce heat and simmer, covered, 20 minutes. Add watercress and simmer until potatoes are softened and watercress is tender, about 5 minutes longer. Remove saucepan from heat; let cool about 5 minutes.
2   Puree soup, in batches if needed, in food processor or blender. Return soup to pot. Stir in half-and-half and reheat over medium heat.

PER SERVING (1⅓ CUPS): 349 grams, 133 Cal, 0 g Total Fat, 0 g Sat Fat, 0 g Trans Fat, 0 mg Chol, 496 mg Sod, 28 g Total Carb, 6 g Total Sugar, 3 g Fib, 6 g Prot, 61 mg Calc.
PointsPlus value: *3*

FYI   Leeks tend to hold sandy dirt between their layers, so it is important to clean them thoroughly. Here's how: Trim the roots, leaving the root ends intact to hold the layers together. Slice lengthwise, fan open the layers, and swish the leeks in a large bowl of cool water to release the sandy dirt.

Food Processor Gazpacho

serves 4

4 plum tomatoes, peeled and sliced
½ cucumber, peeled, seeded, and coarsely
    chopped
½ red bell pepper, cut into chunks
4 scallions, sliced
1 garlic clove, minced
2 tablespoons red wine vinegar
2 cups tomato juice, chilled
¼ teaspoon black pepper
Few drops hot sauce
¼ cup diced cucumber
¼ cup diced red bell pepper
¼ cup diced red onion

1   Combine tomatoes, cucumber, bell pepper, scallions, garlic, and vinegar in food processor; pulse until almost smooth. Pour into large bowl. Stir in tomato juice, black pepper, and hot sauce. Cover and refrigerate until well chilled, at least 4 hours or up to overnight.
2   Ladle gazpacho evenly into 4 chilled soup bowls. Top each serving with 1 tablespoon each diced cucumber, bell pepper, and onion.

PER SERVING (¼ OF SOUP): 272 grams, 60 Cal, 0 g Total Fat, 0 g Sat Fat, 0 g Trans Fat, 0 mg Chol, 441 mg Sod, 12 g Total Carb, 7 g Total Sugar, 3 g Fib, 2 g Prot, 33 mg Calc.
PointsPlus value: *1*

FYI   Here's how to peel tomatoes with ease: Bring a pot of water to a boil. Cut a small shallow × in the bottom of each tomato. Plunge the tomatoes into the water and cook 1 minute. With a slotted spoon, transfer the tomatoes to a bowl of ice water; let cool about 3 minutes. Slip off the skins.

Avgolemono Chicken Soup

serves 4

4 cups reduced-sodium chicken broth or Basic
    Chicken Stock (page 106)
½ pound skinless boneless chicken breasts
2 large eggs
¼ cup lemon juice
1 (10-ounce) package frozen chopped spinach,
    thawed and squeezed dry
2 cups hot cooked brown rice
¼ teaspoon black pepper

1   Combine broth and chicken in large saucepan and bring to boil. Reduce heat and simmer until chicken is cooked through, about 5
minutes. Transfer chicken to plate. When cool
enough to handle, shred chicken or cut into
bite-size pieces. Reserve broth.
2   Whisk together eggs and lemon juice in
medium bowl until frothy; gradually whisk in
1 cup of hot broth.
3   Add spinach to broth and bring to boil.
Reduce heat to low; slowly add egg mixture,
stirring constantly in circular motion. Cook,
whisking constantly, until soup is thickened,
about 3 minutes (do not boil). Stir in chicken,
rice, and pepper; cook until heated through,
about 3 minutes.

PER SERVING (ABOUT 2 CUPS): 488 grams, 248 Cal,
5 g Total Fat, 1 g Sat Fat, 0 g Trans Fat, 140 mg Chol,
739 mg Sod, 28 g Total Carb, 2 g Total Sugar, 4 g Fib,
23 g Prot, 108 mg Calc.
PointsPlus value: **6**

FYI   You can substitute skinless boneless turkey
breast for the chicken, if you like.

Chinese Noodle Soup

serves 6

1 (48-ounce) carton reduced-sodium
    chicken broth or 6 cups Basic Chicken
    Stock (page 106)
2 scallions, sliced on diagonal
1 (1-inch) piece fresh ginger, peeled and
    minced
1 tablespoon reduced-sodium soy sauce
6 baby bok choy, halved
1 cup matchstick-cut carrots
2 cups cooked whole wheat capellini
6 ounces lean cooked pork, cut into
    matchsticks
1 cup lightly packed baby spinach

1   Combine broth, scallions, ginger, and soy
sauce in large saucepan and bring to boil. Reduce heat and simmer until scallions are tender,
about 3 minutes. Add bok choy and carrots;
simmer until barely tender, about 7 minutes.
2   Stir pasta, pork, and spinach into soup;
simmer just until spinach is wilted, about
2 minutes longer.

PER SERVING (1½ CUPS): 369 grams, 137 Cal,
2 g Total Fat, 1 g Sat Fat, 0 g Trans Fat, 823 mg Chol,
743 mg Sod, 17 g Total Carb, 3 g Total Sugar, 3 g Fib,
15 g Prot, 52 mg Calc.
PointsPlus value: **3**

FYI   Order some Chinese roast pork from your
local Chinese take-out restaurant for
this soup or buy a piece of roasted pork loin or
tenderloin from a specialty foods store to use in
this soup.

CHINESE NOODLE SOUP

Hot-and-Sour Soup

serves 8

6 *dried wood ear mushrooms*
4 *cups reduced-sodium chicken broth or Basic*
  Chicken Stock (page 106)
3 *tablespoons unseasoned rice vinegar*
2 *tablespoons reduced-sodium soy sauce*
1 *tablespoon chili garlic sauce*
1 *teaspoon Asian (dark) sesame oil*
½ *pound low-fat firm tofu, drained and diced*
1 *(8-ounce) can bamboo shoots, drained and*
  thinly sliced
3 *tablespoons water*
2½ *tablespoons cornstarch*
1 *large egg white, lightly beaten with 1*
  tablespoon water

1   Put mushrooms in small bowl and add
enough hot water to cover by 2 inches. Let
stand 15 minutes; drain.
2   Combine broth, vinegar, soy sauce, chili
garlic sauce, and sesame oil in large saucepan;
bring to boil. Add mushrooms, tofu, and bamboo shoots. Reduce heat and simmer about 10
minutes.
3   Stir together water and cornstarch in small
bowl until smooth. Whisk in about ¼ cup
of hot broth mixture, then whisk back into
saucepan. Cook, stirring constantly, until soup
bubbles and thickens, about 1 minute. Remove
saucepan from heat; slowly drizzle in egg mixture while stirring in circular motion, 1 minute.

PER SERVING (¾ CUP): 194 grams, 52 Cal, 1 g Total Fat,
0 g Sat Fat, 0 g Trans Fat, 0 mg Chol, 578 mg Sod,
7 g Total Carb, 1 g Total Sugar, 3 g Fib, 5 g Prot,
20 mg Calc.
PointsPlus value: *1*

FYI   Wood ear mushrooms can be found in
Asian grocery stores. They are a traditional
ingredient in hot-and-sour soup.

Bok Choy–Noodle Soup

serves 6

4 *ounces cellophane noodles*
2 *(14½-ounce) cans reduced-sodium chicken*
  broth or 3½ cups Basic Chicken Stock
  (page 106)
1 *(12-ounce) package low-fat extra-firm tofu,*
  cut into ½-inch dice
½ *pound baby bok choy, coarsely chopped*
½ *bunch watercress, trimmed*
2 *scallions, thinly sliced on diagonal*
2 *tablespoons reduced-sodium soy sauce*
1 *teaspoon Asian (dark) sesame oil*
½ *teaspoon black pepper*

1   Put noodles in large bowl and add enough
hot water to cover; let stand until softened,
about 10 minutes; drain. With kitchen scissors,
cut noodles into 3-inch lengths.
2   Pour broth into large saucepan and bring to
boil. Add tofu, bok choy, and watercress; simmer, covered, until vegetables are tender, about
5 minutes. Add noodles, scallions, soy sauce,
sesame oil, and pepper; cook until heated
through, about 2 minutes longer.

PER SERVING (1 CUP): 266 grams, 123 Cal, 2 g Total Fat,
0 g Sat Fat, 0 g Trans Fat, 0 mg Chol, 617 mg Sod,
20 g Total Carb, 1 g Total Sugar, 1 g Fib, 7 g Prot,
67 mg Calc.
PointsPlus value: *3*

FYI   Cellophane noodles (*fun see*) are also
known as glass noodles, bean thread
noodles, and vermicelli. Cellophane
noodles are made from ground mung beans. Once
soaked and cooked, they become translucent and
slippery.

Classic Minestrone

serves 8

2 cups thinly sliced green cabbage
2 onions, chopped
2 carrots, diced
2 celery stalks, diced
1 all-purpose potato, peeled and diced
3 cups reduced-sodium vegetable broth or
    Basic Vegetable Stock (page 107)
3 cups water
1 (14½-ounce) can diced tomatoes
½ teaspoon dried oregano
¼ teaspoon salt
¼ teaspoon black pepper
¼ pound green beans, trimmed and cut into
    ¼-inch pieces
1 zucchini, diced
2 cups cooked small pasta, such as small
    farfalle or elbows
½ cup canned chickpeas, rinsed and drained
½ cup grated Parmesan cheese

1   Combine cabbage, onions, carrots, celery, potato, broth, water, tomatoes with their juice, oregano, salt, and pepper in large pot; bring to boil. Reduce heat and simmer, covered, until carrots begin to soften, about 15 minutes.
2   Stir in green beans and zucchini; cook, covered, until tender, about 8 minutes. Stir in pasta and chickpeas; cook, stirring, until heated through, about 2 minutes longer. Ladle soup evenly into 8 soup bowls and sprinkle evenly with Parmesan.

PER SERVING (ABOUT 1½ CUPS SOUP AND 1 TABLESPOON PARMESAN): 359 grams, 150 Cal, 3 g Total Fat, 1 g Sat Fat, 0 g Trans Fat, 18 mg Chol, 482 mg Sod, 25 g Total Carb, 6 g Total Sugar, 4 g Fib, 8 g Prot, 119 mg Calc.
PointsPlus value: **4**

Ribollita

serves 10

4 teaspoons olive oil
2 onions, chopped
2 slices Canadian bacon, chopped
2 garlic cloves, minced
1 (28-ounce) can whole tomatoes, chopped,
    juice reserved
3 carrots, chopped
3 celery stalks, chopped
1 bunch kale, trimmed and chopped
2 (15½-ounce) cans cannellini (white kidney)
    beans, rinsed and drained
4 (14½-ounce) cans reduced-sodium
    chicken broth or 7 cups Basic Chicken
    Stock (page 106)
8 ounces day-old Italian bread, cut into
    10 slices

1   Heat oil in large pot over medium heat. Add onions, bacon, and garlic; cook until onions are softened, about 5 minutes. Stir in tomatoes with their juice, carrots, and celery. Cook, stirring, until celery and carrot are almost softened, about 10 minutes. Stir in kale, beans, and broth; bring to boil. Reduce heat and simmer, stirring occasionally, until kale is very tender and soup is thickened, about 1 hour.
2   Place 5 slices of bread in bottom of Dutch oven or flameproof casserole in single layer. Spoon a few ladles of soup over the bread, then top with remaining slices of bread. Ladle remaining soup evenly over bread and bring to boil. Reduce heat and simmer until bread is softened, about 10 minutes.

PER SERVING (GENEROUS 1½ CUPS): 438 grams, 198 Cal, 4 g Total Fat, 1 g Sat Fat, 0 g Trans Fat, 2 mg Chol, 874 mg Sod, 33 g Total Carb, 7 g Total Sugar, 6 g Fib, 10 g Prot, 108 mg Calc.
PointsPlus value: **5**

Matzo Ball Soup

serves 4

1 large egg, separated and at room
    temperature
1 large egg white, at room temperature
Pinch cream of tartar
1 tablespoon seltzer water
¼ cup + 2 tablespoons matzo meal
1 tablespoon snipped fresh dill (optional)
2 (14½-ounce) cans reduced-sodium chicken
    broth or 3½ cups Basic Chicken Stock
    (page 106)
2 carrots, thinly sliced

1   With electric mixer on medium-high
speed, beat the 2 egg whites and cream of
tartar in medium bowl until stiff peaks form
when beaters are lifted.
2   With same beaters (no need to wash
them), beat together egg yolk and seltzer in
another medium bowl until mixture is pale and
doubled in volume, about 3 minutes. Fold into
beaten egg whites. Combine matzo meal and
dill, if using, in cup; fold into egg mixture in
three additions just until whites are no longer
visible. Cover bowl and refrigerate matzo mixture at least 30 minutes or up to 2 hours.
3   Meanwhile, bring large pot of salted water
to boil. With damp hands, gently shape matzo
mixture into 8 balls; drop each matzo ball into
boiling water. Simmer, covered, until toothpick
inserted into matzo ball goes in easily, about
30 minutes (do not uncover pot during first 20
minutes).
4   Combine broth and carrots in large saucepan and bring to boil. Reduce heat and simmer,
covered, until carrots are tender, about 8 minutes. With slotted spoon, transfer matzo balls
to soup. Keep hot until ready to serve.

PER SERVING (ABOUT 1 CUP SOUP AND 2 MATZO BALLS):
298 grams, 89 Cal, 2 g Total Fat, 1 g Sat Fat,
0 g Trans Fat, 57 mg Chol, 432 mg Sod, 12 g Total Carb,
4 g Total Sugar, 2 g Fib, 5 g Prot, 29 mg Calc.
PointsPlus value: **2**

FYI   Matzo balls are prized when they are light
and fluffy. In our recipe, the addition of a
bit of seltzer and beaten egg whites ensures that
these matzo balls are perfect every time.

Italian-Style Bean Soup

serves 4

2 teaspoons olive oil
2 garlic cloves, minced
1 (15½-ounce) can cannellini (white kidney)
    beans, rinsed and drained
1 (14½-ounce) can reduced-sodium vegetable
    broth or 1¾ cups Basic Vegetable Stock
    (page 107)
2 teaspoons chopped fresh rosemary
½ teaspoon salt
⅛ teaspoon black pepper
2 tablespoons chopped fresh parsley

1   Heat oil in large saucepan over medium
heat. Add garlic and cook until fragrant, about
30 seconds. Stir in beans, broth, rosemary, salt,
and pepper; bring to boil. Reduce heat and simmer, partially covered, 15 minutes.
2   Remove saucepan from heat. With potato masher, coarsely mash about one-third
of beans. Ladle soup evenly into 4 bowls and
sprinkle with parsley.

PER SERVING (1 CUP): 180 grams, 91 Cal, 3 g Total Fat,
0 g Sat Fat, 0 g Trans Fat, 0 mg Chol, 432 mg Sod,
13 g Total Carb, 1 g Total Sugar, 3 g Fib, 3 g Prot,
36 mg Calc.
PointsPlus value: **2**

Best-Ever Black Bean Soup

serves 4

2 teaspoons olive oil
2 onions, chopped
2 garlic cloves, minced
1 (15½-ounce) can black beans, rinsed and drained
1 (14½-ounce) can reduced-sodium chicken broth or 1¾ cups Basic Chicken Stock (page 106)
1 cup water
1 teaspoon ground cumin
¼ teaspoon black pepper
¼ cup chopped fresh cilantro
2 scallions, thinly sliced
Lime wedges

1   Heat oil in large saucepan over medium heat. Add onions and garlic; cook, stirring, until onions are softened, about 5 minutes. Stir in beans, broth, water, cumin, and pepper; bring to boil. Reduce heat and simmer, covered, 15 minutes. Remove saucepan from heat; let cool 5 minutes.

2   Puree soup, in batches if needed, in food processor or blender. Return soup to saucepan and reheat over medium heat.

3   Ladle soup evenly into 4 bowls and sprinkle evenly with cilantro and scallions. Serve with lime wedges.

PER SERVING (ABOUT 1 CUP): 325 grams, 124 Cal, 3 g Total Fat, 0 g Sat Fat, 0 g Trans Fat, 0 mg Chol, 395 mg Sod, 18 g Total Carb, 6 g Total Sugar, 6 g Fib, 6 g Prot, 52 mg Calc.
PointsPlus value: **3**

Creamy Bean Soup

serves 4

1 (15½-ounce) can cannellini (white kidney) beans, rinsed and drained
1 (15½-ounce) can chickpeas, rinsed and drained
3 cups reduced-sodium vegetable broth or Basic Vegetable Stock (page 107)
2 teaspoons olive oil
1 onion, chopped
2 garlic cloves, minced
½ cup fat-free half-and-half
¼ cup grated Parmesan cheese
⅛ teaspoon black pepper

1   Combine cannellini beans, chickpeas, and ½ cup of broth in food processor or blender and puree.

2   Heat oil in large saucepan over medium heat. Add onion and garlic; cook, stirring, until onion is softened, about 5 minutes. Add remaining 2½ cups broth and the bean puree; bring to boil, stirring occasionally. Reduce heat and simmer, stirring occasionally, about 2 minutes. Stir in half-and-half, Parmesan, and pepper; reheat over medium heat.

PER SERVING (1¼ CUPS): 400 grams, 219 Cal, 5 g Total Fat, 1 g Sat Fat, 0 g Trans Fat, 4 mg Chol, 665 mg Sod, 31 g Total Carb, 8 g Total Sugar, 7 g Fib, 11 g Prot, 186 mg Calc.
PointsPlus value: **5**

FYI   You can use almost any variety of canned beans in this soup to great success. If you prefer a chunkier soup, coarsely mash the beans instead of pureeing them.

Mexican-Style Chicken-Corn Soup

serves 4

2 teaspoons olive oil
1 onion, chopped
1 red bell pepper, diced
2 garlic cloves, minced
3 cups reduced-sodium chicken broth or Basic
    Chicken Stock (page 106)
1 (14½-ounce) can fire-roasted diced
    tomatoes
1 (10-ounce) package frozen corn kernels,
    thawed
1 (4½-ounce) can chopped mild green chiles,
    drained
1 teaspoon chili powder
2 cups shredded cooked chicken breast
½ Hass avocado, pitted, peeled, and cut
    into pieces
¼ cup coarsely chopped fresh cilantro
8 large baked tortilla chips, coarsely broken

1   Heat oil in large saucepan over medium
heat. Add onion, bell pepper, and garlic; cook,
stirring, until onion is softened and lightly
browned, about 8 minutes.
2   Add broth, tomatoes with their juice,
corn, chiles, and chili powder to saucepan;
bring to boil. Add chicken; reduce heat and
simmer until heated through, about 2 minutes.
3   Remove saucepan from heat; stir in avocado and cilantro. Ladle soup evenly into 4
bowls; top evenly with tortilla chips.

**PER SERVING (ABOUT 1½ CUPS SOUP AND 2 TORTILLA
CHIPS):** 540 grams, 295 Cal, 7 g Total Fat, 1 g Sat Fat,
0 g Trans Fat, 59 mg Chol, 851 mg Sod, 33 g Total Carb,
9 g Total Sugar, 7 g Fib, 28 g Prot, 77 mg Calc.
PointsPlus value: **7**

Creamy Corn, Potato, and Bacon Soup

serves 4

2 teaspoons olive oil
1 onion, chopped
½ yellow bell pepper, chopped
1 pound all-purpose potatoes, peeled and
    diced
2½ cups reduced-sodium chicken broth or
    Basic Chicken Stock (page 106)
2 cups fresh or thawed frozen corn kernels
¼ cup fat-free half-and-half
2 slices turkey bacon, crisp cooked and cut
    into ½-inch pieces
2 tablespoons snipped fresh chives

1   Heat oil in large saucepan over medium
heat. Add onion and bell pepper; cook, stirring,
until softened, about 5 minutes. Add potatoes
and broth; bring to boil. Reduce heat and simmer, partially covered, until potatoes are almost
tender, about 10 minutes. Stir in corn and cook
until tender, about 5 minutes longer. Remove
saucepan from heat; let cool 5 minutes.
2   Puree soup, in batches if needed, in food
processor or blender. Return soup to saucepan.
Stir in half-and-half. Reheat over medium heat.
Ladle soup evenly into 4 bowls; sprinkle evenly
with bacon and chives.

PER SERVING (ABOUT 1¼ CUPS): 365 grams, 250 Cal,
4 g Total Fat, 0 g Sat Fat, 0 g Trans Fat, 6 mg Chol,
505 mg Sod, 47 g Total Carb, 7 g Total Sugar, 5 g Fib,
9 g Prot, 40 mg Calc.
PointsPlus value: **7**

FYI Turn this super-easy, super-delicious soup
into chowder by leaving it chunky. This also
saves you the pureeing step.

Yellow Split Pea Soup

serves 6

2 teaspoons olive oil
1 onion, diced
1 carrot, diced
1 celery stalk, diced
2 garlic cloves, minced
1 cup yellow split peas, picked over, rinsed,
     and drained
½ pound red potato, scrubbed and diced
4 cups reduced-sodium chicken broth or Basic
     Chicken Stock (page 106)
½ teaspoon dried oregano
⅛ teaspoon black pepper
1 (¼-pound) slice of roasted turkey breast,
     diced

1   Heat oil in large saucepan over medium
heat. Add onion, carrot, celery, and garlic;
cook, stirring, until onion is softened, about
5 minutes. Add split peas, potato, broth,
oregano, and pepper; bring to boil. Reduce heat
and simmer, covered, until split peas are very
tender, about 1 hour.
2   Stir in turkey and cook until heated
through, about 5 minutes.

PER SERVING (1 CUP): 303 grams, 213 Cal, 2 g Total Fat,
0 g Sat Fat, 0 g Trans Fat, 7 mg Chol, 664 mg Sod,
35 g Total Carb, 6 g Total Sugar, 2 g Fib, 15 g Prot,
25 mg Calc.
PointsPlus value: **6**

African Peanut Soup

serves 4

1 (15½-ounce) can chickpeas, rinsed and
     drained
3 cups reduced-sodium vegetable broth or
     Basic Vegetable Stock (page 107)
3 tablespoons creamy peanut butter
2 onions, chopped
1 (1-inch) piece fresh ginger, peeled and
     minced
2 teaspoons curry powder
1 (14½-ounce) can diced tomatoes
1 tablespoon tomato paste
¼ teaspoon cayenne
¼ cup chopped fresh cilantro
2 scallions, thinly sliced

1   Combine chickpeas, ½ cup of broth, and
the peanut butter in blender or food processor
and puree.
2   Spray large nonstick saucepan or Dutch
oven with olive oil nonstick spray and set over
medium heat. Add onions and ginger; cook,
stirring, until onions are softened, about 5
minutes. Stir in curry powder; cook about 1
minute. Stir in remaining 2½ cups of broth,
the tomatoes with their juice, tomato paste,
cayenne, and chickpea puree; bring to boil.
Reduce heat and simmer, stirring occasionally,
about 5 minutes to allow flavors to blend.
3   Ladle soup evenly into 4 bowls and sprinkle with cilantro and scallions.

PER SERVING (ABOUT 1½ CUPS): 460 grams, 217 Cal,
8 g Total Fat, 1 g Sat Fat, 0 g Trans Fat, 0 mg Chol,
664 mg Sod, 30 g Total Carb, 13 g Total Sugar, 8 g Fib,
9 g Prot, 85 mg Calc.
PointsPlus value: **5**

FYI   Fresh ginger adds a special type of heat to
this soup. If you prefer, however, you can
substitute ½ teaspoon dried ginger for the fresh.

Lentil and Swiss Chard Soup

serves 4

2 teaspoons olive oil
1 onion, chopped
1 garlic clove, minced
1 cup dried brown lentils, picked over, rinsed,
    and drained
4 cups reduced-sodium vegetable broth or
    Basic Vegetable Stock (page 107)
2 cups lightly packed thinly sliced Swiss chard
    leaves
¼ teaspoon salt
⅛ teaspoon black pepper
2 teaspoons lemon juice

1   Heat oil in large saucepan over medium
heat. Add onion and garlic; cook, stirring,
until onion is softened, about 5 minutes. Add
lentils and broth; bring to boil. Reduce heat
and simmer, covered, until lentils are tender,
about 45 minutes.
2   Stir chard, salt, and pepper into soup;
cook, stirring occasionally, until chard is wilted,
about 5 minutes. Stir in lemon juice.

PER SERVING (ABOUT 1½ CUPS): 436 grams, 216 Cal,
3 g Total Fat, 0 g Sat Fat, 0 g Trans Fat, 0 mg Chol,
799 mg Sod, 34 g Total Carb, 6 g Total Sugar, 12 g Fib,
16 g Prot, 46 mg Calc.
PointsPlus value: *5*

▲ HEALTHY EXTRA
Add a 14½-ounce can of drained diced tomatoes
to the soup in step 1 for a bit of bright flavor.

Classic Beef-Barley Soup

serves 4

½ pound round steak, trimmed and cut into
    ½-inch pieces
½ cup pearl barley
5 cups water
1 onion, chopped
2 carrots, diced
2 celery stalks, diced
1 teaspoon salt
⅛ teaspoon black pepper
1 cup frozen baby lima beans, thawed
2 cups sliced white or cremini mushrooms

1   Combine steak, barley, and water in large
saucepan and bring to boil. With slotted spoon,
skim off and discard any foam. Add onion, carrots, celery, salt, and pepper. Reduce heat and
simmer, covered, 30 minutes.
2   Stir lima beans and mushrooms into soup;
cook, covered, until meat is tender, about 15
minutes longer.

PER SERVING (ABOUT 2 CUPS): 532 grams, 180 Cal,
2 g Total Fat, 1 g Sat Fat, 0 g Trans Fat, 29 mg Chol,
665 mg Sod, 24 g Total Carb, 7 g Total Sugar, 6 g Fib,
17 g Prot, 51 mg Calc.
PointsPlus value: *4*

▲ HEALTHY EXTRA
Increase the number of carrots and celery stalks to
3 each.

Quick Gumbo
serves 4

2 teaspoons olive oil
1 green bell pepper, chopped
1 celery stalk, chopped
6 scallions, sliced
1 garlic clove, minced
2 cups reduced-sodium chicken broth or Basic
   Chicken Stock (page 106)
1 (14½-ounce) can crushed tomatoes
1 cup sliced fresh or thawed frozen okra
½ teaspoon dried thyme
1 bay leaf
⅛ teaspoon cayenne
½ cup long-grain white rice
½ pound large shrimp, peeled and deveined
1 (5-ounce) skinless boneless chicken breast,
   cut into ½-inch pieces
1 (¼-pound) piece reduced-fat kielbasa, cut
   into 8 slices

1   Heat oil in large saucepan over medium
heat. Add bell pepper, celery, scallions, and
garlic; cook, stirring, until softened, about 5
minutes. Stir in broth, tomatoes, okra, thyme,
bay leaf, and cayenne; bring to boil. Reduce
heat and simmer, covered, 20 minutes.
2   Stir rice into soup; simmer, covered, 15
minutes. Add shrimp, chicken, and kielbasa.
Simmer, covered, until shrimp are just opaque
in center, chicken is cooked through, and rice
is tender, about 5 minutes. Discard bay leaf.

PER SERVING (ABOUT 1½ CUPS): 387 grams, 293 Cal,
5 g Total Fat, 1 g Sat Fat, 0 g Trans Fat, 114 mg Chol,
527 mg Sod, 38 g Total Carb, 4 g Total Sugar, 5 g Fib,
25 g Prot, 142 mg Calc.
PointsPlus value: **7**

Cioppino
serves 4

2 teaspoons olive oil
1 onion, chopped
½ green bell pepper, chopped
4 garlic cloves, minced
1 (14½-ounce) can crushed tomatoes
1 cup dry red or white wine
½ cup water
¼ cup tomato paste
½ teaspoon dried oregano
½ teaspoon salt
¼ teaspoon red pepper flakes
¾ pound boneless firm white fish, such as
   halibut or red snapper, cut into 1½-inch
   chunks
12 littleneck clams, scrubbed
12 mussels, scrubbed and debearded
¼ pound medium shrimp, peeled and deveined
2 tablespoons chopped fresh basil or parsley

1   Heat oil in Dutch oven or large pot over
medium heat. Add onion, bell pepper, and
garlic; cook, stirring, until softened, about 5
minutes. Stir in tomatoes, wine, water, tomato
paste, oregano, salt, and pepper flakes; bring
to boil. Reduce heat and simmer, covered, 30
minutes.
2   Add fish and simmer, uncovered, 3 minutes. Add clams and mussels; simmer, covered,
3 minutes. Add shrimp and simmer, covered,
until clams and mussels open and shrimp are
just opaque in center, 3–5 minutes longer. Discard any clams or mussels that do not open;
discard bay leaf. Ladle soup evenly into 4 soup
bowls. Sprinkle with basil.

PER SERVING (¼ OF SOUP): 426 grams, 356 Cal,
7 g Total Fat, 1 g Sat Fat, 0 g Trans Fat, 176 mg Chol,
631 mg Sod, 27 g Total Carb, 10 g Total Sugar, 5 g Fib,
45 g Prot, 132 mg Calc.
PointsPlus value: **9**

CIOPPINO

Turkey Mulligatawny

serves 6

2 teaspoons olive oil
1 onion, sliced
1 carrot, sliced
2 celery stalks, sliced
1 red bell pepper, chopped
1 Granny Smith apple, peeled, cored, and
    diced
1/4 cup all-purpose flour
1 tablespoon curry powder
2 cups reduced-sodium chicken broth or Basic
    Chicken Stock (page 106)
1 large tomato, peeled, seeded, and chopped
1/4 teaspoon salt
1/8 teaspoon black pepper
Pinch cayenne
2 cups diced cooked smoked turkey breast

1   Heat oil in large saucepan over medium
heat, Add onion, carrot, celery, bell pepper,
and apple; cook, stirring, until softened, about
8 minutes. Sprinkle with flour and curry powder; cook, stirring, about 2 minutes.
2   Gradually stir broth into vegetable
mixture. Add tomato, salt, pepper, and cayenne: bring to boil. Reduce heat and simmer,
covered, until flavors are blended, about 30
minutes. Add turkey and cook until heated
through, about 5 minutes longer.

PER SERVING (1⅓ CUPS): 257 grams, 133 Cal,
3 g Total Fat, 1 g Sat Fat, 0 g Trans Fat, 20 mg Chol,
713 mg Sod, 17 g Total Carb, 7 g Total Sugar, 3 g Fib,
11 g Prot 35 mg Calc.
PointsPlus value: *3*

▲ **HEALTHY EXTRA**
Ladle each serving of this soup over hot cooked
brown basmati rice (⅔ cup of cooked brown
basmati rice with each serving will increase the
PointsPlus value by *3*).

Smoky Manhattan-Style Clam Chowder

serves 4

2 teaspoons olive oil
1 onion, chopped
1 large garlic clove, minced
1 (½-pound) all-purpose potato, peeled and
    cut into ½-inch dice
1 small zucchini, diced
1 celery stalk, diced
1 carrot, diced
1 (14½-ounce) can fire-roasted diced
    tomatoes
2 (8-ounce) bottles clam juice
½ cup water
½ teaspoon dried oregano
⅛ teaspoon black pepper
1 (6½-ounce) can chopped clams

1   Heat oil in large saucepan over medium
heat. Add onion and garlic; cook, stirring, until
onion is softened, about 5 minutes. Add potato, zucchini, celery, and carrot; cook, stirring,
until onion is softened, about 5 minutes.
2   Add tomatoes with their juice, clam juice,
water, oregano, and pepper; bring to boil. Reduce heat and simmer, partially covered, 15
minutes. Add clams with their juice; cook just
until heated through, about 2 minutes (do not
boil or clams will toughen).

PER SERVING (1½ CUPS): 417 grams, 143 Cal,
3 g Total Fat, 0 g Sat Fat, 0 g Trans Fat, 16 mg Chol,
657 mg Sod, 22 g Total Carb, 8 g Total Sugar, 4 g Fib,
9 g Prot, 61 mg Calc.
PointsPlus value: *4*

Beef, Pork, and Lamb

Beef, Pork, and Lamb

132   Classic Pot Roast
133   Smoky Grilled Brisket
135   Peppered Roast Tenderloin
135   Grilled T-Bone Steak
136   Teriyaki-Flavored Grilled Sirloin
136   London Broil
137   Marinated Flank Steak
137   Argentina-Style Steak and Sauce
139   Middle Eastern Beef Kebabs
139   Our Favorite Meat Loaf
140   Beef Stew
140   Spicy Beef and Broccoli Stir-Fry
141   Stuffed Peppers
141   Beef and Bean Chili
142   Best Grilled Burgers
142   Cheddar-Stuffed Burgers
144   Ragu Bolognese
144   Lasagna with Meat Sauce
145   Classic Spaghetti and Meatballs
147   Pork Roast with Winter Vegetables
147   Caribbean-Style Pork Tenderloin
148   Stir-Fried Pork with Bok Choy and Ginger
148   Barbecued Pork with Mop Sauce
149   Pork with Ginger and Soy
151   Honey-Mustard Pork Chops
151   Spicy Pork Stir-Fry
152   Pork and Black Bean Chili
152   Garlicky Red Beans and Pork
153   Old-World Pasta with Pork and Tomato Sauce
154   Tandoori Lamb with Almond-Apricot Couscous
156   Moroccan-Style Roast Leg of Lamb
156   Rack of Lamb with Herbed Crumb Topping
157   Grilled Lamb Chops with Mixed Herb Pesto
157   Lamb Chops with Yogurt-Mint Sauce
158   Grilled Lamb Chops with Tomato–Bell Pepper Sauce
158   Lamb-Vegetable Stew
159   Venison Chops with Shallot Sauce
160   Venison Steaks with Blackberry Sauce

**BRAISING
MEAT**

1 *Heat small amount of oil in Dutch oven over medium-high heat. Season meat, then brown on all sides.*

2 *Add vegetables, such as chopped onion, celery, carrot, and garlic, to pot and cook until golden.*

3 *Add enough liquid (broth, water, wine) to reach about one-third up side of meat. Bake, covered, in 350°F oven or gently simmer on stovetop until meat is fork-tender.*

Classic Pot Roast

serves 8

4 teaspoons olive oil
1 (2-pound) bottom or top round beef roast, trimmed
2 onions, chopped
1 carrot, chopped
1 celery stalk, chopped
2 garlic cloves, minced
1 teaspoon dried thyme
½ teaspoon dried rosemary
6 juniper berries, crushed (optional)
½ cup dry red wine
1 (14½-ounce) can petite diced tomatoes, drained, juice reserved
1 cup reduced-sodium beef broth or Basic Beef Stock (page 106)
1 teaspoon salt
¼ teaspoon black pepper

1   Heat oil in Dutch oven over medium heat. Add beef and brown on all sides, about 6 minutes; transfer to plate. Add onions, carrot, celery, garlic, thyme, rosemary, and juniper, if using; cook, stirring, until vegetables are softened, about 10 minutes.

2   Increase heat to medium-high. Add wine, scraping any browned bits from bottom of pot. Return beef to pot; add all remaining ingredients and enough of reserved tomato juice to partially cover meat; bring to boil. Reduce heat and simmer, covered, until meat is fork-tender, about 2 hours.

3   Transfer meat to cutting board and thinly slice across grain into 16 slices. Skim off fat from gravy. Return meat to pot and gently reheat over low heat.

PER SERVING (2 SLICES MEAT AND ⅓ CUP GRAVY):
237 grams, 256 Cal, 10 g Total Fat, 3 g Sat Fat,
0 g Trans Fat, 84 mg Chol, 466 mg Sod, 7 g Total Carb,
5 g Total Sugar, 2 g Fib, 30 g Prot, 37 mg Calc.
PointsPlus value: *6*

FYI Here's how to test meat for "fork-tender" doneness. Take a dinner fork or carving fork and stick it into the thickest part of the meat, then pull the fork out. If fork-tender, the fork will go in and out without any resistance.

Smoky Grilled Brisket

serves 8

2 tablespoons smoked paprika
2 tablespoons chili powder
1 tablespoon brown sugar
1 tablespoon onion powder
1 tablespoon garlic powder
1¼ teaspoons salt
1 teaspoon black pepper
¾ cup white wine vinegar
1 tablespoon Worcestershire sauce
1 tablespoon canola oil
1 teaspoon cayenne
1 (2-pound) first-cut brisket, trimmed

1 To make rub, mix together paprika, chili powder, brown sugar, onion powder, garlic powder, salt, and pepper in cup.

2 To make basting sauce, stir together vinegar, Worcestershire sauce, oil, and cayenne in 1-cup glass measure; stir in 1 tablespoon of rub. Transfer ½ cup of sauce to cup; reserve. Pour remaining sauce into large zip-close plastic bag; add brisket. Squeeze out air and seal bag; turn to coat meat. Refrigerate, turning bag occasionally, at least 6 hours or up to overnight.

3 Preheat grill to low or prepare low fire using indirect method.

4 Pat meat dry with paper towels; discard marinade. Pat reserved rub all over meat; put in large foil pan.

5 Put meat in pan on cooler portion of grill rack. Grill, covered, turning occasionally and basting with reserved sauce, until instant-read thermometer inserted into center of meat registers 190°F, 3–3½ hours.

6 Transfer meat to cutting board. Cover loosely with foil; let stand 10 minutes. Thinly slice across grain into 24 slices and arrange on platter. Pour pan juices over brisket.

PER SERVING (ABOUT 3 SLICES): 120 grams, 215 Cal,
8 g Total Fat, 2 g Sat Fat, 0 g Trans Fat, 59 mg Chol,
466 mg Sod, 5 g Total Carb, 2 g Total Sugar, 2 g Fib,
29 g Prot, 28 mg Calc.
PointsPlus value: *5*

▲ **HEALTHY EXTRA**
Enjoy this brisket with bowls of steamed green beans and cooked corn grits (1 cup of quick-cooked corn grits with each serving will increase the *PointsPlus* value by 4).

PEPPERED ROAST TENDERLOIN

Peppered Roast Tenderloin

serves 10

1 (2½-pound) beef tenderloin, trimmed
    and tied
2 garlic cloves, thinly sliced lengthwise
4 teaspoons olive oil
1 tablespoon cracked black peppercorns
2 teaspoons finely chopped fresh rosemary
2 teaspoons finely chopped fresh thyme
2 teaspoons finely chopped fresh sage
½ teaspoon salt

1   Preheat oven to 425°F.
2   With small knife, make small incisions all over tenderloin; insert a slice of garlic into each incision. Rub oil all over meat. Mix together peppercorns, rosemary, thyme, sage, and salt in cup; rub mixture all over tenderloin.
3   Place tenderloin in roasting pan; roast 10 minutes. Reduce oven temperature to 350°F. Roast until instant-read thermometer inserted into center of tenderloin registers 145°F for medium, about 20 minutes longer. Transfer to cutting board; let stand 15 minutes. Cut into 20 slices.

PER SERVING (2 SLICES): 89 grams, 183 Cal, 9 g Total Fat, 3 g Sat Fat, 0 g Trans Fat, 67 mg Chol, 167 mg Sod, 1 g Total Carb, 0 g Total Sugar, 0 g Fib, 24 g Prot, 21 mg Calc.
PointsPlus value: **5**

FYI Crack the peppercorns using a mortar and pestle, or wrap them in a clean kitchen towel and crush by firmly pressing down on them with a meat mallet or the bottom of a heavy skillet or saucepan.

Grilled T-Bone Steak

serves 4

2 teaspoons finely chopped fresh rosemary
2 teaspoons finely chopped fresh sage
1 teaspoon olive oil
½ teaspoon salt
¼ teaspoon black pepper
1 (1¼-pound) T-bone or rib steak, about
    1 inch thick, trimmed

1   Spray grill rack with nonstick spray. Preheat grill to medium-high or prepare medium-high fire using direct method.
2   To make rub, stir together all ingredients except steak in cup. Rub on both sides of steak. Place steak on grill rack and grill until instant-read thermometer inserted into center of steak registers 145°F for medium, about 5 minutes per side. Transfer steak to cutting board; let stand 5 minutes. Cut into 4 equal portions.

PER SERVING (¼ OF STEAK): 109 grams, 213 Cal, 11 g Total Fat, 3 g Sat Fat, 0 g Trans Fat, 58 mg Chol, 366 mg Sod, 0 g Total Carb, 0 g Total Sugar, 0 g Fib, 28 g Prot, 8 mg Calc.
PointsPlus value: **5**

▲ **HEALTHY EXTRA**

Toss together a tasty tomato-corn salad made with 2 cups of raw or cooked corn kernels, a few halved grape tomatoes, and a little chopped red onion dressed with lemon juice and a pinch of salt. This will increase the per-serving *PointsPlus* value by *2*.

Teriyaki-Flavored Grilled Sirloin

serves 4

1/3 cup reduced-sodium soy sauce
3 tablespoons dark brown sugar
2 tablespoons rice wine vinegar
1 tablespoon grated peeled fresh ginger
1 garlic clove, minced
1/4 teaspoon red pepper flakes
1 (1-pound) boneless sirloin steak, about
  1/2 inch thick, trimmed

1   Spray grill rack with nonstick spray. Pre-heat grill to medium-high or prepare medium-high fire using direct method. Or preheat non-stick grill pan over medium-high heat.

2   To make marinade, combine soy sauce, brown sugar, vinegar, ginger, garlic, and pepper flakes in small saucepan and set over medium heat. Bring to simmer and cook 5 minutes. Remove from heat and let cool completely.

3   Transfer cooled marinade to large zip-close plastic bag; add steak. Squeeze out air and seal bag; turn to coat steak. Refrigerate, turning bag occasionally, at least 30 minutes or up to 4 hours.

4   Remove steak from bag; discard marinade. Place steak on grill rack or in grill pan and grill until instant-read thermometer inserted into side of steak registers 145°F for medium, about 5 minutes per side. Transfer steak to cutting board; let stand 5 minutes. Cut across grain into 12 slices.

PER SERVING (3 SLICES): 128 grams, 207 Cal,
5 g Total Fat, 2 g Sat Fat, 0 g Trans Fat, 49 mg Chol,
575 mg Sod, 11 g Total Carb, 9 g Total Sugar, 0 g Fib,
27 g Prot, 22 mg Calc.
PointsPlus value: **5**

London Broil

serves 4

1/2 cup dry red wine
1 garlic clove, minced
1 tablespoon chopped fresh rosemary
1/2 teaspoon salt
1/4 teaspoon black pepper
1 (1-pound) top round or sirloin tip steak,
  trimmed

1   Combine wine, garlic, rosemary, salt, and pepper in large zip-close plastic bag; add steak. Squeeze out air and seal bag; turn to coat steak. Refrigerate, turning bag occasionally, at least 6 hours or up to 1 day.

2   Preheat broiler.

3   Remove steak from bag; discard marinade. Put steak on broiler rack and broil 5 inches from heat until instant-read thermometer inserted into center of steak registers 145°F for medium, about 4 minutes per side. Transfer to cutting board; let stand 5 minutes. Cut across grain into 16 slices.

PER SERVING (4 SLICES): 117 grams, 186 Cal,
5 g Total Fat, 2 g Sat Fat, 0 g Trans Fat, 56 mg Chol,
327 mg Sod, 1 g Total Carb, 0 g Total Sugar, 0 g Fib,
27 g Prot, 12 mg Calc.
PointsPlus value: **5**

▲ HEALTHY EXTRA
Round out the meal with potatoes and steamed broccoli. A cooked 3-ounce red potato and 1 cup of steamed broccoli florets with each serving will increase the *PointsPlus* value by *2*.

Marinated Flank Steak

serves 4

¹/₄ cup reduced-sodium soy sauce
2 tablespoons dry sherry
1 tablespoon honey
1 tablespoon grated peeled fresh ginger
1 tablespoon finely chopped lemongrass
2 garlic cloves, minced
Pinch red pepper flakes
1 (1-pound) flank steak, trimmed
2 teaspoons olive oil
¹/₄ teaspoon black pepper

1   Combine soy sauce, sherry, honey, ginger, lemongrass, garlic, and pepper flakes in large zip-close plastic bag; add steak. Squeeze out air and seal bag. Refrigerate, turning bag occasionally, at least 4 hours or up to 1 day.
2   Meanwhile, preheat broiler.
3   Remove steak from marinade; discard marinade. Pat steak dry with paper towel; rub oil on both sides of steak, then sprinkle with black pepper. Put steak on broiler rack and broil 5 inches from heat until instant-read thermometer inserted into side of steak registers 145°F for medium. Transfer to cutting board; let stand 5 minutes. Cut steak across grain into 12 slices.

PER SERVING (3 SLICES): 123 grams, 219 Cal, 9 g Total Fat, 3 g Sat Fat, 0 g Trans Fat, 42 mg Chol, 530 mg Sod, 8 g Total Carb, 4 g Total Sugar, 0 g Fib, 25 g Prot, 21 mg Calc.
PointsPlus value: **5**

FYI To prepare a stalk of lemongrass, cut off the slender top half of the stalk and discard. Peel away any dry leaves from the bulbous stalk, leaving only the tender inner leaves, and finely chop the stalk.

Argentina-Style Steak and Sauce

serves 4

1 cup lightly packed fresh flat-leaf parsley
    leaves, chopped
¹/₂ cup lightly packed fresh cilantro leaves,
    chopped
1 tablespoon red wine vinegar
1 tablespoon olive oil
¹/₂ teaspoon salt
¹/₄ teaspoon red pepper flakes
1 (1-pound) top round steak, trimmed
¹/₄ teaspoon black pepper

1   Spray grill rack with nonstick spray. Preheat grill to medium-high or prepare medium-high fire using direct method.
2   Meanwhile, to make sauce, combine parsley, cilantro, vinegar, oil, ¹/₄ teaspoon of salt, and the pepper flakes in serving bowl. Add enough cold water to give mixture a saucy consistency, if needed.
3   Sprinkle steak with remaining ¹/₄ teaspoon salt and the black pepper. Place steak on grill rack and grill until instant-read thermometer inserted into center of steak registers 145°F for medium, about 6 minutes per side.
4   Transfer steak to cutting board and let stand 10 minutes. Thinly slice steak across grain into 12 slices. Serve with sauce.

PER SERVING (ABOUT 3 SLICES STEAK AND 1½ TABLESPOONS SAUCE): 110 grams, 197 Cal, 9 g Total Fat, 2 g Sat Fat, 0 g Trans Fat, 65 mg Chol, 480 mg Sod, 2 g Total Carb, 0 g Total Sugar, 0 g Fib, 27 g Prot, 29 mg Calc.
PointsPlus value: **5**

MIDDLE EASTERN BEEF KEBABS

Middle Eastern Beef Kebabs

serves 4

1 onion, coarsely chopped
Grated zest and juice of 1 lemon
2 teaspoons olive oil
2 large garlic cloves, minced
2 teaspoons paprika
1½ teaspoons ground cumin
1 teaspoon dried oregano
Dash cayenne
1 pound beef tenderloin, trimmed and
    cut into 1-inch chunks
1 red onion, cut into 8 wedges
1 red bell pepper, cut into 1-inch pieces
8 white mushrooms
2 cups hot cooked whole wheat couscous

1   To make marinade, combine chopped onion, lemon zest and juice, oil, garlic, paprika, cumin, oregano, and cayenne in food processor or blender and puree.

2   Transfer marinade to large zip-close plastic bag; add beef. Squeeze out air and seal bag. Refrigerate, turning bag occasionally, at least 2 hours or up to overnight.

3   Spray broiler rack with nonstick spray. Preheat broiler.

4   Alternately thread onion wedges, bell pepper, mushrooms, and beef on 4 (12-inch) metal skewers. Put skewers on prepared broiler rack and broil 5 inches from heat, turning, until vegetables are tender and beef is cooked through, about 10 minutes. Serve with couscous.

PER SERVING (1 SKEWER AND ½ CUP COUSCOUS): 292 grams, 309 Cal, 10 g Total Fat, 4 g Sat Fat, 0 g Trans Fat, 71 mg Chol, 58 mg Sod, 27 g Total Carb, 7 g Total Sugar, 5 g Fib, 28 g Prot, 66 mg Calc.
PointsPlus value: **8**

Our Favorite Meat Loaf

serves 4

2 teaspoons canola oil
1 cup finely chopped white mushrooms
1 onion, finely chopped
1 carrot, finely chopped
1 celery stalk, finely chopped
1 pound lean ground beef (7% fat or less)
½ cup quick-cooking (not instant) oats
2 large egg whites
3 tablespoons ketchup
1 tablespoon Worcestershire sauce
2 teaspoons finely chopped fresh thyme or
    ½ teaspoon dried
¼ teaspoon salt
¼ teaspoon black pepper
3 garlic cloves, minced
¼ cup tomato puree or tomato sauce

1   Preheat oven to 350°F.

2   Heat oil in large nonstick skillet over medium heat. Add mushrooms, onion, carrot, and celery; cook, stirring, until onion is softened, about 5 minutes. Transfer to large bowl.

3   Add all remaining ingredients except tomato puree to vegetables in bowl; mix well. Press meat loaf mixture into 4½ × 8½-inch loaf pan.

4   Bake meat loaf 30 minutes. Brush tomato puree on top of loaf. Bake until instant-read thermometer inserted into center of meat loaf registers 160°F for well done, 30–45 minutes longer. Let stand about 5 minutes. Cut into 8 slices.

PER SERVING (2 SLICES): 193 grams, 243 Cal, 8 g Total Fat, 3 g Sat Fat, 0 g Trans Fat, 59 mg Chol, 421 mg Sod, 15 g Total Carb, 5 g Total Sugar, 2 g Fib, 26 g Prot, 35 mg Calc.
PointsPlus value: **6**

Beef Stew

serves 4

2 teaspoons olive oil
1 pound beef round, cut into 1½-inch chunks
1 onion, chopped
1 (14½-ounce) can diced tomatoes
1 cup reduced-sodium beef broth or
     Basic Beef Stock (page 106)
½ cup dry red wine
½ teaspoon dried thyme
½ teaspoon salt
¼ teaspoon black pepper
1 bay leaf
16 frozen pearl onions
4 carrots, cut into 1-inch chunks
4 potatoes, peeled and cut into 1-inch chunks
1 cup frozen green peas
1 tablespoon chopped fresh flat-leaf parsley
1 tablespoon chopped fresh mint

1   Heat oil in nonstick Dutch oven over medium-high heat. Add beef, in batches, and cook until browned on all sides, about 5 minutes. Transfer to bowl. Add onion to pot and cook, stirring, until softened, about 5 minutes.
2   Return beef to pot. Add tomatoes with their juice, broth, wine, thyme, salt, pepper, and bay leaf; bring to boil. Reduce heat and simmer, partially covered, stirring occasionally, 45 minutes.
3   Add pearl onions, carrots, and potatoes to pot; cook, covered, 30 minutes. Stir in peas; cook 10 minutes longer. Stir in parsley and mint; discard bay leaf.

PER SERVING (ABOUT 2 CUPS): 441 grams, 426 Cal, 10 g Total Fat, 2 g Sat Fat, 0 g Trans Fat, 59 mg Chol, 460 mg Sod, 57 g Total Carb, 13 g Total Sugar, 8 g Fib, 27 g Prot, 60 mg Calc.
***PointsPlus* value: 12**

Spicy Beef and Broccoli Stir-Fry

serves 6

3 tablespoons dry sherry
3 tablespoons soy sauce
4 large garlic cloves, minced
1 teaspoon Asian (dark) sesame oil
¼ teaspoon red pepper flakes
½ pound beef tenderloin, trimmed and cut
     into strips
1 teaspoon cornstarch
2 teaspoons canola oil
4 cups broccoli florets
2 cups hot cooked brown rice

1   Stir together sherry, soy sauce, garlic, sesame oil, and pepper flakes in 1-cup glass measure. Transfer ¼ cup of mixture to large zip-close plastic bag; add beef. Squeeze out air and seal bag; turn to coat beef. Refrigerate, turning bag occasionally, at least 1 hour or up to 2 hours.
2   Add cornstarch and enough water to soy sauce mixture in cup to equal ⅓ cup; stir mixture until smooth.
3   Heat nonstick wok or deep large non-stick skillet over high heat until drop of water sizzles in pan; add canola oil and swirl to coat pan. Add beef and stir-fry until no longer pink, about 2 minutes. With slotted spoon, transfer beef to plate. Add broccoli to wok; stir-fry 3 minutes, then cover and cook 1 minute. Re-stir cornstarch mixture; add to wok along with beef. Stir-fry until sauce bubbles and thickens, about 2 minutes. Serve with rice.

PER SERVING (⅙ OF STIR-FRY AND ⅓ CUP RICE): 171 grams, 191 Cal, 6 g Total Fat, 1 g Sat Fat, 0 g Trans Fat, 24 mg Chol, 779 mg Sod, 22 g Total Carb, 1 g Total Sugar, 3 g Fib, 12 g Prot, 455 mg Calc.
***PointsPlus* value: 5**

Stuffed Peppers

serves 4

$\frac{1}{2}$ *pound lean ground beef (7% fat or less)*
1 cup cooked brown rice
1 onion, finely chopped
$\frac{1}{4}$ *cup frozen green peas, thawed*
$\frac{1}{4}$ *cup grated Parmesan cheese*
2 tablespoons tomato paste
3 garlic cloves, minced
1 teaspoon minced fresh thyme
1 teaspoon minced fresh basil
4 green, red, or yellow bell peppers, tops cut
  off and seeded
$\frac{1}{2}$ *cup tomato puree or tomato sauce*

1 Preheat oven to 350°F.
2 Mix together beef, rice, onion, peas, Parmesan, tomato paste, garlic, thyme, and basil in large bowl; spoon evenly into bell peppers. Stand peppers in shallow baking dish or casserole. Pour tomato puree over peppers; add enough water to baking dish to come partway up sides of peppers.
3 Cover baking dish with foil and bake, basting peppers occasionally with tomato liquid, 30 minutes. Uncover and bake until peppers and rice are tender and filling is cooked through, about 20 minutes longer. Let stand 5 minutes before serving.

PER SERVING (1 STUFFED PEPPER): 301 grams, 209 Cal, 5 g Total Fat, 2 g Sat Fat, 0 g Trans Fat, 34 mg Chol, 124 mg Sod, 26 g Total Carb, 7 g Total Sugar, 5 g Fib, 17 g Prot, 93 mg Calc.
PointsPlus value: **5**

Beef and Bean Chili

serves 6

2 teaspoons olive oil
1 large onion, chopped
2 carrots, chopped
2 celery stalks, chopped
1 red bell pepper, chopped
3 large garlic cloves, minced
1 pound lean ground beef (7% fat or less)
1 tablespoon chili powder
2 teaspoons ground cumin
$\frac{1}{2}$ *teaspoon dried oregano*
$\frac{1}{2}$ *teaspoon salt*
$\frac{1}{4}$ *teaspoon black pepper*
1 (14$\frac{1}{2}$-ounce) can fire-roasted diced
  tomatoes
1 (15$\frac{1}{2}$-ounce) can red kidney beans, rinsed
  and drained
6 tablespoons fat-free sour cream
3 cups hot cooked brown rice

1 Heat oil in large nonstick Dutch oven over medium heat. Add onion, carrots, celery, bell pepper, and garlic; cook, stirring, until carrots and celery are softened, about 15 minutes. Add beef and cook, breaking it apart with wooden spoon, until browned, about 7 minutes. Stir in chili powder, cumin, oregano, salt, and black pepper; cook, stirring, 2 minutes.
2 Add tomatoes with their juice and beans to pot; bring to boil. Reduce heat and simmer, partially covered, stirring occasionally, until flavors are blended, about 20 minutes. Serve with sour cream and rice.

PER SERVING (ABOUT 1½ CUPS CHILI, ½ CUP RICE, AND 1 TABLESPOON SOUR CREAM): 396 grams, 373 Cal, 7 g Total Fat, 2 g Sat Fat, 0 g Trans Fat, 47 mg Chol, 452 mg Sod, 52 g Total Carb, 8 g Total Sugar, 11 g Fib, 25 g Prot, 83 mg Calc.
PointsPlus value: **9**

Best Grilled Burgers

serves 4

1 pound lean ground beef (7% fat or less)
½ cup finely chopped scallions
¼ cup fat-free egg substitute
1 tablespoon Worcestershire sauce
½ teaspoon dry mustard
½ teaspoon salt
¼ teaspoon black pepper
*4 whole wheat hamburger buns, split and
     toasted*
4 slices sweet onion, such as Vidalia
4 thick tomato slices
4 lettuce leaves
¼ cup ketchup

1　Spray grill rack with nonstick spray. Preheat grill to medium-high or prepare medium-high fire using direct method.

2　Meanwhile, mix together beef, scallions, egg substitute, Worcestershire sauce, dry mustard, salt, and pepper in large bowl just until well combined. With damp hands, shape mixture into 4 (½-inch-thick) patties.

3　Place patties on grill rack and grill until instant-read thermometer inserted into side of burger registers 160°F for well done, about 5 minutes per side.

4　Place burgers on bottoms of buns and top each with 1 onion slice, 1 tomato slice, and 1 lettuce leaf. Cover with tops of buns and serve with ketchup.

PER SERVING (1 GARNISHED BURGER): 232 grams, 293 Cal, 8 g Total Fat, 3 g Sat Fat, 0 g Trans Fat, 62 mg Chol, 794 mg Sod, 30 g Total Carb, 9 g Total Sugar, 4 g Fib, 28 g Prot, 84 mg Calc.
PointsPlus value: **8**

Cheddar-Stuffed Burgers

serves 4

*1 pound ground buffalo meat or lean ground
     beef (7% fat or less)*
1 small Vidalia onion, finely chopped
1 teaspoon Worcestershire sauce
½ teaspoon salt
⅛ teaspoon black pepper
½ cup shredded reduced-fat Cheddar cheese
4 English muffins, split and toasted
1 cup thinly sliced romaine lettuce
16 small tomato slices

1　Mix together buffalo, onion, Worcestershire sauce, salt, and pepper in large bowl just until well combined. With damp hands, shape mixture into 4 equal balls. With your finger, make deep indentation in center of each ball. Fill each hole with 2 tablespoons of Cheddar. Enclose filling by pinching meat together. Shape into ¾-inch-thick patties.

2　Spray large nonstick skillet with nonstick spray and set over medium-high heat. Place patties in skillet and cook until instant-read thermometer inserted into side of burger registers 145°F for medium, about 4 minutes per side.

3　Place bottoms of muffins on 4 plates. Top each with lettuce, burgers, and tomato slices; cover with tops of muffins.

PER SERVING (1 GARNISHED BURGER): 224 grams, 343 Cal, 12 g Total Fat, 5 g Sat Fat, 0 g Trans Fat, 70 mg Chol, 754 mg Sod, 30 g Total Carb, 2 g Total Sugar, 3 g Fib, 30 g Prot, 257 mg Calc.
PointsPlus value: **9**

FYI　Buffalo meat, sometimes known as bison meat, is very flavorful and has less fat and cholesterol than beef.

Ragu Bolognese

serves 6

2 teaspoons olive oil
¾ *pound lean ground beef (7% fat or less)*
½ *cup dry white wine*
1 onion, *chopped*
1 carrot, *chopped*
1 celery stalk, *chopped*
½ teaspoon dried oregano
½ teaspoon salt
⅛ teaspoon black pepper
1 (28-ounce) can petite diced tomatoes
½ cup low-fat (1%) milk
½ pound whole wheat spaghetti
¼ cup grated Parmesan cheese

1 Heat oil in large deep nonstick skillet over medium-high heat. Add beef and cook, breaking it apart with wooden spoon, until browned, about 5 minutes. Add wine and cook, stirring, until evaporated. Stir in onion, carrot, celery, oregano, salt, and pepper; cook, stirring occasionally, until onion is softened, about 5 minutes. Stir in tomatoes with their juice; bring to a boil. Reduce heat and simmer, stirring occasionally, until slightly thickened, about 12 minutes. Stir in milk and cook, stirring, until creamy and thickened, about 5 minutes longer.
2 Meanwhile, cook spaghetti according to package directions, omitting salt if desired; drain well.
3 Add pasta and Parmesan to skillet and cook, tossing, until heated through, about 2 minutes longer.

PER SERVING (ABOUT 1 CUP): 288 grams, 298 Cal, 6 g Total Fat, 2 g Sat Fat, 0 g Trans Fat, 38 mg Chol, 595 mg Sod, 38 g Total Carb, 8 g Total Sugar, 7 g Fib, 20 g Prot, 112 mg Calc.
PointsPlus value: **7**

Lasagna with Meat Sauce

serves 8

9 lasagna noodles
1 teaspoon fennel seeds
1 teaspoon olive oil
½ *pound lean ground beef (7% fat or less)*
1 onion, *finely chopped*
1 red bell pepper, *chopped*
1 zucchini, *chopped*
1 (26-ounce) jar marinara sauce
1½ cups fat-free ricotta cheese
½ cup shredded part-skim mozzarella cheese
¼ cup grated Pecorino Romano cheese

1 Cook lasagna noodles according to package directions, omitting salt if desired. Drain and rinse noodles. Drain again.
2 Put fennel seeds in small skillet and set over medium-low heat. Cook, stirring constantly, until seeds are lightly browned and fragrant, about 2 minutes. (Watch carefully as seeds can quickly burn.) Transfer seeds to spice grinder or coffee grinder and grind to powder. (Or pulverize using mortar and pestle.)
3 Preheat oven to 375°F.
4 Meanwhile, heat oil in large nonstick skillet over medium-high heat. Add beef, onion, bell pepper, and zucchini. Cook, stirring occasionally, until beef is browned and pan juices are evaporated, about 10 minutes. Stir in marinara sauce and ground fennel seeds; bring to boil. Reduce heat and simmer until sauce is slightly thickened, about 10 minutes.
5 Spread one-fourth of meat sauce in 9 × 13-inch baking dish. Cover with 3 noodles; spread ½ cup of ricotta on top. Repeat layering twice, ending with meat sauce.

6   Cover baking dish with foil. Bake 30 minutes. Remove foil and sprinkle lasagna evenly with mozzarella and Romano. Bake until heated through and cheeses are lightly browned, about 20 minutes longer. Let stand 10 minutes before serving.

PER SERVING (⅛ OF LASAGNA): 235 grams, 207 Cal, 8 g Total Fat, 3 g Sat Fat, 0 g Trans Fat, 28 mg Chol, 767 mg Sod, 18 g Total Carb, 9 g Total Sugar, 3 g Fib, 18 g Prot, 290 mg Calc.
PointsPlus value: **5**

FYI   To make the lasagna ahead, assemble it without the mozzarella and Romano cheeses; cover and refrigerate up to 2 days or freeze up to 2 months. To bake, thaw the lasagna (if frozen) overnight in the refrigerator. Cover with foil and bake 45 minutes; uncover. Sprinkle with the mozzarella and Romano and bake until heated through, about 15 minutes longer.

Classic Spaghetti and Meatballs

serves 6

1 pound lean ground beef (7% fat or less)
⅓ cup seasoned dried bread crumbs
3 tablespoons grated Romano cheese
4 garlic cloves, minced
1 large egg
½ teaspoon salt
¼ + ⅛ teaspoon black pepper
2 teaspoons olive oil
1 onion, chopped
1 teaspoon dried oregano
1 (28-ounce) can whole tomatoes, broken up
½ pound whole wheat spaghetti

1   To make meatballs, mix together beef, bread crumbs, Romano, half of garlic, the egg, ¼ teaspoon of salt, and ¼ teaspoon of pepper in large bowl until well combined. With damp hands, shape mixture into 30 (1-inch) meatballs.
2   Spray large nonstick skillet with nonstick spray and set over medium-high heat. Cook meatballs, in two batches, until browned on all sides, about 4 minutes. Transfer to plate.
3   To make tomato sauce, heat oil in large saucepan over medium-high heat. Add onion, remaining garlic, and the oregano; cook, stirring occasionally, until onion begins to soften, about 3 minutes. Stir in tomatoes with their juice and remaining ¼ teaspoon salt and ⅛ teaspoon pepper; bring to boil. Reduce heat and simmer, covered, 10 minutes. Add meatballs and return to simmer; cook partially covered, stirring occasionally, until meatballs are cooked through and sauce is thickened, about 20 minutes.
4   Meanwhile, cook spaghetti according to package directions, omitting salt if desired; drain well.
5   Divide pasta evenly among 6 shallow bowls and top evenly with meatballs and sauce.

PER SERVING (½ CUP SPAGHETTI, 5 MEATBALLS, AND ½ CUP SAUCE): 269 grams, 343 Cal, 9 g Total Fat, 3 g Sat Fat, 0 g Trans Fat, 85 mg Chol, 713 mg Sod, 44 g Total Carb, 8 g Total Sugar, 7 g Fib, 25 g Prot, 136 mg Calc.
PointsPlus value: **9**

▲ HEALTHY EXTRA
Begin your meal with a classic tricolored salad of sliced radicchio, baby arugula, and sliced Belgian endive dressed with lemon juice and a bit of fresh black pepper.

PORK ROAST WITH WINTER VEGETABLES

Pork Roast with Winter Vegetables

serves 8

2 large garlic cloves, minced
Grated zest of ½ lemon
1 tablespoon chopped fresh rosemary
1½ teaspoons salt
½ teaspoon black pepper
1 (2-pound) boneless center-cut pork loin
    roast, trimmed
½ butternut squash, peeled, seeded, and
    cut into 16 pieces
2 large parsnips, cut into 2-inch lengths
2 large carrots, cut into 2-inch lengths
4 celery stalks, cut into 2-inch lengths
4 teaspoons extra-virgin olive oil

1   Preheat oven to 450°F. Spray large roasting pan with olive oil nonstick spray.
2   Mix together garlic, lemon zest, rosemary, ¾ teaspoon of salt, and ¼ teaspoon of pepper in cup. Rub all over pork. Place pork in roasting pan. Scatter squash, parsnips, carrots, and celery around pork; sprinkle with remaining ¾ teaspoon salt and ¼ teaspoon pepper. Roast until instant-read thermometer inserted into center of pork registers 160°F for medium and vegetables are tender, about 45 minutes.
3   Transfer pork to cutting board and let stand 10 minutes. Cut pork into 16 slices and serve with vegetables.

PER SERVING (2 SLICES PORK AND 1 CUP VEGETABLES): 242 grams, 281 Cal, 14 g Total Fat, 5 g Sat Fat, 0 g Trans Fat, 68 mg Chol, 544 mg Sod, 14 g Total Carb, 4 g Total Sugar, 4 g Fib, 24 g Prot, 76 mg Calc.
PointsPlus value: *7*

Caribbean-Style Pork Tenderloin

serves 4

Grated zest and juice of 1 orange
Grated zest and juice of 1 lime
1 tablespoon olive oil
2 garlic cloves, minced
2 teaspoons ground cumin
½ teaspoon salt
¼ teaspoon black pepper
Pinch cayenne
1 (1-pound) pork tenderloin, trimmed

1   Combine orange zest and juice, lime zest and juice, oil, garlic, cumin, salt, pepper, and cayenne in large zip-close plastic bag; add pork. Squeeze out air and seal bag; turn to coat pork. Refrigerate, turning bag occasionally, at least 2 hours or up to overnight.
2   Preheat oven to 450°F.
3   Lightly spray roasting pan with nonstick spray. Place tenderloin in pan; drizzle marinade over top. Roast 5 minutes. Reduce oven temperature to 350°F and roast until instant-read thermometer inserted into center of tenderloin registers 160°F for medium, 15–18 minutes. Transfer to cutting board and let stand 5 minutes. Cut into 12 slices.

PER SERVING (3 SLICES): 130 grams, 176 Cal, 7 g Total Fat, 2 g Sat Fat, 0 g Trans Fat, 62 mg Chol, 342 mg Sod, 5 g Total Carb, 2 g Total Sugar, 1 g Fib, 23 g Prot, 27 mg Calc.
PointsPlus value: *4*

▲ **HEALTHY EXTRA**
Keep the island feeling of this pork dish by serving it with a plate of thinly sliced fresh pineapple sprinkled with chopped fresh cilantro and a bit of ground cinnamon.

Stir-Fried Pork with Bok Choy and Ginger

serves 4

1 cup reduced-sodium chicken broth or Basic
    Chicken Stock (page 106)
3 tablespoons dry sherry
2 tablespoons reduced-sodium soy sauce
2 tablespoons cornstarch
1 tablespoon sugar
1 pound pork tenderloin, trimmed and cut
    into ¾-inch pieces
1 tablespoon Asian (dark) sesame oil
3 cups sliced bok choy
1 red bell pepper, cut into thin strips
3 garlic cloves, minced
1 tablespoon grated peeled fresh ginger
3 scallions, chopped

1   Stir together broth, 2 tablespoons of
sherry, 1 tablespoon of soy sauce, 1 tablespoon
of cornstarch, and the sugar in small bowl until
very smooth.
2   Toss pork with remaining 1 tablespoon
sherry, 1 tablespoon soy sauce, and 1 tablespoon cornstarch in medium bowl.
3   Heat nonstick wok or deep large nonstick
skillet over medium-high heat until drop of water sizzles in pan; add 1½ teaspoons of sesame
oil and swirl to coat pan. Add pork mixture
and stir-fry until browned, about 5 minutes;
transfer to plate.
4   Heat remaining 1½ teaspoons sesame oil
in wok. Add bok choy and bell pepper; stir-fry
until crisp-tender, about 1 minute. Add garlic
and ginger; stir-fry until fragrant and beginning
to brown, about 1 minute. Return pork mixture to wok; stir-fry, 1 minute.
5   Re-stir cornstarch mixture and add to wok;
stir-fry until sauce bubbles and thickens, about
2 minutes. Serve sprinkled with scallions.

PER SERVING (1 CUP): 258 grams, 267 Cal,
12 g Total Fat, 3 g Sat Fat, 0 g Trans Fat, 56 mg Chol,
411 mg Sod, 14 g Total Carb, 5 g Total Sugar, 2 g Fib,
25 g Prot, 82 mg Calc.
PointsPlus value: *7*

▲ **HEALTHY EXTRA**
Add a side of brown rice to our very tasty stir-fry
(⅔ cup of cooked brown rice with each serving will
increase the *PointsPlus* value by *3*).

Barbecued Pork with Mop Sauce

serves 6

2 tablespoons dark brown sugar
1 tablespoon paprika
1 tablespoon chili powder
1½ teaspoons ground cumin
½ teaspoon salt
¼ teaspoon black pepper
¼ teaspoon cayenne
2 (¾-pound) pork tenderloins, trimmed
⅓ cup ketchup
¼ cup cider vinegar
2 tablespoons dark molasses
2 teaspoons Worcestershire sauce

1   Spray grill rack with nonstick spray. Preheat grill to medium-high or prepare medium-
high fire using indirect method.
2   To make rub, stir together brown sugar,
paprika, chili powder, cumin, salt, pepper, and
cayenne in cup. Rub half of mixture all over
pork; let stand 15 minutes.
3   Meanwhile, to make mop sauce, stir
together ketchup, vinegar, molasses, and
Worcestershire sauce in serving bowl.

4   Rub remaining spice rub all over pork. Place tenderloins on cooler portion of grill rack and grill, covered, 15 minutes. Turn pork over and grill until instant-read thermometer inserted into center of meat registers 160°F for medium, 12–15 minutes longer. Transfer to cutting board and let stand 10 minutes. Cut each tenderloin into 12 slices. Serve with mop sauce.

PER SERVING (4 SLICES PORK AND ABOUT 2 TABLESPOONS SAUCE): 120 grams, 207 Cal, 6 g Total Fat, 2 g Sat Fat, 0 g Trans Fat, 75 mg Chol, 435 mg Sod, 14 g Total Carb, 12 g Total Sugar, 1 g Fib, 25 g Prot, 51 mg Calc.
PointsPlus value: *5*

FYI   Although pork is the meat of choice in this recipe, the tasty spice rub also works well on chicken, beef, and catfish.

Pork with Ginger and Soy

serves 5

1 (1-pound) pork tenderloin, trimmed
3 tablespoons light brown sugar
3 tablespoons reduced-sodium soy sauce
3 garlic cloves, minced
1 tablespoon grated peeled fresh ginger
1 tablespoon unseasoned rice vinegar
2 teaspoons Asian (dark) sesame oil
½ teaspoon salt

1   Cut pork lengthwise in half, cutting almost all the way through, then open meat up like a book. Place pork, cut side down, between 2 pieces of plastic wrap. With meat mallet or rolling pin, pound to ¾-inch thickness.
2   Combine brown sugar, soy sauce, garlic, ginger, vinegar, and sesame oil in large zip-close plastic bag; add pork. Squeeze out air and seal bag; turn to coat pork. Refrigerate, turning bag occasionally, at least 2 hours or up to overnight.
3   Spray grill rack with nonstick spray. Preheat grill to medium or prepare medium fire using direct method.
4   Remove pork from marinade; discard marinade. Sprinkle pork with salt. Place pork on grill rack and grill until well marked and instant-read thermometer inserted into center of pork registers 160°F for medium, about 5 minutes per side. Transfer pork to cutting board and let stand 5 minutes. Cut into 10 slices.

PER SERVING (2 SLICES): 90 grams, 174 Cal, 6 g Total Fat, 2 g Sat Fat, 0 g Trans Fat, 60 mg Chol, 508 mg Sod, 7 g Total Carb, 6 g Total Sugar, 0 g Fib, 17 g Prot, 8 mg Calc.
PointsPlus value: *5*

HONEY-MUSTARD PORK CHOPS

Honey-Mustard Pork Chops

serves 4

¼ cup Dijon mustard
4 teaspoons honey
1 teaspoon cider or white wine vinegar
¼ teaspoon black pepper
4 (5-ounce) bone-in loin pork chops, about 1 inch thick

1   To make marinade, stir together all ingredients except pork in cup.
2   Transfer marinade to large zip-close plastic bag; add pork. Squeeze out air and seal bag; turn to coat meat. Refrigerate, turning bag occasionally, at least 4 hours or up to overnight.
3   Spray broiler rack with nonstick spray. Preheat broiler.
4   Remove chops from bag; discard marinade. Place chops on prepared broiler rack and broil 5 inches from heat until cooked through, about 6 minutes per side.

PER SERVING (1 CHOP): 94 grams, 165 Cal, 5 g Total Fat, 2 g Sat Fat, 0 g Trans Fat, 59 mg Chol, 546 mg Sod, 9 g Total Carb, 5 g Total Sugar, 0 g Fib, 19 g Prot, 17 mg Calc.
PointsPlus value: *4*

▲ **HEALTHY EXTRA**
Serve these delectable chops with steamed fresh kale and steamed thickly sliced ears of corn (½ medium ear of corn per serving will increase the *PointsPlus* value by *1*).

Spicy Pork Stir-Fry

serves 4

2 teaspoons canola oil
1 pound pork tenderloin, trimmed and thinly sliced
1 red bell pepper, cut into thick strips
8 scallions, cut into 2-inch lengths
1 (20-ounce) can pineapple chunks, drained
2 tomatoes, each cut into 8 wedges
1 jalapeño pepper, seeded and minced
2 teaspoons grated peeled fresh ginger
2 garlic cloves, minced
4 teaspoons soy sauce
1 teaspoon Asian (dark) sesame oil
¼ cup chopped fresh cilantro
2 cups hot cooked white rice

1   Heat nonstick wok or deep large nonstick skillet over high heat until drop of water sizzles in pan; add canola oil and swirl to coat pan. Add pork and stir-fry until no longer pink, 1–2 minutes. With slotted spoon, transfer to plate.
2   Add bell pepper to wok and stir-fry 2 minutes. Add scallions and stir-fry 30 seconds. Add pineapple and stir-fry 30 seconds. Return pork to wok along with tomatoes, jalapeño, ginger, garlic, soy sauce, and sesame oil. Stir-fry until heated through, about 2 minutes longer. Sprinkle with cilantro and serve with rice.

PER SERVING (ABOUT 1½ CUPS PORK MIXTURE AND ½ CUP RICE): 430 grams, 419 Cal, 12 g Total Fat, 3 g Sat Fat, 0 g Trans Fat, 56 mg Chol, 491 mg Sod, 52 g Total Carb, 24 g Total Sugar, 4 g Fib, 27 g Prot, 81 mg Calc.
PointsPlus value: *11*

Pork and Black Bean Chili

serves 4

1 onion, chopped
1 red bell pepper, chopped
3 garlic cloves, minced
³/₄ pound pork tenderloin, trimmed and cut
   into ¹/₂-inch pieces
1 (15¹/₂-ounce) can black beans, rinsed and
   drained
1¹/₂ cups reduced-sodium chicken broth or
   Basic Chicken Stock (page 106)
1 (4¹/₂-ounce) can chopped mild green chiles,
   drained
1 tablespoon chili powder
2 teaspoons ground cumin
¹/₂ teaspoon salt
¹/₄ teaspoon black pepper
¹/₄ cup shredded reduced-fat Cheddar cheese
¹/₄ cup fat-free sour cream

1   Spray large nonstick saucepan with nonstick spray and set over medium heat. Add onion, bell pepper, and garlic; cook, stirring, until
onion is softened, about 5 minutes. Add pork
and cook, stirring, until lightly browned, about
3 minutes.
2   Stir beans, broth, chiles, chili powder,
cumin, salt, and pepper into saucepan. Bring
to boil. Reduce heat and simmer, stirring occasionally, until pork is tender and flavors are
blended, about 10 minutes.
3   Ladle chili into 4 bowls and serve with
Cheddar and sour cream.

**PER SERVING (1 CUP CHILI, 1 TABLESPOON CHEDDAR,
AND 1 TABLESPOON SOUR CREAM):** 380 grams, 277 Cal,
7 g Total Fat, 2 g Sat Fat, 0 g Trans Fat, 43 mg Chol,
833 mg Sod, 26 g Total Carb, 6 g Total Sugar, 8 g Fib,
26 g Prot, 137 mg Calc.
PointsPlus value: **6**

Garlicky Red Beans and Pork

serves 4

1 tablespoon olive oil
1 pound boneless pork loin, trimmed and cut
   into 1¹/₂-inch chunks
2 onions, chopped
5 garlic cloves, minced
2 tomatoes, coarsely chopped
1 cup dried red kidney beans, picked over,
   soaked, and drained
1 (4¹/₂-ounce) can chopped mild green chiles,
   drained
¹/₂ cup water
1 teaspoon ground cumin
¹/₂ teaspoon salt
¹/₄ teaspoon black pepper

1   Heat oil in Dutch oven over medium-high
heat. Cook pork, in batches, until browned
on all sides, about 10 minutes. Reduce heat to
medium. Add onions and garlic; cook, stirring,
until onions are softened, about 5 minutes.
2   Return pork to pot along with tomatoes,
beans, chiles, water, cumin, salt, and pepper;
bring to boil. Reduce heat and simmer, covered, until beans are tender, about 1 hour.

PER SERVING (¹/₄ OF BEANS AND PORK): 326 grams,
368 Cal, 11 g Total Fat, 3 g Sat Fat, 0 g Trans Fat,
56 mg Chol, 448 mg Sod, 34 g Total Carb,
6 g Total Sugar, 13 g Fib, 33 g Prot, 121 mg Calc.
PointsPlus value: **8**

FYI   To soak beans, put them in a large bowl
and add enough cold water to cover by at
least 2 inches. Let the beans soak for at least 8
hours or up to overnight, then drain.

Old-World Pasta with Pork and Tomato Sauce

serves 8

1 (28-ounce) can whole tomatoes in juice
1 (14-ounce) can whole tomatoes in juice
2 pounds boneless loin pork chops
    (about ¾-inch thick), trimmed
3 large garlic cloves, minced
2 teaspoons sugar
1 teaspoon dried oregano
1 teaspoon salt
¼ teaspoon black pepper
¼ teaspoon red pepper flakes
1 pound whole wheat penne
Thinly sliced fresh basil

1 Preheat oven to 325°F.
2 Puree (both cans) of tomatoes with their juice, in batches, in blender or food processor.
3 Spray large Dutch oven with nonstick spray and set over medium-high heat. Add pork chops and cook until browned, about 2 minutes per side. Transfer to plate.
4 Reduce heat to medium. Add garlic to pot and cook until fragrant and beginning to color, about 1 minute. Add pureed tomatoes, sugar, oregano, salt, black pepper, and pepper flakes; bring to boil. Return pork to pot.
5 Bake, covered, 1½ hours. Uncover and bake until pork is fork-tender and sauce is slightly thickened, about 30 minutes longer. Transfer pork to cutting board. When cool enough to handle, cut into ½-inch pieces. Return pork to sauce.

6 Meanwhile, cook penne according to package directions, omitting salt if desired; drain. Transfer pasta to large serving bowl and top with half of sauce. Stir to mix well; top with remaining sauce and the basil.

PER SERVING (1½ CUPS PASTA AND GENEROUS ¾ CUP SAUCE): 281 grams, 406 Cal, 9 g Total Fat, 3 g Sat Fat, 0 g Trans Fat, 56 mg Chol, 555 mg Sod, 50 g Total Carb, 6 g Total Sugar, 7 g Fib, 30 g Prot, 87 mg Calc. *PointsPlus* value: *10*

FYI If you like, you can add 1 teaspoon dried basil to the tomato sauce along with the oregano instead of using the fresh basil.

Tandoori Lamb with Almond-Apricot Couscous

serves 8

¾ *cup plain fat-free yogurt*
Juice of 1 lime
½ *small onion, quartered*
1 tablespoon minced peeled fresh ginger
2 large garlic cloves, finely chopped
1 tablespoon paprika
1 teaspoon ground coriander
¼ *teaspoon cayenne*
1 (2-pound) boneless leg of lamb, butterflied
    and trimmed
1 teaspoon salt
1 cup whole wheat couscous
⅓ *cup sliced almonds, toasted*
½ *cup chopped dried apricots*

1 Stir together yogurt, lime juice, onion, ginger, garlic, paprika, coriander, and cayenne in small bowl.

2 Place lamb on work surface; with meat mallet or rolling pin, pound to even thickness. Put lamb in large shallow baking dish and spread yogurt mixture all over. Cover dish with plastic wrap; refrigerate at least 1 hour or up to 4 hours.

3 Spray grill rack with nonstick spray. Preheat grill to medium-high or prepare medium-high fire using direct method.

4 With paper towel, wipe excess yogurt mixture from lamb; sprinkle with salt. Place lamb on grill rack and grill, turning, until instant-read thermometer inserted into thickest part of lamb registers 145°F for medium, about 25 minutes. Transfer to cutting board and let stand 10 minutes.

5 Meanwhile, cook couscous according to package directions. Transfer to serving bowl and top with almonds and apricots. Cut lamb across grain into 32 slices. Serve with couscous.

PER SERVING (4 SLICES LAMB AND SCANT ½ CUP COUSCOUS): 134 grams, 236 Cal, 11 g Total Fat, 4 g Sat Fat, 0 g Trans Fat, 45 mg Chol, 343 mg Sod, 20 g Total Carb, 6 g Total Sugar, 3 g Fib, 15 g Prot, 74 mg Calc.
PointsPlus value: **6**

▲ HEALTHY EXTRA
Toss sliced cucumber, red onion, and chopped parsley with white balsamic vinegar and a sprinkle of salt to serve alongside the lamb.

FYI Couscous, a staple of North African cuisine, is granular semolina. Couscous is also the name of a famous dish in which the couscous is steamed on the top of a special pot, while meat and vegetables are cooked in the bottom.

Moroccan-Style Roast Leg of Lamb

serves 6

2 tablespoons finely chopped fresh mint
3 garlic cloves, minced
1 tablespoon lemon juice
1 tablespoon olive oil
2 teaspoons paprika
1 teaspoon ground cumin
1 teaspoon salt
½ teaspoon black pepper
Pinch cayenne
1 (2-pound) bone-in leg of lamb (preferably sirloin half), trimmed

1   Preheat oven to 375°F.
2   Stir together all ingredients except lamb in cup. Rub mint mixture all over lamb.
3   Place lamb on rack in roasting pan. Roast until instant-read thermometer inserted into thickest part of lamb registers 145°F for medium, about 1½ hours. Transfer to cutting board and let stand 10 minutes. Cut into 12 slices.

PER SERVING (2 SLICES): 123 grams, 272 Cal,
15 g Total Fat, 5 g Sat Fat, 0 g Trans Fat, 119 mg Chol,
484 mg Sod, 1 g Total Carb, 0 g Total Sugar, 0 g Fib,
32 g Prot, 24 mg Calc.
PointsPlus value: **7**

▲ **HEALTHY EXTRA**
Enjoy this lamb the way the locals do in Morocco by serving a bowl of cooked whole wheat couscous sprinkled with chopped fresh mint alongside (⅔ cup of cooked whole wheat couscous with each serving will increase the *PointsPlus* value by *3*).

Rack of Lamb with Herbed Crumb Topping

serves 4

1 (8-rib) rack of lamb (about 1½ pounds), trimmed and frenched
½ teaspoon salt
¼ teaspoon black pepper
½ cup fresh bread crumbs (about 1 slice bread)
1 tablespoon Dijon mustard
2 teaspoons chopped fresh tarragon
1 teaspoon olive oil
1 small garlic clove, minced

1   Spray grill rack with nonstick spray. Preheat grill to medium-high or prepare medium-high fire using direct method.
2   Sprinkle lamb with salt and pepper. Place lamb on grill rack and grill, turning once, until nicely browned, about 10 minutes. Transfer to plate. (Leave grill on.)
3   Stir together all remaining ingredients in small bowl, adding a little water to moisten, if needed. Press crumb mixture on meaty side of lamb; lightly spray crumb mixture with nonstick spray.
4   Return lamb, crumb side up, to grill rack and grill, without turning, until instant-read thermometer inserted into center of rack registers 145°F for medium, about 10 minutes. Transfer to cutting board and let stand 10 minutes. Slice between every other bone to make 4 double chops.

PER SERVING (1 DOUBLE CHOP): 74 grams, 153 Cal,
6 g Total Fat, 2 g Sat Fat, 0 g Trans Fat, 70 mg Chol,
453 mg Sod, 4 g Total Carb, 0 g Total Sugar, 0 g Fib,
18 g Prot, 25 mg Calc.
PointsPlus value: **4**

Grilled Lamb Chops with Mixed Herb Pesto

serves 4

2 garlic cloves, peeled
½ cup lightly packed fresh basil leaves
¼ cup lightly packed fresh flat-leaf parsley
    leaves
Grated zest of ½ lemon
2 tablespoons water
1 tablespoon extra-virgin olive oil
½ teaspoon salt
4 (5-ounce) loin lamb chops, about 1 inch
    thick, trimmed

1   To make pesto, put garlic in food processor and pulse until chopped. Add basil, parsley, and lemon zest; pulse until chopped. Add water, oil, and ¼ teaspoon of salt; process until almost smooth. Transfer to serving dish.

2   Spray grill rack with nonstick spray. Preheat grill to medium-high or prepare medium-high fire using direct method.

3   Sprinkle lamb chops with remaining ¼ teaspoon salt and place on grill rack. Grill, covered, until instant-read thermometer inserted into side of chop registers 145°F for medium, about 4 minutes per side. Serve with pesto.

PER SERVING (1 CHOP AND GENEROUS 1 TABLESPOON PESTO): 83 grams, 165 Cal, 10 g Total Fat, 3 g Sat Fat, 0 g Trans Fat, 57 mg Chol, 344 mg Sod, 1 g Total Carb, 0 g Total Sugar, 0 g Fib, 18 g Prot, 30 mg Calc.
PointsPlus value: *4*

Lamb Chops with Yogurt-Mint Sauce

serves 4

¾ cup plain fat-free yogurt
½ cucumber, peeled, seeded, and chopped
¼ cup lightly packed fresh mint leaves
3 scallions, sliced
1 garlic clove, chopped
¼ teaspoon red pepper flakes
½ teaspoon salt
4 (5-ounce) bone-in loin lamb chops, about
    1 inch thick, trimmed
¼ teaspoon black pepper

1   Spray broiler rack with nonstick spray. Preheat broiler.

2   To make sauce, stir together yogurt, cucumber, mint, scallions, garlic, pepper flakes, and ¼ teaspoon of salt in blender or food processor and puree. Transfer to serving dish.

3   Sprinkle lamb with remaining ¼ teaspoon salt and the black pepper. Place on prepared broiler rack and broil 5 inches from heat until instant-read thermometer inserted into side of chop registers 145°F for medium, about 5 minutes per side. Serve with sauce.

PER SERVING (1 CHOP AND ABOUT ¼ CUP SAUCE): 140 grams, 168 Cal, 7 g Total Fat, 3 g Sat Fat, 0 g Trans Fat, 59 mg Chol, 376 mg Sod, 5 g Total Carb, 4 g Total Sugar, 1 g Fib, 21 g Prot, 112 mg Calc.
PointsPlus value: *4*

Grilled Lamb Chops with Tomato–Bell Pepper Sauce

serves 4

2 red bell peppers, halved and seeded
1 teaspoon olive oil
1 small onion, chopped
2 garlic cloves, minced
½ cup drained canned diced tomatoes
8 pitted Kalamata olives, sliced
2 tablespoons chopped fresh basil
¼ + ⅛ teaspoon black pepper
¼ teaspoon salt
4 (¼-pound) bone-in rib lamb chops, trimmed

1   Spray grill rack with olive oil nonstick spray. Preheat grill to medium-high or prepare medium-high fire using direct method.
2   Place bell peppers, skin side down, on grill rack and grill, turning occasionally, until tender, about 10 minutes. Cut into pieces.
3   Heat oil in large nonstick skillet over medium heat. Add onion and garlic; cook, stirring, until onion is softened, about 5 minutes. Add bell peppers, tomatoes, olives, basil, ⅛ teaspoon of black pepper, and the salt. Simmer, covered, 10 minutes.
4   Sprinkle lamb chops with remaining ¼ teaspoon black pepper. Place chops on grill rack and grill, turning occasionally, until instant-read thermometer inserted into side of chop registers 145°F for medium, about 5 minutes per side. Transfer to platter and serve bell pepper sauce alongside.

PER SERVING (1 LAMB CHOP AND ABOUT ⅓ CUP SAUCE):
207 grams, 247 Cal, 13 g Total Fat, 5 g Sat Fat,
0 g Trans Fat, 68 mg Chol, 415 mg Sod, 8 g Total Carb,
4 g Total Sugar, 2 g Fib, 22 g Prot, 35 mg Calc.
PointsPlus value: *6*

Lamb-Vegetable Stew

serves 4

1 pound boneless leg of lamb, trimmed and cut
    into 1-inch chunks
1 onion, sliced
2 garlic cloves, minced
1 pound baby potatoes, scrubbed and halved
1½ cups baby-cut carrots
1 cup pearl onions, peeled, or frozen pearl
    onions
1 tablespoon paprika
¼ teaspoon dried thyme
1 (14½-ounce) can reduced-sodium beef broth
    or 1¾ cups Basic Beef Stock (page 106)
1 bay leaf
3 cups hot cooked yolk-free egg noodles

1   Spray nonstick Dutch oven with nonstick spray and set over medium-high heat. Add lamb, in batches, and cook until browned on all sides, about 5 minutes. Transfer to bowl.
2   Add onion and garlic to pot; cook, stirring, until onion is softened, about 5 minutes. Add potatoes, carrots, pearl onions, paprika, and thyme; cook, stirring, 2 minutes. Return lamb to pot along with broth and bay leaf; bring to boil. Reduce heat and simmer, covered, until lamb and vegetables are tender, about 35 minutes. Discard bay leaf. Serve with noodles.

PER SERVING (1½ CUPS STEW AND ¾ CUP NOODLES):
449 grams, 404 Cal, 10 g Total Fat, 4 g Sat Fat,
0 g Trans Fat, 89 mg Chol, 310 mg Sod, 47 g Total Carb,
7 g Total Sugar, 4 g Fib, 31 g Prot, 54 mg Calc.
PointsPlus value: *10*

▲ HEALTHY EXTRA
Add 2 zucchini, sliced, to stew during the last 25 minutes of cooking time.

Venison Chops with Shallot Sauce

serves 4

1 onion, chopped
6 garlic cloves, peeled
3 teaspoons olive oil
¾ teaspoon salt
3 tablespoons red wine vinegar
1 cup prepared demi-glace
12 shallots, peeled
¼ teaspoon black pepper
12 small beets, trimmed
4 (3½-ounce) boneless loin venison chops
2 tablespoons chopped fresh parsley

1   Preheat oven to 425°F.
2   To make sauce, toss together onion, garlic, 1 teaspoon of oil, and ¼ teaspoon of salt in small roasting pan. Roast, stirring occasionally, until onion is golden brown, about 25 minutes. Add vinegar, scraping any browned bits from bottom of pan.
3   Transfer onion mixture and pan liquid to medium saucepan. Stir in demi-glace. Bring to a boil over medium-high heat. Reduce heat and simmer, partially covered, 30 minutes. Pour sauce through fine sieve set over medium bowl, pressing hard on solids to extract as much liquid as possible; discard solids. Return sauce to saucepan; keep warm.
4   Wash roasting pan. Toss together shallots, ½ teaspoon of oil, ¼ teaspoon of salt, and pinch of pepper at one end of roasting pan. Toss together beets and ½ teaspoon of oil at other end of roasting pan. Roast until shallots are golden brown, about 30 minutes. Remove shallots from pan; keep warm. Roast beets until tender, about 10 minutes longer.

5   When beets are cool enough to handle, peel. Keep beets and shallots warm.
6   Sprinkle venison chops with remaining ¼ teaspoon salt and remaining pepper. Heat remaining 1 teaspoon oil in large nonstick skillet over high heat. Add venison and cook until browned and instant-read thermometer inserted into side of chop registers 145°F for medium, about 3 minutes per side. Transfer to plate; let stand 5 minutes.
7   To serve, spoon some of sauce onto each of 4 plates; top each with 1 venison chop. Arrange shallots and beets on plates; sprinkle with parsley. Serve remaining sauce alongside.

PER SERVING (1 VENISON CHOP, 3 SHALLOTS, 3 BEETS, AND ABOUT ¼ CUP SAUCE): 596 grams, 401 Cal, 8 g Total Fat, 2 g Sat Fat, 0 g Trans Fat, 84 mg Chol, 928 mg Sod, 54 g Total Carb, 23 g Total Sugar, 8 g Fib, 33 g Prot, 67 mg Calc.
PointsPlus value: **10**

FYI   Demi-glace can be purchased from Williams-Sonoma and D'Artagnan. See Sources (page 10).

Venison Steaks with Blackberry Sauce

serves 4

1 teaspoon olive oil
1 fennel bulb, thinly sliced
1 small radicchio, thinly sliced
1 pint blackberries
½ cup reduced-sodium beef broth or Basic
    Beef Stock (page 106)
2 fresh thyme sprigs
1 tablespoon cornstarch
¼ cup orange juice
2 (6-ounce) venison steaks

1 Heat oil in large nonstick skillet over medium-low heat. Add fennel and radicchio; cook, stirring occasionally, until softened, about 20 minutes.

2 Meanwhile, reserve 8 blackberries. Put remaining berries, the broth, and thyme in small saucepan; bring to boil. Reduce heat and cook until berries are softened, about 2 minutes. Pour mixture through fine-mesh sieve set over medium bowl, pressing hard on berries to extract all the juice; discard solids. Transfer berry puree to saucepan.

3 Stir together cornstarch and orange juice in cup until smooth. Add to berry puree. Cook over medium heat, stirring constantly, until mixture bubbles and thickens, about 2 minutes.

4 Meanwhile, spray broiler rack with nonstick spray. Preheat broiler.

5 Place steaks on prepared broiler rack and broil 5 inches from heat until instant-read thermometer inserted into center of steak registers 145°F for medium, about 1½ minutes per side. Cut into thin slices.

6 To serve, divide vegetables among 4 plates; fan steak slices on top of vegetables and spoon sauce over and around meat. Garnish with reserved berries.

PER SERVING (⅓ CUP VEGETABLES, ½ STEAK, AND ⅓ CUP SAUCE): 245 grams, 178 Cal, 4 g Total Fat, 1 g Sat Fat, 0 g Trans Fat, 71 mg Chol, 184 mg Sod, 15 g Total Carb, 4 g Total Sugar, 6 g Fib, 21 g Prot, 57 mg Calc.
PointsPlus value: *4*

▲ **HEALTHY EXTRA**
A bowl of hot wild rice adds great flavor and elegance to the venison steaks (½ cup of cooked wild rice with each serving will increase the *PointsPlus* value by *2*).

7

Poultry

Poultry

164   Garlic-Roasted Chicken with Gravy
165   Chili-Roasted Chicken and Potatoes
167   Chicken with Rice
167   Chicken with Orange Gremolata
168   Beer Can Chicken
169   Chicken Cacciatore
169   Chicken with Apples and Noodles
170   Barbecue-Sauced Grilled Chicken
170   Spicy Chicken Curry
172   Chicken Breasts with Papaya-Mint Salsa
172   Skillet Chicken with Cherry Tomatoes and Garlic
173   Easy Chicken–Pumpkin Seed Mole
173   Orange-Crumbed Baked Chicken
175   Chicken and Broccoli Rabe with Polenta
175   Chicken Tacos
176   Island Chicken with Pineapple
176   Cumin Chicken Kebabs with Couscous
177   Chicken-Mushroom Hash Casserole
178   Skillet Chicken Paprika
178   Chicken in Lemon-Caper Sauce
180   Spicy Chicken and Broccoli
180   Chicken and Bell Pepper Fajitas
181   Herbed Oven-Fried Chicken
182   Picadillo
182   Chicken and Mushroom Stew
184   Tandoori-Spiced Chicken
184   Chicken with Olives and Dates
185   Chicken and Black Bean Chili
185   Chicken and Vegetable Fried Rice
186   Zesty Chicken-Noodle Casserole
186   Roast Turkey with Onion Gravy
187   Turkey with Feta Topping
188   Mushroom-Stuffed Turkey Breast
189   Turkey Cutlets with Cranberry Sauce
189   Monterey Jack Turkey Burgers
191   Parmesan-Turkey Meat Loaf
191   Easy Enchiladas
192   Cornish Hens Under a Brick
192   Citrus-Glazed Duck Breasts

Garlic-Roasted Chicken with Gravy

serves 4

1 (3½-pound) chicken, giblets discarded
1 lemon, halved
1 onion, halved
4 fresh rosemary sprigs
4 fresh thyme sprigs
6 garlic cloves, peeled
1 cup reduced-sodium chicken broth or Basic
   Chicken Stock (page 106)
2 tablespoons lemon juice
1 tablespoon cornstarch
¼ cup water
3 tablespoons dry white wine
1 shallot, finely chopped
¼ teaspoon dried sage
¼ teaspoon salt

1   Preheat oven to 400°F. Place rack in roasting pan and spray with nonstick spray.
2   Rinse chicken inside and out under cold
running water. Pat dry with paper towels.
Place lemon, onion, rosemary sprigs, thyme
sprigs, and 5 of garlic cloves in body cavity.
Place chicken, breast side up, on prepared rack
in roasting pan. Tuck wings under and tie legs
together with kitchen string.
3   Roast chicken 30 minutes; pour broth and
lemon juice over chicken. Reduce oven temperature to 325°F. Roast, basting, until instant-
read thermometer inserted into thigh (not
touching bone) registers 180°F, about 1 hour
longer. Transfer chicken to cutting board; let
stand 15 minutes.
4   Meanwhile, mince remaining garlic clove.
Pour pan juices into medium saucepan; skim
off any fat and transfer 1 tablespoon of pan
juices to small bowl. Add cornstarch to pan
juices in bowl, whisking until smooth.

5   Add water, wine, minced garlic, shallot,
sage, and salt to pan juices in saucepan; bring
to boil. Reduce heat and simmer 5 minutes.
Whisk in cornstarch mixture; cook, stirring
constantly, until gravy bubbles and thickens,
about 1 minute. Remove lemon, onion, and
herbs from cavity; discard. Carve chicken and
serve with gravy. Remove skin before eating.

PER SERVING (¼ OF CHICKEN AND ¼ CUP GRAVY):
243 grams, 308 Cal, 11 g Total Fat, 3 g Sat Fat,
0 g Trans Fat, 135 mg Chol, 433 mg Sod, 4 g Total Carb,
1 g Total Sugar, 0 g Fib, 45 g Prot, 28 mg Calc.
PointsPlus value: **7**

FYI Refrigerate uncooked chicken in its
original packaging on a low shelf in the
coldest part of the refrigerator for up to 2 days.
For extra protection, place the chicken in a
zip-close plastic bag to prevent any juices from
dripping onto other foods.

Chili-Roasted Chicken and Potatoes

serves 6

1 tablespoon chili powder
2 teaspoons paprika, preferably smoked
1 teaspoon dried oregano
1 teaspoon ground cumin
1 teaspoon salt
2 garlic cloves, minced
1 (3½ -pound) chicken, giblets discarded
3 (10-ounce) baking potatoes, peeled and
    quartered lengthwise

1   Place racks in middle and lower third of oven. Preheat oven to 375°F. Place rack in roasting pan; spray with nonstick spray. Spray 9 × 13-inch baking dish with nonstick spray.

2   To make spice paste, stir together chili powder, paprika, oregano, cumin, ½ teaspoon of salt, and the garlic in cup. Add enough water to form thick paste.

3   Rinse chicken inside and out under cold running water. Pat dry with paper towels. Gently loosen skin on breast and thighs; rub paste on meat under skin. Place chicken, breast side up, on prepared rack in roasting pan. Tuck wings under and tie legs together with kitchen string.

4   Roast chicken on middle oven rack until instant-read thermometer inserted into thigh (not touching bone) registers 180°F, about 1 hour 10 minutes.

5   Meanwhile, put potatoes in prepared baking dish; lightly spray with nonstick spray and sprinkle with remaining ½ teaspoon salt. After chicken has roasted 30 minutes, put potatoes on lower oven rack and roast, turning once or twice, until tender and lightly browned, about 40 minutes.

6   Remove chicken from oven and let stand 10 minutes. Carve chicken and serve with potatoes. Remove skin before eating.

PER SERVING (⅙ OF CHICKEN AND 2 POTATO WEDGES): 227 grams, 308 Cal, 8 g Total Fat, 2 g Sat Fat, 0 g Trans Fat, 90 mg Chol, 494 mg Sod, 26 g Total Carb, 1 g Total Sugar, 3 g Fib, 32 g Prot, 35 mg Calc. *PointsPlus* value: **8**

▲ **HEALTHY EXTRA**
Round out the meal with a Southwest-inspired green bean salad. Toss steamed green beans with enough fat-free tomatillo salsa to coat, then stir in chopped fresh cilantro and a splash of lime juice.

CHICKEN WITH RICE

Chicken with Rice

serves 4

1½ pounds bone-in chicken parts (breasts,
    drumsticks, and thighs), skinned
½ teaspoon salt
¼ teaspoon black pepper
4 teaspoons olive oil
1 red bell pepper, chopped
2 celery stalks, sliced
1 onion, chopped
4 garlic cloves, minced
1 (14½-ounce) can diced tomatoes
½ cup reduced-sodium chicken broth
⅓ cup long-grain white rice
½ teaspoon dried oregano
½ teaspoon saffron threads, crushed
1 cup frozen green peas
¼ cup chopped fresh cilantro

1   Preheat oven to 350°F.
2   Sprinkle chicken with salt and pepper.
Heat oil in large nonstick skillet over medium
heat. Add chicken and cook until browned,
about 4 minutes per side. Transfer to lidded
2-quart casserole dish.
3   Add bell pepper, celery, onion, and garlic
to skillet; cook, stirring, until softened, about 5
minutes. Stir in tomatoes with their juice and
broth; bring to boil. Stir in rice, oregano, and
saffron; add to chicken.
4   Bake, covered, 25 minutes; sprinkle with
peas. Bake, covered, until chicken is cooked
through, rice is tender, and liquid is absorbed,
about 15 minutes. Serve sprinkled with cilantro.

PER SERVING (¼ OF CASSEROLE): 401 grams, 321 Cal,
9 g Total Fat, 2 g Sat Fat, 0 g Trans Fat, 69 mg Chol,
625 mg Sod, 31 g Total Carb, 9 g Total Sugar, 6 g Fib,
29 g Prot, 70 mg Calc.
PointsPlus value: **8**

Chicken with Orange Gremolata

serves 8

½ cup chopped fresh parsley
Grated zest of 1 orange
3 garlic cloves, minced
1 tablespoon olive oil
1 teaspoon ground cumin
3 pounds bone-in chicken parts (breasts,
    drumsticks, and thighs)
1 teaspoon salt
¼ teaspoon black pepper

1   Spray grill rack with nonstick spray. Preheat grill to medium or prepare medium fire
using direct method.
2   Meanwhile, to make gremolata, mix
together parsley, orange zest, garlic, oil, and
cumin in small bowl. Reserve 3 tablespoons of
gremolata in cup.
3   Gently loosen skin on chicken and spread
remaining gremolata on meat under skin. Place
chicken, skin side down, on cooler portion of
grill and grill, covered, turning every 10 minutes, until cooked through, about 30 minutes.
4   Remove skin from chicken. Place chicken
on platter and sprinkle with reserved gremolata.

PER SERVING (1 PIECE CHICKEN): 87 grams, 156 Cal,
6 g Total Fat, 1 g Sat Fat, 0 g Trans Fat, 69 mg Chol,
356 mg Sod, 1 g Total Carb, 0 g Total Sugar, 0 g Fib,
24 g Prot, 22 mg Calc.
PointsPlus value: **4**

FYI   Gremolata (*greh-moh-LAH-tah*) is an Italian
condiment that usually consists of parsley,
garlic, lemon zest, and olive oil. It adds a burst of
flavor to food without much effort. Gremolata can
be sprinkled on almost any meat, fish, or poultry.

SEASONING
CHICKEN

Spreading a spice paste or a mixture
of chopped fresh herbs under the skin
of the breast and leg ensures the meat
will be very flavorful.

1 Make spice paste or herb mixture
as directed.

2 Gently loosen skin on breasts and
leg/thigh, then spread paste over meat.
Pull skin back over meat. Cook as directed. Remove skin before eating.

Beer Can Chicken

serves 6

2 large garlic cloves, minced
1 tablespoon brown sugar
1 tablespoon paprika
2 teaspoons poultry seasoning
1 teaspoon salt
¼ teaspoon black pepper
1 (3½-pound) chicken, giblets discarded
1 (12-ounce) can regular or nonalcoholic beer

1 To make rub, stir together all ingredients
except chicken and beer in cup. Rinse chicken
inside and out under cold running water.
Pat dry. Tuck wings under chicken. Spread 1
tablespoon of rub on meat under skin. Spread
remaining rub over chicken and in body cavity.
Loosely cover; refrigerate at least 30 minutes.
2 Spray grill rack with nonstick spray. Preheat grill to medium or prepare medium fire
using indirect method.
3 Wash unopened beer can with hot, soapy
water; open can. Pour out half of beer and make
two more holes in top of can with can opener.
4 Lower bird onto can of beer (can should
be inside body cavity). Stand chicken on cooler
portion of grill with chicken legs and beer can
forming tripod. Grill, covered, until instant-
read thermometer inserted into thigh (not
touching bone) registers 180°F, 1–1½ hours.
5 Carefully transfer chicken and beer can
to cutting board. Let stand 10 minutes, then
carefully lift chicken off can; discard beer.
Carve chicken. Remove skin before eating.

PER SERVING (⅙ OF CHICKEN): 107 grams, 208 Cal,
8 g Total Fat, 2 g Sat Fat, 0 g Trans Fat, 90 mg Chol,
476 mg Sod, 4 g Total Carb, 2 g Total Sugar, 0 g Fib,
30 g Prot, 26 mg Calc.
PointsPlus value: **5**

Chicken Cacciatore

serves 8

3 pounds bone-in chicken parts (breasts,
    drumsticks, and thighs)
½ teaspoon salt
¼ teaspoon black pepper
1 tablespoon olive oil
1 onion, sliced
3 garlic cloves, minced
2 red bell peppers, cut into ½-inch pieces
¼ pound cremini mushrooms, sliced
2 cups fat-free marinara sauce
½ teaspoon dried oregano
Pinch red pepper flakes

1   Sprinkle chicken with salt and black pepper. Heat 2 teaspoons of oil in large nonstick
skillet over medium-high heat. Add chicken
and cook until browned, about 4 minutes per
side. Transfer to plate.
2   Heat remaining 1 teaspoon oil in same
skillet over medium heat. Add onion and garlic;
cook, stirring, until onion is softened, about 5
minutes. Add bell peppers and mushrooms;
cook, stirring occasionally, until softened, about
5 minutes.
3   Return chicken to skillet. Pour marinara
sauce over chicken; stir in oregano and pepper
flakes; bring to boil. Reduce heat and simmer,
covered, until chicken is cooked through and
vegetables are tender, about 20 minutes longer.
Skim off fat. Remove skin before eating.

**PER SERVING (1 PIECE CHICKEN AND SCANT ½ CUP
VEGETABLES AND SAUCE):** 204 grams, 206 Cal,
6 g Total Fat, 1 g Sat Fat, 0 g Trans Fat, 69 mg Chol,
320 mg Sod, 12 g Total Carb, 7 g Total Sugar, 2 g Fib,
25 g Prot, 41 mg Calc.
PointsPlus value: **5**

FYI   If your skillet is less than 12 inches in
diameter, brown the chicken in 2 batches.

Chicken with Apples and Noodles

serves 4

4 teaspoons olive oil
1 Granny Smith apple, halved, cored, and
    sliced
4 (5-ounce) skinless boneless chicken breasts
½ teaspoon salt
¼ teaspoon black pepper
1 onion, sliced
½ cup reduced-sodium chicken broth
¼ cup cider vinegar
1 tablespoon honey
2 cups hot cooked wide egg noodles

1   Heat 2 teaspoons of oil in large nonstick
skillet over medium heat. Add apple and cook,
stirring, until lightly browned and almost tender, about 5 minutes. Transfer to plate.
2   Sprinkle chicken with salt and pepper.
Heat remaining 2 teaspoons oil in skillet. Add
chicken and cook until browned, about 5 minutes per side. Transfer to plate.
3   Add onion to skillet and cook, stirring, until
softened, about 5 minutes; stir in broth, vinegar,
and honey; cook 2 minutes. Return chicken to
skillet. Simmer, spooning sauce over chicken,
until chicken is cooked through and liquid is
reduced by half, about 5 minutes longer.
4   Return apple to skillet; cook until heated
through, about 2 minutes. Pile noodles on platter; top with chicken mixture.

**PER SERVING (1 CHICKEN BREAST, ¼ CUP SAUCE, AND
½ CUP NOODLES):** 243 grams, 320 Cal, 9 g Total Fat,
2 g Sat Fat, 0 g Trans Fat, 89 mg Chol, 430 mg Sod,
33 g Total Carb, 12 g Total Sugar, 2 g Fib, 28 g Prot,
31 mg Calc.
PointsPlus value: **8**

Barbecue-Sauced Grilled Chicken

serves 6

1 cup ketchup
²/₃ cup strong brewed coffee
½ cup packed light brown sugar
¼ cup cider vinegar
1 teaspoon salt
¼ teaspoon black pepper
Few drops hickory liquid smoke
6 (½-pound) bone-in chicken breasts, skinned

1   Spray grill rack with nonstick spray. Preheat grill to medium-high or prepare medium-high fire using indirect method.
2   Meanwhile, combine ketchup, coffee, brown sugar, vinegar, ½ teaspoon of salt, and the pepper in medium saucepan and set over medium heat. Cook, stirring, until brown sugar is dissolved, about 3 minutes. Bring mixture to boil; reduce heat and simmer 10 minutes. Remove saucepan from heat; stir in liquid smoke. Let sauce cool to room temperature.
3   Sprinkle chicken with remaining ½ teaspoon salt. Place chicken, meaty side down, on cooler portion of grill rack and grill, covered, turning once or twice and brushing with sauce, 15 minutes. Uncover and brush chicken with remaining sauce; grill until cooked through, about 5 minutes longer.

PER SERVING (1 CHICKEN BREAST): 202 grams, 288 Cal, 4 g Total Fat, 1 g Sat Fat, 0 g Trans Fat, 90 mg Chol, 948 mg Sod, 30 g Total Carb, 23 g Total Sugar, 1 g Fib, 34 g Prot, 41 mg Calc.
PointsPlus value: **7**

Spicy Chicken Curry

serves 4

2 garlic cloves, peeled
½ teaspoon salt
1 tablespoon canola oil
2 red onions, thinly sliced
2 teaspoons minced peeled fresh ginger
1 tablespoon garam masala or curry powder
4 (½-pound) bone-in chicken breasts, skinned
1 cup reduced-sodium chicken broth or Basic Chicken Stock (page 106)
⅓ cup plain low-fat yogurt
Fresh cilantro leaves
2 cups hot cooked brown or yellow rice

1   With side of large knife, mash garlic with salt on cutting board until it forms a paste.
2   Heat 2 teaspoons of oil in large nonstick skillet over medium heat. Add onions and cook, stirring, until softened, about 5 minutes. Add garlic paste, ginger, and garam masala; cook, stirring, until fragrant. Transfer to bowl.
3   Add remaining 1 teaspoon oil to skillet. Add chicken and cook, turning, until lightly browned, about 4 minutes per side. Add broth and onion mixture; bring to boil. Reduce heat and simmer, covered, until chicken is cooked through, about 15 minutes. Transfer chicken to platter and keep warm.
4   Bring pan liquid to boil over high heat; boil until reduced by half, about 8 minutes. Remove skillet from heat and whisk in yogurt until blended. Spoon sauce over chicken and sprinkle with cilantro. Serve over rice.

PER SERVING (1 CHICKEN BREAST, ABOUT ¼ CUP SAUCE, AND ½ CUP RICE): 349 grams, 361 Cal, 9 g Total Fat, 2 g Sat Fat, 0 g Trans Fat, 91 mg Chol, 546 mg Sod, 31 g Total Carb, 6 g Total Sugar, 3 g Fib, 38 g Prot, 86 mg Calc.
PointsPlus value: **9**

Chicken Breasts with Papaya-Mint Salsa

serves 4

3 tablespoons lime juice
1 garlic clove, minced
¹/₂ teaspoon salt
4 (5-ounce) skinless boneless chicken breasts
1 papaya, halved, seeded, and diced
1 small Granny Smith apple, unpeeled, cored, and diced
¹/₄ cup finely chopped red onion
3 tablespoons chopped fresh mint
¹/₄ cup whole wheat panko (Japanese bread crumbs)
3 tablespoons sesame seeds

1　Stir together lime juice, garlic, and salt in small bowl. Reserve 1 tablespoon of lime juice mixture in serving bowl; cover and refrigerate. Transfer remaining mixture to large zip-close plastic bag; add chicken. Squeeze out air and seal bag; turn to coat chicken. Refrigerate, turning bag occasionally, at least 30 minutes.
2　To make salsa, stir papaya, apple, onion, and mint into reserved lime juice mixture.
3　Preheat oven to 375°F. Spray shallow baking pan with nonstick spray.
4　Mix together panko and sesame seeds on sheet of wax paper. Coat chicken in crumb mixture. Place in baking pan. Discard any remaining marinade and crumb mixture. Bake until lightly browned and cooked through, about 30 minutes. Serve with salsa.

PER SERVING (1 CHICKEN BREAST AND ½ CUP SALSA): 228 grams, 255 Cal, 8 g Total Fat, 1 g Sat Fat, 0 g Trans Fat, 78 mg Chol, 372 mg Sod, 18 g Total Carb, 9 g Total Sugar, 4 g Fib, 31 g Prot, 54 mg Calc.
PointsPlus value: **7**

Skillet Chicken with Cherry Tomatoes and Garlic

serves 6

6 (5-ounce) skinless boneless chicken breasts
1 teaspoon salt
³/₄ teaspoon black pepper
1 tablespoon olive oil
2 pints red and/or orange cherry tomatoes
3 large garlic cloves, finely chopped
3 tablespoons cider vinegar
2 tablespoons water
2 tablespoons coarsely chopped fresh flat-leaf parsley

1　Sprinkle chicken with ³/₄ teaspoon of salt and ¹/₂ teaspoon of pepper. Spray large heavy skillet with olive oil nonstick spray and set over medium heat. Add half of chicken and cook, turning once, until golden and cooked through, about 12 minutes. Transfer to platter and keep warm. Repeat with remaining chicken.
2　Heat oil in skillet over medium heat. Add tomatoes and garlic; cook, stirring, until garlic is golden, about 2 minutes. Add vinegar, water, parsley, and remaining ¹/₄ teaspoon salt and ¹/₄ teaspoon pepper; cook, stirring, until tomatoes begin to soften, about 2 minutes longer. Spoon over and around chicken.

PER SERVING (1 CHICKEN BREAST AND ABOUT ½ CUP TOMATO MIXTURE): 210 grams, 198 Cal, 6 g Total Fat, 1 g Sat Fat, 0 g Trans Fat, 78 mg Chol, 462 mg Sod, 6 g Total Carb, 0 g Total Sugar, 30 g Fib, 30 g Prot, 31 mg Calc.
PointsPlus value: **5**

Easy Chicken–Pumpkin Seed Mole

serves 4

3 tablespoons shelled pumpkin seeds
4 (¼-pound) thin-sliced chicken breasts
2 teaspoons chili powder
¾ teaspoon salt
2 teaspoons canola oil
1 (14½-ounce) can diced tomatoes
1 teaspoon unsweetened cocoa
1 teaspoon ground cumin
⅛ teaspoon ground cinnamon
2 cups hot cooked brown rice

1   Heat large nonstick skillet over medium-high heat. Add pumpkin seeds and cook, stirring frequently, until toasted, about 1 minute. Transfer seeds to plate; let cool.

2   Sprinkle chicken with 1 teaspoon of chili powder and the salt. Heat oil in same skillet over medium-high heat. Add chicken and cook until browned and cooked through, about 3 minutes per side. Transfer to platter; keep warm.

3   Add tomatoes with their juice, cocoa, cumin, cinnamon, and remaining 1 teaspoon chili powder to skillet; bring to boil over medium-high heat, scraping any browned bits from bottom of skillet. Reduce heat and simmer until sauce is slightly thickened, about 2 minutes. Spoon sauce over chicken and sprinkle with pumpkin seeds. Serve over rice.

PER SERVING (1 PIECE CHICKEN, ¼ CUP SAUCE, SCANT 1 TABLESPOON PUMPKIN SEEDS, AND ½ CUP RICE): 326 grams, 379 Cal, 11 g Total Fat, 2 g Sat Fat, 0 g Trans Fat, 96 mg Chol, 671 mg Sod, 30 g Total Carb, 4 g Total Sugar, 5 g Fib, 40 g Prot, 55 mg Calc.
PointsPlus value: **9**

Orange-Crumbed Baked Chicken

serves 4

2 tablespoons orange juice
2 tablespoons Dijon mustard
¼ teaspoon salt
⅔ cup reduced-fat whole wheat cracker
    crumbs
1 tablespoon grated orange zest
1 shallot, finely chopped
¼ teaspoon black pepper
4 (¼-pound) skinless boneless chicken thighs

1   Preheat oven to 350°F. Spray nonstick baking sheet with nonstick spray.

2   Combine orange juice, mustard, and salt in cup. On sheet of wax paper, mix together cracker crumbs, orange zest, shallot, and pepper. Brush mustard mixture on both sides of chicken, then coat with crumb mixture, pressing firmly so crumbs adhere.

3   Place chicken on prepared baking sheet. Bake 15 minutes; turn chicken over and bake until cooked through, about 20 minutes longer.

PER SERVING (1 CHICKEN THIGH): 115 grams, 239 Cal, 11 g Total Fat, 2 g Sat Fat, 0 g Trans Fat, 74 mg Chol, 480 mg Sod, 13 g Total Carb, 2 g Total Sugar, 1 g Fib, 22 g Prot, 26 mg Calc.
PointsPlus value: **6**

▲ **HEALTHY EXTRA**
Serve a bowl of steamed broccoli crowns alongside the chicken.

**CHICKEN AND
BROCCOLI RABE
WITH POLENTA**

Chicken and Broccoli Rabe with Polenta

serves 4

1 bunch broccoli rabe, chopped
2 teaspoons olive oil
2 (5-ounce) skinless boneless chicken breasts,
    each cut crosswise in half
1 onion, thinly sliced
2 large garlic cloves, minced
½ cup reduced-sodium chicken broth
¼ teaspoon red pepper flakes
2¼ cups water
¾ cup instant polenta or yellow cornmeal
¼ cup grated Parmesan cheese

1   Bring pot of water to boil. Add broccoli
rabe; cook until tender, about 5 minutes; drain.
2   Heat oil in medium nonstick skillet over
medium-high heat. Add chicken and cook until
browned, about 3 minutes per side. Transfer to
plate. Add onion and cook, stirring, until softened, about 5 minutes. Add garlic; cook until
fragrant, about 1 minute. Add broth, pepper
flakes, broccoli rabe, and chicken. Reduce heat
and simmer, covered, until chicken is cooked
through, about 5 minutes.
3   Meanwhile, in medium saucepan, bring
water to boil. Slowly whisk in polenta. Reduce
heat and cook, stirring constantly, 5 minutes.
Remove from heat; stir in half of Parmesan.
Divide polenta evenly among 4 shallow bowls;
spread evenly. Spoon chicken mixture evenly
on top; sprinkle with remaining Parmesan.

PER SERVING (¼ OF CHICKEN MIXTURE AND POLENTA):
272 grams, 288 Cal, 6 g Total Fat, 2 g Sat Fat,
0 g Trans Fat, 43 mg Chol, 239 mg Sod, 36 g Total Carb,
4 g Total Sugar, 4 g Fib, 24 g Prot, 138 mg Calc.
PointsPlus value: *7*

Chicken Tacos

serves 6

4 (5-ounce) skinless boneless chicken breasts
2 teaspoons Mexican or taco seasoning
¼ teaspoon salt
¼ teaspoon black pepper
12 (6-inch) corn tortillas, warmed
1 large tomato, diced
1 Hass avocado, halved, pitted, peeled, and
    diced
1 small onion, thinly sliced
½ cup coarsely chopped fresh cilantro
½ cup fat-free sour cream

1   Sprinkle chicken with Mexican seasoning, salt, and pepper. Spray ridged grill pan
with nonstick spray and set over medium heat.
Place chicken in pan and cook until browned
and cooked through, about 6 minutes per side.
When cool enough to handle, tear chicken into
long, thin strips.
2   Top each tortilla with one-sixth of chicken,
tomato, avocado, onion, cilantro, and sour
cream. Fold tortillas in half.

PER SERVING (2 TACOS): 196 grams, 287 Cal,
8 g Total Fat, 2 g Sat Fat, 0 g Trans Fat, 52 mg Chol,
306 mg Sod, 31 g Total Carb, 3 g Total Sugar, 6 g Fib,
24 g Prot, 131 mg Calc.
PointsPlus value: *7*

Island Chicken with Pineapple

serves 4

1 pound skinless boneless chicken breasts, cut
    into 1-inch chunks
½ teaspoon salt
2 teaspoons olive oil
1 small onion, chopped
1 jalapeño pepper, seeded and minced
3 garlic cloves, minced
1 (15½-ounce) can pinto beans, rinsed and
    drained
½ cup orange juice
½ teaspoon dried oregano
1 cup chopped fresh pineapple
2 tablespoons chopped fresh parsley

1   Sprinkle chicken with ¼ teaspoon of salt.
Heat 1 teaspoon of oil in large nonstick skillet
over medium-high heat. Add chicken and cook,
turning occasionally, until browned and cooked
through, about 5 minutes. Transfer to plate.
2   Add remaining 1 teaspoon oil, the onion,
jalapeño, and garlic to skillet. Reduce heat to
medium; cook, stirring, until onion is softened,
about 5 minutes.
3   Stir in beans, orange juice, oregano, and
remaining ¼ teaspoon salt; bring to boil.
Reduce heat and simmer until flavors are
blended, about 2 minutes. Return chicken to
skillet and cook until heated through, about
1 minute longer. Serve chicken topped with
pineapple and parsley.

PER SERVING (1 CUP CHICKEN MIXTURE AND ¼ CUP
PINEAPPLE): 235 grams, 244 Cal, 5 g Total Fat,
1 g Sat Fat, 0 g Trans Fat, 63 mg Chol, 512 mg Sod,
20 g Total Carb, 8 g Total Sugar, 4 g Fib, 27 g Prot,
51 mg Calc.
PointsPlus value: **6**

Cumin Chicken Kebabs with Couscous

serves 4

¾ cup plain low-fat yogurt
2 garlic cloves, minced
1 tablespoon minced peeled fresh ginger
1 tablespoon ground cumin
2 teaspoons paprika
1 teaspoon turmeric
½ teaspoon salt
⅛–¼ teaspoon cayenne
1 pound skinless boneless chicken breasts, cut
    into 24 pieces
2 large red bell peppers, cut into 1-inch pieces
1 zucchini, cut into ½-inch slices
2 tablespoons chopped fresh cilantro
2 cups hot cooked whole wheat couscous

1   To make marinade, combine yogurt, garlic,
ginger, cumin, paprika, turmeric, salt, and cayenne in large zip-close plastic bag; add chicken.
Squeeze out air and seal bag; refrigerate, turning bag occasionally, at least 30 minutes or up
to overnight.
2   Remove chicken from marinade; discard
marinade. Alternately thread chicken, bell
peppers, and zucchini onto 8 (12-inch) metal
skewers. Spray with nonstick spray.
3   Spray broiler rack with nonstick spray.
Preheat broiler.
4   Place skewers on prepared broiler rack and
broil 5 inches from heat, turning, until chicken
is cooked through, about 12 minutes. Sprinkle
with cilantro and serve over couscous.

PER SERVING (2 SKEWERS AND ½ CUP COUSCOUS):
261 grams, 309 Cal, 4 g Total Fat, 1 g Sat Fat,
0 g Trans Fat, 64 mg Chol, 216 mg Sod, 39 g Total Carb,
4 g Total Sugar, 7 g Fib, 31 g Prot, 77 mg Calc.
PointsPlus value: **8**

Chicken-Mushroom Hash Casserole

serves 4

1 cup fresh whole wheat bread crumbs (about
    2 slices bread)
3 tablespoons grated Romano cheese
2 tablespoons chopped fresh parsley
2 teaspoons olive oil
1 onion, chopped
1 celery stalk, chopped
1 small red bell pepper, diced
1 cup chopped white mushrooms
¾ teaspoon salt
¼ teaspoon black pepper
1 pound skinless boneless chicken breasts, cut
    into ¼-inch pieces
1 tablespoon all-purpose flour
1 teaspoon dried thyme
1 cup fat-free milk

1   Preheat oven to 350°F. Spray shallow 2-quart casserole dish with nonstick spray.
2   To make crumb topping, mix together bread crumbs, Romano cheese, and parsley in small bowl.
3   Heat oil in large nonstick skillet over medium heat. Add onion, celery, and bell pepper; cook, stirring, until softened, about 5 minutes. Add mushrooms and sprinkle with ¼ teaspoon of salt and ⅛ teaspoon of black pepper. Cook, stirring, until mushrooms give up their liquid and liquid is evaporated, about 5 minutes longer.
4   Add chicken to skillet; sprinkle with flour, thyme, remaining ½ teaspoon salt, and remaining ⅛ teaspoon black pepper. Cook, stirring, until chicken is no longer pink, about 5 minutes. Stir in milk; cook, stirring constantly, until sauce bubbles and thickens, about 3 minutes.

5   Spoon hash into prepared casserole; sprinkle evenly with crumb mixture. Bake until golden brown, about 30 minutes.

PER SERVING (GENEROUS 1 CUP): 248 grams, 241 Cal, 6 g Total Fat, 2 g Sat Fat, 0 g Trans Fat, 66 mg Chol, 640 mg Sod, 17 g Total Carb, 7 g Total Sugar, 3 g Fib, 29 g Prot, 137 mg Calc.
PointsPlus value: **6**

▲ HEALTHY EXTRA
Start the meal with a refreshing mixed greens salad with balsamic vinegar.

Skillet Chicken Paprika

serves 4

1 pound skinless boneless chicken thighs, cut
    into 1-inch chunks
1/2 teaspoon salt
1 1/2 teaspoons olive oil
1 large onion, chopped
1 red bell pepper, chopped
2 tablespoons Hungarian paprika
2 tablespoons all-purpose flour
1 (14 1/2-ounce) can diced tomatoes
1 cup reduced-sodium chicken broth or Basic
    Chicken Stock (page 106)
1 garlic clove, minced
2 teaspoons caraway seeds
3 tablespoons light sour cream
3 cups hot cooked yolk-free egg noodles

1   Sprinkle chicken with salt. Heat 1 teaspoon
of oil in large nonstick skillet over medium-
high heat. Add chicken and cook until browned
and cooked through, about 3 minutes per side.
Transfer to plate.
2   Add remaining 1/2 teaspoon oil to skillet.
Add onion and bell pepper; cook stirring, until softened, about 5 minutes. Sprinkle with
paprika and flour; cook, stirring constantly,
1 minute. Stir in tomatoes with their juice,
broth, garlic, and caraway seeds; cook, stirring
constantly, until mixture bubbles and is slightly
thickened, about 2 minutes.
3   Return chicken to skillet and cook over
medium heat until heated through, about 1
minute longer. Remove skillet from heat; stir in
sour cream. Serve over noodles.

PER SERVING (1 1/4 CUPS): 361 grams, 375 Cal,
12 g Total Fat, 3 g Sat Fat, 0 g Trans Fat, 78 mg Chol,
785 mg Sod, 38 g Total Carb, 9 g Total Sugar, 4 g Fib,
28 g Prot, 78 mg Calc.
PointsPlus value: *9*

Chicken in Lemon-Caper Sauce

serves 4

2 tablespoons all-purpose flour
1/2 teaspoon salt
4 (1/4-pound) thin-sliced chicken breasts
2 teaspoons olive oil
1/2 cup reduced-sodium chicken broth
3 tablespoons lemon juice
1 tablespoon capers, drained and chopped
1 teaspoon unsalted butter
2 tablespoons chopped fresh flat-leaf parsley

1   Mix together flour and salt in pie plate.
Dip chicken in seasoned flour, shaking off
excess.
2   Heat oil in large nonstick skillet over
medium-high heat. Add chicken, in batches,
and cook until browned and cooked through,
about 3 minutes per side; transfer to plate.
3   Add broth, lemon juice, and capers to skillet; bring to boil over medium heat. Reduce
heat and simmer until slightly reduced, about
2 minutes. Return chicken to skillet and cook,
turning to coat, until heated through, about 2
minutes. Transfer chicken to platter. Remove
skillet from heat; add butter and parsley. Pour
over chicken.

PER SERVING (1 PIECE CHICKEN AND 2 TABLESPOONS
SAUCE): 127 grams, 170 Cal, 6 g Total Fat, 2 g Sat Fat,
0 g Trans Fat, 65 mg Chol, 488 mg Sod, 4 g Total Carb,
1 g Total Sugar, 0 g Fib, 24 g Prot, 17 mg Calc.
PointsPlus value: *4*

▲ HEALTHY EXTRA
Serve with oven-roasted artichoke wedges and a
blend of whole grain rices (2/3 cup of cooked rice per
serving will increase the *PointsPlus* value by 3).

CHICKEN IN LEMON-CAPER SAUCE

Spicy Chicken and Broccoli

serves 4

1/4 cup + 2 tablespoons water
2 teaspoons cornstarch
4 teaspoons canola oil
1 pound skinless boneless chicken breasts, cut
   into 1/2-inch strips
2 cups small broccoli florets
1 red bell pepper, cut into strips
4 scallions, cut into 1 1/2-inch lengths
1 tablespoon minced peeled fresh ginger
3 garlic cloves, minced
1/2 cup reduced-sodium chicken broth
1/4 cup orange juice
3 tablespoons reduced-sodium soy sauce
1 orange, peeled and sectioned
2 cups hot cooked brown rice

1   Stir together 2 tablespoons of water and the cornstarch in cup until smooth.

2   Heat nonstick wok or deep large nonstick skillet over medium-high heat until drop of water sizzles in pan; add oil and swirl to coat pan. Add chicken and stir-fry until cooked through, about 5 minutes; transfer to plate.

3   Add broccoli and bell pepper to wok; stir-fry, 2 minutes. Add remaining 1/4 cup water; cover and cook until broccoli is crisp-tender, about 4 minutes. Add scallions, ginger, and garlic; stir-fry 1 minute.

4   Re-stir cornstarch mixture. Return chicken to wok. Add broth, orange juice, soy sauce, and cornstarch mixture; stir-fry until sauce bubbles and thickens, about 1 minute. Stir in orange sections. Serve with rice.

PER SERVING (ABOUT 1 1/2 CUPS CHICKEN MIXTURE AND 1/2 CUP RICE): 381 grams, 334 Cal, 8 g Total Fat, 1 g Sat Fat, 0 g Trans Fat, 63 mg Chol, 603 mg Sod, 36 g Total Carb, 7 g Total Sugar, 4 g Fib, 28 g Prot, 61 mg Calc.
PointsPlus* value: *8

FYI   Cornstarch is one of the most commonly used thickening agents. Before being added to a hot liquid, it must be mixed with cold water. If added directly to a hot liquid, it becomes lumpy.

Chicken and Bell Pepper Fajitas

serves 4

2 tablespoons lime juice
1 tablespoon reduced-sodium soy sauce
1/2 teaspoon chili powder
1/2 teaspoon ground cumin
Pinch red pepper flakes
3/4 pound skinless boneless chicken breasts, cut
   on diagonal into thin strips
4 teaspoons canola oil
1 green bell pepper, cut into thin strips
1 red bell pepper, cut into thin strips
1 onion, thinly sliced
4 (6-inch) fat-free flour tortillas, warmed
1/2 cup salsa
1/4 cup fat-free sour cream

1   To make marinade, combine lime juice, soy sauce, chili powder, cumin, and pepper flakes in large zip-close plastic bag; add chicken. Squeeze out air and seal bag; turn to coat chicken. Refrigerate, turning bag occasionally, at least 2 hours or up to overnight. Remove chicken from marinade; discard marinade.

2   Heat 2 teaspoons of oil in large nonstick skillet over medium heat. Add bell peppers and onion; cook, stirring, until softened, about 5 minutes, adding 1 or 2 tablespoons water if skillet becomes dry. Transfer to plate; keep warm.

3   Increase heat to medium-high. Add remaining 2 teaspoons oil in skillet. Add chicken and cook, stirring, until cooked through, about 5 minutes.

4   Place tortillas on work surface; top each with one-fourth of chicken and vegetables. Roll up tortillas to enclose filling. Serve with salsa and sour cream.

PER SERVING (1 FAJITA, 2 TABLESPOONS SALSA, AND 1 TABLESPOON SOUR CREAM): 226 grams, 247 Cal, 7 g Total Fat, 1 g Sat Fat, 0 g Trans Fat, 48 mg Chol, 547 mg Sod, 23 g Total Carb, 7 g Total Sugar, 4 g Fib, 22 g Prot, 87 mg Calc.
PointsPlus value: *6*

Herbed Oven-Fried Chicken
serves 4

½ cup low-fat buttermilk
2 teaspoons paprika
2 teaspoons dried sage, crumbled
2 teaspoons dried rosemary, crumbled
½ cup cornflakes, crushed
3 tablespoons all-purpose flour
4 (½-pound) bone-in chicken breasts, skinned and cut crosswise in half
½ teaspoon salt
¼ teaspoon black pepper

1   Preheat oven to 400°F. Spray heavy shallow baking pan with nonstick spray.

2   Stir together buttermilk, paprika, sage, and rosemary in pie plate. On sheet of wax paper, mix together cornflake crumbs and flour.

3   Sprinkle chicken with salt and pepper. Dip chicken in buttermilk, then coat with cornflake mixture, pressing firmly so it adheres. Place chicken in prepared baking pan; lightly spray with nonstick spray. Bake until crispy and cooked through, about 35 minutes

PER SERVING (2 PIECES CHICKEN): 157 grams, 255 Cal, 4 g Total Fat, 1 g Sat Fat, 0 g Trans Fat, 91 mg Chol, 482 mg Sod, 16 g Total Carb, 3 g Total Sugar, 1 g Fib, 36 g Prot, 68 mg Calc.
PointsPlus value: *6*

▲ HEALTHY EXTRA
Serve this juicy and tender chicken with steamed ears of corn and a plate of thickly sliced tomatoes and sweet onion (1 medium ear of corn, cooked, with each serving will increase the *PointsPlus* value by *2*).

Picadillo

serves 4

2 teaspoons olive oil
2 onions, chopped
2 cups shredded cooked chicken breast
1 Granny Smith apple, peeled, cored, and
    chopped
1 cup canned stewed tomatoes with juice
¼ cup reduced-sodium chicken broth
2 tablespoons dark raisins
2 teaspoons cider vinegar
1 teaspoon minced chipotles en adobo
¼ teaspoon salt
¼ teaspoon black pepper
⅛ teaspoon ground cinnamon

Heat oil in large nonstick skillet over medium
heat. Add onions and cook, stirring, until
lightly browned, about 10 minutes. Stir in
all remaining ingredients; cook, stirring, until
liquid is reduced and flavors are blended, about
10 minutes.

PER SERVING (ABOUT 1 CUP): 273 grams, 221 Cal,
5 g Total Fat, 1 g Sat Fat, 0 g Trans Fat, 60 mg Chol,
440 mg Sod, 21 g Total Carb, 16 g Total Sugar, 4 g Fib,
24 g Prot, 41 mg Calc.
PointsPlus value: **5**

FYI Picadillo is a popular dish in many south-
of-the-border countries, including Mexico
and Cuba. It is usually prepared with ground pork
or beef, but chicken is good too. This flavorful dish
also makes a great filling for tamales or vegetables,
such as bell peppers or zucchini.

Chicken and Mushroom Stew

serves 4

4 (5-ounce) bone-in chicken thighs, skinned
¾ teaspoon salt
¼ teaspoon black pepper
2 teaspoons olive oil
1 large onion, chopped
2 garlic cloves, minced
½ pound mixed mushrooms
1 carrot, thinly sliced
2 celery stalks, sliced
1 cup reduced-sodium chicken broth or Basic
    Chicken Stock (page 106)

1   Sprinkle chicken with salt and pepper.
Spray large nonstick skillet with nonstick spray
and set over medium-high heat. Add chicken
and cook until browned, about 4 minutes per
side. Transfer to plate.
2   Reduce heat to medium. Add oil to skillet.
Add onion and garlic; cook, stirring, until onion
is softened, about 5 minutes. Add mushrooms,
carrot, and celery; cook, stirring, until carrot is
crisp-tender, about 5 minutes. Reduce heat and
cook, stirring, until vegetables are softened,
about 4 minutes.
3   Stir broth into skillet; bring to boil. Add
chicken; reduce heat and simmer, covered,
until cooked through, about 20 minutes.

PER SERVING (1 CHICKEN THIGH AND ½ CUP
VEGETABLES AND SAUCE): 287 grams, 225 Cal,
10 g Total Fat, 3 g Sat Fat, 0 g Trans Fat, 72 mg Chol,
690 mg Sod, 10 g Total Carb, 5 g Total Sugar, 3 g Fib,
23 g Prot, 38 mg Calc.
PointsPlus value: **6**

Tandoori-Spiced Chicken

serves 4

½ cup plain fat-free yogurt
1 tablespoon minced peeled fresh ginger
2 garlic cloves, minced
1 tablespoon paprika
2 teaspoons turmeric
1 teaspoon curry powder
¼ teaspoon ground cinnamon
4 (¼-pound) skinless boneless chicken thighs
½ teaspoon salt
¼ teaspoon black pepper
2 cups hot cooked basmati rice

1   To make marinade, combine yogurt, ginger, garlic, paprika, turmeric, curry powder, and cinnamon in large zip-close plastic bag; add chicken. Squeeze out air and seal bag; turn to coat chicken. Refrigerate, turning bag occasionally, at least 4 hours or up to overnight.
2   Preheat oven to 450°F. Place rack in small roasting pan; spray with canola nonstick spray.
3   Remove chicken from marinade; discard marinade. Place chicken on prepared rack in roasting pan; sprinkle with salt and pepper. Roast until cooked through, about 25 minutes. Serve with rice.

PER SERVING (1 CHICKEN THIGH AND ½ CUP RICE):
135 grams, 298 Cal, 9 g Total Fat, 2 g Sat Fat,
0 g Trans Fat, 75 mg Chol, 369 mg Sod, 33 g Total Carb,
1 g Total Sugar, 1 g Fib, 23 g Prot, 35 mg Calc.
PointsPlus value: **8**

▲ HEALTHY EXTRA
Roast 4 cups of trimmed whole green beans
alongside the chicken.

Chicken with Olives and Dates

serves 4

2 teaspoons olive oil
2 garlic cloves, minced
1 teaspoon minced peeled fresh ginger
1 teaspoon ground cumin
½ teaspoon paprika
¼ teaspoon turmeric
¼ teaspoon ground cinnamon
¼ teaspoon salt
4 (¼-pound) skinless boneless chicken thighs
¼ cup reduced-sodium chicken broth
¼ cup dried apricots, chopped
2 pitted dates, coarsely chopped
10 pitted Kalamata olives, chopped
1 tablespoon grated lemon zest

1   To make marinade, combine oil, garlic, ginger, cumin, paprika, turmeric, cinnamon, and salt in large zip-close plastic bag; add chicken. Squeeze out air and seal bag; turn to coat chicken. Refrigerate about 1 hour. Remove chicken from marinade; discard marinade.
2   Spray large nonstick skillet with nonstick spray and set over medium heat. Add chicken and broth; cook, covered, 15 minutes. Turn chicken over; add all remaining ingredients. Cook, covered, until chicken is cooked through, about 15 minutes longer, adding 1 or 2 tablespoons water, if mixture seems dry.

PER SERVING (1 CHICKEN THIGH AND ABOUT ¼ CUP SAUCE): 131 grams, 250 Cal, 13 g Total Fat, 3 g Sat Fat, 0 g Trans Fat, 76 mg Chol, 403 mg Sod, 10 g Total Carb, 7 g Total Sugar, 1 g Fib, 22 g Prot, 30 mg Calc.
PointsPlus value: **6**

Chicken and Black Bean Chili

serves 4

2 teaspoons olive oil
2 red bell peppers, chopped
1 large onion, chopped
3 garlic cloves, minced
1 pound ground skinless chicken breast
1 (28-ounce) can crushed tomatoes
1 tablespoon chili powder
2 teaspoons ground cumin
$^1/_8$ teaspoon cayenne
1 (15$^1/_2$-ounce) can black beans, rinsed and
    drained

1   Heat oil in nonstick Dutch oven or large
pot over medium heat. Add bell peppers,
onion, and garlic; cook, stirring, until onion is
softened, about 5 minutes. Add chicken; cook,
breaking it apart with wooden spoon, until no
longer pink, about 7 minutes.

2   Add tomatoes, chili powder, cumin, and
cayenne to Dutch oven; bring to boil. Reduce
heat and simmer, stirring, until mixture is
slightly thickened, about 30 minutes. Stir in
beans; simmer until heated through, about 3
minutes longer.

PER SERVING (ABOUT 2 CUPS): 450 grams, 316 Cal,
6 g Total Fat, 1 g Sat Fat, 0 g Trans Fat, 63 mg Chol,
731 mg Sod, 34 g Total Carb, 13 g Total Sugar, 11 g Fib,
32 g Prot, 132 mg Calc.
PointsPlus value: *7*

FYI   This tasty chili works equally well with
ground skinless turkey breast. You can also
use other beans, such as chickpeas, navy beans, or
pinto beans instead of the black beans, if you like.

Chicken and Vegetable Fried Rice

serves 4

$^1/_2$ pound ground skinless chicken
$^1/_4$ cup reduced-sodium chicken broth
1 tablespoon teriyaki sauce
2 teaspoons canola oil
2 large eggs, lightly beaten
2 carrots, finely chopped
1 red bell pepper, diced
6 scallions, cut into 1-inch lengths
2 teaspoons minced peeled fresh ginger
2 garlic cloves, minced
2 cups cold cooked long-grain brown or white
    rice
$^1/_2$ cup frozen green peas, thawed

1   Spray nonstick wok or deep large nonstick
skillet with nonstick spray and heat over
medium-high heat until drop of water sizzles
in pan. Add chicken and stir-fry until browned,
about 5 minutes. Transfer to medium bowl; stir
in broth and teriyaki sauce.

2   Add 1 teaspoon of oil to wok. Add eggs
and stir-fry until set, breaking up eggs as they
cook. Add to chicken in bowl.

3   Add remaining 1 teaspoon oil to wok.
Add carrots, bell pepper, scallions, ginger, and
garlic; stir-fry until tender, about 5 minutes.
Stir in rice and peas; stir-fry until rice begins
to brown, about 4 minutes. Return chicken-egg
mixture to wok; cook until heated through,
about 3 minutes longer.

PER SERVING (ABOUT 1¾ CUPS): 291 grams, 282 Cal,
7 g Total Fat, 2 g Sat Fat, 0 g Trans Fat, 138 mg Chol,
316 mg Sod, 34 g Total Carb, 6 g Total Sugar, 5 g Fib,
20 g Prot, 63 mg Calc.
PointsPlus value: *7*

Zesty Chicken-Noodle Casserole

serves 4

6 ounces wide egg noodles
1 tablespoon olive oil
4 teaspoons all-purpose flour
2 cups fat-free milk
1 tablespoon grated Parmesan cheese
2 cups cubed cooked chicken breast
1 red onion, chopped
2 tablespoons chopped canned mild green chiles
1 tablespoon Dijon mustard
4 teaspoons seasoned dried bread crumbs

1   Preheat oven to 375°F. Spray 2-quart casserole dish with nonstick spray.
2   Cook noodles according to package directions, omitting salt if desired; drain.
3   Heat oil in medium nonstick saucepan over medium heat. Sprinkle with flour; cook, whisking constantly, 2 minutes. Whisk in milk and Parmesan; cook, whisking constantly, until sauce bubbles and thickens, about 3 minutes. Remove saucepan from heat.
4   Stir noodles, chicken, onion, chiles, and mustard into sauce. Transfer to prepared casserole dish; sprinkle evenly with bread crumbs. Bake until browned and bubbling, about 20 minutes.

PER SERVING (GENEROUS 1 CUP): 358 grams, 373 Cal, 9 g Total Fat, 2 g Sat Fat, 0 g Trans Fat, 98 mg Chol, 336 mg Sod, 40 g Total Carb, 9 g Total Sugar, 2 g Fib, 33 g Prot, 217 mg Calc.
***PointsPlus* value: 10**

Roast Turkey with Onion Gravy

serves 12 plus leftovers

1 (9½-pound) turkey, giblets reserved
6 tablespoons lightly packed fresh sage leaves
8 fresh parsley sprigs
8 fresh thyme sprigs
3 onions, thickly sliced
3 cups reduced-sodium chicken broth or Basic Chicken Stock (page 106)
2 tablespoons water
1 tablespoon cornstarch
¼ teaspoon salt
¼ teaspoon black pepper

1   Preheat oven to 350°F. Spray large roasting pan with nonstick spray.
2   Rinse turkey inside and out under cold running water. Pat dry with paper towels. Gently separate skin from meat on breast and thighs. Place 1 tablespoon of sage leaves, 1 parsley sprig, and 1 thyme sprig under skin on each thigh and on each drumstick. Slip 1 tablespoon of sage leaves, 2 parsley sprigs, and 2 thyme sprigs under skin on each breast half.
3   Place turkey in prepared roasting pan; place gizzard, heart, and neck in pan. Scatter onion around turkey. Pour 1 cup of broth into pan.
4   Roast turkey, basting with remaining 2 cups broth every 30 minutes and turning onions occasionally, until instant-read thermometer inserted into thigh (not touching bone) registers 180°F, about 2½ hours. Let turkey stand about 30 minutes.
5   Meanwhile, to make gravy, discard giblets and neck. With slotted spoon, transfer onions to cutting board; coarsely chop. With wooden spoon, scrape up browned bits from bottom of roasting pan. Strain pan juices into 2-cup

glass measure; skim off visible fat. Add enough water to juices to equal 1½ cups. Pour into small saucepan and set over medium heat. Add onions and heat to simmering.

6   Meanwhile, stir together water and cornstarch in cup until smooth. Slowly whisk into pan juices until gravy bubbles and thickens, about 5 minutes. Season with salt and pepper. Carve turkey; serve with gravy.

PER SERVING (2 SLICES WHITE MEAT, 1 SLICE DARK MEAT, AND SCANT ¼ CUP GRAVY): 176 grams, 147 Cal, 3 g Total Fat, 1 g Sat Fat, 0 g Trans Fat, 71 mg Chol, 256 mg Sod, 3 g Total Carb, 2 g Total Sugar, 1 g Fib, 26 g Prot, 22 mg Calc.
PointsPlus value: *3*

FYI   The easiest way to remove all the fat from the pan juices is to use a fat separator. This handy kitchen tool is a clear plastic cup with a long spout that is connected at the very bottom of the cup. The pan juices are poured in and the fat rises to the top. All the juices are slowly poured out until all that is left in the cup is the fat, which is discarded.

Turkey with Feta Topping

serves 4

4 moist-packed sun-dried tomatoes (not
    packed in oil)
½ cup boiling water
⅓ cup crumbled feta cheese
1 shallot, minced
2 garlic cloves, minced
1 tablespoon chopped fresh basil or
    ½ teaspoon dried
¼ teaspoon dried oregano
4 (¼-pound) turkey cutlets

1   Spray broiler rack with nonstick spray. Preheat broiler.
2   Combine sun-dried tomatoes and boiling water in small bowl; let stand 2 minutes. Drain; finely chop tomatoes and return to bowl. Stir in feta, shallot, garlic, basil, and oregano.
3   Place cutlets on prepared broiler rack in single layer. Broil 5 inches from heat 4 minutes. Turn turkey over; top evenly with cheese mixture. Broil until turkey is cooked through and cheese begins to soften, about 5 minutes.

PER SERVING (1 TURKEY CUTLET): 141 grams, 165 Cal, 3 g Total Fat, 2 g Sat Fat, 0 g Trans Fat, 85 mg Chol, 228 mg Sod, 3 g Total Carb, 1 g Total Sugar, 0 g Fib, 29 g Prot, 82 mg Calc.
PointsPlus value: *4*

FYI   This very flavorful dish works equally well with soft or aged goat cheese.

Mushroom-Stuffed Turkey Breast

serves 12

2 tablespoons olive oil
2 onions, chopped
2 cups sliced cremini mushrooms
2 carrots, shredded
2 celery stalks, chopped
1 (10-ounce) package frozen chopped spinach,
    thawed and squeezed dry
½ cup fresh whole wheat bread crumbs (about
    1 slice bread)
⅓ cup grated Parmesan cheese
1 cup reduced-sodium chicken broth or Basic
    Chicken Stock (page 106)
Grated zest of 1 large lemon
1 (3-pound) skinless boneless turkey breast

1   Heat oil in large nonstick skillet over medium heat. Add onions and cook, stirring, until softened, about 5 minutes. Add mushrooms, carrots, and celery; cook, stirring, until carrots are tender, about 5 minutes.

2   Remove skillet from heat. Stir in spinach, bread crumbs, Parmesan, 2 tablespoons of broth, and the lemon zest.

3   Meanwhile, preheat oven to 325°F. Spray 9 × 13-inch roasting pan or baking dish with nonstick spray.

4   Place turkey breast, skinned side down, between two pieces of plastic wrap. With meat mallet or rolling pin, pound to even thickness. Remove top sheet of plastic wrap; spread mushroom mixture over turkey, leaving 2½-inch border. Starting with short side, tightly roll up jelly-roll style. Tightly tie turkey roll at 2-inch intervals with kitchen string. Place, seam side down, in prepared roasting pan; pour remaining broth over turkey and cover loosely with foil.

5   Roast, basting frequently with pan juices, until instant-read thermometer inserted into center of turkey roll registers 170°F, 1–1½ hours. Transfer to cutting board; let stand 10 minutes. Remove string; cut turkey into 12 slices.

PER SERVING (1 SLICE): 195 grams, 184 Cal, 4 g Total Fat, 1 g Sat Fat, 0 g Trans Fat, 76 mg Chol, 184 mg Sod, 7 g Total Carb, 3 g Total Sugar, 2 g Fib, 30 g Prot, 83 mg Calc.
PointsPlus value: *4*

▲ HEALTHY EXTRA

Steam a 1-pound bunch of trimmed asparagus to serve alongside the turkey breast. Just before serving, sprinkle the asparagus with the finely grated zest of half a lemon and a squeeze of lemon juice.

Turkey Cutlets with Cranberry Sauce

serves 4

4 (¼-pound) turkey cutlets
½ teaspoon salt
¼ teaspoon black pepper
1 tablespoon olive oil
1 onion, finely chopped
1 cup cranberry juice cocktail
1 tablespoon dark brown sugar
1 tablespoon red wine vinegar
1 teaspoon drained brine-packed green
    peppercorns
½ teaspoon dried thyme
⅓ cup dried cranberries
2 tablespoons water
1 tablespoon cornstarch

1   Sprinkle cutlets with salt and pepper. Heat oil in large nonstick skillet over medium heat. Add turkey and cook, in batches, until cooked through, about 5 minutes per side. Transfer to platter; keep warm.

2   Add onion to skillet and cook, stirring, until softened, about 5 minutes. Increase heat to medium-high. Add cranberry juice, brown sugar, vinegar, peppercorns, and thyme; bring to boil. Stir in cranberries. Reduce heat and simmer 5 minutes.

3   Meanwhile, stir together water and cornstarch in cup until smooth. Add to skillet; cook, stirring constantly, until sauce bubbles and thickens, about 1 minute. Spoon evenly over turkey.

PER SERVING (1 TURKEY CUTLET AND ¼ CUP SAUCE): 248 grams, 287 Cal, 4 g Total Fat, 1 g Sat Fat, 0 g Trans Fat, 94 mg Chol, 388 mg Sod, 27 g Total Carb, 21 g Total Sugar, 2 g Fib, 35 g Prot, 33 mg Calc.
PointsPlus value: *7*

Monterey Jack Turkey Burgers

serves 4

¾ pound ground skinless turkey breast
1 tablespoon ketchup
2 shallots, minced
1 small garlic clove, minced
½ teaspoon salt
¼ teaspoon black pepper
⅓ cup shredded Monterey Jack cheese
4 slices turkey bacon
4 whole wheat hamburger buns, split and
    toasted
4 thick tomato slices
4 small Boston or butter lettuce leaves

1   Stir together turkey, ketchup, shallots, garlic, salt, and pepper in large bowl until blended but not overmixed; gently stir in Monterey Jack. With damp hands, shape turkey mixture into 4 (½-inch-thick) patties.

2   Spray grill pan with nonstick spray and set over medium-high heat. Place patties in pan and cook until instant-read thermometer inserted into side of burger registers 160°F, about 4 minutes per side. After burgers have cooked for 2 minutes, add bacon to grill pan and cook until crisp, about 3 minutes per side.

3   Place a burger on bottom half of each bun and top with 1 bacon slice, 1 tomato slice, and 1 lettuce leaf. Cover with tops of buns.

PER SERVING (1 GARNISHED BURGER): 184 grams, 294 Cal, 8 g Total Fat, 3 g Sat Fat, 0 g Trans Fat, 77 mg Chol, 802 mg Sod, 27 g Total Carb, 4 g Total Sugar, 4 g Fib, 29 g Prot, 139 mg Calc.
PointsPlus value: *7*

PARMESAN-TURKEY MEAT LOAF

Parmesan-Turkey Meat Loaf

serves 8

1 tablespoon olive oil
1 onion, chopped
1¼ pounds ground skinless turkey breast
2 cups fresh whole wheat bread crumbs (about 4 slices bread)
½ cup fat-free milk
1 large egg white, lightly beaten
3 tablespoons ketchup
2 tablespoons grated Parmesan cheese
1 small garlic clove, minced
½ teaspoon dried basil
¼ teaspoon dried thyme
¼ teaspoon black pepper

1   Preheat oven to 350°F. Spray 5 × 9-inch loaf pan with nonstick spray.
2   Heat oil in medium nonstick skillet over medium heat. Add onion and cook, stirring, until softened, about 5 minutes.
3   Stir together onion and all remaining ingredients in large bowl until well blended but not overmixed. Press turkey mixture into prepared loaf pan. Bake until browned and cooked through, about 1 hour or until instant-read thermometer inserted into center of loaf registers 160°F. Let stand 10 minutes before slicing.

PER SERVING (1 SLICE): 116 grams, 148 Cal,
3 g Total Fat, 1 g Sat Fat, 0 g Trans Fat, 48 mg Chol,
195 mg Sod, 10 g Total Carb, 3 g Total Sugar, 1 g Fib,
20 g Prot, 64 mg Calc.
PointsPlus value: *4*

FYI   To ensure the meat loaf is tender, it is important not to overwork the meat mixture. Mix it with your hands or a wooden spoon just until all the ingredients are well blended.

Easy Enchiladas

serves 4

2 teaspoons canola oil
½ pound hot Italian-style turkey sausage, casings removed
1 red bell pepper, chopped
1 onion, finely chopped
1 teaspoon chili powder
½ teaspoon ground cumin
1 cup canned stewed tomatoes with juice
¾ cup canned black beans, rinsed and drained
¾ cup canned pinto beans, rinsed and drained
⅛ teaspoon black pepper
4 (6-inch) flour tortillas
½ cup shredded fat-free sharp Cheddar cheese

1   Preheat oven to 350°F. Spray shallow 2-quart casserole dish with nonstick spray.
2   Heat oil in large nonstick skillet over medium heat. Add sausage, bell pepper, and onion; cook, breaking sausage apart with wooden spoon, until browned, about 8 minutes. Add chili powder and cumin; cook, stirring, 1 minute. Stir in tomatoes with their juice, black beans, pinto beans, and black pepper. Reduce heat and simmer about 5 minutes.
3   Place tortillas on work surface. Evenly spoon sausage mixture down center of each tortilla; roll up to enclose filling. Place enchiladas, seam side down, in prepared casserole dish; sprinkle evenly with Cheddar.
4   Bake enchiladas until heated through and cheese is melted, about 30 minutes. Let stand 3 minutes before serving.

PER SERVING (1 ENCHILADA): 320 grams, 342 Cal,
10 g Total Fat, 2 g Sat Fat, 0 g Trans Fat, 28 mg Chol,
878 mg Sod, 42 g Total Carb, 6 g Total Sugar, 9 g Fib,
21 g Prot, 230 mg Calc.
PointsPlus value: *8*

Cornish Hens Under a Brick

serves 4

Grated zest and juice of 1 lime
1 tablespoon chopped fresh thyme
2 large garlic cloves, minced
$\frac{1}{2}$ teaspoon salt
$\frac{1}{4}$ teaspoon black pepper
2 (1$\frac{1}{4}$-pound) Cornish hens, giblets discarded

1   To make marinade, stir together lime zest and juice, thyme, garlic, salt, and pepper in cup. Cut each hen in half by cutting along each side of backbone; discard backbone. With fingers, loosen skin over thighs and breast. Rub half of lime mixture under skin; spread remaining mixture over skin. Put hens in large zip-close plastic bag. Squeeze out air and seal bag; refrigerate, turning bag occasionally, up to 4 hours.

2   Meanwhile, spray grill rack with nonstick spray. Preheat grill to medium or prepare medium fire using direct method.

3   Wrap 2 clean bricks in double layer of foil. Remove hens from marinade; discard marinade. Place hen halves, skin side down, on grill rack and place bricks on top. Grill, covered, about 15 minutes. Turn hens. Place bricks back on top of hens. Grill, covered, until instant-read thermometer inserted into thigh (not touching bone) registers 180°F, 12–15 minutes. Transfer hens to platter. Remove skin before eating.

PER SERVING (½ HEN): 135 grams, 162 Cal, 5 g Total Fat, 1 g Sat Fat, 0 g Trans Fat, 122 mg Chol, 363 mg Sod, 3 g Total Carb, 0 g Total Sugar, 1 g Fib, 27 g Prot, 21 mg Calc.
PointsPlus value: *4*

Citrus-Glazed Duck Breasts

serves 4

1$\frac{1}{4}$ cups orange juice
1 teaspoon dried thyme
1 (1$\frac{3}{4}$-pound) boneless duck breast, skin and
    fat removed
$\frac{1}{2}$ cup reduced-sodium chicken broth
$\frac{1}{4}$ cup red wine vinegar
2 small shallots, minced
1 tablespoon grated orange zest
$\frac{1}{2}$ teaspoon salt
$\frac{1}{4}$ teaspoon black pepper

1   Combine 1 cup of orange juice and the thyme in large zip-close plastic bag. Cut duck breast in half and add to bag. Squeeze out air and seal bag; turn to coat duck. Refrigerate, turning bag occasionally, about 2 hours.

2   To make glaze, combine broth, remaining $\frac{1}{4}$ cup orange juice, the vinegar, shallots, orange zest, salt, and pepper in medium saucepan; bring to boil. Reduce heat and simmer, stirring occasionally, until reduced by half, about 15 minutes. Remove from heat.

3   Meanwhile, spray grill rack with nonstick spray. Preheat grill to medium or prepare medium fire using direct method.

4   Remove duck from marinade; discard marinade. Place duck on grill rack and grill, basting with glaze, until juices run clear when duck is pierced with fork, about 8 minutes per side.

5   Transfer duck to cutting board; let cool slightly. Thinly slice on diagonal into 16 slices.

PER SERVING (4 SLICES): 242 grams, 182 Cal, 4 g Total Fat, 2 g Sat Fat, 0 g Trans Fat, 82 mg Chol, 432 mg Sod, 12 g Total Carb, 8 g Total Sugar, 0 g Fib, 22 g Prot, 26 mg Calc.
PointsPlus value: *4*

8

Fish and Shellfish

Fish and Shellfish

197   Grilled Arctic Char Salad
198   Southwestern Salmon
198   Honey-Glazed Salmon with Watermelon-Mint Salsa
199   Salmon with Lemon and Herb Crumbs
199   Grilled Jamaican-Style Halibut
200   Broiled Halibut with Pico de Gallo
200   Braised Halibut with Tomatoes and Orzo
202   Tuna with Black Bean and Corn Salad
202   Teriyaki-Grilled Tuna with Vegetable Skewers
203   Cajun Catfish
205   "Fried" Catfish with Potato Sticks
205   Catfish with Broiled Tomatoes
206   Crispy Catfish with Tartar Sauce
206   Asian Sea Bass
207   Herb-Crusted Tilapia
209   Soft Tacos with Tilapia and Chili-Lime Mayonnaise
209   Greek-Style Haddock
210   Fish Cakes with Creole Rémoulade Sauce
210   Baked Haddock with Ratatouille
211   Bouillabaisse
212   Whole Fish Moroccan Style
212   Trout Amandine
213   Mixed Seafood Skewers with Couscous
213   Paella
214   Seafood Risotto
215   Shrimp Scampi
216   Spaghetti with Spicy Mussels and Shrimp
216   Pappardelle with Shrimp
218   Grilled Spicy Shrimp with Papaya-Lime Salsa
218   Grilled Teriyaki Shrimp
219   Shrimp Creole
219   Scallop Fried Rice
221   Stir-Fried Sea Scallops and Snow Peas
221   Crisped Scallops with Cantaloupe Salsa
222   Maryland Crab Cakes
222   Mussels Marinière
223   Mussels in Saffron-Tomato Sauce
223   Steamed Lobster with Butter Sauce
224   Broiled Stuffed Lobster

GRILLED ARCTIC CHAR AND SALAD

Grilled Arctic Char and Salad

serves 4

1 pound small red potatoes, scrubbed
½ pound haricots verts (slender green beans), trimmed
4 (5-ounce) arctic char fillets
¼ teaspoon salt
¼ teaspoon black pepper
2 tablespoons reduced-sodium chicken broth
2 tablespoons red wine vinegar
2 teaspoons extra-virgin olive oil
1 shallot, minced
1 teaspoon Dijon mustard
4 Boston lettuce leaves
½ cup cherry tomatoes, halved
8 niçoise olives

1   Put potatoes in large saucepan and add enough cold water to cover; bring to boil. Reduce heat and simmer until tender, about 20 minutes. Drain and reserve water. When potatoes are cool enough to handle, halve and slice.
2   Return water to boil. Add haricots verts and cook until tender, about 4 minutes. Drain, then rinse under cold running water.
3   Spray grill rack with olive oil nonstick spray. Preheat grill to medium-high or prepare medium-high fire using direct method.
4   Sprinkle arctic char with salt and pepper; lightly spray with nonstick spray. Place fish on grill rack and grill until just opaque in center, about 4 minutes per side. Transfer fish to cutting board.
5   To make dressing, whisk together broth, vinegar, oil, shallot, and mustard in small bowl. Place arctic char on platter and serve along with potatoes, green beans, tomatoes, lettuce, olives, and dressing. Discard skin before eating.

PER SERVING (1 ARCTIC CHAR FILLET AND ¼ OF SALAD AND DRESSING): 337 grams, 290 Cal, 9 g Total Fat, 2 g Sat Fat, 0 g Trans Fat, 94 mg Chol, 358 mg Sod, 29 g Total Carb, 3 g Total Sugar, 4 g Fib, 23 g Prot, 47 mg Calc.
PointsPlus value: *7*

FYI   Arctic char is similar in flavor and appearance to salmon. Most arctic char sold in the U.S. is farm-raised using ecologically friendly methods, making it a top choice for advocates of sustainable seafood.

Southwestern Salmon

serves 4

1½ cups lightly packed fresh cilantro leaves
¼ cup water
2 tablespoons lime juice
1 teaspoon ground cumin
½ teaspoon salt
¼ teaspoon black pepper
¼ teaspoon hot pepper sauce
2 (½-pound) salmon steaks
1 yellow bell pepper, cut into strips
1 red bell pepper, cut into strips

1   Combine cilantro, water, lime juice, cumin, salt, black pepper, and pepper sauce in food processor or blender and puree. Transfer to large zip-close plastic bag; add salmon. Squeeze out air and seal bag; turn to coat salmon. Refrigerate, turning bag occasionally, about 1 hour.
2   Preheat oven to 400°F. Spray 9-inch square baking dish with nonstick spray.
3   Spread bell peppers in single layer in baking dish. Bake, turning, until almost tender, about 15 minutes.
4   Remove salmon from marinade; discard marinade. Place salmon on top of bell peppers. Bake until salmon is just opaque in center, about 5 minutes per side. Cut salmon steaks in half.

PER SERVING (½ SALMON STEAK AND ABOUT ⅔ CUP
BELL PEPPERS): 168 grams, 201 Cal, 8 g Total Fat,
1 g Sat Fat, 0 g Trans Fat, 72 mg Chol, 133 mg Sod,
4 g Total Carb, 2 g Total Sugar, 1 g Fib, 26 g Prot,
24 mg Calc.
PointsPlus value: **5**

FYI   Choose wild-caught Alaskan salmon over farmed Atlantic salmon. Wild Alaskan salmon come from well-managed populations and are low in contaminants.

Honey-Glazed Salmon with Watermelon-Mint Salsa

serves 4

2 cups diced seedless watermelon
1 scallion, thinly sliced
2 tablespoons chopped fresh mint
1 tablespoon lime juice
¾ teaspoon salt
2 tablespoons honey
2 teaspoons grated lime zest
¼ teaspoon black pepper
4 (¼-pound) salmon fillets

1   To make salsa, mix together watermelon, scallion, mint, lime juice, and ¼ teaspoon of salt in medium bowl.
2   Spray grill rack with nonstick spray. Preheat grill to medium or prepare medium fire using direct method.
3   To make glaze, stir together honey, lime zest, remaining ½ teaspoon salt, and the pepper in cup. Brush on flesh side of fillets.
4   Place salmon, skin side down, on grill rack and grill until just opaque in center, about 5 minutes per side. Brush glaze on flesh side of fillets. Serve with salsa. Remove salmon skin before eating.

PER SERVING (1 SALMON FILLET AND ½ CUP SALSA):
200 grams, 244 Cal, 9 g Total Fat, 1 g Sat Fat,
0 g Trans Fat, 72 mg Chol, 496 mg Sod, 15 g Total Carb,
14 g Total Sugar, 1 g Fib, 26 g Prot, 32 mg Calc.
PointsPlus value: **6**

FYI   You can use other melons in the minted salsa: try cantaloupe, honeydew, Persian, casaba, or Crenshaw.

Salmon with Lemon and Herb Crumbs

serves 4

1 cup fresh whole wheat bread crumbs
    (about 2 slices bread)
Grated zest and juice of ½ lemon
½ teaspoon dried oregano, crumbled
¼ cup fat-free mayonnaise
2 teaspoons Dijon mustard
4 (5-ounce) wild salmon or arctic char fillets
½ teaspoon salt
¼ teaspoon black pepper
Lemon wedges

1   Preheat oven to 400°F. Spray shallow baking pan with olive oil nonstick spray.
2   Stir together bread crumbs, lemon zest,
and oregano in small bowl. Stir together mayonnaise, mustard, and lemon juice in cup.
3   Sprinkle salmon with salt and pepper.
Brush mayonnaise mixture on fish. Top evenly
with bread crumb mixture; spray with nonstick spray. Put fish in prepared pan. Bake
until crumb mixture is golden and fish is just
opaque in center, about 10 minutes. Serve
with lemon wedges.

PER SERVING (1 PIECE SALMON): 158 grams, 218 Cal,
6 g Total Fat, 1 g Sat Fat, 0 g Trans Fat, 68 mg Chol,
607 mg Sod, 9 g Total Carb, 2 g Total Sugar, 1 g Fib,
30 g Prot, 74 mg Calc.
PointsPlus value: *5*

▲ HEALTHY EXTRA
Serve the salmon with baked potatoes and a bowl
of steamed broccoli. A 3-ounce baked potato per
serving will increase the *PointsPlus* value by *2*.

Grilled Jamaican-Style Halibut

serves 4

2 scallions, chopped
2 jalapeño peppers, seeded and minced
2 garlic cloves, halved
2 tablespoons lime juice
1 tablespoon soy sauce
1 tablespoon brown sugar
2 teaspoons olive oil
2 teaspoons chopped fresh thyme
1 teaspoon hot pepper sauce
½ teaspoon ground allspice
½ teaspoon ground cinnamon
½ teaspoon black pepper
1 (1¼-pound) halibut steak, cut into 4 equal
    pieces
Lime wedges

1   To make marinade, combine all ingredients
except halibut and lime wedges in blender and
puree. Transfer to large zip-close plastic bag;
add fish. Squeeze out air and seal bag; turn to
coat fish. Refrigerate, turning bag occasionally,
at least 4 or up to 8 hours. Remove fish from
marinade; discard marinade.
2   Spray grill rack with nonstick spray. Preheat grill to medium-high or prepare medium-
high fire using direct method.
3   Place halibut on grill rack and grill until
just opaque in center, about 5 minutes per
side. Serve with lime wedges.

PER SERVING (1 PIECE OF HALIBUT): 139 grams,
165 Cal, 3 g Total Fat, 0 g Sat Fat, 0 g Trans Fat,
47 mg Chol, 147 mg Sod, 3 g Total Carb, 1 g Total Sugar,
1 g Fib, 31 g Prot, 59 mg Calc.
PointsPlus value: *4*

Broiled Halibut with Pico de Gallo

serves 6

1 large tomato, seeded and chopped
1 small red bell pepper, chopped
1/4 cup finely chopped red onion
1/4 cup chopped fresh cilantro
1 jalapeño pepper, seeded and finely chopped
1 small garlic clove, minced
1 tablespoon lemon juice
1/2 + 1/8 teaspoon salt
2 teaspoons olive oil
6 (5-ounce) halibut steaks
Pinch black pepper

1   To make pico de gallo, mix together tomato, bell pepper, onion, cilantro, jalapeño, garlic, 1 teaspoon of lemon juice, and 1/8 teaspoon of salt in serving bowl.
2   Spray broiler rack with nonstick spray. Preheat broiler.
3   Drizzle remaining 2 teaspoons lemon juice and the oil over halibut. Sprinkle with remaining 1/2 teaspoon salt and the black pepper. Place fish on prepared broiler rack. Broil 5 inches from the heat until fish is just opaque in center, about 4 minutes per side. Serve with pico de gallo. Remove skin before eating.

PER SERVING (1 HALIBUT STEAK AND ABOUT 1/4 CUP PICO DE GALLO): 171 grams, 187 Cal, 5 g Total Fat, 1 g Sat Fat, 0 g Trans Fat, 47 mg Chol, 324 mg Sod, 3 g Total Carb, 2 g Total Sugar, 1 g Fib, 31 g Prot, 74 mg Calc.
PointsPlus value: *4*

FYI   Pico de gallo (*PEE-koh deh Guy-yoh*) is also great with fajitas, tacos, and grilled meat or poultry. This recipe for pico de gallo is easily doubled or tripled.

Braised Halibut with Tomatoes and Orzo

serves 4

2 teaspoons olive oil
1 onion, chopped
2 garlic cloves, minced
2 celery stalks, chopped
1 teaspoon fennel seeds, lightly crushed
1 (14 1/2-ounce) can crushed tomatoes
1 3/4 cups water
1 cup orzo
12 pitted Kalamata olives, halved
1 tablespoon capers, drained
1/4 teaspoon black pepper
1 (1 1/4-pound) halibut fillet, skinned

1   Heat oil in large nonstick skillet over medium-high heat. Add onion and garlic; cook, stirring, until fragrant, about 1 minute. Add celery and fennel seeds; cook, stirring, until celery is slightly softened, about 2 minutes.
2   Add tomatoes, water, orzo, olives, capers, and 1/8 teaspoon of pepper to skillet; bring to boil, stirring occasionally. Reduce heat and simmer, covered, 5 minutes.
3   Season halibut with remaining 1/8 teaspoon pepper. Nestle fish into tomato mixture; simmer, covered, until fish is just opaque in center and orzo is tender, about 12 minutes. Cut halibut into 4 equal pieces.

PER SERVING (1 PIECE OF HALIBUT AND 1 CUP ORZO MIXTURE): 345 grams, 417 Cal, 9 g Total Fat, 1 g Sat Fat, 0 g Trans Fat, 47 mg Chol, 680 mg Sod, 46 g Total Carb, 8 g Total Sugar, 4 g Fib, 40 g Prot, 94 mg Calc.
PointsPlus value: *11*

BRAISED HALIBUT WITH
TOMATOES AND ORZO

Tuna with Black Bean and Corn Salad

serves 4

¼ cup balsamic vinegar
2 tablespoons water
1½ teaspoons Dijon mustard
1 teaspoon salt
¼ teaspoon black pepper
1 (1¼-pound) tuna steak, cut into 4 equal
    pieces
1 (15½-ounce) can black beans, rinsed and
    drained
1 cup frozen corn kernels, thawed
1 cup chopped red bell pepper
1 tomato, chopped
¼ cup chopped fresh cilantro
1 tablespoon lime juice
Few drops hot pepper sauce

1   Combine vinegar, water, mustard, ½ teaspoon of salt, and ⅛ teaspoon of black pepper
in large zip-close plastic bag; add tuna. Squeeze
out air and seal bag; turn to coat tuna. Refrigerate, turning bag occasionally, about 1 hour.
2   Meanwhile, to make black bean and corn
salad, mix together all remaining ingredients
and remaining ½ teaspoon salt and remaining
⅛ teaspoon black pepper in serving bowl.
3   Spray broiler rack with nonstick spray.
Preheat broiler.
4   Remove fish from marinade; discard marinade. Place tuna on prepared broiler rack and
broil 5 inches from heat until browned on outside but still pink on inside, about 3 minutes
per side. Serve with black bean salad.

PER SERVING (1 PIECE OF TUNA AND ABOUT 1 CUP
BEAN SALAD): 314 grams, 281 Cal, 3 g Total Fat,
0 g Sat Fat, 0 g Trans Fat, 66 mg Chol, 626 mg Sod,
24 g Total Carb, 4 g Total Sugar, 6 g Fib, 40 g Prot,
59 mg Calc.
PointsPlus value: **7**

▲ HEALTHY EXTRA
Use 2 tomatoes instead of 1 in the salad.

Teriyaki-Grilled Tuna with Vegetable Skewers

serves 4

¼ cup reduced-sodium soy sauce
2 tablespoons rice wine vinegar
2 tablespoons dry sherry or dry vermouth
3 garlic cloves, minced
1 tablespoon minced peeled fresh ginger
2 teaspoons brown sugar
¼ teaspoon black pepper
1 small red bell pepper, cut into 1-inch pieces
4 white mushrooms, stemmed
1 small zucchini, cut into ¾-inch slices
1 (1¼-pound) tuna steak, cut into 4 equal
    pieces

1   Preheat grill to medium-high or prepare
medium-high fire using direct method.
2   To make basting sauce, whisk together
soy sauce, vinegar, sherry, garlic, ginger, brown
sugar, and black pepper in small bowl.
3   Alternately thread bell pepper, mushrooms,
and zucchini onto 4 (8-inch) metal skewers.

4   Place skewers and tuna on grill rack and grill, turning and brushing with sauce, until tuna is browned on outside but still pink on inside, about 6 minutes, and vegetables are tender, about 8 minutes.

PER SERVING (1 PIECE OF TUNA AND 1 VEGETABLE SKEWER): 212 grams, 195 Cal, 2 g Total Fat, 0 g Sat Fat, 0 g Trans Fat, 66 mg Chol, 662 mg Sod, 7 g Total Carb, 4 g Total Sugar, 1 g Fib, 36 g Prot, 38 mg Calc.
PointsPlus value: *4*

FYI If you prefer to use wooden skewers instead of metal ones, soak them in cold water for at least 30 minutes before using. This will prevent them from charring on the grill.

Cajun Catfish
serves 4

2 garlic cloves, minced
1 shallot, minced
1 tablespoon paprika
1 teaspoon dried oregano
1 teaspoon black pepper
1 teaspoon cayenne
$1/2$ teaspoon dried thyme
$1/2$ teaspoon salt
2 (10-ounce) catfish fillets
1 tablespoon butter, softened
2 tablespoons lemon juice
1 tablespoon snipped fresh chives
1 lemon, cut into wedges

1   Preheat grill to medium-high or prepare medium-high fire using direct method. Tear off 2 (15 × 18-inch) sheets of heavy foil; spray with nonstick spray.
2   Mix together garlic, shallot, paprika, oregano, pepper, cayenne, thyme, and salt in cup.

3   Place 1 catfish fillet, skin side down, on each sheet of foil. Spread butter evenly on flesh side of fish; top evenly with garlic mixture, lemon juice, and chives. To close packets, bring two opposite long sides of foil up to meet in center; fold edges over twice, making $1/2$-inch-wide folds, to seal tightly. Double-fold two remaining open sides, making $1/2$-inch-wide folds, to seal tightly.
4   Place packets on grill rack and grill, covered, until fish is just opaque in center, about 10 minutes. With one or two wide spatulas, transfer packets to cutting board; carefully open, standing back to avoid steam. Cut each fillet in half. Serve with lemon wedges.

PER SERVING (½ CATFISH FILLET): 150 grams, 154 Cal, 6 g Total Fat, 3 g Sat Fat, 0 g Trans Fat, 73 mg Chol, 343 mg Sod, 5 g Total Carb, 1 g Total Sugar, 1 g Fib, 19 g Prot, 43 mg Calc.
PointsPlus value: *4*

▲ **HEALTHY EXTRA**
Enjoy this flavorful fish dish with 2 zucchinis cut lengthwise in half and seasoned with dried oregano, minced garlic, and finely grated lemon zest and grilled or broiled until tender.

"FRIED" CATFISH WITH POTATO STICKS

"Fried" Catfish with Potato Sticks

serves 4

1¼ pounds red potatoes, scrubbed
½ teaspoon salt
½ teaspoon black pepper
1 large egg
¼ cup yellow cornmeal
2 tablespoons finely chopped fresh parsley
4 (5-ounce) catfish fillets
4 lemon wedges

1   Preheat oven to 400°F. Spray 2 baking sheets with nonstick spray.
2   Cut potatoes into ½ × 2-inch sticks; rinse under cold running water and pat dry with paper towels. Spread in single layer on one of prepared baking sheets; spray with nonstick spray. Bake until potatoes are golden brown and crispy, about 30 minutes. Immediately sprinkle with ¼ teaspoon of salt and ¼ teaspoon of pepper.
3   Meanwhile, lightly beat egg in pie plate. Mix together cornmeal, parsley, remaining ¼ teaspoon salt and remaining ¼ teaspoon pepper on sheet of wax paper. Dip catfish, one fillet at a time, in egg, then coat with cornmeal mixture, pressing so it adheres.
4   Place fish on remaining prepared baking sheet; lightly spray with nonstick spray. Bake until golden brown and just opaque in center, about 12 minutes. Serve with potato sticks and lemon wedges.

PER SERVING (1 CATFISH FILLET AND ¼ OF POTATOES): 294 grams, 289 Cal, 5 g Total Fat, 1 g Sat Fat, 0 g Trans Fat, 119 mg Chol, 371 mg Sod, 36 g Total Carb, 3 g Total Sugar, 4 g Fib, 24 g Prot, 44 mg Calc.
PointsPlus value: *7*

Catfish with Broiled Tomatoes

serves 4

4 teaspoons fat-free milk
¼ cup whole wheat flour
1 large egg white, lightly beaten
¾ cup plain dried bread crumbs
4 (5-ounce) catfish fillets
6 plum tomatoes, halved lengthwise
¼ cup grated Parmesan cheese
½ teaspoon dried thyme

1   Spray broiler rack with nonstick spray. Preheat broiler.
2   Put milk, flour, egg white, and ½ cup of bread crumbs in separate shallow bowls or pie plates. Dip catfish fillets, one at a time, into milk, then coat with flour, dip into egg white, and coat with bread crumbs; transfer to prepared broiler rack.
3   Broil fish 5 inches from heat until just opaque in center, about 5 minutes per side. Transfer to platter; keep warm.
4   Place tomatoes, cut side up, in small baking pan. Broil 5 inches from heat until lightly browned, about 5 minutes. Let cool slightly.
5   Meanwhile, mix together remaining ¼ cup bread crumbs, the Parmesan, and thyme in small bowl; sprinkle evenly over tomatoes. Spray crumb mixture with olive oil nonstick spray. Broil until crumb mixture is golden brown, about 3 minutes. Serve alongside fish.

PER SERVING (1 CATFISH FILLET AND 3 TOMATO HALVES): 253 grams, 273 Cal, 6 g Total Fat, 2 g Sat Fat, 0 g Trans Fat, 86 mg Chol, 350 mg Sod, 25 g Total Carb, 4 g Total Sugar, 3 g Fib, 28 g Prot, 145 mg Calc.
PointsPlus value: *7*

Crispy Catfish with Tartar Sauce

serves 4

¾ cup plain fat-free yogurt
1 shallot, finely chopped
2 tablespoons finely chopped fresh parsley
1 tablespoon lemon juice
1 tablespoon fat-free mayonnaise
1 tablespoon pickle relish
2 teaspoons capers, drained and minced
1 teaspoon Worcestershire sauce
¼ teaspoon black pepper
⅛ teaspoon cayenne
¾ cup plain dried bread crumbs
¼ cup almonds, toasted and finely chopped
2 teaspoons dried thyme
Grated zest of 1 lemon
½ cup fat-free buttermilk
4 (5-ounce) catfish fillets
Lemon wedges

1   To make tartar sauce, stir together yogurt, shallot, parsley, lemon juice, mayonnaise, pickle relish, capers, Worcestershire sauce, pepper, and cayenne in serving bowl. Refrigerate, covered, until ready to serve.
2   Preheat oven to 400°F. Spray baking sheet with nonstick spray.
3   Mix together bread crumbs, almonds, thyme, and lemon zest on sheet of wax paper. Pour buttermilk into pie plate. Dip catfish fillets, one at a time, into buttermilk, then coat with bread crumb mixture, pressing gently so crumbs adhere.
4   Place fillets on prepared baking sheet; spray with nonstick spray. Bake until just opaque in center, about 10 minutes. Serve with tartar sauce and lemon wedges.

PER SERVING (1 CATFISH FILLET AND ABOUT ⅓ CUP SAUCE): 240 grams, 284 Cal, 9 g Total Fat, 2 g Sat Fat, 0 g Trans Fat, 70 mg Chol, 403 mg Sod, 25 g Total Carb, 7 g Total Sugar, 2 g Fib, 26 g Prot, 223 mg Calc. *PointsPlus* value: **7**

 HEALTHY EXTRA
Round out the meal with potatoes and Swiss chard. A cooked 3-ounce red potato and 1 cup of steamed Swiss chard with each serving will increase the *PointsPlus* value by **2**.

Asian Sea Bass

serves 4

1 (1-pound) sea bass fillet, cut into 4 equal pieces
6 scallions, thinly sliced
1 tablespoon minced peeled fresh ginger
2 tablespoons reduced-sodium soy sauce
2 teaspoons Asian (dark) sesame oil
2 cups hot cooked brown rice

1   Place rack in deep large skillet and add 1 inch of water; bring to boil.
2   Meanwhile, place sea bass in center of 12 × 18-inch sheet of heavy foil. Sprinkle with half of scallions, the ginger, 1 tablespoon of soy sauce, and the sesame oil. To close packet, bring two opposite long sides of foil up to meet in center; fold edges over twice, making ½-inch-wide folds, to seal tightly. Double-fold two remaining open sides, making ½-inch-wide folds, to seal tightly.

3 Place packet on rack; reduce heat and cook, covered, until fish is just opaque in center, about 10 minutes. With 1 or 2 wide spatulas, transfer packet to cutting board; carefully open, standing back to avoid steam. Divide fish among 4 plates. Pour any cooking juices and remaining 1 tablespoon soy sauce over fillets. Sprinkle with remaining scallions. Serve with rice.

PER SERVING (1 PIECE OF BASS WITH ¼ OF JUICES AND ½ CUP RICE): 222 grams, 256 Cal, 6 g Total Fat, 1 g Sat Fat, 0 g Trans Fat, 49 mg Chol, 392 mg Sod, 25 g Total Carb, 1 g Total Sugar, 2 g Fib, 25 g Prot, 36 mg Calc.
PointsPlus value: **6**

FYI An easy way to remove the skin from the ginger is with a small teaspoon. Use the tip of the spoon to scrape away all the skin.

Herb-Crusted Tilapia
serves 4

½ cup chopped fresh flat-leaf parsley
¼ cup dry white wine
3 tablespoons plain dried bread crumbs
2 teaspoons grated lemon zest
2 tablespoons lemon juice
1 tablespoon finely chopped fresh oregano
1 tablespoon finely chopped fresh thyme
2 teaspoons olive oil
1 garlic clove, minced
¼ teaspoon salt
¼ teaspoon black pepper
1 (1¼-pound) tilapia fillet, cut into
    4 equal pieces
4 carrots, thinly sliced
4 zucchini, thinly sliced
2 teaspoons butter

1 Preheat oven to 375°F. Lightly spray 9 × 13-inch baking dish with nonstick spray.
2 Mix together parsley, wine, bread crumbs, lemon zest and juice, oregano, thyme, oil, garlic, salt, and pepper in small bowl. Let stand until it forms pastelike consistency, about 10 minutes.
3 Place tilapia, skin side down, in prepared baking dish. Spread herb paste over flesh side of fish. Bake until fish is just opaque in center and herb paste forms crust, about 15 minutes.
4 Meanwhile, put carrots in steamer basket; set in medium saucepan over 1 inch boiling water. Cook, covered, 5 minutes; add zucchini and cook until tender, about 3 minutes longer. Transfer vegetables to serving dish; dot with butter. Serve with tilapia.

PER SERVING (1 PIECE OF TILAPIA AND ABOUT 1½ CUPS VEGETABLES): 369 grams, 252 Cal, 8 g Total Fat, 3 g Sat Fat, 0 g Trans Fat, 70 mg Chol, 274 mg Sod, 14 g Total Carb, 6 g Total Sugar, 4 g Fib, 33 g Prot, 82 mg Calc.
PointsPlus value: **6**

▲ **HEALTHY EXTRA**
A bowl of cooked quinoa makes an excellent accompaniment to this tasty fish (⅔ cup cooked quinoa with each serving will increase the *PointsPlus* value by 3).

SOFT TACOS WITH TILAPIA AND
CHILI-LIME MAYONNAISE

Soft Tacos with Tilapia and Chili-Lime Mayonnaise

serves 4

1 teaspoon ground cumin
½ teaspoon salt
⅛ teaspoon black pepper
2 (6-ounce) tilapia fillets
2 teaspoons olive oil
⅓ cup fat-free mayonnaise
Grated zest and juice of ½ lime
2 tablespoons chopped fresh cilantro
1 teaspoon chili powder
8 (6-inch) corn tortillas, warmed
1 cup lightly packed thinly sliced romaine lettuce
1 large tomato, chopped

1   Preheat oven to 450°F. Spray 7 × 11-inch baking dish with nonstick spray.
2   Stir together cumin, salt, and pepper in cup. Sprinkle on tilapia. Place fish, skin side down, in baking dish; drizzle with oil. Cover baking dish with foil; bake until fish is just opaque in center, about 10 minutes.
3   To make chili-lime mayonnaise, stir together mayonnaise, lime zest and juice, cilantro, and chili powder in bowl until mixed.
4   Remove skin from fish and cut into strips. Top each tortilla with about ¼ cup of fish, ¼ cup of lettuce, one-fourth of tomato, and generous 1 tablespoon of mayonnaise. Fold tacos in half.

PER SERVING (2 TACOS): 208 grams, 301 Cal, 12 g Total Fat, 3 g Sat Fat, 0 g Trans Fat, 43 mg Chol, 582 mg Sod, 30 g Total Carb, 2 g Total Sugar, 4 g Fib, 20 g Prot, 114 mg Calc.
PointsPlus value: **8**

Greek-Style Haddock

serves 4

1 tablespoon olive oil
1 onion, chopped
2 garlic cloves, minced
1 (14½-ounce) can diced tomatoes
1 zucchini, diced
8 pitted Kalamata olives, halved
1 tablespoon capers, drained
Pinch red pepper flakes
1 (1½-pound) haddock fillet, cut into 4 equal pieces
¼ cup crumbled fat-free feta cheese

1   Heat oil in large nonstick skillet over medium heat. Add onion and garlic; cook, stirring, until onion is softened, about 5 minutes. Stir in tomatoes with their juice, zucchini, olives, capers, and pepper flakes; bring to boil, stirring occasionally. Reduce heat and simmer until slightly reduced, about 4 minutes.
2   Nestle haddock in tomato mixture, spooning some sauce over. Simmer, covered, until fish is just opaque in center, about 7 minutes. Serve sprinkled with feta.

PER SERVING (1 PIECE OF HADDOCK AND ½ CUP VEGETABLES WITH SAUCE): 297 grams, 246 Cal, 7 g Total Fat, 1 g Sat Fat, 0 g Trans Fat, 98 mg Chol, 547 mg Sod, 10 g Total Carb, 6 g Total Sugar, 3 g Fib, 35 g Prot, 112 mg Calc.
PointsPlus value: **6**

FYI   Buying olives that are already pitted cuts down on your kitchen time, but if you have unpitted olives on hand, here is how to easily remove the pits. Place a couple of olives on a cutting board. With the side of a large knife, press down firmly on the olives, one at a time, until they split, then lift out the pit.

Fish Cakes with Creole Rémoulade Sauce

serves 4

½ cup fat-free mayonnaise
¼ cup + 1 tablespoon chopped fresh flat-leaf parsley
2 shallots, finely chopped
1 scallion, thinly sliced
1 garlic clove, minced
2 tablespoons ketchup
1 tablespoon Creole or other grainy mustard
2 teaspoons hot pepper sauce
⅛ teaspoon black pepper
1 (1-pound) haddock fillet, skinned and cut into chunks
1 teaspoon grated lemon zest
2 tablespoons lemon juice
⅓ cup fat-free egg substitute
¾ cup plain dried bread crumbs

1   To make rémoulade sauce, stir together mayonnaise, 1 tablespoon of parsley, half of shallots, the scallion, garlic, ketchup, mustard, pepper sauce, and pinch of black pepper in serving bowl. Refrigerate, covered, until ready to serve.

2   Put haddock in food processor; pulse until coarsely chopped. Transfer to medium bowl; stir in remaining ¼ cup parsley, remaining shallot, the lemon zest and juice, and remaining pinch black pepper. Add egg substitute, stirring until combined. Stir in ¼ cup of bread crumbs until mixed well.

3   With damp hands, shape fish mixture into 4 (½-inch-thick) patties. Put remaining ½ cup bread crumbs on sheet of wax paper. Gently coat patties with bread crumbs (patties are fragile). Place patties on plate and refrigerate until firm, at least 30 minutes or up to 4 hours.

4   Preheat oven to 200°F.

5   Generously spray large cast-iron or heavy nonstick skillet with nonstick spray and set over medium heat. Add 2 patties to skillet and cook until cooked through and crispy, about 5 minutes per side. Transfer fish cakes to ovenproof platter and keep warm in oven. Wipe skillet clean; repeat with remaining 2 patties. Serve fish cakes with rémoulade sauce.

PER SERVING (1 FISH CAKE AND SCANT ¼ CUP SAUCE):
200 grams, 317 Cal, 12 g Total Fat, 2 g Sat Fat,
0 g Trans Fat, 76 mg Chol, 763 mg Sod, 22 g Total Carb,
3 g Total Sugar, 1 g Fib, 27 g Prot, 91 mg Calc.
PointsPlus value: **8**

FYI   The Creole rémoulade sauce can be made up to three days ahead and refrigerated. Make a double batch of this mayonnaise and use as a sandwich spread, as a dip for vegetables, or as a topping for burgers.

Baked Haddock with Ratatouille

serves 4

2 onions, chopped
4 garlic cloves, minced
1 small eggplant (¾-pound), cut into ½-inch dice
2 red bell peppers, cut into ½-inch dice
1 zucchini, cut into ½-inch dice
2 tomatoes, seeded and chopped
¼ cup thinly sliced fresh basil
½ teaspoon salt
¼ teaspoon black pepper
1 (1-pound) haddock fillet, cut into 4 equal pieces
2 tablespoons tomato paste
1 tablespoon olive oil

1   Preheat oven to 350°F.

2   Spray large skillet with nonstick spray and set over medium heat. Add onions and garlic; cook, stirring, until softened, about 5 minutes. Add eggplant and bell peppers; cook, stirring, until softened, about 5 minutes. Stir in zucchini, tomatoes, basil, salt, and black pepper; cook, stirring, until vegetables are tender, about 5 minutes. Transfer half of vegetables to 2-quart baking dish.

3   Place haddock on top of vegetables. Whisk together tomato paste and oil in small bowl until blended; brush over fish. Top fish with remaining vegetables; bake until fish is just opaque in center, about 20 minutes.

PER SERVING (1 PIECE OF HADDOCK AND ¼ OF RATATOUILLE): 406 grams, 223 Cal, 5 g Total Fat, 1 g Sat Fat, 0 g Trans Fat, 66 mg Chol, 386 mg Sod, 21 g Total Carb, 12 g Total Sugar, 6 g Fib, 25 g Prot, 89 mg Calc.
PointsPlus value: **5**

Bouillabaisse

serves 4

¾ pound red potatoes, scrubbed and cut into ¾-inch pieces
1 large fennel bulb
1 tablespoon olive oil
1 (14½-ounce) can diced tomatoes
2 garlic cloves, minced
3 (1 × 3-inch) strips orange zest
¼ teaspoon saffron threads, lightly crushed
¼ teaspoon dried thyme
3 (8-ounce) bottles clam juice
¾ pound catfish fillet, cut into 1-inch chunks
12 mussels, scrubbed and debearded
½ pound peeled and deveined large shrimp

1   Put potatoes in medium saucepan and add enough water to cover by 2 inches; bring to boil. Cook 5 minutes; remove saucepan from heat. Let stand until potatoes are tender but still hold their shape, about 5 minutes longer; drain.

2   Cut fennel lengthwise in half. Chop one half and cut remaining half into 8 wedges.

3   Heat oil in large pot or Dutch oven over medium heat. Add chopped fennel, tomatoes with their juice, garlic, orange zest, saffron, and thyme; cook, stirring occasionally, until fennel is softened, about 7 minutes. Stir in clam juice. Increase heat to medium-high and bring to boil. Reduce heat and simmer until liquid is reduced to 2½ cups, about 20 minutes. Strain clam juice mixture through sieve set over large bowl, pressing hard on solids to extract as much liquid as possible; discard solids.

4   Return clam juice mixture to pot. Add fennel wedges and simmer until tender, about 8 minutes. With slotted spoon, transfer fennel to large bowl; keep warm. Add catfish to pot; simmer until just opaque in center, about 5 minutes. Transfer to fennel in bowl. Add mussels to pot; simmer, covered, until mussels open, adding shrimp to pot after mussels have cooked 3 minutes. Cook until shrimp is just opaque in center, about 2 minutes. Add mussels and shrimp to bowl. Discard any mussels that do not open.

5   Divide potatoes evenly among 4 large shallow bowls. Put 2 fennel wedges, one-fourth of catfish, one-fourth of shrimp, and 3 mussels in each bowl. Ladle broth over.

PER SERVING (ABOUT 2 CUPS): 576 grams, 300 Cal, 7 g Total Fat, 1 g Sat Fat, 0 g Trans Fat, 149 mg Chol, 800 mg Sod, 28 g Total Carb, 6 g Total Sugar, 5 g Fib, 31 g Prot, 115 mg Calc.
PointsPlus value: **7**

Whole Fish Moroccan Style

serves 4

1 onion, finely chopped
½ cup finely chopped fresh flat-leaf parsley
½ cup finely chopped fresh cilantro
2 garlic cloves, minced
¼ cup lemon juice
4 teaspoons olive oil
1 teaspoon ground cumin
1 teaspoon paprika
½ teaspoon salt
¼ teaspoon turmeric
2 (2-pound) whole fish, such as trout, cleaned

1   Mix together all ingredients except fish in medium bowl.
2   Arrange fish in single layer in nonreactive roasting pan or baking dish. Spoon onion mixture over fish, spreading some into cavity of each fish. Cover pan with plastic wrap and refrigerate, turning once, at least 6 hours or up to overnight.
3   Line broiler rack with foil. Preheat broiler.
4   Wipe off onion mixture from outside of fish. Place fish on prepared broiler rack. Broil 5 inches from heat until just opaque in center, about 10 minutes per side. Cut each fish lengthwise in half.

PER SERVING (½ FISH): 177 grams, 223 Cal, 11 g Total Fat, 2 g Sat Fat, 0 g Trans Fat, 72 mg Chol, 356 mg Sod, 6 g Total Carb, 3 g Total Sugar, 1 g Fib, 25 g Prot, 115 mg Calc.
PointsPlus value: *6*

FYI   Turmeric is prized for the intense yellow color it imparts to food, especially rice.

Trout Amandine

serves 4

3 lemons, 2 juiced and 1 sliced
½ cup dry white wine
¼ cup finely chopped fresh parsley
½ teaspoon salt
½ teaspoon black pepper
4 (5-ounce) trout fillets
¼ cup sliced almonds, toasted

1   Combine ¼ cup of lemon juice, 4 lemon slices, the wine, parsley, salt, and pepper in large nonstick skillet; bring to boil. Place trout fillets in skillet in single layer. Reduce heat and gently simmer, covered, until fillets are just opaque in center, about 5 minutes.
2   Transfer fillets to 4 plates; spoon poaching liquid over. Garnish trout with remaining lemon slices and sprinkle with almonds.

PER SERVING (1 TROUT FILLET, ABOUT 3 TABLESPOONS PAN LIQUID, AND 1 TABLESPOON ALMONDS): 163 grams, 211 Cal, 9 g Total Fat, 2 g Sat Fat, 0 g Trans Fat, 75 mg Chol, 359 mg Sod, 5 g Total Carb, 1 g Total Sugar, 2 g Fib, 26 g Prot, 124 mg Calc.
PointsPlus value: *5*

FYI   Toast the almonds in a dry nonstick skillet over medium-low heat, shaking the pan often. Watch them carefully—since sliced almonds are very thin, they toast in only 2 or 3 minutes and can go from toasty brown to burnt very quickly. Transfer the toasted nuts to a plate as soon as they are done so they don't continue to darken in the hot pan.

▲ HEALTHY EXTRA
Accompany the trout with steamed haricots verts (slender green beans) or regular green beans dressed with lemon juice.

Mixed Seafood Skewers with Couscous

serves 4

2 tablespoons lemon juice
1 tablespoon olive oil
2 garlic cloves, minced
2 teaspoons chopped fresh rosemary
2 teaspoons Dijon mustard
½ teaspoon salt
⅛ teaspoon black pepper
8 large sea scallops (about ¾ pound)
½ pound halibut steak, cut into 1-inch chunks
8 large shrimp, peeled and deveined, tails left on if desired
1 yellow squash, cut into ½-inch slices
1 red bell pepper, cut into 1-inch pieces
2 cups hot cooked whole wheat couscous

1   Spray grill rack with olive oil nonstick spray. Preheat grill to medium-high or prepare medium-high fire using direct method.
2   Meanwhile, whisk together lemon juice, oil, garlic, rosemary, mustard, salt, and black pepper in large bowl. Add scallops, halibut, and shrimp, tossing to coat well. Alternately thread scallops, halibut, shrimp, squash, and bell pepper onto 4 (10-inch) metal skewers.
3   Place skewers on grill rack and grill, turning, until seafood is just opaque in center and vegetables are tender, about 5 minutes. Serve over couscous.

PER SERVING (1 SKEWER AND ½ CUP COUSCOUS): 203 grams, 261 Cal, 3 g Total Fat, 0 g Sat Fat, 0 g Trans Fat, 49 mg Chol, 194 mg Sod, 35 g Total Carb, 2 g Total Sugar, 6 g Fib, 25 g Prot, 60 mg Calc.
PointsPlus value: **6**

Paella

serves 4

2 teaspoons olive oil
1 red bell pepper, coarsely chopped
1 onion, thinly sliced
6 garlic cloves, minced
1 cup long-grain white rice
¼ pound thin-sliced chicken breasts or tenders
3 cups reduced-sodium chicken broth or Basic Chicken Stock (page 106)
1 pound medium shrimp, peeled and deveined, tails left on if desired
¼ teaspoon black pepper
Pinch saffron threads
½ pound medium mussels, scrubbed and debearded
2 tablespoons chopped fresh parsley

1   Heat oil in large nonstick skillet over medium heat. Add bell pepper, onion, and garlic; cook, stirring, until softened, about 5 minutes. Stir in rice and chicken; cook, stirring, until chicken is golden brown, about 2 minutes.
2   Stir broth, shrimp, black pepper, and saffron into skillet; bring to boil. Reduce heat and simmer, covered, until liquid is almost absorbed and rice is tender, about 15 minutes.
3   Add mussels to skillet. Cook, covered, until all liquid is absorbed and mussels open, about 5 minutes longer. Discard any mussels that do not open. Serve sprinkled with parsley.

PER SERVING (¼ OF PAELLA): 508 grams, 373 Cal, 5 g Total Fat, 1 g Sat Fat, 0 g Trans Fat, 189 mg Chol, 728 mg Sod, 48 g Total Carb, 4 g Total Sugar, 2 g Fib, 33 g Prot, 75 mg Calc.
PointsPlus value: **9**

FYI In Spain, paellas are cooked in special double-handled shallow pans, often over a wood fire.

Seafood Risotto

serves 6

4 cups fish broth, vegetable broth, or Basic
   Vegetable Stock (page 107)
1 tablespoon olive oil
1 onion, chopped
4 garlic cloves, minced
1 ¹/₃ cups Arborio or other short-grain white
   rice
¹/₂ cup dry white wine or dry vermouth
³/₄ pound calamari, cleaned
2 cups lightly packed baby spinach
1 cup sliced white mushrooms
³/₄ teaspoon salt
¹/₂ teaspoon black pepper
¹/₂ pound mussels, scrubbed and debearded
¹/₂ pound peeled and deveined medium shrimp
2 tablespoons grated Parmesan cheese

1   Bring broth to simmer in medium saucepan over medium heat; keep at gentle simmer.
2   Heat oil in large nonstick saucepan over
medium heat. Add onion and garlic; cook, stirring, until onion is softened, about 5 minutes.
Add rice and cook, stirring, until coated with
oil, about 1 minute. Add wine and cook, stirring, until absorbed.
3   Add 1 cup of simmering broth to rice;
cook, stirring constantly, until liquid is almost
absorbed. Add ¹/₂ cup of broth; cook, stirring
until liquid is absorbed. Add calamari and ¹/₂
cup of broth; cook, stirring, until broth is almost absorbed. Add spinach, mushrooms, salt,
pepper, and ¹/₂ cup of broth; cook, stirring,
until broth is almost absorbed. Add ¹/₂ cup of
broth; cook, stirring, until almost absorbed.

4   Meanwhile, add mussels to remaining
broth; cook, covered, until mussels open, about
5 minutes. Discard any mussels that do not
open. Add mussels and remaining 1 cup broth
to rice mixture; stir in shrimp. Cook, covered,
until liquid is absorbed and shrimp are just
opaque in center, about 5 minutes longer. Remove saucepan from heat; stir in Parmesan.
Serve at once.

PER SERVING (ABOUT 1¹/₃ CUPS): 348 grams, 326 Cal,
5 g Total Fat, 1 g Sat Fat, 0 g Trans Fat, 159 mg Chol,
761 mg Sod, 48 g Total Carb, 4 g Total Sugar, 3 g Fib,
21 g Prot, 87 mg Calc.
PointsPlus* value: *8

FYI   The key to a great risotto is short-grain
rice, which is shorter and fatter than
regular long-grain rice. Be sure to constantly stir
the risotto to help the rice release its starch and
give the risotto its classic creamy texture. When
properly cooked, the rice should be tender with a
chewy (toothy) center.

Shrimp Scampi

serves 4

4 teaspoons olive oil
1¼ pounds medium shrimp, peeled and
    deveined, tails left on if desired
6 large garlic cloves, minced
½ cup reduced-sodium chicken broth
½ cup dry white wine
¼ cup lemon juice
¼ cup finely chopped fresh parsley
¼ teaspoon salt
¼ teaspoon black pepper

1　Heat oil in large nonstick skillet over
medium-high heat. Add shrimp and cook until
just opaque in center, about 3 minutes. Add garlic and cook, stirring, 30 seconds. With slotted
spoon, transfer shrimp to platter; keep warm.

2　Add all remaining ingredients to skillet;
bring to boil. Boil until sauce is reduced by
half; pour over shrimp.

**PER SERVING (ABOUT 8 SHRIMP AND 3 TABLESPOONS
SAUCE):** 169 grams, 163 Cal, 6 g Total Fat, 1 g Sat Fat,
0 g Trans Fat, 210 mg Chol, 467 mg Sod, 3 g Total Carb,
1 g Total Sugar, 0 g Fib, 23 g Prot, 57 mg Calc.
***PointsPlus* value: 4**

PEELING AND DEVEINING SHRIMP

1　To peel shrimp, tear off all tiny legs
on underside, then pull away shell,
leaving last section of shell and tail
intact, if desired.

2　To devein, with small knife, make
shallow cut all along outer curve just
deep enough to expose dark vein.

3　With tip of knife, remove vein, then
rinse shrimp under cold running water
and pat dry.

Spaghetti with Spicy Mussels and Shrimp

serves 6

½ *pound whole wheat spaghetti*
1 *tablespoon olive oil*
3 *garlic cloves, minced*
¼ *teaspoon red pepper flakes*
4 *plum tomatoes, chopped*
½ *cup bottled clam juice*
Grated zest of ½ *lemon*
½ *teaspoon dried oregano*
½ *teaspoon salt*
¼ *teaspoon black pepper*
12 *mussels, scrubbed and debearded*
½ *pound large shrimp, peeled and deveined*
¼ *cup coarsely chopped fresh flat-leaf parsley*

1   Cook spaghetti according to package directions, omitting salt if desired. Drain and keep warm.
2   Heat oil in large nonstick skillet over medium heat. Add garlic and pepper flakes; cook, stirring, until fragrant, about 1 minute. Add tomatoes, clam juice, lemon zest, oregano, salt, and black pepper; bring to boil.
3   Add mussels and shrimp to skillet; cook, covered, until mussels open and shrimp are just opaque in center, about 5 minutes. Discard any mussels that do not open.
4   Transfer pasta to serving bowl and spoon seafood mixture on top. Sprinkle with parsley.

PER SERVING (1⅓ CUPS): 233 grams, 217 Cal,
4 g Total Fat, 1 g Sat Fat, 0 g Trans Fat, 66 mg Chol,
401 mg Sod, 32 g Total Carb, 3 g Total Sugar, 5 g Fib,
16 g Prot, 49 mg Calc.
PointsPlus value: *6*

Pappardelle with Shrimp

serves 4

6 *ounces pappardelle*
1 *tablespoon olive oil*
1 *garlic clove, minced*
1 *pound medium shrimp, peeled and deveined*
¼ *cup dry white wine*
¾ *cup reduced-sodium chicken broth*
2 *large eggs*
2 *tablespoons grated Parmesan cheese*
¼ *teaspoon black pepper*
3 *tablespoons chopped fresh mint*

1   Cook pappardelle according to package directions, omitting salt if desired; drain.
2   Heat oil in large nonstick skillet over medium heat. Add garlic and cook, stirring, until fragrant, about 1 minute. Add shrimp and cook until just opaque in center, about 3 minutes. Add wine and bring to boil; add broth.
3   Beat eggs, 1 tablespoon of Parmesan, and the pepper in small bowl; slowly whisk in ½ cup of hot broth mixture. Add Parmesan broth mixture to skillet, whisking constantly. Reduce heat and stir in pasta. Cook, stirring constantly, until sauce is thickened and pasta is heated through, about 3 minutes. Transfer to serving bowl; sprinkle evenly with mint and remaining 1 tablespoon Parmesan.

PER SERVING (ABOUT 2 CUPS): 224 grams, 335 Cal,
8 g Total Fat, 2 g Sat Fat, 0 g Trans Fat, 276 mg Chol,
394 mg Sod, 33 g Total Carb, 2 g Total Sugar, 2 g Fib,
29 g Prot, 100 mg Calc.
PointsPlus value: *8*

FYI   Pappardelle are long, flat noodles that are about ½ inch wide. They are usually made with eggs, which makes them very light.

Grilled Spicy Shrimp with Papaya-Lime Salsa

serves 4

1½ teaspoons paprika
½ teaspoon dried thyme
½ teaspoon black pepper
¼ teaspoon salt
⅛ teaspoon cayenne
1¼ pounds large shrimp, peeled and deveined
2 cups diced papaya
3 scallions, thinly sliced
1 lime, peeled and diced

1   Combine paprika, thyme, pepper, salt, and cayenne in large zip-close plastic bag; add shrimp. Squeeze out air and seal bag; turn to coat shrimp. Refrigerate at least 30 minutes or up to 2 hours.
2   Meanwhile, to make salsa, mix together papaya, scallions, and lime in serving bowl.
3   Preheat grill to medium-high or prepare medium-high fire using direct method. Spray grill basket with nonstick spray.
4   Place shrimp in single layer in grill basket and grill until just opaque in center, about 3 minutes per side. Serve with salsa.

PER SERVING (ABOUT 4 SHRIMP AND SCANT ¾ CUP SALSA): 206 grams, 146 Cal, 1 g Total Fat, 0 g Sat Fat, 0 g Trans Fat, 210 mg Chol, 392 mg Sod, 10 g Total Carb, 4 g Total Sugar, 2 g Fib, 23 g Prot, 72 mg Calc.
PointsPlus value: *3*

▲ HEALTHY EXTRA

Serve the shrimp on a bed of cooked brown basmati rice (⅔ cup of hot cooked brown basmati rice with each serving will increase the *PointsPlus* value by *3*).

Grilled Teriyaki Shrimp

serves 4

1¼ pounds large shrimp, peeled and deveined, tails left on if desired
¼ cup Teriyaki Marinade (page 24)
½ pineapple, peeled, cored, and cut into 1-inch chunks
2 red bell peppers, cut into 1-inch pieces
2 cups hot cooked brown rice
2 teaspoons sesame seeds, toasted
4 scallions, sliced

1   Combine shrimp and teriyaki marinade in large zip-close plastic bag. Squeeze out air and seal bag; turn to coat shrimp. Refrigerate, turning bag occasionally, at least 2 hours or up to 4 hours.
2   Meanwhile, spray grill rack with nonstick spray. Preheat grill to medium-high or prepare medium-high fire using direct method.
3   Remove shrimp from marinade; discard marinade. Alternately thread shrimp, pineapple, and bell peppers onto 8 (12-inch) metal skewers. Place skewers on grill rack and grill until shrimp are just opaque in center and peppers are tender, about 4 minutes per side.
4   Put rice in serving bowl; sprinkle with sesame seeds and scallions. Serve with shrimp skewers.

PER SERVING (2 SKEWERS AND ½ CUP RICE): 342 grams, 278 Cal, 3 g Total Fat, 1 g Sat Fat, 0 g Trans Fat, 210 mg Chol, 326 mg Sod, 36 g Total Carb, 9 g Total Sugar, 4 g Fib, 26 g Prot, 72 mg Calc.
PointsPlus value: *7*

▲ HEALTHY EXTRA

A bowl of steamed snow peas makes a light and tasty side to the flavorful teriyaki shrimp.

Shrimp Creole

serves 4

4 teaspoons olive oil
1 onion, chopped
1 red bell pepper, chopped
1 celery stalk, chopped
4 garlic cloves, minced
1 (28-ounce) can stewed tomatoes
2 cups sliced fresh or thawed frozen okra
1 teaspoon chili powder
1 teaspoon dried oregano
½ teaspoon black pepper
Pinch cayenne
1 bay leaf
2 tablespoons water
1 tablespoon cornstarch
1 pound medium shrimp, peeled and deveined
2 cups hot cooked brown rice

1 Heat oil in large nonstick skillet over medium heat. Add onion, bell pepper, celery, and garlic; cook, stirring, until softened, about 5 minutes. Add tomatoes with their juice, okra, chili powder, oregano, black pepper, cayenne, and bay leaf; simmer, covered, until flavors are blended, about 20 minutes.

2 Stir together water and cornstarch in cup until smooth. Add to tomato mixture and cook, stirring, until tomato mixture bubbles and thickens, about 2 minutes. Add shrimp and cook, stirring once or twice, until just opaque in center, about 3 minutes.

3 Discard bay leaf. Spoon rice onto platter. Top with shrimp mixture.

PER SERVING (ABOUT 1½ CUPS SHRIMP MIXTURE AND ½ CUP RICE): 540 grams, 348 Cal, 7 g Total Fat, 1 g Sat Fat, 0 g Trans Fat, 168 mg Chol, 792 mg Sod, 50 g Total Carb, 16 g Total Sugar, 8 g Fib, 24 g Prot, 144 mg Calc.
PointsPlus value: **9**

Scallop Fried Rice

serves 4

2 teaspoons canola oil
2 large eggs, lightly beaten
¾ pound bay scallops
3 scallions, sliced
1 small red bell pepper, diced
1 portobello mushroom, stemmed and diced
1 tablespoon minced peeled fresh ginger
¼ teaspoon salt
¼ teaspoon black pepper
2 cups cold cooked long-grain white or
    brown rice
1 cup frozen baby peas, thawed
1½ teaspoons Asian (dark) sesame oil

1 Heat nonstick wok or deep large nonstick skillet over high heat until drop of water sizzles in pan; add 1 teaspoon of canola oil and swirl to coat pan. Add eggs and stir-fry until set, about 2 minutes. Transfer to plate. Add scallops to wok and stir-fry until just opaque in center, about 3 minutes. Transfer to small bowl.

2 Add remaining 1 teaspoon canola oil to wok. Add bell pepper, mushroom, ginger, salt, and black pepper; stir-fry until vegetables are crisp-tender, about 2 minutes. Add all remaining ingredients and stir-fry until heated through, about 4 minutes.

3 Break up eggs and add to wok along with scallops; stir-fry until mixed well, about 1 minute longer.

PER SERVING (GENEROUS 1 CUP): 249 grams, 281 Cal, 5 g Total Fat, 1 g Sat Fat, 0 g Trans Fat, 42 mg Chol, 459 mg Sod, 32 g Total Carb, 3 g Total Sugar, 3 g Fib, 23 g Prot, 43 mg Calc.
PointsPlus value: **7**

FYI In China, fried rice is a tasty way to use up leftover rice and to create a nourishing meal without a lot of fuss.

**STIR-FRIED SEA SCALLOPS
AND SNOW PEAS**

Stir-Fried Sea Scallops and Snow Peas

serves 4

2 large oranges
2 tablespoons reduced-sodium soy sauce
2 tablespoons reduced-sodium chicken broth
1 tablespoon Worcestershire sauce
½ pound snow peas, trimmed
4 scallions, cut into 2-inch lengths
4 large garlic cloves, slivered
Pinch red pepper flakes
1 pound sea scallops, each sliced horizontally
    into 2 rounds
1 small potato, peeled and finely shredded

1   With vegetable peeler, remove 3 (1 × 4-inch) strips of zest from 1 orange; thinly slice strips on diagonal. Cut off peel and white pith from both oranges, then section each orange over medium bowl, allowing sections and juice to fall into bowl. Stir in orange zest strips, soy sauce, broth, and Worcestershire sauce.
2   Spray nonstick wok or deep large nonstick skillet with nonstick spray and set over medium-high heat until drop of water sizzles in pan. Add snow peas, scallions, garlic, and pepper flakes; stir-fry until snow peas are crisp-tender, about 2 minutes. Add scallops and stir-fry until just opaque in center, about 3 minutes. Add orange mixture and stir-fry until sauce bubbles; cook 30 seconds. Add potato and stir-fry until tender, about 1 minute longer.

PER SERVING (ABOUT 1¼ CUPS): 277 grams, 221 Cal, 1 g Total Fat, 0 g Sat Fat, 0 g Trans Fat, 56 mg Chol, 634 mg Sod, 24 g Total Carb, 9 g Total Sugar, 4 g Fib, 26 g Prot, 93 mg Calc.
PointsPlus value: **5**

Crisped Scallops with Cantaloupe Salsa

serves 4

½ cantaloupe, peeled, seeded, and diced
¼ cup finely chopped red onion
½ jalapeño pepper, seeded and minced
2 tablespoons chopped fresh mint
1 tablespoon lime juice
1½ pounds sea scallops, preferably dry
¼ teaspoon black pepper
4 teaspoons olive oil

1   To make canteloupe salsa, mix together cantaloupe, onion, jalapeño, mint, and lime juice in serving bowl.
2   Sprinkle scallops with black pepper. Heat 2 teaspoons of oil in large nonstick skillet over medium-high heat. Add half of scallops and cook until browned and just opaque in center, about 3 minutes per side. Transfer to plate; keep warm. Repeat with remaining 2 teaspoons oil and the remaining scallops. Serve with salsa.

PER SERVING (ABOUT ½ CUP SCALLOPS AND ½ CUP SALSA): 221 grams, 253 Cal, 6 g Total Fat, 1 g Sat Fat, 0 g Trans Fat, 84 mg Chol, 407 mg Sod, 10 g Total Carb, 6 g Total Sugar, 1 g Fib, 34 g Prot, 47 mg Calc.
PointsPlus value: **6**

FYI   There are two kinds of sea scallops: wet and dry. Wet scallops are treated with a preservative that causes them to absorb water, which is released when the scallops are cooked. Dry scallops are not treated and therefore turn a tempting deep golden brown when cooked and release no liquid.

Maryland Crab Cakes
serves 4

1 pound lump crabmeat, picked over
¾ cup fresh whole wheat bread crumbs (about
  1½ slices)
2 shallots, finely chopped
¼ cup low-fat (1%) milk
3 tablespoons reduced-calorie mayonnaise
2 tablespoons finely chopped fresh parsley
1 teaspoon Old Bay Seasoning
¼ teaspoon black pepper
3 tablespoons all-purpose flour
1 tablespoon butter
1 teaspoon olive oil
3 cups lightly packed mixed baby salad greens
Lemon wedges

1   Gently mix together crabmeat, bread
crumbs, shallots, milk, mayonnaise, parsley,
Old Bay Seasoning, and pepper in large bowl
until mixed well. With damp hands, shape
mixture into 8 patties; cover with plastic wrap
and refrigerate until firm, at least 1 hour or up
to 6 hours.
2   Put flour on sheet of wax paper; lightly
coat each crab cake with flour.
3   Melt butter with oil in large nonstick skillet over medium heat. Add crab cakes and cook
until golden brown and heated through, about 4
minutes per side. Line platter with salad greens;
place crab cakes and lemon wedges on top.

PER SERVING (2 CAKES AND 1¼ CUPS SALAD):
207 grams, 275 Cal, 10 g Total Fat, 3 g Sat Fat,
0 g Trans Fat, 134 mg Chol, 637 mg Sod, 14 g Total Carb,
2 g Total Sugar, 2 g Fib, 30 g Prot, 162 mg Calc.
PointsPlus value: **7**

FYI   German immigrant Gustav Brunn created
Old Bay Seasoning 70 years ago in
Baltimore, where he owned a spice business.

Mussels Marinière
serves 5

1 tablespoon olive oil
4 shallots, thinly sliced
3 large garlic cloves, minced
9 plum tomatoes, chopped
1 tablespoon chopped fresh thyme
3 pounds mussels, scrubbed and debearded
2 cups reduced-sodium chicken broth or Basic
  Chicken Stock (page 106)
¾ cup dry white wine or dry vermouth
⅓ cup chopped fresh basil

1   Heat oil in large pot over medium heat.
Add shallots and garlic; cook, stirring, until
shallots are softened, about 3 minutes. Add
tomatoes and thyme; cook, stirring, until tomatoes are softened, about 5 minutes.
2   Add mussels, broth, and wine to pot; bring
to boil. Reduce heat and simmer, covered, until
mussels open, about 5 minutes. Discard any
mussels that do not open.
3   Divide mussels and tomato mixture evenly
among 4 bowls. Serve sprinkled with basil.

PER SERVING (ABOUT 12 MUSSELS AND ¾ CUP BROTH):
315 grams, 213 Cal, 7 g Total Fat, 1 g Sat Fat,
0 g Trans Fat, 46 mg Chol, 564 mg Sod, 15 g Total Carb,
7 g Total Sugar, 2 g Fib, 22 g Prot, 49 mg Calc.
PointsPlus value: **5**

FYI   Purchase mussels with unbroken, tightly
closed shells or with shells that close when
lightly tapped. The hairy filaments that protrude
from mussels are known as the "beard." Remove
it just before cooking, as removing it kills the
mussel. To remove the beard, grip it between your
thumb and forefinger and pull firmly, or cut
it off with kitchen scissors.

Mussels in Saffron-Tomato Sauce

serves 5

1 tablespoon olive oil
2 garlic cloves, minced
½ cup dry vermouth
1 teaspoon saffron threads
1 (14½-ounce) can diced tomatoes, drained
1 cup bottled clam juice
2 scallions, thinly sliced
3 pounds mussels, scrubbed and debearded
¼ cup finely chopped fresh parsley

1   Heat oil in large pot over medium heat. Add garlic and cook, stirring until fragrant, about 1 minute. Add vermouth and saffron; cook 5 minutes. Add tomatoes, clam juice, and scallions; reduce heat and simmer 3 minutes.

2   Add mussels and cook, covered, until they open, about 5 minutes. Discard any mussels that do not open. Divide mussels evenly among 4 bowls. Spoon saffron broth over mussels and sprinkle with parsley.

PER SERVING (ABOUT 12 MUSSELS AND ⅓ CUP SAUCE): 198 grams, 183 Cal, 6 g Total Fat, 1 g Sat Fat, 0 g Trans Fat, 47 mg Chol, 478 mg Sod, 10 g Total Carb, 5 g Total Sugar, 1 g Fib, 21 g Prot, 52 mg Calc. *PointsPlus* value: *4*

Steamed Lobster with Butter Sauce

serves 4

4 (1½) pound live lobsters
4 tablespoons butter
1 tablespoon lemon juice
1 tablespoon finely chopped fresh parsley
1½ teaspoons finely chopped fresh tarragon
¼ teaspoon black pepper
Lemon wedges

1   Bring very large pot of water to rolling boil; plunge lobsters, head first, into boiling water. Cook, covered, until bright red, about 10 minutes.

2   Meanwhile, to make butter sauce, melt butter in small saucepan over low heat. Add lemon juice, parsley, tarragon, and pepper; cook, stirring, about 1 minute. Remove saucepan from heat; keep warm.

3   With tongs, transfer lobsters to 4 plates. Serve with butter sauce and lemon wedges.

PER SERVING (1 LOBSTER AND ABOUT 1 TABLESPOON SAUCE): 197 grams, 275 Cal, 12 g Total Fat, 7 g Sat Fat, 0 g Trans Fat, 157 mg Chol, 670 mg Sod, 3 g Total Carb, 0 g Total Sugar, 0 g Fib, 36 g Prot, 116 mg Calc. *PointsPlus* value: *7*

FYI   Be sure to select a pot that is large enough to cover the lobsters completely with water. Cookware and department stores sell 19-quart graniteware lobster/clam pots, which are inexpensive and do the job well.

Broiled Stuffed Lobster

serves 4

2 cups low-fat (1%) milk
½ cup dry white wine
1 bouquet garni
¼ cup all-purpose flour
2 cups sliced white mushrooms
2 tablespoons butter
1 teaspoon Dijon mustard
1 large egg yolk
2 tablespoons finely chopped fresh parsley
2 teaspoons lemon juice
½ teaspoon black pepper
4 (1½-pound) live lobsters
¼ cup plain dried bread crumbs
4 teaspoons grated Parmesan cheese
Lemon wedges

1   Combine milk, wine, and bouquet garni
in medium saucepan; bring to boil. Remove
saucepan from heat; let steep, covered, 30
minutes. Discard bouquet garni.

2   Whisk flour into milk mixture until
smooth. Add mushrooms, butter, and mustard;
cook, stirring, over low heat until sauce bubbles
and thickens, about 3 minutes. Remove saucepan from heat. Beat egg yolk in small bowl;
whisk in ½ cup of hot milk mixture, then
whisk mixture back into sauce. Stir in parsley,
lemon juice, and pepper.

3   Meanwhile, bring very large pot of water
to rolling boil; plunge lobsters, head first, into
boiling water. Cook, covered, until bright red,
about 10 minutes. With tongs, transfer lobsters
to cutting board. When cool enough to handle,
remove meat from tails, leaving shells intact.
Cut tail meat into ¾-inch pieces.

4   Preheat broiler.

5   Spoon sauce evenly into empty lobster tail
shells. Top evenly with lobster meat; sprinkle
evenly with bread crumbs and Parmesan.

6   Place lobsters in large shallow roasting
pan. Broil 5 inches from heat until crumbs are
golden brown and stuffing is heated through,
about 4 minutes. Place lobsters on 4 plates;
serve with lemon wedges.

PER SERVING (1 STUFFED LOBSTER): 368 grams,
364 Cal, 11 g Total Fat, 5 g Sat Fat, 0 g Trans Fat,
201 mg Chol, 851 mg Sod, 21 g Total Carb,
7 g Total Sugar, 1 g Fib, 44 g Prot, 305 mg Calc.
PointsPlus value: **9**

FYI   A bouquet garni is a bundle of fresh
herbs, such as parsley, thyme, bay leaves,
and sage, that are either wrapped in a piece of
cheesecloth or tied together with kitchen string.
Wrapping or tying the herbs together makes it easy
to remove them from liquids, such as sauces, stew,
and soups.

Vegetarian Main Dishes

Vegetarian Main Dishes

228   Tofu Burgers
228   Tofu Stir-Fry
230   Marinated Tofu-Vegetable Kebabs
230   Tempeh, Sweet Onion, and Mushroom Chili
231   Tempeh and Vegetable Stir-Fry
232   Soy and Rice Stuffed Cabbage
232   Soy and Bean Chili
233   Wheat Berry and Bean Stew
235   North African Chickpea and Vegetable Tagine
235   Spinach and Bean Burritos
236   Cannellini Bean–Stuffed Peppers
237   Beans and Rice
238   Tex Mex–Style Baked Beans
238   Baked Macaroni and Cheese
240   Winter Vegetable Enchiladas
240   Twice-Baked Potatoes
241   Classic Cheese Soufflé
241   Spanish Tortilla
242   Hearty Vegetable Lasagna
242   Grilled Summer Vegetables with Israeli Couscous
243   Japanese-Style Noodles and Vegetables
245   Pasta with Broccoli and Goat Cheese
245   Pasta with Arugula Pesto and Tomatoes
246   Capellini with Fresh Tomato Sauce
246   Salad Bar Pad Thai
247   Easy Ginger Fried Rice
247   Creamy Polenta with Vegetables
248   Lemony Spring Vegetable Risotto
249   Zucchini Risotto with Sun-Dried Tomatoes
249   Risotto with Swiss Chard
250   Eggplant Rollatini
250   Fiery Falafel
251   Mexicali-Style Stuffed Mushrooms
251   Portobello Mushroom Burgers
252   Potato-Spinach Casserole
252   Spaghetti Squash with Broccoli and Parmesan

Tofu Burgers

serves 4

1 cup brown lentils, picked over, rinsed, and
   drained
6 ounces extra-firm tofu, cubed
¼ cup coarsely chopped fresh parsley
1 garlic clove, minced
1 large egg white, lightly beaten
1 tablespoon unseasoned rice vinegar
1 teaspoon garlic powder
1 teaspoon onion powder
¾ teaspoon salt
¼ teaspoon black pepper
¼ teaspoon hot pepper sauce

1   Bring large pot of water to boil. Add lentils; reduce heat and cook, partially covered, until lentils are tender but still hold their shape, about 25 minutes; drain.

2   Combine lentils and all remaining ingredients in food processor; pulse until mixture forms chunky puree. Shape into 4 patties.

3   Spray large nonstick skillet with nonstick spray and set over medium heat. Add patties and cook until browned and firm, about 3 minutes per side.

PER SERVING (1 BURGER): 201 grams, 196 Cal,
1 g Total Fat, 0 g Sat Fat, 0 g Trans Fat, 0 mg Chol,
491 mg Sod, 30 g Total Carb, 3 g Total Sugar, 11 g Fib,
17 g Prot, 50 mg Calc.
PointsPlus value: *4*

FYI   Tofu, also known as bean curd, has been an important part of Chinese cooking for over 2,000 years. Firm tofu is dense and holds up well in stir-fries and soups. Soft tofu is a good choice when perfect cubes aren't necessary. And silken tofu has a creamy custardlike texture, so it is usually mashed or pureed.

Tofu Stir-Fry

serves 4

1 tablespoon canola oil
1 carrot, sliced on diagonal
2 tablespoons minced peeled fresh ginger
4 garlic cloves, minced
1 pound broccoli crowns, cut into small florets
¼ cup reduced-sodium vegetable broth
1 pound reduced-fat firm tofu, cut into ½-inch
   cubes
8 shiitake mushrooms, stemmed and caps
   thinly sliced
1 red bell pepper, cut into thin strips
1 onion, cut into thin wedges
1 cup snow peas, trimmed
6 scallions, cut into 1½-inch lengths
1 tablespoon + 1½ teaspoons soy sauce
1½ teaspoons Asian (dark) sesame oil
Pinch red pepper flakes

1   Heat nonstick wok or deep large nonstick skillet over high heat until drop of water sizzles in pan; add oil and swirl to coat pan. Add carrot and stir-fry 1 minute. Add ginger and garlic; stir-fry 30 seconds. Add broccoli and broth; cook, covered, 2 minutes.

2   Add tofu, mushrooms, bell pepper, and onion to wok; stir-fry until bell pepper and onion are softened, about 3 minutes. Add all remaining ingredients; stir-fry 1 minute longer.

PER SERVING (GENEROUS 1½ CUPS): 444 grams,
207 Cal, 7 g Total Fat, 1 g Sat Fat, 0 g Trans Fat,
0 mg Chol, 401 mg Sod, 26 g Total Carb,
10 g Total Sugar, 8 g Fib, 14 g Prot, 150 mg Calc.
PointsPlus value: *5*

TOFU STIR-FRY

Marinated Tofu-Vegetable Kebabs

serves 4

¼ cup lemon juice
2 tablespoons reduced-sodium soy sauce
1 teaspoon Asian (dark) sesame oil
1 tablespoon minced peeled fresh ginger
4 garlic cloves, minced
½ teaspoon red pepper flakes
1 pound reduced-fat firm tofu, cut into 1-inch cubes
2 zucchini, cut into ½-inch slices
1 yellow bell pepper, cut into 1-inch pieces
1 onion, cut into 16 wedges
8 small white mushrooms
8 cherry tomatoes

1   Whisk together lemon juice, soy sauce, sesame oil, ginger, garlic, and pepper flakes in large bowl. Add tofu, zucchini, bell pepper, onion, and mushrooms; toss to coat evenly. Let stand at room temperature, stirring occasionally, at least 2 hours or up to 4 hours.

2   Preheat broiler.

3   Beginning and ending with onion wedge, alternately thread marinated vegetables, tofu, and cherry tomatoes onto 8 (12-inch) metal skewers. Place skewers on broiler rack and broil 5 inches from heat, basting with remaining marinade, until vegetables are lightly charred and tender and tofu is browned, about 5 minutes per side. Brush skewers with any remaining marinade before serving.

PER SERVING (2 SKEWERS): 354 grams, 113 Cal, 3 g Total Fat, 0 g Sat Fat, 0 g Trans Fat, 0 mg Chol, 08 mg Sod, 14 g Total Carb, 6 g Total Sugar, 3 g Fib, 11 g Prot, 75 mg Calc.
PointsPlus value: *3*

Tempeh, Sweet Onion, and Mushroom Chili

serves 8

1 (3½-ounce) package dried porcini mushrooms
1 tablespoon olive oil
2 large Vidalia or other sweet onions, chopped
1 green bell pepper, chopped
2 garlic cloves, minced
3 tablespoons chili powder
2 teaspoons ground cumin
1 teaspoon ground cinnamon
¾ pound shiitake mushrooms, stemmed and caps sliced
1 (14½-ounce) can whole peeled tomatoes, broken up, juice reserved
1 (8-ounce) package tempeh, crumbled
2 cups reduced-sodium vegetable broth or Basic Vegetable Stock (page 107)
1 (15½-ounce) can cannellini (white kidney) beans, rinsed and drained
½ cup shredded reduced-fat Monterey Jack cheese
½ cup sliced scallions

1   Put dried porcini mushrooms in small bowl and add enough boiling water to cover by about 2 inches. Let stand 15 minutes; drain. Coarsely chop mushrooms, reserving 1 cup of mushroom liquid.

2   Heat oil in large nonstick pot over medium heat. Add onions, bell pepper, and garlic; cook, stirring, until onion is golden, about 8 minutes. Stir in chili powder, cumin, and cinnamon. Cook, stirring constantly, until fragrant, about 1 minute. Add shiitake mushrooms and cook, stirring occasionally, until tender, about 4 minutes.

3 Add tomatoes with their juice, tempeh, broth, porcini mushrooms, and reserved mushroom liquid to pot; bring to boil. Reduce heat and simmer, covered, until flavors are blended and chili is slightly thickened, about 45 minutes.

4 Stir beans into chili and cook until heated through, about 3 minutes. Serve with bowls of Monterey Jack and scallions.

PER SERVING (GENEROUS 1 CUP CHILI AND 1 TABLESPOON CHEESE): 302 grams, 233 Cal, 7 g Total Fat, 2 g Sat Fat, 0 g Trans Fat, 5 mg Chol, 379 mg Sod, 30 g Total Carb, 5 g Total Sugar, 10 g Fib, 14 g Prot, 138 mg Calc.
PointsPlus value: *6*

Tempeh and Vegetable Stir-Fry

serves 6

2 cups water
1 (8-ounce) package tempeh, cut into ¼-inch
    slices
1 cup reduced-sodium vegetable broth or
    Basic Vegetable Stock (page 107)
¼ cup creamy peanut butter
2 tablespoons reduced-sodium soy sauce
1 tablespoon grated peeled fresh ginger
2 teaspoons canola oil
½ pound green beans, trimmed
½ pound sugar snap peas
1 red bell pepper, cut into thin strips
1 jalapeño pepper, seeded and minced
1 bunch scallions, cut into 2-inch lengths

1 Bring water to boil in medium saucepan. Add tempeh; reduce heat and simmer until softened, about 5 minutes. Drain.

2 Meanwhile, whisk together broth, peanut butter, soy sauce, and ginger in small bowl until smooth.

3 Heat nonstick wok or deep large nonstick skillet over high heat until drop of water sizzles in pan; add oil and swirl to coat pan. Add green beans, sugar snap peas, bell pepper, and jalapeño; stir-fry until vegetables are crisp-tender, about 5 minutes.

4 Add peanut butter mixture and scallions to wok; stir-fry until vegetables are coated and scallions are softened, about 2 minutes.

PER SERVING (1½ CUPS TEMPEH MIXTURE): 211 grams, 207 Cal, 12 g Total Fat, 3 g Sat Fat, 0 g Trans Fat, 0 mg Chol, 342 mg Sod, 15 g Total Carb, 5 g Total Sugar, 4 g Fib, 12 g Prot, 93 mg Calc.
PointsPlus value: *5*

FYI Tempeh, a soy product whose texture resembles ground meat, is fermented soybean cake that is very high in protein. Available in 8-ounce vacuum-sealed packages, it can be found next to the tofu in supermarkets and natural-foods stores. Tempeh is a great substitute for ground beef in this hearty stir-fry.

▲ HEALTHY EXTRA
Add 1 cup of sliced mushrooms—any variety—to the wok along with the green beans in step 3.

Soy and Rice Stuffed Cabbage

serves 4

8 large green cabbage leaves
1 onion, finely chopped
2 celery stalks, thinly sliced
3 garlic cloves, minced
8 ounces frozen soy crumbles
1 cup cooked brown rice
¼ cup raisins, chopped
1½ cups reduced-sodium vegetable broth or
    Basic Vegetable Stock (page 107)
1 (8-ounce) can no-salt-added tomato puree
2 tablespoons cider vinegar
2 tablespoons brown sugar
¼ teaspoon black pepper

1   Preheat oven to 400°F. Spray 9-inch square baking dish with nonstick spray.

2   Meanwhile, bring large pot of water to boil. Add cabbage leaves and return to boil. Cook until cabbage is pliable, about 8 minutes; drain. Rinse cabbage under cold running water; transfer to cutting board. Trim thick ribs at base of leaves.

3   To make filling, spray medium nonstick skillet with nonstick spray and set over medium heat. Add onion and celery; cook, stirring, until softened, about 5 minutes. Add garlic and cook, stirring, until fragrant, about 30 seconds. Transfer vegetables to large bowl; stir in soy crumbles, rice, and raisins.

4   Place ¼ cup of filling in center of each cabbage leaf. Fold sides of cabbage leaves over filling, then roll up to enclose filling. Place cabbage rolls, seam side down, in prepared baking dish.

5   Whisk together all remaining ingredients in small bowl; pour over rolls. Cover baking dish with foil; bake until cabbage is tender, about 1 hour 15 minutes.

PER SERVING (2 ROLLS): 413 grams, 248 Cal, 2 g Total Fat, 0 g Sat Fat, 0 g Trans Fat, 0 mg Chol, 509 mg Sod, 49 g Total Carb, 23 g Total Sugar, 9 g Fib, 18 g Prot, 147 mg Calc.
PointsPlus value: *7*

FYI Soy crumbles, also known as meatless ground burger, are available in the frozen food section of supermarkets. Keep a supply in your freezer and use as a substitute for ground beef or turkey.

Soy and Bean Chili

serves 6

1 tablespoon olive oil
1 large yellow onion, chopped
1 red bell pepper, chopped
1 jalapeño pepper, seeded and minced
3 large garlic cloves, minced
1 small eggplant, unpeeled, diced
1 (28-ounce) can diced tomatoes
1 (12-ounce) package frozen soy crumbles
½ cup water
1 tablespoon chili powder
2 teaspoons dried oregano
1 teaspoon ground cumin
¼ teaspoon salt
2 (15½-ounce) cans pinto beans, rinsed and
    drained
3 cups hot cooked brown rice
1 cup chopped red onion
1 cup shredded reduced-fat sharp Cheddar
    cheese

1   Heat oil in nonstick Dutch oven over medium-high heat. Add yellow onion, bell pepper, jalapeño, and garlic; cook, stirring, until softened, about 5 minutes.

2   Add eggplant, tomatoes with their juice,

soy crumbles, water, chili powder, oregano, cumin, and salt to onion mixture; bring to boil. Reduce heat and simmer, covered, stirring occasionally, 20 minutes. Add beans and simmer, partially covered, until vegetables are softened and flavors are blended, about 20 minutes.

3 Serve chili with bowls of rice, red onion, and Cheddar.

PER SERVING (1⅓ CUPS CHILI, ½ CUP RICE, ABOUT 2½ TABLESPOONS ONION, AND ABOUT 2½ TABLESPOONS CHEESE): 534 grams, 398 Cal, 8 g Total Fat, 3 g Sat Fat, 0 g Trans Fat, 13 mg Chol, 725 mg Sod, 60 g Total Carb, 10 g Total Sugar, 15 g Fib, 27 g Prot, 286 mg Calc.
PointsPlus value: *10*

FYI The hottest part of chile peppers is the pithy white membrane. To keep the heat down, cut away the membrane with a small, sharp knife.

Wheat Berry and Bean Stew

serves 4

1 cup wheat berries
2 teaspoons olive oil
2 onions, finely chopped
1 carrot, finely diced
1 celery stalk, finely chopped
1 garlic clove, minced
3 cups reduced-sodium vegetable broth
2 teaspoons chopped chipotles en adobo
1 (15½-ounce) can red kidney beans, rinsed
    and drained
½ tomato, finely chopped
3 scallions, thinly sliced
1 jalapeño pepper, seeded and finely chopped

1 Put wheat berries in dry medium skillet and set over medium heat. Cook, stirring often, until lightly browned, about 5 minutes.
2 Heat oil in large saucepan over medium heat. Add onions, carrot, and celery; cook, stirring, until onions are golden, about 8 minutes. Add garlic and cook, stirring, until fragrant, about 1 minute.
3 Stir in broth, chipotles en adobo, and wheat berries; bring to boil. Reduce heat and simmer, covered, until wheat berries are tender but still slightly chewy, about 2 hours, adding additional broth or water, if needed. Add beans and cook until heated through, 5 minutes.
4 Mix together tomato, scallions, and jalapeño in small bowl. Serve stew topped with tomato mixture.

PER SERVING (ABOUT 1½ CUPS): 468 grams, 322 Cal, 4 g Total Fat, 0 g Sat Fat, 0 g Trans Fat, 0 mg Chol, 507 mg Sod, 63 g Total Carb, 11 g Total Sugar, 13 g Fib, 12 g Prot, 93 mg Calc.
PointsPlus value: *8*

FYI Chipotles are dried smoked jalapeño peppers; en adobo refers to the thick, very spicy tomato-based sauce they're packed in. Small cans of chipotles en adobo can be found in supermarkets and Latino grocery stores.

NORTH AFRICAN CHICKPEA AND VEGETABLE TAGINE

North African Chickpea and Vegetable Tagine

serves 4

2 teaspoons olive oil
1 onion, chopped
2 garlic cloves, minced
2 teaspoons ground cumin
1 teaspoon turmeric
½ teaspoon ground cinnamon
⅛ teaspoon cayenne
1 (15½-ounce) can chickpeas, rinsed and
    drained
2 large tomatoes (about 1 pound), chopped
2 large carrots, cut on diagonal into
    ½-inch slices
1 (14½-ounce) can reduced-sodium
    vegetable broth
2 zucchini or yellow squash, sliced
3 tablespoons unsalted pistachios, chopped
2 tablespoons chopped fresh mint
2 cups hot cooked whole wheat couscous

1   Heat oil in large nonstick skillet over
medium-high heat. Add onion and cook, stirring frequently, until lightly browned, about 6
minutes. Add garlic, cumin, turmeric, cinnamon, and cayenne; cook, stirring, until fragrant,
about 30 seconds. Add chickpeas, tomatoes,
carrots, and broth; bring to boil.
Reduce heat and simmer, covered, 5 minutes.
2   Stir zucchini into skillet; cook, covered,
stirring occasionally, until tender, about 5 minutes. Transfer tagine to serving bowl; sprinkle
with pistachios and mint. Serve over couscous.

**PER SERVING (ABOUT 1½ CUPS TAGINE AND ½ CUP
COUSCOUS):** 489 grams, 339 Cal, 8 g Total Fat,
1 g Sat Fat, 0 g Trans Fat, 0 mg Chol, 439 mg Sod,
60 g Total Carb, 11 g Total Sugar, 13 g Fib, 13 g Prot,
108 mg Calc.
PointsPlus value: *9*

Spinach and Bean Burritos

serves 4

1 onion, chopped
2 garlic cloves, minced
6 cups lightly packed baby spinach, chopped
1 (15½-ounce) can pinto beans, rinsed and
    drained
¼ cup chunky salsa
1 tablespoon chili powder
2 teaspoons ground cumin
½ teaspoon dried oregano
¼ teaspoon black pepper
4 (8-inch) whole wheat flour tortillas
½ cup shredded reduced-fat Cheddar cheese

1   Spray large nonstick skillet with nonstick
spray and set over medium heat. Add onion
and cook, stirring, until softened, about 5 minutes. Add garlic and cook until fragrant, about
30 seconds. Stir in all remaining ingredients
except tortillas and Cheddar. Cook, covered,
until spinach is wilted and tender, about 4 minutes. Uncover and cook until liquid is evaporated, about 2 minutes longer.
2   Remove skillet from heat and let stand
about 5 minutes. Place one-fourth of spinach
mixture down center of each tortilla; sprinkle
each with 2 tablespoons cheese. Fold each tortilla over to enclose filling.

PER SERVING (1 BURRITO): 236 grams, 255 Cal, 6 g
Total Fat, 2 g Sat Fat, 0 g Trans Fat, 10 mg Chol, 431 mg
Sod, 42 g Total Carb, 5 g Total Sugar, 8 g Fib, 12 g Prot,
284 mg Calc.
PointsPlus value: *7*

FYI You can use other beans in this burrito,
including black beans, red kidney beans, or
chickpeas, if you like.

PEELING GARLIC

1 Place garlic clove(s) on cutting board. With flat side of large chef's knife, press down on each clove just enough to lightly crush it and split skin.

2 With your fingers, remove skin, then slice or mince garlic as directed.

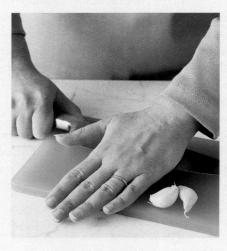

Cannellini Bean–Stuffed Peppers

serves 4

1 (15½-ounce) can cannellini (white kidney) beans, rinsed and drained
2 celery stalks, finely chopped
1 onion, finely chopped
2 tablespoons dry white wine
1 tablespoon balsamic vinegar
1 tablespoon red wine vinegar
2 teaspoons olive oil
1 teaspoon dried oregano
1 teaspoon dried thyme
1 teaspoon dried basil
¼ teaspoon salt
¼ teaspoon black pepper
4 red bell peppers, halved lengthwise and seeded

1   Preheat oven to 425°F.
2   Mix together all ingredients except bell peppers in medium bowl.
3   Place bell peppers, cut side up, in baking dish just large enough to hold them. Cover baking dish with foil; roast until crisp-tender, about 20 minutes. Uncover and roast just until bell peppers are softened, about 15 minutes longer. Drain off any liquid; let peppers cool to room temperature.
4   Fill peppers evenly with bean mixture. Serve at room temperature.

PER SERVING (2 STUFFED PEPPER HALVES): 269 grams, 134 Cal, 3 g Total Fat, 0 g Sat Fat, 0 g Trans Fat, 0 mg Chol, 263 mg Sod, 24 g Total Carb, 6 g Total Sugar, 7 g Fib, 5 g Prot, 72 mg Calc.
PointsPlus value: *3*

Beans and Rice

serves 4

1 tablespoon olive oil
1 green bell pepper, finely chopped
1 onion, finely chopped
6 garlic cloves, minced
1 (15½-ounce) can black beans, rinsed and
    drained
1 (14½-ounce) can diced tomatoes
1½ cups reduced-sodium vegetable broth or
    Basic Vegetable Stock (page 107)
2 teaspoons chopped fresh thyme or ½
    teaspoon dried
½ teaspoon salt
¼ teaspoon hot pepper sauce
1 bay leaf
2 tablespoons chopped fresh cilantro
4 cups hot cooked brown rice

1   Heat oil in medium nonstick saucepan
over medium heat. Add bell pepper, onion, and
garlic; cook until onion is very soft and golden,
about 15 minutes.
2   Stir in beans, tomatoes with their juice,
broth, thyme, salt, pepper sauce, and bay leaf;
bring to boil. Reduce heat and simmer, stirring
occasionally, until sauce is thickened and vegetables are tender, about 45 minutes. If mixture
becomes too thick, add a little water.
3   Stir in cilantro; discard bay leaf. Serve over
brown rice.

PER SERVING (1 CUP BEAN MIXTURE AND 1 CUP RICE):
547 grams, 369 Cal, 6 g Total Fat, 1 g Sat Fat,
0 g Trans Fat, 0 mg Chol, 764 mg Sod, 68 g Total Carb,
8 g Total Sugar, 11 g Fib, 11 g Prot, 88 mg Calc.
PointsPlus value: *10*

FYI Meat, fish, poultry, eggs, soybean products,
and milk and milk products are good
sources of complete proteins because they contain
all of the essential amino acids. Beans, grains,
and nuts are incomplete proteins because they
lack one or more of the essential amino acids.
When beans and grains are eaten together, such as
in this bean and rice dish, they form a complete
protein.

▲ HEALTHY EXTRA
Begin your meal with a lettuce, tomato, and red
onion salad dressed with lemon juice and sprinkled
with fat-free feta cheese (1 ounce of crumbled fat-
free feta cheese with each serving will increase the
PointsPlus value by *1*).

Tex Mex–Style Baked Beans

serves 4

2 (15½-ounce) cans great northern beans,
  rinsed and drained
1 (14½-ounce) can fire-roasted diced
  tomatoes
1 (14½-ounce) can reduced-sodium vegetable
  broth or 1¾ cups Basic Vegetable Stock
  (page 107)
¼ cup strong brewed coffee
¼ cup cider vinegar
1 onion, chopped
¼ cup packed dark brown sugar
1 teaspoon dry mustard
½ teaspoon red pepper flakes
¼ cup shredded reduced-fat Cheddar cheese

1   Preheat oven to 350°F.
2   Mix together all ingredients except
Cheddar in large Dutch oven or lidded casserole dish. Bake, covered, until thick sauce is
formed, about 2 hours. (If sauce gets too thick,
add water.) Serve topped with cheese.

**PER SERVING (ABOUT 1½ CUPS BEAN MIXTURE AND
1 TABLESPOON CHEESE):** 440 grams, 252 Cal,
3 g Total Fat, 1 g Sat Fat, 0 g Trans Fat, 5 mg Chol,
731 mg Sod, 45 g Total Carb, 21 g Total Sugar, 10 g Fib,
11 g Prot, 154 mg Calc.
PointsPlus value: **6**

FYI   Fire-roasted canned tomatoes get their
tempting smoky flavor from a blend of
natural hardwoods that are used in the searing and
smoking process.

Baked Macaroni and Cheese

serves 6

8 ounces whole wheat penne
2 tablespoons canola oil
2 tablespoons all-purpose flour
2 cups fat-free milk
2⅓ cups shredded fat-free Cheddar cheese
¼ teaspoon salt
¼ teaspoon black pepper

1   Preheat oven to 350°F.
2   Cook penne according to package directions, omitting salt if desired. Drain in colander, then rinse under cold running water; drain.
3   Heat oil in large saucepan over medium
heat. Add flour and cook, whisking constantly,
2 minutes. Gradually add milk, whisking until
smooth. Increase heat to medium-high and
bring to boil; boil 1 minute.
4   Remove saucepan from heat; add 2 cups
of Cheddar, the salt, and pepper, stirring until
cheese is melted. Stir in pasta. Pour into shallow 2-quart baking dish or 6 individual baking
dishes; sprinkle with remaining ⅓ cup cheese.
Bake until lightly browned and bubbly, about
25 minutes for a 2-quart baking dish and about
15 minutes for individual baking dishes. Let
stand 5 minutes before serving.

PER SERVING (ABOUT ¾ CUP): 165 grams, 267 Cal,
5 g Total Fat, 1 g Sat Fat, 0 g Trans Fat, 9 mg Chol,
521 mg Sod, 36 g Total Carb, 5 g Total Sugar, 3 g Fib,
21 g Prot, 466 mg Calc.
PointsPlus value: **7**

BAKED MACARONI AND CHEESE

Winter Vegetable Enchiladas

serves 4

1 large acorn squash
2 large carrots, cut into ½-inch slices
12 Brussels sprouts, thinly sliced lengthwise
    and separated into shreds
2 tablespoons chili powder
½ teaspoon dried oregano
¼ teaspoon salt
⅛ teaspoon cayenne
8 (8-inch) reduced-fat whole wheat tortillas
½ cup shredded reduced-fat Cheddar cheese
1 cup enchilada sauce

1   Preheat oven to 400°F.
2   Cut squash lengthwise into quarters; scoop out seeds. With vegetable peeler, peel skin from ridges. Put squash and carrots in large baking dish; lightly spray with nonstick spray. Roast, stirring once or twice, until lightly browned and tender, about 40 minutes.
3   Reduce oven temperature to 350°F.
4   With small knife, peel remaining skin from squash; cut squash into chunks. Return squash and carrots to baking dish along with Brussels sprouts, chili powder, oregano, salt, and cayenne. Toss until mixed well.
5   Lay tortillas on work surface. Spoon one-eighth of vegetable mixture down center of each tortilla; sprinkle each with 1 tablespoon of Cheddar, then roll tortillas up to enclose filling.
6   Place enchiladas, seam side down, in same baking dish. Pour enchilada sauce on top. Bake until sauce forms glaze, about 20 minutes.

PER SERVING (2 ENCHILADAS): 362 grams, 334 Cal,
7 g Total Fat, 2 g Sat Fat, 0 g Trans Fat, 10 mg Chol,
748 mg Sod, 73 g Total Carb, 10 g Total Sugar, 13 g Fib,
13 g Prot, 218 mg Calc.
PointsPlus value: *10*

Twice-Baked Potatoes

serves 4

4 baking potatoes, scrubbed
3 cups chopped broccoli crowns
¼ cup fat-free milk
1 cup shredded extra-sharp Cheddar cheese
¼ cup light sour cream
1 teaspoon Dijon mustard
¾ teaspoon salt
⅛ teaspoon cayenne

1   Preheat oven to 425°F.
2   Prick potatoes in several places with fork. Bake until toothpick inserted into center of potato goes in easily, about 1 hour. Reduce oven temperature to 375°F.
3   Put broccoli in steamer basket; set in medium saucepan over 1 inch boiling water. Cook, covered, until tender, about 5 minutes. Remove steamer basket from saucepan.
4   Cut potatoes lengthwise in half. With teaspoon, scoop out pulp into medium bowl, leaving ¼-inch shell. Mash potatoes with milk until smooth. Stir in Cheddar, sour cream, mustard, salt, and cayenne; fold in broccoli.
5   Spoon potato mixture evenly into potato shells. Place on baking sheet; bake until heated through, about 10 minutes.

PER SERVING (2 STUFFED POTATO HALVES): 285 grams,
282 Cal, 8 g Total Fat, 5 g Sat Fat, 0 g Trans Fat,
25 mg Chol, 517 mg Sod, 42 g Total Carb,
4 g Total Sugar, 5 g Fib, 15 g Prot, 302 mg Calc.
PointsPlus value: *8*

FYI   For a super-crispy top, broil the potatoes 5 inches from the heat after baking them.

Classic Cheese Soufflé

serves 4

1 cup fat-free milk
3 tablespoons all-purpose flour
1½ cups shredded reduced-fat Cheddar
    cheese
½ teaspoon salt
⅛ teaspoon cayenne
2 large eggs, separated, at room temperature
2 large egg whites, at room temperature

1   Preheat oven to 350°F.
2   Whisk together milk and flour in heavy
medium saucepan until smooth; set over low
heat. Cook, stirring, until mixture bubbles and
thickens, about 5 minutes. Remove saucepan
from heat; stir in Cheddar, ¼ teaspoon of salt,
and the cayenne.
3   Lightly beat the 2 egg yolks in small bowl.
Gradually whisk in ½ cup of hot cheese sauce,
then whisk back into sauce until smooth.
4   With electric mixer on medium speed,
beat 4 egg whites and remaining ¼ teaspoon
salt in large bowl just until stiff peaks form
when beaters are lifted. With rubber spatula,
stir one-fourth of egg whites into cheese mixture to lighten it, then fold in remaining whites
just until no longer visible.
5   Gently pour soufflé mixture into ungreased 3-quart soufflé dish. Bake until puffed
and cooked through, about 35 minutes. Serve
at once.

PER SERVING (¼ OF SOUFFLÉ): 149 grams, 209 Cal,
12 g Total Fat, 7 g Sat Fat, 0 g Trans Fat, 138 mg Chol,
382 mg Sod, 10 g Total Carb, 4 g Total Sugar, 0 g Fib,
18 g Prot, 390 mg Calc.
PointsPlus value: *6*

▲ **HEALTHY EXTRA**

An endive and apple salad makes a tasty
accompaniment to this elegant cheese soufflé.

Spanish Tortilla

serves 4

2 (½-pound) red potatoes, peeled and cut
    into scant ¼-inch slices
1 large red bell pepper, cut into matchsticks
1 large onion, thinly sliced
½ teaspoon salt
¼ teaspoon black pepper
2 cups fat-free egg substitute
1 tablespoon olive oil

1   Mix together all ingredients except egg
substitute and oil in medium bowl. Spoon into
8-inch nonstick skillet and set over very low
heat. Cook, stirring once and shaking pan occasionally, until potatoes are tender, about 20
minutes (potatoes should not brown).
2   Transfer potato mixture to large bowl.
Add egg substitute and toss to coat evenly.
Wipe skillet clean. Add oil to skillet and set
over medium heat; add potato mixture. With
wide spatula, press potato mixture to form
compact cake. Reduce heat to very low. Cook,
smoothing edge of tortilla with silicone spatula
occasionally, until tortilla is almost dry on top,
about 15 minutes.
3   Place flat plate on top of skillet and invert pan. Lift off pan and slide tortilla back
into skillet. Cook until set on bottom, about 8
minutes longer. Remove skillet from heat and
let stand 5 minutes. Slide tortilla onto serving
plate; cut into 4 wedges.

PER SERVING (1 WEDGE): 309 grams, 213 Cal,
4 g Total Fat, 1 g Sat Fat, 0 g Trans Fat, 0 mg Chol,
552 mg Sod, 29 g Total Carb, 7 g Total Sugar, 3 g Fib,
15 g Prot, 60 mg Calc.
PointsPlus value: *5*

Hearty Vegetable Lasagna

serves 4

1 small eggplant (about 1 pound), peeled and cut into ¼-inch rounds
1 large zucchini, cut on diagonal into ¼-inch slices
¼ teaspoon black pepper
2 teaspoons olive oil
2 large garlic cloves, minced
2 (14½-ounce) cans fire-roasted tomatoes
1 (8-ounce) package cremini mushrooms, sliced
1 large red bell pepper, chopped
¼ cup thinly sliced fresh basil
5 (6½ × 7-inch) sheets no-boil lasagna noodles
1 cup shredded part-skim mozzarella cheese
¼ cup grated Parmesan cheese

1   Preheat oven to 400°F. Spray 8-inch square baking dish and 2 baking sheets with nonstick spray.

2   Place eggplant and zucchini on prepared baking sheets, overlapping slices if necessary. Spray with nonstick spray and sprinkle with ⅛ teaspoon of black pepper. Bake until vegetables are tender, about 15 minutes.

3   Meanwhile, heat oil in large nonstick skillet over medium-high heat. Add garlic and cook, stirring, until fragrant, about 30 seconds. Add tomatoes with their juice, mushrooms, bell pepper, basil, and remaining ⅛ teaspoon black pepper. Reduce heat and cook until sauce is bubbling but not thickened, about 10 minutes longer.

4   Spread ½ cup of sauce in prepared baking dish. Cover with 1 lasagna noodle and top with one-fourth of eggplant and zucchini. Cover with ½ cup of sauce and sprinkle with 2 tablespoons of mozzarella and 1 tablespoon of Parmesan. Repeat to make 4 more layers, ending with noodle topped with sauce. If any sauce remains, spoon over lasagna.

5   Cover baking dish with foil and bake until bubbly, about 35 minutes. Uncover and bake until sauce is absorbed, about 10 minutes longer. Let stand about 5 minutes before serving.

PER SERVING (¼ OF LASAGNA): 537 grams, 291 Cal, 9 g Total Fat, 4 g Sat Fat, 0 g Trans Fat, 20 mg Chol, 696 mg Sod, 39 g Total Carb, 13 g Total Sugar, 7 g Fib, 17 g Prot, 320 mg Calc.
PointsPlus value: *8*

Grilled Summer Vegetables with Israeli Couscous

serves 6

2 large onions, cut into ½-inch rounds
2 yellow squash, cut into 1-inch slices
2 yellow or orange bell peppers, cut into thick strips
½ pound asparagus, trimmed and cut into 2-inch lengths
1 small eggplant (about 1 pound), quartered lengthwise and cut into ½-inch slices
½ teaspoon dried savory or thyme
½ teaspoon salt
½ teaspoon black pepper
1 cup Israeli couscous
½ cup crumbled reduced-fat feta cheese

1   Preheat grill to medium or prepare medium fire using direct method.

2   Spray vegetable grill topper with nonstick spray and place on grill rack. Place vegetables on grill topper, in batches if necessary, and spray with nonstick spray. Grill, turning, until tender and lightly charred, about 8 minutes. Transfer vegetables to large bowl. Sprinkle with savory, salt, and black pepper, tossing to mix.

3   Meanwhile, bring small saucepan of water to boil; add couscous. Reduce heat and cook, covered, until tender, about 8 minutes; drain.

4   Divide couscous evenly among 6 plates. Top with vegetables; sprinkle with feta.

PER SERVING (½ CUP COUSCOUS, ABOUT 1⅓ CUPS VEGETABLES, AND GENEROUS 1 TABLESPOON CHEESE): 254 grams, 182 Cal, 2 g Total Fat, 1 g Sat Fat, 0 g Trans Fat, 3 mg Chol, 324 mg Sod, 36 g Total Carb, 7 g Total Sugar, 4 g Fib, 8 g Prot, 53 mg Calc.
PointsPlus value: **5**

Japanese-Style Noodles and Vegetables

serves 4

½ pound egg noodles
2 tablespoons unseasoned rice vinegar
4 teaspoons canola oil
1 tablespoon Dijon mustard
1 tablespoon yellow miso
1 cup snow peas, thinly sliced on diagonal
1 cup small broccoli florets
½ red bell pepper, cut into thin strips
½ cup canned straw mushrooms, drained
2 scallions, thinly sliced

1   Cook egg noodles according to package directions, omitting salt if desired. Drain in colander, then rinse under cold running water; drain again. Transfer to serving bowl.

2   To make sauce, combine vinegar, oil, mustard, and miso in blender or mini food processor and puree.

3   Put snow peas, broccoli, and bell pepper in steamer basket; set in medium saucepan over 1 inch boiling water. Cook, covered, until vegetables are tender, about 5 minutes. Remove steamer basket from saucepan. Transfer vegetables to colander and rinse under cold running water; drain.

4   Add vegetables and sauce to noodles in bowl. Toss to mix well. Add mushrooms and scallions; gently toss to combine.

PER SERVING (ABOUT 1½ CUPS): 260 grams, 272 Cal, 8 g Total Fat, 1 g Sat Fat, 0 g Trans Fat, 46 mg Chol, 384 mg Sod, 42 g Total Carb, 4 g Total Sugar, 4 g Fib, 10 g Prot, 55 mg Calc.
PointsPlus value: **7**

FYI Miso, fermented soybean paste, is a basic flavoring ingredient in Japanese cooking. White miso is very mild, while yellow miso is a bit stronger and used for flavoring most foods. Red miso and brown miso are even more strongly flavored and are best used for stews and heartier dishes.

PASTA WITH BROCCOLI AND GOAT CHEESE

Pasta with Broccoli and Goat Cheese

serves 4

¹/₂ *pound whole wheat spaghetti*
4 teaspoons olive oil
3 large garlic cloves, thinly sliced
2 cups small broccoli florets
Grated zest of 1 lemon
¹/₂ *teaspoon salt*
¹/₄ *teaspoon red pepper flakes*
¹/₃ *cup crumbled reduced-fat soft goat cheese*

1   Cook spaghetti according to package directions, omitting salt if desired. Drain, reserving ¹/₄ cup of pasta cooking water. Transfer pasta to serving bowl; keep warm.
2   Meanwhile, heat oil in large nonstick skillet over medium heat. Add garlic and cook, stirring, until fragrant, about 30 seconds. Add broccoli and cook, stirring, until tender, about 5 minutes. Add broccoli, lemon zest, salt, and pepper flakes to pasta; toss, adding just enough of reserved pasta water to moisten. Sprinkle with goat cheese.

PER SERVING (1½ CUPS): 110 grams, 265 Cal,
7 g Total Fat, 1 g Sat Fat, 0 g Trans Fat, 2 mg Chol,
349 mg Sod, 46 g Total Carb, 3 g Total Sugar, 6 g Fib,
10 g Prot, 45 mg Calc.
PointsPlus value: **7**

▲ **HEALTHY EXTRA**
Use 3 cups of broccoli florets instead of 2 cups
for a more substantial dish. Be sure to add a little
more red pepper flakes and grated lemon zest to
keep the flavors bright.

Pasta with Arugula Pesto and Tomatoes

serves 4

¹/₂ *pound farfalle (bow-tie pasta)*
4 teaspoons olive oil
6 plum tomatoes, chopped
¹/₂ *teaspoon salt*
¹/₄ *teaspoon black pepper*
2 cups lightly packed baby arugula
¹/₂ *cup lightly packed flat-leaf parsley leaves*
2 large garlic cloves, minced
¹/₄ *cup grated Parmesan cheese*

1   Cook farfalle according to package directions, omitting salt if desired; drain. Transfer pasta to serving bowl; keep warm.
2   Heat 2 teaspoons of oil in medium nonstick skillet over medium heat. Add tomatoes, ¹/₄ teaspoon of salt and ¹/₈ teaspoon of pepper; cook, stirring, until tomatoes are softened, about 4 minutes. Remove skillet from heat.
3   To make pesto, combine arugula, parsley, remaining 2 teaspoons oil, the garlic, and remaining ¹/₄ teaspoon salt and ¹/₈ teaspoon pepper in food processor or blender and puree. Add Parmesan and pulse to combine.
4   Add pesto and tomatoes to pasta; toss to mix well.

PER SERVING (ABOUT 1 CUP): 179 grams, 296 Cal,
7 g Total Fat, 2 g Sat Fat, 0 g Trans Fat, 4 mg Chol,
402 mg Sod, 48 g Total Carb, 5 g Total Sugar, 3 g Fib,
11 g Prot, 114 mg Calc.
PointsPlus value: **8**

  If you can't find baby arugula, use regular
arugula and tear it into small pieces.

Capellini with Fresh Tomato Sauce

serves 4

½ pound whole wheat capellini
4 tomatoes, seeded and chopped
1 small onion, finely chopped
¼ cup chopped fresh basil
2 garlic cloves, minced
1 tablespoon red wine vinegar
2 teaspoons olive oil
½ teaspoon sugar
½ teaspoon salt
¼ teaspoon black pepper
¼ cup grated Parmesan cheese

1   Cook capellini according to package directions, omitting salt if desired; drain.
2   Meanwhile, mix together tomatoes, onion, basil, garlic, vinegar, oil, and sugar in serving bowl. Add pasta, salt, and pepper; toss to mix well. Sprinkle with Parmesan.

PER SERVING (ABOUT 1½ CUPS): 361 grams, 283 Cal, 5 g Total Fat, 2 g Sat Fat, 0 g Trans Fat, 4 mg Chol, 405 mg Sod, 52 g Total Carb, 8 g Total Sugar, 9 g Fib, 12 g Prot, 108 mg Calc.
PointsPlus value: *7*

FYI   The tasty fresh tomato sauce is also excellent spooned over steamed green beans, zucchini, or grilled eggplant slices.

Salad Bar Pad Thai

serves 4

¼ pound rice sticks (rice vermicelli)
¼ cup unseasoned rice vinegar
2 tablespoons reduced-sodium soy sauce
1 tablespoon sugar
¼ teaspoon red pepper flakes
2 teaspoons canola oil
8 scallions, sliced
1 garlic clove, chopped
1½ cups cooked snow peas, halved crosswise
1 tomato, cut into ¾-inch chunks
1 cup bean sprouts
3 hard-cooked large eggs, finely chopped
½ cup chopped fresh cilantro
½ cup chopped fresh mint
½ cup chopped fresh basil
3 tablespoons unsalted dry-roasted peanuts, finely chopped

1   Place rice sticks in large bowl; add enough hot water to cover and let soak until softened, about 10 minutes; drain. (If using spaghetti, cook according to package directions.)
2   Whisk together vinegar, soy sauce, sugar, and chili garlic sauce in small bowl.
3   Heat nonstick wok or deep large nonstick skillet over high heat until drop of water sizzles in pan; add oil and swirl to coat pan. Add scallions and garlic; stir-fry until scallions begin to soften, about 2 minutes. Add rice sticks and toss to coat. Stir in vinegar mixture; stir-fry until heated through, about 2 minutes. Add snow peas, tomato, and bean sprouts; stir-fry 1 minute. Spoon pad thai into serving bowl. Top with eggs, cilantro, mint, basil, and peanuts.

PER SERVING (GENEROUS 1½ CUPS): 264 grams, 298 Cal, 10 g Total Fat, 2 g Sat Fat, 0 g Trans Fat, 159 mg Chol, 378 mg Sod, 40 g Total Carb, 8 g Total Sugar, 6 g Fib, 13 g Prot, 118 mg Calc.
PointsPlus value: *8*

Easy Ginger Fried Rice

serves 4

1 tablespoon canola oil
¾ cup fat-free egg substitute
4 scallions, cut into 1-inch pieces
2 tablespoons minced peeled fresh ginger
1 (16-ounce) bag frozen mixed vegetables, thawed
4 cups cold cooked brown rice
½ cup reduced-sodium vegetable broth
3 tablespoons reduced-sodium soy sauce
¼ teaspoon black pepper

1   Heat nonstick wok or deep large nonstick skillet and set over medium-high heat until drop of water sizzles in pan; add 2 teaspoons of oil and swirl to coat pan. Add egg substitute and cook, gently stirring, until set, about 1 minute. Transfer to small bowl.

2   Add remaining 1 teaspoon oil to wok. Add scallions and ginger; stir-fry until scallions are softened, about 2 minutes. Add mixed vegetables and stir-fry until crisp-tender, about 1 minute.

3   Add rice to wok and stir-fry until heated through, about 3 minutes. Add broth and soy sauce; stir-fry until liquid is absorbed, about 1 minute longer. Return egg substitute to wok and sprinkle with pepper; stir-fry until mixed.

PER SERVING (1½ CUPS): 417 grams, 360 Cal,
6 g Total Fat, 1 g Sat Fat, 0 g Trans Fat, 0 mg Chol,
671 mg Sod, 64 g Total Carb, 2 g Total Sugar, 9 g Fib,
15 g Prot, 76 mg Calc.
PointsPlus value: *9*

Creamy Polenta with Vegetables

serves 4

8 large shiitake mushrooms, stemmed and caps thinly sliced
1 (10-ounce) package frozen green peas, thawed
½ cup dry vermouth or dry white wine
½ teaspoon salt
½ teaspoon black pepper
4 cups water
1 cup instant polenta
¼ cup grated Parmesan cheese

1   Spray large skillet with nonstick spray and set over medium-high heat. Add mushrooms and cook until softened, about 2 minutes. Add peas and cook 1 minute. Add vermouth and bring to boil. Cook until slightly reduced, about 1 minute. Stir in ¼ teaspoon of salt and ¼ teaspoon of pepper. Remove skillet from heat; keep warm.

2   Meanwhile, to make polenta, combine water and remaining ¼ teaspoon salt in medium saucepan; bring to boil over medium-high heat. Reduce heat to medium; whisk in polenta in thin, steady stream. Cook, stirring constantly with wooden spoon, until polenta is thick but not stiff, about 5 minutes. Remove saucepan from heat and stir in Parmesan and remaining ¼ teaspoon pepper.

3   Divide polenta evenly among 4 plates; top evenly with vegetable mixture. Serve at once.

PER SERVING (1 CUP POLENTA AND ½ CUP VEGETABLE MIXTURE): 413 grams, 261 Cal, 2 g Total Fat,
1 g Sat Fat, 0 g Trans Fat, 4 mg Chol, 454 mg Sod,
52 g Total Carb, 4 g Total Sugar, 9 g Fib, 10 g Prot,
93 mg Calc.
PointsPlus value: *6*

Lemony Spring Vegetable Risotto

serves 8

1 pound asparagus, trimmed and cut into
    1-inch pieces
1 teaspoon salt
5 cups reduced-sodium vegetable broth or
    Basic Vegetable Stock (page 107)
1 tablespoon olive oil
2 leeks (white and light green part only),
    chopped
3 garlic cloves, minced
2 teaspoons chopped fresh thyme or
    $1/2$ teaspoon dried
$1^1/2$ cups Arborio rice
$1/3$ cup dry white wine
1 cup frozen baby peas, thawed
1 teaspoon grated lemon zest
3 tablespoons lemon juice
$1/2$ cup grated Parmesan cheese
$1/4$ teaspoon black pepper

1   Bring large pot of water to boil. Add asparagus and salt; cook until asparagus are bright green, about 2 minutes. Drain in colander, then rinse under cold running water; drain again.

2   Bring broth to simmer in medium saucepan over medium heat; keep at gentle simmer.

3   Heat oil in large nonstick saucepan over medium heat. Add leeks, garlic, and thyme; cook, stirring, until leeks begin to soften, about 3 minutes. Add rice and cook, stirring, until coated with oil, about 1 minute. Add wine and cook, stirring, until absorbed.

4   Add simmering broth to rice, $1/2$ cup at a time, stirring until broth is absorbed before adding more; cook until rice is tender but slightly chewy in center. Stir in asparagus, peas, and lemon zest and juice with last addition of simmering broth. Stir in Parmesan and pepper. Serve at once.

PER SERVING (1⅓ CUPS): 266 grams, 241 Cal, 5 g Total Fat, 2 g Sat Fat, 0 g Trans Fat, 4 mg Chol, 696 mg Sod, 42 g Total Carb, 4 g Total Sugar, 3 g Fib, 9 g Prot, 105 mg Calc.
PointsPlus value: **6**

FYI To clean leeks, trim the roots and green tops, leaving the root ends intact to hold the layers together. Slice the leeks lengthwise and fan the layers open; swish in a large bowl of cool water. Let the leeks stand a few minutes to allow the grit to fall to the bottom of the bowl, then lift them out.

Zucchini Risotto with Sun-Dried Tomatoes

serves 4

3¹/₂ *cups reduced-sodium vegetable broth or*
    Basic Vegetable Stock (page 107)
¹/₂ *cup tomato juice*
1 *tablespoon olive oil*
6 *shallots, finely chopped*
4 *zucchini, cut into* ¹/₄*-inch dice*
¹/₂ *cup dry white wine*
1¹/₃ *cups Arborio rice*
16 *moist-packed sun-dried tomatoes (not*
    packed in oil), finely chopped
¹/₂ *cup chopped fresh parsley*
2 *tablespoons grated Parmesan cheese*
¹/₄ *teaspoon black pepper*

1   Combine broth and tomato juice in medium saucepan and bring to simmer over medium heat; keep at gentle simmer.
2   Heat oil in medium nonstick saucepan over medium heat. Add shallots and cook, stirring, until softened, about 5 minutes. Add zucchini and wine; cook until zucchini is softened, about 5 minutes. Add rice; cook, stirring, until coated with oil, about 1 minute.
3   Add 1 cup of simmering broth mixture, the sun-dried tomatoes, and parsley to rice; cook, stirring, until liquid is absorbed. Add remaining broth mixture, ¹/₂ cup at a time, stirring until broth is absorbed before adding more, until rice is tender but slightly chewy in center. Stir in Parmesan and pepper. Serve at once.

PER SERVING (1½ CUPS): 566 grams, 419 Cal,
7 g Total Fat, 2 g Sat Fat, 0 g Trans Fat, 2 mg Chol,
742 mg Sod, 79 g Total Carb, 10 g Total Sugar, 6 g Fib,
14 g Prot, 123 mg Calc.
PointsPlus value: *11*

Risotto with Swiss Chard

serves 4

3¹/₂ *cups reduced-sodium vegetable broth or*
    Basic Vegetable Stock (page 107)
1 *tablespoon olive oil*
1 *onion, finely chopped*
1¹/₃ *cups Arborio rice*
¹/₂ *cup dry white wine*
1 *bunch Swiss chard, trimmed and chopped*
2 *tablespoons grated Parmesan cheese*
¹/₄ *teaspoon black pepper*
¹/₄ *teaspoon ground nutmeg*

1   Bring broth to simmer in medium saucepan over medium heat; keep at gentle simmer.
2   Heat oil in large nonstick saucepan over medium heat. Add onion and cook, stirring, until softened, about 5 minutes. Add rice and cook, stirring, until coated with oil, about 1 minute. Add wine; cook, stirring, until absorbed.
3   Add 1 cup of simmering broth to rice; cook, stirring, until broth is absorbed. Stir in handful of chard. Add remaining broth, ¹/₂ cup at a time along with handful of chard, stirring until broth is absorbed before adding more and cooking until rice is tender but slightly chewy in center. Stir in Parmesan, pepper, and nutmeg. Serve at once.

PER SERVING (1½ CUPS): 437 grams, 376 Cal,
6 g Total Fat, 2 g Sat Fat, 0 g Trans Fat, 2 mg Chol,
639 mg Sod, 70 g Total Carb, 6 g Total Sugar, 5 g Fib,
12 g Prot, 126 mg Calc.
PointsPlus value: *10*

 FYI   You can use either green or red Swiss chard in this risotto.

Eggplant Rollatini

serves 4

2 eggplants (about 1½ pounds each), peeled
  and each cut lengthwise into 4 slices
2 teaspoons olive oil
2 onions, chopped
3 garlic cloves, minced
1 cup fat-free ricotta cheese
2 tablespoons chopped fresh parsley
¾ teaspoon dried oregano
1 cup fat-free marinara sauce
¼ teaspoon cayenne
⅓ cup shredded fontina cheese
2 tablespoons grated Parmesan cheese

1   Preheat broiler. Line 2 baking sheets with
foil; spray with olive oil nonstick spray. Arrange
eggplant slices on prepared baking sheets. Broil
5 inches from heat, without turning, until deep
golden brown, about 6 minutes; let cool.
2   Preheat oven to 375°F. Spray 9 × 13-inch
baking dish with nonstick spray. Heat oil in large
nonstick skillet over medium heat. Add onions
and garlic; cook, stirring, about 5 minutes.
3   Stir together ricotta, parsley, and ¼ teaspoon of oregano in medium bowl; stir in onion
mixture. Spread about ¼ cup of ricotta mixture over pale side of each eggplant slice and
roll up to enclose filling. Place eggplant rolls,
seam side down, in prepared baking dish.
4   Stir together marinara sauce, remaining
½ teaspoon oregano, and the cayenne in small
bowl; spoon over eggplant rolls. Sprinkle with
fontina and Parmesan. Bake until eggplant is
browned and sauce is bubbly, about 30 minutes.

PER SERVING (2 EGGPLANT ROLLS): 500 grams, 259 Cal,
7 g Total Fat, 3 g Sat Fat, 0 g Trans Fat, 22 mg Chol,
305 mg Sod, 38 g Total Carb, 22 g Total Sugar, 10 g Fib,
13 g Prot, 251 mg Calc.
PointsPlus value: *6*

Fiery Falafel

serves 8

1 (10-ounce) package falafel mix
1¼ cups water
6 tablespoons reduced-fat mayonnaise
2 teaspoons minced chipotles en adobo
4 teaspoons olive oil
4 (6-inch) onion or whole wheat pita breads,
  halved
8 small romaine lettuce leaves

1   Stir together falafel mix and water in medium bowl until combined well; let stand according to package directions.
2   Meanwhile, stir together mayonnaise and
chipotles en adobo in small bowl.
3   Drop falafel mixture by 2 tablespoonfuls
onto large sheet of wax paper, making total of
20 mounds.
4   Heat 1 teaspoon of oil in very large nonstick skillet over medium-high heat. Shape 5
mounds of falafel mixture into 2-inch patties
and add to skillet as they are shaped. Cook
until golden and firm, about 2 minutes per
side. Transfer patties to plate and keep warm.
Repeat with remaining oil and falafel mixture.
5   Spread 1½ teaspoons of chipotle mayonnaise inside each pita half. Cut 4 falafel patties
in half. Fill each pita half with 2½ falafel patties and 1 lettuce leaf.

PER SERVING (1 FALAFEL-STUFFED PITA): 129 grams,
251 Cal, 8 g Total Fat, 1 g Sat Fat, 0 g Trans Fat,
4 mg Chol, 862 mg Sod, 37 g Total Carb, 4 g Total Sugar,
8 g Fib, 14 g Prot, 59 mg Calc.
PointsPlus value: *7*

FYI   Falafel, street food in Middle Eastern
countries, are highly seasoned chickpea
balls that are tucked into pita bread along with
lettuce, tomato, and yogurt sauce.

Mexicali-Style Stuffed Mushrooms

serves 4

12 (4-inch) portobello mushrooms
1 small red bell pepper, chopped
1 onion, chopped
3 large garlic cloves, minced
2 (15½-ounce) cans pinto beans, rinsed and
    drained
1 teaspoon dried oregano
½ teaspoon salt
¼ teaspoon red pepper flakes
1 cup frozen baby corn kernels, thawed
½ cup shredded reduced-fat Cheddar cheese

1   Preheat oven to 400°F.
2   Remove stems from mushrooms and
coarsely chop; reserve. Place mushroom caps,
stemmed side up, in jelly-roll pan.
3   To make filling, spray large nonstick skillet
with nonstick spray and set over medium heat.
Add bell pepper and onion; cook, stirring, until
softened, 5 minutes. Add garlic and cook until
fragrant. Add chopped mushroom stems and
cook, stirring, until softened, about 2 minutes.
Transfer mushroom mixture to large bowl.
Stir in beans, oregano, salt, and pepper flakes.
Spoon half of mushroom mixture into food
processor and puree; stir back into remaining
mushroom mixture. Add corn.
4   Spoon mushroom mixture evenly into
mushroom caps, mounding in center. Cover
loosely with foil and bake 15 minutes. Uncover
and sprinkle evenly with Cheddar; bake until
and cheese is melted, about 5 minutes longer.

PER SERVING (3 STUFFED MUSHROOMS): 503 grams,
296 Cal, 4 g Total Fat, 2 g Sat Fat, 0 g Trans Fat,
8 mg Chol, 662 mg Sod, 47 g Total Carb, 8 g Total Sugar,
13 g Fib, 18 g Prot, 162 mg Calc.
PointsPlus value: **7**

Portobello Mushroom Burgers

serves 4

4 large portobello mushrooms, stemmed
2 tablespoons + 2 teaspoons fat-free balsamic
    dressing
¼ teaspoon salt
¼ teaspoon black pepper
4 multigrain hamburger buns, split
1 cup lightly packed mixed baby salad greens
4 thick tomato slices
4 thick onion slices, preferably sweet
2 ounces soft goat cheese, crumbled

1   Spray grill rack with nonstick spray. Preheat grill to high or prepare hot fire using direct
method. (Or spray ridged grill pan with nonstick spray and set over medium-high heat.)
2   Brush portobellos with 2 tablespoons of
balsamic dressing; sprinkle with salt and pepper. Place mushrooms on grill rack (or in grill
pan) and grill until softened, about 6 minutes
per side.
3   Place 1 mushroom on bottom of each bun
and drizzle evenly with remaining 2 teaspoons
dressing. Top each with ¼ cup of greens, 1
tomato slice, and 1 onion slice. Sprinkle evenly
with goat cheese and cover with tops of buns.

PER SERVING (1 GARNISHED BURGER): 243 grams,
228 Cal, 6 g Total Fat, 3 g Sat Fat, 0 g Trans Fat,
7 mg Chol, 582 mg Sod, 35 g Total Carb,
10 g Total Sugar, 4 g Fib, 10 g Prot, 86 mg Calc.
PointsPlus value: **6**

▲ HEALTHY EXTRA
Serve the burgers with carrot and celery sticks for
some satisfying crunch.

Potato-Spinach Casserole

serves 4

1 onion, chopped
2 garlic cloves, minced
1 jalapeño pepper, seeded and minced
¼ teaspoon salt
¼ teaspoon black pepper
Pinch cayenne
2 large Yukon Gold potatoes, peeled and very
    thinly sliced
1 (10-ounce) package frozen chopped spinach,
    thawed and squeezed dry
¼ cup shredded reduced-fat Monterey Jack
    cheese
⅔ cup reduced-sodium vegetable broth

1   Preheat oven to 375°F. Spray 8-inch
square baking dish with nonstick spray.
2   Spray large nonstick skillet with nonstick
spray and set over medium heat. Add onion
and garlic; cook, stirring, until onion is softened, about 5 minutes. Add jalapeño, salt,
black pepper, and cayenne; cook, stirring constantly, until fragrant, about 30 seconds.
3   Spread half of potatoes in prepared baking
dish. Top with half of onion mixture, the spinach, and Monterey Jack. Cover with remaining
potatoes and onion mixture. With wide spatula, gently press down; pour broth over top.
4   Cover baking dish with foil and bake 1
hour. Uncover and bake until casserole is lightly browned and potatoes are tender, about 15
minutes longer.

PER SERVING (2 CUPS): 261 grams, 153 Cal,
2 g Total Fat, 1 g Sat Fat, 0 g Trans Fat, 5 mg Chol,
338 mg Sod, 28 g Total Carb, 3 g Total Sugar, 4 g Fib,
7 g Prot, 145 mg Calc.
PointsPlus value: *4*

Spaghetti Squash with Broccoli and Parmesan

serves 4

1 (3-pound) spaghetti squash, pricked several
    times with fork
1 tablespoon olive oil
1 red onion, thinly sliced
4 garlic cloves, minced
1 (15½-ounce) can small white beans, rinsed
    and drained
¾ pound broccoli crowns, cut into small florets
6 moist-packed sun-dried tomatoes
    (not packed in oil), chopped
½ teaspoon salt
½ cup reduced-sodium vegetable broth
¼ cup grated Parmesan cheese

1   Preheat oven to 350°F.
2   Place squash in roasting pan or baking dish
and bake until tender, about 1 hour.
3   When cool enough to handle, cut squash
lengthwise in half and scoop out seeds; discard.
With fork, scrape out pulp into medium bowl.
4   Heat oil in large nonstick skillet over medium heat. Add onion and garlic; cook, stirring,
until onion is softened, about 5 minutes. Add
beans and broccoli; cook, stirring, 1 minute.
Stir in sun-dried tomatoes and salt. Add broth.
5   Reduce heat and simmer, covered, stirring
occasionally, until broccoli is tender, about 5
minutes. Add squash and cook, stirring occasionally, until heated through, about 2 minutes
longer. Serve sprinkled with Parmesan.

**PER SERVING (2 CUPS SQUASH MIXTURE AND 1
TABLESPOON PARMESAN):** 483 grams, 238 Cal,
7 g Total Fat, 2 g Sat Fat, 0 g Trans Fat, 4 mg Chol,
601 mg Sod, 38 g Total Carb, 5 g Total Sugar, 10 g Fib,
10 g Prot, 207 mg Calc.
PointsPlus value: *6*

10

Vegetable Sides

Vegetable Sides

256   Creamy Mashed Potatoes
257   Olive Oil and Lemon Smashed Potatoes
257   Potato Pancakes
259   Scalloped Potatoes with Cheese
259   Hash Brown Potatoes
260   Oven Fries
260   Sweet Potato Wedges with Chipotle Mayonnaise
262   Oven-Baked Onion Rings
262   Sweet Potato Casserole
263   Corn Pudding
264   Oven-Roasted Corn on the Cob
264   Broccoli with Garlic
265   Lemon-Butter Broccoli Spears
265   Pan-Braised Broccoli Rabe
266   Roasted Asparagus and Red Peppers
266   Oven-Roasted Beets and Garlic
267   Red Cabbage with Ginger
267   Dilled Carrots
269   Oven-Roasted Brussels Sprouts and Carrots
269   Cauliflower with Curried Tomato Sauce
270   Eggplant Parmesan Stacks
270   Sweet-and-Sour Grilled Fennel
271   Lemony Green Beans with Parsley
271   Kale with Balsamic Vinegar
272   Wild Mushrooms with Fresh Thyme
272   Creole-Style Okra
273   Ratatouille Casserole
274   Cherry Tomatoes with Thyme
274   Provençal-Style Stuffed Tomatoes
276   Roasted Peppers with Orange Zest and Olives
276   Classic Roasted Vegetables
277   Skillet Summer Squash
277   "Creamed" Spinach
278   Spicy Stir-Fried Sesame Spinach
278   Spaghetti Squash Primavera
279   Maple and Butter–Glazed Acorn Squash Wedges
279   Summertime Succotash
280   Swiss Chard au Gratin
280   Mixed Pickled Vegetables

Creamy Mashed Potatoes

serves 6

*2 pounds baking potatoes, peeled and cut into
    1-inch chunks*
¾ cup reduced-fat (2%) milk, warmed
1½ tablespoons olive oil
½ teaspoon salt
Pinch black pepper

1   Combine potatoes and enough water to
cover by 1 inch in large saucepan; bring to boil.
Reduce heat and simmer until tender, about 12
minutes; drain. Remove saucepan from heat.
2   With potato masher, mash potatoes until
smooth. With wooden spoon, beat in milk, oil,
salt, and pepper.

PER SERVING (⅔ CUP): 151 grams, 153 Cal,
4 g Total Fat, 1 g Sat Fat, 0 g Trans Fat, 2 mg Chol,
215 mg Sod, 27 g Total Carb, 3 g Total Sugar, 2 g Fib,
3 g Prot, 43 mg Calc.
PointsPlus value: *4*

Variations

Roasted Garlic Mashed Potatoes

Remove loose papery skin from 1 head of
garlic, leaving head intact. Wrap garlic in foil.
Place in small baking dish and roast in 350°F
oven until softened, about 1 hour. When cool
enough to handle, separate cloves and squeeze
soft garlic from each clove into small bowl. Stir
garlic into potatoes along with milk. (Garlic
can be roasted up to 3 days ahead and refrigerated, tightly covered.)

PER SERVING (⅔ CUP): 157 grams, 162 Cal,
4 g Total Fat, 1 g Sat Fat, 0 g Trans Fat, 2 mg Chol,
216 mg Sod, 29 g Total Carb, 4 g Total Sugar, 2 g Fib,
4 g Prot, 54 mg Calc.
PointsPlus value: *4*

Celery Root and Mashed Potatoes

Substitute 1 pound trimmed peeled celery root
that has been cut into scant ½-inch pieces for 1
pound of potatoes. Prepare as directed.

PER SERVING (⅔ CUP): 158 grams, 127 Cal,
4 g Total Fat, 1 g Sat Fat, 0 g Trans Fat, 2 mg Chol,
277 mg Sod, 20 g Total Carb, 4 g Total Sugar, 2 g Fib,
3 g Prot, 68 mg Calc.
PointsPlus value: *3*

Horseradish Mashed Potatoes

Prepare potatoes as directed, stirring 2 tablespoons drained prepared white horseradish into
potatoes along with milk.

▲ HEALTHY EXTRA
Stir 1 cup of steamed chopped spinach into the
mashed potatoes in step 2.

Olive Oil and Lemon Smashed Potatoes

serves 6

2 pounds Yukon Gold potatoes, scrubbed and
  cut into 1-inch chunks
1½ tablespoons extra-virgin olive oil
2 teaspoons grated lemon zest
2 tablespoons lemon juice
½ teaspoon salt
¼ teaspoon black pepper

1   Combine potatoes and enough water to
cover by 1 inch in large saucepan; bring to boil.
Reduce heat and simmer until tender, about 12
minutes; drain. Remove saucepan from heat.
2   With potato masher, coarsely mash potatoes. With wooden spoon, beat in oil, lemon
zest and juice, salt, and pepper.

PER SERVING (⅔ **CUP**): 161 grams, 156 Cal,
3 g Total Fat, 1 g Sat Fat, 0 g Trans Fat, 0 mg Chol,
203 mg Sod, 27 g Total Carb, 0 g Total Sugar, 2 g Fib,
4 g Prot, 2 mg Calc.
PointsPlus value: *4*

FYI   You can prepare the potatoes up to 2 hours
ahead. Transfer them to a bowl and cover
tightly with plastic wrap. When ready to serve, vent
the plastic wrap and microwave on Medium until
heated through, about 3 minutes. Or set the bowl
of potatoes over a pot of simmering water for up to
30 minutes, stirring occasionally.

Potato Pancakes

serves 6

1¼ pounds baking potatoes, peeled and
  shredded
2 scallions, minced
2 large egg whites
3 tablespoons all-purpose flour
¼ teaspoon salt
2 tablespoons canola oil

1   Put potatoes in large bowl and add enough
cold water to cover. Soak 30 minutes; drain
and pat dry with paper towels or clean towel.
2   Meanwhile, preheat oven to 375°F.
3   Stir together potatoes, scallions, egg
whites, flour, and salt in medium bowl until
well combined. Divide mixture into 12 equal
portions and place in jelly-roll pan.
4   Heat 2 teaspoons of oil in large nonstick
skillet over medium heat. Add 4 portions of
potato mixture to skillet and flatten with wide
spatula. Cook until golden, about 3 minutes
per side. Transfer to ungreased baking sheet.
Repeat with remaining oil and potato mixture.
5   Transfer potato pancakes to oven and bake
until crisp and cooked through, about 5 minutes.

PER SERVING (2 PANCAKES): 97 grams, 130 Cal,
5 g Total Fat, 1 g Sat Fat, 0 g Trans Fat, 0 mg Chol,
313 mg Sod, 19 g Total Carb, 2 g Total Sugar, 2 g Fib,
3 g Prot, 8 mg Calc.
PointsPlus value: *3*

FYI   In this recipe, it's preferable to use starchy
potatoes, such as russets or Idahos. But
you can also use Yukon Gold potatoes, which are
an all-purpose potato that have a medium amount
of starch.

Scalloped Potatoes with Cheese

serves 8

2 tablespoons all-purpose flour
1 teaspoon salt
¼ teaspoon black pepper
6 red potatoes (about 2 pounds), peeled
9 tablespoons shredded reduced-fat Gruyère
    or Cheddar cheese
2 cups fat-free half-and-half

1   Preheat oven to 350°F. Spray 8-inch
square baking dish with nonstick spray.
2   Stir together flour, salt, and pepper in cup.
3   Cut potatoes crosswise into ¼-inch slices.
Arrange one-third of potatoes in overlapping
layer in prepared baking dish. Sprinkle with half
of seasoned flour and 3 tablespoons Gruyère.
Top with half of remaining potatoes; sprinkle
with remaining seasoned flour and 3 tablespoons cheese. Arrange remaining potatoes on
top and sprinkle with remaining 3 tablespoons
cheese. Pour half-and-half over all.
4   Cover baking dish with foil; bake 45 minutes. Reduce oven temperature to 325°F. Uncover and bake until top is golden brown and
potatoes are tender, about 1 hour longer.

PER SERVING (½ CUP): 182 grams, 180 Cal,
3 g Total Fat, 2 g Sat Fat, 0 g Trans Fat, 8 mg Chol,
375 mg Sod, 30 g Total Carb, 6 g Total Sugar, 2 g Fib,
7 g Prot, 191 mg Calc.
PointsPlus value: *5*

FYI   Before layering the potatoes, pat them dry
with paper towels or a clean kitchen towel.

Hash Brown Potatoes

serves 4

2 teaspoons canola oil
1¼ pounds all-purpose potatoes, cooked and
    cut into ½-inch pieces
2 onions, finely chopped
½ cup reduced-sodium chicken broth
½ teaspoon salt
⅛ teaspoon black pepper

Heat oil in large nonstick skillet over medium-
high heat. Add potatoes and onions; cook,
stirring, until lightly browned, about 5 minutes.
Add broth, salt, and pepper. Reduce heat and
cook, flattening mixture with spatula and
turning it over when it forms a crust, about 15
minutes longer.

PER SERVING (¼ OF HASH BROWNS): 227 grams,
158 Cal, 2 g Total Fat, 1 g Sat Fat, 0 g Trans Fat,
3 mg Chol, 382 mg Sod, 31 g Total Carb, 6 g Total Sugar,
4 g Fib, 4 g Prot, 34 mg Calc.
PointsPlus value: *4*

▲ **HEALTHY EXTRA**
Grilled arctic char fillets and steamed green beans
turn these hash browns into a complete meal
(a 3-ounce portion of cooked arctic char fillet with
each serving will increase the *PointsPlus* value
by *4*).

Oven Fries

serves 4

1 1/4 *pounds baking potatoes, peeled and cut*
  into 1/2-*inch slices*
3/4 *teaspoon salt*
1/2 *teaspoon sugar*
4 *teaspoons canola oil*
1 *teaspoon paprika*

1   Preheat oven to 450°F. Spray nonstick baking sheet with nonstick spray.
2   Combine potatoes, 1/4 teaspoon of salt, and the sugar with enough cold water to cover in large bowl. Soak 15 minutes; drain and pat dry with paper towels or clean kitchen towel.
3   Toss together potatoes, oil, and paprika in large bowl until evenly coated. Spread in single layer on prepared baking sheet. Bake, turning potatoes over as they brown, until cooked through and crisp, about 45 minutes. Sprinkle with remaining 1/2 teaspoon salt.

PER SERVING (1/4 OF OVEN FRIES): 116 grams, 146 Cal, 5 g Total Fat, 0 g Sat Fat, 0 g Trans Fat, 0 mg Chol, 442 mg Sod, 24 g Total Carb, 2 g Total Sugar, 2 g Fib, 2 g Prot, 7 mg Calc.
PointsPlus value: **4**

FYI   Sugar on french fries? Absolutely! Soaking the cut-up potatoes in sugar (and salt) helps to remove some of their liquid which makes them much crispier when baked.

Sweet Potato Wedges with Chipotle Mayonnaise

serves 4

4 (6-*ounce*) *sweet potatoes, scrubbed*
1/4 *cup fat-free mayonnaise*
1/4 *cup chipotle salsa*

1   Preheat oven to 425°F. Spray baking sheet with nonstick spray.
2   Slice potatoes lengthwise in half and cut each half into 4 wedges. Place wedges, cut side down, on prepared baking sheet. Roast 15 minutes; turn potatoes over. Roast until tender and nicely browned along edges, about 20 minutes.
3   Meanwhile, stir together mayonnaise and salsa in serving bowl until blended. Serve alongside potatoes.

PER SERVING (8 POTATO WEDGES AND 2 TABLESPOONS MAYONNAISE): 135 grams, 124 Cal, 1 g Total Fat, 0 g Sat Fat, 0 g Trans Fat, 2 mg Chol, 205 mg Sod, 28 g Total Carb, 12 g Total Sugar, 4 g Fib, 2 g Prot, 33 mg Calc.
PointsPlus value: **3**

→
FROM TOP: SWEET POTATO WEDGES
WITH CHIPOTLE MAYONNAISE, OVEN-BAKED
ONION RINGS (PAGE 262), OVEN FRIES

Oven-Baked Onion Rings

serves 6

1/3 cup all-purpose flour
1/2 teaspoon salt
1/8 teaspoon cayenne
3 large egg whites
1/4 cup plain dried bread crumbs
1 large Spanish onion, cut into 1/4-inch rounds

1   Place rack in upper third of oven. Preheat oven to 400°F. Spray nonstick baking sheet with nonstick spray.
2   Mix together flour, salt, and cayenne on sheet of wax paper. Lightly beat egg whites in pie plate. Put bread crumbs on separate sheet of wax paper.
3   Separate onion slices into double rings with one ring inside the other. Coat rings with seasoned flour; dip in egg whites, then coat with bread crumbs.
4   Place onion rings on prepared baking sheet. Bake until browned, about 10 minutes. Turn onion rings over; bake until browned, about 8 minutes longer.

PER SERVING (ABOUT 6 ONION RINGS): 94 grams, 108 Cal, 1 g Total Fat, 0 g Sat Fat, 0 g Trans Fat, 0 mg Chol, 339 mg Sod, 20 g Total Carb, 4 g Total Sugar, 2 g Fib, 5 g Prot, 44 mg Calc.
PointsPlus value: *3*

Sweet Potato Casserole

serves 6

2 sweet-tart apples, peeled, cored, and thinly
   sliced
1 pound sweet potatoes, peeled and thinly
   sliced
1 teaspoon finely chopped crystallized ginger
1/2 teaspoon salt
1/4 cup thawed frozen apple juice concentrate
1/4 cup water
2 tablespoons dark brown sugar
2 teaspoons lemon juice
1/4 teaspoon ground cinnamon
1/8 teaspoon ground cloves
1 tablespoon butter

1   Preheat oven to 375°F. Spray 8-inch square baking dish with nonstick spray.
2   Place half of apples in prepared baking dish; top with half of potatoes and sprinkle with 1/2 teaspoon of ginger and 1/4 teaspoon of salt. Repeat layers once.
3   Mix together apple juice concentrate, water, brown sugar, lemon juice, cinnamon, and cloves in small bowl; pour over potatoes. Cover with foil. Bake 45 minutes; dot with butter. Bake, covered, until apples and potatoes are tender and apple juice mixture is lightly browned, about 15 minutes.

PER SERVING (ABOUT 2/3 CUP): 120 grams, 128 Cal, 2 g Total Fat, 1 g Sat Fat, 0 g Trans Fat, 5 mg Chol, 107 mg Sod, 27 g Total Carb, 19 g Total Sugar, 3 g Fib, 1 g Prot, 24 mg Calc.
PointsPlus value: *3*

FYI Sweet potatoes are a tuber belonging to the morning glory family. The two most common varieties are a pale-skinned sweet potato and a darker-skinned variety that is usually labeled yams but technically is not.

Corn Pudding

serves 4

2 cups fresh or frozen corn kernels
1 teaspoon canola oil
1 onion, finely chopped
¹/₂ red bell pepper, finely chopped
¹/₂ cup fat-free evaporated milk
2 tablespoons all-purpose flour
¹/₃ cup shredded Gruyère cheese
2 tablespoons grated Parmesan cheese
¹/₂ teaspoon salt
¹/₈ teaspoon cayenne
3 large egg whites

1   Preheat oven to 350°F. Spray 1-quart souf-flé dish with nonstick spray.

2   Bring 1 inch of water to boil in small saucepan. Add corn; cook, covered, until tender, about 4 minutes. Drain; reserve liquid.

3   Heat oil in medium nonstick saucepan over medium heat. Add onion and bell pepper; cook, stirring, about 5 minutes. Remove saucepan from heat. Whisk in reserved corn cooking liquid, the evaporated milk, and flour until smooth. Cook, stirring, until mixture bubbles and thickens, about 5 minutes. Remove saucepan from heat; stir in Gruyère, Parmesan, salt, cayenne, and corn.

4   With electric mixer on medium speed, beat egg whites in medium bowl until stiff peaks form. With rubber spatula, fold beaten whites into corn mixture; pour into prepared dish. Bake until pudding is browned and puffed and knife inserted near center comes out almost clean, about 1 hour. Serve pudding at once.

PER SERVING (¼ OF PUDDING): 210 grams, 196 Cal, 6 g Total Fat, 3 g Sat Fat, 0 g Trans Fat, 13 mg Chol, 458 mg Sod, 26 g Total Carb, 7 g Total Sugar, 3 g Fib, 12 g Prot, 231 mg Calc.
PointsPlus value: *5*

CUTTING KERNELS FROM EARS OF CORN

1   *Remove husk and silk from corn.*

2   *Stand an ear of corn on cutting board. With sharp knife, slice down to cut off kernels, cutting as close to cob as possible. Turn ear of corn and repeat to remove all kernels.*

Oven-Roasted Corn on the Cob

serves 4

2 tablespoons finely chopped fresh cilantro
2 tablespoons lime juice
1 tablespoon water
4 teaspoons butter, melted
4 ears of corn, husks and silk removed

1   Preheat oven to 450°F. Tear off four 12-inch sheets of heavy foil.
2   Stir together cilantro, lime juice, water, and butter in cup; brush over ears of corn. Place 1 ear of corn on each sheet of foil and wrap tightly; place directly on oven rack. Roast corn, turning occasionally, until tender, about 35 minutes.

PER SERVING (1 EAR OF CORN): 107 grams, 113 Cal,
5 g Total Fat, 3 g Sat Fat, 0 g Trans Fat, 10 mg Chol,
14 mg Sod, 18 g Total Carb, 6 g Total Sugar, 3 g Fib,
3 g Prot, 4 mg Calc.
PointsPlus value: *3*

FYI   When selecting fresh corn, check the silk strands at the tops of the ears. The silk should be smooth, shiny, and damp. If it is dry, the corn is not freshly picked and will not be sweet and tender when cooked.

Broccoli with Garlic

serves 4

1 bunch broccoli, coarsely chopped
2 teaspoons olive oil
3 garlic cloves, minced
¼ teaspoon dried oregano
¼ cup jarred roasted red bell pepper (not packed in oil), chopped

1   Bring ½ inch of water to boil in large non-stick skillet. Add broccoli and cook, covered, until crisp-tender, about 5 minutes; drain. Wipe skillet dry.
2   Add oil to skillet and set over medium heat. Add broccoli, garlic, and oregano; cook, stirring, until garlic is golden, about 2 minutes. Stir in roasted pepper; cook, stirring, until heated through, about 1 minute longer.

PER SERVING (ABOUT 1 CUP): 90 grams, 49 Cal,
3 g Total Fat, 0 g Sat Fat, 0 g Trans Fat, 0 mg Chol,
47 mg Sod, 6 g Total Carb, 2 g Total Sugar, 2 g Fib,
2 g Prot, 40 mg Calc.
PointsPlus value: *1*

▲ **HEALTHY EXTRA**
Turn this vegetable side dish into a main course by serving it over whole wheat spaghetti (1 cup of cooked whole wheat spaghetti with each serving will increase the *PointsPlus* value by *4*).

Lemon-Butter Broccoli Spears

serves 4

1 bunch broccoli, trimmed and cut into thin
    spears
1 tablespoon unsalted butter
2 teaspoons lemon juice
Grated zest of 1 lemon
1/2 teaspoon salt
1/8 teaspoon black pepper

1   Put broccoli in steamer basket; set in large
pot over 1 inch boiling water. Cook, covered,
until crisp-tender, about 3 minutes. Remove
pot from heat.
2   Melt butter in large nonstick skillet over
medium-high heat. When butter foams, add
lemon juice; cook 30 seconds. Add broccoli,
lemon zest, salt, and pepper; cook, tossing
occasionally, until broccoli is heated through,
about 1 minute longer.

PER SERVING (1 CUP): 78 grams, 46 Cal, 3 g Total Fat,
2 g Sat Fat, 0 g Trans Fat, 8 mg Chol, 310 mg Sod,
4 g Total Carb, 2 g Total Sugar, 2 g Fib, 2 g Prot,
36 mg Calc.
PointsPlus value: *1*

FYI   To prepare this tasty dish in even less
time, cook frozen broccoli spears according
to the package directions, then follow the recipe
as directed.

Pan-Braised Broccoli Rabe

serves 4

1 bunch broccoli rabe, trimmed
1 tablespoon olive oil
3 garlic cloves, minced
1/4 teaspoon fennel seeds, crushed
2/3 cup reduced-sodium chicken broth
1/2 teaspoon salt

1   Bring large pot of water to boil. Add broccoli rabe and return water to boil; cook until
broccoli rabe is crisp-tender, about 2 minutes.
Drain in colander, then rinse under cold running water; drain again.
2   Heat oil in large nonstick skillet over
medium-high heat. Add garlic and fennel
seeds; cook, stirring, until fragrant, about 1
minute. Add broccoli rabe and cook 1 minute.
Add broth and salt; bring to boil. Reduce heat
and simmer until broccoli rabe is tender, about
3 minutes longer.

PER SERVING (1/4 CUP): 159 grams, 70 Cal, 3 g Total Fat,
1 g Sat Fat, 0 g Trans Fat, 0 mg Chol, 428 mg Sod,
6 g Total Carb, 2 g Total Sugar, 2 g Fib, 5 g Prot,
59 mg Calc.
PointsPlus value: *2*

FYI   Broccoli rabe, also called broccoli raab or
rapini, is a dark leafy green vegetable that
is related to the cabbage family. To tone down its
distinctly bitter flavor, it is usually first blanched
in boiling water, as we have done here.

Roasted Asparagus and Red Peppers

serves 4

1 pound asparagus, trimmed and bottom third
of spears peeled
1 large red bell pepper, cut into thick strips
1 tablespoon lemon juice
2 teaspoons olive oil
½ teaspoon salt
¼ teaspoon red pepper flakes
1 teaspoon grated lemon zest

1   Preheat oven to 400°F. Spray nonstick baking sheet with nonstick spray.
2   Put asparagus and bell pepper in large bowl. Add lemon juice, oil, salt, and pepper flakes; toss to coat evenly. Spread vegetables in single layer on prepared baking sheet. Roast, shaking pan occasionally, until tender, about 15 minutes. Transfer vegetables to serving bowl; sprinkle with lemon zest.

PER SERVING (ABOUT ⅔ CUP): 105 grams, 46 Cal,
3 g Total Fat, 0 g Sat Fat, 0 g Trans Fat, 0 mg Chol,
298 mg Sod, 6 g Total Carb, 2 g Total Sugar, 2 g Fib,
2 g Prot, 16 mg Calc.
PointsPlus value: *1*

FYI   Roasting vegetables is an easy way to maximize flavor without adding a lot of fat: The high heat helps to caramelize the natural sugars in the vegetables, which brings out all their sweetness.

Oven-Roasted Beets and Garlic

serves 4

4 large beets, trimmed, peeled, and quartered
6 garlic cloves, quartered
1 tablespoon minced fresh thyme
2 teaspoons olive oil
½ cup orange juice

1   Preheat oven to 375°F.
2   Toss together beets, garlic, 1½ teaspoons of thyme, and the oil in 9 × 13-inch baking dish. Drizzle with orange juice. Cover baking dish with foil; roast until beets are almost tender when pierced with knife, about 45 minutes. Remove foil and sprinkle beets with remaining 1½ teaspoons thyme; roast until beets are tender, about 10 minutes longer.

PER SERVING (ABOUT ½ CUP): 114 grams, 74 Cal,
3 g Total Fat, 0 g Sat Fat, 0 g Trans Fat, 0 mg Chol,
60 mg Sod, 12 g Total Carb, 8 g Total Sugar, 2 g Fib,
2 g Prot, 26 mg Calc.
PointsPlus value: *2*

FYI   The fresher the beets are, the less time it will take for them to cook until tender.

Red Cabbage with Ginger

serves 4

2 teaspoons olive oil
½ red onion, thinly sliced
2 tablespoons minced peeled fresh ginger
4 cups thinly sliced red cabbage
⅔ cup reduced-sodium chicken broth

Heat oil in large skillet over medium heat. Add onion and ginger; cook, stirring, until fragrant, about 1 minute. Stir in cabbage and broth. Reduce heat and simmer, covered, stirring occasionally, until cabbage is tender, about 20 minutes longer.

PER SERVING (ABOUT ¼ CUP): 129 grams, 49 Cal, 3 g Total Fat, 0 g Sat Fat, 0 g Trans Fat, 0 mg Chol, 112 mg Sod, 6 g Total Carb, 4 g Total Sugar, 2 g Fib, 2 g Prot, 39 mg Calc.
PointsPlus value: *1*

▲ **HEALTHY EXTRA**
Add a very thinly sliced peeled, quartered, and cored Granny Smith apple to the skillet along with the cabbage.

Dilled Carrots

serves 4

4 carrots, sliced
½ teaspoon salt
2 bay leaves
1 (3-inch) cinnamon stick
¼ cup lemon juice
2 tablespoons snipped fresh dill
4 teaspoons olive oil
1 teaspoon sugar
⅛ teaspoon cayenne

1   Combine carrots, salt, bay leaves, and cinnamon stick in large skillet. Add enough water to cover and bring to boil. Reduce heat and simmer until carrots are tender, about 10 minutes. Drain; discard bay leaves and cinnamon stick.
2   Whisk together all remaining ingredients in medium bowl. Add carrots and toss to coat. Let stand until flavors are blended, about 1 hour. Serve at room temperature.

PER SERVING (½ CUP): 100 grams, 83 Cal, 5 g Total Fat, 1 g Sat Fat, 0 g Trans Fat, 0 mg Chol, 331 mg Sod, 10 g Total Carb, 7 g Total Sugar, 2 g Fib, 1 g Prot, 22 mg Calc.
PointsPlus value: *2*

OVEN-ROASTED BRUSSELS
SPROUTS AND CARROTS

Oven-Roasted Brussels Sprouts and Carrots

serves 4

3 carrots, cut lengthwise in half, then on
    diagonal into long slices
2 cups Brussels sprouts, trimmed and halved
1 tablespoon olive oil
¼ teaspoon salt
Pinch black pepper

1   Preheat oven to 425°F.
2   Toss together all ingredients in large shallow baking pan. Spread vegetables in single
layer; roast, stirring every 10 minutes, until
browned and tender, about 40 minutes.

PER SERVING (¼ CUP): 137 grams, 89 Cal, 4 g Total Fat,
1 g Sat Fat, 0 g Trans Fat, 0 mg Chol, 200 mg Sod,
13 g Total Carb, 7 g Total Sugar, 3 g Fib, 2 g Prot,
38 mg Calc.
PointsPlus value: *2*

FYI Remove any wilted outer leaves from the
Brussels sprouts, and when trimming them
be sure to leave the core intact to help hold the
halves together. If the Brussels sprouts are large,
cut them into quarters.

Cauliflower with Curried Tomato Sauce

serves 4

1 teaspoon olive oil
1 onion, finely chopped
2 teaspoons minced peeled fresh ginger
2 teaspoons curry powder
½ teaspoon ground cumin
1 cup tomato puree
½ cup water
1 cauliflower, cut into small florets
1 tablespoon chopped fresh parsley

1   Heat oil in large nonstick skillet over medium heat. Add onion and ginger; cook, stirring, until onion is softened, about 5 minutes.
Stir in curry powder and cumin; cook, stirring,
1 minute.
2   Stir tomato puree and water into onion
mixture. Reduce heat and simmer, covered,
stirring occasionally, 15 minutes. Remove skillet from heat; let cool slightly.
3   Meanwhile, bring ½ inch of water to boil
in large saucepan. Add cauliflower and cook,
covered, until tender, about 5 minutes; drain.
4   Transfer cauliflower to serving bowl; top
with sauce and sprinkle with parsley.

PER SERVING (GENEROUS ½ CUP): 280 grams, 92 Cal,
2 g Total Fat, 0 g Sat Fat, 0 g Trans Fat, 0 mg Chol,
296 mg Sod, 18 g Total Carb, 10 g Total Sugar, 6 g Fib,
5 g Prot, 59 mg Calc.
PointsPlus value: *2*

FYI When you trim the cauliflower, save the
stems for some good eating. Cut the core
and stems into chunks and steam until tender,
about 5 minutes.

Eggplant Parmesan Stacks

serves 4

1 eggplant (about 1¼ pounds), cut into 8
    rounds, about ½ inch thick
½ teaspoon salt
¼ teaspoon black pepper
2 large tomatoes
4 large fresh basil leaves, very thinly sliced
1 teaspoon olive oil
½ teaspoon red wine vinegar
½ cup shredded part-skim mozzarella cheese
2 tablespoons grated Parmesan cheese

1   Preheat oven to 425°F. Spray large baking
sheet with nonstick spray.
2   Place eggplant slices in single layer on prepared baking sheet; sprinkle with ¼ teaspoon
of salt and ⅛ teaspoon of pepper. Roast until
eggplant is tender, about 15 minutes.
3   Reduce oven temperature to 375°F.
4   Cut 1 tomato into 4 slices. Seed and
coarsely chop remaining tomato. Mix chopped
tomato, basil, oil, vinegar, and remaining ¼ teaspoon salt and ⅛ teaspoon pepper in bowl.
5   Top each of 4 largest eggplant slices with
1 tomato slice and 1 tablespoon of mozzarella.
Top each with another eggplant slice, 1 tablespoon of mozzarella, and 1½ teaspoons of Parmesan. Place eggplant stacks on baking sheet.
Bake until heated through, about 20 minutes.
Transfer to 4 plates. Spoon chopped tomato
mixture on top.

PER SERVING (1 EGGPLANT STACK): 253 grams, 118 Cal,
5 g Total Fat, 3 g Sat Fat, 0 g Trans Fat, 10 mg Chol,
445 mg Sod, 14 g Total Carb, 8 g Total Sugar, 5 g Fib,
7 g Prot, 150 mg Calc.
PointsPlus value: *3*

Sweet-and-Sour Grilled Fennel

serves 4

3 large fennel bulbs
2 tablespoons balsamic vinegar
2 tablespoons light brown sugar
½ teaspoon salt
⅛ teaspoon black pepper
Chopped fresh parsley

1   Spray grill rack with nonstick spray. Preheat grill to medium or prepare medium fire
using direct method.
2   Meanwhile, cut fennel bulbs lengthwise
into ½-inch slices. Combine 1 tablespoon
of vinegar, the brown sugar, salt, and pepper
in cup.
3   Spray fennel with nonstick spray. Place
on grill rack and grill until tender and lightly
browned, about 4 minutes per side. Brush with
vinegar mixture; grill 1 minute longer.
4   Transfer fennel to serving bowl; drizzle
with the remaining 1 tablespoon vinegar and
sprinkle with parsley. Serve hot, warm, or at
room temperature.

PER SERVING (¼ OF FENNEL): 192 grams, 86 Cal,
0 g Total Fat, 0 g Sat Fat, 0 g Trans Fat, 0 mg Chol,
387 mg Sod, 21 g Total Carb, 8 g Total Sugar, 6 g Fib,
2 g Prot, 96 mg Calc.
PointsPlus value: *2*

FYI If the fennel bulbs come with their feathery
tops still attached, snip some of them
and use to sprinkle on the finished dish instead of
the parsley.

Lemony Green Beans with Parsley

serves 4

2 teaspoons olive oil
1 pound green beans, trimmed and cut into
    2-inch lengths
2 tablespoons water
1 tablespoon lemon juice
2 tablespoons chopped fresh parsley

Heat oil in large nonstick skillet over medium heat. Add green beans and cook, stirring, until bright green, about 3 minutes. Stir in water and lemon juice. Reduce heat and cook, covered, 2 minutes. Uncover and cook, stirring, until beans are crisp-tender, about 2 minutes longer. Sprinkle with parsley.

PER SERVING (1 CUP): 127 grams, 60 Cal, 3 g Total Fat,
3 g Sat Fat, 0 g Trans Fat, 0 mg Chol, 5 mg Sod,
9 g Total Carb, 2 g Total Sugar, 4 g Fib, 2 g Prot,
54 mg Calc.
PointsPlus value: *2*

FYI You can substitute haricots verts (slender green beans) for the regular green beans, if you like. Be sure to reduce the cooking time by about 2 minutes.

Kale with Balsamic Vinegar

serves 4

4 cups chopped kale (about 1 pound)
2 teaspoons olive oil
6 shallots, finely chopped
$1/4$ cup water
1 tablespoon balsamic vinegar
$1/2$ teaspoon Dijon mustard
$1/8$ teaspoon salt
$1/8$ teaspoon black pepper

1   Bring $1/2$ inch of water to boil in large nonstick skillet. Add kale and cook, covered, until wilted and tender, about 5 minutes. Drain in colander. Wipe skillet dry.
2   Heat oil in same skillet over medium heat. Add shallots and cook, stirring, until softened, about 5 minutes. Add water, vinegar, and mustard; bring to boil. Cook, stirring constantly, 1 minute. Return kale to skillet and sprinkle with salt and pepper; cook, stirring, until heated through, about 2 minutes.

PER SERVING (SCANT 1 CUP): 122 grams, 65 Cal,
3 g Total Fat, 0 g Sat Fat, 0 g Trans Fat, 0 mg Chol,
110 mg Sod, 10 g Total Carb, 2 g Total Sugar, 2 g Fib,
2 g Prot, 64 mg Calc.
PointsPlus value: *2*

FYI Kale, a member of the cabbage family, is available year-round but is at its best during the colder months. Choose bunches that are deeply colored without any yellowing or wilting. Kale can be stored in a plastic bag in the crisper drawer of your refrigerator for up to 3 to 4 days. If you can't find kale in your supermarket, substitute mustard greens or collard greens.

Wild Mushrooms with Fresh Thyme

serves 4

1 tablespoon olive oil
1 shallot, minced
1 large garlic clove, minced
¼ pound mixed mushrooms, such as white,
    cremini, and oyster, thickly sliced
¼ teaspoon salt
1 teaspoon reduced-sodium soy sauce
1 teaspoon fresh thyme leaves
Pinch black pepper
1 tablespoon chopped fresh flat-leaf parsley

1   Heat oil in large nonstick skillet over medium heat. Add shallot and cook, stirring frequently, until softened, about 3 minutes. Add garlic and cook, stirring constantly, until fragrant, about 1 minute.

2   Add mushrooms and salt to skillet; cook, stirring frequently, until mushrooms release their liquid, about 7 minutes. Stir in soy sauce, thyme, and pepper; cook, stirring occasionally, until pan liquid is almost evaporated, about 3 minutes. Stir in parsley.

PER SERVING (½ CUP): 97 grams, 57 Cal, 4 g Total Fat, 1 g Sat Fat, 0 g Trans Fat, 0 mg Chol, 200 mg Sod, 5 g Total Carb, 1 g Total Sugar, 1 g Fib, 3 g Prot, 10 mg Calc.
PointsPlus value: *2*

FYI Cooking mushrooms until they release their liquid and it evaporates greatly intensifies their earthy flavor. Allowing the edges of the mushroom to brown slightly makes them even tastier.

Creole-Style Okra

serves 6

2 teaspoons olive oil
1 onion, finely chopped
1 celery stalk, finely chopped
4½ cups fresh okra, trimmed, or thawed
    frozen whole okra
1 (14½-ounce) can crushed tomatoes
¼ cup water
2 slices turkey bacon, crisp cooked and
    crumbled
⅛ teaspoon cayenne
⅛ teaspoon black pepper
1 bay leaf
⅛ teaspoon filé powder

1   Heat oil in large nonstick skillet over medium heat. Add onion and celery; cook, stirring, until onion is golden, about 8 minutes.

2   Add okra, tomatoes, water, bacon, cayenne, pepper, and bay leaf to skillet; bring to boil. Reduce heat and simmer, covered, until okra is just tender, about 10 minutes. Remove skillet from heat and discard bay leaf; stir in filé powder.

PER SERVING (1 CUP): 193 grams, 88 Cal, 3 g Total Fat, 1 g Sat Fat, 0 g Trans Fat, 4 mg Chol, 284 mg Sod, 14 g Total Carb, 6 g Total Sugar, 3 g Fib, 4 g Prot, 63 mg Calc.
PointsPlus value: *2*

FYI Filé powder is made from dried sassafras leaves. It is used to flavor and thicken Creole and Cajun dishes. Always stir it in after you have removed the pot from the heat, since filé powder becomes tough and stringy if overheated.

Ratatouille Casserole

serves 6

1 small eggplant, peeled, quartered lengthwise,
    and sliced
2 zucchini, sliced
3 teaspoons olive oil
1 red bell pepper, cut into thin strips
1 onion, very thinly sliced
3 garlic cloves, very thinly sliced
½ cup water
¼ cup tomato paste
2 tablespoons chopped fresh parsley
2 tablespoons chopped fresh basil
2 teaspoons chopped fresh thyme
¼ teaspoon salt
¼ teaspoon black pepper
1 tomato, thinly sliced

1   Place racks in upper and lower thirds of
oven. Preheat oven to 400°F. Spray 2 large nonstick baking sheets and 1-quart baking dish or
casserole dish with nonstick spray.
2   Place eggplant and zucchini in single layer
on prepared baking sheets; brush with 2 teaspoons of oil. Roast 12 minutes; turn vegetables
and roast until tender, about 8 minutes longer.
3   Reduce oven temperature to 350°F. Heat
remaining 1 teaspoon oil in large nonstick skillet over medium heat. Add bell pepper, onion,
and garlic; cook, stirring, until softened, about
5 minutes. Cook, covered, shaking skillet occasionally, 5 minutes longer.
4   Whisk together water, tomato paste,
parsley, basil, thyme, salt, and black pepper in
small bowl. Toss roasted vegetables, bell pepper mixture, and tomato paste mixture in prepared baking dish; spread to form even layer.
Top with tomato slices. Cover baking dish with
foil. Bake until vegetables are tender, about
50 minutes. Uncover and bake until lightly
browned on top, about 15 minutes longer.

PER SERVING (⅙ OF RATATOUILLE): 193 grams, 73 Cal,
3 g Total Fat, 0 g Sat Fat, 0 g Trans Fat, 0 mg Chol,
110 mg Sod, 12 g Total Carb, 6 g Total Sugar, 3 g Fib,
3 g Prot, 29 mg Calc.
PointsPlus value: *2*

FYI   Ratatouille originated in the south of
France in the region of Provence. It
classically contains eggplant, tomatoes, onion, bell
peppers, zucchini, and fresh herbs. Ratatouille
makes an excellent side dish for chicken, lamb,
or fish and is often served as an appetizer
accompanied by bread toasts. It can be served hot,
warm, or at room temperature.

Cherry Tomatoes with Thyme

serves 4

1 teaspoon olive oil
1 pint red cherry tomatoes
1 pint yellow cherry tomatoes
1 tablespoon fresh thyme leaves
¼ teaspoon salt
⅛ teaspoon black pepper
2 tablespoons chopped fresh parsley

1   Heat oil in large nonstick skillet over medium heat.
2   Add cherry tomatoes, thyme, salt, and pepper to skillet. Cook, shaking skillet occasionally, until tomatoes are blistered and shiny, about 5 minutes. Sprinkle with parsley.

PER SERVING (ABOUT 1 CUP): 149 grams, 38 Cal, 2 g Total Fat, 0 g Sat Fat, 0 g Trans Fat, 0 mg Chol, 170 mg Sod, 6 g Total Carb, 3 g Total Sugar, 2 g Fib, 1 g Prot, 17 mg Calc.
PointsPlus value: *1*

▲ **HEALTHY EXTRA**
Cut the cherry tomatoes in half and cook until softened, then serve over broiled or grilled chicken breasts. A 3-ounce portion of cooked skinless, boneless chicken breast per serving will increase the *PointsPlus* value by *3*.

Provençal-Style Stuffed Tomatoes

serves 4

⅓ cup whole wheat panko (Japanese bread crumbs)
3 tablespoons chopped fresh parsley
2 tablespoons grated Parmesan cheese
2 teaspoons herbes de Provence
1 garlic clove, minced
¼ teaspoon salt
4 assorted color tomatoes, cut crosswise in half

1   Preheat oven to 425°F. Spray large baking dish with olive oil nonstick spray.
2   Stir together all ingredients except tomatoes in small bowl.
3   Place tomato halves, cut side up, in prepared baking dish. Top each tomato half with heaping tablespoon of crumb mixture; lightly spray with nonstick spray. Bake until tomatoes are soft and topping is browned, about 30 minutes.

PER SERVING (2 TOMATO HALVES): 163 grams, 70 Cal, 3 g Total Fat, 1 g Sat Fat, 0 g Trans Fat, 2 mg Chol, 215 mg Sod, 13 g Total Carb, 6 g Total Sugar, 3 g Fib, 4 g Prot, 62 mg Calc.
PointsPlus value: *2*

 In place of the herbes de Provence, you can substitute 1 teaspoon dried thyme, 1 teaspoon dried basil, and ¼ teaspoon fennel seeds, crushed.

Roasted Peppers with Orange Zest and Olives

serves 4

4 large bell peppers, quartered lengthwise and
    seeded
1 tablespoon olive oil
3 large garlic cloves, thinly sliced
2 tablespoons red wine vinegar
12 pitted brine-cured olives, halved
1 tablespoon capers, drained and rinsed
Grated zest of ½ navel orange
½ teaspoon dried oregano

1   Spray grill rack with nonstick spray. Preheat grill to medium or prepare medium fire
using direct method.
2   Place bell peppers on grill rack and grill
until peppers are softened and skins are blackened, about 6 minutes per side. Put peppers
in large zip-close plastic bag and seal bag; let
steam 10 minutes.
3   Meanwhile, put oil and garlic in small
skillet and set over low heat. Cook, stirring
frequently, until garlic softens and turns golden
brown along edges, about 5 minutes; remove
skillet from heat.
4   When cool enough to handle, peel peppers
and pile on platter. Add vinegar, olives, capers,
orange zest, and oregano to garlic in skillet,
stirring to combine; spoon over peppers. Let
stand at least 15 minutes or up to 1 hour to
allow flavors to develop. Peppers can be refrigerated in covered container up to 2 days.

PER SERVING (4 PIECES OF PEPPER): 194 grams,
106 Cal, 6 g Total Fat, 1 g Sat Fat, 0 g Trans Fat,
0 mg Chol, 177 mg Sod, 13 g Total Carb, 4 g Total Sugar,
4 g Fib, 2 g Prot, 24 mg Calc.
PointsPlus value: *3*

Classic Roasted Vegetables

serves 4

2 red bell peppers, quartered lengthwise and
    seeded
1 zucchini, sliced on diagonal
1 yellow squash, sliced on diagonal
1 Vidalia or other sweet onion, root end left
    intact, cut into 8 wedges
1 pound jumbo asparagus, trimmed and cut
    into 2-inch lengths
3 garlic cloves, minced
4 teaspoons extra-virgin olive oil
1 teaspoon balsamic vinegar
½ teaspoon dried basil
¼ teaspoon salt
¼ teaspoon black pepper

1   Place racks in upper and lower thirds of
oven. Preheat oven to 450°F. Spray 2 baking
sheets with nonstick spray.
2   Cut each piece of bell pepper on diagonal
to form 2 triangles. Toss together bell peppers
and all remaining ingredients in large bowl. Divide between prepared baking sheets.
3   Roast vegetables, tossing occasionally, until
tender and lightly browned, about 30 minutes.
Serve hot, warm, or at room temperature.

PER SERVING (ABOUT 1 CUP): 260 grams, 106 Cal,
5 g Total Fat, 1 g Sat Fat, 0 g Trans Fat, 0 mg Chol,
448 mg Sod, 14 g Total Carb, 7 g Total Sugar, 5 g Fib,
4 g Prot, 53 mg Calc.
PointsPlus value: *3*

▲ HEALTHY EXTRA

Serve the roasted vegetables over a bed of cooked
whole wheat pasta for a flavor-packed vegetarian
meal (1 cup of cooked whole wheat penne with each
serving will increase the *PointsPlus* value by *4*).

Skillet Summer Squash

serves 4

2 teaspoons olive oil
3 yellow squash, sliced
½ teaspoon grated lemon zest
1 tablespoon lemon juice
1 teaspoon minced fresh thyme
¼ teaspoon salt
⅛ teaspoon black pepper

Heat oil in large nonstick skillet over medium heat. Add squash and cook, stirring occasionally, until golden brown, about 5 minutes. Stir in all remaining ingredients and cook, stirring occasionally, until heated through, about 3 minutes longer.

PER SERVING (ABOUT ¼ CUP): 154 grams, 51 Cal, 3 g Total Fat, 0 g Sat Fat, 0 g Trans Fat, 0 mg Chol, 148 mg Sod, 7 g Total Carb, 3 g Total Sugar, 3 g Fib, 2 g Prot, 31 mg Calc.
PointsPlus value: *1*

"Creamed" Spinach

serves 4

2 (10-ounce) bags spinach
⅔ cup low-fat (1%) cottage cheese
¼ cup low-fat (1%) milk
1 tablespoon grated Parmesan cheese
½ garlic clove, minced
⅛ teaspoon black pepper

1   Put spinach in steamer basket; set in large pot containing 1 inch boiling water. Cook, covered, until spinach is bright green and wilted, about 3 minutes. Lift out steamer basket. Let spinach cool about 5 minutes; squeeze to remove any excess liquid. Chop spinach.

2   Combine all remaining ingredients in food processor or blender and puree. Add one-fourth of spinach and puree.

3   Combine remaining spinach with cottage cheese mixture in large nonstick skillet and set over medium heat. Cook, stirring occasionally, until heated through, about 5 minutes.

PER SERVING (ABOUT ¼ CUP): 182 grams, 92 Cal, 1 g Total Fat, 1 g Sat Fat, 0 g Trans Fat, 3 mg Chol, 404 mg Sod, 16 g Total Carb, 1 g Total Sugar, 7 g Fib, 9 g Prot, 142 mg Calc.
PointsPlus value: *2*

Spicy Stir-Fried Sesame Spinach

serves 4

2 (10-ounce) bags spinach
2 teaspoons Asian (dark) sesame oil
1 large garlic clove, minced
1 teaspoon grated peeled fresh ginger
¼ teaspoon red pepper flakes
1 tablespoon reduced-sodium soy sauce
1 teaspoon sugar
1 teaspoon sesame seeds

1   Put spinach in steamer basket; set in large pot containing 1 inch boiling water. Cook, covered, until spinach is bright green and wilted, about 3 minutes. Lift out steamer basket. Let spinach cool about 5 minutes; squeeze to remove any excess liquid.
2   Heat sesame oil in large nonstick skillet over medium-high heat. Add garlic, ginger, and pepper flakes; stir-fry until fragrant, about 30 seconds. Add spinach and stir-fry 1 minute. Stir in soy sauce and sugar; stir-fry until heated through, 1 minute. Sprinkle with sesame seeds.

PER SERVING (⅓ CUP): 152 grams, 91 Cal, 3 g Total Fat, 0 g Sat Fat, 0 g Trans Fat, 0 mg Chol, 378 mg Sod, 17 g Total Carb, 1 g Total Sugar, 7 g Fib, 4 g Prot, 103 mg Calc.
PointsPlus value: *2*

FYI   To save time, use two 10-ounce packages thawed frozen spinach in place of the fresh. Just be sure to squeeze out the excess liquid before cooking.

Spaghetti Squash Primavera

serves 4

1 (2-pound) spaghetti squash
2 teaspoons olive oil
2 scallions, thinly sliced
2 garlic cloves, minced
½ cup reduced-sodium chicken broth
½ teaspoon dried marjoram
½ teaspoon grated lemon zest
¼ teaspoon salt
12 asparagus spears, trimmed and cut into
     2-inch lengths
1 cup frozen green peas, thawed
2 teaspoons lemon juice

1   Preheat oven to 350°F.
2   Cut squash lengthwise in half; scoop out seeds and discard. Place, cut side down, in 7 × 11-inch baking dish. Add enough water to come ½ inch up sides of squash. Cover baking dish with foil; bake until squash is tender, about 45 minutes. Transfer to cutting board; let stand until cool enough to handle. With fork, scoop pulp out into medium bowl.
3   Heat oil in large nonstick skillet over medium heat. Add scallions and garlic; cook, stirring, until fragrant, about 1 minute. Add broth, marjoram, lemon zest, and salt; bring to boil, then add asparagus and peas. Reduce heat and simmer, covered, 2 minutes. Stir in squash and lemon juice; cook, stirring, until heated through, about 3 minutes.

PER SERVING (¼ OF SPAGHETTI SQUASH MIXTURE): 282 grams, 114 Cal, 3 g Total Fat, 1 g Sat Fat, 0 g Trans Fat, 0 mg Chol, 286 mg Sod, 19 g Total Carb, 3 g Total Sugar, 5 g Fib, 5 g Prot, 63 mg Calc.
PointsPlus value: *3*

Maple and Butter–Glazed Acorn Squash Wedges

serves 6

1 acorn squash (about 2½ pounds)
⅓ cup pure maple syrup
1 tablespoon butter, melted
Pinch cayenne

1   Preheat oven to 400°F. Spray large baking pan with olive oil nonstick spray.
2   Slice acorn squash lengthwise in half; scoop out seeds and discard. Place squash, cut side down, on cutting board. Cut each half lengthwise in half, then cut each piece lengthwise into thirds, making total of 12 wedges.
3   Place squash wedges, cut side down, in prepared baking pan. Roast 15 minutes.
4   Meanwhile, stir together all remaining ingredients in small bowl. Turn squash over; brush with glaze. Roast 10 minutes, then brush with remaining glaze. Roast squash until tender, about 10 minutes longer.

PER SERVING (2 SQUASH WEDGES): 149 grams, 135 Cal, 2 g Total Fat, 1 g Sat Fat, 0 g Trans Fat, 5 mg Chol, 7 mg Sod, 31 g Total Carb, 16 g Total Sugar, 6 g Fib, 1 g Prot, 69 mg Calc.
PointsPlus value: *3*

Summertime Succotash

serves 4

1 cup frozen lima beans
4 teaspoons olive oil
1 green bell pepper, diced
1 zucchini, diced
½ red onion, chopped
1 garlic clove, minced
2 large plum tomatoes, chopped
1 cup fresh or thawed frozen corn kernels
½ teaspoon salt
¼ teaspoon black pepper
2 tablespoons chopped fresh basil
2 tablespoons chopped fresh cilantro

1   Cook lima beans according to package directions; drain.
2   Heat oil in medium nonstick skillet over medium heat. Add bell pepper, zucchini, onion, and garlic; cook, stirring, until bell pepper and zucchini are tender, about 8 minutes. Add tomatoes and cook, stirring, 2 minutes.
3   Add beans, corn, salt, and black pepper to zucchini mixture. Reduce heat and simmer, covered, until flavors are blended, about 10 minutes. Stir in basil and cilantro.

PER SERVING (GENEROUS 1 CUP): 209 grams, 139 Cal, 5 g Total Fat, 1 g Sat Fat, 0 g Trans Fat, 0 mg Chol, 308 mg Sod, 21 g Total Carb, 5 g Total Sugar, 5 g Fib, 5 g Prot, 31 mg Calc.
PointsPlus value: *4*

 HEALTHY EXTRA
Use 4 plum tomatoes instead of 2.

Swiss Chard au Gratin

serves 4

2 cups sliced Swiss chard stalks
4 1/2 cups lightly packed thinly sliced Swiss
    chard leaves
1/3 cup shredded reduced-fat Jarlsberg cheese
1 tablespoon grated Parmesan cheese
1 garlic clove, minced
1/4 teaspoon black pepper

1   Place rack in upper third of oven. Preheat
oven to 400°F. Spray 1-quart baking dish or
casserole dish with nonstick spray.
2   Bring large saucepan of water to boil; add
Swiss chard stalks. Cook 5 minutes; add Swiss
chard leaves and cook until tender, about 3
minutes longer; drain.
3   Place half of chard stalks and leaves in prepared baking dish; top with half of Jarlsberg,
Parmesan, garlic, and pepper. Repeat layers
once. Bake until cheese is melted and bubbling,
about 20 minutes.

PER SERVING (ABOUT 1 CUP): 65 grams, 35 Cal,
1 g Total Fat, 1 g Sat Fat, 0 g Trans Fat, 1 mg Chol,
152 mg Sod, 3 g Total Carb, 0 g Total Sugar, 1 g Fib,
4 g Prot, 117 mg Calc.
PointsPlus value: **1**

FYI   Swiss chard is widely available from spring
through fall and, like spinach, it freezes
well. Here's how to prepare it: Drop the cleaned
leaves into boiling water for about 2 minutes, then
chill in ice water. Drain the leaves, put into an
airtight container, and freeze.

Mixed Pickled Vegetables

serves 24

2 cups cider vinegar
1 cup water
1/4 cup sugar
2 tablespoons mustard seeds
2 teaspoons turmeric
1 teaspoon salt
1/2 teaspoon red pepper flakes
1 (1-pound) bag baby-cut carrots
1 small cauliflower, cut into small florets
1/2 pound green beans, trimmed and halved
2 cups fresh corn kernels
1 onion, chopped

1   Combine vinegar, water, sugar, mustard
seeds, turmeric, salt, and pepper flakes in
Dutch oven and bring to boil. Add carrots and
return to boil. Reduce heat and simmer, covered, 5 minutes.
2   Add cauliflower, green beans, corn, and
onion to Dutch oven; return to boil. Reduce
heat and simmer, covered, until vegetables are
crisp-tender, about 8 minutes.
3   Pack hot vegetable mixture into hot steril-
ized ball jars to within 1/4 inch of tops. Wipe jar
rims and threads clean; cover quickly with lids
and screw bands on securely but not too tightly.
Immerse jars in deep kettle with enough boiling
water to cover jars by 1 inch. Cover and simmer 15 minutes. Carefully lift jars from water
and let cool completely. Store in cool, dark
place up to 6 months.

PER SERVING (2/3 CUP): 69 grams, 37 Cal, 0 g Total Fat,
0 g Sat Fat, 0 g Trans Fat, 0 mg Chol, 111 mg Sod,
9 g Total Carb, 4 g Total Sugar, 2 g Fib, 1 g Prot,
15 mg Calc.
PointsPlus value: **1**

11

Grain and Bean Sides

Grain and Bean Sides

284 Tomato Rice with Chiles and Corn
284 Herbed Brown Rice
285 Five-Vegetable Fried Rice
285 Curried Basmati Rice
286 Venetian-Style Rice and Peas
286 Brown and Wild Rice with Walnuts and Cranberries
287 Sausage and Rice Dressing
288 Wild Rice and Mushroom Dressing
288 Risotto Milanese
290 Cornbread, Apricot, and Cranberry Dressing
292 Noodles with Spicy Peanut Sauce
292 Orzo with Grilled Eggplant and Tomato
293 Broccoli with Pasta and White Beans
293 Couscous with Lime and Scallion
295 Barley, Leek, and Rosemary Gratin
296 Spinach, Mushroom, and Bulgur Pilaf
296 Kasha Varnishkes
297 Cremini Mushrooms with Quinoa and Thyme
297 Creamy Blue Cheese Polenta
298 Lentils with Spiced Vegetables
298 Baked Beans
299 Smoky Black Beans
299 Cuban-Style Rice and Beans
300 New Orleans Red Beans and Rice
300 Summery Pasta with Chickpeas and Tomatoes
302 Chickpeas and Chunky Vegetables
302 Skillet Asparagus with Pinto Beans and Tomatoes

Tomato Rice with Chiles and Corn

serves 8

1 tablespoon olive oil
1 onion, chopped
1 cup white rice
2 garlic cloves, minced
2 teaspoons chili powder
1 (14½-ounce) can reduced-sodium chicken
    broth or 1¾ cups Basic Chicken Stock
    (page 106)
½ cup water
1 carrot, diced
1 celery stalk, diced
¼ teaspoon salt
1 (14½-ounce) can diced tomatoes with
    jalapeños, drained
⅔ cup frozen corn kernels

1   Heat oil in medium saucepan over
medium-high heat. Add onion and cook,
stirring, until softened, about 5 minutes. Add
rice and cook, stirring, until golden, about 4
minutes. Add garlic and chili powder; cook, stirring frequently, until fragrant, about 30 seconds.
2   Stir broth, water, carrot, celery, and salt
into rice mixture. Reduce heat and simmer,
covered, 15 minutes. Stir in tomatoes and
corn; return to simmer. Cook, covered, until
rice is tender and liquid is absorbed, about 10
minutes. Fluff with fork before serving.

PER SERVING (¾ CUP): 243 grams, 149 Cal,
2 g Total Fat, 0 g Sat Fat, 0 g Trans Fat, 0 mg Chol,
467 mg Sod, 29 g Total Carb, 4 g Total Sugar, 2 g Fib,
4 g Prot, 38 mg Calc.
PointsPlus value: *4*

HEALTHY EXTRA
Stir 2 cups of sliced white or cremini mushrooms
into the rice mixture along with the carrots in step 2.

Herbed Brown Rice

serves 6

2 tablespoons olive oil
1 onion, chopped
3 garlic cloves, minced
1 red bell pepper, finely chopped
1 celery stalk, finely chopped
1 cup instant brown rice
1½ cups water
½ teaspoon salt
½ cup chopped fresh flat-leaf parsley

1   Heat oil in large nonstick saucepan over
medium heat. Add onion and garlic; cook,
stirring, just until garlic is golden, about 3 minutes. Add bell pepper and celery; cook, stirring,
until crisp-tender, about 3 minutes.
2   Stir in rice, water, and salt; bring to boil.
Reduce heat and simmer, covered, 5 minutes.
Remove saucepan from heat; stir in parsley. Let
stand 5 minutes before serving.

PER SERVING (GENEROUS ½ CUP): 140 grams, 118 Cal,
5 g Total Fat, 1 g Sat Fat, 0 g Trans Fat, 0 mg Chol,
212 mg Sod, 16 g Total Carb, 2 g Total Sugar, 2 g Fib,
2 g Prot, 21 mg Calc.
PointsPlus value: *3*

FYI   This easy and flavorful rice dish makes
an excellent side to many poultry, meat,
and seafood dishes, as well as making a delicious
stuffing for chicken or Cornish hens.

Five-Vegetable Fried Rice

serves 6

1 cup thinly sliced baby-cut carrots
1 small red bell pepper, cut into thin strips
12 scallions, thinly sliced
8 shiitake mushrooms, stemmed and caps
    sliced
1 cup bean sprouts
3 large eggs, lightly beaten
3 cups hot cooked brown rice
2 tablespoon reduced-sodium soy sauce
2 teaspoons Asian (dark) sesame oil
1/4 teaspoon black pepper

1   Spray nonstick wok or deep large nonstick skillet with nonstick spray and set over
high heat until drop of water sizzles in pan.
Add carrots, bell pepper, scallions, mushrooms, and bean sprouts; stir-fry until carrots
are crisp-tender, about 3 minutes. Transfer to
medium bowl.

2   Spray wok with nonstick spray. Add eggs
and cook, stirring to break up eggs, until set,
about 2 minutes. Return vegetables to wok
along with all remaining ingredients. Stir-fry
until heated through, about 2 minutes longer.

PER SERVING (ABOUT 1 CUP): 222 grams, 198 Cal,
5 g Total Fat, 1 g Sat Fat, 0 g Trans Fat, 106 mg Chol,
53 mg Sod, 32 g Total Carb, 3 g Total Sugar, 4 g Fib,
7 g Prot, 49 mg Calc.
PointsPlus value: *5*

▲ HEALTHY EXTRA
Double the amount of shiitake mushrooms.

Curried Basmati Rice

serves 6

8 cremini or white mushrooms, sliced
2 onions, chopped
1/2 red bell pepper, chopped
1/2 green bell pepper, chopped
1 cup basmati rice
1 1/2 teaspoons curry powder
1/4 teaspoon salt
1 1/2 cups water

1   Spray large nonstick saucepan with nonstick spray and set over medium heat. Add
mushrooms, onions, and bell peppers; cook,
stirring, until softened, about 5 minutes.

2   Stir all remaining ingredients into vegetable mixture; bring to boil. Reduce heat and
simmer, covered, until rice is tender and liquid
is absorbed, about 20 minutes.

PER SERVING (ABOUT 1 CUP): 189 grams, 153 Cal,
0 g Total Fat, 0 g Sat Fat, 0 g Trans Fat, 0 mg Chol,
102 mg Sod, 33 g Total Carb, 4 g Total Sugar, 3 g Fib,
4 g Prot, 31 mg Calc.
PointsPlus value: *4*

FYI   Basmati rice is considered a luxury food
in India and Pakistan, where it was first
cultivated. The word *basmati*, which means
"queen of fragrance," is an apt name for this
very aromatic rice.

Venetian-Style Rice and Peas

serves 8

2 (14½-ounce) cans reduced-sodium chicken
    broth or 3½ cups Basic Chicken Stock
    (page 106)
1¼ cups water
2 teaspoons unsalted butter
2 teaspoons olive oil
2 celery stalks, finely chopped
1 small onion, finely chopped
1 cup Arborio rice
2 cups fresh green peas (about 1½ pounds
    unshelled) or thawed frozen green peas
½ cup grated Parmesan cheese
2 tablespoons chopped fresh flat-leaf parsley

1   Combine broth and water in medium
saucepan and bring to simmer over medium
heat; keep at gentle simmer.
2   Melt butter with oil in large nonstick skillet over medium heat. Add celery and onion;
cook, stirring, until onion is golden, about 8
minutes. Add rice and cook, stirring, until
coated, about 1 minute.
3   Add 1 cup of simmering broth to rice, stirring until absorbed. Continue to add broth, ½
cup at a time, stirring until broth is absorbed
before adding more, until rice is tender but still
chewy in center, adding peas after 10 minutes
of cooking time. Stir in Parmesan and parsley.
Serve at once.

PER SERVING (½ CUP): 229 grams, 183 Cal,
4 g Total Fat, 2 g Sat Fat, 0 g Trans Fat, 7 mg Chol,
381 mg Sod, 29 g Total Carb, 3 g Total Sugar, 3 g Fib,
8 g Prot, 88 mg Calc.
PointsPlus value: *5*

FYI This classic dish—also known as *risi e
bisi*—is a close relative of risotto but with
a soupier texture. It is comfort food par excellence
and a great way to enjoy freshly shelled garden
peas or sugar snap peas. Be sure to use only
short-grain Italian rice varieties, such as Arborio or
Carnaroli, which release their starch as they cook,
giving this dish its classic creamy texture.

Brown and Wild Rice with Walnuts and Cranberries

serves 8

2 teaspoons canola oil
6 shallots, chopped (about ½ cup)
2 garlic cloves, minced
½ cup brown rice
½ cup wild rice
3 cups reduced-sodium vegetable broth or
    Basic Vegetable Stock (page 107)
⅛ teaspoon salt
⅛ teaspoon red pepper flakes
⅔ cup dried cranberries
⅓ cup chopped walnuts
¼ cup chopped fresh parsley
Grated zest of ½ navel orange

1   Heat oil in large saucepan over medium
heat. Add shallots and garlic; cook, stirring,
until softened, about 3 minutes. Add brown
rice and wild rice; cook, stirring, until lightly
toasted and fragrant, about 3 minutes.

2   Add broth, salt, and pepper flakes to rice; bring to boil. Reduce heat and simmer, covered, until rice is almost tender, about 30 minutes. Add cranberries and cook until rice is tender but slightly chewy, about 10 minutes longer. Transfer to serving bowl; stir in walnuts, parsley, and orange zest.

PER SERVING (½ CUP): 198 grams, 177 Cal, 5 g Total Fat, 1 g Sat Fat, 0 g Trans Fat, 0 mg Chol, 215 mg Sod, 31 g Total Carb, 9 g Total Sugar, 3 g Fib, 4 g Prot, 26 mg Calc.
PointsPlus value: **5**

FYI   Brown rice and wild rice are well suited for cooking together, as they each take about 40 minutes to become tender. Dried cranberries, a touch of orange zest, fresh parsley, and walnuts add flavor, color, and crunch to this perfect-for-Thanksgiving side dish.

Sausage and Rice Dressing
serves 8

¹⁄₄ *pound sweet Italian-Style turkey sausages, casings removed*
1 *tablespoon butter*
2 *celery stalks, chopped*
1 *onion, chopped*
¹⁄₂ *cup chopped fennel*
2 *garlic cloves, minced*
3 *cups cooked brown rice*
¹⁄₄ *cup reduced-sodium chicken broth*
2 *tablespoons chopped fresh sage*
1 *tablespoon grated lemon zest*
¹⁄₂ *teaspoon salt*
¹⁄₄ *teaspoon black pepper*

1   Preheat oven to 325°F. Spray 2-quart baking dish or casserole dish with nonstick spray.
2   Put sausage in large nonstick skillet and set over medium heat. Cook, breaking it apart with wooden spoon, until browned, about 5 minutes. With slotted spoon, transfer sausage to plate.
3   Add butter to skillet. When melted, add celery, onion, fennel, and garlic. Cook, stirring, until softened, about 5 minutes. Return sausage to skillet along with all remaining ingredients. Reduce heat to low and cook until broth is absorbed, about 5 minutes.
4   Transfer rice mixture to prepared baking dish. Bake until heated through and golden, about 45 minutes.

PER SERVING (ABOUT ²⁄₃ CUP): 131 grams, 132 Cal, 4 g Total Fat, 2 g Sat Fat, 0 g Trans Fat, 10 mg Chol, 251 mg Sod, 20 g Total Carb, 2 g Total Sugar, 2 g Fib, 4 g Prot, 27 mg Calc.
PointsPlus value: **3**

▲ **HEALTHY EXTRA**
Serve this robust dressing along with your Thanksgiving turkey. Two 2-ounce slices of skinless roasted turkey breast with each serving will increase the *PointsPlus* value by **4**.

Wild Rice and Mushroom Dressing

serves 8

1 cup reduced-sodium chicken broth or
    Basic Chicken Stock (page 106)
1 cup water
²/₃ cup wild rice
1 tablespoon olive oil
2 cups thinly sliced shiitake mushroom caps
1 red bell pepper, cut into thin strips
1 celery stalk, chopped
6 shallots, chopped
1 teaspoon dried thyme
¹/₂ teaspoon salt
¹/₄ teaspoon black pepper
¹/₄ cup dry white wine or dry vermouth
1 cup lightly packed chopped spinach

1   Combine broth and water in small saucepan and bring to boil; stir in rice. Reduce heat and simmer, covered, until liquid is absorbed, about 40 minutes. Remove from heat.
2   Preheat oven to 325°F. Spray 2-quart baking dish or casserole dish with nonstick spray.
3   Heat oil in large nonstick skillet over medium heat. Add mushrooms, bell pepper, celery, shallots, thyme, salt, and black pepper; cook, stirring, until vegtables are softened, about 5 minutes; add wine. Reduce heat and simmer until wine is almost absorbed, about 3 minutes. Remove skillet from heat; stir in spinach and rice. Spoon dressing into prepared baking dish. Bake until heated through, about 40 minutes.

PER SERVING (¹/₈ OF DRESSING): 191 grams, 109 Cal, 2 g Total Fat, 0 g Sat Fat, 0 g Trans Fat, 0 mg Chol, 240 mg Sod, 21 g Total Carb, 2 g Total Sugar, 3 g Fib, 4 g Prot, 19 mg Calc.
PointsPlus value: *3*

Risotto Milanese

serves 8

3¹/₂ cups reduced-sodium chicken broth or
    Basic Chicken Stock (page 106)
Pinch saffron threads
1 tablespoon olive oil
1 onion, chopped
1 cup Arborio rice
¹/₂ cup dry white wine
2 tablespoons grated Parmesan cheese
2 teaspoons butter
2 teaspoons grated lemon zest
¹/₈ teaspoon black pepper
Chopped fresh parsley

1   Bring broth to simmer in small saucepan over medium heat; stir in saffron. Keep at gentle simmer.
2   Heat oil in large nonstick saucepan over medium heat. Add onion and cook, stirring, until softened, about 5 minutes. Add rice and cook, stirring, until coated with oil, about 1 minute. Add wine and cook, stirring, until almost absorbed.
3   Add simmering broth to rice, ¹/₂ cup at a time, stirring until broth is absorbed before adding more and cooking until rice is tender but still chewy in center. Stir in 1 tablespoon of Parmesan, the butter, lemon zest, and pepper. Serve sprinkled with remaining 1 tablespoon Parmesan and the parsley.

PER SERVING (¹/₂ CUP): 157 grams, 146 Cal, 4 g Total Fat, 1 g Sat Fat, 0 g Trans Fat, 4 mg Chol, 297 mg Sod, 24 g Total Carb, 2 g Total Sugar, 1 g Fib, 5 g Prot, 24 mg Calc.
PointsPlus value: *4*

FYI   Saffron and lemon zest give this risotto its regal quality and lovely hue. Risotto Milanese is traditionally paired with osso buco (braised veal shanks).

RISOTTO MILANESE

Cornbread, Apricot, and Cranberry Dressing

serves 12

¹/₂ cup + 2 tablespoons yellow cornmeal
¹/₂ cup + 1 tablespoon all-purpose flour
1 tablespoon sugar
¹/₂ teaspoon baking powder
¹/₂ teaspoon baking soda
¹/₄ teaspoon salt
3 scallions, thinly sliced
2 tablespoons snipped fresh dill
3 large egg whites
¹/₂ cup fat-free milk
2 tablespoons canola oil
1 cup apple juice
¹/₂ cup chopped dried apricots
¹/₄ cup dried cranberries
1 (3-inch) cinnamon stick
4 slices day-old whole wheat bread, cut into
    ¹/₂-inch cubes

1 Preheat oven to 425°F. Spray 8-inch square baking pan with nonstick spray.

2 To make cornbread, whisk together cornmeal, flour, sugar, baking powder, baking soda, and salt in large bowl. Stir in scallions and dill. Beat 2 egg whites, the milk, and oil in small bowl. Add milk mixture to cornmeal mixture, stirring just until cornmeal mixture is moistened.

3 Scrape batter into prepared baking dish and spread evenly. Bake until edges are golden and toothpick inserted into center of cornbread comes out clean, 12–15 minutes. Let cool in pan on wire rack 10 minutes. Remove cornbread from pan and let cool completely on rack.

4 Meanwhile, combine apple juice, apricots, cranberries, and cinnamon stick in small sauce-pan; bring to boil. Reduce heat and simmer until apple juice is reduced by half, 5–10 minutes; discard cinnamon stick.

5 Preheat oven to 325°F. Spray 2-quart baking dish or casserole dish with nonstick spray.

6 Crumble cornbread into large bowl. Add apple juice mixture, remaining egg white and the bread cubes; stir until mixed well. Spoon into prepared baking dish. Bake until golden, 40–50 minutes.

PER SERVING (¹/₁₂ **OF DRESSING**): 76 grams, 133 Cal, 3 g Total Fat, 0 g Sat Fat, 0 g Trans Fat, 0 mg Chol, 182 mg Sod, 24 g Total Carb, 9 g Total Sugar, 2 g Fib, 4 g Prot, 33 mg Calc.
PointsPlus value: **4**

FYI **Prepare the cornbread at least 1 day ahead for the best results. Or bake it up to 3 months ahead and freeze in a large zip-close plastic bag. Thaw at room temperature.**

CORNBREAD, APRICOT, AND
CRANBERRY DRESSING

Noodles with Spicy Peanut Sauce

serves 6

½ pound whole wheat spaghetti
¼ cup Thai peanut sauce
⅓ cup reduced-fat (2%) milk
2 teaspoons minced peeled fresh ginger
½ teaspoon salt
½ cup very thinly sliced scallions
½ small red bell pepper, cut into thin strips

1 Cook spaghetti according to package directions, omitting salt if desired. Drain in colander; rinse under cool running water. Drain.
2 To make dressing, combine peanut sauce, milk, ginger, and salt in blender and puree.
3 Toss together noodles, dressing, scallions, and bell pepper in serving bowl.

PER SERVING (⅔ CUP): 148 grams, 172 Cal,
4 g Total Fat, 1 g Sat Fat, 0 g Trans Fat, 1 mg Chol,
229 mg Sod, 31 g Total Carb, 2 g Total Sugar, 5 g Fib,
8 g Prot, 41 mg Calc.
PointsPlus value: **5**

FYI The spaghetti and peanut sauce can be prepared up to several hours ahead. It is best, however, not to toss them together until just before serving or the sauce will be absorbed into the pasta.

Orzo with Grilled Eggplant and Tomato

serves 8

6 ounces orzo
1 small eggplant (about ¾ pound), cut into ½-inch rounds
1 small red bell pepper, quartered lengthwise and seeded
1 large tomato, seeded and chopped
½ cup diced fat-free feta cheese
8 pitted Kalamata olives, coarsely chopped
2 scallions, sliced
¼ cup chopped snipped dill
¼ cup chopped fresh parsley
Grated zest and juice of 1 lemon
1 tablespoon extra-virgin olive oil
¼ teaspoon black pepper

1 Cook orzo according to package directions, omitting salt if desired; drain. Transfer to bowl.
2 Spray grill rack with nonstick spray. Preheat grill to medium or prepare medium fire using direct method.
3 Spray eggplant with nonstick spray. Place eggplant and bell pepper on grill rack and grill until tender, about 4 minutes per side.
4 Cut eggplant and bell pepper into ½-inch pieces. Add to orzo along with all remaining ingredients; toss to mix well.

PER SERVING (¾ CUP): 121 grams, 134 Cal,
3 g Total Fat, 1 g Sat Fat, 0 g Trans Fat, 0 mg Chol,
182 mg Sod, 22 g Total Carb, 3 g Total Sugar, 3 g Fib,
5 g Prot, 44 mg Calc.
PointsPlus value: **3**

FYI You can substitute almost any vegetables you like for the eggplant and bell pepper, including zucchini, red onion, or cherry tomatoes.

Broccoli with Pasta and White Beans

serves 6

1 bunch broccoli, cut into florets
½ pound whole wheat capellini
1 tablespoon olive oil
3 large garlic cloves, minced
1 (15½-ounce) can cannellini (white kidney) beans, rinsed and drained
¼ teaspoon salt
¼ teaspoon red pepper flakes
⅓ cup grated Parmesan cheese

1   Bring large pot of water to boil. Add broccoli and cook 3 minutes; with slotted spoon, transfer to medium bowl. Return water to boil; stir in pasta. Cook according to package directions, omitting salt if desired. Drain, reserving 1 cup of cooking water.

2   Meanwhile, heat oil in large nonstick skillet over medium-low heat. Add garlic and cook, stirring, until golden, about 2 minutes.

3   Add broccoli to skillet. Increase heat to medium-high and cook, stirring frequently, until broccoli is tender, about 5 minutes. Stir in beans, salt, pepper flakes, and ¾ cup of reserved cooking water. Increase heat to high and cook, stirring frequently, until beans are heated through, about 2 minutes.

4   Add pasta to skillet and cook, stirring, until heated through, about 1 minute, adding remaining ¼ cup cooking water if mixture seems dry. Remove skillet from heat; add Parmesan and toss to coat.

PER SERVING (1 CUP): 206 grams, 220 Cal, 5 g Total Fat, 1 g Sat Fat, 0 g Trans Fat, 4 mg Chol, 253 mg Sod, 37 g Total Carb, 2 g Total Sugar, 8 g Fib, 11 g Prot, 116 mg Calc.
PointsPlus value: *6*

Couscous with Lime and Scallion

serves 6

1½ cups water
1 cup whole wheat couscous
1 teaspoon extra-virgin olive oil
½ teaspoon salt
1 red bell pepper, finely chopped
1 carrot, finely chopped
8 scallions, thinly sliced
¼ cup lime juice
¼ cup finely chopped fresh parsley
⅛ teaspoon black pepper

1   Bring water to boil in medium saucepan; add couscous, oil, and salt. Remove saucepan from heat; let stand until water is absorbed, about 5 minutes. Fluff couscous with fork.

2   Combine all remaining ingredients in serving bowl. Add couscous and toss to mix well.

PER SERVING (ABOUT ⅔ CUP): 151 grams, 164 Cal, 2 g Total Fat, 0 g Sat Fat, 0 g Trans Fat, 0 mg Chol, 206 mg Sod, 34 g Total Carb, 2 g Total Sugar, 6 g Fib, 6 g Prot, 30 mg Calc.
PointsPlus value: *4*

▲ HEALTHY EXTRA
Use 2 carrots instead of 1 and toss with ¼ cup of chopped fresh cilantro.

BARLEY, LEEK, AND ROSEMARY GRATIN

Barley, Leek, and Rosemary Gratin

serves 8

2 cups reduced-sodium vegetable broth or
    Basic Vegetable Stock (page 107)
²/₃ cup pearl barley, rinsed
1 tablespoon butter
1 tablespoon olive oil
3 leeks (white and light green part only),
    halved lengthwise and sliced
1 tablespoon chopped fresh rosemary
¼ teaspoon salt
¼ teaspoon black pepper
½ cup shredded Comté or Gruyère cheese

1   Bring broth to boil in large saucepan; add barley. Reduce heat and simmer, covered, until tender, about 25 minutes.

2   Preheat oven to 375°F. Lightly spray 2-quart baking dish with nonstick spray.

3   Meanwhile, melt butter with oil in large nonstick skillet over medium heat. Add leeks and cook, stirring, until softened, about 10 minutes. Stir in barley, rosemary, salt, and pepper.

4   Transfer barley mixture to prepared baking dish. Sprinkle evenly with Comté; bake until barley mixture is heated through and cheese is melted, about 15 minutes.

PER SERVING (½ CUP): 121 grams, 143 Cal, 6 g Total Fat, 3 g Sat Fat, 0 g Trans Fat, 11 mg Chol, 219 mg Sod, 19 g Total Carb, 2 g Total Sugar, 4 g Fib, 5 g Prot, 99 mg Calc.
PointsPlus value: *4*

FYI   Barley has a temptingly chewy texture and earthy flavor that goes well with the leeks, while Comté cheese crowns this casserole perfectly. Comté is made in a region of France that bears the same name. This cheese is in the same family as Gruyère so it melts beautifully.

CLEANING LEEKS

1 *Cut off dark green portion and root end and discard.*

2 *Insert knife about 1 inch from root end and cut leek in half, leaving root end intact.*

3 *Hold leek by root end and swish thoroughly in a bowl of cool water to release grit between leaves. Swish again, if needed. Chop or slice leek as directed in recipe.*

Spinach, Mushroom, and Bulgur Pilaf

serves 6

1 pound plum tomatoes, quartered lengthwise
1 large onion, sliced
3 garlic cloves, minced
1 tablespoon olive oil
1 (15½-ounce) can cannellini (white kidney) beans, rinsed and drained
1 (8-ounce) package white mushrooms, sliced
2½ cups reduced-sodium chicken broth or Basic Chicken Stock (page 106)
¼ teaspoon black pepper
2 cups bulgur
2 cups tightly packed baby spinach

1   Preheat oven to 400°F. Spray roasting pan with olive oil nonstick spray.
2   Put tomatoes, onion, garlic, and oil in prepared pan and toss until mixed well. Spread to form single layer. Roast, stirring once, 30 minutes. Stir in beans and mushrooms; roast until vegetables are evenly browned, about 15 minutes longer.
3   With slotted spoon, transfer roasted vegetables to large saucepan. Add 1 cup of broth to roasting pan, stirring to scrape up any browned bits from bottom of pan. Add to saucepan.
4   Add remaining 1½ cups broth and the pepper to saucepan; bring to boil. Stir in bulgur. Reduce heat and simmer, covered, until bulgur is tender and liquid is absorbed, about 10 minutes. Stir in spinach and cook until wilted, about 2 minutes longer.

PER SERVING (1 CUP): 330 grams, 259 Cal, 3 g Total Fat, 1 g Sat Fat, 0 g Trans Fat, 0 mg Chol, 444 mg Sod, 50 g Total Carb, 5 g Total Sugar, 12 g Fib, 11 g Prot, 49 mg Calc.
PointsPlus value: *6*

Kasha Varnishkes

serves 6

½ cup medium or coarse kasha (buckwheat groats)
1 large egg, lightly beaten
1 cup reduced-sodium chicken broth, Basic Chicken Stock (page 106), or water
1 tablespoon canola oil
1 onion, thinly sliced
2 cups thinly sliced white mushrooms
1½ cups hot cooked farfalle (bow ties)
⅛ teaspoon black pepper

1   Stir together kasha and egg in small bowl until grains are coated evenly.
2   Spray medium nonstick saucepan with nonstick spray and set over medium heat. Add kasha and cook, stirring constantly with wooden spoon, until grains are separated, about 3 minutes. Add broth and bring to boil. Reduce heat and simmer, covered, until kasha is tender, about 10 minutes.
3   Meanwhile, heat oil in large nonstick skillet over medium heat. Add onion and cook, stirring, until golden, about 8 minutes. Add mushrooms and cook, stirring, until softened, about 3 minutes longer. Stir in kasha, farfalle, and pepper.

PER SERVING (ABOUT 1 CUP): 140 grams, 143 Cal, 4 g Total Fat, 1 g Sat Fat, 0 g Trans Fat, 35 mg Chol, 117 mg Sod, 23 g Total Carb, 3 g Total Sugar, 3 g Fib, 6 g Prot, 14 mg Calc.
PointsPlus value: *4*

FYI   The combination of kasha and farfalle pasta is a classic, but kasha is also excellent served on its own.

Cremini Mushrooms with Quinoa and Thyme

serves 6

1 tablespoon olive oil
2 cups sliced cremini mushrooms
2 shallots, finely chopped
2 garlic cloves, chopped
2 teaspoons chopped fresh thyme
1 cup quinoa, rinsed and drained
2 cups reduced-sodium chicken broth or Basic
    Chicken Stock (page 106)

1   Heat oil in medium saucepan over medium heat. Add mushrooms, shallots, garlic, and thyme; cook, stirring occasionally, until mushrooms are softened, about 5 minutes.
2   Stir quinoa and broth into mushroom mixture; bring to boil. Reduce heat and simmer, covered, until liquid is absorbed, 15–20 minutes. Fluff with fork.

PER SERVING (⅔ CUP): 140 grams, 143 Cal,
4 g Total Fat, 1 g Sat Fat, 0 g Trans Fat, 0 mg Chol,
215 mg Sod, 22 g Total Carb, 1 g Total Sugar, 2 g Fib,
6 g Prot, 24 mg Calc.
PointsPlus value: *4*

FYI   Quinoa (*KEEN-wah*), an ancient grain with a mild flavor and slightly chewy texture, is a nutrition powerhouse. It is considered a complete protein, as it contains all the essential amino acids comparable to those found in meat, poultry, and fish. Look for quinoa in the supermarket or in your local natural-foods store.

Creamy Blue Cheese Polenta

serves 6

3 cups water
2 cups low-fat (1%) milk
¾ teaspoon salt
¼ teaspoon black pepper
1 cup instant polenta
½ cup crumbled reduced-fat blue cheese
2 tablespoons grated Parmesan cheese

Combine water, milk, salt, and pepper in large saucepan; bring to boil over medium-high heat. Add polenta in thin, steady stream, whisking constantly. Cook, stirring constantly with wooden spoon, until polenta is thick and creamy, about 5 minutes. Stir in blue cheese and Parmesan. Serve at once.

PER SERVING (⅔ CUP): 252 grams, 158 Cal,
1 g Total Fat, 1 g Sat Fat, 0 g Trans Fat, 6 mg Chol,
412 mg Sod, 28 g Total Carb, 4 g Total Sugar, 3 g Fib,
7 g Prot, 144 mg Calc.
PointsPlus value: *4*

FYI   For the most delicious Parmesan, choose Parmigiano-Reggiano, the long-aged cow's milk cheese from northern Italy famed for its rich, sharp flavor and granular texture. It is usually sold in wedges with Parmigiano-Reggiano stenciled on the rind. Avoid jarred grated Parmesan cheese, as it often contains hydrogenated oil and stabilizers.

Lentils with Spiced Vegetables

serves 6

2 teaspoons olive oil
2 onions, sliced
2 (14½-ounce) cans reduced-sodium chicken
    broth or 3½ cups Basic Chicken Stock
    (page 106)
1 cup brown lentils, picked over, rinsed,
    and drained
3 garlic cloves, minced
1 tablespoon minced peeled fresh ginger
2 teaspoons ground cumin
1 teaspoon ground coriander
¼ teaspoon black pepper
2 carrots, thinly sliced
1 (1-pound) bag frozen mixed vegetables

1 Heat oil in medium nonstick skillet over
medium heat. Add onions and cook, stirring,
until very soft and deep golden brown, about
20 minutes.
2 Meanwhile, combine broth, lentils, garlic,
ginger, cumin, coriander, and pepper in large
skillet and set over high heat; bring to boil. Reduce heat and simmer, covered, 15 minutes.
3 Stir carrots into lentil mixture; top with
frozen vegetables and bring to boil. Reduce
heat and simmer, covered, until lentils and
vegetables are tender, about 10 minutes. Serve
topped with onions.

**PER SERVING (1 CUP LENTIL MIXTURE AND
ABOUT 3 TABLESPOONS ONIONS):** 375 grams, 211 Cal,
3 g Total Fat, 1 g Sat Fat, 0 g Trans Fat, 0 mg Chol,
415 mg Sod, 37 g Total Carb, 7 g Total Sugar, 12 g Fib,
14 g Prot, 62 mg Calc.
PointsPlus value: **5**

Baked Beans

serves 4

1 onion, finely chopped
2 tablespoons ketchup
1 tablespoon dark brown sugar
1 tablespoon cider vinegar
1 tablespoon pure maple syrup
2 teaspoons dark molasses
¾ teaspoon mustard powder
¼ teaspoon ground ginger
¼ teaspoon black pepper
Pinch ground cloves
1 cup water
1 (15½-ounce) can navy or great northern
    beans, rinsed and drained
¼ teaspoon salt

1 Preheat oven to 275°F.
2 Combine onion, ketchup, brown sugar,
vinegar, maple syrup, molasses, mustard powder, ginger, pepper, and cloves in flameproof
2½-quart lidded casserole dish. Stir in water
and bring to boil. Reduce heat and simmer,
stirring occasionally, until thickened, about 20
minutes.
3 Stir beans and salt into onion mixture.
Bake, covered, stirring occasionally, 1 hour,
adding a little water if beans look dry. If there
is too much liquid after 1 hour, uncover and
bake until excess liquid is evaporated.

PER SERVING (¼ OF BEANS): 195 grams, 143 Cal,
1 g Total Fat, 0 g Sat Fat, 0 g Trans Fat, 0 mg Chol,
288 mg Sod, 30 g Total Carb, 13 g Total Sugar, 5 g Fib,
6 g Prot, 60 mg Calc.
PointsPlus value: **4**

Smoky Black Beans

serves 10

1 (16-ounce) package black beans, picked
    over, rinsed, and drained
1 tablespoon olive oil
1 large onion, chopped
2 jalapeño peppers, seeded and finely chopped
2 large garlic cloves, finely chopped
1½ teaspoons dried oregano
1 teaspoon ground cumin
1 (6-ounce) smoked ham hock
1 (48-ounce) can reduced-sodium chicken
    broth or 6 cups Basic Chicken Stock
    (page 106)
1 (12-ounce) can beer
½ teaspoon salt
¼ teaspoon black pepper

1 Soak beans according to package directions; drain.
2 Preheat oven to 300°F.
3 Heat oil in Dutch oven over medium-high heat. Add onion and cook, stirring, until lightly browned, about 8 minutes. Add jalapeño, garlic, oregano, and cumin; cook, stirring constantly, until fragrant, about 30 seconds. Stir in ham hock, beans, broth, beer, salt, and black pepper; bring to boil. Bake until beans are tender, about 1½ hours. Discard ham hock.

PER SERVING (1 CUP): 271 grams, 180 Cal,
2 g Total Fat, 1 g Sat Fat, 0 g Trans Fat, 2 mg Chol,
470 mg Sod, 28 g Total Carb, 4 g Total Sugar, 10 g Fib,
12 g Prot, 40 mg Calc.
PointsPlus value: *4*

▲ **HEALTHY EXTRA**

Grilled large or extra-large shrimp make a quick and tasty accompaniment to these boldly flavored black beans (4 ounces of cooked shrimp with each serving will increase the *PointsPlus* value by *2*).

Cuban-Style Rice and Beans

serves 6

1 cup quick-cooking brown rice
1 tablespoon olive oil
1 onion, chopped
2 garlic cloves, minced
1 red bell pepper, chopped
1 teaspoon dried oregano
1 bay leaf
2 tomatoes, chopped
1 tablespoon white vinegar
2 (15½-ounce) cans black beans, rinsed and
    drained
½ teaspoon salt
¼ teaspoon black pepper
¼ cup chopped fresh cilantro

1 Cook rice according to package directions; keep warm.
2 Meanwhile, heat oil in large saucepan over medium-high heat. Add onion and garlic; cook, stirring, until onion is slightly softened, about 2 minutes. Add bell pepper, oregano, and bay leaf; cook, stirring occasionally, until bell pepper is slightly softened, about 2 minutes. Add tomatoes and vinegar; cook, stirring, until tomatoes are slightly softened, about 2 minutes.
3 Stir beans, salt, and black pepper into vegetable mixture. Reduce heat and simmer, covered, until vegetables are softened and mixture is creamy, about 8 minutes. Discard bay leaf. Sprinkle with cilantro. Serve over rice.

PER SERVING (⅔ CUP BEAN MIXTURE AND ½ CUP RICE):
219 grams, 204 Cal, 4 g Total Fat, 0 g Sat Fat,
0 g Trans Fat, 0 mg Chol, 375 mg Sod, 35 g Total Carb,
4 g Total Sugar, 8 g Fib, 8 g Prot, 56 mg Calc.
PointsPlus value: *5*

New Orleans Red Beans and Rice

serves 4

¾ cup quick-cooking rice
1½ tablespoons olive oil
2 celery stalks, chopped
1 onion, chopped
1 green bell pepper, chopped
3 garlic cloves, minced
1 (14½-ounce) can diced tomatoes
1 teaspoon ground cumin
½ teaspoon hot pepper sauce
1 (15½-ounce) can pinto beans,
   rinsed and drained

1   Cook rice according to package directions, omitting salt if desired; keep warm.
2   Heat oil in large nonstick skillet over medium-high heat. Add celery, onion, bell pepper, and garlic; cook, stirring frequently, until vegetables are softened, about 5 minutes.
3   Add tomatoes with their juice, cumin, and pepper sauce to skillet; bring to boil. Reduce heat and simmer until slightly thickened, about 4 minutes. Add beans and simmer until heated through, about 2 minutes longer. Serve over rice.

PER SERVING (SCANT ½ CUP RICE AND 1 CUP BEANS): 342 grams, 220 Cal, 5 g Total Fat, 1 g Sat Fat, 0 g Trans Fat, 0 mg Chol, 301 mg Sod, 36 g Total Carb, 7 g Total Sugar, 7 g Fib, 7 g Prot, 72 mg Calc.
PointsPlus value: **5**

FYI   In New Orleans, many dishes begin with celery, onion, and green bell pepper, a combination known as the holy trinity.

Summery Pasta with Chickpeas and Tomatoes

serves 8

3 cups whole wheat pasta, such as gemelli,
   shells, or elbows
1 (15½-ounce) can chickpeas, rinsed and
   drained
1 each red and yellow tomato, seeded and
   diced
2 celery stalks, sliced
¼ cup lightly packed fresh flatleaf parsley
   leaves
2 tablespoons red wine vinegar
1 tablespoon olive oil
½ teaspoon dried oregano
½ teaspoon salt
¼ teaspoon black pepper
⅛ teaspoon red pepper flakes
⅓ cup coarsely crumbled reduced-fat feta
   cheese

1   Cook pasta according to package directions, omitting salt if desired. Drain in colander and rinse under cold running water; drain again.
2   Toss together pasta and all remaining ingredients except feta in serving bowl. Sprinkle with cheese.

PER SERVING (ABOUT ½ CUP): 122 grams, 200 Cal, 3 g Total Fat, 1 g Sat Fat, 0 g Trans Fat, 2 mg Chol, 288 mg Sod, 37 g Total Carb, 2 g Total Sugar, 5 g Fib, 9 g Prot, 0 g Alcohol, 0 g Sugar Alcohol, 43 mg Calc.
PointsPlus value: **5**

FYI   Changing the number of servings to 4 turns this boldly flavored pasta dish into a hearty vegetarian main dish.

Chickpeas and Chunky Vegetables

serves 4

1 (15½-ounce) can chickpeas, rinsed and
    drained
1 cup matchstick-cut carrots
1 cup halved cherry tomatoes
½ cup diced mini (Persian) cucumber
¼ cup diced red onion
¼ cup chopped fresh cilantro
¼ cup chopped fresh parsley
1 tablespoon lime juice
1 tablespoon extra-virgin olive oil
1 garlic clove, minced
1 teaspoon ground cumin
1 teaspoon paprika
½ teaspoon salt
⅛ teaspoon black pepper

1   Toss together chickpeas, carrots, tomatoes, cucumber, onion, cilantro, and parsley in serving bowl.
2   To make dressing, whisk together all remaining ingredients in small bowl. Drizzle over chickpea mixture and toss to coat well.

PER SERVING (ABOUT 1 CUP): 179 grams, 126 Cal,
5 g Total Fat, 1 g Sat Fat, 0 g Trans Fat, 0 mg Chol,
435 mg Sod, 18 g Total Carb, 5 g Total Sugar, 5 g Fib,
5 g Prot, 48 mg Calc.
PointsPlus value: *3*

FYI   If you happen to be growing mint in your garden or in a window box, you can use some in addition to the cilantro and parsley or instead of one or both of them, if you prefer. Exact amounts are not critical to the success of this tasty dish.

Skillet Asparagus with Pinto Beans and Tomatoes

serves 4

1 tablespoon olive oil
2 garlic cloves, minced
1½ cups fresh or frozen corn kernels
1 pound asparagus, trimmed and cut into 1-
    inch pieces
1 (15½-ounce) can pinto beans, rinsed and
    drained
1 cup grape tomatoes, halved
3 scallions, thinly sliced
1 tablespoon capers, drained
½ teaspoon salt
¼ teaspoon black pepper

1   Heat oil in large nonstick skillet over medium-high heat. Add garlic and cook, stirring, until fragrant, about 30 seconds. Add corn and cook, stirring until lightly browned, about 2 minutes.
2   Add asparagus and cook, stirring frequently, until bright green, about 3 minutes. Add beans and cook until asparagus is tender, about 2 minutes. Stir in all remaining ingredients.

PER SERVING (1 CUP): 236 grams, 171 Cal, 4 g Total Fat,
1 g Sat Fat, 0 g Trans Fat, 0 mg Chol, 496 mg Sod,
27 g Total Carb, 3 g Total Sugar, 7 g Fib, 7 g Prot,
49 mg Calc.
PointsPlus value: *4*

▲ HEALTHY EXTRA
Serve trout fillets alongside this unusual bean dish. A 6-ounce portion of broiled or grilled rainbow trout fillet with each serving will increase the *PointsPlus* value by *6*.

12

Slow-Cooker Classics

Slow-Cooker Classics

306   Beef Stew with Carrots and Peas
306   Corned Beef and Cabbage
307   Blanquette de Veau
307   Savory Lamb Stew
308   Lamb Shanks with White Beans
308   Pork Roast with Sauerkraut and Apples
310   Bigos
310   Pork and Broccoli "Stir-Fry"
311   Chicken and Turkey Sausage Gumbo
312   Garlicky Chicken Stew
312   Tuscan Chicken and Sausage Stew
313   Best-Ever Chicken Loaf
313   Chicken Soup
314   Kielbasa and Bean Soup
314   Vegetable-Barley Soup
316   Turkey Chowder
316   Smoky Turkey Chili
318   Manhattan Clam Chowder
318   Dal Soup

Beef Stew with Carrots and Peas

serves 4

1 pound beef round, cut into 1½-inch chunks
3 tablespoons all-purpose flour
4 teaspoons olive oil
1 onion, chopped
4 all-purpose potatoes, peeled and cut into
    1-inch chunks
2 large carrots, cut into 1-inch chunks
1 cup frozen green peas
8 frozen pearl onions
1 cup canned diced tomatoes with juice
½ cup dry red wine
½ teaspoon dried thyme
½ teaspoon salt
¼ teaspoon black pepper
1 bay leaf

1   Toss together beef and flour in large bowl until coated evenly.
2   Heat oil in large nonstick skillet over medium heat. Add onion and cook, stirring, until softened, about 5 minutes. Transfer to 5- or 6-quart slow cooker.
3   Increase heat under skillet to medium-high. Add beef, in batches, and cook until browned on all sides, about 10 minutes, transferring beef to slow cooker as it is browned.
4   Stir all remaining ingredients into slow cooker. Cover and cook until beef and vegetables are tender, 4–5 hours on high or 8–10 hours on low. Discard bay leaf.

PER SERVING (ABOUT 1½ CUPS): 441 grams, 426 Cal, 10 g Total Fat, 2 g Sat Fat, 1 g Trans Fat, 59 mg Chol, 460 mg Sod, 57 g Total Carb, 13 g Total Sugar, 8 g Fib, 27 g Prot, 60 mg Calc.
PointsPlus value: *11*

Corned Beef and Cabbage

serves 8

2 large onions, sliced
1 (1¾-pound) lean corned beef brisket,
    trimmed
4 carrots, cut into 2-inch chunks
4 all-purpose potatoes (about 1 pound), peeled
    and cut into 2-inch chunks
2 fresh thyme sprigs
1 (1½-pound) head green cabbage, cored and
    cut into 8 wedges
1¼ cups reduced-sodium chicken broth or
    Basic Chicken Stock (page 106)
1 teaspoon dry mustard

1   Put onions in bottom of 5- or 6-quart slow cooker; place corned beef on top. Scatter carrots and potatoes around meat; top with thyme sprigs. Place cabbage wedges on top of vegetables. Pour broth over and sprinkle with dry mustard.
2   Cover and cook until meat and vegetables are fork-tender, 4–5 hours on high or 8–10 hours on low.
3   Transfer corned beef to platter and cut into 16 slices. With slotted spoon, remove vegetables from pot and place around meat.

PER SERVING (2 SLICES CORNED BEEF, ½ CARROT, ½ POTATO, 1 WEDGE CABBAGE): 308 grams, 286 Cal, 14 g Total Fat, 5 g Sat Fat, 1 g Trans Fat, 73 mg Chol, 984 mg Sod, 22 g Total Carb, 8 g Total Sugar, 4 g Fib, 17 g Prot 65 mg Calc.
PointsPlus value: *7*

▲ **HEALTHY EXTRA**
Begin your meal with a chopped escarole salad dressed with lemon juice, a pinch of salt, and a bit of black pepper.

Blanquette de Veau

serves 4

1 pound boneless veal shoulder, cut into 1½-inch chunks
1 (8-ounce) package white mushrooms, quartered
16 frozen pearl onions
1 cup reduced-sodium chicken broth or Basic Chicken Stock (page 106)
¼ cup dry vermouth
¾ teaspoon dried thyme
¼ teaspoon salt
¼ teaspoon white pepper
3 tablespoons all-purpose flour
3 tablespoons cold water
1 cup frozen baby peas

1   Combine veal, mushrooms, and onions in 5- or 6-quart slow cooker. Stir in broth, vermouth, thyme, salt, and pepper. Cover and cook until veal and vegetables are fork-tender, 4–5 hours on high or 8–10 hours on low.
2   About 30 minutes before cooking time is up, whisk together flour and water in small bowl until smooth; whisk in ¼ cup of hot stew liquid until blended. Stir flour mixture and peas into slow cooker. Cover and cook until mixture bubbles and thickens, about 30 minutes longer.

PER SERVING (1¼ CUPS): 297 grams, 223 Cal, 5 g Total Fat, 1 g Sat Fat, 2 g Trans Fat, 99 mg Chol, 404 mg Sod, 19 g Total Carb, 6 g Total Sugar, 4 g Fib, 26 g Prot, 57 mg Calc.
PointsPlus value: **5**

FYI   Blanquette de veau, which means "white veal" in French, is an apt name for this creamy, pale, delicately flavored stew. Like most stews and braises, it tastes even better a day or two later.

Savory Lamb Stew

serves 4

1 pound boneless leg of lamb, trimmed and cut into 1½-inch chunks
3 tablespoons all-purpose flour
4 teaspoons olive oil
1 onion, finely chopped
1 carrot, finely chopped
1 celery stalk, finely chopped
2 garlic cloves, minced
½ cup dry white wine
1 (14½-ounce) can whole tomatoes, broken up, juice reserved
½ cup water
2 all-purpose potatoes, peeled and cut into ¾-inch cubes
½ pound green beans, trimmed and cut into 1-inch pieces
2 teaspoons chopped fresh thyme
½ teaspoon salt
½ teaspoon black pepper

1   Toss together lamb and flour in large bowl.
2   Heat oil in large nonstick skillet over medium heat. Add onion, carrot, celery, and garlic; cook until onion is softened, 5 minutes. Transfer to 5- or 6-quart slow cooker.
3   Increase heat under skillet to medium-high. Add lamb, in batches, and cook until browned on all sides, about 10 minutes, transferring lamb to slow cooker as it is browned. Add wine to skillet and cook, scraping up browned bits; add to slow cooker. Add all remaining ingredients to slow cooker. Cover and cook until lamb and vegetables are tender, 4–5 hours on high or 8–10 hours on low.

PER SERVING (ABOUT 1½ CUPS): 429 grams, 345 Cal, 11 g Total Fat, 3 g Sat Fat, 0 g Trans Fat, 65 mg Chol, 523 mg Sod, 37 g Total Carb, 9 g Total Sugar, 6 g Fib, 26 g Prot, 95 mg Calc.
PointsPlus value: **9**

Lamb Shanks with White Beans

serves 4

2 garlic cloves, minced
1 teaspoon olive oil
½ teaspoon salt
½ teaspoon black pepper
4 (7-ounce) lamb shanks, trimmed
1 large onion, chopped
1 carrot, chopped
1 (14½-ounce) can diced tomatoes
1 cup reduced-sodium beef broth
⅔ cup dry white wine
2 teaspoons chopped fresh rosemary
2 (15½-ounce) cans cannellini (white kidney) beans, rinsed and drained

1   Stir together garlic, ½ teaspoon of oil, the salt, and ¼ teaspoon of pepper in cup; rub all over lamb shanks.

2   Heat remaining ½ teaspoon oil in large nonstick skillet over medium-high heat. Add lamb shanks, in batches, and cook until browned on all sides, about 8 minutes, transferring lamb to plate as it is browned.

3   Combine onion and carrot in 5- or 6-quart slow cooker; place lamb shanks on top. Pour tomatoes with their juice, broth, and wine around lamb; sprinkle with rosemary. Cover and cook until lamb and vegetables are tender, 4–5 hours on high or 8–10 hours on low. About 35 minutes before cooking time is up, skim off fat and discard; stir in beans. Cover and cook until heated through, about 30 minutes longer.

PER SERVING (1 LAMB SHANK AND 1½ CUPS VEGETABLES WITH BEANS): 431 grams, 261 Cal, 5 g Total Fat, 1 g Sat Fat, 0 g Trans Fat, 47 mg Chol, 764 mg Sod, 32 g Total Carb, 7 g Total Sugar, 9 g Fib, 22 g Prot, 94 mg Calc.
PointsPlus value: **6**

Pork Roast with Sauerkraut and Apples

serves 6

½ teaspoon dried thyme
½ teaspoon black pepper
⅛ teaspoon salt
1 (1½-pound) boneless pork loin roast, trimmed
2 teaspoons canola oil
1 (2-pound) package sauerkraut, rinsed and drained
1 large red onion, sliced
1 McIntosh or Cortland apple, peeled, cored, and diced
2 teaspoons caraway seeds
½ cup dry white wine
Chopped fresh parsley

1   Sprinkle thyme, pepper, and salt over pork. Heat oil in large nonstick skillet over medium-high heat. Add pork and cook until browned on all sides, about 6 minutes.

2   Combine sauerkraut, onion, apple, and caraway seeds in 5- or 6-quart slow cooker. Place pork on top of vegetables; pour wine over. Cover and cook until pork and vegetables are fork-tender, 4–5 hours on high or 8–10 hours on low.

3   Transfer pork to platter and cut into 6 slices. Spoon sauerkraut mixture around pork. Sprinkle with parsley.

PER SERVING (1 SLICE PORK AND ¾ CUP SAUERKRAUT MIXTURE): 247 grams, 224 Cal, 9 g Total Fat, 3 g Sat Fat, 0 g Trans Fat, 63 mg Chol, 589 mg Sod, 11 g Total Carb, 4 g Total Sugar, 5 g Fib, 23 g Prot, 76 mg Calc.
PointsPlus value: **5**

PORK ROAST
WITH SAUERKRAUT
AND APPLES

Bigos

serves 10

1 ounce dried mushrooms
1 cup boiling water
1¼ pounds lean boneless pork loin, trimmed
    and cut into 1-inch chunks
4 slices turkey bacon, cut into pieces
1 red onion, sliced
1 (32-ounce) bag fresh sauerkraut, rinsed well
    and drained
2 large carrots, thickly sliced
2 Golden Delicious or Braeburn apples,
    unpeeled and cut into chunks
3 large pitted dried plums, quartered
1 cup reduced-sodium chicken broth
3 tablespoons tomato paste
1 pound turkey kielbasa sausage, sliced

1   Combine mushrooms and boiling water in
small bowl; let stand about 10 minutes.
2   Meanwhile, heat large nonstick skillet over
medium-high heat. Add pork, in batches, and
cook until browned, about 6 minutes per batch.
Transfer to 5- or 6-quart slow cooker. Add
bacon and onion to skillet; cook, stirring, until
onion is softened and bacon is crisp, about 5
minutes. Add onion mixture, sauerkraut, carrots, apples, and dried plums to slow cooker.
3   Transfer soaked mushrooms and liquid to
sieve set over bowl. Chop mushrooms; add to
slow cooker. Whisk mushroom liquid, broth,
and tomato paste; add to slow cooker. Top
with sausage. Cover and cook until pork and
vegetables are fork-tender, 4–5 hours on high
or 8–10 hours on low.

PER SERVING (ABOUT 1 CUP): 399 grams, 303 Cal,
8 g Total Fat, 2 g Sat Fat, 0 g Trans Fat, 75 mg Chol,
934 mg Sod, 31 g Total Carb, 13 g Total Sugar, 7 g Fib,
27 g Prot, 78 mg Calc.
PointsPlus value: **7**

Pork and Broccoli "Stir-Fry"

serves 6

1½ pounds lean boneless pork loin, trimmed
    and cut into 1½-inch chunks
2 tablespoons minced peeled fresh ginger
4 garlic cloves, minced
2½ cups reduced-sodium chicken broth or
    Basic Chicken Stock (page 106)
¼ cup hoisin sauce
3 tablespoons reduced-sodium soy sauce
1 tablespoon cornstarch
1 (1-pound) bag frozen broccoli and
    cauliflower
½ pound mixed mushrooms, such as shiitake,
    oyster, and cremini, sliced (remove stems
    if using shiitakes)
1 large red bell pepper, cut into strips
1 onion, cut into thin wedges

1   Combine pork, ginger, and garlic in 5- or
6-quart slow cooker. Stir together broth and
hoisin sauce in small bowl; pour over pork.
Cover and cook until pork is fork-tender, 4–5
hours on high or 8–10 hours on low.
2   Transfer pork to bowl. Whisk soy sauce
and cornstarch in cup until smooth. Gradually
stir into slow cooker. Cover and cook on high
until mixture simmers, about 10 minutes.
3   Stir in broccoli and cauliflower, mushrooms, bell pepper, and onion. Cover and cook
on high until vegetables are tender, about 45
minutes. Add pork; cook 10 minutes longer.

PER SERVING (ABOUT 1 CUP): 369 grams, 235 Cal,
6 g Total Fat, 2 g Sat Fat, 0 g Trans Fat, 67 mg Chol,
741 mg Sod, 17 g Total Carb, 7 g Total Sugar, 4 g Fib,
26 g Prot, 68 mg Calc.
PointsPlus value: **5**

Chicken and Turkey Sausage Gumbo

serves 6

1 onion, chopped
1 green bell pepper, chopped
2 celery stalks, chopped
¾ pound skinless boneless chicken thighs, cut
    into 1½-inch chunks
¾ pound sweet or hot Italian-style turkey
    sausages, cut into 1½ -inch chunks
1 tablespoon Cajun seasoning
2 cups reduced-sodium chicken broth or Basic
    Chicken Stock (page 106)
1 (14½-ounce) can fire-roasted diced
    tomatoes
3 tablespoons all-purpose flour
3 tablespoons cold water
1 (10-ounce) package frozen sliced okra
1 cup frozen corn kernels

1   Combine onion, bell pepper, and celery in
5- or 6-quart slow cooker. Place chicken and
sausages on top of vegetables; sprinkle with
Cajun seasoning. Top with broth and tomatoes
with their juice. Cover and cook until chicken,
sausages, and vegetables are fork-tender, 4–5
hours on high or 8–10 hours on low.

2   About 45 minutes before cooking time is
up, whisk together flour and water in small bowl
until smooth; whisk in ¼ cup of hot gumbo
liquid. Stir flour mixture into slow cooker;
stir in okra and corn. Cover and cook on high
until mixture bubbles and thickens, about 45
minutes longer.

PER SERVING (GENEROUS 1½ CUPS): 397 grams,
271 Cal, 11 g Total Fat, 3 g Sat Fat, 0 g Trans Fat,
72 mg Chol, 815 mg Sod, 21 g Total Carb,
6 g Total Sugar, 4 g Fib, 24 g Prot, 69 mg Calc.
PointsPlus value: **7**

DICING BELL PEPPERS

1   Cut pepper lengthwise in half; cut
off stem and scrape out seeds.

2   With large chef's knife, cut pepper
half into ¼- to ½-inch-thick strips.
Gather strips into a pile and cut
across to form dice.

3   Repeat with other pepper half.

Garlicky Chicken Stew

serves 8

1 (3½-pound) chicken, cut into 8 pieces and
    skinned
½ cup dry white wine
3 tablespoons tomato paste
1 (14½-ounce) can reduced-sodium chicken
    broth or 1¾ cups Basic Chicken Stock
    (page 106)
5 large garlic cloves, chopped
1 teaspoon dried thyme
½ teaspoon salt
½ teaspoon black pepper
3 tablespoons red wine vinegar
2 tablespoons all-purpose flour
1 (9-ounce) package frozen green beans
3 tomatoes, halved and sliced
2 tablespoons chopped fresh parsley

1   Put chicken in 5- or 6-quart slow cooker.
Whisk together wine and tomato paste in small
bowl until smooth. Pour over chicken. Add 1
½ cups of broth, the garlic, thyme, salt, and
pepper to slow cooker. Cover and cook until
chicken is fork-tender, 4–5 hours on high or
8–10 hours on low.
2   Meanwhile, refrigerate remaining broth.
3   About 40 minutes before cooking time is
up, whisk together remaining broth, vinegar,
and flour in small bowl until smooth. Whisk in
about ¼ cup of hot stew liquid until blended.
Gradually stir broth mixture into slow cooker.
4   Add green beans and tomatoes to slow
cooker. Cover and cook on high until stew
simmers and green beans are tender, about 35
minutes. Serve sprinkled with parsley.

PER SERVING (1 PIECE CHICKEN WITH ½ CUP SAUCE):
257 grams, 166 Cal, 3 g Total Fat, 1 g Sat Fat,
0 g Trans Fat, 67 mg Chol, 390 mg Sod, 8 g Total Carb,
2 g Total Sugar, 2 g Fib, 23 g Prot, 45 mg Calc.
PointsPlus value: *4*

Tuscan Chicken and Sausage Stew

serves 6

3/4 pound skinless boneless chicken thighs, cut
    into 2-inch chunks
1 pound sweet or hot Italian-style turkey
    sausage, cut into 2-inch pieces
2 cups cremini mushrooms, halved or
    quartered if large
1 red onion, chopped
3 large garlic cloves, minced
1 teaspoon dried oregano
1/2 teaspoon salt
1/4 teaspoon black pepper
Pinch red pepper flakes
1 (9-ounce) package frozen artichoke hearts
1 large red bell pepper, diced
1 cup reduced-sodium chicken broth or Basic
    Chicken Stock (page 106)

1   Spray large nonstick skillet with olive oil
nonstick spray and set over medium-high heat.
Add chicken and cook, stirring, until browned,
about 5 minutes; transfer to 5- or 6-quart slow
cooker. Add sausage to skillet and cook, stirring, until browned, about 5 minutes. Add to
slow cooker.
2   Add mushrooms, onion, and garlic to slow
cooker. Sprinkle with oregano, salt, black pepper, and pepper flakes. Layer artichokes and
bell pepper on top. Pour broth over. Cover and
cook until chicken and vegetables are fork-tender, 4–5 hours on high or 8–10 hours on low.

PER SERVING (¼ OF STEW): 274 grams, 258 Cal,
13 g Total Fat, 1 g Sat Fat, 0 g Trans Fat, 82 mg Chol,
838 mg Sod, 10 g Total Carb, 3 g Total Sugar, 4 g Fib,
26 g Prot, 45 mg Calc.
PointsPlus value: *6*

Best-Ever Chicken Loaf

serves 6

3 slices bread, cut into 1-inch pieces
1/3 cup fat-free milk
3 large carrots
1 onion, halved
1 large celery stalk, cut into chunks
1 pound ground skinless chicken breast
1 large egg
3 tablespoons ketchup
1 tablespoon Dijon mustard
1 tablespoon Worcestershire sauce
1/2 teaspoon salt
6 small red potatoes, scrubbed and halved
1/2 pound cremini mushrooms, thickly sliced

1   Toss together bread and milk in large bowl until coated evenly. Let stand 10 minutes.
2   Meanwhile, slice 1 carrot and cut remaining 2 carrots into 2-inch chunks. Coarsely chop 1 onion half and slice remaining half. Reserve carrot chunks and sliced onion.
3   Combine sliced carrot, sliced onion, and celery in food processor. Add to bread with all ingredients except potatoes and mushrooms. Mix well. Shape mixture into oval loaf; place in 5- or 6-quart slow cooker.
4   Scatter potatoes, mushrooms, and reserved carrot and onion around loaf. Cover and cook until loaf is cooked through and vegetables are tender, 4–5 hours on high or 8–10 hours on low. Cut loaf into 6 slices. Serve with vegetables.

PER SERVING (1 SLICE CHICKEN LOAF, 2 POTATO HALVES, AND 1/6 OF VEGETABLES): 348 grams, 306 Cal, 4 g Total Fat, 1 g Sat Fat, 0 g Trans Fat, 78 mg Chol, 537 mg Sod, 45 g Total Carb, 9 g Total Sugar, 5 g Fib, 23 g Prot, 83 mg Calc.
PointsPlus value: **8**

Chicken Soup

serves 8

2 parsnips, diced
2 carrots, diced
2 celery stalks, diced
1 onion, chopped
4 fresh parsley sprigs
2 tablespoons snipped fresh dill
3/4 teaspoon dried thyme
1/4 teaspoon black pepper
1 pound bone-in chicken breasts, skinned
1 pound bone-in chicken thighs, skinned
7 cups reduced-sodium chicken broth or Basic Chicken Stock (page 106)

1   Combine parsnips, carrots, celery, onion, parsley, dill, thyme, and pepper in 5- or 6-quart slow cooker. Place chicken breasts and thighs on top of vegetables. Add broth; cover and cook 4–5 hours on high or 8–10 hours on low.
2   About 1 hour before cooking time is up, transfer chicken to plate.
3   When cool enough to handle, separate chicken meat from bones and cut into bite-size pieces. Return chicken to slow cooker; cover and cook 45 minutes.

PER SERVING (1½ CUPS): 361 grams, 177 Cal, 4 g Total Fat, 1 g Sat Fat, 0 g Trans Fat, 54 mg Chol, 616 mg Sod, 13 g Total Carb, 6 g Total Sugar, 3 g Fib, 21 g Prot, 41 mg Calc.
PointsPlus value: **4**

 If you are not partial to the taste of parsnips, leave them out and use 3 carrots and 3 celery stalks instead.

Kielbasa and Bean Soup

serves 8

¾ *pound turkey kielbasa, sliced*
½ *bunch kale, trimmed and chopped*
    (about 4 cups)
1 *onion, chopped*
1 *carrot, chopped*
1 *celery stalk, chopped*
2 *garlic cloves, minced*
3 *cups reduced-sodium chicken broth or Basic*
    Chicken Stock (page 106)
1 *(15½-ounce) can red kidney beans, rinsed*
    and drained
1 *(15½-ounce) can great northern beans,*
    rinsed and drained
1 *(14½-ounce) can diced tomatoes*
½ *cup dry red wine or water*
1 *teaspoon dried basil*
½ *teaspoon dried oregano*

Combine all ingredients in 5- or 6-quart slow
cooker. Cover and cook until vegetables are
tender, 4–5 hours on high or 8–10 hours on low.

PER SERVING (1 CUP): 329 grams, 159 Cal, 4 g Total Fat,
1 g Sat Fat, 0 g Trans Fat, 0 mg Chol, 797 mg Sod,
19 g Total Carb, 5 g Total Sugar, 6 g Fib, 13 g Prot,
70 mg Calc.
PointsPlus value: **4**

FYI You can use almost any variety of beans in
this hearty soup, including black beans,
cannellini (white kidney beans), chickpeas, or pinto
beans. Other dark, leafy greens, such as mustard
greens, collard greens, spinach, or escarole, can be
used instead of the kale, if you like.

Vegetable-Barley Soup

serves 8

1 *(8-ounce) package white mushrooms,*
    quartered
2 *carrots, sliced*
1 *large zucchini, diced*
1 *yellow squash, halved lengthwise and sliced*
1 *small fennel bulb, chopped*
1 *celery stalk, chopped*
1 *onion, chopped*
4 *garlic cloves, thinly sliced*
4 *cups reduced-sodium vegetable broth or*
    Basic Vegetable Stock (page 107)
1 *(14½-ounce) can Italian-seasoned diced*
    tomatoes
1 *cup frozen lima beans*
¾ *cup quick-cooking barley*
1 *teaspoon dried basil*
¼ *teaspoon salt*
½ *teaspoon black pepper*

Combine all ingredients in 5- or 6-quart slow
cooker. Cover and cook until vegetables are
tender, 4–5 hours on high or 8–10 hours on
low.

PER SERVING (1½ CUPS): 344 grams, 141 Cal,
1 g Total Fat, 0 g Sat Fat, 0 g Trans Fat, 0 mg Chol,
445 mg Sod, 30 g Total Carb, 9 g Total Sugar, 6 g Fib,
6 g Prot, 72 mg Calc.
PointsPlus value: **4**

FYI Be sure to make a batch of this soup in the
summer when vegetables are at their peak
of flavor. Cook the soup as directed, then cool and
freeze in 2- to 4-cup covered freezer containers for
up to 6 months. Thaw overnight in the refrigerator
and reheat.

VEGETABLE-BARLEY SOUP

Turkey Chowder

serves 8

4 slices turkey bacon, crisp cooked and
    chopped
1 pound turkey breast cutlets, cut into ½-inch
    pieces
1 baking potato, peeled and diced
2 carrots, diced
1 onion, chopped
1 celery stalk, diced
2 (10¾-ounce) cans low-fat condensed cream
    of mushroom soup
2 cups reduced-sodium chicken broth or Basic
    Chicken Stock (page 106)
½ teaspoon dried thyme
½ teaspoon dried sage

Combine all ingredients in 5- or 6-quart slow
cooker. Cover and cook until soup is thickened
and turkey and vegetables are tender, 4–5
hours on high or 8–10 hours on low.

PER SERVING (1 CUP): 253 grams, 161 Cal, 4 g Total Fat,
2 g Sat Fat, 0 g Trans Fat, 47 mg Chol, 792 mg Sod,
14 g Total Carb, 4 g Total Sugar, 2 g Fib, 17 g Prot,
35 mg Calc.
PointsPlus value: **4**

Smoky Turkey Chili

serves 8

1 pound ground skinless turkey breast
1 large onion, chopped
1 red bell pepper, chopped
4 garlic cloves, chopped
3 (15½-ounce) cans small white beans, rinsed
    and drained
1 (14½-ounce) can diced tomatoes
1 cup ketchup
1 (4½-ounce) can chopped mild green chiles
3 tablespoons chili powder
2 tablespoons honey
1 tablespoon ground cumin
2 teaspoons instant espresso powder
1 teaspoon dried oregano
¼ teaspoon hickory liquid smoke
Chopped fresh parsley

Combine turkey, onion, bell pepper, and
garlic in 5- or 6-quart slow cooker. Stir in
all remaining ingredients. Cover and cook
until flavors are blended and chili is slightly
thickened, 4–5 hours on high or 8–10 hours on
low. Serve sprinkled with parsley.

PER SERVING (1¼ CUPS): 302 grams, 232 Cal,
2 g Total Fat, 0 g Sat Fat, 0 g Trans Fat, 47 mg Chol,
673 mg Sod, 32 g Total Carb, 8 g Total Sugar, 8 g Fib,
23 g Prot, 96 mg Calc.
PointsPlus value: **5**

▲ **HEALTHY EXTRA**

Top each serving of chili with sour cream and
Cheddar cheese (2 tablespoons fat-free sour cream
and 2 tablespoons shredded fat-free Cheddar
cheese per serving will increase the *PointsPlus*
value by *1*).

SMOKY TURKEY CHILI

Manhattan Clam Chowder

serves 6

2 teaspoons olive oil
2 celery stalks, finely chopped
2 carrots, finely chopped
1 onion, chopped
2 garlic cloves, minced
1 baking potato, peeled and diced
2 (6½-ounce) cans chopped clams with
  their juice
2 bay leaves
1 (14½-ounce) can diced tomatoes
1 (8-ounce) bottle clam juice
1 teaspoon dried oregano
¾ teaspoon dried thyme
4 slices turkey bacon, crisp cooked and
  broken into pieces

1   Heat oil in large nonstick skillet over medium heat. Add celery, carrots, onion, and garlic; cook, stirring, until onion is softened, about 5 minutes. Transfer to 5- or 6-quart slow cooker.
2   Add all remaining ingredients except bacon to slow cooker, stirring to combine. Cover and cook until vegetables are tender, 4–5 hours on high or 8–10 hours on low. Discard bay leaves. Ladle chowder evenly into 6 soup bowls and sprinkle with bacon.

PER SERVING (1½ CUPS SOUP WITH ⅙ OF BACON):
274 grams, 137 Cal, 4 g Total Fat, 1 g Sat Fat,
0 g Trans Fat, 27 mg Chol, 654 mg Sod, 15 g Total Carb,
6 g Total Sugar, 3 g Fib, 12 g Prot, 48 mg Calc.
PointsPlus value: *4*

FYI   To save time, skip cooking the vegetables in the skillet. Instead, put all the ingredients—except the bacon—in the slow cooker and cook as directed.

Dal Soup

serves 8

1 tablespoon canola oil
2 carrots, chopped
2 onions, chopped
3 garlic cloves, minced
1 tablespoon grated peeled fresh ginger
2 teaspoons ground cumin
2 teaspoons ground coriander
1 pound red lentils, picked over, rinsed, and
  drained
6 cups reduced-sodium chicken broth or Basic
  Chicken Stock (page 106)
1 tablespoon unsalted butter
½ teaspoon turmeric

1   Heat oil in large nonstick skillet over medium heat. Add carrots, onions, and garlic; cook, stirring, until carrots are crisp-tender, about 5 minutes. Stir in ginger, cumin, and coriander; cook, stirring, until fragrant, about 2 minutes longer. Transfer to 5- or 6-quart slow cooker.
2   Add all remaining ingredients to slow cooker, stirring to combine. Cover and cook until lentils are softened and vegetables are tender, 4–5 hours on high or 8–10 hours on low.

PER SERVING (1 CUP): 300 grams, 259 Cal,
4 g Total Fat, 1 g Sat Fat, 0 g Trans Fat, 4 mg Chol,
499 mg Sod, 41 g Total Carb, 7 g Total Sugar, 11 g Fib,
17 g Prot, 74 mg Calc.
PointsPlus value: *6*

FYI   Dal (or dahl) is an Indian dish that is usually made with lentils and spices and served as a side dish to complement a buffet of Indian foods. Here, we have kept the traditional seasonings and made it into a soup.

13

Pizzas, Calzones, and
Sandwiches

Pizzas, Calzones, and Sandwiches

322   Whole Wheat Pizza Dough
323   Basic Cheese Pizza
323   Pizza Margherita
324   Easy Clam Pizza
324   Caramelized Onion, Fig, and Stilton Pizza
326   Greek Pizza
327   Mushroom, Bacon, and Gruyère Pizza
329   Sicilian Sausage–Stuffed Pizza
330   Mushroom-Spinach Calzones
331   Pissaladière with Tomato Coulis and Goat Cheese
331   Greek-Style Grilled Lamb Burger Sandwiches
333   Grilled Steak Sandwiches with Golden Onions
333   Roast Beef Sandwiches with Horseradish Mayonnaise
334   California Hummus Sandwiches
334   Egg Salad Sandwiches with Curry and Cilantro
335   Middle Eastern–Style Chicken Sandwiches
336   Vietnamese-Style Grilled Chicken Sandwiches
338   Turkey BLTs
338   Sicilian-Style Sausage and Pepper Heroes
339   Classic Tuna Salad Sandwiches
339   Grilled Shrimp, Basil, and Goat Cheese Sandwiches
340   Crab Cake Sandwiches
340   Lobster Rolls

Whole Wheat Pizza Dough

serves 12

¾ *cup warm water (105°–115°F)*
½ *package (1 rounded teaspoon) active dry*
    yeast
½ *teaspoon sugar*
2 *teaspoons olive oil*
2¼ *cups white whole wheat flour*
¾ *teaspoon salt*

1   Combine water, yeast, and sugar in 1-cup
glass measure, stirring to dissolve. Let stand
until foamy, about 5 minutes. Stir in oil.

2   Combine flour and salt in food processor;
pulse until mixed well. With machine running,
scrape yeast mixture through feed tube; pulse
until dough forms a ball. Turn dough out onto
lightly floured work surface and knead until
smooth and elastic, about 10 minutes.

3   Spray large bowl with nonstick spray; place
dough in bowl, turning to coat. Cover bowl
with plastic wrap and let dough rise in warm
place (80°–85°F) until doubled in volume,
about 1 hour.

4   Punch down dough, then cut in half. Use
as directed in recipe. Can be refrigerated up
to 1 day or frozen in floured zip-close plastic
freezer bag up to 6 months.

PER SERVING (¹⁄₁₂ OF DOUGH): 41 grams, 91 Cal,
1 g Total Fat, 0 g Sat Fat, 0 g Trans Fat, 0 mg Chol,
146 mg Sod, 19 g Total Carb, 0 g Total Sugar, 3 g Fib,
3 g Prot, 1 mg Calc.
PointsPlus value: *2*

FYI To mix the dough by hand, combine the
water, yeast, and sugar in a large bowl. Set
aside until foamy. Stir in the oil, flour, and salt
until the dough gathers around the spoon. Turn the
dough out onto a lightly floured work surface and
knead until smooth and elastic, about 10 minutes.

Variations

Cornmeal Pizza Dough

Substitute 1 cup cornmeal for 1 cup of white
whole wheat flour.

PER SERVING (¹⁄₁₂ OF DOUGH): 42 grams, 97 Cal,
1 g Total Fat, 0 g Sat Fat, 0 g Trans Fat, 0 mg Chol,
147 mg Sod, 19 g Total Carb, 0 g Total Sugar, 5 g Fib,
3 g Prot, 1 mg Calc.
PointsPlus value: *2*

Semolina Pizza Dough

Substitute 1½ cups semolina flour (or
farina cereal) for 1½ cups of white whole
wheat flour.

PER SERVING (¹⁄₁₂ OF DOUGH): 46 grams, 111 Cal,
1 g Total Fat, 0 g Sat Fat, 0 g Trans Fat, 0 mg Chol,
147 mg Sod, 22 g Total Carb, 1 g Total Sugar, 2 g Fib,
4 g Prot, 4 mg Calc.
PointsPlus value: *3*

Basic Cheese Pizza

serves 6

½ recipe (about 1 pound) Whole Wheat Pizza
   Dough (opposite), at room temperature
2 cups Classic Tomato Sauce (page 12) or
   fat-free marinara sauce
¾ cup shredded part-skim mozzarella cheese
2 tablespoons grated Parmesan cheese
1 tablespoon extra-virgin olive oil

1   Place rack on lowest rung of oven. Preheat
oven to 450°F. Spray nonstick pizza pan or baking sheet with nonstick spray.
2   Turn dough out onto lightly floured work
surface and briefly knead. With lightly floured
rolling pin, roll dough into 12-inch round.
Transfer to prepared pizza pan.
3   Spread tomato sauce evenly over dough,
then sprinkle with mozzarella and Parmesan.
Drizzle with oil. Bake until crust is golden and
mozzarella is melted, about 15 minutes.

PER SERVING (⅙ OF PIZZA): 143 grams, 201 Cal,
6 g Total Fat, 2 g Sat Fat, 0 g Trans Fat, 10 mg Chol,
390 mg Sod, 29 g Total Carb, 7 g Total Sugar, 4 g Fib,
9 g Prot, 142 mg Calc.
PointsPlus value: **5**

▲ **HEALTHY EXTRA**

Turn this pizza from light to robust by topping it
with 1 cup each of sliced white mushrooms and
zucchini after sprinkling on the mozzarella.

Pizza Margherita

serves 6

1 tablespoon cornmeal
2 pints grape tomatoes, halved
1 red onion, thinly sliced
2 large garlic cloves, thinly sliced
1 tablespoon balsamic vinegar
¼ teaspoon salt
¼ teaspoon black pepper
½ recipe (about 1 pound) Semolina Pizza
   Dough (opposite)
¾ cup shredded reduced-fat mozzarella cheese
12 fresh basil leaves, thinly sliced

1   Place racks in middle and on lowest rung
of oven. Preheat oven to 450°F. Spray nonstick
baking sheet and nonstick pizza pan with nonstick spray.
2   Spread tomatoes, onion, and garlic in
single layer on prepared baking sheet. Sprinkle
with vinegar, salt, and pepper. Roast on middle
rack, stirring once or twice, until tomatoes are
lightly browned, about 35 minutes.
3   Turn dough out onto lightly floured work
surface and briefly knead. With lightly floured
rolling pin, roll dough into 12-inch round.
Transfer to prepared pizza pan.
4   Spoon tomato mixture evenly over dough,
leaving 1-inch border; sprinkle with mozzarella.
Bake on bottom rack until crust is golden and
cheese is melted, about 15 minutes. Sprinkle
with basil.

PER SERVING (⅙ OF PIZZA): 169 grams, 193 Cal,
3 g Total Fat, 2 g Sat Fat, 0 g Trans Fat, 8 mg Chol,
310 mg Sod, 32 g Total Carb, 7 g Total Sugar, 3 g Fib,
9 g Prot, 104 mg Calc.
PointsPlus value: **5**

Easy Clam Pizza

serves 6

2 (6½-ounce) cans chopped clams, drained
¼ cup moist-packed sun-dried tomatoes (not
packed in oil), chopped
2 large garlic cloves, minced
1 tablespoon olive oil
¼ teaspoon red pepper flakes
¼ teaspoon black pepper
1 (10-ounce) prebaked thin whole wheat pizza
crust
1½ cups shredded part-skim mozzarella
cheese
2 tablespoons grated Parmesan cheese
2 tablespoons chopped fresh parsley

1   Place rack on lowest rung of oven. Preheat oven to 450°F. Spray nonstick pizza pan or baking sheet with nonstick spray.
2   Mix together clams, sun-dried tomatoes, garlic, oil, and pepper flakes in medium bowl.
3   Place pizza crust on prepared pizza pan. Spread clam mixture evenly over crust; sprinkle with mozzarella and Parmesan. Bake until mozzarella is melted, about 10 minutes. Sprinkle with parsley.

PER SERVING (⅙ OF PIZZA): 132 grams, 258 Cal, 10 g Total Fat, 5 g Sat Fat, 0 g Trans Fat, 31 mg Chol, 705 mg Sod, 25 g Total Carb, 3 g Total Sugar, 5 g Fib, 19 g Prot, 262 mg Calc.
PointsPlus value: **7**

▲ **HEATHY EXTRA**
Intensify the tomato flavor in this pizza by adding 1 cup halved grape tomatoes to the clam mixture in step 2.

Caramelized Onion, Fig, and Stilton Pizza

serves 6

2 teaspoons olive oil
3 Vidalia or other sweet onions, thinly sliced
6 dried figs, stemmed and sliced
1 (10-ounce) prebaked thin whole wheat pizza
crust
3 ounces Stilton cheese, crumbled

1   Place rack on lowest rung of oven. Preheat oven to 450°F. Spray nonstick pizza pan or baking sheet with nonstick spray or line with parchment paper.
2   Heat oil in large nonstick skillet over medium heat. Add onions and cook, stirring, until softened, about 5 minutes. Reduce heat to low; add figs and cook, stirring occasionally, until onions are golden brown and figs are softened, about 12 minutes longer.
3   Place pizza crust on prepared pizza pan. Spoon onion mixture evenly over crust; sprinkle with Stilton. Bake until topping is heated through and cheese is softened, about 15 minutes.

PER SERVING (⅙ OF PIZZA): 140 grams, 258 Cal, 8 g Total Fat, 4 g Sat Fat, 0 g Trans Fat, 11 mg Chol, 434 mg Sod, 40 g Total Carb, 16 g Total Sugar, 8 g Fib, 9 g Prot, 163 mg Calc.
PointsPlus value: **7**

FYI Stilton is considered one of the world's greatest cheeses. There are only six dairies licensed to produce this special cheese, and it can only be made in the English counties of Derbyshire, Leicestershire, and Nottingham. Stilton takes its name from the village where it was first made.

CARAMELIZED ONION, FIG,
AND STILTON PIZZA

Greek Pizza

serves 6

1 tablespoon olive oil
1 onion, chopped
1 (10-ounce) package frozen chopped spinach,
   thawed and squeezed dry
1 cup fat-free ricotta cheese
⅓ cup crumbled reduced-fat feta cheese
4 scallions, thinly sliced
¼ cup snipped fresh dill
½ teaspoon black pepper
½ recipe (about 1 pound) Cornmeal Pizza
   Dough (page 322)

1   Place rack on lowest rung of oven. Preheat
oven to 450°F. Spray nonstick pizza pan or baking sheet with nonstick spray.
2   Heat oil in large nonstick skillet over
medium-high heat. Add onion and cook, stirring, until softened, about 5 minutes. Stir in
spinach and cook, stirring, until flavors are
blended, about 3 minutes. Transfer to large
bowl; stir in all remaining ingredients except
dough.
3   Turn dough out onto lightly floured work
surface; cut in half. Briefly knead each piece of
dough until smooth. With lightly floured rolling
pin, roll one piece of dough into 12-inch round.
Transfer to prepared pizza pan.
4   Spread spinach mixture evenly over
dough, leaving 1-inch border. Lightly brush
edge of dough with water. Roll remaining piece
of dough into 12-inch round. Place on top of
spinach filling; crimp edge to seal tightly. Cut
4 slashes in top of dough to allow steam to
escape. Bake until filling is heated through and
crust is golden, about 25 minutes.

PER SERVING (⅙ OF PIZZA): 174 grams, 181 Cal,
4 g Total Fat, 1 g Sat Fat, 0 g Trans Fat, 7 mg Chol,
328 mg Sod, 28 g Total Carb, 3 g Total Sugar, 5 g Fib,
9 g Prot, 156 mg Calc.
PointsPlus value: *6*

▲ **HEALTHY EXTRA**
A classic Greek salad is the perfect way to begin
your meal. Toss together thick cucumber slices,
wedges of tomatoes, and red onion slices and
sprinkle with fat-free feta cheese (1 ounce of
crumbed fat-free feta cheese with each serving will
increase the *PointsPlus* value by *1*).

Mushroom, Bacon, and Gruyère Pizza

serves 6

2 teaspoons olive oil
3 cups sliced cremini mushrooms
1 large red onion, thinly sliced
1 teaspoon dried thyme
½ teaspoon salt
¼ teaspoon black pepper
¼ cup dry red wine
1 (10-ounce) prebaked thin whole wheat pizza
   crust
4 slices turkey bacon, crisp cooked and
   crumbled
½ cup shredded Gruyère cheese

1　Place rack on lowest rung of oven. Preheat oven to 450°F. Spray nonstick pizza pan or baking sheet with nonstick spray.

2　Heat oil in large nonstick skillet over medium-high heat. Add mushrooms and cook, stirring, until mushroom liquid is released and it evaporates, about 10 minutes. Stir in onion, thyme, salt, and pepper. Cook, stirring, until onion is softened, about 5 minutes. Add wine and cook, stirring, until evaporated, about 3 minutes longer.

3　Place pizza crust on prepared pizza pan. Spoon mushroom mixture evenly over crust. Sprinkle with bacon and Gruyère. Bake until topping is heated through and cheese is melted, about 15 minutes.

PER SERVING (⅙ OF PIZZA): 123 grams, 216 Cal, 9 g Total Fat, 4 g Sat Fat, 0 g Trans Fat, 18 mg Chol, 573 mg Sod, 26 g Total Carb, 3 g Total Sugar, 5 g Fib, 10 g Prot, 155 mg Calc.
PointsPlus value: **6**

CHOPPING ONIONS

1　With large chef's knife, cut off stem end of onion. Cut onion in half through root end; remove brown peel.

2　Place onion half, cut side down, on cutting board. Make cuts, ¼ inch apart, up to root end. Keeping root end intact, make cuts across, ¼ inch apart, to form ¼-inch pieces.

3　Repeat with other half.

SICILIAN SAUSAGE-STUFFED PIZZA

Sicilian Sausage–Stuffed Pizza

serves 8

½ *pound fully cooked smoked chicken*
sausages, coarsely chopped
1 *pound cremini or white mushrooms, sliced*
1 *onion, chopped*
1 *tomato, chopped*
1 *large garlic clove, minced*
½ *cup shredded part-skim mozzarella cheese*
¼ *cup part-skim ricotta cheese*
¼ *cup grated Romano or Parmesan cheese*
½ *recipe (about 1 pound) Whole Wheat Pizza*
Dough (page 322)

1 Place rack on lowest rung of oven. Preheat oven to 450°F. Spray nonstick pizza pan or baking sheet with nonstick spray.

2 Spray large nonstick skillet with nonstick spray and set over medium-high heat. Add sausages and cook, stirring, until lightly browned, about 5 minutes; transfer to large bowl.

3 Add mushrooms and onion to skillet; cook, stirring, until mushroom liquid is released and it evaporates, about 10 minutes. Stir in tomato and garlic; cook 1 minute longer. Add mushroom mixture to sausages in bowl; let cool. Stir in mozzarella, ricotta, and Romano.

4 Turn dough out onto lightly floured work surface and knead until smooth; cut in half. With lightly floured rolling pin, roll one piece of dough into 12-inch round. Transfer dough to prepared pizza pan. Spread mushroom filling evenly over dough, leaving ¾-inch border. Lightly brush edge of dough with water.

5 Roll remaining piece of dough into 12-inch round; place on top of filling. Press edges together to seal; crimp edge. Cut 5 slits in top of dough to allow steam to escape. Bake until crust is golden, about 15 minutes. Let cool 5–10 minutes and serve hot, or transfer to wire rack and serve warm or at room temperature. Cut into 8 wedges.

PER SERVING (1 WEDGE): 153 grams, 168 Cal, 6 g Total Fat, 2 g Sat Fat, 0 g Trans Fat, 30 mg Chol, 387 mg Sod, 19 g Total Carb, 3 g Total Sugar, 3 g Fib, 12 g Prot, 109 mg Calc.
PointsPlus value: *4*

▲ HEALTHY EXTRA
Enjoy this stuffed pizza with a crisp radicchio, endive, and arugula salad tossed with red wine vinegar and a pinch of salt.

Mushroom-Spinach Calzones

serves 4

²/₃ cup warm water (105°–115°F)
1 package quick-rise yeast
¼ teaspoon sugar
1 cup bread flour
½ cup whole wheat flour
½ teaspoon salt
1 onion, chopped
1 teaspoon dried oregano
3 cups coarsely chopped white or cremini
    mushrooms
½ (10-ounce) package frozen chopped
    spinach, thawed and squeezed dry
¾ cup shredded part-skim mozzarella cheese

1   Spray baking sheet with nonstick spray.
2   Combine water, yeast, and sugar in small bowl, stirring to dissolve. Let stand until foamy, about 5 minutes.
3   Combine bread flour, whole wheat flour, and salt in food processor; pulse until mixed well. With machine running, scrape yeast mixture through feed tube, processing just until dough forms a ball. Knead dough by pulsing until smooth and elastic, about 3 minutes.
4   Spray large bowl with nonstick spray; place dough in bowl, turning to coat. Cover bowl with plastic wrap and let dough rise in warm place (80°–85°F) until doubled in volume, 30–45 minutes.
5   Meanwhile, spray large nonstick skillet with nonstick spray and set over medium heat. Add onion and oregano; cook, stirring, until onion is softened, about 5 minutes. Transfer to plate. Add mushrooms to skillet and cook, stirring occasionally, until mushrooms release their liquid and it evaporates, about 15 minutes. Remove skillet from heat; stir in onion and spinach.

6   Punch down dough in bowl. Turn dough out onto lightly floured work surface; cut into 4 equal pieces. With lightly floured rolling pin, roll out each piece of dough into 7-inch round. Place one-fourth of vegetable mixture in center of each dough round; top each with 3 tablespoons of mozzarella. Fold dough over filling to form half-moon shape; press edges together firmly to seal. Place calzones on prepared baking sheet. Cover loosely with plastic wrap and let rise in warm place (80°–85°F) 30 minutes.
7   Meanwhile, place racks in upper and lower thirds of oven. Place roasting pan on lower rack; add enough hot water to come 2 inches up sides of pan. Preheat oven to 400°F.
8   Bake calzones on upper rack until lightly browned, about 20 minutes.

PER SERVING (1 CALZONE): 243 grams, 200 Cal, 4 g Total Fat, 2 g Sat Fat, 0 g Trans Fat, 12 mg Chol, 424 mg Sod, 31 g Total Carb, 4 g Total Sugar, 4 g Fib, 13 g Prot, 195 mg Calc.
PointsPlus value: **5**

FYI   Calzones, individual half moon–shaped filled pizzas, originated in Naples. The filling can be sausages, vegetables, or poultry along with cheese; they can be deep-fried or baked as we have done here.

Pissaladière with Tomato Coulis and Goat Cheese

serves 6

1 tablespoon +2 teaspoons olive oil
2 onions, thinly sliced
¼ teaspoon salt
4 large tomatoes, chopped (about 4 cups)
1 teaspoon sugar
1 tablespoon balsamic vinegar
½ recipe (about 1 pound) Whole Wheat Pizza
    Dough (page 322)
4 ounces reduced-fat soft goat cheese
10 niçoise olives, pitted and chopped
1 teaspoon dried thyme

1   Place rack on lowest rung of oven. Preheat
oven to 450°F. Spray 10½ × 15½-inch nonstick jelly-roll pan with nonstick spray.
2   Heat 1 tablespoon of oil in large nonstick
skillet over medium heat. Add onions and salt;
cook, stirring, until onions are golden, about 15
minutes. Transfer to plate.
3   To make tomato coulis, heat remaining
2 teaspoons oil in same skillet. Add tomatoes
and sugar; cook, stirring, until liquid is almost
evaporated, about 10 minutes. Add vinegar
and simmer until evaporated, about 1 minute.
4   With floured hands, stretch and press
dough onto bottom of prepared jelly-roll pan.
Spread onions evenly over dough; spoon tomato coulis over. Sprinkle evenly with goat
cheese, olives, and thyme. Bake until crust is
golden and cheese is softened, about 20 minutes. Cut into 6 squares. Serve warm.

PER SERVING (1 SQUARE): 252 grams, 241 Cal,
11 g Total Fat, 2 g Sat Fat, 0 g Trans Fat, 3 mg Chol,
410 mg Sod, 31 g Total Carb, 8 g Total Sugar, 5 g Fib,
6 g Prot, 23 mg Calc.
PointsPlus value: *6*

Greek-Style Grilled Lamb Burger Sandwiches

serves 4

1 pound lean ground lamb
1 scallion, finely chopped
¼ cup chopped fresh cilantro
1 large egg white
½ teaspoon salt
¼ teaspoon black pepper
1⅓ cups lightly packed thinly sliced
    romaine lettuce
2 tomatoes, sliced
¼ cup lightly packed fresh mint leaves
4 (6-inch) whole wheat pita breads, warmed
⅓ cup plain fat-free yogurt

1   Mix together lamb, scallion, cilantro, egg
white, salt, and pepper in medium bowl just
until combined well. With damp hands, shape
into 4 (½-inch-thick) patties.
2   Spray grill rack with nonstick spray. Preheat grill to medium-high or prepare medium-
high fire using direct method.
3   Place patties on grill rack and grill until
instant-read thermometer inserted into side
of burger registers 145°F for medium, about 5
minutes per side.
4   Fill each pita bread with 1 lamb burger
and one-fourth of lettuce, tomatoes, and mint;
drizzle evenly with yogurt.

PER SERVING (1 BURGER-STUFFED PITA): 268 grams,
346 Cal, 8 g Total Fat, 2 g Sat Fat, 0 g Trans Fat,
65 mg Chol, 712 mg Sod, 42 g Total Carb,
4 g Total Sugar, 6 g Fib, 30 g Prot, 72 mg Calc.
PointsPlus value: *9*

GRILLED STEAK SANDWICHES WITH GOLDEN ONIONS

Grilled Steak Sandwiches with Golden Onions

serves 4

1 teaspoon olive oil
2 large onions, thinly sliced
2 teaspoons sugar
2 teaspoons red wine vinegar
¼ teaspoon salt
¼ teaspoon black pepper
1 (1-pound) flank steak, trimmed
2 tablespoons Dijon mustard
8 slices whole grain bread
1 cup lightly packed baby arugula

1   Heat oil in medium nonstick skillet over medium-high heat. Add onions and sugar; cook, stirring, until onions are golden, about 10 minutes. Add vinegar, ⅛ teaspoon of salt, and ⅛ teaspoon of pepper; cook, stirring constantly, until vinegar is evaporated, about 30 seconds. Remove skillet from heat.
2   Meanwhile, spray broiler rack with non-stick spray. Preheat broiler.
3   Sprinkle steak with remaining ⅛ teaspoon salt and ⅛ teaspoon pepper. Put steak on prepared broiler rack and broil 5 inches from heat until instant-read thermometer inserted into side of steak registers 145°F for medium, about 5 minutes per side. Let stand 5 minutes. Cut against grain into 12 slices.
4   Spread mustard evenly on 4 slices of bread; top evenly with arugula. Place 3 slices of steak in each sandwich; top each with ¼ cup of onion. Cover with remaining bread.

PER SERVING (1 SANDWICH): 206 grams, 350 Cal, 12 g Total Fat, 4 g Sat Fat, 1 g Trans Fat, 54 mg Chol, 661 mg Sod, 33 g Total Carb, 9 g Total Sugar, 5 g Fib, 29 g Prot, 87 mg Calc.
PointsPlus value: **9**

Roast Beef Sandwiches with Horseradish Mayonnaise

serves 4

¼ cup reduced-fat mayonnaise
1 tablespoon prepared horseradish, drained
⅛ teaspoon salt
⅛ teaspoon black pepper
4 Boston or butter lettuce leaves
8 slices whole wheat bread
½ pound thinly sliced fat-free roast beef
1 large tomato, thinly sliced
8 thin slices red onion

1   To make sauce, stir together mayonnaise, horseradish, salt, and pepper in cup.
2   Place 1 lettuce leaf on each of 4 slices of bread. Top each with one-fourth of roast beef, one-fourth of tomato, 2 onion slices, and remaining slices of bread.

PER SERVING (1 SANDWICH): 203 grams, 136 Cal, 6 g Total Fat, 1 g Sat Fat, 0 g Trans Fat, 40 mg Chol, 699 mg Sod, 30 g Total Carb, 6 g Total Sugar, 5 g Fib, 21 g Prot, 136 mg Calc.
PointsPlus value: **6**

▲ **HEALTHY EXTRA**
Add a slice of fat-free Swiss cheese to each sandwich for even more great flavor. One (¾-ounce) slice of fat-free Swiss cheese per serving will increase the *PointsPlus* value by *1*.

California Hummus Sandwiches

serves 4

*1 cup (8 ounces) store-bought hummus,
   or 1 cup Hummus (page 57)*
8 slices whole grain bread
8 thick tomato slices
1 cup shredded carrots
1 cup lightly packed tender watercress sprigs
1 cup alfalfa, pea, or broccoli sprouts

Spread 2 tablespoons of hummus on each slice
of bread. Layer each of 4 slices of bread with
2 tomato slices, ¼ cup of carrots, ¼ cup of
watercress, and ¼ cup of alfalfa sprouts. Cover
with remaining slices of bread.

PER SERVING (1 SANDWICH): 199 grams, 257 Cal,
8 g Total Fat, 1 g Sat Fat, 0 g Trans Fat, 0 mg Chol,
507 mg Sod, 38 g Total Carb, 6 g Total Sugar, 9 g Fib,
11 g Prot, 93 mg Calc.
PointsPlus value: **6**

Egg Salad Sandwiches with Curry and Cilantro

serves 4

7 hard-cooked large eggs, peeled and halved
¼ cup fat-free mayonnaise
1 scallion, chopped
3 tablespoons chopped fresh cilantro
2 teaspoons curry powder
⅛ teaspoon black pepper
8 slices whole grain bread
4 Boston or butter lettuce leaves

1   Remove and discard 3 egg yolks (or reserve
for another use). Chop or grate remaining 4
eggs and 3 egg whites; put in medium bowl.
Stir in all remaining ingredients except bread
and lettuce.
2   Spread ½ cup of egg salad on each of 4
slices of bread. Top each with 1 lettuce leaf
and cover with remaining slices of bread.

PER SERVING (1 SANDWICH): 156 grams, 235 Cal,
8 g Total Fat, 2 g Sat Fat, 0 g Trans Fat, 214 mg Chol,
480 mg Sod, 28 g Total Carb, 6 g Total Sugar, 4 g Fib,
15 g Prot, 84 mg Calc.
PointsPlus value: **6**

 HEALTHY EXTRA
Add thick slices of ripe tomato to the sandwiches.

Middle Eastern–Style Chicken Sandwiches

serves 4

1 tablespoon white wine vinegar
2 teaspoons olive oil
½ teaspoon salt
¼ teaspoon black pepper
4 (5-ounce) skinless boneless chicken breasts
1 small garlic clove, chopped
1 cup plain fat-free yogurt
1 kirby cucumber, unpeeled and shredded
2 tablespoons finely chopped fresh mint
4 (6-inch) pocketless pita breads
2 cups lightly packed thinly sliced romaine
    lettuce
½ small red onion, thinly sliced

1   To make marinade, combine vinegar, oil, ¼ teaspoon of salt, and ⅛ teaspoon of pepper in large zip-close plastic bag; add chicken. Squeeze out air and seal bag; turn to coat chicken. Refrigerate, turning bag occasionally, at least 2 hours or up to 4 hours.

2   Meanwhile, spray grill rack with nonstick spray. Preheat grill to medium or prepare medium fire using direct method.

3   To make raita, with side of large knife, mash garlic with remaining ¼ teaspoon salt on cutting board until it forms a paste. Stir together yogurt, cucumber, mint, garlic paste, and remaining ⅛ teaspoon pepper in serving bowl.

4   Remove chicken from bag; discard marinade. Place chicken on grill rack and grill until cooked through, about 5 minutes per side. When cool enough to handle, cut on diagonal into ½-inch slices.

5   Place pitas on work surface; top each with ½ cup of lettuce and one-fourth of chicken and onion. Top each with 2 tablespoons of raita. Gently fold in sides of sandwiches; wrap bottom half of each sandwich in foil or parchment. Serve remaining raita alongside.

PER SERVING (1 SANDWICH): 290 grams, 377 Cal, 6 g Total Fat, 1 g Sat Fat, 0 g Trans Fat, 80 mg Chol, 719 mg Sod, 41 g Total Carb, 5 g Total Sugar, 3 g Fib, 38 g Prot, 165 mg Calc.
PointsPlus value: **9**

▲ **HEALTHY EXTRA**
Serve clusters of seedless red or green grapes alongside the sandwiches.

Vietnamese-Style Grilled Chicken Sandwiches

serves 4

1/4 cup lime juice
2 teaspoons canola oil
Pinch cayenne
4 (5-ounce) skinless boneless chicken breasts
1 cup matchstick-cut carrots
1/2 cup seasoned rice vinegar
1 teaspoon sugar
1/2 cup fat-free mayonnaise
1 tablespoon ketchup
1/4 teaspoon chili powder
1 (10-ounce) whole grain baguette, cut into
      4 equal pieces
12 baby romaine lettuce leaves
20 thin slices peeled cucumber
24 fresh cilantro leaves

1   To make marinade, combine lime juice, oil, and cayenne in large zip-close plastic bag; add chicken. Squeeze out air and seal bag; turn to coat chicken. Refrigerate, turning bag occasionally, at least 1 hour or up to 4 hours.

2   Meanwhile, mix together carrots, vinegar, and sugar in small bowl; let stand about 15 minutes. Stir together mayonnaise, ketchup, and chili powder in another small bowl.

3   Spray grill rack with nonstick spray. Preheat grill to medium or prepare medium fire using direct method. (Or spray nonstick ridged grill pan with nonstick spray and set over medium heat.) Remove chicken from bag; discard marinade. Place chicken on grill rack (or in grill pan) and grill until cooked through, about 5 minutes per side. Transfer to plate; let stand 5 minutes. Cut on diagonal into 1/2-inch slices.

4   Drain carrots. Cut each piece of bread lengthwise in half, cutting almost all the way through. Spread mayonnaise mixture on bottom half of bread. Layer each sandwich with 3 romaine leaves, 5 cucumber slices, 1/4 cup of carrots, one-fourth of chicken, and 6 cilantro leaves.

PER SERVING (1 SANDWICH): 295 grams, 396 Cal, 7 g Total Fat, 1 g Sat Fat, 0 g Trans Fat, 82 mg Chol, 689 mg Sod, 48 g Total Carb, 8 g Total Sugar, 6 g Fib, 37 g Prot, 55 mg Calc.
PointsPlus value: *10*

FYI   If the fresh cilantro you purchase comes with the stems attached, do not throw them away after trimming. They are jam-packed with flavor. Wash and pat them dry, then chop and use in your favorite soup, salad, or marinade.

VIETNAMESE-STYLE GRILLED CHICKEN SANDWICHES

Turkey BLTs

serves 4

8 slices turkey bacon, crisp cooked
½ cup fat-free mayonnaise
¼ teaspoon black pepper
8 slices whole grain bread, toasted
8 thick tomato slices
8 Boston or butter lettuce leaves

1   Break each bacon slice in half. Stir together mayonnaise and pepper in small bowl.
2   Spread 1 tablespoon of seasoned mayonnaise on each slice of bread. Layer each of 4 slices of bread with 4 pieces of bacon, 2 tomato slices, and 1 lettuce leaf. Cover with remaining slices of bread.

PER SERVING (1 SANDWICH): 178 grams, 238 Cal, 9 g Total Fat, 2 g Sat Fat, 0 g Trans Fat, 29 mg Chol, 735 mg Sod, 32 g Total Carb, 7 g Total Sugar, 5 g Fib, 10 g Prot, 69 mg Calc.
PointsPlus value: **6**

Sicilian-Style Sausage and Pepper Heroes

serves 4

¾ pound sweet Italian-style turkey sausages
2 red bell peppers, halved and seeded
1 large onion, thickly sliced
1 tablespoon balsamic vinegar
½ teaspoon dried oregano
¼ teaspoon black pepper
Pinch red pepper flakes
4 (8-inch) whole wheat hero rolls, split

1   Spray grill rack with nonstick spray. Preheat grill to medium-high or prepare medium-high fire using direct method.
2   Place sausages, bell peppers, and onion on grill rack and grill, turning, until sausages are cooked through, bell peppers are blackened, and onion is lightly browned and softened, about 20 minutes.
3   Put bell peppers in large zip-close plastic bag; seal bag and let steam 10 minutes.
4   When cool enough to handle, peel bell peppers and cut into wide strips. Transfer to large bowl. When cool enough to handle, cut sausages on diagonal into ½-inch slices. Add to bell peppers in bowl. Separate onion into rings and add to bowl along with vinegar, oregano, black pepper, and pepper flakes; toss to mix well.
5   With your fingers, remove bready centers from rolls; discard. Fill each roll with one-fourth of sausage mixture.

PER SERVING (1 SANDWICH): 241 grams, 363 Cal, 11 g Total Fat, 3 g Sat Fat, 0 g Trans Fat, 38 mg Chol, 820 mg Sod, 51 g Total Carb, 8 g Total Sugar, 8 g Fib, 19 g Prot, 106 mg Calc.
PointsPlus value: **9**

Classic Tuna Salad Sandwiches

serves 4

1 (5-ounce) package water-packed white tuna
1 (2.5-ounce) package water-packed white tuna
6 tablespoons fat-free mayonnaise
2 small celery stalks with leaves, thinly sliced
2 scallions, thinly sliced
2 tablespoons chopped fresh parsley
Pinch salt
Pinch black pepper
8 slices whole grain bread
8 thick tomato slices
8 small lettuce leaves

1   Flake tuna in medium bowl. Stir in mayonnaise, celery, scallions, parsley, salt, and pepper.
2   Spread scant ½ cup of tuna mixture on each of 4 slices of bread. Top each with 2 tomato slices and 2 lettuce leaves. Cover with remaining slices of bread.

PER SERVING (1 SANDWICH): 220 grams, 233 Cal, 5 g Total Fat, 1 g Sat Fat, 0 g Trans Fat, 25 mg Chol, 684 mg Sod, 31 g Total Carb, 7 g Total Sugar, 5 g Fib, 19 g Prot, 77 mg Calc.
PointsPlus value: *6*

▲ HEALTHY EXTRA

A crunchy carrot salad is a great way to get more vitamins. Toss together packaged matchstick-cut carrots, some finely chopped fresh parsley, lemon juice, and a pinch each of salt and black pepper.

Grilled Shrimp, Basil, and Goat Cheese Sandwiches

serves 4

1 pound large shrimp, peeled and deveined
8 fresh basil leaves, thinly sliced
1 tablespoon extra-virgin olive oil
¼ teaspoon salt
⅛ teaspoon black pepper
8 slices whole grain country-style bread
1 (4¼-ounce) package light garlic and herb cheese spread
20 arugula leaves
2 tomatoes, each cut into 4 thick slices

1   Toss together shrimp, basil, oil, salt, and pepper in large bowl; marinate in refrigerator 20 minutes.
2   Meanwhile, spray grill rack with nonstick spray. Preheat grill to medium or prepare medium fire using direct method.
3   Thread shrimp onto 4 (10-inch) metal skewers. Discard marinade. Place shrimp and slices of bread on grill rack and grill, turning, until shrimp are just opaque in center and bread is golden brown and nicely marked, 3–5 minutes.
4   Spread cheese spread evenly on slices of bread. Top each of 4 slices of bread with 5 arugula leaves, 2 tomato slices, and one-fourth of shrimp. Cover with remaining slices of bread.

PER SERVING (1 SANDWICH): 257 grams, 309 Cal, 9 g Total Fat, 3 g Sat Fat, 0 g Trans Fat, 173 mg Chol, 737 mg Sod, 29 g Total Carb, 5 g Total Sugar, 4 g Fib, 28 g Prot, 130 mg Calc.
PointsPlus value: *8*

▲ HEALTHY EXTRA

For dessert, serve a bowl of large strawberries, preferably with their stems still attached.

Crab Cake Sandwiches

serves 4

2 tablespoons lemon juice
4 teaspoons olive oil
2 teaspoons Dijon mustard
¾ pound crabmeat, picked over
¼ cup fat-free mayonnaise
¼ cup minced shallots
¼ cup + 3 tablespoons plain dried bread
    crumbs
1 large egg white, lightly beaten
2 whole wheat English muffins, split and
    toasted
1 cup lightly packed baby romaine lettuce

1   To make dressing, combine lemon juice, oil, and mustard.

2   Spray broiler rack with nonstick spray. Preheat broiler.

3   To make crab cakes, mix crabmeat, mayonnaise, shallots, 3 tablespoons of bread crumbs, and the egg white in bowl. Shape mixture into 4 patties. Coat with remaining ¼ cup bread crumbs.

4   Place patties on broiler rack; spray with nonstick spray and broil until golden, about 4 minutes per side. Put English muffin half on each of 4 plates; top with lettuce, 1 crab cake, and dressing.

PER SERVING (1 SANDWICH): 194 grams, 269 Cal,
8 g Total Fat, 1 g Sat Fat, 0 g Trans Fat, 61 mg Chol,
777 mg Sod, 19 g Total Carb, 6 g Total Sugar, 3 g Fib,
24 g Prot, 177 mg Calc.
PointsPlus value: **7**

▲ **HEALTHY EXTRA**
Place a large slice of tomato and a thin slice of red onion on top of the lettuce.

Lobster Rolls

serves 4

1 pound cooked lobster meat, coarsely
    chopped
¼ cup reduced-fat mayonnaise
2 scallions, thinly sliced
1 celery stalk, chopped
Juice of ½ lemon
¼ teaspoon black pepper
4 split-top hot dog buns, split and toasted

Mix together all ingredients except buns in medium bowl. Fill each bun with one-fourth of lobster mixture.

PER SERVING (1 SANDWICH): 199 grams, 288 Cal,
8 g Total Fat, 2 g Sat Fat, 0 g Trans Fat, 86 mg Chol,
806 mg Sod, 26 g Total Carb, 4 g Total Sugar, 2 g Fib,
27 g Prot, 124 mg Calc.
PointsPlus value: **7**

FYI As delectable as these rolls are with lobster, they are equally delicious when prepared with lump crabmeat. Just be sure to pick over the crabmeat to remove all the bits of cartilage.

14

Yeast Breads, Quick Breads, and Muffins

Yeast Breads, Quick Breads, and Muffins

344   No-Knead Whole Wheat Bread
344   No-Knead Dried Tomato and Herb Bread
345   Honey-Wheat Crescent Rolls
346   Whole Wheat Focaccia
346   Food Processor Wheat Bread with Honey
347   Bran Bread
348   Holiday Stollen
350   Panettone
351   Classic Sticky Buns
352   Hot Cross Buns
353   Sweet Brown Bread
353   Irish Soda Bread
354   Quick Naan Flatbread
354   Classic Corn Bread
355   Pepper Jack and Chile Corn Bread
355   Banana-Applesauce Bread
356   Carrot-Pecan Bread
356   Cranberry-Orange Bread
357   Jumbo Bran Muffins
357   Buttermilk-Blueberry Corn Muffins
358   Whole Grain Breakfast Muffins
360   Baking Powder Biscuits
361   Orange and Sage Biscuits
361   Yogurt Biscuits
363   Double Grain Blueberry Scones
364   Whole Wheat–Buttermilk Scones

No-Knead Whole Wheat Bread
serves 12

3 cups whole wheat flour
½ cup steel-cut oats
2 teaspoons salt
1 package quick-rise yeast
1½ cups water

1   Generously spray 5 × 9-inch loaf pan with nonstick spray.
2   Stir together flour, oats, salt, and yeast in large bowl. Add water, stirring until blended (dough will be very sticky). Cover bowl with plastic wrap; let dough rise in warm place (80°–85°F) until covered with popped bubbles, about 4 hours.
3   Turn dough out onto lightly floured work surface. With floured hands, punch down dough and fold over onto itself twice (dough will be sticky). Shape dough into rectangle and transfer to prepared pan, pressing dough into corners and sides. Loosely cover pan with plastic wrap; let rise in warm place (80°–85°F) 1 hour.
4   Meanwhile, preheat oven to 375°F.
5   Remove plastic wrap; bake until browned, about 40 minutes. Remove bread from pan and let cool completely on wire rack.

PER SERVING (¹⁄₁₂ **OF LOAF**): 68 grams, 128 Cal, 1 g Total Fat, 0 g Sat Fat, 0 g Trans Fat, 0 mg Chol, 391 mg Sod, 27 g Total Carb, 1 g Total Sugar, 4 g Fib, 5 g Prot, 15 mg Calc.
PointsPlus value: *3*

FYI   Quick-rise yeast (also known as rapid-rise yeast and instant yeast) makes baking with yeast simpler. Unlike active dry yeast, quick-rise yeast is mixed directly into the flour mixture, since it does not need to be combined with water to start working.

No-Knead Dried Tomato and Herb Bread
serves 12

3 cups bread flour
1 package quick-rise yeast
2 teaspoons dried thyme
1 teaspoon salt
1 cup water
½ cup grated Parmesan cheese
5 moist-packed sun-dried tomatoes
    (not packed in oil), coarsely chopped

1   Whisk together flour, yeast, thyme, and salt in large bowl. Stir in water. Stir in Parmesan and sun-dried tomatoes. Cover bowl with plastic wrap; let dough rise in warm place (80°–85°F) until covered with bubbles, about 4 hours.
2   Turn dough out onto lightly floured work surface. Punch down dough and fold over onto itself twice. Transfer to clean bowl and cover; let rest 30 minutes.
3   Meanwhile, place heavy ovenproof lidded 3-quart saucepan, Dutch oven, or casserole dish in oven. Preheat oven to 450°F.
4   With lightly floured hands, shape dough into ball with same diameter as saucepan. Sprinkle cornmeal all over dough.
5   Wearing oven mitts, remove saucepan from oven. Carefully place dough, bottom facing up, in saucepan. Cover and bake 30 minutes. Uncover and bake until dark brown, about 30 minutes longer. Remove bread from pan and let cool completely on wire rack.

PER SERVING (¹⁄₁₂ **OF LOAF**): 41 grams, 146 Cal, 2 g Total Fat, 1 g Sat Fat, 0 g Trans Fat, 3 mg Chol, 274 mg Sod, 26 g Total Carb, 1 g Total Sugar, 1 g Fib, 6 g Prot, 57 mg Calc.
PointsPlus value: *4*

Honey-Wheat Crescent Rolls

makes 12

1 cup warm water (105°–115°F)
2 tablespoons honey
1 package active dry yeast
1½ cups all-purpose flour
1 cup whole wheat flour
1½ teaspoons salt

1   Combine water, honey, and yeast in 2-cup glass measure, stirring to dissolve. Let stand until foamy, about 5 minutes.

2   Combine all-purpose flour, whole wheat flour, and salt in food processor. With machine running, scrape yeast mixture through feed tube; pulse until dough forms a ball, about 1 minute. Turn dough out onto lightly floured work surface; knead just until smooth, about 2 minutes.

3   Spray large bowl with nonstick spray; place dough in bowl, turning to coat. Cover bowl with plastic wrap and let dough rise in warm place (80°–85°F) until doubled in volume, about 35 minutes.

4   Spray baking sheet with nonstick spray.

5   Punch dough down in bowl. Turn dough out onto lightly floured work surface; cut in half. Roll one piece of dough into 10-inch round. With pizza cutter or long, thin knife, cut into 6 wedges. Roll each wedge up from wide side. Place rolls, pointed end down, 1 inch apart, on prepared baking sheet. Repeat with remaining dough, making total of 12 rolls. Cover loosely with plastic wrap and let rise in warm place (80°–85°F) until doubled in volume, about 35 minutes.

6   Meanwhile, preheat oven to 375°F.

7   Bake until rolls are golden brown and sound hollow when tapped on bottom, about 15 minutes. Transfer to wire rack. Serve warm or at room temperature.

PER SERVING (1 ROLL): 50 grams, 103 Cal, 0 g Total Fat, 0 g Sat Fat, 0 g Trans Fat, 0 mg Chol, 293 mg Sod, 22 g Total Carb, 3 g Total Sugar, 2 g Fib, 3 g Prot, 7 mg Calc.
PointsPlus value: *3*

FYI   To mix the rolls by hand, in a large bowl, stir together the water, honey, and yeast; set aside until foamy. Stir in the all-purpose flour, whole-wheat flour, and salt until the dough starts to gather around the spoon. Turn the dough out onto a lightly floured work surface and knead until smooth and elastic, about 10 minutes. Proceed as directed.

Whole Wheat Focaccia

serves 12

1 1/2 cups all-purpose flour
1/2 cup whole wheat flour
1 package quick-rise yeast
1 teaspoon sugar
1 teaspoon salt
1 cup warm water (105°–115°F)
1 1/2 tablespoons olive oil

1   Spray large bowl and large baking sheet with olive oil nonstick spray. Lightly sprinkle baking sheet with cornmeal.
2   Combine all-purpose flour, whole wheat flour, yeast, sugar, and salt in food processor; pulse until mixed well. With machine running, pour water through feed tube, processing just until dough forms a ball. Knead dough by pulsing until smooth and elastic, about 3 minutes. Turn dough out onto lightly floured work surface; knead 1 minute. Transfer dough to prepared bowl, turning to coat. Cover bowl with plastic wrap; let dough rise in warm place (80°–85°F) until doubled in volume, about 40 minutes.
3   Turn dough out onto lightly floured work surface. Punch down dough and shape into 8 × 12-inch rectangle; transfer to prepared baking sheet. Cover loosely with clean kitchen towel; let rise 30 minutes.
4   Meanwhile, preheat oven to 425°F.
5   With your fingers, poke dough all over to create dimples; lightly brush with oil. Bake until browned, about 20 minutes. Let cool 5 minutes on baking sheet on wire rack. Cut focaccia into 12 pieces. Serve warm.

PER SERVING (1 PIECE): 44 grams, 92 Cal, 2 g Total Fat, 0 g Sat Fat, 0 g Trans Fat, 0 mg Chol, 195 mg Sod, 16 g Total Carb, 1 g Total Sugar, 1 g Fib, 3 g Prot, 5 mg Calc.
PointsPlus value: *2*

Variations

Fresh Rosemary and Coarse Salt Focaccia

Lightly press about 1 tablespoon fresh rosemary leaves into dough after brushing with oil; sprinkle with 1/2 teaspoon coarse sea salt or kosher salt and proceed as directed.

Red Onion Focaccia

Sprinkle dough with 1/3 cup very thinly sliced red onion after brushing with oil; proceed as directed.

Sun-Dried Tomato and Olive Focaccia

Sprinkle dough with 3 tablespoons chopped moist-packed sun-dried tomatoes (not packed in oil) and 3 tablespoons chopped pitted Kalamata olives after brushing with oil; proceed as directed.

PER SERVING (1 PIECE): 46 grams, 99 Cal, 3 g Total Fat, 0 g Sat Fat, 0 g Trans Fat, 0 mg Chol, 244 mg Sod, 17 g Total Carb, 1 g Total Sugar, 1 g Fib, 3 g Prot, 7 mg Calc.
PointsPlus value: *3*

Food Processor Wheat Bread with Honey

serves 12

1 cup warm water (105°–115°F)
1 tablespoon + 1 teaspoon honey
1 package active dry yeast
1 1/4 cups all-purpose flour
1/4 cup whole wheat flour
1 teaspoon salt

1   Stir together water, honey, and yeast in 2-cup glass measure, stirring to dissolve. Let stand until foamy, about 5 minutes.

2   Combine all-purpose flour, whole wheat flour, and salt in food processor; pulse until mixed well. With machine running, scrape yeast mixture through feed tube, processing just until dough forms a ball. Knead dough by pulsing until smooth and elastic, about 3 minutes.

3   Spray large bowl with nonstick spray; place dough in bowl, turning to coat. Cover bowl with plastic wrap; let dough rise in warm place (80°–85°F) until doubled in volume, about 1 hour. Punch down dough. Turn dough out onto lightly floured surface; pat into 8 × 12-inch rectangle. Fold lengthwise into thirds, pinching seams to seal; shape into 8-inch loaf.

4   Spray 4½ × 8½-inch loaf pan with non-stick spray. Place dough, seam side down, in pan. Cover loosely with clean kitchen towel; let rise in warm place (80°–85°F) until doubled in volume, about 1 hour.

5   Meanwhile, preheat oven to 350°F.

6   Bake until bread sounds hollow when tapped on bottom, about 1 hour. Remove from pan and let cool completely on wire rack.

PER SERVING (¹⁄₁₂ OF LOAF): 39 grams, 65 Cal, 0 g Total Fat, 0 g Sat Fat, 0 g Trans Fat, 0 mg Chol, 195 mg Sod, 14 g Total Carb, 2 g Total Sugar, 1 g Fib, 2 g Prot, 4 mg Calc.
PointsPlus value: *2*

FYI   Using a food processor to knead dough makes baking bread fast and easy. But if you enjoy kneading, follow the recipe until the dough is formed, then turn it out onto a lightly floured work surface and knead until smooth and elastic, about 10 minutes.

▲ HEALTHY EXTRA

Turn a slice of our hearty bread into a healthful breakfast by serving it with 1 cup each of fat-free cottage cheese and sweet cherries (1 cup of fat-free cottage cheese with each serving will increase the *PointsPlus* value by *3*).

Bran Bread

serves 12

1 package active dry yeast
1¹⁄₃ cups warm water (105°–115°F)
2 cups all-purpose flour
1 cup unprocessed wheat bran
¾ cup whole wheat flour
2 teaspoons salt

1   Sprinkle yeast over water in 2-cup glass measure, stirring to dissolve. Let stand until foamy, about 5 minutes.

2   Combine all-purpose flour, wheat bran, whole wheat flour, and salt in food processor; pulse until mixed well. With machine running, scrape yeast mixture through feed tube, processing just until dough forms a ball. Knead dough by pulsing until smooth and elastic.

3   Spray large bowl with nonstick spray; place dough in bowl, turning to coat. Cover bowl; let dough rise in warm place (80°–85°F) until doubled in volume, about 1 hour. Punch down dough. Cover bowl; let dough rise in warm place (80°–85°F) 30 minutes.

4   Punch down dough. Turn dough out onto lightly floured work surface; pat into 8 × 12-inch rectangle. Fold lengthwise into thirds, pinching seams to seal; shape into 8-inch loaf. Spray 4½ × 8½-inch loaf pan with nonstick spray. Place loaf, seam side down, in pan. Cover and let rise until dough is 1 inch above rim of pan, about 1 hour.

5   Meanwhile, preheat oven to 375°F.

6   Bake until bread sounds hollow when tapped on bottom, 45–50 minutes. Remove from pan and let cool completely on wire rack.

PER SERVING (¹⁄₁₂ OF LOAF): 59 grams, 110 Cal, 1 g Total Fat, 0 g Sat Fat, 0 g Trans Fat, 0 mg Chol, 390 mg Sod, 24 g Total Carb, 1 g Total Sugar, 3 g Fib, 4 g Prot, 9 mg Calc.
PointsPlus value: *3*

Holiday Stollen

serves 16

¹/₂ cup golden raisins
¹/₃ cup candied fruit, such as cherries,
*   citron, orange peel, or lemon peel or a*
*   combination, chopped*
¹/₄ cup dried currants
¹/₄ cup dark rum or apple juice
3¹/₄–3¹/₂ cups all-purpose flour
³/₄ cup fat-free milk, warmed (105°–115°F)
¹/₃ cup + 1 teaspoon granulated sugar
1 package active dry yeast
¹/₃ cup slivered almonds
1 teaspoon salt
¹/₂ teaspoon ground cardamom
1 large egg
5 tablespoons unsalted butter, melted and
*   cooled*
¹/₂ teaspoon vanilla extract
3 tablespoons confectioners' sugar

1   Combine raisins, candied fruit, currants, and rum in small saucepan and set over medium heat. Bring to simmer; remove saucepan from heat and let stand 30 minutes. Drain fruit, discarding liquid. Toss together fruit and ¹/₄ cup of flour in small bowl until coated.

2   Combine milk, 1 teaspoon of granulated sugar, and the yeast in large bowl of electric mixer, stirring to dissolve. Let stand 5 minutes. Combine 3 cups of flour, the remaining ¹/₃ cup granulated sugar, the almonds, salt, and cardamom in medium bowl. Add flour mixture, dried fruit mixture, egg, butter, and vanilla to yeast mixture and beat on medium-low speed until sticky dough forms.

3   Turn dough out onto well-floured work surface and knead, adding enough of remaining flour, 1 tablespoon at a time, until dough becomes smooth and elastic, about 10 minutes. Spray large bowl with nonstick spray. Place dough in bowl, turning to coat. Cover bowl with plastic wrap and let dough rise in warm place (80°–85°F), until indentation made with your index finger remains, about 1¹/₂ hours (dough will not be doubled in volume).

4   Spray baking sheet with nonstick spray.

5   Punch down dough in bowl; let rest 10 minutes. Turn dough out onto lightly floured work surface; roll into 9 × 15-inch oval. Fold dough lengthwise almost in half, allowing about 1 inch of bottom half to protrude. Transfer dough to prepared baking sheet. Cover loosely with plastic wrap and let dough rise in warm place (80°–85°F) until doubled in volume, about 1 hour.

6   Meanwhile, preheat oven to 350°F.

7   Remove plastic wrap. Bake until stollen is lightly browned and sounds hollow when tapped on bottom, 25–30 minutes. Immediately sprinkle with confectioners' sugar. Transfer to wire rack to cool completely.

PER SERVING (¹/₁₆ OF LOAF): 64 grams, 204 Cal, 5 g Total Fat, 2 g Sat Fat, 0 g Trans Fat, 23 mg Chol, 14 mg Sod, 35 g Total Carb, 12 g Total Sugar, 2 g Fib, 4 g Prot, 31 mg Calc.
PointsPlus value: **5**

FYI Stollen is a traditional German fruit bread usually eaten at Christmas. It is thought to have originated in the city of Dresden in 1474. At that time, in preparation for Christmas, the use of milk and butter was forbidden, making stollen heavy and somewhat tasteless. In Dresden today, there are 150 bakers designated as official stollen bakers.

HOLIDAY STOLLEN

Panettone

serves 16

$^1/_3$ *cup fat-free milk*
1 package active dry yeast
$^1/_2$ *cup bread flour*
2 cups +2 tablespoons all-purpose flour
$^1/_4$ *cup sugar*
2 teaspoons grated lemon zest
$^1/_2$ *teaspoon salt*
$^3/_4$ *cup golden raisins*
$^1/_2$ *cup finely chopped candied fruit peel*
2 large eggs, lightly beaten
4 tablespoons unsalted butter, melted
    and cooled
$^1/_4$ *cup water*
1 teaspoon vanilla extract
$^1/_4$ *teaspoon anise extract (optional)*

1   Heat milk over medium-low heat in small saucepan until warm (105°–115°F). Remove saucepan from heat and sprinkle in yeast, whisking until dissolved.

2   Put bread flour in large bowl. Add yeast mixture, stirring until paste is formed. Cover bowl with plastic wrap and let rise in warm place (80°–85°F) until doubled in volume, about 1 hour 15 minutes.

3   Combine 2 cups of all-purpose flour, the sugar, lemon zest, and salt in food processor fitted with plastic blade; pulse until mixed well. Add raisins and candied fruit peel. With machine running, scrape yeast mixture and all remaining ingredients through feed tube, processing until dough forms.

4   Turn dough out onto lightly floured work surface and knead in remaining 2 tablespoons all-purpose flour. Spray large bowl with nonstick spray; place dough in bowl, turning to coat.

5   Cover bowl with plastic wrap and let dough rise in warm place (80°–85°F) until

doubled in volume, about 1 hour 30 minutes. Punch down dough.

6   Lightly spray panettone mold or 6-inch soufflé dish with nonstick spray. Put dough in mold. Lightly spray piece of plastic wrap with nonstick spray; place, sprayed side down, on top of panettone. Let rise in warm place (80°–85°F) until doubled in volume, about 1½ hours.

7   Meanwhile, preheat oven to 375°F.

8   With single-edge razor blade or very sharp small knife, cut × in top of panettone. Bake until well browned and toothpick inserted into center of panettone comes out clean, about 40 minutes. Cool in mold on wire rack 15 minutes; unmold and let cool completely on rack.

PER SERVING (¹⁄₁₆ **OF PANETTONE):** 56 grams, 164 Cal, 4 g Total Fat, 2 g Sat Fat, 0 g Trans Fat, 34 mg Chol, 91 mg Sod, 29 g Total Carb, 12 g Total Sugar, 0 g Fib, 4 g Prot, 24 mg Calc.
PointsPlus value: **5**

FYI   Grated orange zest can be substituted for the lemon zest, and dark raisins or currants can be used instead of the golden raisins, if you like.

Classic Sticky Buns

makes 8

1 package active dry yeast
2 tablespoons warm water (105°–115°F)
½ cup fat-free milk, warmed (105°–115°F)
1 large egg
1 tablespoon unsalted butter, melted
2¼ cups all-purpose flour
3 tablespoons granulated sugar
1½ teaspoons ground cinnamon
½ teaspoon salt
½ cup dark raisins
2 teaspoons fat-free milk
¼ cup confectioners' sugar
1½ teaspoons water
½ teaspoon vanilla extract

1   Sprinkle yeast over water in cup, stirring to dissolve. Let stand until foamy, about 5 minutes.
2   Stir together 2 tablespoons of warm milk, the egg, and butter in small bowl. Combine flour, granulated sugar, cinnamon, and salt in food processor. With machine running, scrape yeast mixture through feed tube, then pour in remaining warm milk, processing until dough forms a ball. Knead dough by pulsing until smooth and elastic, about 3 minutes.
3   Spray large bowl with nonstick spray. Place dough in bowl, turning to coat. Cover bowl with plastic wrap and let dough rise in warm place (80°–85°F) until doubled in volume, 30–45 minutes.
4   Spray 8-inch round cake pan with nonstick spray. Punch down dough. Turn dough out onto lightly floured work surface; knead in raisins. Divide dough into 8 equal pieces. Roll each piece of dough into 8-inch rope, then coil each rope to form bun. Place buns in prepared pan; cover pan loosely with plastic wrap. Let rise until doubled in volume, 35–40 minutes.

5   Meanwhile, preheat oven to 375°F.
6   Brush tops of buns with 2 teaspoons milk. Bake until lightly browned, 20–25 minutes.
7   Stir together confectioners' sugar, water, and vanilla in small bowl until smooth. With small spatula, spread icing over hot buns. Serve warm or at room temperature.

PER SERVING (1 BUN): 80 grams, 205 Cal, 3 g Total Fat, 1 g Sat Fat, 0 g Trans Fat, 31 mg Chol, 166 mg Sod, 40 g Total Carb, 13 g Total Sugar, 2 g Fib, 6 g Prot, 38 mg Calc.
PointsPlus value: **6**

FYI You can substitute golden raisins for the dark raisins and apple pie spice for the cinnamon, if you like.

Hot Cross Buns

makes 12

¾ *cup + 2 tablespoons warm water*
    (105°–115°F)
2 tablespoons + 1 teaspoon granulated sugar
1 package active dry yeast
2¾ *cups all-purpose flour*
¼ *cup whole wheat flour*
1 teaspoon salt
1 teaspoon ground cinnamon
½ *teaspoon ground nutmeg*
½ *teaspoon ground cloves*
1 large egg, lightly beaten
1 tablespoon unsalted butter, melted
¼ *cup dried currants or raisins*
2 tablespoons mixed diced candied fruit
¼ *cup confectioners' sugar*
1 teaspoon lemon juice

1   Combine water, 1 teaspoon of granulated sugar, and the yeast in 2-cup glass measure, stirring to dissolve. Let stand until foamy, about 5 minutes.
2   Combine all-purpose flour, whole wheat flour, remaining 2 tablespoons granulated sugar, the salt, cinnamon, nutmeg, and cloves in food processor; pulse until mixed well. With machine running, scrape yeast mixture, egg, and butter through feed tube, pulsing until dough forms a ball, about 1 minute. Turn dough out onto lightly floured work surface; knead in currants and candied fruit.
3   Spray large bowl with nonstick spray; place dough in bowl, turning to coat. Cover bowl loosely with plastic wrap; let dough rise in warm place (80°–85°F) until doubled in volume, about 1 hour.

4   Spray baking sheet with nonstick spray. Punch down dough in bowl. Turn out onto lightly floured work surface and knead just until smooth, about 2 minutes. Divide dough into 12 equal pieces; shape each piece into ball. Place balls about 2 inches apart on prepared baking sheet. Cover loosely with plastic wrap; let rise in warm place (80°–85°F) until doubled in volume, about 30 minutes.
5   Meanwhile, preheat oven to 375°F.
6   Remove plastic wrap. Bake until buns sound hollow when tapped on bottom, about 20 minutes. Transfer to wire rack and let cool completely.
7   Stir together confectioners' sugar and lemon juice in small bowl until smooth. Spoon into small plastic bag; snip off one corner and pipe cross on each bun.

PER SERVING (1 BUN): 65 grams, 163 Cal, 2 g Total Fat, 1 g Sat Fat, 0 g Trans Fat, 20 mg Chol, 202 mg Sod, 33 g Total Carb, 8 g Total Sugar, 2 g Fib, 4 g Prot, 14 mg Calc.
PointsPlus value: *4*

FYI Eating these spiced buns on Good Friday is a custom that dates back to the early 1700s in England. At that time, a law was introduced that allowed these buns to be eaten only on that particular holiday.

Sweet Brown Bread

serves 12

1¼ cups whole wheat flour
1 teaspoon baking powder
1 teaspoon grated orange or lemon zest
½ teaspoon ground cinnamon
½ teaspoon baking soda
⅛ teaspoon salt
½ cup low-fat buttermilk
1 large egg
3 tablespoons dark molasses
2 tablespoons dark brown sugar

1   Preheat oven to 375°F. Spray 4½ × 8½-inch loaf pan with nonstick spray.
2   Whisk together flour, baking powder, orange zest, cinnamon, baking soda, and salt in medium bowl. Whisk together buttermilk, egg, molasses, and brown sugar in small bowl until blended. Add buttermilk mixture to flour mixture, stirring just until flour mixture is moistened (do not overmix). Pour batter into prepared pan.
3   Bake until toothpick inserted into center of bread comes out clean, 35–40 minutes. Let cool in pan on wire rack 10 minutes. Remove bread from pan and let cool completely on rack.

PER SERVING (¹⁄₁₂ OF LOAF): 35 grams, 75 Cal, 1 g Total Fat, 0 g Sat Fat, 0 g Trans Fat, 18 mg Chol, 128 mg Sod, 16 g Total Carb, 6 g Total Sugar, 2 g Fib, 3 g Prot, 39 mg Calc.
PointsPlus value: *2*

▲ HEALTHY EXTRA
Enjoy a slice of this slightly sweet, delicately spiced bread with ⅔ cup fat-free ricotta cheese and some sliced strawberries, and increase the *PointsPlus* value by *3*.

Irish Soda Bread

serves 10

1½ cups + 1 tablespoon all-purpose flour
½ cup whole wheat flour
½ cup dried currants
2 teaspoons caraway seeds
2 teaspoons grated lemon zest
1 teaspoon baking soda
½ teaspoon salt
1 cup low-fat buttermilk
3 tablespoons honey
1 teaspoon sugar

1   Set rack in upper third of oven. Preheat oven to 350°F. Spray baking sheet with nonstick spray.
2   Whisk together all-purpose flour, whole wheat flour, currants, caraway seeds, lemon zest, baking soda, and salt in large bowl. Whisk together buttermilk and honey in small bowl until blended. Add buttermilk mixture to flour mixture, stirring just until flour mixture is moistened (do not overmix).
3   Turn dough out onto lightly floured work surface. With floured hands, gently knead 7 times. Shape dough into 7-inch round loaf; place on prepared baking sheet. With single-edge razor blade or very sharp knife, cut × in top of bread; sprinkle with sugar.
4   Bake until browned and toothpick inserted into center of bread comes out clean, 40–45 minutes. Transfer to wire rack. Serve warm or at room temperature.

PER SERVING (¹⁄₁₀ OF LOAF): 66 grams, 144 Cal, 1 g Total Fat, 0 g Sat Fat, 0 g Trans Fat, 1 mg Chol, 270 mg Sod, 32 g Total Carb, 12 g Total Sugar, 2 g Fib, 4 g Prot, 44 mg Calc.
PointsPlus value: *4*

Quick Naan Flatbread

makes 8

2 cups all-purpose flour
1½ teaspoons baking powder
1 teaspoon sugar
¼ teaspoon salt
⅛ teaspoon baking soda
½ cup fat-free milk
1 large egg

1   Combine flour, baking powder, sugar, salt, and baking soda in food processor; pulse until mixed well. Beat milk and egg in small bowl. With machine running, pour milk mixture through feed tube, processing just until dough forms a ball. Knead dough by pulsing until smooth and elastic, about 3 minutes.
2   Spray large bowl with nonstick spray; place dough in bowl, turning to coat. Cover bowl with plastic wrap; let dough rise in warm place (80°–85°F) until doubled in volume, about 3 hours.
3   Preheat oven to 450°F. Lightly spray large baking sheet with olive oil nonstick spray or line with sheet of parchment paper.
4   Punch down dough in bowl. Turn dough out onto lightly floured work surface. Divide dough into 8 equal pieces; shape each piece into ⅜-inch-thick teardrop shape. Transfer to prepared baking sheet. Bake until firm, 10–12 minutes. Transfer to wire rack and let cool completely.

PER SERVING (1 NAAN): 54 grams, 130 Cal, 1 g Total Fat, 0 g Sat Fat, 0 g Trans Fat, 27 mg Chol, 180 mg Sod, 25 g Total Carb, 2 g Total Sugar, 1 g Fib, 5 g Prot, 42 mg Calc.
PointsPlus value: *3*

FYI   Naan is traditionally made with yeast. This easy version uses baking powder as the raising agent.

Classic Corn Bread

serves 12

1¼ cups yellow cornmeal
¾ cup all-purpose flour
4 teaspoons sugar
2½ teaspoons baking powder
½ teaspoon salt
1 cup + 2 tablespoons low-fat buttermilk
1 large egg

1   Preheat oven to 400°F. Spray 8-inch square baking pan with nonstick spray.
2   Whisk together cornmeal, flour, sugar, baking powder, and salt in large bowl. Beat buttermilk and egg in small bowl until blended. Add buttermilk mixture to flour mixture, stirring just until flour mixture is moistened (do not overmix). Pour batter into prepared pan and spread evenly.
3   Bake until golden brown and toothpick inserted into center of corn bread comes out clean, 20–25 minutes. Let cool in pan on wire rack 10 minutes. Cut into 12 pieces. Serve warm.

PER SERVING (1 PIECE): 52 grams, 102 Cal, 1 g Total Fat, 0 g Sat Fat, 0 g Trans Fat, 19 mg Chol, 206 mg Sod, 20 g Total Carb, 3 g Total Sugar, 1 g Fib, 3 g Prot, 47 mg Calc.
PointsPlus value: *3*

FYI   For corn bread with an extra-crispy crust, spray an 8-inch cast-iron skillet with nonstick spray and preheat in the oven. Wearing oven mitts, remove the hot skillet from the oven and pour in the batter, spreading evenly. Bake as directed.

Pepper Jack and Chile Corn Bread

serves 12

1 cup all-purpose flour
¾ cup yellow cornmeal
1 tablespoon sugar
1 teaspoon salt
1 teaspoon baking powder
¼ teaspoon baking soda
1 cup low-fat buttermilk
1 large egg, lightly beaten
2 large egg whites, lightly beaten
1 (4½-ounce) can diced mild green chiles,
    drained
3 tablespoons canola oil
½ cup shredded reduced-fat pepper Jack
    cheese

1   Preheat oven to 425°F. Spray 8-inch square baking pan with nonstick spray.
2   Whisk together flour, cornmeal, sugar, salt, baking powder, and baking soda in large bowl. Beat buttermilk, egg, egg whites, chiles, and oil in medium bowl until blended. Add buttermilk mixture to flour mixture, stirring just until flour mixture is moistened (do not overmix). Gently stir in pepper Jack. Pour batter into prepared pan and spread evenly.
3   Bake until edges are golden and toothpick inserted into center of corn bread comes out clean, about 20 minutes. Let cool in pan on wire rack 10 minutes. Cut into 12 pieces. Serve warm.

PER SERVING (1 PIECE): 67 grams, 138 Cal, 5 g Total Fat, 1 g Sat Fat, 0 g Trans Fat, 22 mg Chol, 334 mg Sod, 18 g Total Carb, 3 g Total Sugar, 1 g Fib, 5 g Prot, 68 mg Calc.
PointsPlus value: *4*

Banana-Applesauce Bread

serves 12

1¼ cups all-purpose flour
1 cup whole wheat flour
½ teaspoon baking soda
½ teaspoon salt
6 very ripe small bananas
1 cup sugar
½ cup fat-free egg substitute
⅓ cup canola oil
¼ cup unsweetened applesauce
1 teaspoon vanilla extract

1   Preheat oven to 350°F. Spray 5 × 9-inch loaf pan with nonstick spray; dust with flour, shaking out excess.
2   Whisk all-purpose flour, whole wheat flour, baking soda, and salt in medium bowl.
3   Mash bananas in large bowl; whisk in sugar, egg substitute, oil, applesauce, and vanilla until blended. Add banana mixture to flour mixture, stirring just until flour mixture is moistened (do not overmix). Scrape batter into prepared pan and spread evenly.
4   Bake until deep golden brown and toothpick inserted into center of bread comes out clean, about 1 hour 15 minutes. Let cool in pan on wire rack 10 minutes. Remove bread from pan and let cool completely on rack.

PER SERVING (1/12 OF LOAF): 112 grams, 255 Cal, 7 g Total Fat, 1 g Sat Fat, 0 g Trans Fat, 0 mg Chol, 172 mg Sod, 46 g Total Carb, 27 g Total Sugar, 3 g Fib, 4 g Prot, 12 mg Calc.
PointsPlus value: *7*

Carrot-Pecan Bread

serves 16

1 1/2 cups white whole wheat flour
1 cup all-purpose flour
1 1/2 teaspoons ground cinnamon
1 teaspoon baking powder
1 teaspoon baking soda
1/2 teaspoon salt
1/4 teaspoon ground nutmeg
3/4 cup plain fat-free yogurt
1/2 cup packed dark brown sugar
1/2 cup applesauce
1/4 cup canola oil
2 large egg whites
2 1/2 cups shredded carrots
1/2 cup pecans, chopped
1/2 cup dried cranberries, chopped

1   Preheat oven to 350°F. Spray 5 × 9-inch loaf pan with nonstick spray.
2   Whisk together white whole wheat flour, all-purpose flour, cinnamon, baking powder, baking soda, salt, and nutmeg in large bowl. Whisk together yogurt, brown sugar, apple-sauce, oil, and egg whites in medium bowl until blended. Add applesauce mixture to flour mixture, stirring just until flour mixture is moistened (do not overmix). Stir in carrots, pecans, and cranberries just until blended. Scrape batter into prepared pan and spread evenly.
3   Bake until toothpick inserted into center of bread comes out clean, 50–60 minutes. Let cool in pan on wire rack 10 minutes. Remove bread from pan and let cool completely on rack.

PER SERVING (1/16 OF LOAF): 78 grams, 182 Cal, 7 g Total Fat, 1 g Sat Fat, 0 g Trans Fat, 0 mg Chol, 197 mg Sod, 29 g Total Carb, 12 g Total Sugar, 3 g Fib, 4 g Prot, 37 mg Calc.
PointsPlus value: **5**

Cranberry-Orange Bread

serves 20

2 1/4 cups all-purpose flour
1/4 cup whole wheat flour
2 teaspoons baking powder
1/2 teaspoon baking soda
1/2 teaspoon salt
6 tablespoons butter, softened
1 cup sugar
2 large eggs
1 tablespoon grated orange zest
1/2 cup orange juice
2 teaspoons vanilla extract
1 1/2 cups fresh or frozen cranberries, chopped
1/2 cup chopped walnuts

1   Preheat oven to 350°F. Lightly spray 5 × 9-inch loaf pan with nonstick spray; dust with flour, shaking out excess.
2   Whisk both flours, the baking powder, the baking soda, and the salt in large bowl.
3   With electric mixer on medium speed, beat butter and sugar in large bowl until light and fluffy. Add eggs, one at a time. Reduce mixer speed to low; beat in half of flour mixture just until blended. Add orange zest and juice and vanilla, beating until blended. Beat in remaining flour mixture just until blended. Stir in cranberries and walnuts. Scrape batter into prepared pan and spread evenly.
4   Bake until toothpick inserted into center of bread comes out clean, about 55 minutes. Let cool in pan on wire rack 10 minutes. Remove loaf from pan and let cool completely on rack. Cut into 10 slices; cut each slice in half.

PER SERVING (1/2 SLICE): 54 grams, 160 Cal, 6 g Total Fat, 3 g Sat Fat, 0 g Trans Fat, 30 mg Chol, 135 mg Sod, 24 g Total Carb, 11 g Total Sugar, 1 g Fib, 3 g Prot, 19 mg Calc.
PointsPlus value: **4**

Jumbo Bran Muffins

makes 6

¼ cup + 2 tablespoons all-purpose flour
2 tablespoons light brown sugar
2 tablespoons butter, cut into pieces
2 tablespoons chopped walnuts
1½ cups unprocessed wheat bran
1 cup white whole wheat flour
1 teaspoon baking soda
½ teaspoon baking powder
¼ teaspoon salt
1 large egg
2 large egg whites
⅓ cup granulated sugar
2 tablespoons dark molasses
1 cup low-fat buttermilk
⅔ cup golden raisins

1   Preheat oven to 375°F. Spray nonstick 6-cup jumbo muffin pan with nonstick spray.
2   To make crumb topping, combine 2 tablespoons of all-purpose flour and the brown sugar in medium bowl. With pastry blender, cut in butter. Stir in walnuts.
3   To make batter, whisk bran, white whole wheat flour, remaining ¼ cup all-purpose flour, the baking soda, baking powder, and salt in large bowl. With electric mixer, beat egg, egg whites, sugar, and molasses in separate large bowl until blended. Reduce mixer speed; beat in buttermilk. Add bran mixture, beating just until blended. Stir in raisins. Spoon batter into prepared cups. Sprinkle evenly with topping.
4   Bake until toothpick inserted into center of muffin comes out clean, about 25 minutes. Cool 5 minutes. Remove from pan; cool.

PER SERVING (½ MUFFIN): 76 grams, 174 Cal,
4 g Total Fat, 2 g Sat Fat, 0 g Trans Fat, 24 mg Chol,
211 mg Sod, 33 g Total Carb, 18 g Total Sugar, 5 g Fib,
6 g Prot, 54 mg Calc.
PointsPlus value: **5**

Buttermilk-Blueberry Corn Muffins

makes 12

1 cup all-purpose flour
½ cup white whole wheat flour
½ cup yellow cornmeal, preferably
    stone ground
⅓ cup granulated sugar
1½ teaspoons baking powder
½ teaspoon baking soda
½ teaspoon ground cinnamon
¼ teaspoon salt
1 cup low-fat buttermilk
¼ cup canola oil
1 large egg
1½ cups fresh or frozen blueberries
2 tablespoons turbinado (raw) sugar

1   Preheat oven to 400°F. Line 12-cup muffin pan with paper liners.
2   Whisk together all-purpose flour, white whole wheat flour, cornmeal, granulated sugar, baking powder, baking soda, cinnamon, and salt in large bowl. Beat buttermilk, oil, and egg in small bowl until blended. Add buttermilk mixture to flour mixture, stirring just until flour mixture is moistened (do not overmix). Gently stir in blueberries. Spoon batter evenly into prepared cups; sprinkle with turbinado sugar.
3   Bake until muffin springs back when lightly pressed, 15–20 minutes. Let cool in pan on wire rack 5 minutes. Remove muffins from pan and let cool on rack.

PER SERVING (1 MUFFIN): 77 grams, 172 Cal,
6 g Total Fat, 1 g Sat Fat, 0 g Trans Fat, 19 mg Chol,
177 mg Sod, 28 g Total Carb, 11 g Total Sugar, 2 g Fib,
4 g Prot, 42 mg Calc.
PointsPlus value: **5**

Whole Grain Breakfast Muffins

makes 12

1½ cups whole wheat flour
½ cup all-purpose flour
⅓ cup sugar
¼ cup + 2 teaspoons toasted wheat germ
1 tablespoon baking powder
½ teaspoon salt
¾ cup reduced-fat (2%) milk
⅓ cup canola oil
¼ cup fat-free egg substitute

1   Preheat oven to 400°F. Line 12-cup muffin pan with paper liners.
2   Whisk together whole wheat flour, all-purpose flour, sugar, ¼ cup of wheat germ, the baking powder, and salt in medium bowl. Beat milk, oil, and egg substitute in small bowl until blended. Add milk mixture to flour mixture, stirring just until flour mixture is moistened (do not overmix). Spoon batter into prepared cups, filling them about two-thirds full. Sprinkle with remaining 2 teaspoons wheat germ.
3   Bake until browned and toothpick inserted into center of muffin comes out clean, about 25 minutes. Cool muffins in pan on wire rack 3 minutes; remove muffins from pan and serve warm.

PER SERVING (1 MUFFIN): 56 grams, 166 Cal, 7 g Total Fat, 1 g Sat Fat, 0 g Trans Fat, 1 mg Chol, 211 mg Sod, 23 g Total Carb, 7 g Total Sugar, 2 g Fib, 4 g Prot, 48 mg Calc.
PointsPlus value: **5**

Variations

Jam-Filled Whole Wheat Muffins

Fill muffin cups evenly with half of batter. Top each with 1 teaspoon of raspberry or strawberry jam. Cover evenly with remaining batter; bake as directed.

PER SERVING (1 MUFFIN): 63 grams, 183 Cal, 7 g Total Fat, 1 g Sat Fat, 0 g Trans Fat, 1 mg Chol, 211 mg Sod, 27 g Total Carb, 11 g Total Sugar, 2 g Fib, 4 g Prot, 48 mg Calc.
PointsPlus value: **5**

Ginger and Golden Raisin Muffins

Stir 1 tablespoon finely chopped crystallized ginger and ¼ cup finely chopped golden raisins into batter.

PER SERVING (1 MUFFIN): 60 grams, 180 Cal, 7 g Total Fat, 1 g Sat Fat, 0 g Trans Fat, 1 mg Chol, 212 mg Sod, 26 g Total Carb, 10 g Total Sugar, 3 g Fib, 5 g Prot, 50 mg Calc.
PointsPlus value: **5**

Orange-Spice Muffins

Add ½ teaspoon pumpkin pie spice and 1 teaspoon grated orange zest to flour mixture.

PER SERVING (1 MUFFIN): 56 grams, 167 Cal, 7 g Total Fat, 1 g Sat Fat, 0 g Trans Fat, 1 mg Chol, 211 mg Sod, 23 g Total Carb, 7 g Total Sugar, 2 g Fib, 4 g Prot, 48 mg Calc.
PointsPlus value: **5**

WHOLE GRAIN BREAKFAST MUFFINS

TESTING FOR DONENESS

1 Insert toothpick or cake tester into center of baked good; it should come out clean (unless recipe states otherwise).

2 For muffins, begin testing 5 minutes before suggested minimum baking time. Quick breads and cakes should be tested 10 minutes before suggested minimum baking time and then every 5 minutes.

Baking Powder Biscuits
makes 12

1 cup whole wheat flour
¾ cup all-purpose flour
3 tablespoons toasted wheat germ
2 teaspoons baking powder
½ teaspoon baking soda
½ teaspoon salt
3 tablespoons cold unsalted butter, cut into
   pieces
¾ cup low-fat buttermilk

1   Preheat oven to 400°F.
2   Whisk together whole wheat flour, all-purpose flour, wheat germ, baking powder, baking soda, and salt in medium bowl. With pastry blender or two knives used scissors-style, cut butter into flour mixture until mixture resembles coarse crumbs. Add buttermilk in 2 additions, stirring with fork until very moist dough forms.
3   Turn dough out onto lightly floured work surface and knead 6 times. Pat dough into 7-inch round. With floured 2-inch round cutter, cut out biscuits without twisting cutter. Gather scraps and reroll, making total of 12 biscuits. Place biscuits about 1 inch apart on ungreased baking sheet.
4   Bake until golden brown, 12–15 minutes. Serve hot or warm.

PER SERVING (2 BISCUITS): 79 grams, 201 Cal, 7 g Total Fat, 4 g Sat Fat, 0 g Trans Fat, 17 mg Chol, 460 mg Sod, 30 g Total Carb, 3 g Total Sugar, 3 g Fib, 7 g Prot, 75 mg Calc.
PointsPlus value: **5**

FYI   When you knead the dough, be sure to use just enough flour to prevent the dough from being too sticky. A moist dough is a bit harder to work with, but the resulting biscuits will be very, very tender.

Orange and Sage Biscuits
makes 12

1 cup all-purpose flour
¾ cup white whole wheat flour
1½ teaspoons baking powder
2 teaspoons dried sage
1 teaspoon salt
½ teaspoon baking soda
5 tablespoons cold unsalted butter, cut into
    pieces
¾ cup low-fat buttermilk
2 teaspoons grated orange zest

1   Whisk together all-purpose flour, white whole wheat flour, baking powder, sage, salt, and baking soda in large bowl. With pastry blender or two knives used scissors-style, cut butter into flour mixture until mixture resembles coarse crumbs.
2   Stir together buttermilk and orange zest in glass measure. Add to flour mixture, stirring with fork just until blended. Knead mixture in bowl once or twice to form soft dough. Shape dough into disk; wrap in plastic wrap and re-frigerate about 15 minutes.
3   Meanwhile, preheat oven to 425°F. Spray large baking sheet with nonstick spray.
4   On lightly floured work surface, roll dough to scant ½-inch thickness. With floured 2-inch round cutter, cut out biscuits without twist-ing cutter. Gather scraps and reroll, making total of 12 biscuits. Place biscuits, about 1 inch apart, on prepared baking sheet.
5   Bake until golden brown, 12–15 minutes. Serve hot or warm.

PER SERVING (1 BISCUIT): 13 grams, 119 Cal,
5 g Total Fat, 3 g Sat Fat, 0 g Trans Fat, 13 mg Chol,
332 mg Sod, 15 g Total Carb, 1 g Total Sugar, 1 g Fib,
3 g Prot, 36 mg Calc.
PointsPlus value: *3*

Yogurt Biscuits
makes 16

2 cups all-purpose flour
1 cup plain fat-free yogurt
1 teaspoon sugar
2 teaspoons baking powder
½ teaspoon baking soda
½ teaspoon salt

1   Stir together 1 cup of flour and the yogurt in large bowl until blended and very smooth; sprinkle with sugar. Cover bowl loose-ly with plastic wrap and let rest in warm place (80°–85°F) at least 4 hours or up to overnight.
2   Preheat oven to 425°F. Spray baking sheet with nonstick spray.
3   Whisk together remaining 1 cup flour, the baking powder, baking soda, and salt in medium bowl. Stir into yogurt mixture until well blended.
4   Turn dough out onto lightly floured work surface; pat into 6 × 8-inch rectangle. With pizza cutter or long, thin knife, cut dough lengthwise into 4 strips, then cut each strip crosswise into 4 pieces, making total of 16 bis-cuits. Place biscuits 1 inch apart on prepared baking sheet.
5   Bake 10 minutes. Reduce oven tempera-ture to 400°F. Bake until golden brown, about 10 minutes longer. Transfer biscuits to wire rack; serve warm.

PER SERVING (1 BISCUIT): 31 grams, 64 Cal,
0 g Total Fat, 0 g Sat Fat, 0 g Trans Fat, 0 mg Chol,
168 mg Sod, 13 g Total Carb, 1 g Total Sugar, 0 g Fib,
2 g Prot, 31 mg Calc.
PointsPlus value: *2*

FYI   If you prefer your biscuits to contain some whole grains, substitute white whole wheat flour for half of the all-purpose flour.

DOUBLE GRAIN BLUEBERRY SCONES

Double Grain Blueberry Scones

makes 12

1 ½ *cups white whole wheat flour*
½ *cup old-fashioned oats*
¼ *cup ground flaxseed*
¼ *cup packed brown sugar*
1 ½ *teaspoons baking powder*
½ *teaspoon baking soda*
½ *teaspoon salt*
4 *tablespoons cold unsalted butter, cut into*
    pieces
1 *cup fresh or frozen blueberries*
¾ *cup low-fat buttermilk*
1 *large egg white*
1 *tablespoon turbinado (raw) sugar*

1   Preheat oven to 375°F. Spray baking sheet with nonstick spray.

2   Whisk together flour, oats, flaxseed, brown sugar, baking powder, baking soda, and salt in large bowl. With pastry blender or two knives used scissors-style, cut in butter until mixture resembles coarse crumbs. Gently stir in blueberries. Reserve 1 tablespoon of buttermilk. Beat remaining buttermilk and the egg white in small bowl until blended. Add to flour mixture, stirring just until flour mixture is moistened (dough will be soft).

3   Gather dough into ball and place on lightly floured work surface; cut in half. Knead each piece of dough 2 times. Place portions of dough about 5 inches apart on prepared baking sheet. Pat each piece of dough into 6-inch round. Spray long, thin knife with nonstick spray; cut each round into 6 wedges (do not separate wedges). Brush scones with reserved buttermilk and sprinkle evenly with turbinado sugar.

4   Bake until toothpick inserted into center of scone comes out clean, 15–20 minutes. Let cool on baking sheet on wire rack 5 minutes. With pancake spatula, slide each scone round onto rack and let cool completely. Separate wedges to serve.

PER SERVING (1 SCONE): 64 grams, 152 Cal, 6 g Total Fat, 3 g Sat Fat, 0 g Trans Fat, 11 mg Chol, 221 mg Sod, 23 g Total Carb, 8 g Total Sugar, 3 g Fib, 4 g Prot, 44 mg Calc.
PointsPlus value: *4*

FYI   Turbinado sugar is raw sugar that has been steam cleaned. Its slightly coarse, pale amber crystals have a subtle molasses flavor. Turbinado is most often used to sweeten coffee and tea, but it is also used to add shine and texture to the tops of baked goods. It can be found in the baking aisle of supermarkets.

Whole Wheat–Buttermilk Scones

makes 12

1¹/₂ cups whole wheat flour
1¹/₂ cups all-purpose flour
1 tablespoon sugar
1 tablespoon baking powder
¹/₂ teaspoon baking soda
¹/₂ teaspoon salt
2 tablespoons cold unsalted butter, cut into
*   pieces*
1 cup low-fat buttermilk

1   Preheat oven to 400°F.
2   Whisk together whole wheat flour, all-purpose flour, sugar, baking powder, baking soda, and salt in medium bowl. With pastry blender or two knives used scissors-style, cut butter into flour mixture until mixture resembles coarse crumbs. Add buttermilk to flour mixture, stirring just until moist dough forms.
3   With floured hands, knead dough 6–8 times in bowl to bring dough together (dough will be shaggy).
4   Turn dough out onto lightly floured work surface and pat to ¹/₂-inch thickness. With floured 2¹/₂-inch round cutter, cut out 10 rounds without twisting cutter. Gather scraps and reroll, making total of 12 scones. Place scones 1 inch apart on ungreased baking sheet.
5   Bake until golden brown, about 12 minutes. Transfer to wire rack; serve warm.

PER SERVING (1 SCONE): 56 grams, 137 Cal,
3 g Total Fat, 1 g Sat Fat, 0 g Trans Fat, 6 mg Chol,
267 mg Sod, 25 g Total Carb, 3 g Total Sugar, 2 g Fib,
4 g Prot, 52 mg Calc.
PointsPlus value: *4*

Variations

Chocolate-Cherry Scones

Increase sugar to ¹/₃ cup. Substitute ¹/₄ cup unsweetened cocoa for ¹/₄ cup of the whole wheat flour. Stir ¹/₃ cup mini semisweet chocolate chips and ¹/₄ cup finely chopped dried sour cherries into batter in step 2.

PER SERVING (1 SCONE): 67 grams, 181 Cal,
4 g Total Fat, 2 g Sat Fat, 0 g Trans Fat, 6 mg Chol,
268 mg Sod, 34 g Total Carb, 11 g Total Sugar,
3 g Fib, 5 g Prot, 56 mg Calc.
PointsPlus value: *5*

Lemon-Blueberry Scones

Increase sugar to ¹/₄ cup. Stir ³/₄ cup fresh or frozen blueberries and 1 teaspoon grated lemon zest into batter in step 2.

PER SERVING (1 SCONE): 68 grams, 154 Cal,
3 g Total Fat, 1 g Sat Fat, 0 g Trans Fat, 6 mg Chol,
268 mg Sod, 29 g Total Carb, 7 g Total Sugar, 3 g Fib,
4 g Prot, 53 mg Calc.
PointsPlus value: *4*

Dried Peach–Pecan Scones

Increase sugar to ¹/₄ cup. Stir ¹/₄ cup finely chopped toasted pecans and ¹/₄ cup finely chopped dried peaches into batter in step 2.

PER SERVING (1 SCONE): 65 grams, 174 Cal,
4 g Total Fat, 2 g Sat Fat, 0 g Trans Fat, 6 mg Chol,
267 mg Sod, 30 g Total Carb, 7 g Total Sugar, 3 g Fib,
5 g Prot, 55 mg Calc.
PointsPlus value: *5*

15

Cakes, Pies, and More

Cakes, Pies, and More

368   Sour Cream Coffee Cake
368   Chocolate-Buttermilk Bundt Cake
370   Flourless Chocolate Cake
371   Bûche de Noël
372   Yellow Layer Cake with Cocoa Frosting
372   Rolled Orange Sponge Cake
374   Lemon Angel Food Cake with Berries
375   Carrot Cake
375   Pumpkin Spice Cake
376   Caramel Cake with Bourbon-Pear Sauce
377   Dark Fruit Cake
378   Honey Cake
378   Citrus Passover Cake
379   Triple Ginger Gingerbread
381   Mahogany Velvet Cupcakes with Cream Cheese Frosting
382   Lemon Cheesecake with Blueberry Sauce
383   Pie Dough for Single Crust
383   Classic Apple Pie
384   Big Blueberry Pie
384   Cherry Pie
385   Triple Citrus Pie
385   Sweet Potato Pie
386   Peach Crumb Pie
387   Strawberry-Rhubarb Pie
388   Sour Cream Pumpkin Pie
388   Pecan Pie
390   Coconut Cream Pie
391   Neapolitan Easter Pie
392   French Lemon Tart
393   Rugelach
394   Brownies
394   Lemon Poppy Seed Crisps
396   Chocolate Chip Cookies
396   Peanut Butter Cookies
397   Linzer Thumbprint Jewel Cookies
397   Cranberry-Oatmeal Cookies
398   Gingerbread Cookies
399   Mocha Meringues
399   Macadamia Coconut Meringues
400   Chocolate-Espresso Biscotti
401   Double Chocolate–Hazelnut Biscotti
402   Coconut Macaroons
402   Ginger Spice Cookies

Sour Cream Coffee Cake

serves 12

CAKE

2 cups all-purpose flour
1 tablespoon baking powder
1/2 teaspoon five-spice powder
3/4 cup granulated sugar
1 large egg
2 tablespoons canola oil
1/2 cup light sour cream
1/3 cup low-fat buttermilk
1 1/2 cups fresh or frozen blueberries

TOPPING

1/3 cup all-purpose flour
1/4 cup packed dark brown sugar
1 teaspoon grated orange zest
2 tablespoons butter, softened

1   Preheat oven to 350°F. Spray 7 × 11-inch baking dish with nonstick spray.
2   To make cake, whisk together flour, baking powder, and five-spice powder in large bowl. Whisk together granulated sugar, egg, and oil in small bowl until pale, then whisk in sour cream and buttermilk until blended. Add egg mixture to flour mixture, stirring just until blended and smooth. Pour batter into prepared baking dish and spread evenly; scatter blueberries on top.
3   To make topping, mix flour, brown sugar, and orange zest in bowl. With fingertips, blend in butter until mixture resembles coarse crumbs; sprinkle over blueberries.
4   Bake until toothpick inserted into center of cake comes out clean, about 45 minutes. Let cool in baking dish on wire rack. Serve warm.

PER SERVING (1/12 OF CAKE): 87 grams, 224 Cal, 6 g Total Fat, 2 g Sat Fat, 0 g Trans Fat, 26 mg Chol, 133 mg Sod, 40 g Total Carb, 20 g Total Sugar, 1 g Fib, 4 g Prot, 60 mg Calc.
PointsPlus value: **6**

Chocolate-Buttermilk Bundt Cake

serves 24

2 cups all-purpose flour
1 1/4 cups sugar
2 teaspoons baking powder
1/2 teaspoon baking soda
1/2 teaspoon salt
1/2 cup unsweetened cocoa
1 ounce semisweet chocolate, finely chopped
1/2 cup boiling water
1 cup low-fat buttermilk
1/3 cup canola oil
1 large egg
1 large egg white
1 tablespoon vanilla extract
3/4 cup mini semisweet chocolate chips

1   Preheat oven to 325°F. Spray 10-inch Bundt pan with nonstick spray.
2   Whisk together flour, sugar, baking powder, baking soda, and salt in medium bowl. Combine cocoa and chopped chocolate in small bowl. Pour boiling water over cocoa mixture, stirring until chocolate is melted.
3   Whisk together buttermilk, oil, egg, egg white, and vanilla in large bowl; stir in cocoa mixture. Add flour mixture, stirring just until no longer visible. Stir in chocolate chips. Pour batter into prepared pan.
4   Bake until toothpick inserted into center of cake comes out clean, 45–50 minutes. Let cool in pan on wire rack 10 minutes. Invert and remove pan. Let cool completely.

PER SERVING (1/24 OF CAKE): 52 grams, 150 Cal, 6 g Total Fat, 2 g Sat Fat, 0 g Trans Fat, 9 mg Chol, 123 mg Sod, 24 g Total Carb, 14 g Total Sugar, 1 g Fib, 3 g Prot, 26 mg Calc.
PointsPlus value: **4**

CHOCOLATE-BUTTERMILK
BUNDT CAKE

Flourless Chocolate Cake

serves 10

1 cup granulated sugar
4 ounces good-quality bittersweet chocolate,
    finely chopped
½ cup + 3 tablespoons unsweetened Dutch-
    process cocoa
½ cup water
2 large egg yolks
2 teaspoons vanilla extract
⅛ teaspoon almond extract
4 large egg whites, at room temperature
¼ teaspoon cream of tartar
½ cup unsalted matzo meal
3 tablespoons confectioners' sugar

1   Preheat oven to 375°F. Line bottom of
8-inch springform pan with wax paper; spray
with nonstick spray.

2   Combine ¾ cup of granulated sugar, the
chocolate, cocoa, and water in heavy medium
saucepan and set over medium-low heat. Cook,
stirring constantly, until chocolate is melted
and mixture is smooth, about 8 minutes. Transfer to large bowl; whisk in egg yolks, vanilla,
and almond extract; let cool slightly.

3   With electric mixer on medium-high
speed, beat egg whites and cream of tartar in
large bowl until soft peaks form when beaters
are lifted. Gradually sprinkle in remaining ¼
cup granulated sugar, 1 tablespoon at a time,
beating until stiff, glossy peaks form when
beaters are lifted.

4   Stir matzo meal into chocolate mixture.
With rubber spatula, stir one-fourth of beaten
egg whites into chocolate mixture to lighten it,
then gently fold in remaining egg whites until
no streaks of white remain. Scrape batter into
prepared pan and smooth top.

5   Bake until cake is puffy and toothpick inserted into center comes out with a few moist
crumbs clinging, about 30 minutes. Let cool
completely in pan on wire rack (cake will sink
as it cools).

6   Unmold cake by sliding thin knife around
side of cake to loosen it from pan, then release
and remove pan side. Dust top of cake with
confectioners' sugar just before serving.

PER SERVING (¹⁄₁₀ **OF CAKE**): 73 grams, 192 Cal,
7 g Total Fat, 3 g Sat Fat, 0 g Trans Fat, 43 mg Chol,
25 mg Sod, 35 g Total Carb, 26 g Total Sugar, 3 g Fib,
4 g Prot, 13 mg Calc.
PointsPlus value: *6*

FYI   For this delicious cake to be its most
decadent, it is important to use the best
chocolate available. Choose an imported chocolate
with a minimum of 70% cocoa solids.

Bûche de Noël

serves 18

CAKE

¾ *cup cake flour*
⅓ *cup unsweetened cocoa*
½ *teaspoon ground cinnamon*
½ *teaspoon baking powder*
¼ *teaspoon baking soda*
⅛ *teaspoon salt*
3 *large eggs*
¾ *cup granulated sugar*
1½ *teaspoons vanilla extract*
½ *cup fat-free milk, at room temperature*
¼ *cup confectioners' sugar*
2 *cups thawed frozen fat-free whipped topping*

FROSTING

1 *(8-ounce) tub reduced-fat cream cheese*
1 *cup confectioners' sugar*
⅓ *cup unsweetened cocoa*
1 *teaspoon vanilla extract*
2 *ounces semisweet chocolate, melted and*
   cooled

1   Preheat oven to 375°F. Spray 10½ × 15½-inch jelly-roll pan with nonstick spray. Line bottom with parchment paper or wax paper; spray with nonstick spray. Dust pan with flour, shaking out excess.

2   To make cake, whisk together flour, cocoa, cinnamon, baking powder, baking soda, and salt in medium bowl. With electric mixer on medium speed, beat eggs, granulated sugar, and vanilla in large bowl until light and fluffy. Reduce mixer speed to low. Alternately add flour mixture and milk, beginning and ending with flour mixture and beating just until blended. Pour batter into prepared pan and spread evenly.

3   Bake until toothpick inserted into center of cake comes out clean, 8–10 minutes. Spread clean kitchen towel on work surface and top with sheet of wax paper; dust with confectioners' sugar. Run knife around edges of cake to loosen from pan; invert cake onto wax paper. Lift off pan and peel off wax paper. Starting at long side closest to you, gently roll up cake with towel. Place on wire rack and let cool completely, about 45 minutes.

4   Meanwhile, to make frosting, with electric mixer on low speed, beat together cream cheese, confectioners' sugar, cocoa, and vanilla in medium bowl until combined; increase speed to high and beat until smooth. Reduce mixer speed to low. Beat in melted chocolate until blended; increase speed to high and beat until smooth, about 2 minutes longer.

5   Gently unroll cooled cake; remove wax paper and towel. With narrow metal spatula, spread whipped topping over cake almost to edges; reroll. Place cake, seam side down, on platter. With long serrated knife, cut off 3-inch-thick diagonal wedge of cake, starting cut about 1 inch from end of cake.

6   Spread cut side of cake wedge with 3 tablespoons of frosting and place, frosted side down, on top of cake, slightly off to one side and near one end to resemble a branch. Spread remaining frosting on cake and branch. With tines of fork, etch circles on ends of cake and on top of branch to resemble bark. Draw tines of fork along length of cake to resemble bark. Refrigerate at least 3 hours or up to overnight.

PER SERVING (1/18 OF CAKE): 64 grams, 161 Cal,
5 g Total Fat, 3 g Sat Fat, 0 g Trans Fat, 42 mg Chol,
140 mg Sod, 27 g Total Carb, 18 g Total Sugar,
1 g Fib, 4 g Prot, 38 mg Calc.
PointsPlus value: *5*

Yellow Layer Cake with Cocoa Frosting

serves 12

CAKE

1 cup + 2 tablespoons cake flour
1 teaspoon baking soda
¼ teaspoon salt
¼ cup + 2 tablespoons granulated sugar
2 tablespoons + 1 teaspoon unsalted butter, softened
1 large egg
2 teaspoons vanilla extract
½ cup fat-free milk

FROSTING

1¼ cups part-skim ricotta cheese
¼ cup unsweetened cocoa
¼ cup packed dark brown sugar
2 teaspoons unsalted butter, softened
½ teaspoon vanilla extract

1   Preheat oven to 350°F. Spray two 8-inch round cake pans with nonstick spray.

2   To make cake, whisk together flour, baking soda, and salt in small bowl.

3   With electric mixer on high speed, beat granulated sugar and butter in medium bowl until light and fluffy. Add egg and vanilla, beating until well blended. Reduce mixer speed to low. Alternately add flour mixture and milk, beginning and ending with flour mixture and beating just until blended. Scrape batter into prepared pans, dividing evenly.

4   Bake until toothpick inserted into center of cake comes out clean, 15–20 minutes. Let cake cool in pans on wire racks 5 minutes. Remove cake from pans and let cool completely on racks.

5   Meanwhile, to make frosting, combine all frosting ingredients in food processor and process until smooth.

6   Place one cake layer on cake plate. With narrow metal spatula, spread thin layer of frosting over cake; top with remaining cake layer. Spread remaining frosting over top and side of cake.

PER SERVING (¹⁄₁₂ OF CAKE): 68 grams, 155 Cal, 6 g Total Fat, 3 g Sat Fat, 0 g Trans Fat, 34 mg Chol, 199 mg Sod, 22 g Total Carb, 12 g Total Sugar, 1 g Fib, 5 g Prot, 93 mg Calc.
PointsPlus value: *4*

FYI When frosting cake layers, place the first layer, rounded side down, on the cake plate. Frost this layer, then top with the second layer, rounded side up.

Rolled Orange Sponge Cake

serves 10

2 tablespoons confectioners' sugar
4 large eggs, separated and at room temperature
3 large egg whites, at room temperature
¾ cup granulated sugar
2 tablespoons grated orange zest
1 tablespoon lemon juice
⅛ teaspoon salt
¾ cup + 3 tablespoons sifted cake flour
½ cup + 2 tablespoons orange spreadable fruit

1   Preheat oven to 350°F. Line 10½ × 15½-inch jelly-roll pan with wax paper. Dust clean kitchen towel with 1 tablespoon of confectioners' sugar.

2   With electric mixer on medium speed, beat the 7 egg whites in medium bowl until soft peaks form when beaters are lifted.

3   With electric mixer on high speed (no need to wash beaters), beat egg yolks in large bowl until thickened; gradually add granulated sugar, beating until mixture is very thick and pale. Beat in orange zest, lemon juice, and salt. Reduce mixer speed to low. Gradually add flour, beating just until blended. With rubber spatula, stir one-fourth of beaten egg whites into batter to lighten it, then gently fold in remaining egg whites just until no streaks of white remain. Scrape batter into prepared pan and spread evenly.

4   Bake until cake is golden and top springs back when lightly pressed, 12–15 minutes.

5   Run knife around edges of cake to loosen from pan; invert onto prepared towel. Lift pan and peel off wax paper. Beginning at a short side, gently roll up cake with towel. Place on wire rack and let cool completely, about 45 minutes.

6   Gently unroll cooled cake and remove wax paper and towel. Spread spreadable fruit over cake; gently reroll. Place cake, seam side down, on platter; dust with remaining 1 tablespoon confectioners' sugar.

PER SERVING (¹⁄₁₀ **OF CAKE**): 79 grams, 177 Cal, 2 g Total Fat, 1 g Sat Fat, 0 g Trans Fat, 85 mg Chol, 71 mg Sod, 35 g Total Carb, 25 g Total Sugar, 0 g Fib, 4 g Prot, 14 mg Calc.
PointsPlus value: *5*

MEASURING DRY INGREDIENTS

1   *With fork or whisk, stir flour, cocoa, or confectioners' sugar to aerate. With large spoon, lightly spoon ingredient into dry measuring cup to overflowing. (Do not tap cup on counter or shake it as that will pack down the ingredient and give an inaccurate measure.)*

2   *Use straight edge of knife to sweep across top of measuring cup to remove any excess.*

Lemon Angel Food Cake with Berries

serves 12

1½ *cups sugar*
1 *cup + 2 tablespoons sifted cake flour*
¼ *teaspoon salt*
12 *large egg whites, at room temperature*
1¼ *teaspoons cream of tartar*
1 *tablespoon + 1 teaspoon grated lemon zest*
    (about 2 large lemons)
1 *teaspoon vanilla extract*
2 *(6-ounce) containers raspberries*
2 *cups sliced hulled strawberries*
2 *tablespoons raspberry liqueur (framboise)*

1   Place rack in lower third of oven. Preheat oven to 375°F.

2   Sift ¾ cup of sugar, the flour, and salt into small bowl.

3   With electric mixer on medium-high speed, beat egg whites and cream of tartar in large bowl until soft peaks form when beaters are lifted. Add remaining ¾ cup sugar, 2 tablespoons at a time, beating until sugar is dissolved and egg whites form stiff, glossy peaks when beaters are lifted. Beat in 1 tablespoon of lemon zest and the vanilla.

4   Sift flour mixture, one-third at a time, over beaten egg whites; fold in with rubber spatula just until flour mixture is no longer visible, scraping down side and along bottom of bowl (do not overmix). Gently scrape batter into ungreased 9- or 10-inch tube pan; gently smooth surface.

5   Bake until toothpick inserted into center of cake comes out clean, 25–35 minutes. Invert cake pan onto its legs or neck of bottle. Let cool completely.

6   Meanwhile, combine raspberries, strawberries, liqueur, and remaining 1 teaspoon lemon zest in medium bowl; let stand 30 minutes.

7   Run thin knife around edge of pan and center tube to loosen cake. With knife, loosen cake from bottom of pan. Lift out cake; invert onto cake plate. Using angel food cake cutter or long serrated knife, cut cake into 12 wedges. Serve cake wedges topped with berry mixture.

PER SERVING (1 WEDGE OF CAKE AND ABOUT ⅓ CUP BERRY MIXTURE): 129 grams, 181 Cal, 0 g Total Fat, 0 g Sat Fat, 0 g Trans Fat, 0 mg Chol, 104 mg Sod, 40 g Total Carb, 28 g Total Sugar, 3 g Fib, 5 g Prot, 15 mg Calc.
PointsPlus value: *5*

FYI   To be sure that the sugar is dissolved in the beaten egg whites, rub a little of the mixture between your thumb and forefinger. It should feel smooth—not gritty. An angel food cake cutter resembles a comb with long sharp tines and an offset handle. This inexpensive kitchen tool gently cuts angel food cake into neat slices.

Carrot Cake

serves 12

CAKE

¾ cup all-purpose flour
½ cup yellow cornmeal
1½ teaspoons baking powder
½ teaspoon ground cinnamon
¼ teaspoon salt
½ cup thawed frozen apple juice concentrate
¼ cup fat-free milk
2 tablespoons + 2 teaspoons canola oil
1 large egg
2 tablespoons brown sugar
1 cup shredded carrots
½ cup raisins

FROSTING

½ cup light cream cheese (Neufchâtel), at
    room temperature
1 tablespoon honey

1   Preheat oven to 375°F. Spray 9-inch Bundt
pan with nonstick spray.
2   To make cake, whisk flour, cornmeal, baking powder, cinnamon, and salt in bowl.
3   With electric mixer, beat apple juice concentrate, milk, oil, egg, and brown sugar in large
bowl until combined; beat in carrots and raisins.
Reduce mixer speed. Add flour mixture, beating
until blended. Scrape into prepared pan.
4   Bake until toothpick inserted into center
of cake comes out clean, 35–40 minutes. Let
cool completely in pan on wire rack.
5   Combine cream cheese and honey in food
processor; process until smooth. Invert cake
onto cake plate. With narrow metal spatula,
spread frosting over cake.

PER SERVING (¹⁄₁₂ OF CAKE): 63 grams, 155 Cal,
5 g Total Fat, 1 g Sat Fat, 0 g Trans Fat, 21 mg Chol,
133 mg Sod, 26 g Total Carb, 15 g Total Sugar, 1 g Fib,
3 g Prot, 33 mg Calc.
PointsPlus value: *4*

Pumpkin Spice Cake

serves 20

CAKE

3 cups all-purpose flour
2 cups granulated sugar
1 tablespoon pumpkin pie spice
1 tablespoon baking powder
¼ teaspoon salt
1 (15-ounce) can pumpkin puree
4 large eggs
½ cup canola oil
½ cup fat-free milk
2 teaspoons vanilla extract

GLAZE

¾ cup confectioners' sugar
1½ tablespoons lemon juice

1   Preheat oven to 375°F. Spray 10-inch
Bundt pan with nonstick spray. Lightly dust
with flour, shaking out excess.
2   To make cake, whisk together flour,
granulated sugar, pumpkin pie spice, baking
powder, and salt in large bowl. Whisk together
pumpkin puree and eggs in medium bowl until
blended. Gradually whisk in oil, milk, and
vanilla until blended. Add pumpkin mixture to
flour mixture, stirring just until flour mixture
is moistened. Pour batter into prepared pan.
3   Bake until toothpick inserted into center
of cake comes out clean, 55–60 minutes. Let
cake cool in pan on wire rack 10 minutes.
Remove from pan and let cool on rack until
warm, about 30 minutes.
4   Meanwhile, to make glaze, stir together
confectioners' sugar and lemon juice in small
bowl until smooth; drizzle over warm cake.

PER SERVING (¹⁄₂₀ OF CAKE): 89 grams, 239 Cal,
7 g Total Fat, 1 g Sat Fat, 0 g Trans Fat, 43 mg Chol,
104 mg Sod, 41 g Total Carb, 25 g Total Sugar, 2 g Fib,
4 g Prot, 33 mg Calc.
PointsPlus value: *6*

Caramel Cake with Bourbon-Pear Sauce

serves 12

SYRUP

½ cup granulated sugar
1 tablespoon cold water
½ cup boiling water

CAKE

2¼ cups all-purpose flour
1 teaspoon baking powder
1 teaspoon baking soda
¼ teaspoon salt
3 tablespoons unsalted butter, softened
¾ cup low-fat buttermilk, at room
  temperature
½ cup fat-free egg substitute, at room
  temperature
½ cup packed dark brown sugar
½ teaspoon vanilla extract
3 large firm-ripe Bosc pears, peeled, cored,
  and cut into large dice
1 tablespoon bourbon or dark rum

1   To make caramel syrup, combine granulated sugar and cold water in heavy medium saucepan and set over medium heat. Cook, washing down pan side with brush dipped in cold water and swirling pan occasionally, until syrup turns amber, about 6 minutes (do not stir). Remove saucepan from heat and carefully stir in boiling water. Return saucepan to heat and cook, stirring constantly, until sugar is completely dissolved. Remove saucepan from heat and let cool.

2   Preheat oven to 350°F. Spray 9-inch round cake pan with nonstick spray.

3   To make cake, whisk together flour, baking powder, baking soda, and salt in medium bowl.

4   With electric mixer on high speed, beat butter in large bowl until creamy. Beat in buttermilk, egg substitute, brown sugar, vanilla, and ¼ cup of caramel syrup until well blended. Reduce mixer speed to low. Gradually add flour mixture, beating just until blended. Scrape batter into prepared pan and spread evenly.

5   Bake until toothpick inserted into center of cake comes out clean, 25–30 minutes. Let cake cool in pan on wire rack 5 minutes. Remove cake from pan and let cool completely on rack.

6   Meanwhile, add pears to remaining caramel syrup in saucepan and bring to boil. Reduce heat and simmer, covered, 15 minutes. Remove saucepan from heat. With fork or potato masher, lightly mash pears until mixture resembles chunky applesauce; stir in bourbon. Transfer to serving bowl; let cool slightly. Serve with cake.

PER SERVING (¹⁄₁₂ OF CAKE AND ABOUT ¼ CUP PEAR SAUCE): 121 grams, 203 Cal, 3 g Total Fat, 2 g Sat Fat, 0 g Trans Fat, 8 mg Chol, 228 mg Sod, 39 g Total Carb, 20 g Total Sugar, 1 g Fib, 4 g Prot, 42 mg Calc.
PointsPlus value: *5*

Dark Fruit Cake

serves 36

2 cups dark raisins
1½ cups golden raisins
1 cup dried currants
2 tablespoons brandy, port, or vanilla extract
1 tablespoon grated lemon zest
2 cups all-purpose flour
2 teaspoons baking powder
1 teaspoon ground cinnamon
½ teaspoon ground nutmeg
½ teaspoon ground ginger
½ teaspoon ground allspice
½ teaspoon salt
½ cup (1 stick) butter, softened
1 cup packed dark brown sugar
2 tablespoons dark molasses
4 large eggs
6 ounces sliced almonds, finely chopped
¼ cup unsweetened applesauce

1   Mix together dark raisins, golden raisins, currants, brandy, and lemon zest in large bowl. Let macerate, stirring once or twice, about 20 minutes.

2   Preheat oven to 300°F. Spray 9-inch springform pan with nonstick spray. Line bottom of pan with round of wax paper and side of pan with strip of wax paper.

3   Whisk together flour, baking powder, cinnamon, nutmeg, ginger, allspice, and salt in medium bowl.

4   With electric mixer on high speed, beat butter and brown sugar in large bowl until light and fluffy. Add molasses and beat 1 minute. Add eggs, one at a time, beating well after each addition. Reduce mixer speed to low. Add flour mixture and beat just until blended. Add fruit mixture and any liquid, the almonds, and applesauce, beating just until mixed well. Scrape batter into prepared pan and spread evenly.

5   Bake 1½ hours. Reduce oven temperature to 250°F. Bake until toothpick inserted into center of cake comes out clean, about 1½ hours longer. Let cool in pan on wire rack 15 minutes. Remove pan side and let cool completely on rack.

PER SERVING (⅟₃₆ OF CAKE): 46 grams, 159 Cal, 6 g Total Fat, 2 g Sat Fat, 0 g Trans Fat, 30 mg Chol, 68 mg Sod, 26 g Total Carb, 19 g Total Sugar, 2 g Fib, 3 g Prot, 35 mg Calc.
PointsPlus value: **4**

FYI   You can use other dried fruits instead of the currants in this special cake. Try dried cranberries, dried cherries, or dried blueberries.

Honey Cake

serves 16

CAKE

3 large eggs
1 cup honey
2/3 cup orange juice
1/4 cup sugar
3 tablespoons canola oil
1 tablespoon grated orange zest
1 tablespoon grated lemon zest
1 teaspoon vanilla extract
2 1/2 cups all-purpose flour
3/4 teaspoon ground cinnamon
3/4 teaspoon baking soda
1/4 teaspoon salt

SYRUP

1/2 cup honey
1/3 cup water
2 1/2 tablespoons sugar
2 tablespoons orange juice
1 tablespoon lemon juice

1   Place rack in lower third of oven. Preheat oven to 350°F. Spray 10-inch Bundt pan with nonstick spray. Lightly dust with flour, shaking out excess.

2   To make cake, lightly beat eggs in large bowl. Whisk in honey, orange juice, sugar, oil, orange zest, lemon zest, and vanilla until blended. Whisk together flour, cinnamon, baking soda, and salt in medium bowl. Add flour mixture to honey mixture, stirring just until blended. Pour into prepared pan.

3   Bake until toothpick inserted into center comes out clean, 50–55 minutes. Let cool in pan on wire rack.

4   Meanwhile, to make syrup, combine all syrup ingredients in small saucepan. Bring to boil over high heat; cook 1 minute. Remove saucepan from heat; let cool 15 minutes. Slowly pour syrup over warm cake in pan; let soak 30 minutes. Place inverted cake plate on top of cake. Invert cake with pan; lift off pan (all of syrup may not get absorbed).

PER SERVING (1/16 OF CAKE): 88 grams, 232 Cal, 4 g Total Fat, 1 g Sat Fat, 0 g Trans Fat, 40 mg Chol, 110 mg Sod, 48 g Total Carb, 32 g Total Sugar, 1 g Fib, 4 g Prot, 14 mg Calc.
***PointsPlus* value: 7**

FYI   The color and flavor of honey depends upon the nectar source (the blossoms). The color ranges from almost colorless to dark brown and the flavor from delicate to deep and bold. Keep in mind that the darker the honey, the deeper the flavor. Honey varieties include acacia, autumn wildflower, blackberry, buckwheat, cactus, raspberry, catnip, goldenrod, and tupelo.

Citrus Passover Cake

serves 12

1 1/2 cups matzo meal
1/4 cup sliced almonds
1/4 teaspoon salt
1/2 navel orange, unpeeled and cut into chunks
1 tablespoon lemon juice
5 large eggs, at room temperature
8 large egg whites, at room temperature
1 1/2 cups granulated sugar
2 tablespoons confectioners' sugar

1   Place rack in middle of oven. Preheat oven to 350°F.

2   Combine matzo meal, almonds, and salt in food processor; pulse until nuts are finely ground. Transfer to small bowl. Combine orange chunks and lemon juice in food processor (no need to clean bowl); pulse until orange is finely chopped.

3   With electric mixer on medium speed, beat eggs and egg whites in large bowl until thick and foamy. Gradually add granulated sugar, beating until very thick, about 5 minutes. With rubber spatula, alternately fold matzo meal mixture and orange mixture into egg mixture until well blended. Scrape batter into ungreased 10-inch tube pan with removable bottom (not nonstick).

4   Bake until cake springs back when lightly pressed and toothpick inserted into center comes out clean, 45–55 minutes. Let cake cool completely in pan on wire rack.

5   Run thin knife around edge of pan and center tube to loosen cake. With knife, loosen cake from bottom of pan. Lift out cake; invert onto cake plate. Using angel food cake cutter or long serrated knife, cut cake into 12 wedges. Dust with confectioners' sugar.

PER SERVING (1/12 OF CAKE): 89 grams, 196 Cal, 3 g Total Fat, 1 g Sat Fat, 0 g Trans Fat, 89 mg Chol, 112 mg Sod, 36 g Total Carb, 27 g Total Sugar, 1 g Fib, 7 g Prot, 21 mg Calc.
PointsPlus value: *5*

▲ HEALTHY EXTRA

Serve a mix of diced fresh fruit alongside each serving of this perennial favorite.

Triple Ginger Gingerbread

serves 12

1¼ cups all-purpose flour
1 cup whole wheat flour
1 teaspoon baking powder
1 teaspoon baking soda
½ teaspoon salt
4 tablespoons unsalted butter, softened
½ cup packed dark brown sugar
1 tablespoon grated peeled fresh ginger
2 teaspoons ground ginger
¼ teaspoon ground cloves
1 cup low-fat buttermilk
½ cup fat-free egg substitute
2 tablespoons chopped crystallized ginger
1 teaspoon vanilla extract
¼ cup + 2 tablespoons golden raisins

1   Preheat oven to 350°F. Spray 8-inch square baking pan with nonstick spray.

2   Whisk together all-purpose flour, whole wheat flour, baking powder, baking soda, and salt in medium bowl.

3   With electric mixer on high speed, beat butter in large bowl until creamy. Add brown sugar, fresh ginger, ground ginger, and cloves, beating until light and fluffy. Reduce mixer speed to medium and beat in buttermilk, egg substitute, crystallized ginger, and vanilla. Reduce mixer speed to low and beat in flour mixture; stir in raisins. Scrape into prepared pan.

4   Bake until toothpick inserted into center of cake comes out clean, 25–30 minutes. Let cool completely in pan on wire rack.

PER SERVING (1/12 OF CAKE): 76 grams, 187 Cal, 4 g Total Fat, 3 g Sat Fat, 0 g Trans Fat, 11 mg Chol, 283 mg Sod, 33 g Total Carb, 15 g Total Sugar, 2 g Fib, 5 g Prot, 54 mg Calc.
PointsPlus value: *5*

Mahogany Velvet Cupcakes with Cream Cheese Frosting

makes 12

CUPCAKES

1¼ *cups all-purpose flour*
1 *cup granulated sugar*
3 *tablespoons unsweetened cocoa*
1½ *teaspoons baking soda*
¼ *teaspoon salt*
1 *(8¼-ounce) can whole beets, drained and pureed in blender*
½ *cup low-fat buttermilk*
¼ *cup canola oil*
2 *large eggs*
1 *teaspoon white vinegar*

FROSTING

1 *(8-ounce) package cold fat-free cream cheese*
1 *cup confectioners' sugar, sifted*
1 *teaspoon grated lemon zest*

1   Preheat oven to 350°F. Line 12-cup muffin pan with paper liners.
2   To make cake, whisk together flour, granulated sugar, cocoa, baking soda, and salt in medium bowl. Whisk together beet puree, buttermilk, oil, eggs, and vinegar in another medium bowl. Add buttermilk mixture to flour mixture, stirring just until flour mixture is moistened (do not overmix). Pour batter into prepared muffin cups, filling them about two-thirds full.
3   Bake until cupcakes spring back when lightly pressed, about 20 minutes. Let cool completely in pan on wire rack.

4   Meanwhile, to make frosting, with electric mixer on medium speed, beat cream cheese and confectioners' sugar in medium bowl until smooth. Beat in lemon zest.
5   Remove cupcakes from muffin pan. With narrow metal spatula, spread about 1 tablespoon frosting over each cupcake.

PER SERVING (1 CUPCAKE): 97 grams, 234 Cal, 6 g Total Fat, 1 g Sat Fat, 0 g Trans Fat, 37 mg Chol, 355 mg Sod, 40 g Total Carb, 27 g Total Sugar, 1 g Fib, 6 g Prot, 57 mg Calc.
PointsPlus value: *6*

FYI   Traditionally, red velvet cupcakes—or cakes—get their deep red color from a hefty amount of red food color. Our cupcakes get their deep, dark color from beets, which contribute rich color and some vegetable goodness instead of artificial ingredients.

Lemon Cheesecake with Blueberry Sauce

serves 32

CRUST

1½ *cups reduced-fat graham cracker crumbs (about 10 crackers)*
1 *tablespoon unsalted butter, melted*
1 *tablespoon light corn syrup*

TOPPING

2 *cups fat-free sour cream*
¼ *cup sugar*

CAKE

4 *(8-ounce) packages light cream cheese (Neufchâtel), softened*
1¼ *cups sugar*
2 *large eggs*
2 *large egg whites*
1 *tablespoon grated lemon zest (about 2 large lemons)*
1 *tablespoon lemon juice*
2 *teaspoons vanilla extract*

SAUCE

¼ *cup sugar*
1 *tablespoon cornstarch*
2 *cups fresh or thawed frozen blueberries*
1 *tablespoon water*
1 *tablespoon lemon juice*

1   Preheat oven to 350°F. Spray 10-inch springform pan with nonstick spray.

2   To make crust, stir together cracker crumbs, butter, and corn syrup in medium bowl until moistened. Press crumb mixture firmly onto bottom of prepared pan; refrigerate.

3   To make topping, stir together sour cream and sugar in bowl; cover and refrigerate.

4   To make cake, with electric mixer on medium speed, beat cream cheese in large bowl until very smooth. Gradually add sugar, beating until fluffy. Add eggs, one at a time, beating well after each addition. Beat in egg whites, lemon zest and juice, and vanilla until blended. Pour batter over crust.

5   Bake until center of cheesecake jiggles slightly, 55–60 minutes. Let cool in pan on wire rack 15 minutes. Spoon sour cream topping over cake; spread evenly with narrow metal spatula. Refrigerate at least 8 hours or up to 2 days.

6   To make sauce, stir together sugar and cornstarch in medium saucepan. Add blueberries and water; cook over medium heat, stirring, until berries soften and sauce bubbles and thickens, about 4 minutes. Remove saucepan from heat and stir in lemon juice. Transfer sauce to serving bowl and refrigerate until cool.

7   To serve, with thin knife dipped into hot water, cut cake into 32 wedges, dipping knife between cuts and shaking off excess water. Serve cake wedges topped with blueberry sauce.

PER SERVING (¹⁄₃₂ OF CAKE AND ABOUT 1 TABLESPOON SAUCE): 76 grams, 158 Cal, 8 g Total Fat, 5 g Sat Fat, 0 g Trans Fat, 36 mg Chol, 164 mg Sod, 18 g Total Carb, 15 g Total Sugar, 1 g Fib, 5 g Prot, 62 mg Calc. *PointsPlus* value: 4

FYI To crush graham crackers, break them up and put into a food processor. Process until finely and evenly crushed into crumbs.

Pie Dough for Single Crust

makes 1 (9-inch) crust

1 cup all-purpose flour
2 teaspoons sugar
1/8 teaspoon salt
2 tablespoons cold unsalted butter, cut
    into pieces
2 tablespoons cold vegetable shortening
1 teaspoon cider vinegar
3–4 tablespoons ice water

1   Whisk together flour, sugar, and salt in large bowl. With pastry blender or two knives used scissors-style, cut butter and shortening into flour mixture until mixture resembles coarse crumbs. With fork, stir in vinegar and water, 1 tablespoon at a time, until dough begins to form.
2   Press dough together and shape into disk. Wrap in plastic wrap and refrigerate at least 1 hour or up to overnight. (If refrigerating overnight, let stand at room temperature about 20 minutes before rolling out.)

Variation

Pie Dough for Double Crust

Prepare as directed in step 1, but doubling the recipe. Divide the dough in half. Shape each piece of dough into disk and wrap in plastic wrap; refrigerate at least 1 hour or up to overnight. (If refrigerating overnight, let stand at room temperature about 20 minutes before rolling out.)

 Look for trans fat–free vegetable shortening in your supermarket.

Classic Apple Pie

serves 16

1/2 cup + 2 teaspoons sugar
1 1/2 tablespoons all-purpose flour
1/2 teaspoon ground cinnamon
3 pounds Golden Delicious apples, peeled,
    cored, and thinly sliced
1 tablespoon lemon juice
1 teaspoon vanilla extract
Pie Dough for Double Crust (left)
1 large egg white, lightly beaten

1   Preheat oven to 450°F.
2   To make filling, stir together 1/2 cup of sugar, the flour, and cinnamon in large bowl. Add apples, lemon juice, and vanilla.
3   On lightly floured work surface with lightly floured rolling pin, roll one disk of dough into 12-inch round. Gently fold dough in quarters and ease into 9-inch pie plate, pressing dough against side of pie plate. Trim edge, leaving 1-inch overhang. Spoon in apple filling.
4   Roll remaining disk of dough into 12-inch round. Fold in quarters and place on top of filling. Trim edge to 1-inch overhang. Tuck edge under and decoratively crimp. Brush pie with beaten egg white and sprinkle with remaining 2 teaspoons sugar. With tip of small knife, make several 1-inch slits in top of pie.
5   Place pie on baking sheet to catch any drips. Bake 15 minutes. Reduce oven temperature to 350°F. Bake until pie is golden and filling is bubbling in center, 45–50 minutes. Let cool completely on wire rack.

PER SERVING (1/16 OF PIE): 113 grams, 190 Cal, 7 g Total Fat, 3 g Sat Fat, 0 g Trans Fat, 8 mg Chol, 41 mg Sod, 32 g Total Carb, 18 g Total Sugar, 2 g Fib, 2 g Prot, 8 mg Calc.
PointsPlus value: *5*

Big Blueberry Pie

serves 16

¾ cup + 1 tablespoon sugar
¼ cup cornstarch
⅛ teaspoon salt
3 pints blueberries
1 tablespoon lemon juice
Pie Dough for Double Crust (page 383)
1 large egg white, lightly beaten

1   Preheat oven to 425°F.
2   To make filling, stir together ¾ cup of sugar, the cornstarch, and salt in large bowl. Add blueberries and lemon juice; toss to mix well.
3   On lightly floured work surface with lightly floured rolling pin, roll one disk of dough into 12-inch round. Gently fold dough in quarters and ease into 9-inch pie plate, pressing it against side of pie plate. Trim edge, leaving 1-inch overhang. Spoon blueberry filling into pie shell.
4   Roll remaining disk of dough into 12-inch round. Fold in quarters and place on top of filling. Tuck edge under and decoratively crimp. Brush pie with beaten egg white and sprinkle with remaining 1 tablespoon sugar. With tip of small knife, make several 1-inch slits in top of pie to allow steam to escape.
5   Place pie on baking sheet to catch any drips. Bake 20 minutes. Reduce oven temperature to 375°F. Bake until crust is golden and filling is bubbling in center, about 25 minutes longer. Loosely cover pie with foil during last 30 minutes of baking to prevent overbrowning, if needed. Let cool on wire rack about 1 hour to serve warm or let cool completely.

PER SERVING (¹⁄₁₆ OF PIE): 98 grams, 192 Cal, 7 g Total Fat, 3 g Sat Fat, 0 g Trans Fat, 8 mg Chol, 62 mg Sod, 32 g Total Carb, 17 g Total Sugar, 2 g Fib, 2 g Prot, 7 mg Calc.
PointsPlus value: **5**

Cherry Pie

serves 16

¾ cup sugar
¼ cup cornstarch
⅛ teaspoon salt
2 (14½-ounce) cans sour cherries packed in
    water, drained, juice reserved
1 tablespoon lemon juice
¼ teaspoon almond extract
Pie Dough for Double Crust [page 383]

1   Preheat oven to 425°F.
2   To make filling, stir together sugar, cornstarch, and salt in large bowl. Add cherries, ½ cup of reserved cherry juice, the lemon juice, and almond extract, gently stirring to mix well.
3   On lightly floured work surface with lightly floured rolling pin, roll one disk of dough into 12-inch round. Gently fold dough in quarters and ease into 9-inch pie plate, pressing it against side of pie plate. Trim edge, leaving 1-inch overhang. Spoon cherry filling into pie shell.
4   Roll remaining disk of dough into 12-inch round. Fold in quarters and place on top of filling. Tuck edges under and decoratively crimp. With tip of small knife, make several 1-inch slits in top of pie to allow steam to escape.
5   Place pie on baking sheet to catch any drips. Bake 20 minutes. Reduce oven temperature to 375°F. Bake until crust is golden and filling is bubbling in center, about 25 minutes longer. Loosely cover pie with foil during last 30 minutes of baking to prevent overbrowning, if needed. Let cool on wire rack about 1 hour to serve warm, or let cool completely.

PER SERVING (¹⁄₁₆ OF PIE): 93 grams, 176 Cal, 7 g Total Fat, 2 g Sat Fat, 0 g Trans Fat, 8 mg Chol, 60 mg Sod, 29 g Total Carb, 14 g Total Sugar, 1 g Fib, 2 g Prot, 9 mg Calc.
PointsPlus value: **5**

Triple Citrus Pie

serves 10

Pie Dough for Single Crust (page 383)
¼ cup lemon juice
¼ cup lime juice
2 teaspoons unflavored gelatin
1 (14-ounce) can sweetened condensed milk
Grated zest of ½ orange
1½ cups thawed frozen fat-free whipped
    topping

1   On floured work surface, roll dough into
12-inch round. Fold dough in quarters and ease
into 9-inch pie plate. Trim edge, leaving 1-inch
overhang. Crimp edge. Freeze until firm.
2   Meanwhile, preheat oven to 400°F.
3   Line pie shell with sheet of foil; fill with
dried beans or rice. Bake until crust is set,
about 10 minutes; remove foil with beans.
Bake until golden, 10–12 minutes longer, pressing dough down with back of spoon if puffed.
Let cool completely on wire rack.
4   To make filling, combine lemon juice
and lime juice in small saucepan and sprinkle
gelatin over; let stand until softened, about 2
minutes. Set over low heat and cook, stirring
constantly, just until gelatin is dissolved, about
2 minutes. Add condensed milk and cook, stirring, until heated through, about 5 minutes.
Pour mixture into large bowl; refrigerate until
filling begins to set, about 30 minutes.
5   Whisk filling until smooth; whisk in orange
zest. Fold in whipped topping. Pour into pie
shell; refrigerate until firm, at least 3 hours.

PER SERVING (¹⁄₁₀ OF PIE): 87 grams, 225 Cal,
5 g Total Fat, 2 g Sat Fat, 0 g Trans Fat, 11 mg Chol,
78 mg Sod, 39 g Total Carb, 27 g Total Sugar, 0 g Fib,
5 g Prot, 107 mg Calc.
PointsPlus value: *6*

Sweet Potato Pie

serves 8

2 large sweet potatoes (about 1 1/2 pounds)
Pie Dough for Single Crust (page 383)
2 large eggs
3 large egg whites
½ cup packed light brown sugar
¾ cup fat-free evaporated milk
1 teaspoon ground cinnamon
¾ teaspoon ground ginger
½ teaspoon salt
¼ teaspoon ground nutmeg

1   Put potatoes in saucepan with enough
water to cover; bring to boil. Reduce heat and
simmer until tender, about 35 minutes; drain
and let cool.
2   On floured work surface, roll dough into
12-inch round. Fold dough in quarters and ease
into 9-inch pie plate. Trim edge, leaving 1-inch
overhang. Crimp edge. Freeze until firm.
3   Preheat oven to 375°F.
4   To make filling, peel potatoes and cut into
large pieces. Mash potatoes in large bowl until
smooth. Measure out 1¹⁄₃ cups of potato puree. Whisk all remaining ingredients into puree.
5   Line pie shell with sheet of foil; fill with
dried beans or rice. Bake until crust is set,
about 10 minutes; remove foil with beans. Bake
until golden, 10–12 minutes longer. Let cool.
6   Reduce oven temperature to 350°F. Pour
filling into pie shell. Bake until center of pie
jiggles slightly, 35–40 minutes. Let cool.

PER SERVING (⅛ OF PIE): 138 grams, 249 Cal,
7 g Total Fat, 3 g Sat Fat, 0 g Trans Fat, 62 mg Chol,
267 mg Sod, 39 g Total Carb, 20 g Total Sugar, 2 g Fib,
7 g Prot, 111 mg Calc.
PointsPlus value: *7*

Peach Crumb Pie

serves 12

FILLING

3½ *pounds peaches, halved, pitted, and*
  cut into wedges (about 7 cups)
¾ *cup packed light brown sugar*
1½ *tablespoons cornstarch*
½ *teaspoon ground cinnamon*
¼ *teaspoon ground ginger*
1 *teaspoon vanilla extract*

TOPPING

⅔ *cup old-fashioned oats*
½ *cup packed light brown sugar*
¼ *cup all-purpose flour*
¼ *teaspoon salt*
2 *tablespoons unsalted butter, melted*
1 *tablespoon lemon juice*
1 *teaspoon water*

Pie Dough for Single Crust (page 383)

1   Preheat oven to 375°F.
2   To make filling, gently toss together all fill-ing ingredients in large bowl until combined.
3   To make crumb topping, stir together oats, brown sugar, flour, and salt in medium bowl. Add butter, lemon juice, and water, stirring un-til mixed well. With your hands, press crumb mixture together to form large clumps.
4   On lightly floured work surface with lightly floured rolling pin, roll dough into 12-inch round. Gently fold dough in quarters and ease into 9-inch pie plate, pressing it against side of pie plate. Trim edge, leaving 1-inch overhang. Decoratively crimp edge of dough. Spoon peach filling into pie shell. Break up crumb topping clumps and place on top of filling.

5   Place pie on baking sheet to catch any drips. Bake 40 minutes; loosely cover with sheet of foil to prevent overbrowning. Bake until filling is bubbling in center, 40–45 minutes longer. Let cool completely on wire rack.

PER SERVING (1/12 OF PIE): 155 grams, 254 Cal, 6 g Total Fat, 3 g Sat Fat, 0 g Trans Fat, 10 mg Chol, 83 mg Sod, 48 g Total Carb, 32 g Total Sugar, 3 g Fib, 3 g Prot, 31 mg Calc.
PointsPlus value: *7*

FYI   In this pie, we use peaches with their skins left on. If you prefer to use peeled peaches, drop them into a large pot of boiling water for 1 minute. Plunge the peaches into a bowl of ice water for 1 minute, then slip off their skins.

Strawberry-Rhubarb Pie

serves 12

FILLING

1½ pounds rhubarb, trimmed and cut
into ½-inch pieces
1 (1-pound) container strawberries,
hulled and quartered
1 cup sugar
¼ cup instant tapioca
2 teaspoons lemon juice
½ teaspoon ground nutmeg
¼ teaspoon salt

TOPPING

⅔ cup old-fashioned oats
½ cup sugar
¼ cup all-purpose flour
¼ teaspoon ground cinnamon
¼ teaspoon salt
2 tablespoons unsalted butter, melted
1 tablespoon orange juice
1 teaspoon water

Pie Dough for Single Crust (page 383)

1   Preheat oven to 375°F.
2   To make filling, toss together all filling ingredients in large bowl until mixed well. Let stand 15 minutes.
3   Meanwhile, to make oat topping, stir together oats, sugar, flour, cinnamon, and salt in medium bowl. Add butter, orange juice, and water, stirring until combined. With your hands, press crumb mixture together to form large clumps.

4   On lightly floured work surface with floured rolling pin, roll dough into 12-inch round. Gently fold dough in quarters and ease into 9-inch pie plate, pressing it against side of pie plate. Trim edge, leaving 1-inch overhang. Decoratively crimp edge of dough. Spoon strawberry-rhubarb filling into pie shell. Break up crumb topping clumps and place on top of filling.
5   Place pie on baking sheet to catch any drips. Bake until filling is bubbling in center, about 1 hour 20 minutes. Loosely cover pie with foil during last 30 minutes of baking to prevent overbrowning, if needed. Let cool completely on wire rack.

PER SERVING (¹⁄₁₂ OF PIE): 141 grams, 251 Cal, 7 g Total Fat, 3 g Sat Fat, 0 g Trans Fat, 10 mg Chol, 125 mg Sod, 47 g Total Carb, 28 g Total Sugar, 3 g Fib, 3 g Prot, 49 mg Calc.
PointsPlus value: *7*

Sour Cream Pumpkin Pie
serves 12

Pie Dough for Single Crust (page 383)
1 (15-ounce) can pumpkin puree
²/₃ cup light sour cream
½ cup sugar
½ cup fat-free egg substitute
1 teaspoon ground cinnamon
½ teaspoon ground ginger
¼ teaspoon ground cloves
¼ teaspoon ground nutmeg

1   On lightly floured work surface with lightly floured rolling pin, roll dough into 12-inch round. Gently fold dough in quarters and ease into 9-inch pie plate, pressing it against side of pie plate. Trim edge, leaving 1-inch overhang. Decoratively crimp edge of dough. Freeze until firm, about 15 minutes.
2   Meanwhile, preheat oven to 400°F.
3   Whisk together pumpkin and sour cream in large bowl until blended. Whisk in all remaining ingredients until mixed well. Pour into pie shell.
4   Bake pie 15 minutes. Reduce oven temperature to 350°F. Bake until center of pie jiggles slightly, about 40 minutes longer. Let cool completely on wire rack.

PER SERVING (¹⁄₁₂ OF PIE): 88 grams, 143 Cal,
5 g Total Fat, 3 g Sat Fat, 0 g Trans Fat, 9 mg Chol,
61 mg Sod, 22 g Total Carb, 11 g Total Sugar, 2 g Fib,
3 g Prot, 33 mg Calc.
PointsPlus value: *4*

Pecan Pie
serves 20

Pie Dough for Single Crust (page 383)
3 large egg whites
1 large egg
1 cup light corn syrup
½ cup granulated sugar
¹/₃ cup packed dark brown sugar
1 teaspoon vanilla extract
¹/₈ teaspoon salt
1 cup pecans

1   On lightly floured work surface with lightly floured rolling pin, roll dough into 12-inch round. Gently fold dough in quarters and ease into 9-inch pie plate, pressing it against side of pie plate. Trim edge, leaving 1-inch overhang. Decoratively crimp edge of dough. Freeze until firm, about 15 minutes.
2   Meanwhile, preheat oven to 425°F.
3   Whisk together all remaining ingredients except pecans in large bowl; stir in pecans. Pour into pie shell and spread evenly.
4   Bake pie 15 minutes. Reduce oven temperature to 350°F. Bake until edges are set and filling is jiggly in center, 30–35 minutes longer. Loosely cover pie with foil to prevent overbrowning, if needed. Let cool completely on wire rack.

PER SERVING (¹⁄₂₀ OF PIE): 50 grams, 169 Cal,
6 g Total Fat, 2 g Sat Fat, 0 g Trans Fat, 14 mg Chol,
62 mg Sod, 27 g Total Carb, 18 g Total Sugar, 1 g Fib,
2 g Prot, 10 mg Calc.
PointsPlus value: *5*

FYI   If you have a 9-inch fluted pie dish, roll the dough into an 11-inch circle and fit into the dish.

PECAN PIE

Coconut Cream Pie

serves 12

Pie Dough for Single Crust (page 383)
¾ *teaspoon unflavored gelatin*
3 *tablespoons water*
⅓ *cup sugar*
2 *tablespoons cornstarch*
⅛ *teaspoon salt*
1 *cup low-fat (1%) milk*
½ *cup light (reduced-fat) coconut milk*
2 *large egg yolks*
2 *teaspoons vanilla extract*
⅛ *teaspoon coconut extract*
½ *cup thawed frozen fat-free whipped topping*
2 *tablespoons flaked sweetened coconut,*
   toasted

1   On lightly floured work surface with lightly floured rolling pin, roll dough into 12-inch round. Gently fold dough in quarters and ease into 9-inch pie plate, pressing it against side of pie plate. Trim edge, leaving 1-inch overhang. Decoratively crimp edge of dough. Freeze until firm, about 15 minutes.

2   Meanwhile, preheat oven to 400°F.

3   Line pie shell with sheet of foil; fill with dried beans or rice. Bake until crust is set, about 10 minutes; remove foil with beans. Bake until golden, 10–12 minutes longer, pressing dough down with back of spoon if puffed. Let cool completely on wire rack.

4   Meanwhile, sprinkle gelatin over water in small saucepan; let stand until softened, about 2 minutes. Set over low heat; cook, stirring constantly, just until dissolved, about 2 minutes. Remove saucepan from heat.

5   Whisk together sugar, cornstarch, and salt in medium saucepan. Whisk in low-fat milk, coconut milk, and egg yolks until smooth. Set over medium heat and cook, stirring frequently, until mixture begins to bubble and thicken,

about 8 minutes; cook, stirring, 1 minute longer. Remove saucepan from heat; stir in dissolved gelatin, vanilla, and coconut extract.

6   Pour filling into pie shell; spread evenly. Press piece of plastic wrap directly onto surface to prevent skin from forming. Let cool to room temperature, then refrigerate until firm, at least 2 hours or up to overnight.

7   Just before serving, carefully remove plastic wrap. Cut pie into 12 wedges. Top each serving with dollop of whipped topping and sprinkling of coconut.

PER SERVING (¹⁄₁₂ OF PIE, 2 TEASPOONS WHIPPED
TOPPING, AND SCANT ½ TEASPOON COCONUT):
69 grams, 138 Cal, 6 g Total Fat, 3 g Sat Fat,
0 g Trans Fat, 41 mg Chol, 67 mg Sod, 18 g Total Carb,
8 g Total Sugar, 1 g Fib, 3 g Prot, 31 mg Calc.
PointsPlus value: *4*

Variation

Banana Cream Pie

Thinly slice 2 small bananas and toss with 1 tablespoon lemon juice. Prepare custard as directed, substituting fat-free evaporated milk for the coconut milk and omitting coconut and coconut extract. Spread half of custard in pie shell and top with layer of sliced bananas (reserve 12 slices for garnish). Spread remaining custard evenly over bananas and chill as directed. Top each wedge of pie with whipped topping and banana slice just before serving.

PER SERVING (¹⁄₁₂ OF PIE AND 2 TEASPOONS WHIPPED
TOPPING): 87 grams, 156 Cal, 5 g Total Fat, 3 g Sat Fat,
0 g Trans Fat, 41 mg Chol, 79 mg Sod, 23 g Total Carb,
13 g Total Sugar, 1 g Fib, 3 g Prot, 59 mg Calc.
PointsPlus value: *4*

Neapolitan Easter Pie

serves 12

½ cup wheat berries
1 (15-ounce) container part-skim ricotta
  cheese
1 cup fat-free egg substitute
⅔ cup sugar
½ teaspoon ground cinnamon
¼ teaspoon salt
¼ cup chopped candied citron
¼ cup chopped candied orange peel
2 teaspoons grated orange zest
Pie Dough for Single Crust (page 383)

1 Put wheat berries in small bowl and add enough cold water to cover. Cover bowl with plastic wrap; let soak in refrigerator at least 6 hours or up to overnight; drain.

2 Transfer wheat berries to medium saucepan and add enough cold water to cover by 1 inch. Bring to boil over medium-high heat. Reduce heat and simmer, partially covered, stirring occasionally, until tender, 30–45 minutes. Drain; let cool completely.

3 Preheat oven to 350°F. Spray 9-inch springform pan with nonstick spray.

4 With wooden spoon, beat together ricotta, egg substitute, sugar, cinnamon, and salt in large bowl until blended. Stir in wheat berries, citron, candied orange peel, and orange zest. Scrape into prepared pan and spread evenly.

5 On lightly floured work surface with lightly floured rolling pin, roll dough into 10-inch round. With fluted pastry cutter, cut dough into ½-inch-wide strips. Arrange half of strips, ½ inch apart, over filling, then top with remaining strips to form crisscross pattern. Trim strips to ½ inch overhang and tuck ends under.

6 Bake until lightly browned and toothpick inserted into center of pie comes out clean, about 1 hour. Let cool completely in pan on wire rack. Run thin knife around edge of pie to loosen from pan. Remove side of pan and place pie on serving plate. Serve or cover loosely with plastic wrap and refrigerate up to 3 days.

PER SERVING (1/12 OF PIE): 102 grams, 225 Cal, 7 g Total Fat, 4 g Sat Fat, 0 g Trans Fat, 16 mg Chol, 167 mg Sod, 33 g Total Carb, 16 g Total Sugar, 2 g Fib, 8 g Prot, 112 mg Calc.
PointsPlus value: *6*

FYI Wheat berries—whole wheat kernels—are a traditional ingredient in this holiday cheesecake. Found in natural-foods stores, wheat berries have a slightly chewy texture when cooked.

French Lemon Tart

serves 12

FILLING

¾ teaspoon unflavored gelatin
3 tablespoons water
1 cup sugar
1 (2-inch) strip lemon zest, removed
    with vegetable peeler
1 cup lemon juice (about 4 large lemons)
2 large eggs
1 large egg white
1 teaspoon vanilla extract

CRUST

1¼ cups cake flour
1 teaspoon sugar
⅛ teaspoon salt
4 tablespoons cold unsalted butter, cut into
    pieces
1 large egg yolk
2 tablespoons ice water

1   To make filling, sprinkle gelatin over water in cup and let stand until softened, about 2 minutes.

2   Bring 1 inch of water to simmer in bottom of double boiler.

3   Whisk together sugar, lemon zest and juice, eggs, and egg white in top of double boiler. Set over simmering water and cook, stirring constantly, until mixture begins to thicken, about 8 minutes.

4   Stir in softened gelatin and cook, stirring, until gelatin is dissolved, about 1 minute. Remove saucepan from heat; stir in vanilla. Pour lemon filling through sieve set over medium bowl. Press piece of plastic wrap directly onto surface to prevent skin from forming. Let cool to room temperature. Refrigerate until chilled, at least 4 hours or up to 2 days.

5   To make crust, whisk together flour, sugar, and salt in large bowl. With pastry blender or two knives used scissors-style, cut in butter until mixture resembles coarse crumbs. Stir in egg yolk, then add water, 1 tablespoon at a time, stirring until dough begins to form. Turn dough out onto work surface. With heel of your hand, briefly knead dough, then shape into disk. Wrap in plastic wrap and refrigerate at least 1 hour or up to overnight. (If refrigerating overnight, let stand at room temperature about 20 minutes before rolling out.)

6   On lightly floured work surface with lightly floured rolling pin, roll dough into 12-inch round. Gently fold dough in quarters and ease into 9-inch removable bottom tart pan, pressing it against side of pan; trim edge. Freeze until firm, about 15 minutes.

7   Meanwhile, preheat oven to 400°F.

8   Line dough with sheet of foil; fill with dried beans or rice. Bake until crust is set, about 10 minutes; remove foil with beans. Bake until golden, 10–12 minutes longer, pressing dough down with back of spoon if puffed. Let cool completely on wire rack.

9   Just before serving, scrape cooled filling into tart shell and spread evenly.

PER SERVING (1⁄12 OF TART): 75 grams, 167 Cal, 5 g Total Fat, 3 g Sat Fat, 0 g Trans Fat, 63 mg Chol, 46 mg Sod, 28 g Total Carb, 17 g Total Sugar, 0 g Fib, 3 g Prot, 11 mg Calc.
PointsPlus value: **5**

FYI Don't have a double boiler? Use a medium bowl set over a medium saucepan of simmering water. Make sure that the bottom of the bowl is over—not in—the water.

Rugelach

makes 32

DOUGH

2 cups all-purpose flour
¼ teaspoon salt
1 (8-ounce) container fat-free cottage cheese
4 ounces light cream cheese (Neufchâtel),
    softened
½ cup granulated sugar
2 tablespoons unsalted butter, softened

FILLING

½ cup packed dark brown sugar
⅓ cup walnuts, chopped
⅓ cup dried currants
¾ teaspoon ground cinnamon

1   To make dough, whisk together flour and
salt in medium bowl.
2   With electric mixer on medium speed, beat
cottage cheese, cream cheese, granulated sugar,
and butter in large bowl until light and fluffy.
Reduce mixer speed to low. Gradually add flour
mixture, beating until dough forms. Divide
dough in half and shape each piece into disk.
Wrap in plastic wrap and freeze 20 minutes.
3   Meanwhile, to make filling, stir together
all filling ingredients in small bowl.
4   Preheat oven to 350°F. Line 2 large baking
sheets with parchment paper.
5   On lightly floured work surface with lightly
floured rolling pin, roll one disk of dough into
11-inch round. Sprinkle half of filling over
dough. Place sheet of wax paper on top of
filling and lightly press down to help brown
sugar mixture adhere. With pizza cutter or
long, thin knife, cut dough into 16 wedges.
Roll wedges up beginning with wide end. Bend
ends in slightly to form crescents, if desired.

Place rugelach, 1 inch apart, on prepared baking sheet. Repeat with remaining dough and
filling, making total of 32 rugelach.
6   Bake until lightly golden, 30–35 minutes,
rotating baking sheets after 15 minutes. With
spatula, transfer rugelach to wire rack and let
cool completely.

PER SERVING (1 RUGELACH): 29 grams, 86 Cal,
2 g Total Fat, 1 g Sat Fat, 0 g Trans Fat, 5 mg Chol,
59 mg Sod, 14 g Total Carb, 8 g Total Sugar, 0 g Fib,
2 g Prot, 15 mg Calc.
PointsPlus value: *2*

FYI   Rugelach freeze very well. Store them
between layers of wax paper in an airtight
freezer container up to 3 months. Thaw at room
temperature.

Brownies

makes 16

³/₄ cup all-purpose flour
¹/₃ cup unsweetened cocoa
1 teaspoon baking powder
¹/₈ teaspoon ground cinnamon
¹/₈ teaspoon salt
2 ounces semisweet chocolate, chopped
4 tablespoons unsalted butter
1 cup sugar
2 large eggs
1 large egg white
1¹/₂ teaspoons vanilla extract

1   Preheat oven to 350°F. Spray 8-inch square baking pan with nonstick spray.
2   Whisk together flour, cocoa, baking powder, cinnamon, and salt in medium bowl.
3   Melt chocolate and butter in small heavy saucepan over low heat. Scrape into medium bowl; let cool 1 minute. With wooden spoon, stir in sugar, then add eggs, egg white, and vanilla, stirring until blended. Add chocolate mixture to flour mixture, stirring until well combined. Scrape batter into prepared pan and spread evenly.
4   Bake until toothpick inserted into center of brownies comes out with a few moist crumbs clinging, 20–22 minutes. Let cool completely in pan on wire rack. Cut into 16 brownies.

PER SERVING (1 BROWNIE): 36 grams, 127 Cal,
5 g Total Fat, 3 g Sat Fat, 0 g Trans Fat, 34 mg Chol,
54 mg Sod, 20 g Total Carb, 12 g Total Sugar, 1 g Fib,
2 g Prot, 15 mg Calc.
PointsPlus value: *4*

Lemon Poppy Seed Crisps

makes 32

³/₄ cup all-purpose flour
1 tablespoon poppy seeds
¹/₄ cup sugar
3 tablespoons unsalted butter, softened
1 teaspoon grated lemon zest
Pinch salt

1   Preheat oven to 350° F. Spray nonstick baking sheet with nonstick cooking spray.
2   Whisk together flour and poppy seeds in small bowl.
3   With electric mixer on medium speed, beat sugar, butter, lemon zest, and salt in large bowl until light and fluffy. Reduce mixer speed to low. Gradually add flour mixture, beating just until blended. Shape dough into ball and cut in half. Shape each piece of dough into disk and wrap in plastic wrap. Refrigerate until firm, at least 30 minutes or up to several hours.
4   Roll one piece of dough between two sheets of wax paper into 7-inch round. With fluted pastry wheel or pizza cutter, cut dough round into 16 wedges. With spatula, place wedges, 1 inch apart, on prepared baking sheet. Repeat with remaining piece of dough.
5   Bake until cookies are golden, 10–12 minutes, rotating baking sheet after 5 minutes. Let cool on baking sheet on wire rack 5 minutes. With spatula, transfer cookies to rack and let cool completely.

PER SERVING (4 COOKIES): 25 grams, 110 Cal,
5 g Total Fat, 3 g Sat Fat, 0 g Trans Fat, 12 mg Chol,
19 mg Sod, 16 g Total Carb, 6 g Total Sugar, 0 g Fib,
1 g Prot, 19 mg Calc.
PointsPlus value: *3*

→
FROM LEFT: LEMON POPPY SEED CRISPS,
CRANBERRY-OATMEAL COOKIES (PAGE 397),
PEANUT BUTTER COOKIES (PAGE 396)

Chocolate Chip Cookies

makes 24

½ cup quick-cooking (not instant) oats
1 cup white whole wheat flour
½ teaspoon baking soda
¼ teaspoon salt
*4 tablespoons unsalted butter, melted and
    cooled*
¾ cup packed light brown sugar
1 large egg
1 teaspoon vanilla extract
1 cup semisweet chocolate chips (6 ounces)

1   Place racks in upper and lower thirds of
oven. Preheat oven to 350°F. Spray 2 baking
sheets with nonstick spray.
2   Put oats in blender or food processor and
process until finely ground. Whisk together
oats, flour, baking soda, and salt in small bowl.
With electric mixer on medium speed, beat
butter, brown sugar, egg, and vanilla in large
bowl until well blended. Reduce mixer speed
to low. Gradually add flour mixture, beating
just until blended. Stir in chocolate chips. Drop
dough by level tablespoonfuls, 2 inches apart,
on prepared baking sheets, making total of 24
cookies. With bottom of glass dipped into flour,
press each mound to form 2-inch cookies.
3   Bake until cookies are browned along edges,
9–11 minutes, rotating baking sheets after 5
minutes. Let cool on baking sheets on wire
racks about 1 minute. With spatula, transfer
cookies to racks and let cool completely.

PER SERVING (1 COOKIE): 26 grams, 104 Cal,
4 g Total Fat, 3 g Sat Fat, 0 g Trans Fat, 14 mg Chol,
57 mg Sod, 16 g Total Carb, 11 g Total Sugar, 1 g Fib,
2 g Prot, 11 mg Calc.
PointsPlus value: *3*

Peanut Butter Cookies

makes 24

½ cup + 2 tablespoons all-purpose flour
½ cup white whole wheat flour
½ teaspoon baking soda
½ teaspoon salt
4 tablespoons butter, softened
¼ cup natural chunky peanut butter
⅓ cup packed dark brown sugar
1 large egg
1 teaspoon vanilla extract
½ cup peanut butter chips

1   Preheat oven to 350°F. Spray 2 baking
sheets with nonstick spray.
2   Whisk together all-purpose flour, white
whole wheat flour, baking soda, and salt in
small bowl. With electric mixer on medium
speed, beat butter and peanut butter in large
bowl until creamy. Gradually beat in brown
sugar, egg, and vanilla until light and fluffy. Reduce mixer speed to low. Gradually add flour
mixture, beating just until blended. Stir in
peanut butter chips. Drop dough by generous
tablespoonfuls, about 1 inch apart, on prepared
baking sheets, making total of 24 cookies. With
back of fork, lightly press each cookie to form
crisscross pattern.
3   Bake until cookies are browned on bottom,
12–15 minutes, rotating baking sheets after
6 minutes. Let cool on baking sheet on wire
racks about 1 minute. With spatula, transfer
cookies to racks and let cool completely.

PER SERVING (1 COOKIE): 22 grams, 96 Cal,
5 g Total Fat, 3 g Sat Fat, 0 g Trans Fat, 14 mg Chol,
90 mg Sod, 11 g Total Carb, 5 g Total Sugar, 1 g Fib,
3 g Prot, 11 mg Calc.
PointsPlus value: *3*

Linzer Thumbprint Jewel Cookies

makes 24

¾ cup all-purpose flour
¼ cup quick-cooking (not instant) oats
¼ cup finely chopped almonds
¼ cup flaked sweetened coconut
¼ teaspoon salt
6 tablespoons unsalted butter, softened
2 tablespoons granulated sugar
2 tablespoons confectioners' sugar
¼ cup seedless raspberry jam

1   Preheat oven to 325°F.
2   Mix together flour, oats, almonds, coconut, and salt in medium bowl. With electric mixer on medium speed, beat butter and granulated sugar in large bowl until light and fluffy. Reduce mixer speed to low. Gradually add flour mixture, beating just until blended. Shape dough into 24 balls and place 1½ inches apart on ungreased large baking sheets. With your thumb or end of wooden spoon, make small indentation in each cookie.
3   Bake until cookies are lightly golden along edges, about 20 minutes, rotating baking sheets after 10 minutes. With spatula, transfer cookies to wire racks and let cool completely.
4   Dust cookies with confectioners' sugar; fill each indentation with ½ teaspoon of jam.

PER SERVING (1 COOKIE): 15 grams, 68 Cal,
4 g Total Fat, 2 g Sat Fat, 0 g Trans Fat, 8 mg Chol,
27 mg Sod, 8 g Total Carb, 4 g Total Sugar, 1 g Fib,
1 g Prot, 5 mg Calc.
PointsPlus value: *2*

FYI   You can use other jams in these cookies, including apricot, strawberry, or black raspberry.

Cranberry-Oatmeal Cookies

makes 24

½ cup white whole wheat flour
½ teaspoon ground cinnamon
¼ teaspoon ground nutmeg
¼ teaspoon baking soda
¼ teaspoon salt
1½ cups old-fashioned oats, preferably toasted
4 tablespoons butter, softened
¼ cup packed light brown sugar
1 apple, peeled, cored, and grated
1 large egg
½ teaspoon vanilla extract
½ cup dried cranberries

1   Place racks in upper and lower thirds of oven. Preheat oven to 350°F. Spray 2 baking sheets with nonstick spray.
2   Whisk together flour, cinnamon, nutmeg, baking soda, and salt in large bowl. Stir in oats.
3   With electric mixer on medium speed, beat butter and brown sugar in separate large bowl until light and fluffy. Add apple, egg, and vanilla, beating until mixed well. Reduce mixer speed to low. Gradually beat in oat mixture until blended. Stir in cranberries. Drop dough by tablespoonfuls, about 1 inch apart, on prepared baking sheets, making total of 24 cookies. With back of spoon, flatten each cookie.
4   Bake until cookies are lightly browned, 12–15 minutes. Let cool on baking sheets on wire racks. Transfer to wire racks and let cool completely.

PER SERVING (2 COOKIES): 45 grams, 136 Cal,
5 g Total Fat, 3 g Sat Fat, 0 g Trans Fat, 28 mg Chol,
83 mg Sod, 21 g Total Carb, 9 g Total Sugar, 2 g Fib,
3 g Prot, 14 mg Calc.
PointsPlus value: *4*

Gingerbread Cookies

makes 26

COOKIE DOUGH

2¹/₂ cups all-purpose flour
1¹/₂ teaspoons ground cinnamon
1 teaspoon ground ginger
1 teaspoon baking soda
¹/₂ teaspoon ground cloves
¹/₂ teaspoon salt
²/₃ cup packed dark brown sugar
¹/₄ cup canola oil
3 tablespoons unsalted butter, softened
¹/₂ cup dark molasses
1 large egg
1 teaspoon grated orange or lemon zest

ICING

1¹/₂ cups confectioners' sugar
2–3 tablespoons hot water
¹/₈ teaspoon vanilla, orange, or lemon extract
1–2 drops food coloring (optional)

1   To make cookie dough, whisk together flour, cinnamon, ginger, baking soda, cloves, and salt in medium bowl.
2   With electric mixer on medium speed, beat brown sugar, oil, and butter in large bowl until light and fluffy. Beat in molasses, egg, and orange zest until blended and smooth. Reduce mixer speed to low. Gradually add flour mixture, beating until blended. Divide dough in half. Shape each piece of dough into disk and wrap in plastic wrap. Refrigerate until firm, at least 2 hours or up to overnight.
3   Preheat oven to 375°F. Spray 2 baking sheets with nonstick spray.
4   Roll out one piece of dough on lightly floured work surface to ¹/₄-inch thickness. Cut out gingerbread girls or boys with lightly floured 3-inch cutter. Place 1 inch apart on prepared baking sheets. Repeat with remaining dough, gathering and rolling out scraps, making total of 26 cookies.
5   Bake until cookies are firm to touch, 9–11 minutes, rotating baking sheets after 5 minutes. With spatula, transfer to wire racks and let cool completely.
6   To make icing, stir together confectioners' sugar, water, and extract in medium bowl until smooth. If icing is too thick, add a few more drops of water. Tint with food coloring, if using. With narrow metal spatula, spread icing over cooled cookies. Let icing set, about 20 minutes.

PER SERVING (1 COOKIE): 38 grams, 143 Cal, 4 g Total Fat, 1 g Sat Fat, 0 g Trans Fat, 12 mg Chol, 101 mg Sod, 26 g Total Carb, 16 g Total Sugar, 0 g Fib, 2 g Prot, 23 mg Calc.
PointsPlus value: *4*

FYI To measure the confectioners' sugar, lightly spoon it into dry measuring cups without packing it down.

Mocha Meringues
makes 42

2 teaspoons vanilla extract
1¼ teaspoons instant espresso powder
4 large egg whites, at room temperature
¼ teaspoon cream of tartar
¼ teaspoon salt
1 cup sugar
2 tablespoons unsweetened cocoa

1   Place racks in upper and lower thirds of oven. Preheat oven to 250°F. Line 2 baking sheets with parchment paper.
2   Stir together vanilla extract and espresso powder in cup until espresso is dissolved. With electric mixer on medium-high speed, beat egg whites, cream of tartar, and salt in large bowl until soft peaks form when beaters are lifted. Gradually sprinkle in sugar, 2 tablespoons at a time, beating until stiff, glossy peaks form when beaters are lifted. Beat in vanilla mixture. Reduce mixer speed to very low; stir in cocoa until just combined.
3   Spoon meringue into pastry bag with ½-inch opening or spoon into zip-close plastic bag and cut off one corner to form ½-inch opening. Pipe meringue to form 1-inch diameter "kisses," 1½ inches apart, on prepared baking sheets.
4   Bake until meringues are dry, 50–55 minutes, rotating baking sheets after 25 minutes. Turn off oven; prop open oven door with wooden spoon. Let meringues cool completely in oven, about 1 hour. Carefully peel meringues off paper. Store in airtight container up to several weeks.

PER SERVING (2 COOKIES): 17 grams, 42 Cal, 0 g Total Fat, 0 g Sat Fat, 0 g Trans Fat, 0 mg Chol, 38 mg Sod, 10 g Total Carb, 9 g Total Sugar, 0 g Fib, 1 g Prot, 1 mg Calc.
PointsPlus value: *1*

Macadamia Coconut Meringues
makes 36

3 large egg whites, at room temperature
Pinch salt
½ cup sugar
¼ cup flaked sweetened coconut
1 teaspoon coconut extract
18 macadamia nuts, halved

1   Preheat oven to 250°F. Line large baking sheet with parchment paper.
2   With electric mixer on medium-high speed, beat egg whites and salt in large bowl until soft peaks form when beaters are lifted. Gradually sprinkle in sugar, 1 tablespoon at a time, beating until stiff, glossy peaks form when beaters are lifted. With rubber spatula, fold in coconut and coconut extract.
3   Spoon meringue into pastry bag fitted with large star tip. Pipe 36 rosettes, about 1 inch apart, on prepared baking sheet. Place macadamia half in center of each cookie.
4   Bake until edges of meringues begin to dry and meringues are lightly browned, about 40 minutes. Turn off oven; prop open oven door with wooden spoon. Let cookies dry completely in oven until crisp, at least 3 hours or up to overnight. Carefully peel meringues off paper. Store in airtight container up to several weeks.

PER SERVING (2 COOKIES): 30 grams, 96 Cal, 5 g Total Fat, 1 g Sat Fat, 0 g Trans Fat, 0 mg Chol, 39 mg Sod, 13 g Total Carb, 12 g Total Sugar, 1 g Fib, 2 g Prot, 6 mg Calc.
PointsPlus value: *3*

Chocolate-Espresso Biscotti

makes 80

2 cups all-purpose flour
$1/3$ cup unsweetened cocoa
$2^1/2$ tablespoons ground coffee
2 teaspoons baking powder
$3/4$ teaspoon ground cinnamon
$1/4$ teaspoon salt
$1/2$ cup slivered almonds
1 cup sugar
2 large eggs
3 tablespoons strong brewed coffee
$1^1/2$ teaspoons vanilla extract

1   Preheat oven to 350°F. Spray baking sheet with nonstick spray.

2   Whisk together flour, cocoa, ground coffee, baking powder, cinnamon, and salt in large bowl; stir in almonds. Beat sugar, eggs, brewed coffee, and vanilla in medium bowl until mixed well. With electric mixer on low speed, add sugar mixture to flour mixture, beating until dry dough forms. Cut dough in half.

3   On lightly floured work surface, shape each piece of dough into log about 15 inches long, 1 inch high, and $1^3/4$ inches wide. Transfer to prepared baking sheet. Press logs until $3/4$ inch high and 2 inches wide.

4   Bake until toothpick inserted into center of log comes out clean, 20–25 minutes, rotating baking sheet after 10 minutes. Let cool about 10 minutes.

5   Meanwhile, reduce oven temperature to 300°F. With two spatulas, transfer 1 log to cutting board. Using long serrated knife, cut log into $1/4$-inch slices. Repeat with remaining log, making total of 80 biscotti. Place biscotti, cut side down, on baking sheet. Bake 10 minutes per side. Let cool completely on wire racks. (Biscotti will continue to crisp as they cool.)

PER SERVING (1 BISCOTTI): 9 grams, 28 Cal, 1 g Total Fat, 0 g Sat Fat, 0 g Trans Fat, 5 mg Chol, 18 mg Sod, 5 g Total Carb, 3 g Total Sugar, 0 g Fib, 1 g Prot, 6 mg Calc.
PointsPlus value: *1*

▲ HEALTHY EXTRA

Serve the biscotti the way they do in Italy: with cups of freshly brewed espresso or cappuccino and a bowl of fresh fruit, such as grapes, berries, or figs. A cappuccino made with 1 cup of fat-free milk will increase the *PointsPlus* value by *2*.

Double Chocolate–Hazelnut Biscotti

makes 80

¾ cup hazelnuts, chopped
1¾ cups all-purpose flour
¾ cup mini semisweet chocolate chips
½ cup unsweetened Dutch-process cocoa
1 tablespoon instant espresso or coffee powder
1 teaspoon baking soda
¼ teaspoon salt
1 cup sugar
2 large eggs
2 large egg whites
1 tablespoon vanilla extract

1   Place racks in upper and lower thirds of oven. Preheat oven to 350°F. Line 2 large baking sheets with foil; spray with nonstick spray.
2   Spread hazelnuts in jelly-roll pan; bake, shaking pan once or twice, until lightly browned, about 8 minutes. Wrap hot nuts in clean kitchen towel and rub nuts together to remove as much of the skins as possible. Let cool.
3   Combine 2 tablespoons of hazelnuts, the flour, 2 tablespoons of chocolate chips, the cocoa, espresso powder, baking soda, and salt in food processor. Pulse until nuts are finely ground; transfer to large bowl.
4   Combine sugar, eggs, egg whites, and vanilla in food processor (no need to clean bowl); process until slightly thickened, about 2 minutes. Add to flour mixture, stirring until blended well. Stir in remaining hazelnuts and chocolate chips. Spoon one-fourth of batter (about ¾ cup) along one side of prepared baking sheet to form log about 14 inches long and 1½ inches wide; repeat with remaining batter, forming 2 logs on each baking sheet.

5   Bake until toothpick inserted into center of log comes out clean, about 15 minutes, rotating baking sheets after 8 minutes. Let cool on baking sheets on wire racks 10 minutes.
6   Reduce oven temperature to 300°F. With two spatulas, transfer 1 log to cutting board. With long serrated knife, cut log on diagonal into ½-inch slices. Repeat with remaining logs, making total of 80 biscotti. Stand slices, about 1 inch apart, on prepared baking sheets. Bake until dry to touch, 20–25 minutes. Let cool completely on wire racks. (Biscotti will continue to crisp as they cool.)

PER SERVING (1 BISCOTTI): 22 grams, 76 Cal, 3 g Total Fat, 1 g Sat Fat, 0 g Trans Fat, 11 mg Chol, 53 mg Sod, 13 g Total Carb, 7 g Total Sugar, 1 g Fib, 2 g Prot, 7 mg Calc.
PointsPlus value: *2*

FYI   Biscotti, twice-baked cookies, are first baked as a log, then sliced and baked again until crisp and crunchy, making them ideal for dunking into espresso or milk.

Coconut Macaroons

makes 24

2/3 cup fat-free sweetened condensed milk
1 large egg white
2 teaspoons vanilla extract
1/8 teaspoon coconut extract
1/8 teaspoon salt
2 cups crisp rice cereal
1 cup flaked sweetened coconut

1   Preheat oven to 300°F. Line 2 baking
sheets with parchment paper.
2   Stir together condensed milk, egg white,
vanilla, coconut extract, and salt in large bowl;
stir in cereal and coconut. Drop batter by tablespoonfuls, about 2 inches apart, on prepared
baking sheets. (Batter may not hold together;
moisten your fingers with water and press
mounds to re-shape, if needed.)
3   Bake until cookies are lightly browned,
about 18 minutes, rotating baking sheets after 8
minutes. Let cool completely on baking sheets
on wire racks. Carefully peel macaroons off
paper. Store in airtight container up to 3 days.

PER SERVING (2 COOKIES): 30 grams, 89 Cal,
2 g Total Fat, 2 g Sat Fat, 0 g Trans Fat, 1 mg Chol,
84 mg Sod, 16 g Total Carb, 13 g Total Sugar, 0 g Fib,
2 g Prot, 50 mg Calc.
PointsPlus value: *2*

Ginger-Spice Cookies

makes 36

1 1/2 cups all-purpose flour
1/2 cup white whole wheat flour
1 teaspoon cinnamon
1 teaspoon ground ginger
1 teaspoon baking soda
1/4 teaspoon black pepper
1/4 cup canola oil
1/4 cup dark molasses
1 large egg
1 cup + 3 tablespoons sugar

1   Place racks in upper and lower thirds of
oven. Preheat oven to 350°F. Line two large
baking sheets with parchment paper.
2   Whisk together all-purpose flour, white
whole wheat flour, cinnamon, ginger, baking
soda, and pepper in medium bowl. Whisk together oil, molasses, and egg in large bowl until
smooth; whisk in 1 cup of sugar. Add flour
mixture and stir until blended. Let dough rest
10 minutes.
3   Spread remaining 3 tablespoons sugar on
small plate. Shape dough into 1-inch balls. Dip
tops of balls in sugar and place, sugared side up,
about 2 inches apart, on prepared baking sheets.
4   Bake until cookies are cracked, soft in
center, and firm along edge, 10–12 minutes.
Let cool on baking sheets on wire racks about 2
minutes. Transfer cookies to racks and let cool
completely.

PER SERVING (1 COOKIE): 17 grams, 61 Cal, 2 g Total Fat,
0 g Sat Fat, 0 g Trans Fat, 6 mg Chol, 38 mg Sod,
11 g Total Carb, 6 g Total Sugar, 0 g Fib, 0 g Prot,
14 mg Calc.
PointsPlus value: *2*

FYI   You can add other warm spices to these
cookies, including ground cloves, mace, or
allspice. Use up to 1/2 teaspoon total.

16

Fruit and Frozen Desserts,
Puddings, and Sauces

Fruit and Frozen Desserts, Puddings, and Sauces

406	Double Apple Strudel
408	Apple Brown Betty
408	Spiced Double Berry Crisp
409	Strawberry Shortcakes
410	Classic Crêpes Suzette
411	Peaches in Red Wine
411	Peach Melba
412	Roasted Strawberries and Sorbet
412	Black and White Strawberries
413	Frozen Mango-Lime Mousse
413	Vanilla Frozen Yogurt
415	Raspberry-Orange Frozen Yogurt
415	Real Mint Ice Cream
416	Double Chocolate Sorbet
416	Watermelon Sorbet
417	Honeydew Sorbet
417	Grapefruit-Strawberry Granita
418	Summer Pudding
418	Coconut Bread Pudding with Chocolate Sauce
419	Rice Pudding with Golden Raisins
420	Old-Fashioned Butterscotch Pudding
420	Classic Chocolate Mousse
422	Toasted Coconut Custard
422	Best Blueberry Sauce
423	Raspberry Sauce
424	Rich Chocolate Sauce
424	Hot Fudge Sauce

Double Apple Strudel

serves 16

3 Golden Delicious apples, peeled, cored,
    and cut into ¾-inch chunks
18 dried apple slices, coarsely chopped
½ cup water
⅓ cup dark raisins
⅓ cup sugar
2 tablespoons cornstarch
½ teaspoon ground cinnamon
1 teaspoon vanilla extract
¾ cup walnuts
4 gingersnap cookies
4 tablespoons unsalted butter, melted
12 (12 × 17-inch) sheets frozen phyllo
    dough, thawed

1   To make filling, combine fresh and dried apples, water, raisins, sugar, cornstarch, and cinnamon in large nonstick skillet. Cook, covered, stirring occasionally, until apples are very tender and mixture is slightly thickened. Stir in vanilla. Remove skillet from heat and let cool completely.

2   Combine walnuts and gingersnaps in food processor; pulse until finely ground.

3   Preheat oven to 375°F. Spray large baking sheet with nonstick spray or line with parchment paper.

4   To assemble strudel, reserve 2 teaspoons of butter. Place 1 sheet of phyllo on clean kitchen towel and lightly brush with some of remaining butter. (Keep remaining phyllo covered with damp paper towel to prevent it from drying out.) Top with another sheet of phyllo; lightly brush with butter and sprinkle with 1 tablespoon of cookie crumb mixture. Repeat layering with phyllo, crumb mixture, and butter, ending with phyllo. Spoon apple filling over phyllo leaving 2-inch border. Using towel

to help lift edges of phyllo and starting at long side, roll strudel up jelly-roll style to enclose filling. Cut strudel in half.

5   Place strudel halves, seam side down, on prepared baking sheet; brush with reserved butter. With small sharp knife, make 7 evenly spaced cuts through top layers of phyllo (do not cut through to filling) in each strudel. Bake until golden, 40–45 minutes. Let cool 10 minutes in pan on wire rack. Transfer one strudel to cutting board. With serrated knife, slice strudel through cuts. Repeat with remaining strudel.

PER SERVING (1 SLICE): 70 grams, 160 Cal, 7 g Total Fat, 2 g Sat Fat, 0 g Trans Fat, 8 mg Chol, 101 mg Sod, 24 g Total Carb, 14 g Total Sugar, 2 g Fib, 2 g Prot, 12 mg Calc.
PointsPlus value: *4*

FYI You can vary this strudel by substituting golden raisins, dried cranberries, blueberries, or cherries for the dark raisins and pecans or almonds for the walnuts.

DOUBLE APPLE STRUDEL

Apple Brown Betty

serves 4

4 slices reduced-calorie whole wheat or
    multigrain bread, lightly toasted and
    torn into pieces
2 tablespoons light brown sugar
1 teaspoon ground cinnamon
4 Golden Delicious apples, peeled, cored,
    and sliced
2 teaspoons butter, cut into pieces
$^1/_3$ cup water

1   Preheat oven to 375°F. Spray 1½-quart
shallow casserole dish with nonstick spray.
2   Put toast in food processor or blender;
pulse until coarse crumbs form. Transfer to
small bowl. Add brown sugar and cinnamon,
tossing to combine well. Spread half of apples
in prepared casserole; sprinkle evenly with half
of crumb mixture. Spread remaining apples on
top and cover with remaining crumb mixture.
Dot evenly with butter and drizzle water over.
3   Bake until top is crisp and fruit is bubbling, about 45 minutes. Serve hot or warm.

PER SERVING (¼ OF BETTY): 188 grams, 177 Cal,
3 g Total Fat, 1 g Sat Fat, 0 g Trans Fat, 5 mg Chol,
94 mg Sod, 40 g Total Carb, 24 g Total Sugar, 8 g Fib,
3 g Prot, 79 mg Calc.
PointsPlus value: *5*

FYI   For more flavor interest, use a variety
of apples, such as Fuji, Braeburn, and
Granny Smith.

Spiced Double Berry Crisp

serves 6

FILLING
1 pint blueberries
2 (6-ounce) containers raspberries or
    blackberries
Grated zest of $^1/_2$ orange
$^1/_3$ cup granulated sugar
1 tablespoon cornstarch
$^1/_4$ teaspoon salt

TOPPING
$^1/_2$ cup old-fashioned oats
$^1/_4$ cup white whole wheat flour
$^1/_4$ cup packed light brown sugar
1 teaspoon ground cinnamon
$^1/_4$ teaspoon ground nutmeg
1 tablespoon unsalted butter, melted
1 tablespoon canola oil
Pinch salt

1   Preheat oven to 375°F. Spray 1½-quart
baking dish with nonstick spray.
2   To make filling, toss together all filling ingredients in large bowl; spoon into baking dish.
3   To make topping, stir together all topping
ingredients in medium bowl until moistened.
Squeeze mixture together to form loose ball,
then break into small pieces and sprinkle evenly
over filling. Bake until filling is bubbling and
topping is golden, about 20 minutes, loosely
covering crisp with foil to prevent overbrowning, if needed.

PER SERVING (⅙ OF CRISP): 144 grams, 220 Cal,
5 g Total Fat, 2 g Sat Fat, 0 g Trans Fat, 5 mg Chol,
128 mg Sod, 43 g Total Carb, 28 g Total Sugar, 7 g Fib,
3 g Prot, 33 mg Calc.
PointsPlus value: *6*

Strawberry Shortcakes

makes 8

1 (1-pound) container strawberries,
    hulled and halved
½ cup granulated sugar
2 teaspoons lemon juice
1¾ cups all-purpose flour
2 teaspoons baking powder
¼ teaspoon salt
4 tablespoons cold unsalted butter, cut
    into pieces
⅔ cup low-fat buttermilk
2 tablespoons fat-free milk
1 tablespoon turbinado (raw) sugar
¾ cup plain fat-free Greek yogurt

1   Preheat oven to 425°F. Spray baking sheet
with nonstick spray.
2   Toss strawberries, ¼ cup of granulated
sugar, and the lemon juice in medium bowl.
3   Whisk together flour, remaining ¼ cup
granulated sugar, the baking powder, and salt in
large bowl. With pastry blender or two knives
used scissors-style, cut butter into flour mixture until it resembles coarse crumbs. Gradually add buttermilk, stirring until flour mixture
is moistened. Gather dough into ball and knead
just until it holds together.
4   Turn dough out onto lightly floured
work surface and pat to ½-inch thickness.
With floured 2½-inch round cutter, cut out
shortcakes; gather scraps and reroll to cut
out additional shortcakes, making total of 8
shortcakes. Place shortcakes on prepared baking sheet. Brush with milk and sprinkle with
turbinado sugar.

5   Bake until golden brown, 12–15 minutes,
rotating baking sheet after 6 minutes. Transfer
shortcakes to wire rack and let cool completely.
6   To serve, cut shortcakes horizontally
in half. Place shortcake bottom on each of 8
plates; top each with ¼ cup of berries and
1½ tablespoons of yogurt. Cover with tops
of shortcakes.

PER SERVING (1 FILLED SHORTCAKE): 153 grams,
242 Cal, 6 g Total Fat, 4 g Sat Fat, 0 g Trans Fat,
16 mg Chol, 202 mg Sod, 41 g Total Carb,
19 g Total Sugar, 2 g Fib, 6 g Prot, 78 mg Calc.
PointsPlus value: *6*

FYI   To ensure that the shortcakes are as flaky
as possible, don't overwork the dough;
knead it just until it holds together.

SECTIONING CITRUS FRUIT

1 Cut slice off top and bottom of fruit.

2 Stand fruit upright on cutting board. Following curve of fruit, cut away peel and white pith, from top to bottom.

3 Holding fruit over bowl to catch juice, cut between each membrane to release sections.

Classic Crêpes Suzette

serves 8

½ cup orange juice
¼ cup sugar
3 oranges, peeled and sectioned, juice reserved
8 Crêpes (page 49)
3 tablespoons Grand Marnier
2 tablespoons unsalted butter
2 teaspoons grated orange zest

1   Combine orange juice, sugar, and orange juice in large nonstick skillet and set over medium heat. Cook, stirring, until sugar is dissolved and mixture is hot.

2   Fold each crêpe in quarters and place in skillet, overlapping them, if needed. Cook, turning once, until heated through, about 2 minutes. Transfer crêpes to platter. Add orange segments and Grand Marnier to skillet and bring to boil; cook 30 seconds. Remove skillet from heat and swirl in butter until melted; stir in zest. Pour sauce and orange segments over crêpes. Serve at once.

PER SERVING (1 CRÊPE AND ⅛ OF ORANGE SEGMENTS WITH SAUCE): 130 grams, 141 Cal, 4 g Total Fat, 2 g Sat Fat, 0 g Trans Fat, 61 mg Chol, 106 mg Sod, 22 g Total Carb, 14 g Total Sugar, 2 g Fib, 4 g Prot, 70 mg Calc.
PointsPlus value: *4*

Peaches in Red Wine

serves 4

4 large peaches, pitted and sliced
1 cup dry red wine
2 teaspoons sugar
4 fresh mint sprigs

Toss together peaches, wine, and sugar in medium bowl. Let stand at room temperature 30 minutes. Divide peaches and wine sauce evenly among 4 dessert dishes and garnish each serving with mint sprig.

PER SERVING (1 PEACH WITH ¼ CUP SAUCE):
218 grams, 118 Cal, 0 g Total Fat, 0 g Sat Fat,
0 g Trans Fat, 0 mg Chol, 3 mg Sod, 21 g Total Carb,
16 g Total Sugar, 3 g Fib, 1 g Prot, 13 mg Calc.
PointsPlus value: **5**

FYI This easy and delectable dessert also works well with a dry white wine, such as pinot grigio or sauvignon blanc.

▲ **HEALTHY EXTRA**
Sprinkle each serving with fresh raspberries or blackberries.

Peach Melba

serves 4

2 large peaches, peeled, halved, and pitted
2 teaspoons lemon juice
2 (6-ounce) containers raspberries
2 teaspoons sugar
1 pint vanilla low-fat frozen yogurt

1   Toss together peaches and lemon juice in medium bowl.
2   To make raspberry sauce, with fork, crush half of raspberries in small bowl; stir in sugar. Gently stir in remaining raspberries.
3   To serve, place peach half, cut side up, in each of 4 dessert dishes. Top each with ½-cup scoop of yogurt. Spoon raspberry sauce evenly around yogurt. Serve at once.

PER SERVING (1 DESSERT): 284 grams, 176 Cal,
2 g Total Fat, 1 g Sat Fat, 0 g Trans Fat, 5 mg Chol,
62 mg Sod, 37 g Total Carb, 29 g Total Sugar, 7 g Fib,
6 g Prot, 174 mg Calc.
PointsPlus value: **5**

FYI This classic dessert was created in the late 19th century by a French chef in homage to the very popular Australian opera singer Nelly Melba.

Roasted Strawberries and Sorbet

serves 4

1 (1-pound) container strawberries, hulled
    and halved if large
1 tablespoon sugar
¼ teaspoon black pepper
1 pint strawberry sorbet

1   Preheat oven to 425°F.
2   Spread strawberries in jelly-roll pan;
sprinkle with sugar and pepper. Roast, without
turning, until softened, about 20 minutes. Set
aside until warm.
3   To serve, place ½-cup scoop of sorbet in
each of 4 dessert dishes. Spoon strawberries
evenly around sorbet. Serve at once.

PER SERVING (1 DESSERT): 210 grams, 126 Cal,
1 g Total Fat, 0 g Sat Fat, 0 g Trans Fat, 0 mg Chol,
5 mg Sod, 31 g Total Carb, 28 g Total Sugar, 3 g Fib,
2 g Prot, 21 mg Calc.
PointsPlus value: *4*

Black and White Strawberries

serves 6

¼ cup + 2 tablespoons semisweet chocolate
    chips
1½ teaspoons raspberry liqueur (framboise)
1½ teaspoons water
½ ounce white chocolate, chopped, or 2
    tablespoons white chocolate chips
2 cups unhulled strawberries

1   Line large baking sheet with sheet of wax
paper. Combine semisweet chocolate, liqueur,
and water in small microwavable bowl. Microwave on High, stirring twice, until chocolate is
melted and mixture is smooth, about 1½ minutes. Holding a berry by its hull, dip halfway
into chocolate, allowing excess to drip back
into bowl; place strawberry on wax paper. Repeat with remaining berries and chocolate.
2   Put white chocolate in another cup. Microwave on High, stirring once, until melted
and smooth, about 1 minute. Dip tines of fork
into white chocolate; drizzle over strawberries
in zigzag fashion. Refrigerate until chocolate is
set, about 20 minutes.

PER SERVING (ABOUT 4 STRAWBERRIES): 63 grams,
81 Cal, 4 g Total Fat, 3 g Sat Fat, 0 g Trans Fat,
1 mg Chol, 4 mg Sod, 12 g Total Carb, 9 g Total Sugar,
2 g Fib, 1 g Prot, 15 mg Calc.
PointsPlus value: *2*

FYI   Other fruits, including kiwifruit, pineapple,
pear wedges, or apple slices, can also be
dipped. Arrange them in rows on a platter for an
elegant presentation.

Frozen Mango-Lime Mousse

serves 4

2 mangoes, peeled, pitted, and diced
½ cup part-skim ricotta cheese
¼ cup sugar
1 teaspoon grated lime zest
2 tablespoons lime juice
1 package unflavored gelatin
¼ cup cold water
1 cup low-fat (1%) milk

1   Combine mangoes, ricotta, sugar, and lime zest and juice in food processor or blender and puree.

2   Sprinkle gelatin over water in cup; let stand until softened, about 2 minutes. Add to mango mixture in food processor.

3   Bring milk just to boil in small saucepan. Add to mango mixture and puree. Pour mousse into four 8-ounce ramekins, dividing evenly; cover with plastic wrap. Freeze until set, at least 2 hours or up to overnight.

PER SERVING (1 MOUSSE): 218 grams, 192 Cal,
3 g Total Fat, 2 g Sat Fat, 0 g Trans Fat, 12 mg Chol,
76 mg Sod, 35 g Total Carb, 31 g Total Sugar, 2 g Fib,
8 g Prot, 172 mg Calc.
PointsPlus value: **5**

Vanilla Frozen Yogurt

serves 8

2 cups plain low-fat yogurt
2 cups fat-free half-and-half
1 cup sugar
2 teaspoons vanilla extract
Pinch salt

1   Whisk together all ingredients in large bowl until sugar is dissolved.

2   Pour yogurt mixture into ice-cream maker and freeze according to manufacturer's instructions. Transfer yogurt to freezer container and freeze until firm, at least 2 hours or up to 6 hours. Yogurt is best served within 1 day.

PER SERVING (½ CUP): 146 grams, 178 Cal,
1 g Total Fat, 1 g Sat Fat, 0 g Trans Fat, 4 mg Chol,
111 mg Sod, 35 g Total Carb, 33 g Total Sugar, 0 g Fib,
5 g Prot, 192 mg Calc.
PointsPlus value: **5**

FYI   Make this frozen yogurt even more delectable by using a vanilla bean instead of the vanilla extract. With a small, sharp knife, split the bean lengthwise in half, then scrape all the tiny seeds into the yogurt mixture in step 1.

RASPBERRY-ORANGE
FROZEN YOGURT

Raspberry-Orange Frozen Yogurt

serves 8

3 (6-ounce) containers raspberries
1 cup sugar
Grated zest of ½ orange
2 tablespoons orange juice
Pinch salt
1 cup vanilla low-fat yogurt
1 cup fat-free half-and-half

1   Combine raspberries, sugar, orange zest and juice, and salt in medium bowl; let stand, stirring occasionally, 30 minutes.

2   Meanwhile, whisk together yogurt and half-and-half in large bowl until smooth; stir in raspberry mixture until combined well. Cover and refrigerate until thoroughly chilled, about 2 hours.

3   Pour yogurt mixture into ice-cream maker and freeze according to manufacturer's instructions. Transfer to freezer container and freeze until firm, at least 2 hours or up to 6 hours. Yogurt is best served within 1 day.

PER SERVING (½ CUP): 153 grams, 177 Cal,
1 g Total Fat, 0 g Sat Fat, 0 g Trans Fat, 2 mg Chol,
63 mg Sod, 40 g Total Carb, 34 g Total Sugar, 4 g Fib,
3 g Prot, 108 mg Calc.
PointsPlus value: **5**

FYI   Chilling the yogurt mixture before putting it into the ice-cream maker cuts down on the freezing time.

Real Mint Ice Cream

serves 10

1 quart fat-free half-and-half
2 cups lightly packed fresh mint leaves
½ cup sugar
1 cup fat-free egg substitute
Pinch salt
Few drops green food coloring

1   Combine half-and-half, mint, and sugar in large saucepan and set over medium-high heat. Bring just to boil, stirring until sugar is dissolved. Remove saucepan from heat; cover and let stand 10 minutes. Pour mint mixture through sieve set over large bowl, pressing hard on solids to extract as much liquid as possible; discard solids.

2   Whisk together egg substitute and salt in medium bowl. Whisk in ½ cup of hot half-and-half mixture. Whisk into half-and-half mixture in saucepan and set over medium-low heat. Cook, whisking slowly and constantly, until custard is thickened and coats back of spoon, about 5 minutes (do not let boil).

3   Pour custard through fine-mesh sieve set over large bowl. Let cool to room temperature, whisking occasionally. Cover and refrigerate until thoroughly chilled, at least 3 hours or up to overnight.

4   Pour custard mixture into ice-cream maker and freeze according to manufacturer's instructions. Transfer ice cream to freezer container and freeze until firm, about 3 hours. Ice cream is best served within 1 day.

PER SERVING (½ CUP): 146 grams, 123 Cal,
0 g Total Fat, 0 g Sat Fat, 0 g Trans Fat, 0 mg Chol,
150 mg Sod, 22 g Total Carb, 17 g Total Sugar, 1 g Fib,
6 g Prot, 172 mg Calc.
PointsPlus value: **3**

Double Chocolate Sorbet
serves 4

2 cups water
½ cup sugar
⅓ cup unsweetened cocoa
¼ cup honey
*½ ounce (½ square) unsweetened chocolate,
    chopped*
½ teaspoon instant espresso or coffee powder

1   Stir together ½ cup of water, the sugar, cocoa, honey, chocolate, and espresso in medium saucepan and set over medium heat. Bring to simmer and cook, stirring, until sugar is dissolved, about 3 minutes. Remove saucepan from heat; stir in remaining 1½ cups water.
2   Pour chocolate mixture into 9 × 13-inch baking pan. Cover pan with foil; freeze until chocolate mixture is frozen along edges, about 1 hour. With fork, scrape icy edges in toward center. Repeat every 30 minutes until sorbet is semifirm, about 2 hours.
3   Transfer sorbet to food processor and puree. Scrape into freezer container with tight-fitting lid; freeze until firm, about 3 hours longer.

PER SERVING (GENEROUS ½ CUP): 175 grams, 196 Cal, 3 g Total Fat, 2 g Sat Fat, 0 g Trans Fat, 0 mg Chol, 7 mg Sod, 47 g Total Carb, 41 g Total Sugar, 3 g Fib, 2 g Prot, 16 mg Calc.
PointsPlus value: **6**

▲ **HEALTHY EXTRA**
Surround each serving of this very chocolaty sorbet with sliced fresh strawberries and diced mango.

Watermelon Sorbet
serves 4

4 cups seedless watermelon chunks
¼ cup superfine sugar
2 tablespoons lime juice

1   Combine all ingredients in blender or food processor and puree. Transfer to freezer container with tight-fitting lid; freeze, covered, until mixture resembles set gelatin, 4–6 hours.
2   Puree watermelon mixture, in batches, in blender or food processor; return to container. Freeze, covered, overnight. Let sorbet stand at room temperature 5 minutes before serving.

PER SERVING (ABOUT ½ CUP): 160 grams, 91 Cal, 0 g Total Fat, 0 g Sat Fat, 0 g Trans Fat, 0 mg Chol, 5 mg Sod, 27 g Total Carb, 25 g Total Sugar, 1 g Fib, 1 g Prot, 11 mg Calc.
PointsPlus value: **3**

FYI   Superfine sugar dissolves quickly, an essential quality when making this refreshing sorbet. If unavailable, you can process granulated sugar in a blender until it is finely ground, about 30 seconds.

Honeydew Sorbet

serves 8

¹/₂ cup water
¹/₂ cup sugar
2 (3-inch) strips lime zest
Pinch salt
1 tablespoon lime juice
1 chilled ripe honeydew (3¹/₂ pounds), peeled,
    halved, seeded, and chopped

1   To make sugar syrup, combine water, sugar, lime zest, and salt in small saucepan and set over high heat. Bring to boil, stirring until sugar is dissolved. Reduce heat and simmer 5 minutes; stir in lime juice. Pour syrup through sieve set over small bowl; discard solids. Cover and refrigerate until thoroughly chilled, about 30 minutes.
2   Meanwhile, puree honeydew, in batches, in blender or food processor. Transfer to medium bowl and whisk in sugar syrup. Pour melon mixture through sieve set over large bowl, pressing hard on solids to extract as much as liquid as possible; discard solids.
3   Transfer melon mixture to ice-cream maker and freeze according to manufacturer's instructions. Transfer sorbet to freezer container and freeze until firm, at least 2 hours or up to overnight. This sorbet is best served within 1 day.

PER SERVING (½ CUP): 121 grams, 81 Cal, 0 g Total Fat, 0 g Sat Fat, 0 g Trans Fat, 0 mg Chol, 27 mg Sod, 21 g Total Carb, 20 g Total Sugar, 1 g Fib, 0 g Prot, 6 mg Calc.
PointsPlus value: *2*

FYI   You can substitute cantaloupe, Crenshaw, or casaba melon for the honeydew to create flavorful variations.

Grapefruit-Strawberry Granita

serves 6

1¹/₂ cups thickly sliced hulled strawberries
2 cups ruby red grapefruit juice
¹/₂ cup superfine sugar

1   Puree strawberries in blender or food processor. Pour strawberry puree and grapefruit juice through sieve set over large bowl to remove seeds, pressing hard to extract as much liquid as possible; discard solids. Stir in sugar.
2   Transfer grapefruit mixture to 9 × 13-inch baking pan. Cover pan with foil and freeze until frozen along edges, about 1 hour. With fork, scrape icy edges in toward center. Repeat every 30 minutes until granita is semifirm, about 2 hours.
3   Use a fork to scrape across the surface of granita, transferring ice shards to 6 dessert dishes. Serve at once.

PER SERVING (ABOUT ½ CUP): 141 grams, 124 Cal, 0 g Total Fat, 0 g Sat Fat, 0 g Trans Fat, 0 mg Chol, 9 mg Sod, 31 g Total Carb, 29 g Total Sugar, 1 g Fib, 1 g Prot, 13 mg Calc.
PointsPlus value: *3*

Summer Pudding

serves 6

1 pint blueberries
1 (6-ounce) container blackberries
1 (6-ounce) container raspberries
1/3 cup sugar
2 tablespoons water
2 (3-inch) strips lemon zest
2 cups chopped hulled strawberries
10 slices firm-textured white bread, crusts
    removed

1   Combine blueberries, blackberries, raspberries, sugar, and water in large saucepan and
set over medium heat. Cook, stirring, until
berries begin to release their juice, about 3
minutes. Bring to simmer and cook, stirring
occasionally, until slightly thickened, about 5
minutes. Remove saucepan from heat; stir in
strawberries.

2   Line 2-quart bowl with two pieces of
overlapping plastic wrap, allowing excess to
extend over rim of bowl by about 4 inches.
Line bottom and side of bowl with bread, cutting to fit as needed. Spoon berry mixture into
bowl. Cover with layer of bread, cutting to fit
as needed. Fold plastic wrap over top of pudding. Place plate, slightly smaller than bowl,
on top of pudding and weight with about 4
cans of food. Refrigerate at least 8 hours or up
to 2 days.

3   To serve, fold back plastic wrap and invert
pudding onto serving plate. Lift off bowl and
remove plastic wrap. Cut pudding into 6
wedges and put on plates or spoon into bowls.

PER SERVING (1 WEDGE): 196 grams, 168 Cal,
1 g Total Fat, 0 g Sat Fat, 0 g Trans Fat, 0 mg Chol,
111 mg Sod, 39 g Total Carb, 23 g Total Sugar, 7 g Fib,
3 g Prot, 48 mg Calc.
PointsPlus value: **4**

FYI   This beautiful and luscious warm-weather
dessert can be prepared with a variety of
berries or with only one kind, if you prefer.

Coconut Bread Pudding with Chocolate Sauce

serves 12

1/2 cup sweetened flaked coconut
1 (20-ounce) can pineapple chunks in
    juice, drained
3 large eggs
2 large egg whites
1/2 cup sugar
1 teaspoon salt
2 1/4 cups fat-free milk
1 cup light (reduced-fat) coconut milk
1 teaspoon vanilla extract
5 cups (3/4-inch) French or Italian bread cubes
2 ounces bittersweet or semisweet chocolate,
    chopped
2 teaspoons unsweetened cocoa

1   Preheat broiler.

2   Spread coconut in small shallow baking
pan. Broil 5 inches from heat, stirring once or
twice, until lightly toasted, about 3 minutes.
Transfer to plate. Spread pineapple in same
baking pan; broil, turning once, until lightly
browned, about 3 minutes. Let cool.

3   Preheat oven to 350°F.

4   Beat eggs, egg whites, sugar, and salt until well combined. Stir in 2 cups of fat-free milk, the coconut milk, and vanilla. Add bread and stir until coated. Let soak 10 minutes. Stir in coconut and pineapple.

5   Pour pudding mixture into 7 × 11-inch baking dish. Bake until puffed and lightly browned, about 40 minutes. Let cool slightly.

6   Meanwhile, to make chocolate sauce, combine chocolate, cocoa, and remaining ¼ cup milk in 1-cup glass measure. Microwave on High 45 seconds; stir until chocolate is melted and mixture is smooth. Serve alongside bread pudding.

PER SERVING (¹⁄₁₂ OF PUDDING AND SCANT 1 TABLESPOON SAUCE): 144 grams, 173 Cal, 6 g Total Fat, 3 g Sat Fat, 0 g Trans Fat, 54 mg Chol, 327 mg Sod, 26 g Total Carb, 17 g Total Sugar, 1 g Fib, 5 g Prot, 77 mg Calc.
PointsPlus value: **5**

FYI   The coconut can also be toasted in a skillet: Spread the coconut in a medium skillet and cook over medium heat, stirring often, until golden. Transfer to a plate.

Rice Pudding with Golden Raisins

serves 4

2 cups fat-free milk
¼ cup sugar
2 tablespoons water
⅓ cup Arborio or other short-grain rice
2 large eggs
¼ cup golden raisins
1 teaspoon vanilla extract
Pinch cinnamon
4 teaspoons butter

1   Combine 1½ cups of milk, the sugar, and water in small saucepan; bring to boil. Stir in rice. Reduce heat and simmer, stirring occasionally, 30 minutes.

2   Preheat oven to 325°F. Spray 1½-quart baking dish with nonstick spray.

3   Combine remaining ½ cup milk, the eggs, raisins, vanilla, and cinnamon in medium bowl; stir in rice. Pour into prepared baking dish; dot with butter. Bake, stirring twice, 25 minutes.

PER SERVING (¼ OF PUDDING): 196 grams, 234 Cal, 6 g Total Fat, 4 g Sat Fat, 0 g Trans Fat, 120 mg Chol, 114 mg Sod, 36 g Total Carb, 22 g Total Sugar, 2 g Fib, 8 g Prot, 190 mg Calc
PointsPlus value: **6**

Old-Fashioned Butterscotch Pudding

serves 6

²/₃ *cup packed dark brown sugar*
2 tablespoons cornstarch
2 cups fat-free half-and-half
3 large egg yolks
¹/₄ *teaspoon salt*
2 teaspoons vanilla extract

1   Whisk together brown sugar and cornstarch in medium saucepan. Slowly whisk in half-and-half until smooth; set over medium heat. Cook, whisking, until mixture bubbles and thickens, about 10 minutes. Remove saucepan from heat.
2   Whisk together egg yolks and salt in medium bowl. Whisk about ½ cup of hot half-and-half mixture into egg mixture. Whisk into half-and-half mixture in saucepan. Reduce heat to low and cook, stirring, until pudding is thickened and smooth, about 2 minutes.
3   Pour pudding through sieve set over medium bowl; whisk in vanilla. Divide pudding evenly among 6 dessert dishes; let cool to room temperature. Refrigerate until chilled and set, at least 2 hours or up to overnight.

PER SERVING (½ CUP): 117 grams, 202 Cal,
7 g Total Fat, 4 g Sat Fat, 0 g Trans Fat, 106 mg Chol,
150 mg Sod, 29 g Total Carb, 27 g Total Sugar, 0 g Fib,
4 g Prot, 139 mg Calc.
PointsPlus value: **5**

FYI   If you prefer pudding without a skin on top, press a piece of plastic wrap or wax paper directly onto the surface of each pudding before putting in the refrigerator.

Classic Chocolate Mousse

serves 16

8 ounces bittersweet chocolate, chopped
3 tablespoons hazelnut liqueur
2 tablespoons light corn syrup
¹/₄ *cup powdered egg whites*
³/₄ *cup warm water*
¹/₂ *cup sugar*
¹/₂ *cup candied orange slivers*

1   Fill medium saucepan with 1 inch of water and bring to simmer over medium heat. Put chocolate in medium bowl and set over simmering water. Cook, stirring, until chocolate is melted and smooth, about 5 minutes. Remove bowl from saucepan.
2   Combine chocolate, liqueur, and corn syrup in large bowl. Whisk together powdered egg whites and warm water until egg white powder is completely dissolved, about 2 minutes. With electric mixer on low speed, beat egg white mixture until foamy. Increase speed to medium-high and beat until soft peaks form when beaters are lifted. Add sugar, 2 tablespoons at a time, beating until stiff, glossy peaks form when beaters are lifted.
3   With rubber spatula, stir about one-third of meringue into chocolate mixture to lighten it. Fold remaining meringue into chocolate mixture in two batches just until whites are no longer visible. Spoon mousse into 16 dishes. Refrigerate, until firm, at least 3 hours.

**PER SERVING (¹/₁₆ OF MOUSSE AND ½ TABLESPOON
CANDIED ORANGE):** 38 grams, 170 Cal, 8 g Total Fat,
4 g Sat Fat, 0 g Trans Fat, 0 mg Chol, 39 mg Sod,
26 g Total Carb, 21 g Total Sugar, 2 g Fib, 3 g Prot,
8 mg Calc.
PointsPlus value: **5**

Toasted Coconut Custard

serves 4

1 cup low-fat (1%) milk
1/3 cup instant nonfat dry milk powder
2 tablespoons sugar
1 teaspoon coconut extract
2 large eggs
1 teaspoon vanilla extract
2 tablespoons sweetened flaked coconut,
    toasted

1   Preheat oven to 350°F. Spray four 6-ounce custard cups or ramekins with nonstick spray.
2   Combine milk, milk powder, sugar, and coconut extract in medium saucepan and set over medium-high heat. Cook, stirring frequently, until mixture boils and sugar is dissolved, 3–4 minutes. Whisk eggs in medium bowl; gradually whisk in hot milk mixture and vanilla. Divide evenly among prepared custard cups; sprinkle evenly with coconut. Put custards in roasting pan and place in oven; pour enough hot (not boiling) water into pan to come halfway up sides of cups.
3   Bake until knife inserted into center of custard comes out clean, 20–25 minutes. Transfer to wire rack and let cool to room temperature. Refrigerate custards until chilled, at least 4 hours or up to overnight.

PER SERVING (1 CUSTARD): 103 grams, 124 Cal, 4 g Total Fat, 2 g Sat Fat, 0 g Trans Fat, 109 mg Chol, 102 mg Sod, 14 g Total Carb, 13 g Total Sugar, 0 g Fib, 8 g Prot, 169 mg Calc.
PointsPlus value: *3*

FYI   Stirring nonfat dry milk powder into the low-fat milk lends it a creamy richness, eliminating the need to use whole milk, which is standard in custard.

Best Blueberry Sauce

serves 6 (makes 1½ cups)

1 pint blueberries
½ cup confectioners' sugar
2 tablespoons water
2 teaspoons lime juice

Combine blueberries, confectioners' sugar, and water in large saucepan and set over medium heat. Cook, stirring occasionally, until berries soften and mixture thickens, about 5 minutes. Stir in lime juice. Cool to room temperature. Transfer to covered container; refrigerate up to 1 week.

PER SERVING (¼ CUP): 65 grams, 66 Cal, 0 g Total Fat, 0 g Sat Fat, 0 g Trans Fat, 0 mg Chol, 3 mg Sod, 17 g Total Carb, 15 g Total Sugar, 1 g Fib, 0 g Prot, 3 mg Calc.
PointsPlus value: *2*

▲ **HEALTHY EXTRA**
Spoon this sauce over plain fat-free yogurt (1 cup of plain fat-free yogurt with each serving will increase the *PointsPlus* value by *3*).

Raspberry Sauce

serves 4 (makes 1 cup)

1 (6-ounce) container raspberries
¼ cup raspberry spreadable fruit
1 tablespoon honey
¾ teaspoon vanilla extract

Puree raspberries in food processor or blender. Press raspberries through sieve set over medium bowl, pressing hard on solids to extract as much liquid as possible; discard seeds. Combine pureed raspberries, spreadable fruit, honey, and vanilla in blender and puree.

PER SERVING (¼ CUP): 68 grams, 79 Cal, 0 g Total Fat, 0 g Sat Fat, 0 g Trans Fat, 0 mg Chol, 0 mg Sod, 19 g Total Carb, 14 g Total Sugar, 3 g Fib, 0 g Prot, 10 mg Calc.
PointsPlus value: *2*

FYI During raspberry season, which begins in early July, take advantage of their abundance, fresh flavor, and low price by freezing them to enjoy later. Use the berries in our flavorful sauce—no need to thaw them.

HEALTHY EXTRA
Drizzle this very raspberry sauce over a bowl of mixed fresh fruit, such as peaches, raspberries, and nectarines.

FREEZING RASPBERRIES

1 *Discard any stems, leaves, or blemished berries. Do not wash them.*

2 *Spread berries in single layer in jelly-roll pan lined with wax paper. Freeze until hard, about 2 hours.*

3 *Transfer berries to zip-close freezer plastic bag. Squeeze out air and seal bag. Return to freezer for up to 6 months.*

Rich Chocolate Sauce

serves 16 (makes 2 cups)

8 ounces semisweet chocolate, finely chopped
1 cup water
1 teaspoon vanilla extract

1 Fill medium saucepan with 1½ inches of water and set over medium-low heat; bring to gentle simmer. Put chocolate and water in medium bowl and set over simmering water. Cook, stirring, until chocolate is melted and mixture is smooth.

2 Remove bowl from saucepan; whisk in vanilla. Use immediately or cool to room temperature. Transfer sauce to covered container; refrigerate up to 1 month. Stir well and serve chilled or gently reheat.

PER SERVING (2 TABLESPOONS): 29 grams, 68 Cal,
6 g Total Fat, 3 g Sat Fat, 0 g Trans Fat, 0 mg Chol,
1 mg Sod, 7 g Total Carb, 0 g Total Sugar, 0 g Fib,
0 g Prot, 9 mg Calc.
PointsPlus value: *2*

FYI For a deeper, richer chocolate flavor, use bittersweet chocolate with 60–70% cocoa solids.

Hot Fudge Sauce

serves 12 (makes 1½ cups)

1 cup fat-free half-and-half
2 tablespoons dark corn syrup
8 ounces semisweet chocolate, chopped
1 teaspoon vanilla extract

1 Combine half-and-half and corn syrup in heavy medium saucepan and set over medium heat. Bring to boil, whisking until smooth. Remove saucepan from heat. Add chocolate, stirring until melted and smooth.

2 Bring chocolate mixture to boil over medium-high heat. Boil 30 seconds, whisking constantly. Remove saucepan from heat; stir in vanilla. Use or cool to room temperature. Transfer to covered container; refrigerate up to 3 weeks.

PER SERVING (2 TABLESPOONS): 32 grams, 112 Cal,
5 g Total Fat, 3 g Sat Fat, 0 g Trans Fat, 0 mg Chol,
14 mg Sod, 16 g Total Carb, 12 g Total Sugar, 1 g Fib,
2 g Prot, 14 mg Calc.
PointsPlus value: *3*

Index

Page numbers in *italics* indicate
illustrations.

A

Acorn Squash, Wedges, Maple and Butter–
Glazed, 279
African Peanut Soup, 124
All-American Potato Salad, 92, *93*
Almond(s)
-Apricot Couscous, Tandoori Lamb
with, 154, *155*
-Cranberry Granola, 40
Trout Amandine, 212
Angel Food Cake, Lemon, with Berries,
374
Antipasto Platter, 73
Apple(s)
Beet, and Watercress Salad, 84
Brown Betty, 408
with Chicken and Noodles, 169
Pie, Classic, 383
and Sauerkraut, Pork Roast with, 308,
309
Strudel, Double, 406, *407*
Applesauce, -Banana Bread, 355
Apricot
-Almond Couscous, Tandoori Lamb
with, 154, *155*
Corn Bread, and Cranberry Dressing,
290, *291*
Arctic Char, Grilled, with Salad, *196*, 197
Argentina-Style Steak and Sauce, 137
Arugula
and Ham Crêpes, Creamy, *48*, 49
Pesto, and Tomatoes, Pasta with, 245
Roast Beef Salad with, 97
Asian
Sea Bass, 206
Vinaigrette, 30
Asparagus
Canadian Bacon, and Scallion
Omelette, 43
and Red Peppers, Roasted, 266
Skillet, with Pinto Beans and Tomatoes,
302
Avgolemono Chicken Soup, 116

B

Baba Ghanoush, 57
Baby Romaine with Clementines and
Pecans, 85
Bacon
Canadian, Asparagus, and Scallion
Omelette, 43
Corn, and Potato Soup, 123
Mushroom, and Gruyère Pizza, 327
Baked Beans, 298
Baked Fruit–Cinnamon Oatmeal, 42
Baked Haddock with Ratatouille, 210
Baked Macaroni and Cheese, 238, *239*
Baking Powder Biscuits, 360
Balsamic Vinegar, Kale with, 271
Banana
-Applesauce Bread, 355
Cream Pie, 390
Barbecued Pork with Mop Sauce, 148
Barbecue Sauce
Grilled Chicken, 170
Smoky, 14, *15*
Barley
Beef Soup, Classic, 125
Leek, and Rosemary Gratin, *294*, 295
-Vegetable Soup, 314, *315*
Basic Beef Stock, 106

Basic Cheese Pizza, 323
Basic Chicken Stock, 106
Basic Dry Rub, 26
Basic Marinade, 23
Basic Omelette, 43
Basic Pancakes, 39
Basic Vegetable Stock, 107
Basil
Grilled Shrimp, and Goat Cheese
Sandwiches, 339
Pesto, 16
-Roasted Tomato Sauce, 13
-Tomato Soup, Fresh, 113
Bean(s). *See also* Black Bean(s); Cannellini
Beans; Pinto Bean(s); Red Bean(s);
White Bean(s)
Baked, 298
Baked, Tex Mex–Style, 238
and Beef Chili, 141
and Kielbasa Soup, 314
and Rice, 237
and Rice, Cuban-Style, 299
Soup, Creamy, 121
Soup, Italian (-Style), 120
and Soy Chili, 232
and Spinach Burritos, 235
and Wheat Berry Stew, 233
Beef. *See also* Burgers; Roast Beef; Steak
Barley Soup, Classic, 125
and Bean Chili, 141
Brisket, Smoky, Grilled, 133
and Broccoli Stir-Fry, Spicy, 140
Corned, and Cabbage, 306
Kebabs, Middle-Eastern, *138*, 139
London Broil, 136
Meat Loaf, Our Favorite, 139
Picadillo in Lettuce Leaves, 76
Pot Roast, Classic, 132
Salad, Thai, Grilled, *96*, 97
Stew, 140
Stew with Carrots and Peas, 306
Stock, Basic, 106
Tenderloin, Peppered, Roast, *134*, 135
Beer Can Chicken, 168
Beet(s)
Apple, and Watercress Salad, 84
and Garlic, Oven-Roasted, 266
Bell Pepper(s)
Cannellini Bean–Stuffed, 236
and Chicken Fajitas, 180
–Nectarine Salsa, *20*, 21
Red, and Asparagus, Roasted, 266
Stuffed, 141
–Tomato Sauce, Grilled Lamb Chops
with, 158
White Bean, and Olive Pizzas, 70
Bell Pepper(s), Roasted
with Orange Zest and Olives, 276
Red, Coulis, 17
–Tomato Soup, 113
Tomato–Stuffed Eggplant Rollups, 73
Berry(ies). *See also* Blackberry;
Blueberry(ies); Raspberry(ies);
Strawberry(ies)
Double, Spice Crisp, 408
Lemon Angel Food Cake with, 374
Best Blueberry Sauce, 422
Best-Ever Black Bean Soup, 121
Best-Ever Chicken Loaf, 313
Best Grilled Burgers, 142
Big Blueberry Pie, 383
Biscotti
Chocolate-Espresso, 400
Double Chocolate–Hazelnut, 401
Biscuits
Baking Powder, 360

Orange and Sage, 361
Yogurt, 361
Black and White Strawberries, 412
Black Bean(s)
and Chicken Chili, 185
and Corn Salad, Tuna with, 202
and Mango Salsa, 19, *20*
and Pork Chili, 152
Quinoa, and Shrimp Salad, 101
Salad, Southwestern, 94
Smoky, 299
Soup, Best-Ever, 121
Black Pepper(ed)
Dry Rub, 27
Fennel and Lemon Rub, 26
Roast Tenderloin, *134*, 135
Blanquette de Veau, 307
BLTs, Turkey, 338
Blueberry(ies)
-Buttermilk Corn Muffins, 357
Double Grain Scones, *362*, 363
-Lemon Scones, 364
Pancakes, 39
Pie, Big, 384
Sauce, Best, 422
Sauce, Lemon Cheesecake with, 382
Blue Cheese
Dressing, 32
Polenta, Creamy, 297
Bok Choy
and Ginger, Pork Stir-Fry with, 148
–Noodle Soup, 118
Borscht, 108
Bouillabaisse, 211
Bourbon, -Pear Sauce, Caramel Cake with,
376
Braised Halibut with Tomatoes and Orzo,
200, *201*
Bran
Bread, 347
Muffins, Jumbo, 357
Bread. *See also* Corn Bread; Sweet Bread(s)
Bran, 347
Dried Tomato and Herb, No-Knead, 344
Focaccia, Whole Wheat, 346
Irish Soda, 353
Naan Flatbread, Quick, 354
Wheat, with Honey, Food Processor,
346
Wheat-Honey Crescent Rolls, 350
Whole Wheat, No-Knead, 344
Bread Pudding, Coconut, with Chocolate
Sauce, 418
Breakfast Tostadas, 50, *51*
Brisket, Smoky Grilled, 133
Broccoli
and Beef Stir-Fry, Spicy, 140
and Chicken, Spicy, 180
with Garlic, 264
and Goat Cheese, Pasta with, *244*, 245
and Parmesan, Spaghetti Squash with,
252
with Pasta and White Beans, 293
and Pork Stir-Fry, 310
Spears, Lemon-Butter, 265
Broccoli Rabe
and Chicken with Polenta, *174*, 175
Pan Braised, 265
Broiled Halibut with Pico de Gallo, 200
Broiled Stuffed Lobster, 224
Brown and Wild Rice with Walnuts and
Cranberries, 286
Brown Betty, Apple, 408
Brownies, 394
Bruschetta
Portobello and Ham, *67*, 68
White Bean, 68

Brussels Sprouts, and Carrots, Oven-
Roasted, *268*, 269
Bûche de Noël, 371
Buckwheat Pancakes, 39
Bulgur, Pilaf, Spinach and Mushroom, 296
Bundt Cake, Chocolate-Buttermilk, 368,
369
Buns
Hot Cross, 352
Sticky, Classic, 351
Burgers
Best Grilled, 142
Cheddar-Stuffed, 142, *143*
Lamb, Grilled, Greek-Style
Sandwiches, 331
Portobello Mushroom, 251
Tofu, 228
Turkey, Monterey Jack, 189
Burritos, Spinach and Bean, 235
Butter
-Lemon Broccoli Spears, 265
and Maple–Glazed Acorn Squash
Wedges, 279
Sauce, Steamed Lobster with, 223
Buttermilk
-Blueberry Corn Muffins, 357
-Chocolate Bundt Cake, 368, *369*
–Whole Wheat Scones, 364
–Whole Wheat Waffles, 38
Butternut Squash and Sage Soup, 114
Butterscotch Pudding, Old-Fashioned, 420

C
Cabbage
and Corned Beef, 306
Radicchio, and Jicama Slaw, 91
Red, with Ginger, 267
Stuffed, Rice and Soy, 232
Caesar Salad, Whole Leaf, with Golden
Croutons, 84
Cajun
Catfish, 203
Dry Rub, 27
Cake
Bûche de Noël, 371
Bundt, Chocolate-Buttermilk, 368, *369*
Caramel, with Bourbon-Pear Sauce,
376
Carrot, 375
Cheesecake, Lemon, with Blueberry
Sauce, 382
Chocolate, Flourless, 370
Citrus Passover, 378
Dark Fruit, 377
Honey, 378
Lemon Angel Food, with Berries, 374
Orange Sponge, Rolled, 372
Pumpkin Spice, 375
Sour Cream Coffee, 368
Strawberry Shortcakes, 409
Triple Ginger Gingerbread, 379
Yellow Layer, with Cocoa Frosting, 372
California
Greens Salad with Baked Goat Cheese,
88
Hummus Sandwiches, 334
Seafood Salad, 101
Sushi Rolls, 72
Calzones, Mushroom-Spinach, 330
Canadian Bacon, Asparagus, and Scallion
Omelette, 43
Cannellini Bean–Stuffed Peppers, 236
Cantaloupe, Salsa, Crisped Scallops with,
221
Capellini with Fresh Tomato Sauce, 246
Capers, -Lemon Sauce, Chicken in, 178,
179

Caponata, 59
Caramel Cake with Bourbon-Pear Sauce,
376
Caramelized
Garlic Toasts, 66, *67*
Onion, Fig, and Stilton Pizza, 324, *325*
Caribbean-Style Pork Tenderloin, 147
Carrot(s)
and Brussels Sprouts, Oven-Roasted,
268, 269
Cake, 375
Dilled, 267
-Ginger Dressing, 31
and Peas, Beef Stew with, 306
-Pecan Bread, 356
Casserole(s)
Chicken-Mushroom Hash, 177
Chicken-Noodle, Zesty, 186
Ratatouille, 273
Spinach-Potato, 252
Sweet Potato, 262
Catfish
with Broiled Tomatoes, 205
Cajun, 203
Crispy, with Tartar Sauce, 206
"Fried," with Potato Sticks, *204*, 205
Cauliflower with Curried Tomato Sauce,
269
Caviar Eggs, 62
Celery Root and Mashed Potatoes, 256
Cereal. *See* Granola; Oatmeal; Porridge
Cheddar-Stuffed Burgers, 142, *143*
Cheese. *See also* Blue Cheese; Feta; Goat
Cheese; Parmesan
Cheddar-Stuffed Burgers, 142, *143*
Crisps, 60
and Macaroni, Baked, 238, *239*
Monterey Jack Turkey Burgers, 189
Pepper Jack and Chile Corn Bread, 355
pizza with. *see* Pizza
Quiche, 52
Ricotta Salata, Watermelon-Peach Salad
with, *86*, 87
Sauce, Rich, 14
Scalloped Potatoes with, *258*, 259
Soufflé, Classic, 241
and Spinach Quiche, 52
Straws, 60, *61*
Cheesecake, Lemon, with Blueberry Sauce,
382
Cherry(ies)
-Chocolate Scones, 364
Pie, 384
Cherry Tomato(es)
and Garlic, Skillet Chicken with, 172
with Thyme, 274
Chicken
with Apples and Noodles, 169
Baked, Orange-Crumbed, 173
Barbecue-Sauced, Grilled, 170
Beer Can, 168
and Bell Pepper Fajitas, 180
and Black Bean Chili, 185
Breasts with Papaya-Mint Salsa, 172
and Broccoli, Spicy, 180
and Broccoli Rabe with Polenta, *174*,
175
Cacciatore, 169
Skillet Chicken with Cherry Tomatoes
and Garlic, 172
Cumin Kebabs, with Couscous, 176
Curry, Spicy, 170, *171*
Garlic-Roasted, with Gravy, 164
in Lemon-Caper Sauce, 178, *179*
Loaf, Best-Ever, 313
-Mushroom Hash Casserole, 177
and Mushroom Stew, 182, *183*

-Noodle Casserole, Zesty, 186
with Olives and Dates, 184
with Orange Gremolata, 167
Oven-Fried, Herbed, 181
Paprika, Skillet, 178
Picadillo, 182
with Pineapple, Island, 176
and Potatoes, Chili-Roasted, 165
–Pumpkin Seed Mole, Easy, 173
with Rice, *166*, 167
Sandwiches, Grilled, Vietnamese-Style,
336, *337*
Sandwiches, Middle Eastern-Style, 335
Satay with Peanut Sauce, 76
and Sausage Stew, Tuscan, 312
Stew, Garlicky, 312
Stock, Basic, 106
Tacos, 175
Tandoori Spiced, 184
and Turkey Sausage Gumbo, 311
and Vegetable Fried Rice, 185
Chicken Salad
Chinese, 98
Classic, 99
Crispy Buffalo-Style, 98
Chicken Soup, 313
Avgolemono, 116
-Corn, Mexican-Style, *122*, 123
Chickpea(s)
Cakes, Hot-and-Spicy, 65
and Chunky Vegetables, 302
and Tomatoes, Summery Pasta with,
300, *301*
and Vegetable Tagine, North African,
234, 235
Chile(s)
and Corn, Tomato Rice with, 284
and Pepper Jack Corn Bread, 355
Chili
Beef and Bean, 141
Chicken and Black Bean, 185
Pork and Black Bean, 152
Smoky Turkey, 316, *317*
Soy and Bean, 232
Tempeh, Sweet Onion, and Mushroom,
230
Chili (Powder)
-Lime Mayonnaise, Soft Tacos with
Tilapia and, *208*, 209
-Roasted Chicken and Potatoes, 165
Chilled Cucumber-Yogurt Soup, 109
Chimichurri Sauce, 17
Chinese
Chicken Salad, 98
Noodle Soup, 116, *117*
Chipotle Mayonnaise, Sweet Potato
Wedges with, 260, *261*
Chives, Yellow Squash Soup with,
Creamy, 111
Chocolate
Brownies, 394
-Buttermilk Bundt Cake, 368, *369*
Cake, Flourless, 370
-Cherry Scones, 364
Chip Cookies, 396
Cocoa Frosting, Yellow Layer Cake
with, 372
Double, –Hazelnut Biscotti, 401
Double, Sorbet, 416
-Espresso Biscotti, 400
Hot Fudge Sauce, 424
Mocha Meringues, 399
Mousse, Classic, 420, *421*
Sauce, Coconut Bread Pudding with,
418
Sauce, Rich, 424

Chowder
  Clam, Manhattan, 318
  Clam, Smoky Manhattan-Style, 128
  Turkey, 316
Chutney, Mango, 22
Cilantro, and Curry, Egg Salad Sandwich with, 334
Cinnamon, –Baked Fruit Oatmeal, 42
Cioppino, 126, *127*
Citrus
  Dressing, Orange and Red Onion Salad with, 88
  -Glazed Duck Breasts, 192
  Marinade, 25
  Passover Cake, 378
  Triple, Pie, 385
Clam
  Chowder, Manhattan, 318
  Chowder, Smoky Manhattan-Style, 128
  Pizza, Easy, 324
Classic
  Apple Pie, 383
  Beef Barley Soup, 125
  Cheese Soufflé, 241
  Chicken Salad, 99
  Chocolate Mousse, 420, *421*
  Corn Bread, 354
  Crêpes Suzette, 410
  Guacamole, 56
  Minestrone, 119
  Pot Roast, 132
  Roasted Vegetables, 276
  Spaghetti and Meatballs, 145
  Sticky Buns, 351
  Tomato Sauce, 12
  Tuna Salad Sandwiches, 339
  Vinaigrette, 30
Clementines, and Pecans, Baby Romaine with, 85
Coconut
  Bread Pudding with Chocolate Sauce, 418
  Cream Pie, 390
  Macadamia Meringues, 399
  Macaroons, 402
  Toasted, Custard, 422
Coffee
  Chocolate-Espresso Biscotti, 400
  Mocha Meringues, 399
Coffee Cake, Sour Cream, 368
Condiments
  Cranberry-Walnut Relish, 22
  Mango Chutney, 22
Cookies
  Chocolate Chip, 396
  Chocolate-Espresso Biscotti, 400
  Cranberry-Oatmeal, *395*, 397
  Double Chocolate–Hazelnut Biscotti, 401
  Gingerbread, 398
  Ginger-Spice, 402
  Lemon Poppy Seed Crisps, 394, *395*
  Linzer Thumbprint Jewel, 397
  Macadamia Coconut Meringues, 399
  Mocha Meringues, 399
  Peanut Butter, *395*, 396
  Rugelach, 393
Corn
  and Black Bean Salad, Tuna with, 202
  -Chicken Soup, Mexican-Style, *122*, 123
  and Chiles, Tomato Rice with, 284
  on the Cob, Oven-Roasted, 264
  Potato, and Bacon Soup, Creamy, 123
  Pudding, 263
  Soup, Summertime Grilled, 108
Corn Bread
  Apricot, and Cranberry Dressing, 290, *291*

Classic, 354
  Pepper Jack and Chile, 355
Corned Beef and Cabbage, 306
Cornish Hens under a Brick, 192
Cornmeal Pizza Dough, 322
Corn Muffins, Blueberry-Buttermilk, 357
Coulis
  Roasted Red Pepper, 17
  Tomato, and Goat Cheese, Pissaladière with, 331
Couscous
  Almond-Apricot, Tandoori Lamb with, 154, *155*
  Cumin Chicken Kebabs with, 176
  Israeli, Grilled Summer Vegetables with, 242
  with Lime and Scallion, 293
  Seafood Skewers, Mixed, with, 213
Crab
  Cakes, Maryland, 222
  Cake Sandwiches, Open-Face, 340
Cranberry(ies)
  -Almond Granola, 41
  Corn Bread, and Apricot Dressing, 290, *291*
  -Oatmeal Cookies, *395*, 397
  -Orange Bread, 356
  and Pecans, Wild Rice Salad with, 94
  Sauce, Turkey Cutlets with, 189
  -Walnut Relish, 22
  and Walnuts, Brown and Wild Rice with, 286
Cream Cheese, Frosting, Mahogany Velvet Cupcakes with, *380*, 381
"Creamed" Spinach, 277
Creamy
  Bean Soup, 121
  Blue Cheese Polenta, 297
  Corn, Potato, and Bacon Soup, 123
  Ham and Arugula Crêpes, *48*, 49
  Mashed Potatoes, 256
  Polenta with Vegetables, 247
  Yellow Squash Soup with Chives, 111
Cremini Mushrooms with Quinoa and Thyme, 297
Creole (-Style)
  Okra, 272
  Rémoulade Sauce, Fish Cakes with, 210
  Shrimp, 219
Crêpes, 49
  Ham and Arugula, Creamy, *48*, 49
Crisp, Spice Double Berry, 408
Crisped Scallops with Cantaloupe Salsa, 221
Crispy Buffalo-Style Chicken Salad, 98
Crispy Catfish with Tartar Sauce, 206
Crostini, Roasted Vegetable, 66, 67
Croutons, Golden, Whole Leaf Caesar Salad with, 84
Cuban-Style Rice and Beans, 299
Cucumber, -Yogurt Soup, Chilled, 109
Cumin Chicken Kebabs with Couscous, 176
Cupcakes, Mahogany Velvet, with Cream Cheese Frosting, *380*, 381
Curry(ied)
  Basmati Rice, 285
  Chicken, Spicy, 170, *171*
  and Cilantro, Egg Salad Sandwich with, 334
  Deviled Eggs, 62
  Tomato Sauce, Cauliflower with, 269
Custard, Toasted Coconut, 422

D
Dal Soup, 318

Dark Fruit Cake, 377
Dates, and Olives, Chicken with, 184
Dessert Sauce(s)
  Blueberry, Best, 422
  Blueberry, Lemon Cheesecake with, 382
  Bourbon-Pear, Caramel Cake with, 376
  Chocolate, Coconut Bread Pudding with, 418
  Chocolate, Rich, 424
  Hot Fudge Sauce, 424
  Raspberry, 423
Deviled Eggs, 62
  Caviar, 62
  Curried, 62
  Horseradish, 62
Dijon-Herb Marinade, 24
Dill(ed)
  Carrots, 267
  Scrambled Eggs with Smoked Salmon and, 42
Dip(s). *See also* Spreads
  Roasted Red Pepper, 58
  White Bean, 58
Double Apple Strudel, 406, *407*
Double Chocolate–Hazelnut Biscotti, 401
Double Chocolate Sorbet, 416
Double Grain Blueberry Scones, *362*, 363
Double Maple Waffles, 38
Dressing, Salad. *See* Salad Dressing
Dressing(s)
  Citrus, Orange and Red Onion Salad with, 88
  Corn Bread, Apricot, and Cranberry, 290, *291*
  Sausage and Rice, 287
  Wild Rice and Mushroom, 288
Dried Peach–Pecan Scones, 364
Dry Rub(s)
  Basic, 26
  Cajun, 27
  Fennel, Lemon, and Black Pepper, 26
  Jamaican Jerk Paste, 28
  Pepper, 27
Duck
  Breasts, Citrus-Glazed, 192
  and Goat Cheese Quesadillas, 77

E
Easy Chicken–Pumpkin Seed Mole, 173
Easy Clam Pizza, 324
Easy Enchiladas, 191
Easy Ginger Fried Rice, 247
Eggplant
  Grilled, Orzo and Tomatoes with, 292
  Parmesan Stacks, 270
  Rollatini, 250
  Roll-Ups, Roasted Pepper and Tomato–Stuffed, 73
Egg(s). *See also* Deviled Eggs; Frittata; Omelettes
  Fried, Tex Mex–Style, 46
  Salad Sandwiches with Curry and Cilantro, 334
  Scrambled, with Smoked Salmon and Dill, 42
  Tomato, and Parmesan–Topped Pizza, 47
  Vegetable Scrambled, 44
Enchiladas
  Easy, 191
  Winter Vegetable, 240
Espresso, -Chocolate Biscotti, 400

F
Fajitas, Chicken and Bell Pepper, 180

Falafel, Fiery, 250
Fennel
    Grilled, Sweet-and-Sour, 270
    Lemon, and Black Pepper Rub, 26
Feta
    and Spinach, Greek Pita Pizza, 50
    Topping, Turkey with, 187
Fiery Falafel, 250
Fig, Caramelized Onion, and Stilton Pizza, 324, *325*
Fish. *See also* Catfish; Haddock; Halibut; Salmon; Tilapia; Tuna
    Cakes with Creole Rémoulade Sauce, 210
    Grilled Arctic Char and Salad, *196*, 197
    Sea Bass, Asian, 206
    Trout Amandine, 212
    Whole, Moroccan-Style, 212
Five-Vegetable Fried Rice, 285
Flank Steak, Marinated, 137
Flatbread
    Lemon-Thyme Zucchini on, 69
    Naan, Quick, 354
Flourless Chocolate Cake, 370
Focaccia
    Fresh Rosemary and Coarse Salt, 346
    Red Onion, 346
    Sun-Dried Tomato and Olive, 346
    Whole Wheat, 346
Food Processor Gazpacho, 115
Food Processor Wheat Bread with Honey, 346
French
    Lemon Tart, 392
    Onion Soup, *110*, 111
French Toast
    Stuffed, 36, *37*
    Whole Grain, 36
Fresh Tomato-Basil Soup, 113
"Fried" Catfish with Potato Sticks, *204*, 205
Fried Eggs Tex Mex–Style, 46
Frittata
    Potato-Onion, 45
    Roman Rice, 44
    Shrimp, Mushroom, and Tomato, 46
Frosting
    Cocoa, Yellow Layer Cake with, 372
    Cream Cheese, Mahogany Velvet Cupcakes with, *380*, 381
Frozen Mango-Lime Mousse, 413
Fruit. *See also specific fruits*
    Baked, –Cinnamon Oatmeal, 42
    -Quinoa Salad, 95
    and Wheat Berries, Smoked Turkey with, 99
Fruit Cake, Dark, 377

G

Garlic
    and Beets, Oven-Roasted, 266
    Broccoli with, 264
    Roasted, Mashed Potatoes, 256
    -Roasted Chicken with Gravy, 164
    Shrimp Tapas, 78, *79*
    Toasts, Caramelized, 66, *67*
Garlicky Chicken Stew, 312
Garlicky Red Beans and Pork, 152
Gazpacho, Food Processor, 115
German Potato Salad, 92
Ginger
    and Bok Choy, Pork Stir-Fry with, 148
    -Carrot Dressing, 31
    Fried Rice, Easy, 247
    and Golden Raisin Muffins, 358
    -Hoisin Marinade, 23
    Red Cabbage with, 267

and Soy, Pork with, 149
    -Spice Cookies, 402
Gingerbread
    Cookies, 398
    Triple Ginger, 379
Goat Cheese
    Baked, Greens Salad with, California, 88
    and Broccoli, Pasta with, *244*, 245
    and Duck Quesadillas, 77
    Grilled Shrimp, and Basil Sandwiches, 339
    and Tomato Coulis, Pissaladière with, 331
    Tomatoes, and Sweet Onion Salad, 87
    and Tomato Omelette, 43
Granita, Strawberry-Grapefruit, 417
Granola
    Almond-Cranberry, 41
    Walnut-Raisin, *40*, 41
Grapefruit-Strawberry Granita, 417
Gratin, Barley, Leek, and Rosemary, *294*, 295
Gravy
    Garlic-Roasted Chicken with, 164
    Onion, Roast Turkey with, 186–187
Greek (-Style)
    Grilled Lamb Burger Sandwiches, 331
    Haddock, 209
    Islands Salad, 85
    Pita Pizzas with Spinach and Feta, 50
    Pizza, 326
Green Beans, with Parsley, Lemony, 271
Green Goddess Dressing, 28, *29*
Green Sauce, 18
Gremolata, Orange, Chicken with, 167
Grilled Arctic Char and Salad, *196*, 197
Grilled Jamaican-Style Halibut, 199
Grilled Lamb Chops with Mixed Herb Pesto, 157
Grilled Lamb Chops with Tomato–Bell Pepper Sauce, 158
Grilled Shrimp, Basil, and Goat Cheese Sandwiches, 339
Grilled Spicy Shrimp with Papaya-Lime Salsa, 218
Grilled Steak Sandwiches with Golden Onions, *332*, 333
Grilled Summer Vegetables with Israeli Couscous, 242
Grilled T-Bone Steak, 135
Grilled Teriyaki Shrimp, 218
Grilled Thai Beef Salad, *96*, 97
Gruyère, Mushroom, and Bacon Pizza, 327
Guacamole, Classic, 56
Gumbo
    Chicken and Turkey Sausage, 311
    Quick, 126

H

Haddock
    Greek-Style, 209
    with Ratatouille, Baked, 210
Halibut
    Braised, with Tomatoes and Orzo, 200, *201*
    Broiled, with Pico de Gallo, 200
    Grilled Jamaican-Style, 199
Ham
    and Arugula Crêpes, Creamy, *48*, 49
    and Portobello Bruschetta, *67*, 68
Hash Brown Potatoes, 259
Hazelnut, –Double Chocolate Biscotti, 401
Hearty Vegetable Lasagna, 242
Herb(ed). *See also* Cilantro; Dill(ed); Mint(ed); Parsley; Rosemary
    Brown Rice, 284

Crumb Topping, Rack of Lamb with, 156
    -Crusted Tilapia, 207
    -Dijon Marinade, 24
    and Dried Tomato No-Knead Bread, 344
    and Lemon Crumbs, Salmon with, 199
    –Mixed Mushroom Omelette, 43
    Oven-Fried Chicken, 181
    Pesto, Mixed, Grilled Lamb Chops with, 157
Hoisin-Ginger Marinade, 23
Holiday Stollen, 348, *349*
Honey
    Cake, 378
    -Glazed Salmon with Watermelon-Mint Salsa, 198
    Wheat Bread with, Food-Processor, 346
    -Wheat Crescent Rolls, 345
Honeydew Sorbet, 417
Honey-Mustard
    Dressing, 31
    Pork Chops, *150*, 151
Horseradish
    Deviled Eggs, 62
    Mashed Potatoes, 256
    Mayonnaise, Roast Beef Sandwiches with, 333
    Salmon Salad with, 89
    Sauce, Shrimp Cocktail with, 80
Hot-and-Soup Soup, 118
Hot-and-Spicy Chickpea Cakes, 65
Hot Cross Buns, 352
Hot Fudge Sauce, 424
Hummus, 57
    Sandwich, California, 334

I

Ice Cream, Mint, Real, 415
Irish Soda Bread, 353
Island Chicken with Pineapple, 176
Italian (-Style)
    Bean Soup, 120
    Dressing, 30
    Stuffed Mushrooms, 62

J

Jamaican Jerk Paste, 28
Jam-Filled Whole Wheat Muffins, 358
Japanese-Style Noodles and Vegetables, 243
Jerk Paste, Jamaican, 28
Jicama, Radiccio, and Cabbage Slaw, 91
Jumbo Bran Muffins, 357

K

Kale with Balsamic Vinegar, 271
Kasha Varnishkes, 296
Kebabs and Skewers
    Beef, Middle-Eastern, *138*, 139
    Cumin Chicken, with Couscous, 176
    Korean Steak on a Stick, 74, *75*
    Seafood, Mixed, with Couscous, 213
    Teriyaki-Grilled Tuna with Vegetable, 202
    Tofu-Vegetable, Marinated, 230
Keema Samosas, 64
Kielbasa and Bean Soup, 314
Korean Steak on a Stick, 74, *75*

L

Lamb
    Burger Sandwiches, Grilled, Greek-Style, 331
    Chops, Grilled, With Mixed Herb Pesto, 157
    Chops, Grilled, With Tomato–Bell

Pepper Sauce, 158
Chops with Yogurt-Mint Sauce, 157
Rack of, with Herbed Crumb Topping, 156
Roast Leg of, Moroccan-Style, 156
Shanks with White Beans, 308
Stew, Savory, 307
Tandoori, Almond-Apricot Couscous with, 154, *155*
-Vegetable Stew, 158
Lasagna
with Meat Sauce, 144
Vegetable, Hearty, 242
Leek(s), Barley, and Rosemary Gratin, *294*, 295
Lemon
Angel Food Cake with Berries, 374
-Blueberry Scones, 364
-Butter Broccoli Spears, 265
-Caper Sauce, Chicken in, 178, *179*
Cheesecake with Blueberry Sauce, 382
Chicken, Grilled, 172
Fennel, and Black Pepper Rub, 26
and Herb Crumbs, Salmon, 199
and Olive Oil Smashed Potatoes, 257
Poppy Seed Crisps, 394, *395*
Tart, French, 392
-Thyme Zucchini on Flatbread, 69
Lemony Green Beans with Parsley, 271
Lemony Spring Vegetable Risotto, 248
Lentil(s)
with Spiced Vegetables, 298
and Swiss Chard Soup, 125
Lettuce Leaves, Picadillo in, 76
Lime
-Chile Mayonnaise, Soft Tacos with Tilapia and, *208*, 209
-Mango Mousse, Frozen, 413
-Papaya Salsa, Grilled Spicy Shrimp with, 218
and Scallions, Couscous with, 293
Linzer Thumbprint Jewel Cookies, 397
Lobster
Rolls, 340
Salad, 100
Steamed, with Butter Sauce, 223
Stuffed, Broiled, 224
Summer Rolls with Dipping Sauce, Vietnamese, 79, 80
London Broil, 136

M

Macadamia Coconut Meringues, 399
Macaroni, and Cheese, Baked, 238, *239*
Macaroons, Coconut, 402
Mahogany Velvet Cupcakes with Cream Cheese Frosting, *380*, 381
Mango
and Black Bean Salsa, 19, *20*
Chutney, 22
-Lime Mousse, Frozen, 413
Manhattan Clam Chowder, 318
Manhattan-Style Clam Chowder, Smoky, 128
Maple
and Butter–Glazed Acorn Squash Wedges, 279
Double, Waffles, 38
Marinade
Basic, 23
Citrus, 25
Dijon-Herb, 24
Hoisin-Ginger, 23
Tandoori Yogurt, 25
Teriyaki, 24
Marinated Flank Steak, 137
Marinated Tofu-Vegetable Kebabs, 230

Maryland Crab Cakes, 222
Matzo Ball Soup, 120
Mayonnaise
Chile-Lime, Soft Tacos with Tilapia and, *208*, 209
Chipotle, Sweet Potato Wedges with, 260, *261*
Horseradish, Roast Beef Sandwiches with, 333
Meatballs, and Spaghetti, Classic, 145
Meat Loaf
Chicken Loaf, Best-Ever, 313
Our Favorite, 139
Turkey-Parmesan, *190*, 191
Meringues
Coconut Macadamia, 399
Mocha, 399
Mexicali-Style Stuffed Mushrooms, 251
Mexican-Style Chicken-Corn Soup, *122*, 123
Middle Eastern (-Style)
Beef Kebabs, *138*, 139
Chicken Sandwiches, 335
Milanese-Style Tuna Spread, 59
Mint(ed)
Ice Cream, Real, 415
-Papaya Salsa, Chicken Breasts with, 172
Tabbouleh, 95
-Watermelon Salsa, Honey-Glazed Salmon with, 198
-Yogurt Sauce, Lamb Chops with, 157
Mixed Grain Porridge, 41
Mixed Mushroom–Herb Omelette, 43
Mixed Mushroom Soup, 112
Mixed Pickled Vegetables, 280
Mixed Seafood Skewers with Couscous, 213
Mocha Meringues, 399
Mole, Chicken–Pumpkin Seed, Easy, 173
Monterey Jack Turkey Burgers, 189
Moroccan-Style
Roast Leg of Lamb, 156
Whole Fish, 212
Mousse
Chocolate, Classic, 420, *421*
Mango-Lime, Frozen, 413
Muffins
Bran, Jumbo, 357
Buttermilk-Blueberry Corn, 357
Ginger and Golden Raisin, 358
Jam-Filled Whole Wheat, 358
Orange-Spice, 358
Whole Grain Breakfast, 358, *359*
Mulligatawny, Turkey, 128
Mushroom(s)
Bacon, and Gruyère Pizza, 327
-Chicken Hash Casserole, 177
and Chicken Stew, 182, *183*
Cremini, with Quinoa and Thyme, 297
Mixed,–Herb Omelette, 43
Mixed, Soup, 112
Portobello and Ham Bruschetta, 67, 68
Portobello Burgers, 251
Shrimp, and Tomato Frittata, 46
Spinach, and Bulgur Pilaf, 296
-Spinach Calzones, 330
Spinach-Stuffed, 63
Stuffed, Italian-Style, 62
Stuffed, Mexicali-Style, 251
-Stuffed Turkey Breast, 188
Tempeh, and Sweet Onion Chili, 230
Wild, with Fresh Thyme, 272
and Wild Rice Dressing, 288

Mussels
Marinière, 222
in Saffron-Tomato Sauce, 223
and Shrimp, Spicy, Spaghetti with, 216
Mustard. *See also* Honey-Mustard; Dijon-Herb Marinade, 24

N

Naan Flatbread, Quick, 354
Nachos Grandes, 70, *71*
Neapolitan Easter Pie, 391
Nectarine–Bell Pepper Salsa, *20*, 21
New Orleans Red Beans and Rice, 300
Niçoise, Salad, 89
No-Cook Summer Tomato Sauce, 13
No-Knead Dried Tomato and Herb Bread, 344
No-Knead Whole Wheat Bread, 344
Noodle(s)
–Bok Choy Soup, 118
with Chicken and Apples, 169
-Chicken Casserole, Zesty, 186
Soup, Chinese, 116, *117*
with Spicy Peanut Sauce, 292
and Vegetables, Japanese-Style, 243
North African Chickpea and Vegetable Tagine, *234*, 235

O

Oatmeal
Baked Fruit–Cinnamon, 42
-Cranberry Cookies, *395*, 397
Okra, Creole-Style, 272
Old-Fashioned Butterscotch Pudding, 420
Old-World Pasta with Pork and Tomato Sauce, 153
Olive Oil and Lemon Smashed Potatoes, 257
Olive(s)
and Dates, Chicken with, 184
and Orange Zest, Roasted Peppers with, 276
and Sun-Dried Tomato Focaccia, 346
White Bean, and Bell Pepper Pizza, 70
Omelette(s)
Basic, 43
Canadian Bacon, Asparagus, and Scallion, 43
Mixed Mushroom–Herb, 43
Tomato and Goat Cheese, 43
Onion(s)
Caramelized, Fig, and Stilton Pizza, 324, *325*
Golden, Grilled Steak Sandwiches with, *332*, 333
Gravy, Roast Turkey with, 186
-Potato Frittata, 45
Red, and Orange Salad with Citrus Dressing, 88
Red, Focaccia, 346
Rings, Oven-Baked, *261*, 262
Soup, French, *110*, 111
Sweet, Tempeh and Mushroom Chili, 230
Sweet, Tomatoes, and Goat Cheese Salad, 87
Tartlets, Smoky, 69
Open-Face Crab Cake Sandwiches, 340
Orange(s)
-Cranberry Bread, 356
-Crumbed Baked Chicken, 173
Gremolata, Chicken with, 167
-Raspberry Frozen Yogurt, *414*, 415
and Red Onion Salad with Citrus Dressing, 88
and Sage Biscuits, 361
-Spice Muffins, 358

Orange *(continued)*
  Sponge Cake, Rolled, 372
  Waffles, 38
  Zest, and Olives, Roasted Peppers with, 276
Orzo
  with Grilled Eggplant and Tomato, 292
  and Tomatoes, Braised Halibut with, 200, *201*
Our Favorite Meat Loaf, 139
Oven-Baked Onion Rings, *261*, 262
Oven-Fried Chicken, Herbed, 181
Oven Fries, 260, *261*
Oven-Roasted Beets and Garlic, 266
Oven-Roasted Brussels Sprouts and Carrots, *268*, 269
Oven-Roasted Corn on the Cob, 264

P
Pad Thai, Salad Bar, 246
Paella, 213
Pan-Braised Broccoli Rabe, 265
Pancakes
  Basic, 39
  Blueberry, 39
  Buckwheat, 39
  Potato, 257
  Whole Wheat, 39
Panettone, 350
Panzanella, Tuscan, 102
Papaya
  -Lime Salsa, Grilled Spicy Shrimp with, 218
  -Mint Salsa, Chicken Breasts with, 172
Pappardelle with Shrimp, 216, *217*
Paprika, Chicken, Skillet, 178
Parmesan
  and Broccoli, Spaghetti Squash with, 252
  Eggplant Stacks, 270
  Tomato, and Egg–Topped Pizza, 47
  -Turkey Meat Loaf, *190*, 191
Parsley, Green Beans with, Lemony, 271
Passover Cake, Citrus, 378
Pasta. *See also* Noodle(s)
  with Arugula Pesto and Tomatoes, 245
  with Broccoli and Goat Cheese, *244*, 245
  with Broccoli and White Beans, 293
  Capellini with Fresh Tomato Sauce, 246
  with Chickpeas and Tomatoes, Summery, 300, *301*
  Lasagna, Hearty Vegetable, 242
  Lasagna with Meat Sauce, 144
  Macaroni and Cheese, Baked, 238, *239*
  Old-World, with Pork and Tomato Sauce, 153
  Pappardelle with Shrimp, 216, *217*
  Salad Primavera, 102
  Spaghetti and Meatballs, Classic, 145
  Spaghetti with Spicy Mussels and Shrimp, 216
Pastry, Apple Strudel, Double, 406, *407*
Peach(es)
  Crumb Pie, 386
  –Dried Peach Scones, 364
  Melba, 411
  in Red Wine, 411
  -Watermelon Salad, with Ricotta Salata, *86*, 87
Peanut Butter Cookies, *395*, 396
Peanut(s)
  Sauce, Chicken Satay with, 76
  Sauce, Spicy, Noodles with, 292
  Soup, African, 124

Pear(s), -Bourbon Sauce, Caramel Cake with, 376
Peas
  and Carrots, Beef Stew with, 306
  and Rice, Venetian-Style, 286
Pecan(s)
  Baby Romaine with Clementines and, 85
  -Carrot Bread, 356
  and Cranberries, Wild Rice Salad with, 94
  –Dried Peach Scones, 364
  Pie, 388, *389*
Pepper Dry Rub, 27
Peppered Roast Tenderloin, *134*, 135
Pepper Jack and Chile Corn Bread, 355
Peppers. *See* Bell Pepper(s); Chile(s)
Pesto
  Arugula, and Tomatoes, Pasta with, 245
  Basil, 16
  Mixed Herb, Grilled Lamb Chops with, 157
Picadillo, 182
  in Lettuce Leaves, 76
Pickled Vegetables, Mixed, 280
Pico de Gallo, *20*, 21
  Broiled Halibut with, 200
Pie(s)
  Apple, Classic, 383
  Banana Cream, 390
  Blueberry, Big, 384
  Cherry, 384
  Citrus, Triple, 385
  Coconut Cream, 390
  Dough, for Single and Double Crust, 383
  Neapolitan Easter, 391
  Peach Crumb, 386
  Pecan, 388, *389*
  Sour Cream Pumpkin, 388
  Strawberry-Rhubarb, 387
  Sweet Potato, 385
Pineapple, Chicken with, Island, 176
Pinto Bean(s), and Tomatoes, Skillet Asparagus with, 302
Pissaladière with Tomato Coulis and Goat Cheese, 331
Pita, Greek Pizza, Spinach and Feta, 50
Pizza
  Caramelized Onion, Fig, and Stilton, 324, *325*
  Cheese, Basic, 323
  Clam, Easy, 324
  Greek, 326
  Margherita, 323
  Mushroom, Bacon, and Gruyère, 327
  Pita with Spinach and Feta, Greek, 50
  Sicilian Sausage–Stuffed, *328*, 329
  Tomato, Parmesan, and Egg–Topped, 47
  White Bean, Bell Pepper, and Olive, 70
Pizza Dough
  Cornmeal, 322
  Semolina, 322
  Whole Wheat, 322
Polenta
  Blue Cheese, Creamy, 297
  Chicken and Broccoli Rabe with, *174*, 175
  with Vegetables, Creamy, 247
Poppy Seed, Lemon Crisps, 394, *395*
Pork. *See also* Ham
  Barbecue, with Mop Sauce, 148
  Bigos, 310
  and Black Bean Chili, 152
  and Broccoli Stir Fry, 310
  Chops, Honey-Mustard, *150*, 151
  with Ginger and Soy, 149

and Red Beans, Garlicky, 152
  Roast, with Sauerkraut and Apples, 308, *309*
  Roast, with Winter Vegetables, *146*, 147
  Stir-Fry, Spicy, 151
  Stir-Fried with Bok Choy and Ginger, 148
  Tenderloin, Caribbean-Style, 147
  and Tomato Sauce, Old-World Pasta with, 153
Porridge, Mixed Grain, 41
Portobello
  and Ham Bruschetta, *67*, 68
  Mushroom Burgers, 251
Potato(es)
  and Celery Root, Mashed, 256
  and Chili-Roasted Chicken, 165
  Corn, and Bacon Soup, Creamy, 123
  Hash Brown, 259
  Horseradish Mashed, 256
  Olive Oil and Lemon Smashed, 257
  -Onion Frittata, 45
  Oven Fries, 260, *261*
  Pancakes, 257
  Roasted Garlic Mashed, 256
  Scalloped with Cheese, *258*, 259
  -Spinach Casserole, 252
  Sticks, "Fried" Catfish with, *204*, 205
  Twice Baked, 240
  -Watercress Soup, 115
Potato Salad
  All-American, 92, *93*
  German, 92
Pot Roast, Classic, 132
Provençal-Style Stuffed Tomatoes, 274, *275*
Pudding
  Bread, Coconut, with Chocolate Sauce, 418
  Butterscotch, Old-Fashioned, 420
  Corn, 263
  Rice, with Golden Raisins, 419
  Summer, 418
Pumpkin
  Soup, South American–Style, 112
  Sour Cream Pie, 388
  Spice Cake, 375
Pumpkin Seeds, –Chicken Mole, Easy, 173

Q
Quesadillas, Duck and Goat Cheese, 77
Quiche
  Cheese, 52
  Spinach and Cheese, 52
Quick Gumbo, 126
Quick Naan Flatbread, 354
Quinoa
  Black Bean, and Shrimp Salad, 101
  -Fruit Salad, 95
  and Thyme, Cremini Mushrooms with, 297

R
Rack of Lamb with Herbed Crumb Topping, 156
Radicchio, Cabbage, and Jicama Slaw, 91
Ragu Bolognese, 144
Rainbow Slaw, *90*, 91
Raisin(s)
  Golden, and Ginger Muffins, 358
  Golden, Rice Pudding with, 419
  -Walnut Granola, *40*, 41
Raita, 18
Raspberry(ies)
  -Orange Frozen Yogurt, *414*, 415
  Sauce, 423

Ratatouille
Baked Haddock with, 210
Casserole, 273
Real Mint Ice Cream, 415
Red Bean(s)
and Pork, Garlicky, 152
and Rice, New Orleans, 300
Red Cabbage with Ginger, 267
Red Wine, Peaches in, 411
Relish, Cranberry-Walnut, 22
Rhubarb, -Strawberry Pie, 387
Ribollita, 119
Rice. See also Risotto; Wild Rice
Basmati, Curried, 285
and Beans, 237
and Beans, Cuban Style, 299
Brown, Herbed, 284
Brown and Wild, with Walnuts and
Cranberries, 286
Chicken with, 166, 167
Fried, Five-Vegetable, 285
Frittata, Roman, 44
Ginger Fried, Easy, 247
and Peas, Venetian-Style, 286
Pudding with Golden Raisins, 419
and Red Beans, New Orleans, 300
and Sausage Dressing, 287
Scallop Fried, 219
and Soy Stuffed Cabbage, 232
Tomato, with Chiles and Corn, 284
Vegetable Fried, Chicken and, 185
Rich Cheese Sauce, 14
Rich Chocolate Sauce, 424
Ricotta Salata, Watermelon-Peach Salad
with, 86, 87
Risotto
Lemony Spring Vegetable, 248
Milanese, 288, 289
Seafood, 214
with Swiss Chard, 249
Zucchini, with Sun-Dried Tomatoes,
249
Roast Beef
Salad, Thai-Style, 74
Salad with Arugula, 97
Sandwiches with Horseradish
Mayonnaise, 333
Roasted Asparagus and Red Peppers, 266
Roasted Garlic Mashed Potatoes, 256
Roasted Pepper and Tomato–Stuffed
Eggplant Rollups, 73
Roasted Peppers with Orange Zest and
Olives, 276
Roasted Red Pepper Coulis, 17
Roasted Red Pepper Dip, 58
Roasted Tomato-Basil Sauce, 13
Roasted Tomato–Bell Pepper Soup, 113
Roasted Vegetable Crostini, 66, 67
Roasted Vegetable Stock, 107
Roast Turkey with Onion Gravy, 186
Rolled Orange Sponge Cake, 372
Rolls, Crescent, Wheat-Honey, 345
Romaine, Baby, with Clementines and
Pecans, 85
Roman Rice Frittata, 44
Rosemary
Barley, and Leek Gratin, 294, 295
Fresh, and Course Salt Focaccia, 346
Rubs. See Dry Rub(s)
Rugelach, 393

S
Saffron, -Tomato Sauce, Mussels in, 223
Sage
and Butternut Squash Soup, 114
and Orange Biscuits, 361
Salad Dressing

Asian Vinaigrette, 30
Blue Cheese, 32
Carrot-Ginger, 31
Classic Vinaigrette, 30
Green Goddess, 28, 29
Honey-Mustard, 31
Italian, 30
Thousand Island, 32
Salad(s). See also Chicken Salad; Potato
Salad
Baby Romaine, with Clementines and
Pecans, 85
Bar, Pad Thai, 246
Beet, Apple, and Watercress, 84
Black Bean, Southwestern, 94
Black Bean and Corn, Tuna with, 202
Egg, Sandwiches, with Curry and
Cilantro, 334
Greens with Baked Goat Cheese,
California, 88
Grilled Arctic Char and, 196, 197
Islands, Greek, 85
Lobster, 100
Niçoise, 89
Orange and Red Onion, with Citrus
Dressing, 88
Pasta Primavera, 102
Quinoa, Black Bean, and Shrimp, 101
Quinoa-Fruit, 95
Roast Beef, Thai-Style, 74
Roast Beef with Arugula, 97
Salmon with Horseradish, 89
Seafood, California, 101
Thai Beef, Grilled, 96, 97
Tomatoes, Sweet Onion, and Goat
Cheese, 87
Tuna and White Bean, 100
Tuna, Sandwiches, Classic, 339
Tuscan Panzanella, 102
Watermelon-Peach, with Ricotta Salata,
86, 87
Whole Leaf Caesar, with Golden
Croutons, 84
Wild Rice, with Pecans and
Cranberries, 94
Salmon
Honey-Glazed, with Watermelon-Mint
Salsa, 198
with Lemon and Herb Crumbs, 199
Salad with Horseradish, 89
Smoked, Scrambled Eggs and Dill
with, 42
Southwestern, 198
Salsa
Cantaloupe, Crisped Scallops with, 221
Mango and Black Bean, 19, 20
Nectarine–Bell Pepper, 20, 21
Papaya-Lime, Grilled Spicy Shrimp
with, 218
Papaya-Mint, Chicken Breasts with,
172
Pico de Gallo, 20, 21
Watermelon-Mint, Honey-Glazed
Salmon with, 198
Sandwich(es)
Chicken, Grilled, Vietnamese-Style,
336, 337
Chicken, Middle Eastern-Style, 335
Crab Cake, Open-Face, 340
Egg Salad, with Curry and Cilantro,
334
Grilled Shrimp, Basil, and Goat
Cheese, 339
Grilled Steak, with Golden Onions,
332, 333
Hummus, California, 334

Lamb Burger, Grilled, Greek-Style,
331
Roast Beef with Horseradish
Mayonnaise, 333
Tuna Salad, Classic, 339
Sauce(s). See also Dessert Sauce(s);
Mayonnaise; Salsa; Tomato Sauce
Barbecue, Grilled Chicken, 170
Barbecue, Smoky, 14, 15
Blackberry, Venison Steaks with, 160
Butter, Steamed Lobster with, 223
Cheese, Rich, 14
Chimichurri, 17
Cranberry, Turkey Cutlets with, 189
Creole Rémoulade, Fish Cakes with,
210
Green, 18
Lemon-Caper, Chicken in, 178, 179
Raita, 18
Shallot, Venison Chops with, 159
Spicy Peanut, Noodles with, 292
Tartar, 19
Tartar, Crispy Catfish with, 206
Vietnamese Dipping, Lobster Summer
Rolls with, 79, 80
Yogurt-Mint, Lamb Chops with, 157
Sauerkraut, and Apples, Roast Pork with,
308, 309
Sausage(s)
and Chicken Stew, Tuscan, 312
and Pepper Heroes, Sicilian, 338
and Rice Dressing, 287
–Stuffed Pizza, Sicilian, 328, 329
Turkey, and Chicken Gumbo, 311
Savory Lamb Stew, 307
Scallion(s)
Canadian Bacon, and Asparagus
Omelette, 43
and Lime, Couscous with, 293
Scalloped Potatoes with Cheese, 258, 259
Scallop(s)
Crisped, Cantaloupe Salsa with, 221
Fried Rice, 219
Sea, and Snow Peas, Stir-Fried, 220,
221
Scones
Blueberry, Double Grain, 362, 363
Chocolate-Cherry, 364
Dried Peach–Pecan Scones, 364
Lemon-Blueberry, 364
Whole Wheat–Buttermilk, 364
Scrambled Eggs with Smoked Salmon and
Dill, 42
Sea Bass, Asian, 206
Seafood. See also Clam; Lobster; Scallops;
Shrimp
Bouillabaisse, 211
Paella, 213
Risotto, 214
Salad, California, 101
Skewers, Mixed, with Couscous, 213
Semolina Pizza Dough, 322
Sesame, Spinach, Spicy Stir-Fried, 278
Seviche, Tuna, 78
Shellfish. See Seafood
Shortcakes, Strawberry, 409
Shrimp
Cocktail with Horseradish Sauce, 80
Creole, 219
Garlic Tapas, 78, 79
Grilled, Basil, and Goat Cheese
Sandwiches, 339
Grilled Spicy, with Papaya-Lime Salsa,
218
Mushroom, and Tomato Frittata, 46
Parpardelle with, 216, 217
Quinoa, and Black Bean Salad, 101

Shrimp *(continued)*
    Scampi, 215
    and Spicy Mussels, Spaghetti with, 216
    Teriyaki, Grilled, 218
Sicilian
    Caramelized Onion, and Fig Pizza, *324, 325*
    Sausage and Pepper Heroes, 338
    Sausage–Stuffed Pizza, *328, 329*
Skewered foods. *See* Kebabs and Skewers
Skillet Asparagus with Pinto Beans and Tomatoes, 302
Skillet Chicken with Cherry Tomatoes and Garlic, 172
Skillet Chicken Paprika, 178
Skillet Summer Squash, 277
Slaw
    Radicchio, Cabbage, and Jicama, 91
    Rainbow, *90*, 91
Smoked Salmon, Scrambled Eggs and Dill with, 42
Smoky Barbecue Sauce, 14, *15*
Smoky Black Beans, 299
Smoky Grilled Brisket, 133
Smoky Manhattan-Style Clam Chowder, 128
Smoky Onion Tartlets, 69
Smoky Turkey Chili, 316, *317*
Snow Peas, and Sea Scallops, Stir-Fried, *220,* 221
Soft Tacos with Tilapia and Chili-Lime Mayonnaise, *208, 209*
Sorbet
    Double Chocolate, 416
    Honeydew, 417
    Roasted Strawberries and, 412
    Watermelon, 416
Soup(s). *See also* Chowder
    African Peanut, 124
    Avgolemono Chicken, 116
    Bean, Creamy, 121
    Bean, Italian-Style, 120
    Beef Barley, Classic, 125
    Black Bean, Best-Ever, 121
    Bok Choy–Noodle, 118
    Borscht, 108
    Butternut Squash and Sage, 114
    Chicken, 313
    Chicken-Corn, Mexican-Style, *122,* 123
    Cioppino, 126, *127*
    Corn, Potato, and Bacon, Creamy, 123
    Cucumber-Yogurt, Chilled, 109
    Dal, 318
    Gazpacho, Food Processor, 115
    Gumbo, Quick, 126
    Hot-and-Sour, 118
    Kielbasa and Bean, 314
    Lentil and Swiss Chard, 125
    Matzo Ball, 120
    Minestrone, Classic, 119
    Mushroom, Mixed, 112
    Noodle, Chinese, 116, *117*
    Onion, French, *110,* 111
    Potato-Watercress, 115
    Ribollita, 119
    Roasted Tomato–Bell Pepper, 113
    South American–Style Pumpkin, 112
    Summertime Grilled Corn, 108
    Tomato-Basil, Fresh, 113
    Turkey Mulligatawny, 128
    Vegetable-Barley, 314, *315*
    Yellow Split Pea, 124
    Yellow Squash with Chives, Creamy, 111
Sour Cream

Coffee Cake, 368
    Pumpkin Pie, 388
South American–Style Pumpkin Soup, 112
Southwestern
    Black Bean Salad, 94
    Salmon, 198
Soy
    and Bean Chili, 232
    and Ginger, Pork with, 149
    and Rice Stuffed Cabbage, 232
Spaghetti
    and Meatballs, Classic, 145
    with Spicy Mussels and Shrimp, 216
Spaghetti Squash
    with Broccoli and Parmesan, 252
    Primavera, 278
Spanakopita Triangles, 64
Spanish Tortilla, 241
Spice(d). *See also* Black Pepper(ed); Chili (Powder); Cumin; Curry(ied); Dry Rub(s); Paprika
    Double Berry Crisp, 408
    -Ginger Cookies, 402
    -Orange Muffins, 358
    Pumpkin, Cake, 375
Spicy Beef and Broccoli Stir-Fry, 140
Spicy Chicken and Broccoli, 180
Spicy Chicken Curry, 170, *171*
Spicy Pork Stir-Fry, 151
Spicy Stir-Fried Sesame Spinach, 278
Spicy Tomato Sauce, 12
Spinach
    and Bean Burritos, 235
    and Cheese Quiche, 52
    "Creamed," 277
    and Feta, Greek Pita Pizza, 50
    Mushroom, and Bulgur Pilaf, 296
    -Mushroom Calzones, 330
    Potato Casserole, 252
    Sesame, Spicy Stir-Fried, 278
    -Stuffed Mushrooms, 63
Split Pea Soup, Yellow, 124
Sponge Cake, Orange, Rolled, 372
Spreads
    Caponata, 59
    Milanese-Style Tuna, 59
Squash. *See also* Zucchini
    Acorn, Maple and Butter–Glazed Wedges, 279
    Butternut and Sage Soup, 114
    Spaghetti, Primavera, 278
    Spaghetti, with Broccoli and Parmesan, 252
    Summer, Skillet, 277
    Yellow, Soup with Chives, Creamy, 111
Steak
    Argentina-Style, and Sauce, 137
    Flank, Marinated, 137
    Sandwiches, Grilled, with Golden Onions, *332,* 333
    Sirloin, Grilled, Teriyaki-Flavored, 136
    on a Stick, Korean, *74, 75*
    T-Bone, Grilled, 135
Steamed Lobster with Butter Sauce, 223
Stew(s)
    Beef, 140
    Beef, with Carrots and Peas, 306
    Chicken, Garlicky, 312
    Chicken and Mushroom, 182, *183*
    Chicken and Sausage, Tuscan, 312
    Lamb, Savory, 307
    Lamb-Braised, 158
    Wheat Berry and Bean, 233
Sticky Buns, Classic, 351
Stilton, Caramelized Onion, and Fig Pizza, *324, 325*

Stir-Fry
    Beef and Broccoli, Spicy, 140
    Pork, Spicy, 151
    Pork with Bok Choy and Ginger, 148
    Pork and Broccoli, 310
    Sea Scallops with Snow Peas, *220,* 221
    Spicy Sesame Spinach, 278
    Tempeh and Vegetable, 231
    Tofu, 228, *229*
Stock
    Beef, Basic, 106
    Chicken, Basic, 106
    Roasted Vegetable, 107
    Vegetable, Basic, 107
Stollen, Holiday, 348, *349*
Strawberry(ies)
    Black and White, 412
    -Grapefruit Granita, 417
    -Rhubarb Pie, 387
    Shortcakes, 409
    and Sorbet, Roasted, 412
Strudel, Apple, Double, 406, *407*
Stuffed French Toast, 36, *37*
Stuffed Peppers, 141
Stuffed Turkey Rollups, 77
Succotash, Summertime, 279
Summer Pudding, 418
Summertime Grilled Corn Soup, 108
Summertime Succotash, 279
Summery Pasta with Chickpeas and Tomatoes, 300, *301*
Sushi Rolls, California, 72
Sweet Bread(s). *See also* Buns
    Banana-Applesauce, 355
    Brown, 353
    Carrot-Pecan, 356
    Cranberry-Orange, 356
    Holiday Stollen, 348, *349*
    Panettone, 350
Sweet Potato(es)
    Casserole, 262
    Pie, 385
    Wedges with Chipotle Mayonnaise, 260, *261*
Sweet-and-Sour Grilled Fennel, 270
Swiss Chard
    au Gratin, 280
    and Lentil Soup, 125
    Risotto with, 249

T
Tabbouleh, Minted, 95
Tacos
    Chicken, 175
    Soft, with Tilapia and Chili-Lime Mayonnaise, *208,* 209
Tagine, Chickpea and Vegetable, North African, *234,* 235
Tandoori
    Lamb with Almond-Apricot Couscous, 154, *155*
    -Spiced Chicken, 184
    Yogurt Marinade, 25
Tapas, Garlic Shrimp, 78, *79*
Tartar Sauce, 19
    Crispy Catfish with, 206
Tempeh
    Sweet Onion, and Mushroom Chili, 230
    and Vegetable Stir-Fry, 231
Teriyaki
    -Flavored Grilled Sirloin, 136
    -Grilled Tuna with Vegetable Skewers, 202
    Marinade, 24
    Shrimp, Grilled, 218
Tex Mex–Style Baked Beans, 238

Thai-Style Roast Beef Salad, 74
Thousand Island Dressing, 32
Thyme
    Cherry Tomatoes with, 274
    Fresh, Wild Mushrooms with, 272
    -Lemon Zucchini on Flatbread, 69
    and Quinoa, Cremini Mushrooms with, 297
Tilapia
    Herb-Crusted, 207
    Soft Tacos, and Chili-Lime Mayonnaise, 208, 209
Toasted Coconut Custard, 422
Tofu
    Burgers, 228
    Stir-Fry, 228, 229
    -Vegetable Kebabs, Marinated, 230
Tomato(es)
    and Arugula Pesto, Pasta with, 245
    -Basil Soup, Fresh, 113
    Broiled, Catfish with, 205
    Cherry, with Thyme, 274
    and Chickpeas, Summery Pasta with, 300, 301
    Coulis, and Goat Cheese, Pissaladière with, 331
    Dried, and Herb, No-Knead Bread, 344
    and Goat Cheese Omelette, 43
    and Orzo, Braised Halibut with, 200, 201
    Orzo and Grilled Eggplant with, 292
    Parmesan, and Egg-Topped Pizza, 47
    and Pinto Beans, Skillet Asparagus with, 302
    Rice, with Chiles and Corn, 284
    Roasted, -Bell Pepper Soup, 113
    and Roasted Pepper-Stuffed Eggplant Rollups, 73
    Shrimp, and Mushroom Frittata, 46
    Stuffed, Provençal-Style, 274, 275
    Sun-Dried, Focaccia, 346
    Sun-Dried, Zucchini Risotto with, 249
    Sweet Onion, and Goat Cheese Salad, 87
Tomato Sauce
    -Basil, Roasted, 13
    -Bell Pepper, Grilled Lamb Chops with, 158
    Classic, 12
    Curried, Cauliflower with, 269
    Fresh, Capellini with, 246
    Meat, Lasagna with, 144
    No-Cook Summer, 13
    and Pork, Old-World Pasta with, 153
    Ragu Bolognese, 144
    -Saffron, Mussels in, 223
    Spicy, 12
Tortilla, Spanish, 241
Tostadas, Breakfast, 50, 51
Triple Citrus Pie, 385
Triple Ginger Gingerbread, 379
Trout Amandine, 212
Tuna
    with Black Bean and Corn Salad, 202
    Salad Sandwiches, Classic, 339
    Seviche, 78
    Spread, Milanese-Style, 59
    Teriyaki-Grilled, with Vegetable Skewers, 202
    and White Bean Salad, 100
Turkey
    BLTs, 338
    Breast, Mushroom-Stuffed, 188
    Burgers, Monterey Jack, 189
    Chowder, 316
    Cutlets with Cranberry Sauce, 189
    with Feta Topping, 187

Mulligatawny, 128
    -Parmesan Meat Loaf, 190, 191
    Roast, with Onion Gravy, 186
    Rollups, Stuffed, 77
    Sausage, and Chicken Gumbo, 311
    Smoked, with Wheat Berries and Fruit, 99
    Smoky, Chili, 316, 317
Tuscan Chicken and Sausage Stew, 312
Tuscan Panzanella, 102
Twice-Baked Potatoes, 240

V
Vanilla
    Frozen Yogurt, 413
    Waffles, 38
Veal, Blanquette de, 307
Vegetable(s). See also specific vegetables
    -Barley Soup, 314, 315
    and Chickpea Tagine, North African, 234, 235
    Chunky, Chickpeas and, 302
    Five-, Fried Rice,, 285
    Fried Rice, Chicken and, 185
    -Lamb Stew, 158
    Lasagna, Hearty, 242
    Mixed, Pickled, 280
    and Noodles, Japanese-Style, 243
    Polenta with, Creamy, 247
    Roasted, Classic, 276
    Roasted, Crostini, 66, 67
    Roasted, Stock, 107
    Scrambled Eggs, 44
    Skewers, Teriyaki-Grilled Tuna with, 202
    Spiced, Lentils with, 298
    Spring, Lemony Risotto, 248
    Stock, Basic, 107
    Summer, Grilled, with Israeli Couscous, 242
    and Tempeh Stir-Fry, 231
    -Tofu Kebabs, Marinated, 230
    Winter, Enchiladas, 240
    Winter, Pork Roast with, 146, 147
Venetian-Style Rice and Peas, 286
Venison
    Chops with Shallot Sauce, 159
    Steaks with Blackberry Sauce, 160
Vietnamese (-Style)
    Grilled Chicken Sandwiches, 336, 337
    Lobster Summer Rolls with Dipping Sauce, 79, 80
Vinaigrette. See Salad Dressing

W
Waffles
    Double Maple, 38
    Orange, 38
    Vanilla, 38
    Whole Wheat-Buttermilk, 38
Walnut(s)
    and Cranberries, Brown and Wild Rice with, 286
    Cranberry Relish, 22
    -Raisin Granola, 40, 41
Watercress
    Beet, and Apple Salad, 84
    -Potato Soup, 115
Watermelon
    -Mint Salsa, Honey-Glazed Salmon with, 198
    -Peach Salad with Ricotta Salata, 86, 87
    Sorbet, 416
Wheat. See also Whole Wheat
    Bread, with Honey, Food-Processor, 346
    -Honey Crescent Rolls, 345

Wheat Berry(ies)
    and Bean Stew, 233
    with Smoked Turkey and Fruit, 99
White Bean(s)
    Bell Pepper, and Olive Pizzas, 70
    and Broccoli, Pasta with, 293
    Bruschetta, 68
    Dip, 58
    Lamb Shanks with, 308
    and Tuna Salad, 100
Whole Fish Moroccan Style, 212
Whole Grain
    Breakfast Muffins, 358, 359
    French Toast, 36
Whole Leaf Caesar Salad with Golden Croutons, 84
Whole Wheat
    Bread, No-Knead, 344
    -Buttermilk Scones, 364
    -Buttermilk Waffles, 38
    Focaccia, 346
    Muffins, Jam-Filled, 358
    Pancakes, 39
    Pizza Dough, 322
Wild Mushrooms with Fresh Thyme, 272
Wild Rice
    and Brown, with Walnuts and Cranberries, 286
    and Mushroom Dressing, 288
    Salad with Pecans and Cranberries, 94
Winter Vegetable Enchiladas, 240

Y
Yellow Layer Cake with Cocoa Frosting, 372
Yellow Split Pea Soup, 124
Yogurt
    Biscuits, 361
    -Cucumber Soup, Chilled, 109
    Frozen, Raspberry-Orange, 414, 415
    Frozen, Vanilla, 413
    -Mint Sauce, Lamb Chops with, 157
    Tandoori Marinade, 25

Z
Zesty Chicken-Noodle Casserole, 186
Zucchini
    Lemon-Thyme, on Flatbread, 69
    Risotto with Sun-Dried Tomatoes, 249

Recipes by *PointsPlus* value

0 PointsPlus value
Basic Beef Stock, 106
Basic Dry Rub, 26
Cajun Dry Rub, 27
Pepper Dry Rub, 27
Pico de Gallo, 21

1 PointsPlus value
Asian Vinaigrette, 31
Basic Chicken Stock, 106
Basic Omelette, 43
Basic Vegetable Stock, 107
Beet, Apple, and Watercress Salad, 84
Broccoli with Garlic, 264
Caponata, 59
Carrot-Ginger Dressing, 31
Cheese Crisps, 60
Cherry Tomatoes with Thyme, 274
Chimichurri Sauce, 17
Chocolate-Espresso Biscotti, 400
Citrus Marinade, 25
Classic Tomato Sauce, 12
Dijon-Herb Marinade, 24
Fennel, Lemon, and Black Pepper
  Rub, 26
Food Processor Gazpacho, 115
Garlic Shrimp Tapas, 78
Green Goddess Dressing, 28
Green Sauce, 18
Hoisin-Ginger Marinade, 23
Hot-and-Soup Soup, 118
Italian Dressing, 30
Lemon-Butter Broccoli Spears, 265
Mixed Mushroom–Herb Omelette, 43
Mixed Pickled Vegetables, 280
Mocha Meringues, 399
Nectarine–Bell Pepper Salsa, 21
Radicchio, Cabbage, and Jicama Slaw,
  91
Raita, 18
Red Cabbage with Ginger, 267
Roasted Asparagus and Red Peppers,
  266
Roasted Vegetable Stock, 107
Skillet Summer Squash, 277
Smoky Onion Tartlets, 69
Spicy Tomato Sauce, 12
Swiss Chard au Gratin, 280
Tandoori Yogurt Marinade, 25
Tartar Sauce, 19
Teriyaki Marinade, 24

2 PointsPlus value
Baba Ghanoush, 57
Baby Romaine with Clementines and
  Pecans, 85
Basic Marinade, 23
Basil Pesto, 16
Best Blueberry Sauce, 422
Black and White Strawberries, 412
Blue Cheese Dressing, 32
Borscht, 108
California Greens Salad with Baked
  Goat Cheese, 88
Canadian Bacon, Asparagus, and
  Scallion Omelette, 43
Cauliflower with Curried Tomato
  Sauce, 269
Cheese Straws, 60
Chicken Satay with Peanut Sauce, 76
Chilled Cucumber-Yogurt Soup, 109
Classic Guacamole, 56
Classic Vinaigrette, 30
Coconut Macaroons, 402
Cornmeal Pizza Dough, 322

Cranberry-Walnut Relish, 22
"Creamed" Spinach, 277
Creole-Style Okra, 272
Crêpes, 49
Dilled Carrots, 267
Double Chocolate–Hazelnut Biscotti,
  401
Food Processor Wheat Bread with
  Honey, 346
Fresh Rosemary and Coarse Salt
  Focaccia, 346
Ginger Spice Cookies, 402
Greek Islands Salad, 85
Honeydew Sorbet, 417
Honey-Mustard Dressing, 31
Hummus, 57
Italian-Style Bean Soup, 120
Italian-Style Stuffed Mushrooms, 62
Jamaican Jerk Paste, 28
Kale with Balsamic Vinegar, 271
Keema Samosas, 64
Lemony Green Beans with Parsley, 271
Linzer Thumbprint Jewel Cookies, 397
Mango and Black Bean Salsa, 19
Matzo Ball Soup, 120
Mixed Mushroom Soup, 112
No-Cook Summer Tomato Sauce, 13
Oven-Roasted Beets and Garlic, 266
Oven-Roasted Brussels Sprouts and
  Carrots, 269
Pan-Braised Broccoli Rabe, 265
Picadillo in Lettuce Leaves, 76
Provençal-Style Stuffed Tomatoes, 274
Rainbow Slaw, 91
Raspberry Sauce, 423
Ratatouille Casserole, 273
Red Onion Focaccia, 346
Rich Cheese Sauce, 14
Rich Chocolate Sauce, 424
Roasted Red Pepper Coulis, 17
Roasted Red Pepper Dip, 58
Roasted Tomato-Basil Sauce, 13
Rugelach, 393
South American–Style Pumpkin Soup,
  112
Spicy Stir-Fried Sesame Spinach, 278
Sweet-and-Sour Grilled Fennel, 270
Sweet Brown Bread, 353
Thousand Island Dressing, 32
Tomato, Sweet Onion, and Goat
  Cheese Salad, 87
Tomato and Goat Cheese Omelette, 43
Vietnamese Lobster Summer Rolls with
  Dipping Sauce, 80
White Bean Dip, 58
Whole Leaf Caesar Salad with Golden
  Croutons, 84
Whole Wheat Focaccia, 346
Whole Wheat Pizza Dough, 322
Wild Mushrooms with Fresh Thyme,
  272
Yogurt Biscuits, 361

3 PointsPlus value
All-American Potato Salad, 92
Antipasto Platter, 73
Best-Ever Black Bean Soup, 121
Bok Choy–Noodle Soup, 118
Bran Bread, 347
Cannellini Bean–Stuffed Peppers, 236
Caramelized Garlic Toasts, 66
Caviar Eggs, 62
Celery Root and Mashed Potatoes, 256
Chickpeas and Chunky Vegetables, 302
Chinese Noodle Soup, 116
Chocolate Chip Cookies, 396
Classic Corn Bread, 354

Classic Roasted Vegetables, 276
Creamy Yellow Squash Soup with
  Chives, 111
Curried Deviled Eggs, 62
Deviled Eggs, 62
Eggplant Parmesan Stacks, 270
Fresh Tomato-Basil Soup, 113
German Potato Salad, 92
Grapefruit-Strawberry Granita, 417
Grilled Spicy Shrimp with Papaya-
  Lime Salsa, 218
Herbed Brown Rice, 284
Honey-Wheat Crescent Rolls, 345
Horseradish Deviled Eggs, 62
Hot Fudge Sauce, 424
Hot-and-Spicy Chickpea Cakes, 65
Lemon Poppy Seed Crisps, 394
Macadamia Coconut Meringues, 399
Mango Chutney, 22
Maple and Butter–Glazed Acorn
  Squash Wedges, 279
Marinated Tofu-Vegetable Kebabs, 230
Milanese-Style Tuna Spread, 59
Nachos Grandes, 70
No-Knead Whole Wheat Bread, 344
Orange and Red Onion Salad with
  Citrus Dressing, 88
Orange and Sage Biscuits, 361
Orzo with Grilled Eggplant and
  Tomato, 292
Oven-Baked Onion Rings, 262
Oven-Roasted Corn on the Cob, 264
Peanut Butter Cookies, 396
Portobello and Ham Bruschetta, 68
Potato Pancakes, 257
Potato-Watercress Soup, 115
Quick Naan Flatbread, 354
Real Mint Ice Cream, 415
Roasted Pepper and Tomato–Stuffed
  Eggplant Rollups, 73
Roasted Peppers with Orange Zest and
  Olives, 276
Roasted Tomato–Bell Pepper Soup, 113
Roast Turkey with Onion Gravy, 186
Roman Rice Frittata, 44
Sausage and Rice Dressing, 287
Scrambled Eggs with Smoked Salmon
  and Dill, 42
Semolina Pizza Dough, 322
Shrimp Cocktail with Horseradish
  Sauce, 80
Smoky Barbecue Sauce, 14
Spaghetti Squash Primavera, 278
Spanakopita Triangles, 64
Spinach-Stuffed Mushrooms, 63
Stuffed Turkey Rollups, 77
Summertime Grilled Corn Soup, 108
Sun-Dried Tomato and Olive Foccacia,
  346
Sweet Potato Casserole, 262
Sweet Potato Wedges with Chipotle
  Mayonnaise, 260
Toasted Coconut Custard, 422
Tuna Seviche, 78
Turkey Mulligatawny, 128
Vegetable Scrambled Eggs, 44
Watermelon Sorbet, 416
Wild Rice and Mushroom Dressing,
  288

4 PointsPlus value
Baked Beans, 298
Banana Cream Pie, 390
Barley, Leek, and Rosemary Gratin, 295
Breakfast Tostadas, 50
Broiled Halibut with Pico de Gallo, 200
Brownies, 394

Cajun Catfish, 203
Caribbean-Style Pork Tenderloin, 147
Carrot Cake, 375
Chicken in Lemon-Caper Sauce, 178
Chicken Soup, 313
Chicken with Orange Gremolata, 167
Chocolate-Buttermilk Bundt Cake, 368
Citrus-Glazed Duck Breasts, 192
Classic Beef-Barley Soup, 125
Classic Crêpes Suzette, 410
Classic Minestrone, 119
Coconut Cream Pie, 390
Cornbread, Apricot, and Cranberry
  Dressing, 290
Cornish Hens under a Brick, 192
Couscous with Lime and Scallion, 293
Cranberry-Oatmeal Cookies, 397
Cranberry-Orange Bread, 356
Creamy Blue Cheese Polenta, 297
Creamy Mashed Potatoes, 256
Cremini Mushrooms with Quinoa and
  Thyme, 297
Curried Basmati Rice, 285
Dark Fruit Cake, 377
Double Apple Strudel, 406
Double Grain Blueberry Scones, 363
Duck and Goat Cheese Quesadillas, 77
Garlicky Chicken Stew, 312
Gingerbread Cookies, 398
Grilled Jamaican-Style Halibut, 199
Grilled Lamb Chops with Mixed Herb
  Pesto, 157
Grilled Thai Beef Salad, 97
Hash Brown Potatoes, 259
Honey-Mustard Pork Chops, 151
Horseradish Mashed Potatoes, 256
Hot Cross Buns, 352
Irish Soda Bread, 353
Kasha Varnishkes, 296
Kielbasa and Bean Soup, 314
Korean Steak on a Stick, 74
Lamb Chops with Yogurt-Mint Sauce,
  157
Lemon-Blueberry Scones, 364
Lemon Cheesecake with Blueberry
  Sauce, 382
Lemon-Thyme Zucchini on Flatbread, 69
Manhattan Clam Chowder, 318
Minted Tabbouleh, 95
Mushroom-Stuffed Turkey Breast, 188
Mussels in Saffron-Tomato Sauce, 223
No-Knead Dried Tomato and Herb
  Bread, 344
Olive Oil and Lemon Smashed Potatoes,
  257
Oven Fries, 260
Parmesan-Turkey Meat Loaf, 191
Pepper Jack and Chile Corn Bread, 355
Potato-Onion Frittata, 45
Potato-Spinach Casserole, 252
Quinoa-Fruit Salad, 95
Rack of Lamb with Herbed Crumb
  Topping, 156
Risotto Milanese, 288
Roast Beef Salad with Arugula, 97
Roasted Garlic Mashed Potatoes, 256
Roasted Strawberries with Sorbet, 412
Roasted Vegetable Crostini, 66
Shrimp Scampi, 215
Sicilian Sausage–Stuffed Pizza, 329
Skillet Asparagus with Pinto Beans and
  Tomatoes, 302
Smoky Black Beans, 299
Smoky Manhattan-Style Clam Chowder,
  128
Sour Cream Pumpkin Pie, 388
Southwestern Black Bean Salad, 94

Summer Pudding, 418
Summertime Succotash, 279
Teriyaki-Grilled Tuna with Vegetable
  Skewers, 202
Thai-Style Roast Beef Salad, 74
Tofu Burgers, 228
Tomato Rice with Chiles and Corn, 284
Tuna and White Bean Salad, 100
Turkey Chowder, 316
Turkey with Feta Topping, 187
Vegetable-Barley Soup, 314
Venison Steaks with Blackberry Sauce,
  160
Watermelon-Peach Salad with Ricotta
  Salata, 87
White Bean Bruschetta, 68
Whole Wheat–Buttermilk Scones, 364
Yellow Layer Cake with Cocoa
  Frosting, 372

5 *PointsPlus* value
African Peanut Soup, 124
Almond-Cranberry Granola, 41
Apple Brown Betty, 408
Argentina-Style Steak and Sauce, 137
Baked Haddock with Ratatouille, 210
Baking Powder Biscuits, 360
Barbecued Pork with Mop Sauce, 148
Basic Cheese Pizza, 323
Beer Can Chicken, 168
Big Blueberry Pie, 384
Blanquette de Veau, 307
Brown and Wild Rice with Walnuts and
  Cranberries, 286
Bûche de Noël, 371
Buttermilk-Blueberry Corn Muffins,
  357
Butternut Squash and Sage Soup, 114
California Sushi Rolls, 72
Caramel Cake with Bourbon-Pear
  Sauce, 376
Carrot-Pecan Bread, 356
Cherry Pie, 384
Chicken Cacciatore, 169
Chocolate-Cherry Scones, 364
Citrus Passover Cake, 378
Classic Apple Pie, 383
Classic Chicken Salad, 99
Classic Chocolate Mousse, 420
Coconut Bread Pudding with Chocolate
  Sauce, 418
Corn Pudding, 263
Creamy Bean Soup, 121
Creamy Ham and Arugula Crêpes, 49
Cuban-Style Rice and Beans, 299
Double Maple Waffles, 38
Dried Peach–Pecan Scones, 364
Five-Vegetable Fried Rice, 285
French Lemon Tart, 392
French Onion Soup, 111
Frozen Mango-Lime Mousse, 413
Ginger and Golden Raisin Muffins, 358
Grilled Summer Vegetables with Israeli
  Couscous, 242
Grilled T-Bone Steak, 135
Holiday Stollen, 348
Jam-Filled Whole Wheat Muffins, 358
Jumbo Bran Muffins, 357
Lasagna with Meat Sauce, 144
Lemon Angel Food Cake with Berries,
  374
Lentil and Swiss Chard Soup, 125
Lentils with Spiced Vegetables, 298
London Broil, 136
Marinated Flank Steak, 137
Mixed Grain Porridge, 41
Mushroom-Spinach Calzones, 330

Mussels Marinière, 222
New Orleans Red Beans and Rice, 300
Noodles with Spicy Peanut Sauce, 292
Old-Fashioned Butterscotch Pudding,
  420
Orange-Spice Muffins, 358
Orange Waffles, 38
Panettone, 345
Pasta Salad Primavera, 102
Peaches in Red Wine, 411
Peach Melba, 411
Pecan Pie, 388
Peppered Roast Tenderloin, 135
Picadillo, 182
Pizza Margherita, 323
Pork and Broccoli "Stir Fry," 310
Pork with Ginger and Soy, 149
Pork Roast with Sauerkraut and Apples,
  308
Raspberry-Orange Frozen Yogurt, 415
Ribollita, 119
Rolled Orange Sponge Cake, 372
Salmon with Lemon and Herb Crumbs,
  199
Scalloped Potatoes with Cheese, 259
Skillet Chicken with Cherry Tomatoes
  and Garlic, 172
Smoky Grilled Brisket, 133
Smoky Turkey Chili, 316
Southwestern Salmon, 198
Spanish Tortilla, 241
Spicy Beef and Broccoli Stir-Fry, 140
Spinach and Cheese Quiche, 52
Stir-Fried Sea Scallops and Snow Peas,
  221
Stuffed Peppers, 141
Summery Pasta with Chickpeas and
  Tomatoes, 300
Tempeh and Vegetable Stir-Fry, 231
Teriyaki-Flavored Grilled Sirloin, 136
Tofu Stir-Fry, 228
Triple Ginger Gingerbread, 379
Trout Amandine, 212
Vanilla Frozen Yogurt, 413
Vanilla Waffles, 38
Venetian-Style Rice and Peas, 286
Walnut-Raisin Granola, 41
White Bean, Bell Pepper, and Olive
  Pizzas, 70
Whole Grain Breakfast Muffins, 358
Whole Grain French Toast, 36
Whole Wheat–Buttermilk Waffles, 38
Wild Rice Salad with Pecans and
  Cranberries, 94

6 *PointsPlus* value
Asian Sea Bass, 206
Avgolemono Chicken Soup, 116
Broccoli with Pasta and White Beans,
  293
California Hummus Sandwiches, 334
Cheese Quiche, 52
Chicken and Bell Pepper Fajitas, 180
Chicken and Mushroom Stew, 182
Chicken-Mushroom Hash Casserole,
  177
Chicken with Olives and Dates, 184
Chinese Chicken Salad, 98
Classic Cheese Soufflé, 241
Classic Pot Roast, 132
Classic Sticky Buns, 351
Classic Tuna Salad Sandwiches, 339
Creamy Polenta with Vegetables, 247
Crisped Scallops with Cantaloupe Salsa,
  221
Crispy Buffalo-Style Chicken Salad, 98
Dal Soup, 318

Double Chocolate Sorbet, 416
Eggplant Rollatini, 250
Egg Salad Sandwiches with Curry and
  Cilantro, 334
Flourless Chocolate Cake, 370
Greek Pita Pizzas with Spinach and
  Feta, 50
Greek Pizza, 326
Greek-Style Haddock, 209
Grilled Lamb Chops with Tomato–Bell
  Pepper Sauce, 158
Herb-Crusted Tilapia, 207
Herbed Oven-Fried Chicken, 181
Honey-Glazed Salmon with
  Watermelon-Mint Salsa, 199
Island Chicken with Pineapple, 176
Lamb Shanks with White Beans, 308
Lemony Spring Vegetable Risotto, 248
Mahogany Velvet Cupcakes with Cream
  Cheese Frosting, 381
Mixed Seafood Skewers with Couscous,
  213
Mushroom, Bacon, and Gruyère Pizza,
  327
Neapolitan Easter Pie, 391
Orange-Crumbed Baked Chicken, 173
Our Favorite Meat Loaf, 139
Pissaladière with Tomato Coulis and
  Goat Cheese, 331
Pork and Black Bean Chili, 152
Portobello Mushroom Burgers, 251
Pumpkin Spice Cake, 375
Rice Pudding with Golden Raisins, 419
Roast Beef Sandwiches with Horseradish
  Mayonnaise, 333
Shrimp, Mushroom, and Tomato Frittata,
  46
Sour Cream Coffee Cake, 368
Spaghetti Squash with Broccoli and
  Parmesan, 252
Spaghetti with Spicy Mussels and
  Shrimp, 216
Spiced Double Berry Crisp, 408
Spinach, Mushroom, and Bulgur Pilaf,
  296
Strawberry Shortcakes, 409
Tandoori Lamb with Almond-Apricot
  Couscous, 154
Tempeh, Sweet Onion, and Mushroom
  Chili, 230
Tex Mex–Style Baked Beans, 238
Triple Citrus Pie, 385
Turkey BLTs, 338
Tuscan Chicken and Sausage Stew, 312
Whole Fish Moroccan Style, 212
Yellow Split Pea Soup, 124

7 PointsPlus value
Baked Fruit–Cinnamon Oatmeal, 42
Baked Macaroni and Cheese, 238
Banana-Applesauce Bread, 355
Barbecue-Sauced Grilled Chicken, 170
Basic Pancakes, 39
Bigos, 310
Blueberry Pancakes, 39
Bouillabaisse, 211
Buckwheat Pancakes, 39
California Seafood Salad, 101
Capellini with Fresh Tomato Sauce,
  246
Caramelized Onion, Fig, and Stilton
  Pizza, 324
Catfish with Broiled Tomatoes, 205
Chicken and Black Bean Chili, 185
Chicken and Broccoli Rabe with
  Polenta, 175
Chicken and Turkey Sausage Gumbo,

311
Chicken and Vegetable Fried Rice, 185
Chicken Breasts with Papaya-Mint
  Salsa, 172
Chicken Tacos, 175
Corned Beef and Cabbage, 306
Crab Cake Sandwiches, 340
Creamy Corn, Potato, and Bacon Soup,
  123
Crispy Catfish with Tartar Sauce, 206
Easy Clam Pizza, 324
Fiery Falafel, 250
"Fried" Catfish with Potato Sticks, 205
Garlic-Roasted Chicken with Gravy,
  164
Grilled Arctic Char and Salad, 197
Grilled Teriyaki Shrimp, 218
Honey Cake, 378
Japanese-Style Noodles and Vegetables,
  243
Lobster Rolls, 340
Maryland Crab Cakes, 222
Mexicali-Style Stuffed Mushrooms,
  251
Mexican-Style Chicken-Corn Soup,
  123
Monterey Jack Turkey Burgers, 189
Moroccan-Style Roast Leg of Lamb,
  156
Pasta with Broccoli and Goat Cheese,
  245
Peach Crumb Pie, 386
Pork Roast with Winter Vegetables, 147
Quick Gumbo, 126
Ragu Bolognese, 144
Scallop Fried Rice, 219
Soy and Rice Stuffed Cabbage, 232
Spinach and Bean Burritos, 235
Steamed Lobster with Butter Sauce,
  223
Stir-Fried Pork with Bok Choy and
  Ginger, 148
Strawberry-Rhubarb Pie, 387
Sweet Potato Pie, 385
Tuna with Black Bean and Corn Salad,
  202
Turkey Cutlets with Cranberry Sauce,
  189
Tuscan Panzanella, 102
Whole Wheat Pancakes, 39

8 PointsPlus value
Best-Ever Chicken Loaf, 313
Best Grilled Burgers, 142
Chicken with Apples and Noodles, 169
Chicken with Rice, 167
Chili-Roasted Chicken and Potatoes,
  165
Cumin Chicken Kebabs with Couscous,
  176
Easy Enchiladas, 191
Fish Cakes with Creole Rémoulade
  Sauce, 210
Garlicky Red Beans and Pork, 152
Grilled Shrimp, Basil, and Goat Cheese
  Sandwiches, 339
Hearty Vegetable Lasagna, 242
Lobster Salad, 100
Middle Eastern Beef Kebabs, 139
Pappardelle with Shrimp, 216
Pasta with Arugula Pesto and Tomatoes,
  245
Salad Bar Pad Thai, 246
Salmon Salad with Horseradish, 89
Seafood Risotto, 214
Soft Tacos with Tilapia and Chili-Lime
  Mayonnaise, 209

Spicy Chicken and Broccoli, 180
Stuffed French Toast, 36
Tandoori-Spiced Chicken, 184
Twice-Baked Potatoes, 240
Wheat Berries with Smoked Turkey
  and Fruit, 99
Wheat Berry and Bean Stew, 233

9 PointsPlus value
Beef and Bean Chili, 141
Broiled Stuffed Lobster, 224
Cheddar-Stuffed Burgers, 142
Cioppino, 126
Classic Spaghetti and Meatballs, 145
Easy Chicken–Pumpkin Seed Mole,
  173
Easy Ginger Fried Rice, 247
Fried Eggs Tex Mex–Style, 46
Greek-Style Grilled Lamb Burger
  Sandwiches, 331
Grilled Steak Sandwiches with Golden
  Onions, 333
Middle Eastern–Style Chicken
  Sandwiches, 335
North African Chickpea and Vegetable
  Tagine, 235
Paella, 213
Salad Niçoise, 89
Savory Lamb Stew, 307
Shrimp Creole, 219
Sicilian-Style Sausage and Pepper
  Heroes, 338
Skillet Chicken Paprika, 178
Spicy Chicken Curry, 170

10 PointsPlus value
Beans and Rice, 237
Lamb-Vegetable Stew, 158
Old-World Pasta with Pork and Tomato
  Sauce, 153
Quinoa, Black Bean, and Shrimp Salad,
  101
Risotto with Swiss Chard, 249
Soy and Bean Chili, 232
Tomato, Parmesan, and Egg–Topped
  Pizza, 47
Venison Chops with Shallot Sauce, 159
Vietnamese-Style Grilled Chicken
  Sandwiches, 336
Winter Vegetable Enchiladas, 240
Zesty Chicken-Noodle Casserole, 186

11 PointsPlus value
Beef Stew with Carrots and Peas, 306
Braised Halibut with Tomatoes and
  Orzo, 200
Spicy Pork Stir-Fry, 151
Zucchini Risotto with Sun-Dried
  Tomatoes, 249

12 PointsPlus value
Beef Stew, 140